Linux+ and LPIC-1 Guide to Linux Certification

Fifth Edition

Jason W. Eckert
triOS College

Linux+ and LPIC-1 Guide to Linux Certification, 5th edition
Jason Eckert and triOS College

SVP, Higher Education & Skills Product: Erin Joyner

VP, Product Management: Mike Schenk

Product Director: Lauren Murphy

Product Team Manager: Kristin McNary

Product Manager: Amy Savino

Product Assistant: Thomas Benedetto

Director, Learning Design: Rebecca von Gillern

Senior Manager, Learning Design: Leigh Hefferon

Learning Designer: Natalie Onderdonk

Vice President, Marketing – Science, Technology, & Math: Jason Sakos

Senior Marketing Director: Michele McTighe

Associate Marketing Manager: Cassie Cloutier

Product Specialist: Mackenzie Paine

Director, Content Creation: Juliet Steiner

Senior Manager, Content Creation: Patty Stephan

Senior Content Manager: Brooke Greenhouse

Director, Digital Production Services: Krista Kellman

Digital Delivery Lead: Jim Vaughey

Designer: Erin Griffin

Cover Designer: Joseph Villanova

Cover image: iStock.com/kotkoa

Technical Editor: Danielle Shaw

Developmental Editor: Lisa Ruffalo

Production Service/Composition: SPi Global

For product information and technology assistance, contact us at
Cengage Customer & Sales Support, 1-800-354-9706 or support.cengage.com.

For permission to use material from this text or product, submit all requests online at **www.cengage.com/permissions.**

Library of Congress Control Number: 2019935400

ISBN: 978-1-337-56979-8
LLF IBSN: 978-1-337-68441-5

Cengage
20 Channel Center Street
Boston, MA 02210
USA

Cengage is a leading provider of customized learning solutions with employees residing in nearly 40 different countries and sales in more than 125 countries around the world. Find your local representative at **www.cengage.com.**

Cengage products are represented in Canada by Nelson Education, Ltd.

To learn more about Cengage platforms and services, register or access your online learning solution, or purchase materials for your course, visit **www.cengage.com.**

Notice to the Reader

Publisher does not warrant or guarantee any of the products described herein or perform any independent analysis in connection with any of the product information contained herein. Publisher does not assume, and expressly disclaims, any obligation to obtain and include information other than that provided to it by the manufacturer. The reader is expressly warned to consider and adopt all safety precautions that might be indicated by the activities described herein and to avoid all potential hazards. By following the instructions contained herein, the reader willingly assumes all risks in connection with such instructions. The publisher makes no representations or warranties of any kind, including but not limited to, the warranties of fitness for particular purpose or merchantability, nor are any such representations implied with respect to the material set forth herein, and the publisher takes no responsibility with respect to such material. The publisher shall not be liable for any special, consequential, or exemplary damages resulting, in whole or part, from the readers' use of, or reliance upon, this material. https://mail.yahoo.com/d/folders/50

Printed in the United States of America
Print Number: 01   Print Year: 2019

Brief Contents

Table of Contents

CHAPTER 4

Linux Filesystem Management 147

CHAPTER 7

Working with the BASH Shell... 339

CHAPTER 8

System Initialization, X Windows, and Localization 413

CHAPTER 12

Network Configuration 621

APPENDIX A

Certification 821

APPENDIX B

GNU Public License 827

APPENDIX C

Finding Linux Resources on the Internet 841

APPENDIX D

Applying Your Linux Knowledge to macOS 847

Introduction

"In a future that includes competition from open source, we can expect that the eventual destiny of any software technology will be to either die or become part of the open infrastructure itself."

Eric S. Raymond, *The Cathedral and the Bazaar*

As Eric S. Raymond reminds us, open source software will continue to shape the dynamics of the computer software industry for the next long while, just as it has for the last two decades. Coined and perpetuated by hackers, the term "open source software" refers to software in which the source code is freely available to anyone who wants to improve it (usually through collaboration). At the heart of the open source software movement lies Linux—an operating system whose rapid growth has shocked the world by demonstrating the nature and power of the open source model.

However, as Linux continues to grow, so must the number of Linux-educated users, administrators, developers, and advocates. We now find ourselves in a time in which Linux education is of great importance to the information technology industry. Key to demonstrating Linux skills and knowledge is the certification process. This book, *Linux+ and LPIC-1 Guide to Linux® Certification,* uses carefully constructed examples, questions, and practical exercises to prepare readers with the necessary information to achieve the latest version of the sought-after Linux+ certification from CompTIA, as well as the latest version of the LPIC-1 certification from the Linux Professional Institute (LPI). Whatever your ultimate goal, you can be assured that reading this book in combination with study, creativity, and practice will make the open source world come alive for you as it has for many others.

Intended Audience

Simply put, this book is intended for those who want to learn the Linux operating system and master the topics tested on the Linux+ certification exam from CompTIA or the LPIC-1 certification exams from LPI. It does not assume any prior knowledge of

Linux. Although the topics introduced in this book and associated certification exams are geared toward systems administration, they are also well suited for those who will use or develop programs for Linux systems, or want to pursue a career in cloud computing, supercomputing, cybersecurity, blockchain development, or Internet of Things (IoT) technology, where Linux knowledge is a prerequisite.

Chapter Descriptions

Chapter 1, "Introduction to Linux," introduces operating systems as well as the features, benefits, and uses of the Linux operating system. This chapter also discusses the history and development of Linux and open source software.

Chapter 2, "Linux Installation and Usage," outlines the procedures necessary to prepare for and install Linux on a typical computer system. This chapter also describes how to interact with a Linux system via a terminal and enter basic commands into a Linux shell, such as those used to obtain help and to properly shut down the system.

Chapter 3, "Exploring Linux Filesystems," outlines the Linux filesystem structure and the types of files that you find within it. This chapter also discusses commands you can use to view and edit the content of those files.

Chapter 4, "Linux Filesystem Management," covers the commands you can use to locate and manage files and directories on a Linux filesystem. This chapter also discusses how to link files, as well as interpret and set file and directory permissions, special permissions, and attributes.

Chapter 5, "Linux Filesystem Administration," discusses how to create, mount, and manage filesystems in Linux. This chapter also discusses the files that identify storage devices, the various filesystems available for Linux systems, as well as the partitions and logical volumes used to host filesystems.

Chapter 6, "Linux Server Deployment," introduces the types of hardware and storage configurations used within server environments, as well as the considerations for installing a Linux server. This chapter also discusses device driver support, common problems that may occur during installation, system rescue, as well as configuring Linux server storage (SAN, RAID, ZFS, and BTRFS).

Chapter 7, "Working with the BASH Shell," covers the major features of the BASH shell, including redirection, piping, variables, aliases, and environment files. This chapter also explores the syntax of basic shell scripts and the use of Git to provide version control for shell scripts.

Chapter 8, "System Initialization, X Windows, and Localization," covers the GRUB bootloader that you use to start the Linux kernel. This chapter also discusses how to start daemons during system initialization as well as how to start and stop them afterwards. Finally, this chapter discusses the structure and configuration of Linux graphical user interfaces, as well as setting up time, time zone, and locale information.

Chapter 9, "Managing Linux Processes," covers types of processes as well as how to view their attributes, run them in the background, change their priority, and kill them. This chapter also discusses how to schedule processes to occur in the future using various utilities.

Chapter 10, "Common Administrative Tasks," details three important areas of system administration: printer administration, log file administration, and user administration.

Chapter 11, "Compression, System Backup, and Software Installation," describes utilities that are commonly used to compress and back up files on a Linux filesystem. This chapter also discusses how to install software from source code, as well as how to use the Red Hat Package Manager and the Debian Package Manager.

Chapter 12, "Network Configuration," introduces networks, network utilities, and the IP protocol, as well as how to configure the IP protocol on a NIC or PPP interface. This chapter also explains how to set up name resolution, IP routing, network services, and the technologies you can use to administer Linux servers remotely.

Chapter 13, "Configuring Network Services and Cloud Technologies," details the configuration of key infrastructure, Web, file sharing, email, and database network services. This chapter also examines how virtualization and containers are used within cloud environments, the configuration of Docker containers, and the tools and processes used to perform continuous deployment of apps to cloud environments.

Chapter 14, "Security, Troubleshooting, and Performance," discusses the utilities and processes used to provide security for Linux systems. This chapter also explores the utilities used to monitor system performance, as well as the troubleshooting procedures for solving performance, hardware, application, filesystem, and network problems.

Additional information is contained in the appendices at the rear of the book. Appendix A discusses the certification process, with emphasis on the Linux+ and LPIC-1 certifications. It also explains how the objective lists for the Linux+ and LPIC-1 certifications match each chapter in the textbook. Appendix B provides a copy of the GNU Public License. Appendix C explains how to find Linux resources on the Internet and lists some common resources by category. Appendix D applies the Linux concepts introduced within this book to the macOS UNIX operating system from Apple.

Features

To ensure a successful learning experience, this book includes the following pedagogical features:

- *Chapter objectives*—Each chapter in this book begins with a detailed list of the concepts to be mastered within the chapter. This list provides you with a quick reference to chapter contents as well as a useful study aid.

- *Illustrations and tables*—Numerous illustrations of server screens and components aid you in visualizing common setup steps, theories, and concepts. In addition, many tables provide details and comparisons of both practical and theoretical information and can be used for a quick review of topics.
- *End-of-chapter material*—The end of each chapter includes the following features to reinforce the material covered in the chapter:
  - *Summary*—A bulleted list gives a brief but complete summary of the chapter.
  - *Key Terms list*—This section lists all new terms in the chapter. Definitions for each key term can be found in the Glossary.
  - *Review Questions*—A list of review questions tests your knowledge of the most important concepts covered in the chapter.
  - *Hands-On Projects*—Hands-On Projects help you to apply the knowledge gained in the chapter.
  - *Discovery Exercises*—Additional projects that guide you through real-world scenarios and advanced topics.

New to This Edition

This edition has been updated to include the concepts and procedures tested on the latest certification exams from CompTIA and the Linux Professional Institute (LPI). More specifically, this edition contains:

- Content that maps to the latest CompTIA Linux+ (XK0-004) and LPIC-1: System Administrator (101-500, 102-500) certification exams
- Updated information pertinent to the latest Linux distributions and technologies
- New material on server storage technologies, network tools, Git, cloud technologies, Docker containers, and devop workflows
- Expanded material on troubleshooting and security practices, concepts, and technologies
- Continued focus on Linux server administration, including key network services (FTP, NFS, Samba, Apache, DNS, DHCP, NTP, Postfix, SSH, VNC, and SQL)
- Hands-On Projects designed for Fedora Linux, as well as modern and legacy Ubuntu Server Linux installed on the same computer
- Appendices that map the latest Linux+ and LPIC-1 certification objectives to each chapter, identify key Linux-related Internet resources, and apply the Linux administration topics covered within the book to Apple macOS

Text and Graphic Conventions

Wherever appropriate, additional information and exercises have been added to this book to help you better understand what is being discussed in the chapter. Special headings throughout the text alert you to additional materials:

> ### Note
>
> The Note heading is used to present additional helpful material related to the subject being described.

> ### Hands-On Projects
>
> The Hands-On Project heading indicates that the projects following it give you a chance to practice the skills you learned in the chapter and acquire hands-on experience.

Instructor Resources

MindTap

MindTap activities for *Linux+ and LPIC-1 Guide to Linux® Certification, Fifth Edition*, are designed to help students master the skills they need in today's workforce. Research shows that employers need critical thinkers, troubleshooters, and creative problem-solvers to stay relevant in this fast-paced, technology-driven world. MindTap helps you achieve this goal with assignments and activities that provide hands-on practice and real-life relevance. Students are guided through assignments that help them master basic knowledge and understanding before moving on to more challenging problems.

All MindTap activities and assignments are tied to defined unit learning objectives. Live virtual machine labs offer real-life application and practice. Readings and dynamic visualizations support the lecture, and a post-course assessment measures exactly how much students have learned. MindTap supplies the analytics and reporting to see easily where the class stands in terms of progress, engagement, and completion rates. Use the content and learning path as they are, or choose how these materials wrap around yours. You control what students see and when they see it. Learn more at *http://www.cengage.com/mindtap/*.

Instructor Companion Site

The following teaching tools are available for download at the companion site for this book. Simply search for this book's title, author, or ISBN at *www.cengagebrain.com* and click Instructor Downloads. An instructor login is required.

- *Instructor's Manual*—The Instructor's Manual that accompanies this book includes additional instructional material to assist in class preparation, including items such as overviews, chapter objectives, teaching tips, quick quizzes, class discussion topics, additional projects, additional resources, and key terms. A sample syllabus is also available.

- *Test bank*—Cengage Testing Powered by Cognero is a flexible, online system that allows you to do the following:
  - Author, edit, and manage test bank content from multiple Cengage solutions.
  - Create multiple test versions in an instant.
  - Deliver tests from your LMS, your classroom, or wherever you want.
- *PowerPoint presentations*—This book provides PowerPoint slides to accompany each chapter. Slides can be used to guide classroom presentations, to make available to students for chapter review, or to print as classroom handouts. Files are also supplied for every figure in the book. Instructors can use these files to customize PowerPoint slides, illustrate quizzes, or create handouts.
- *Solutions*—Solutions to all end-of-chapter review questions and projects are available.

Student Resources

MindTap for Linux+ and LPIC-1 Guide to Linux Certification, Fifth Edition, helps you learn on your terms.

- Instant access in your pocket: Take advantage of the MindTap Mobile App to learn on your terms. Read or listen to textbooks and study with the aid of instructor notifications, flashcards, and practice quizzes.
- MindTap helps you create your own potential. Gear up for ultimate success: Track your scores and stay motivated toward your goals. Whether you have more work to do or are ahead of the curve, you'll know where you need to focus your efforts. The MindTap Green Dot will charge your confidence along the way.
- MindTap helps you own your progress. Make your textbook yours; no one knows what works for you better than you. Highlight key text, add notes, and create custom flashcards. When it's time to study, everything you've flagged or noted can be gathered into a guide you can organize.

About the Author

Jason W. Eckert is an experienced technical trainer, consultant, and best-selling author in the Information Technology (IT) industry. With 45 industry certifications, 30 years of IT experience, 4 published apps, and 24 published textbooks covering topics such as UNIX, Linux, Security, Windows Server, Microsoft Exchange Server, PowerShell, BlackBerry Enterprise Server, and Video Game Development, Mr. Eckert brings his expertise to every class that he teaches at triOS College, and to his role as the Dean of Technology. For more information about Mr. Eckert, visit *jasoneckert.net*.

Acknowledgments

First, I would like to thank the staff at Cengage for an overall enjoyable experience writing a textbook on Linux that takes a fundamentally different approach than traditional textbooks. Additionally, I wish to thank Lisa Ruffolo, Danielle Shaw, Brooke Greenhouse, Natalie Onderdonk, and Hemalatha Loganathan for working extremely hard to pull everything together and ensure that the book provides a magnificent Linux experience. I also wish to thank Frank Gerencser of triOS College for providing me with the opportunity to write five editions of a book on a topic that I'm very passionate about over the past two decades. Finally, I wish to thank the Starbucks Coffee Company for keeping me ahead of schedule, and my dog Pepper for continually reminding me that taking a break is always a good idea.

Readers are encouraged to email comments, questions, and suggestions regarding *Linux+ and LPIC-1 Guide to Linux® Certification* to Jason W. Eckert: jason.eckert@trios.com.

Before You Begin

Linux can be a large and intimidating topic if studied in a haphazard way. So, as you begin your study of Linux, keep in mind that each chapter in this book builds on the preceding one. To ensure that you gain a solid understanding of core Linux concepts, read the chapters in consecutive order. You should also participate in a local Linux Users Group (LUG) and explore the Internet for websites, forums, YouTube videos, and social media articles that will expand your knowledge of Linux.

Lab Requirements

The following hardware is required at minimum for the Hands-On Projects at the end of each chapter:

- A 64-bit CPU
- 8 GB RAM (12 GB RAM recommended)
- 120 GB hard disk or SSD
- Internet connection

Similarly, the following lists the software required for the Hands-On Projects at the end of each chapter:

- Fedora 28 Live Installation Media
- Ubuntu Server 14 Installation Media
- Ubuntu Server 18 Installation Media

## CHAPTER 1

INTRODUCTION TO LINUX

After completing this chapter, you will be able to:

Explain the purpose of an operating system

Outline the key features of the Linux operating system

Describe the origins of the Linux operating systems

Identify the characteristics of various Linux distributions and where to find them

Explain the common uses of Linux in industry today

Linux technical expertise is essential in today's computer workplace as more and more companies switch to Linux to meet their computing needs. Thus, it is important to understand how Linux can be used, what benefits Linux offers to a company, and how Linux has developed and continues to develop. In the first half of this chapter, you will learn about operating system terminology and features of the Linux operating system, as well as the history and development of Linux. Later in this chapter, you will learn about the various types of Linux and about the situations in which Linux is used.

Operating Systems

Every computer has two fundamental types of components: hardware and software. You are probably familiar with these terms, but it's helpful to review their meanings so you can more easily understand how Linux helps them work together.

Hardware consists of the physical components inside a computer that are electrical in nature; they contain a series of circuits that manipulate the flow of information. A computer can contain many pieces of hardware, including the following:

- A processor (also known as the central processing unit or CPU), which computes information
- Physical memory (also known as random access memory, or RAM), which stores information needed by the processor
- Hard disk and solid state disk drives, which store most of the information that you use
- CD/DVD drives, which read and write information to and from CD/DVD discs
- Flash memory card readers, which read and write information to and from removable memory cards, such as Secure Digital (SD) cards
- Sound cards, which provide audio to external speakers
- Video cards, which display results to the display screen
- Network adapter cards, which provide access to wired and wireless (Wi-Fi or Bluetooth) networks
- Ports (such as USB, eSATA, GPIO, and Thunderbolt), which provide access to external devices including keyboards, mice, printers, and storage devices
- Mainboards (also known as motherboards), which provide the circuitry (also known as a bus) for interconnecting all other components

Software, on the other hand, refers to the sets of instructions or **programs** that allow the hardware components to manipulate data (or files). When a bank teller types information into the computer behind the counter at a bank, for example, the bank teller is using a program that understands what to do with your bank records. Programs and data are usually stored on hardware media, such as hard disks or solid state disks, although they can also be stored on removable media or even embedded in computer chips. These programs are loaded into parts of your computer hardware (such as your computer's memory and processor) when you first turn on your computer and when you start additional software, such as word processors or Internet browsers. After a program is executed on your computer's hardware, that program is referred to as a **process**. In other words, a program is a file stored on your computer, whereas a process is that file in action, performing a certain task.

There are two types of programs. The first type, **applications** (or **apps**), includes those programs designed for a specific use and with which you commonly interact, such as word processors, computer games, graphical manipulation programs, and computer system utilities. The second type, **operating system (OS)** software, consists of a set of software components that control the hardware of your computer. Without an operating system, you would not be able to use your computer. Turning on a computer loads the operating system into computer hardware, which then loads and centrally controls all other application software in the background. At this point, the **user** (the person using the computer) is free to interact with the applications, perhaps by typing on the keyboard or clicking with a mouse. Applications take the information the user supplies and relay it to the operating system, which uses the computer hardware to carry out the requests. The relationship between users, application software, operating system software, and computer hardware is illustrated in Figure 1-1.

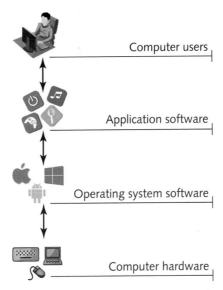

Computer users

Application software

Operating system software

Computer hardware

Figure 1-1   The role of operating system software

The operating system carries out many tasks by interacting with different types of computer hardware. For the operating system to accomplish the tasks, it must contain the appropriate device driver software for every hardware device in your computer. Each **device driver** tells the operating system how to use that specific device. The operating system also provides a **user interface**, which is a program that accepts user input indicating what to do, forwards this input to the operating system for completion, and, after it is completed, gives the results back to the user. The user interface can be a command-line prompt, in which the user types commands, or it can be a **graphical user interface (GUI)**, which consists of menus, dialog boxes, and symbols (known as icons) that the user can interact with via the keyboard or the mouse. A typical Linux GUI is shown in Figure 1-2.

Finally, operating systems offer **system services**, which are applications that handle system-related tasks, such as printing, scheduling programs, and network access. These system services determine most of the functionality in an operating system. Different operating systems offer different system services, and many operating systems allow users to customize the services they offer.

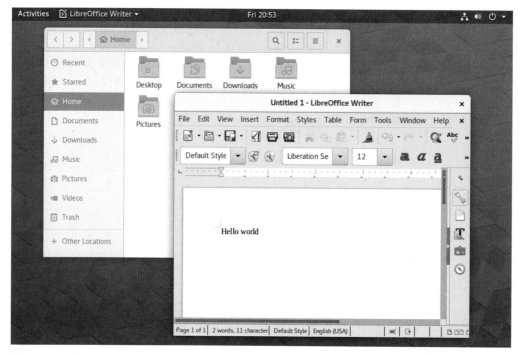

Figure 1-2   A Linux graphical user interface

The Linux Operating System

Linux (pronounced "Lih-nucks") is an operating system you use to run applications on a variety of hardware. Similar to other operating systems, Linux loads into computer memory when you first power on your computer and initializes (or activates) all of the hardware components. Next, it loads the programs that display the interface. From within the interface, you can execute commands that tell the operating system and other applications to perform specific tasks. The operating system then uses the computer hardware to perform the tasks required by the applications.

Linux can manage thousands of tasks at the same time, including allowing multiple users to access the system simultaneously. Hence, Linux is referred to as a **multiuser** and **multitasking** operating system.

Versions of the Linux Operating System

The core component of the Linux operating system is called the Linux **kernel**. The Linux kernel and supporting software (called function libraries) are written almost entirely in the C programming language, which is one of the most common languages that software developers use when creating programs.

Although you can use a variety of software to modify the appearance of Linux, the underlying kernel is common to all types of Linux. The Linux kernel is developed continuously; thus, you should understand the version numbers of the Linux kernel to decide which kernel version is appropriate for your needs. Because the Linux kernel is directly responsible for controlling the computer's hardware (via device drivers), you might sometimes need to upgrade the kernel after installing Linux to take advantage of new technologies or to fix problems (also known as bugs) related to your computer's hardware. Consequently, you need a good understanding of your system's hardware to decide which kernel to use.

> **Note**
>
> For a complete list of kernels, kernel versions, and their improvements, see *www.kernel.org*.

In some cases, you can use updates in the form of a kernel module or a kernel patch to provide or fix hardware supported by the kernel. Kernel modules and kernel patches are discussed later in this book.

Identifying Kernel Versions

Linux kernel versions are made up of the following three components:

- Major number
- Minor number
- Revision number

Let's look at a sample Linux kernel version, 4.17.6. In this example, the **major number** is the number 4, which indicates the major version of the Linux kernel. The **minor number**, represented by the number 17, indicates the minor revision of the Linux kernel. As new features are added to the Linux kernel over time, the minor number is incremented. The major number is usually incremented when a major kernel feature is implemented, when the minor number versioning reaches a high number, or to signify a major event; for example, the 3.0 kernel was introduced to commemorate the twentieth anniversary of Linux.

Linux kernel changes occur frequently. Very minor changes are represented by a **revision number** indicating the most current changes to the version of the particular kernel that is being released. For example, a 4.17.6 kernel has a revision number of 6. This kernel is the sixth release of the 4.17 kernel. Some kernels have over 100 revisions as a result of developers making constant improvements to the kernel code.

> **Note**
>
> Sometimes, a fourth number is added to a kernel version to indicate a critical security or bug patch. For example, a 4.17.6.1 kernel is a 4.17.6 kernel with a critical patch number of 1.

Modern Linux kernels that have a major, minor, and revision number are referred to as **production kernels**; they have been thoroughly tested by several Linux developers and are declared stable. **Developmental kernels** are not fully tested and imply instability; they are tested for vulnerabilities by people who develop Linux software. Most developmental kernels append the minor number with the letters -rc (release candidate) followed by a number that represents the version of the developmental kernel. For example, the 4.18-rc3 developmental kernel is the third release candidate for the 4.18 kernel; if Linux developers declare it stable after being thoroughly tested, it will become the 4.18.0 production kernel.

Note 📎

Until Linux kernel 2.6.0, an odd-numbered minor number was used to denote a development kernel, and an even-numbered minor number was used to denote a production kernel.

Note 📎

When choosing a kernel for a mission-critical computer such as a **server**, ensure that you choose a production kernel. This reduces the chance that you will encounter a bug in the kernel, which saves you the time needed to change kernels.

Table 1-1 shows some sample kernel versions released since the initial release of Linux.

Table 1-1   Sample Linux kernel version history

Kernel version	Date released	Type
0.01	September 1991	First Linux kernel
0.12	January 1992	Production (stable)
0.95	March 1992	Developmental
0.98.6	December 1992	Production (stable)
0.99.15	March 1994	Developmental
1.0.8	April 1994	Production (stable)
1.3.100	May 1996	Developmental
2.0.36	November 1998	Production (stable)
2.3.99	May 2000	Developmental

Table 1-1   Sample Linux kernel version history *(continued)*

Kernel version	Date released	Type
2.4.17	December 2001	Production (stable)
2.5.75	July 2003	Developmental
2.6.35	August 2010	Production (stable)
3.0.0	July 2011	Production (stable)
3.2.21	June 2012	Production (stable)
3.10.4	July 2013	Production (stable)
3.15.10	August 2014	Production (stable)
4.0.0	April 2015	Production (stable)
4.6.3	March 2016	Production (stable)
4.12.5	August 2017	Production (stable)
4.18-rc3	July 2018	Developmental

Licensing Linux

Companies often choose Linux as their operating system because of the rules governing Linux licensing. Unlike most other operating systems, Linux is freely developed and continuously improved by a large community of software developers. For this reason, it is referred to as **Open Source Software (OSS)**.

To understand OSS, you must first understand how source code is used to create programs. **Source code** refers to the list of instructions that a software developer writes to make up a program; an example of source code is shown in Figure 1-3.

```
#define MODULE
#include <linux/module.h>
int init_module(void){
        printk("My module has been activated.\n");
        return 0;
}
void cleanup_module(void){
        printk("My module has been deactivated.");
}
```

Figure 1-3   Source code

After the software developer finishes writing the instructions, the source code is compiled into a format (called machine language) that only your computer's processor can understand and execute. To edit an existing program, the software developer must edit the source code and then recompile it.

The format and structure of source code follows certain rules defined by the **programming language** in which it was written. Programmers write Linux source code in many programming languages. After being compiled into machine language, all programs look the same to the computer operating system, regardless of the programming language in which they were written. As a result, software developers choose a programming language to create source code based on ease of use, functionality, and comfort level.

The fact that Linux is an OSS operating system means that software developers can read other developers' source code, modify that source code to make the software better, and redistribute that source code to other developers who might improve it further. Like all OSS, Linux source code must be distributed free of charge, regardless of the number of modifications made to it. People who develop OSS commonly use the Internet to share their source code, manage software projects, and submit comments and fixes for bugs (flaws). In this way, the Internet acts as the glue that binds together Linux developers in particular and OSS developers in general.

Note

To read the complete open source definition, visit *opensource.org*.

Here are some implications of the OSS way of developing software:

- Software is developed rapidly through widespread collaboration.
- Software bugs (errors) are noted and promptly fixed.
- Software features evolve quickly, based on users' needs.
- The perceived value of the software increases because it is based on usefulness and not on price.

As you can imagine, sharing ideas and source code is beneficial to software developers. However, a software company's business model changes drastically when OSS enters the picture. The main issue is this: How can a product that is distributed freely generate revenue? After all, without revenue any company will go out of business.

The OSS process of software development was never intended to generate revenue directly. Its goal was to help people design better software by eliminating many of the problems associated with traditional software development, which is typically driven by predefined corporate plans and rigid schedules. By contrast, OSS development assumes that software creation is an art in which a particular problem can be solved in many ways. One software developer might create a program that measures widgets using four pages of source code, while another developer might create a program that does the same task in one page of source code. You might think that this openness to multiple ways of solving a problem would result in a haphazard software development process, but the sharing of ideas that is the heart of OSS development keeps developers focused on the best possible solutions. Also, while OSS developers contribute their strengths to a project, they learn new techniques from other developers at the same time.

Because the selling of software for profit discourages the free sharing of source code, OSS generates revenue indirectly. Companies usually make money by selling computer hardware that runs OSS, by selling customer support for OSS, or by creating **closed source software** programs that run on open source products such as Linux.

The OSS development process is, of course, not the only way to develop and license software. Table 1-2 summarizes the types of software you are likely to encounter. The following section explains these types in more detail.

Table 1-2   Software types

Type	Description
Open source	Software in which the source code and software can be obtained free of charge and optionally modified to suit a particular need
Closed source	Software in which the source code is not available; although this type of software might be distributed free of charge, it is usually quite costly and commonly referred to as commercial software
Freeware	Closed source software that is given out free of charge; it is sometimes referred to as freemium software
Shareware	Closed source software that is initially given out free of charge but that requires payment after a certain period of use

Types of Open Source Licenses

Linux adheres to the **GNU General Public License (GPL)**, which was developed by the **Free Software Foundation (FSF)**. The GPL stipulates that the source code of any software published under its license must be freely available. If someone modifies that source code, that person must also redistribute that source code freely, thereby keeping the source code free forever.

Note

"**GNU**" stands for "GNUs Not UNIX."

Note

The GPL is freely available at *www.gnu.org* and in this book's Appendix B, "GNU General Public License."

Another type of open source license is the **artistic license**, which ensures that the source code of the program is freely available yet allows the original author of the source code some control over the changes made to it. Thus, if one developer obtains and improves the source code of a program, the original author has the right to reject those improvements. As a result of this restriction, artistic licenses are rarely used because many developers do not want to work on potentially futile projects.

In addition to the two open source licenses mentioned are other types of open source licenses that differ only slightly from one another. Those licenses must adhere to the open source definition but might contain extra conditions that the open source definition does not.

Note

For a list of approved open source licenses, visit *opensource.org*.

Types of Closed Source Licenses

Closed source software can be distributed for free or for a cost; either way, the source code for the software is unavailable from the original developers. The majority of closed source software is sold commercially and bears the label of its manufacturer. Each of these software packages can contain a separate license that restricts free distribution of the program and its source code in many ways.

Note

Examples of closed source software are software created by companies such as Microsoft, Apple, and Electronic Arts (EA).

Another type of closed source software is **freeware**, in which the software program is distributed free of charge, yet the source code is unavailable. Freeware might also contain licenses that restrict the distribution of source code. Another approach to this style of closed source licensing is **shareware**, which is distributed free of charge, yet after a certain number of hours of usage or to gain certain features of the program, payment is required. Although freeware and shareware do not commonly distribute their source code under an open source license, some people incorrectly refer to freeware as OSS, assuming that the source code is free as well.

Linux Advantages

The main operating systems in use today include Linux, Microsoft Windows, UNIX, and macOS. Notably, Linux is the fastest growing operating system released to date. Although Linux was only created in 1991, the number of Linux users estimated by Red Hat in 1998 was 7.5 million, and the number of Linux users estimated by Google in

2010 was over 40 million (including the number of Linux-based Android smartphone and device users). In 2013, LinuxCounter.net (*http://linuxcounter.net*) estimated that the number of Linux users was over 70 million, and Google estimated that over 900 million Linux-based Android devices had shipped by then. Since 1998, many large companies, including IBM, Hewlett-Packard, Intel, and Dell, have announced support for Linux and OSS. In the year 2000, IBM announced plans to spend one billion dollars on Linux and Linux development alone.

People have begun using Linux for many reasons. The following advantages are examined in the sections that follow:

- Risk reduction
- Meeting business needs
- Stability and security
- Flexibility for different hardware platforms
- Ease of customization
- Ease of obtaining support
- Cost reduction

Risk Reduction

Companies need software to perform mission-critical tasks, such as database tracking, Internet business (e-commerce), and data manipulation. However, changes in customer needs and market competition can cause the software a company uses to change frequently. Keeping the software up to date can be costly and time-consuming, but is a risk that companies must take. Imagine that a fictitious company, ABC Inc., buys a piece of software from a fictitious software vendor, ACME Inc., to integrate its sales and accounting information with customers via the Internet. What would happen if ACME went out of business or stopped supporting the software due to lack of sales? In either case, ABC would be using a product that had no software support, and any problems that ABC had with the software after that time would go unsolved and could result in lost revenue. In addition, all closed source software is eventually retired after it is purchased, forcing companies to buy new software every so often to obtain new features and maintain software support.

If ABC instead chose to use an OSS product and the original developers became unavailable to maintain it, then the ABC staff would be free to take the source code, add features to it, and maintain it themselves provided the source code was redistributed free of charge. Also, most OSS does not retire after a short period of time because collaborative open source development results in constant software improvement geared to the needs of the users.

Meeting Business Needs

Recall that Linux is merely one product of open source development. Many thousands of OSS programs are available, and new ones are created daily by software developers worldwide. Most open source Internet tools have been developed for quite some time now, and the focus in the Linux community in the past few years has been on developing application software, cloud technologies, and security-focused network services that run on Linux. Almost all of this software is open source and freely available, compared to other operating systems, in which most software is closed source and costly.

OSS is easy to locate on the Web, at sites such as SourceForge (*sourceforge.net*), GitHub (*github.com*), and GNU Savannah (*savannah.gnu.org*). New software is published to these sites daily. SourceForge alone hosts over 430,000 software development projects.

Common software available for Linux includes but is not limited to the following:

- Scientific and engineering software
- Software emulators
- Web servers, Web browsers, and e-commerce suites
- Desktop productivity software (e.g., word processors, presentation software, spreadsheets)
- Graphics manipulation software
- Database software
- Security software

In addition, companies that run the UNIX operating system (including macOS, which is a flavor of UNIX) might find it easy to migrate to Linux. For those companies, Linux supports most UNIX commands and standards, which eases a transition to Linux because the company likely would not need to purchase additional software or retrain staff. For example, suppose a company that tests scientific products has spent time and energy developing custom software that runs on the UNIX operating system. If this company transitions to another operating system, its staff would need to be retrained or hired, and much of the custom software would need to be rewritten and retested, which could result in a loss of customer confidence. If, however, that company transitions to Linux, the staff would require little retraining, and little of the custom software would need to be rewritten and retested, hence saving money and minimizing impact on consumer confidence.

Companies that need to train staff on Linux usage and administration can take advantage of several educational resources and certification exams for various Linux skill levels. Certification benefits as well as the CompTIA Linux+ and LPIC-1 certifications are discussed in this book's Appendix A, "Certification."

In addition, for companies that require a certain development environment or need to support custom software developed in the past, Linux provides support for most programming languages.

Stability and Security

OSS is developed by people who have a use for it. This collaboration among several developers with a common need speeds up software creation, and when bugs in the software are found by these users, bug fixes are created quickly. Often, the users who identify the bugs can fix the problem because they have the source code, or they can provide detailed descriptions of their problems so that other developers can fix them.

By contrast, customers using closed source operating systems must rely on the operating system vendor to fix any bugs. Users of closed source operating systems must report the bug to the manufacturer and wait for the manufacturer to develop, test, and release a solution to the problem, known as a **hot fix**. This process might take weeks or even months, which is slow and costly for most companies and individuals. The thorough and collaborative open source approach to testing software and fixing software bugs increases the stability of Linux; it is not uncommon to find a Linux system that has been running continuously for months or even years without being turned off.

Security, a vital concern for most companies and individuals, is another Linux strength. Because Linux source code is freely available and publicly scrutinized, security loopholes are quickly identified and fixed by several developers. In contrast, the source code for closed source operating systems is not released to the public for scrutiny, which means customers must rely on the OS vendor to provide security. A security breach unnoticed by the vendor can be exploited by the wrong person. Every day, new malicious software (destructive programs that exploit security loopholes, such as viruses and malware) is unleashed on the Internet with the goal of infiltrating closed source operating systems, such as Windows. By contrast, the number of viruses that can affect Linux is exceedingly low. As of April 2008, Linux had fewer than 100 known viruses, whereas Windows had more than 1,000,000 known viruses. Compared to other systems, the amount of malicious software for Linux systems remains incredibly low, and nearly all of it is designed to breach older versions of unprotected Linux-based Android smartphones. As a result, most desktop and server Linux systems that run antivirus and antimalware software today do so because they host files that may be shared with Windows computers.

Note 📎

For a list of recent malicious software, visit *securelist.com*.

Flexibility for Different Hardware Platforms

Another important feature of Linux is that it can run on a variety of computer **hardware platforms** frequently found in different companies. Although Linux is most commonly installed on the Intel x86/x64 platforms, it can also be installed on other types of hardware, such as the POWER platform from IBM that runs on many of the largest supercomputers in the world. Companies can run Linux on very large and expensive hardware for big tasks, such as graphics rendering or chemical molecular modeling, as well as on smaller systems, such as point-of-sale terminals and inventory scanners. Few other operating systems run on more than two hardware platforms, making Linux the ideal choice for companies that use different types of or specialized hardware.

Here is a partial list of hardware platforms on which Linux can run:

- Intel x86/x64
- Itanium
- Mainframe (S/390, z/Architecture)
- ARM
- MIPS
- SPARC/Ultra-SPARC
- PowerPC/POWER

In addition to the platforms in the preceding list, Linux can be customized to work on most hardware. Thousands of high-tech companies rely on embedded operating system technology to drive their systems. NASA spacecrafts, Internet routers and firewalls, Google Android smartphones and tablets, Amazon Kindle eBook readers, TomTom GPS navigation systems, smart thermostats, and Wi-Fi access points all run Linux. This focus on mobile and embedded devices will become more important as the need for new functionality increases. The rich set of OSS developers at work today makes Linux an attractive choice for manufacturers of mobile and embedded devices.

Ease of Customization

The ease of controlling the inner workings of Linux is another attractive feature, particularly for companies that need their operating system to perform specialized functions. If you want to use Linux as a Web server, you can simply recompile the Linux kernel to include only the support needed to be a Web server. This results in a much smaller and faster kernel.

Note 📎

A small kernel performs faster than a large kernel because it contains less code for the processor to analyze. On high-performance systems, you should remove any unnecessary features from the kernel to improve performance.

Today, customizing and recompiling the Linux kernel is a well-documented and easy process; however, it is not the only way to customize Linux. Only software packages necessary to perform certain tasks need to be installed; thus, each Linux system can have a unique configuration and set of applications available to the user. Linux also supports several system programming languages, such as Shell and PERL, which you can use to automate tasks or create custom tasks.

Consider a company that needs an application to copy a database file from one computer to another computer, yet also needs to manipulate the database file (perhaps by checking for duplicate records), summarize the file, and finally print it as a report. This might seem like a task that would require expensive software; however, in Linux, you can write a short PERL script that uses common Linux commands and programs to perform these tasks. This type of customization is invaluable to companies because it allows them to combine several existing applications to perform a certain task, which might be specific only to that company and, hence, not previously developed by another free software developer. Most Linux configurations present hundreds of small utilities, which, when combined with Shell or PERL programming, can make new programs that meet many business needs.

Ease of Obtaining Support

For those who are new to Linux, the Internet offers a world of Linux documentation. **Frequently asked questions (FAQs)** and instructions known as **HOWTO** documents are arranged by topic and are available to anyone. HOWTO documents are maintained by their authors yet are centrally collected by the **Linux Documentation Project (LDP)**, which has several hundred websites worldwide that allow you to search or download HOWTO documents.

A search of the word "HOWTO" on a typical Internet **search engine** such as *www.google.com* displays thousands of results, or you can download the worldwide collection of HOWTO documents at *www.tldp.org*.

In addition, several Internet **newsgroups** allow Linux users to post messages and reply to previously posted messages. If you have a specific problem with Linux, you can post your problem on an Internet newsgroup and receive help from those who know the solution. Linux newsgroups are posted to frequently; thus, you can usually expect a solution to a problem within hours. A list of common Linux newsgroups can be found at *http://groups.google.com*.

An alternative to Internet newsgroups include Linux-focused Facebook groups and website forums. Appendix C, "Finding Linux Resources on the Internet," describes how to navigate Internet resources and lists some resources that you might find useful.

Although online support is the typical method of getting help, other methods are available. Most Linux distributions provide professional telephone support services for a modest fee, and many organizations give free support to those who ask. The most common of these groups are referred to as **Linux User Groups (LUGs)**, and most large cities across the globe have at least one. LUGs are groups of Linux users who meet regularly to discuss Linux-related issues and problems. An average LUG meeting consists of several new Linux users (also known as Linux newbies), administrators, developers, and experts (also known as Linux gurus). LUG meetings are a resource to solve problems and learn about the local Linux community. Most LUGs host websites that contain a multitude of Linux resources, including summaries of past meetings and discussions. One common activity seen at a LUG meeting is referred to as an Installfest; several members bring in their computer equipment to install Linux and other Linux-related software. This approach to transferring knowledge is very valuable to LUG members because concepts can be demonstrated and the solutions to problems can be modeled by more experienced Linux users.

> **Note** 🖉
>
> To find a list of available LUGs in your region, search for the words "LUG cityname" on an Internet search engine such as *www.google.com* (substituting your city's name for "cityname"). When searching for a LUG, keep in mind that LUGs might go by several different names; for example, the LUG in Hamilton, Ontario, Canada is known as HLUG (Hamilton Linux Users Group). Many LUGs today are managed using Facebook groups or meeting sites such as *www.meetup.com*.

Cost Reduction

Linux is less expensive than other operating systems such as Windows because there is no cost associated with acquiring the software. In addition, a wealth of OSS can run on different hardware platforms running Linux, and a large community of developers is available to diagnose and fix bugs in a short period of time for free. While Linux and the Linux source code are distributed freely, implementing Linux is not cost free. Costs include purchasing the computer hardware necessary for the computers hosting Linux, hiring people to install and maintain Linux, and training users of Linux software.

The largest costs associated with Linux are the costs associated with hiring people to maintain the Linux system. However, closed source operating systems have this cost in addition to the cost of the operating system itself. The overall cost of using a particular operating system is known as the **total cost of ownership (TCO)**. Table 1-3 shows an example of the factors involved in calculating the TCO for operating systems.

Table 1-3   Calculating the total cost of ownership

Costs	Linux	Closed source operating system
Operating system cost	$0	Greater than $0
Cost of administration	Low: Stability is high and bugs are fixed quickly by open source developers.	Moderate/high: Bug fixes are created by the vendor of the operating system, which could result in costly downtime.
Cost of additional software	Low/none: Most software available for Linux is also open source.	Moderate/high: Most software available for closed source operating systems is also closed source.
Cost of software upgrades	Low/none	Moderate/high: Closed source software is eventually retired, and companies must buy upgrades or new products to gain functionality and stay competitive.

The History of Linux

Linux is based on the UNIX operating system developed by Ken Thompson and Dennis Ritchie of AT&T Bell Laboratories in 1969 and was developed through the efforts of many people as a result of the hacker culture that formed in the 1980s. Therefore, to understand how and why Linux emerged on the operating system market, you must first understand UNIX and the hacker culture. Figure 1-4 illustrates a timeline representing the history of the UNIX and Linux operating systems.

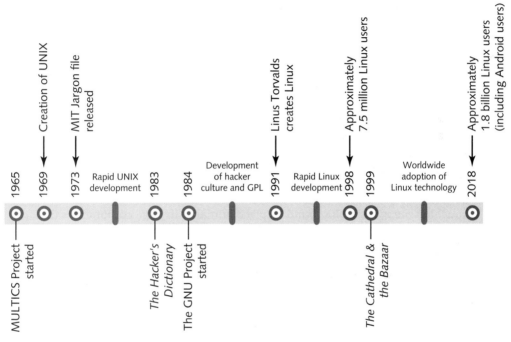

Figure 1-4   Timeline of UNIX and Linux development

UNIX

The UNIX operating system has roots running back to 1965, when the Massachusetts Institute of Technology (MIT), General Electric, and AT&T Bell Laboratories began developing an operating system called **Multiplexed Information and Computing Service (MULTICS)**. MULTICS was a test project intended to reveal better ways of developing time-sharing operating systems, in which the operating system regulates the amount of time each process has to use the processor. The project was abandoned in 1969. However, Ken Thompson, who had worked on the MULTICS operating system, continued to experiment with operating systems. In 1969, he developed an operating system called **UNIX** that ran on the DEC (Digital Equipment Corporation) PDP-7 computer.

Shortly thereafter, Dennis Ritchie invented the C programming language that was used on Ken Thompson's UNIX operating system. The C programming language was a revolutionary language. Most programs at the time needed to be written specifically for the hardware of the computer, which involved referencing volumes of information regarding the hardware in order to write a simple program. However, the C programming language was much easier to use to write programs, and it was possible to run a program on different machines without having to rewrite the code. The UNIX operating system was rewritten in the C programming language, and by the late-1970s, the UNIX operating system ran on different hardware platforms, something that the computing world had never seen until that time. Hence, people called UNIX a portable operating system.

Unfortunately, the company Ken Thompson and Dennis Ritchie worked for (AT&T) was restricted by a federal court order from marketing UNIX. In an attempt to keep UNIX viable, AT&T sold the UNIX source code to several companies, encouraging them to agree to standards among them. Each of these companies developed its own variety, or **flavor**, of UNIX yet adhered to standards agreed upon by all. AT&T also gave free copies of the UNIX source code to certain universities to promote widespread development of UNIX. One result was a UNIX version developed at the University of California, Berkeley in the early 1980s known as **BSD (Berkeley Software Distribution)**. In 1982, one of the companies to whom AT&T sold UNIX source code (Sun Microsystems) marketed UNIX on relatively inexpensive hardware and sold thousands of computers that ran UNIX to companies and universities.

Throughout the 1980s, UNIX found its place primarily in large corporations that had enough money to purchase the expensive computing equipment needed to run UNIX (usually a DEC PDP-11, VAX, or Sun Microsystems computer). A typical UNIX system in the 1980s could cost over $100,000, yet it performed thousands of tasks for client computers (also known as dumb terminals). Today, UNIX still functions in that environment; many large companies employ different flavors of UNIX for their heavy-duty, mission-critical tasks, such as e-commerce and database hosting. Common flavors of UNIX today include BSD, Hewlett-Packard's **HP-UX**, IBM's **AIX**, as well as Apple's **macOS** and **iOS** operating systems.

The Hacker Culture

The term **hacker** refers to a person who attempts to expand his knowledge of computing through experimentation. It should not be confused with the term **cracker**, which refers to someone who illegally uses computers for personal benefit or to cause damage.

In the early days of UNIX, hackers came primarily from engineering or scientific backgrounds, because those were the fields in which most UNIX development occurred. Fundamental to hacking was the idea of sharing knowledge. A famous hacker, Richard Stallman, promoted the free sharing of ideas while he worked at the Artificial Intelligence Laboratory at MIT. He believed that free sharing of all knowledge in the computing industry would promote development. In the mid-1980s, Stallman formed the Free Software Foundation (FSF) to encourage free software development.

This movement was quickly accepted by the academic community in universities around the world, and many university students and other hackers participated in making free software, most of which ran on UNIX. As a result, the hacker culture was commonly associated with the UNIX operating system.

Unfortunately, UNIX was not free software, and by the mid-1980s some of the collaboration seen earlier by UNIX vendors diminished and UNIX development fragmented into different streams. As a result, UNIX did not represent the ideals of the FSF, and so Stallman founded the **GNU Project** in 1984 to promote free development for a free operating system that was not UNIX.

Note

For a description of the FSF and GNU, visit *www.gnu.org*.

This development eventually led to the publication of the GNU Public License (GPL), which legalized free distribution of source code and encouraged collaborative development. Any software published under this license must be freely available with its source code; any modifications made to the source code must then be redistributed free as well, keeping the software development free forever.

As more and more hackers worked together developing software, a hacker culture developed with its own implied rules and conventions. Most developers worked together without ever meeting each other; they communicated primarily via newsgroups and email. *The Hacker's Dictionary*, published by MIT in 1983, detailed the terminology regarding computing and computing culture that had appeared since the mid-1970s. Along with the FSF, GNU, and GPL, it served to codify the goals and ideals of the hacker culture. But it wasn't until the publication of Eric S. Raymond's *The Cathedral and the Bazaar*, in 1999, that the larger world was introduced to this thriving culture. Raymond, a hacker himself, described several aspects of the hacker culture:

- Software users are treated as codevelopers.
- Software is developed primarily for peer recognition and not for money.
- The original author of a piece of software is regarded as the owner of that software and coordinates the cooperative software development.
- The use of a particular piece of software determines its value, not its cost.
- Attacking the author of source code is never done. Instead, bug fixes are either made or recommended.
- Developers must understand the implied rules of the hacker culture before being accepted into it.

This hacker culture proved to be very productive, with several thousand free tools and applications created in the 1980s, including the famous Emacs editor, which is a common tool used in Linux today. During this time, many programming function libraries and UNIX-like commands also appeared as a result of the work on the GNU Project. Hackers became accustomed to working together via newsgroup and email correspondence. In short, the UNIX hacker culture, which supported free sharing of source code and collaborative development, set the stage for Linux.

Linux

Although Richard Stallman started the GNU Project to make a free operating system, the GNU operating system never took off. Much of the experience gained by hackers developing the GNU Project was later pooled into Linux. A Finnish student named **Linus Torvalds** first developed Linux in 1991 when he was experimenting with improving **MINIX** (Mini-UNIX, a small educational version of UNIX developed by Andrew Tannenbaum) for the Intel x86 platform. The Intel x86 platform was fast becoming standard in homes and businesses around the world and was a good choice for any free development at the time. The key feature of the Linux operating system that attracted the development efforts of the hacker culture was that Torvalds had published Linux under the GNU Public License.

Since 1991, when the source code for Linux was released, the number of software developers dedicated to improving Linux has increased each year. The Linux kernel was developed collaboratively and was centrally managed; however, many Linux add-on packages were developed freely worldwide by those members of the hacker culture who were interested in their release. Linux was a convenient focal point for free software developers. During the early-to-mid-1990s, Linux development proceeded at full speed, with hackers contributing their time to what turned into a large-scale development project. All of this effort resulted in several distributions of Linux. A **distribution** of Linux is a collection or bundle of software containing the commonly developed Linux operating system kernel and libraries, combined with add-on software specific to a certain use. Well-known distributions of Linux include **Red Hat**, **openSUSE**, **Debian**, **Ubuntu**, **Gentoo**, **Linux Mint**, and **Arch**.

This branding of Linux did not imply the fragmentation that UNIX experienced in the late-1980s. All distributions of Linux had a common kernel and utilities. Their blend of add-on packages simply made them look different on the surface. Linux still derived its usefulness from collaborative development.

Linux development continued to expand throughout the late-1990s as more developers grew familiar with the form of collaborative software development advocated by the hacker culture. By 1998, when the term "OSS" first came into use, there were already many thousands of OSS developers worldwide. Small companies formed to offer Linux solutions for business. People invested in these companies by buying stock in them. Unfortunately, this trend was short-lived. By the year 2000, most of these companies had vanished. At the same time, the OSS movement caught the attention and support of large companies (such as IBM, Compaq, Dell, and Hewlett-Packard), and there was a shift in Linux development over the following decade to support the larger computing environments and mobile devices.

It is important to note that Linux is a by-product of OSS development. Recall that the OSS developers are still members of the hacker culture and, as such, are intrinsically motivated to develop software that has an important use. Thus, OSS development has changed over time; in the 1980s, the hacker culture concentrated on developing Internet and programming tools, whereas in the 1990s, it focused on developing the Linux operating system. Since 2000, interest has grown in embedded Linux (Linux OSes that run on smaller hardware devices such as mobile devices) and developing cloud- and security-focused application programs for use on the Linux operating system. Because Linux is currently very well developed, even more application development can be expected from the OSS community in the next decade.

Note

For more information on the free software movement and the development of Linux, watch the 2001 television documentary *Revolution OS* (available on YouTube). It features interviews with Linus Torvalds, Richard Stallman, and Eric S. Raymond.

Linux Distributions

It is time-consuming and inefficient to obtain Linux by first downloading and installing the Linux kernel and then adding desired OSS packages. Instead, it's more common to download a distribution of Linux containing the Linux kernel, common function libraries, and a series of OSS packages.

Note

Remember that although Linux distributions appear different on the surface, they run the same kernel and contain many of the same packages.

Despite the fact that varied distributions of Linux are essentially the same under the surface, they do have important differences. Different distributions might support different hardware platforms. Also, Linux distributions include predefined sets of software; some Linux distributions include many server-related tools, such as Web servers and database servers, whereas others include numerous workstation and development software applications. Still others might include a complete set of open source tools that you can use to customize a Linux system to perform specific functions. In that case, you simply choose the open source tools you want to install. For example, you might choose to install a database server.

While Linux distributions use the same Linux kernel versions that are community developed, they can modify those kernels in order to provide fixes and optimizations that are specific to the distribution and used for long-term support. These are called **distribution kernels**, and list a patch version and distribution identifier following the major, minor, and revision number. For example, the 4.17.6-100.fc28.x86_64 kernel is distribution release 100 of the Linux 4.17.6 production kernel used on a 64-bit (x86_64) version of the Fedora Linux 28 distribution (fc28).

Linux distributions that include many specialized tools might not contain a GUI; an example of this is a Linux distribution that fits within a single small flash memory chip and can be used as a home Internet **router**. Most distributions, however, do include a GUI that can be further customized to suit the needs of the user.

The core component of the GUI in Linux is referred to as **X Windows**. The original implementation of X Windows on Linux was called XFree86 but has since been replaced by X.org and Wayland. X.org is the latest implementation of X Windows based on the original MIT X Windows project that was released as OSS in 2004, and Wayland is an alternative to X.org that was designed to be easier to develop and maintain. In addition to X Windows, several Linux window managers and desktop environments are available, which together affect the look and feel of the Linux GUI. X Windows in combination with a window manager and desktop environment is referred to as a **GUI environment**. The two main competing GUI environments available in Linux are the **GNU Network Object Model Environment (GNOME)** and the **K Desktop Environment (KDE)**. These two GUI environments are more or less comparable in functionality, although users might have a personal preference for one desktop over the other. This is often the case when a company wants to do a great deal of software development in the GUI environment; the GNOME desktop, written in the C programming language, uses the widely available gtk toolkit, whereas the KDE desktop, written in the C++ programming language, uses the qt toolkit. The language and toolkit that best fits a company's need will be the one preferred at that time. Most common Linux distributions ship with both GNOME and KDE GUI environments, whereas others offer support for both so that either GUI environment can be easily downloaded and installed. Figures 1-5 and 1-6 compare these two GUI environments.

Note 🖉

In addition to GNOME and KDE, several other desktop environments are available to Linux systems. One example is Cinnamon, which is a desktop derived from GNOME that is particularly easy to use. Another example is XFCE, which is a lightweight desktop environment designed for Linux systems with few CPU and RAM resources.

Although the differences between Linux distributions can help narrow the choice of Linux distributions to install, one of the most profound reasons companies choose one distribution over another is support for package managers. A **package manager**

Figure 1-5   The GNOME desktop

Figure 1-6   The KDE desktop

is a software system that installs and maintains software. It keeps track of installed software, requires a standard format and documentation, and can manage and remove software from a system by recording all relevant software information in a central software database on your computer.

Note

A package manager in Linux is similar to the Apps and Features or Programs and Features section in the Windows Settings or Control Panel apps, respectively.

One of the most widely supported package managers is the Red Hat Package Manager (RPM). Most Linux software is available in RPM format, and the RPM is standard on many Linux distributions that were originally derived from the Red Hat Linux distribution. The Debian Package Manager (DPM) is also very common today; it offers the same advantages as the RPM but for systems that were originally derived from the Debian Linux distribution. Other, less common package managers available for Linux include Pacman (Arch Linux), Zypper (openSUSE Linux), and Portage (Gentoo Linux). In addition to obtaining software in package manager format, you can download software in tarball format. A **tarball** is a compressed archive of files, like WinZip or RAR files, usually containing scripts that install the software contents to the correct location on the system, or source code that can be compiled into a working program and copied to the system. Unfortunately, tarballs do not update a central software database and, as a result, are very difficult to manage, upgrade, or remove from the system. Traditionally, most Linux software was available in tarball format, but package managers have since become the standard method for installing software.

Note

For a list of common Linux distributions, visit *www.linux.org*.

Anyone can create a Linux distribution by packaging OSS with the Linux kernel. As a result, over 500 Linux distributions are publicly registered. Many are small, specialized distributions designed to fulfill certain functions, but some are mainstream Linux distributions used widely throughout the computing world. Typically, a distribution is associated with a website from which the distribution can be downloaded for free. In addition, most Linux distributions can be obtained from other websites, such as *iso.linuxquestions.org*. Some distributions of Linux are also available on DVDs for a small fee from computer stores and websites; however, downloading from the Internet is the most common method of obtaining Linux.

Table 1-4 briefly describes some mainstream Linux distributions, their features, and where to find them on the Internet.

Table 1-4	Common Linux distributions		
Distribution	**Features**	**Platforms**	**Location**
Red Hat	One of the earliest Linux distributions, and one that is commonly used within organizations today. Two distributions of Red Hat are available: the Enterprise distribution geared for enterprise environments and the Fedora distribution geared for all environments (servers, desktops, laptops, etc.). Both editions ship with the RPM package manager and GNOME as the default desktop environment.	x86/x64 PPC/POWER Mainframe ARM	*www.redhat.com* *getfedora.org*
openSUSE	Originally developed primarily in Europe, openSUSE is the oldest business-focused Linux distribution. Novell purchased the distribution to replace its NetWare OS and distributes enterprise versions of openSUSE.	x86/x64 PPC/POWER ARM	*www.opensuse.org* *www.suse.com*
Debian	Offering the largest number of customization options of all Linux distributions, Debian Linux contains software packages for any use and supports nearly all languages and hardware platforms.	x86/x64 PPC/POWER Mainframe ARM MIPS	*www.debian.org*
Ubuntu	A Debian-based distribution that is widely used in all environments, Ubuntu is designed to be easy to use and supports nearly all hardware, including mobile computing devices.	x86/x64 PPC/POWER Mainframe ARM	*www.ubuntu.com*
Gentoo	A Linux distribution that focuses on hardware and software optimization. Each program and part of the operating system on a Gentoo system is compiled specifically for the hardware on the particular system and optimized for that hardware during the process.	x86/x64 PPC/POWER ARM	*www.gentoo.org*
Linux Mint	A relatively new and easy-to-use Linux distribution that is focused on providing desktop and mobile user capabilities.	x86/x64	*www.linuxmint* *.com*
Arch	A very lightweight and customizable Linux distribution. Due to its focus on simplicity and customization, it is often used within specialized environments and on small footprint systems.	x86/x64	*www.archlinux.org*

Common Uses of Linux

As discussed earlier, an important feature of Linux is its versatility. Linux can provide services meeting the needs of differing companies in a variety of situations. Furthermore, configuring these services is straightforward given the wide range of documentation freely available on the Internet; you can choose the services that are required and then customize Linux to provide those services. These services can be used on a local computer **workstation**, or you can configure a service to allow other computers to connect to it across a network. Services that are used on the local computer are referred to as **workstation services**, whereas services that are made available for other computers across a network are known as **server services**.

> ### Note
>
> A computer that hosts a server service is commonly referred to as a server.

Although you can use thousands of server and workstation services to customize Linux, Linux configurations commonly used today include the following:

- Internet servers
- File and print servers
- Application servers
- Cloud systems
- Supercomputers
- Scientific workstations
- Office/personal workstations
- Cybersecurity workstations
- Mobile devices

Internet Servers

Linux hosts a wide range of Internet services, and it was from these services that Linux gained its popularity in the 1990s. All of these services are available free of charge and, like all OSS, undergo constant improvement, which makes Linux an attractive choice when a company is planning for the use of Internet services. Companies that use services on a computer to serve client computers are said to have an Internet server. Linux contains hundreds of network services that provide the framework for an Internet server; the most common of these services include the following:

- Web services
- DNS services
- DHCP services
- Time services
- Mail services

- FTP services
- Authentication services
- Certificate services
- Routing services
- Firewall and proxy services
- Advanced security services

Many of these applications are discussed in more detail later in this book.

Web Services

Although many Internet tools and services are available, the most popular is the Internet browser, which can connect client computers to servers worldwide hosting information of many types: text, pictures, music, binary data, video, and much more. The community of servers that hosts this information is known as the World Wide Web (WWW), and a server hosting information is known as a Web server. On a basic level, a Web server is just a server using Hypertext Transfer Protocol (HTTP) to provide information to requesting Web browsers running on client computers; however, Web servers can also process programs known as Common Gateway Interface (CGI) scripts and provide secure connections such as Secure Sockets Layer (SSL) or Transport Layer Security (TLS). A CGI is a program that runs on the Web server and enables connection to a resource running on another server on the network not connected to the Internet such as a database. This is very useful, as not all information provided over the Internet needs to reside on Web servers. CGIs can be written in several programming languages, including C and C++, making them readily compatible with Linux. SSL and TLS are secure methods of communicating with a Web server in which the information passing between the client computer and the Web server is encrypted to keep it secure. This form of transmission is widely used any time confidentiality is required, such as in Internet banking or in transferring a client's credit card information in e-commerce. You can tell SSL/TLS is in use when the http:// in the browser's address bar changes to https://.

Note

Many open source Web server software packages are available for Linux. The most widely used is the Apache Web Server. For more information about the Apache Web Server, visit *httpd.apache.org*.

DNS Services

Each computer on a network needs a unique way to identify itself and to refer to other computers. This is accomplished by assigning each computer a number called an **Internet Protocol (IP) address**. An IP address is a long string of numbers that would be very hard for the typical person to remember. Thus, IP addresses are often associated with more user-friendly names. In particular, servers are identified by names like *www.linux.org*, which are known as fully qualified domain names (FQDNs). When you use a Web browser such as Google Chrome or Mozilla Firefox to request information from a Web server, you typically type the Web server's FQDN (e.g., *www.linux.org*) into your browser's address bar. However, FQDNs exist only for the convenience of the human beings who use computer networks. The computers themselves rely on IP addresses. Thus, before your browser can retrieve the requested information from the Web server, it needs to know the IP address associated with the FQDN you typed into the address bar. Your browser gets this information by contacting a server hosting a Domain Name Space (DNS) service. The DNS server maintains a list of the proper FQDN to IP mappings, and quickly returns the requested IP address to your browser. Your browser can then use this IP address to connect to the target website.

For companies wanting to create a DNS server, Linux is an inexpensive solution, as many distributions of Linux ship with a Domain Name Service known as BIND (Berkeley Internet Name Daemon).

Note

Each computer participating on the Internet must have an IP address.

Note

Names for computers on the Internet, such as *www.linux.org*, are also known as fully qualified domain names (FQDNs).

Note

You can find the latest version of BIND at the Internet Systems Consortium website, *www.isc.org*.

DHCP Services

Recall that each computer on the Internet must have an IP address. While an administrator typically configures this address on servers, it is impractical to do the same to the plethora of workstations and other systems on the Internet. As a result, most computers on the Internet automatically receive an IP address and related configuration from a Dynamic Host Configuration Protocol (DHCP) server by broadcasting an IP address request on the network. This is normally performed at system startup and periodically afterward. Any Linux computer can function as a DHCP server by adding and configuring the DHCP daemon, dhcpd.

Time Services

Most system components and network services require the correct date and time in order to function properly. The BIOS (Basic Input Output System) on each computer contains a system clock that stores the current date and time. Operating systems can choose to use the time from this system clock or obtain time information from other servers on the Internet or local network using the **Network Time Protocol (NTP)**. A Linux system can obtain time information from an NTP server or provide time information to other systems using NTP via the NTP daemon (ntpd) or Chrony NTP daemon (chronyd).

Mail Services

In the 1980s and early 1990s, email was a service that was found primarily in universities. Today, almost every Internet user has an email account and uses email on a regular basis. Email addresses are easy to acquire and can be obtained free of charge.

Email is distributed via a network of email servers, also known as **Mail Transfer Agents (MTAs)**. Many MTAs are freely available for Linux, including sendmail, postfix, and exim. Before the user can access his email, it must be downloaded from an MTA; the service that provides this is known as a **Mail Delivery Agent (MDA)**. Linux also provides several of these services; getmail and mpop are two of the most common. Finally, the user views her email using a program known as a **Mail User Agent (MUA)**. Common MUAs available for Linux include mutt, Alpine, Mozilla Thunderbird, and Claws Mail.

FTP Services

The most common and efficient method for transferring files over the Internet is by using the File Transfer Protocol (FTP). In addition, FTP is commonplace when transferring files on an internal company network because it is very quick and robust. A user starts the FTP service on her computer (now known as an FTP server) and allows users to connect; users on other computers then connect to this server using an FTP client program and download any desired files. Most FTP servers available on the Internet allow any user to connect and are, hence, called anonymous FTP servers. Furthermore, most operating systems, such as Linux, UNIX, Microsoft Windows, and macOS, are distributed with an FTP client program, making it easy for users to connect to these FTP servers.

Note

Although several FTP service software programs are available for Linux, the most commonly used is the Very Secure FTP Server, which can be downloaded at *security.appspot.com/vsftpd.html*.

Authentication Services

To access any computer securely, you must log in using a valid username and password before gaining access to the user interface. This process is called **authentication**. However, users today often need to securely access resources on several servers within their organization, and each of these computers requires that you authenticate before access is granted. To ensure that you do not need to enter your username and password on every network computer that you access within your organization, you can configure your computer to log into an authentication service on a network server using a protocol, such as **Kerberos**. After you log into an authentication service using Kerberos successfully, you receive a Kerberos ticket that your computer presents to all other computers within your organization to prove your identity. Microsoft Active Directory is one of the most common Kerberos-based authentication services, and every Linux computer can be easily configured to log into it. However, organizations can install other alternate authentication services on Linux servers, including the Kerberos-based Apache Directory.

Note

You can learn more about Apache Directory at *directory.apache.org*.

Certificate Services

Because data is frequently passed across networks to other computers, the data within them could easily be intercepted and read by crackers. To prevent this, many technologies use an encryption algorithm to protect the data before it is transmitted on the network. An encryption algorithm uses a series of mathematical steps in sequence to scramble data. Because the steps within encryption algorithms are widely known, nearly all encryption algorithms use a random component called a **key** to modify the steps within the algorithm. **Symmetric encryption** algorithms are reversible; data can be decrypted by reversing the algorithm using the same key that was used to encrypt it. Unfortunately, it is difficult for two computers on a network to communicate this key. As a result, network technologies typically use **asymmetric encryption** to protect the data that travels across the network. Asymmetric encryption uses a pair of keys that are uniquely generated on each system: a **public key** and a **private key**. You can think of a public key as the opposite of a private key. If you encrypt data using a public key, that data can only be decrypted using the matching private key. Alternatively, if you encrypt data using a private key, that data can only be decrypted using the matching public key. Each system must contain at least one public/private key pair. The public key is freely distributed to any other host on the network, whereas the private key is used only by the system and never distributed.

Say, for example, that you want to send an encrypted message from your computer (host A) to another computer (host B). Your computer would first obtain the public key from host B and use it to encrypt the message. Next, your computer will send the encrypted message across the network to host B, at which point host B uses its private key to decrypt the message. Because host B is the only computer on the network with the private key that matches the public key you used to encrypt the message, host B is the only computer on the network that can decrypt the message.

You can also use private keys to authenticate a message. If host A encrypts a message using its private key and sends that message to host B, host B (and any other host on the network) can easily obtain the matching public key from host A to decrypt the message. By successfully decrypting the message, host B has proved that it must have been encrypted using host A's private key. Because host A is the only computer on the network that possesses this private key, host B has proven that the message was sent by host A and not another computer that has impersonated the sender.

> **Note** 🖉
>
> A message that has been encrypted using a private key is called a **digital signature**.

> **Note** 🖉
>
> Most network technologies use symmetric encryption to encrypt data that is sent on a network, and asymmetric encryption to securely communicate the symmetric encryption key between computers on the network.

> **Note** 🖉
>
> Common symmetric encryption algorithms include AES, 3DES, and RC4. Common asymmetric encryption algorithms include DH, RSA, and ECC.

Because public keys are transmitted across a network, a cracker could substitute her own public key in place of another public key to hijack encrypted communications. To prevent this, nearly all public keys are digitally signed by a trusted third-party computer called a **Certification Authority (CA)**. Many commercial CAs digitally sign certificates for a fee, including Verisign, GeoTrust, eTrust, and Comodo. Alternatively, an organization can install its own CA to digitally sign public keys for use by its own computers when communicating across networks and the Internet. Common CA software packages for Linux include OpenSSL and OpenXPKI.

Note

A public key that has been digitally signed by a CA is called a **certificate**.

Note

An organization that installs one or more CAs is said to have a **Public Key Infrastructure (PKI)**.

Note

You can learn more about OpenSSL at *www.openssl.org*. To learn more about OpenXPKI, visit *www.openxpki.org*.

Routing Services

Routing is a core service that is necessary for the Internet to function. The Internet is merely a large network of interconnected networks; in other words, it connects company networks, home networks, and institutional networks so that they can communicate with each other. A router is a computer or a special hardware device that provides this interconnection; it contains information regarding the structure of the Internet and sends information from one network to another. Companies can use routers to connect their internal networks to the Internet as well as to connect their networks together inside the company. Linux is a good choice for this service as it provides support for routing and is easily customizable; many Linux distributions, each of which can fit within a few megabytes of flash storage, provide routing capabilities.

Firewall and Proxy Services

The term "firewall" describes the structures that prevent a fire from spreading. In the automobile industry, a firewall protects the passengers in a car if a fire breaks out in the engine compartment. Just as an automobile firewall protects passengers, a computer firewall protects companies from outside intruders on the Internet. Most firewalls are computers that are placed between the company network and the company's connection to the Internet; all traffic must then pass through this firewall, allowing the company to control traffic at the firewall, based on a complex set of rules. Linux has firewall support built directly into the kernel. Utilities such as netfilter/iptables, which are included with nearly all Linux distributions, can be used to configure the rules necessary to make a system a firewall.

Note

You can find out more about using netfilter/iptables to configure Linux firewalls at *netfilter.org*.

Because firewalls are usually located between a company's internal network and the Internet, they often provide other services that allow computers inside the company easy access to the Internet. The most common of these services are known as proxy services. A **proxy server** requests Internet resources, such as websites and FTP sites, on behalf of the computer inside the company. In other words, a workstation computer inside the company sends a request to the proxy server connected to the Internet. The proxy server then obtains and returns the requested information to the workstation computer. One proxy server can allow thousands of company workstation computers access to the Internet simultaneously without lengthy configuration of the workstation computers; proxy servers keep track of the information passed to each client by maintaining a Network Address Translation (NAT) table. Although netfilter/iptables can perform NAT capabilities, Squid is the most common fully featured proxy server used on Linux. Squid retains a copy of any requested Internet resources (via a process known as caching) so that it can respond more quickly to future requests for the same resources.

Note

To obtain or find information regarding the Squid proxy server, visit *www.squid-cache.org*.

Advanced Security Services

Today, organizations use specialized server hardware running Linux that may provide routing, firewall, and proxy services alongside additional advanced security services. These servers are called **security appliances** and are used to provide security between an organization's network and the Internet. Many Linux-based commercial security appliances and security appliance software suites for Linux provide one or more of the following services:

- Malware and virus filtering
- Spam filtering
- Bot protection
- Intrusion detection
- Advanced traffic throttling
- Virtual Private Network (VPN) functionality

- Centralized event logging for network devices using Simple Network Management Protocol (SNMP)
- Security Information and Event Management (SIEM) for centralized network and security monitoring

---

Note

Security appliances that provide multiple security functions are often called **Next Generation Firewall (NGFW)** or **Unified Threat Management (UTM)** appliances.

Note

A common open source SIEM security appliance that runs on Linux is AlienVault OSSIM, which is available at *www.alienvault.com/ossim*.

Note

Some routers, firewalls, and security appliances can also separate requests for a specific resource, such as a website, across several servers that provide the same service; this feature is called **load balancing**, and can be used to provide fast, fault-tolerant access to specific services.

File and Print Servers

Networks were created to share resources, primarily printers and information. In business, it is not cost-effective to purchase and install a printer on the computer of every user who needs to print. It is far easier and cheaper to install one central printer on a server and let multiple users print to it across the computer network. Often, information must also be commonly available to users to allow them to collaborate on projects or perform their daily jobs. Duplicating data on every user machine would consume too much hard drive space and coordinating changes to this data would be nearly impossible. By employing a network, this information can be made available to all who need it and kept up to date. Another benefit to this central storage of information is that a user can access data regardless of the computer that he logs into. Central storage also allows a company to safeguard its information by using devices to back up or make copies of stored data on a regular basis in case of computer failure. Most companies perform backups of data at least every week to ensure that if data is lost on the central server, it can be restored from a back-up copy quickly.

Linux is well suited to the task of centrally sharing resources. It is inherently a fast, light operating system, and a distribution suited to the task can be installed on the central server. Linux can share information with other Linux, UNIX, and macOS machines using services such as Network File System (NFS) and Common UNIX Printing System (CUPS), and share resources with computers running other operating systems, such as Microsoft Windows. Client computers can access a shared resource on a server running Linux provided that server has the appropriate service available. The most common service used to allow Windows clients to connect to shared information and printers on a Linux server is Samba.

Note 🖉

Samba can be found at *www.samba.org*.

Application Servers

An application server is a computer running a program that acts as an intermediary between a client computer and the information, normally stored in a database, the client computer needs. A **database** is an organized collection of data that is arranged into tables of related information. The client requests some data to change or view, and the application server interacts with the database to manipulate and retrieve the required information. This is often described as a front-end/back-end relationship. The front end runs on the client computer and is the interface the user sees and interacts with to request data. The front end takes this request, formulates it so that the server can understand it, and passes the request along to the back-end application running on the server. The back-end application interacts with the database and returns the results to the front-end application on the client computer, which displays it in a user-friendly format for the user.

With the rapid development of the Internet in the 1990s, many companies centralized their key software elements on Internet application servers, making it possible to serve client computers worldwide. This approach saves both time and money when changes need to be made to the software. It also means only one central database needs to be maintained. **Database management systems (DBMSs)** are a collection of programs and tools designed to allow for the creation, modification, manipulation, maintenance, and access of information from databases.

Several free open source DBMS programs and tools facilitate creating, managing, and retrieving data from a database as well as interacting with closed source databases, including those from Microsoft and Oracle.

The most popular and widely used DBMSs available for Linux today are PostgreSQL, MySQL (My Structured Query Language), and MariaDB (based on MySQL). All three are powerful, fast, and light, and they can interact with other databases such as Oracle. They can also be integrated with most Web servers via CGI scripts for use as an application server on the Internet and are supported by most other open source technologies.

Note

To learn more about PostgreSQL, visit *www.postgresql.org*. To learn more about MySQL, visit *www.mysql.com*. To learn more about MariaDB, visit *mariadb.org*.

Application servers need not only be used for interaction with databases; they can provide management functionality as well, allowing access and administration from anywhere in the world via the Internet. Management interfaces have taken advantage of the comprehensive development surrounding client Web browsers and Internet technologies and now offer a full range of computer management capabilities from the comfortable and standard interface of the client Web browser. One common open source management interface for Linux is Webmin, a customizable application server that allows users to manage almost all services available in Linux from anywhere on the Internet.

Note

Webmin can be found at *www.webmin.com*.

Cloud Systems

Simply put, the **cloud** is just another term for the Internet. Organizations are moving their data to servers that are hosted within data centers accessible across the Internet. This process is often referred to as "moving data to the cloud."

Cloud servers offer the advantage of accessing their data from anywhere on the Internet. Because the cost of a data center can be shared by many organizations, data can be made fault tolerant at a lower cost. Organizations may even host their own private data center that is accessible to other computers across the Internet; this is often called a **private cloud**, and the organization is referred to as a **cloud provider**. Regardless of whether it is public or private, there are three main approaches to hosting data and services within the cloud: SaaS, PaaS, and IaaS.

Software as a Service (SaaS) refers to hosting a service (and the associated data) within a cloud environment, where users can access the service across the Internet. Facebook, Twitter, PayPal, Dropbox, and Microsoft Office 365 are all examples of SaaS.

Platform as a Service (PaaS) differs from SaaS in that companies can create their own Web apps and services that are hosted by another cloud provider. Companies need to ensure that their Web apps and services adhere to the rules set by the cloud provider. Common PaaS cloud providers include Amazon Web Services (AWS), IBM Bluemix, Google App Engine, and Microsoft Azure.

Infrastructure as a Service (IaaS) differs from both SaaS and PaaS in that the cloud provider provides the hardware and storage within a data center only, and companies install, manage, and access their own virtualized operating systems within that data center via **cloud platform** software. OpenStack is one of the most popular open source cloud platform software suites and is supported by nearly all major Linux distributions.

Note

You can find more information about OpenStack at *www.openstack.org*.

Note

A virtualized operating system used by IaaS can be either an entire operating system or a subset of an existing operating system (called a **container**) that provides a unique service on the network. Virtual operating systems and containers have a unique name and IP address, and appear as separate servers to other computers on the network. Many PaaS providers also use containers to host the Web apps and services for organizations within the cloud.

Because Linux is OSS and doesn't require expensive licensing, it is often used to implement SaaS, PaaS, and IaaS and to be hosted within a virtualized IaaS cloud platform. In fact, Linux comprised over 90 percent of the public cloud in 2017, which is often reflected by posts on websites and social media sites as shown in Figure 1-7.

Figure 1-7 A Reddit post regarding Linux cloud market share
Source: Reddit

Supercomputers

Many companies and institutions use computers to perform extraordinarily large calculations for which most computers would be unsuitable. To accomplish these tasks, companies either buy computers with multiple processors or use specialized services to combine several smaller computers in a way that allows them to function as one large supercomputer. Combining several smaller computers is called **clustering**. Companies and individuals requiring this type of computing make up the supercomputing community, which is growing quickly as technology advances in new directions.

Although it might seem logical to purchase computers with many processors, the performance of a computer relative to the number of processors decreases as you add processors to a computer. In other words, a computer with 64 processors does not handle 64 times as much work as one processor because of physical limitations within the computer hardware itself; a computer with 64 processors might only perform 50 times as much work as a single processor. The ability for a computer to increase workload as the number of processors increases is known as **scalability**, and most computers, regardless of the operating system used, do not scale well with more than 32 processors. As a result of this limitation, many people in the supercomputing community **cluster** small computers to work as one large computer. This approach results in much better scalability; 64 computers with one processor each working toward a common goal can handle close to 64 times as much as a single processor.

Most of the supercomputing community has focused on Linux when developing clustering technology; the most common method of Linux clustering is known as **Beowulf clustering**, which is easy to configure and well documented. One way to implement a Beowulf cluster is to have one master computer send instructions to several slave computers, which compute parts of the calculation concurrently and send their results back to the master computer using a **Message Passing Interface (MPI)** software framework such as OpenMPI. This type of supercomputing breaks tasks into smaller units and executes them in parallel on many machines at once; thus, it is commonly referred to as parallel supercomputing. Many free programs are written to run on parallelized computers. Beowulf parallel supercomputer technology has been aggressively developed since the mid-1990s and has been tested in various environments; currently, institutions, companies, and universities host thousands of Beowulf clusters worldwide.

> **Note**
>
> You can find more information about OpenMPI at *www.open-mpi.org*.

> **Note**
>
> Clustering can also be used on a smaller scale to provide fault tolerance for two or more Internet, file and print, or application servers that host the same data and services. By installing a cluster service on these servers, you can provide a single identity for the services on the servers that other computers can access. If one of the clustered servers fails, the other servers within the cluster will seamlessly respond to requests sent to this single identity.

Scientific/Engineering Workstations

Many developers from Richard Stallman's Free Software Foundation came from the scientific and engineering community, which needed to develop programs to run analyses. In the 1980s and early 1990s, this scientific and engineering community largely developed software for the UNIX operating system that was common in universities around the world; today, this community is focusing on developing software for Linux. Any software previously made for UNIX can be ported to Linux easily. Scientists and engineers often use parallel supercomputers to compute large tasks, and OSS developers, with a background in scientific computing, have done much of the development on Beowulf technology. One example is SHARCnet

(Shared Hierarchical Academic Research Computing Network) in Ontario, Canada, in which several universities have developed and tested supercomputing technology and parallel programs for use in the scientific and engineering fields.

Note

You can find more information about SHARCnet at *www.sharcnet.ca*.

Often, the programs that are required by the scientific and engineering community must be custom developed to suit the needs of the people involved; however, many OSS programs, which you can use or modify, are freely available in scientific and engineering fields, including, but not limited to the following list:

- Physics, Astrophysics, and Biophysics
- Fluid Dynamics and Geophysics
- Biocomputation
- Materials and Polymer Chemistry
- General Mathematics and Optimization
- Data Mining
- Number Theory
- Computer/Linear/Array Algebra
- Mathematical Visualization and Modeling
- Statistics and Regression Analysis
- Data Plotting and Processing
- Computer Graphics Generation
- Computer Modeling
- Paleontology
- Molecular Modeling
- Electrical Engineering
- Artificial Intelligence
- Geographic Modeling and Earth Sciences
- Oceanography

Office/Personal Workstations

Server services for Linux were the primary focus of OSS development for Linux in the 1990s, but since 2000, this focus has been expanded to other types of software, including workstation software designed to benefit users in the office and home environments. By definition, a workstation is a single-user computer, more powerful than a typical home system; however, people often call any single-user computer that is not a server a workstation. It is where users work and interact, running programs and connecting to servers. Today, you find Linux on desktop and laptop computers running OSS packages that allow the user to create, organize, and manipulate office documents and graphic art, including but not limited to the following:

- Graphics editing software (such as Gimp)
- Desktop publishing software (such as Scribus)
- Media software (such as VLC)
- Financial software (such as Gnucash)
- Office productivity suites (such as Apache OpenOffice)
- Bittorrent clients (such as qBitTorrent)

Cybersecurity Workstations

Organizations need security to protect their data on systems and networks. The technologies and processes used to analyze existing security and provide data protections are collectively referred to as **cybersecurity**. Those who work within a cybersecurity field must use specialized tools to scan key computers and networks for security vulnerabilities (called a **vulnerability assessment**) as well as attempt to break into systems to test the strength of their security measures (called a **penetration test**). Additionally, cybersecurity workers must continually monitor the security of systems and networks to determine when a system has been breached, as well as perform forensic analysis to investigate the nature of the breach and the damage incurred.

Most of the tools for performing a vulnerability assessment and penetration test, as well as the tools for detecting and investigating security breaches are exclusively for Linux systems. Thus, anyone working within a cybersecurity field will use a Linux workstation. Several cybersecurity-focused Linux distributions, such as Kali Linux, ship with most of these tools preinstalled for cybersecurity use.

Note

You can obtain and learn more about Kali Linux at *www.kali.org*.

Mobile Devices

In the past decade, mobile devices such as tablets and smartphones have grown tremendously in popularity. Today, mobile computing is the primary means of communication for millions of people worldwide.

Following the introduction of the Apple iPhone in 2007, several Linux-based smartphone and tablet operating systems started to appear on the market. The most notable of these was Google **Android** in 2008. Linux provides the core architecture used on Google Android devices, and an additional Android framework provides for user functionality. Android was acquired by Google in 2005 and is currently developed by Google's Open Handset Alliance, which consists of nearly 100 hardware and software manufacturers.

Due to its open nature and number of associated smartphone manufacturers, consumer, professional, and developer support for Android has grown exponentially in recent years. Today, you can find Android on many other devices that provide specialized user interfaces, such as televisions, storage systems, cars, watches, and eyeglasses. By 2017, Android was installed on over 85 percent of smartphones in the world, and the Google Play Store (Google's Android app store) hosted more than 3.5 million apps and provided over 85 billion downloads.

Although Google Android is the most successful mobile application of Linux, you may find other Linux distributions on mobile devices, including but not limited to the following:

- AsteroidOS
- postmarketOS
- Sailfish OS
- SHR
- Tizen
- Ubuntu Touch

Chapter Summary

- Linux is an operating system whose kernel and associated software packages are freely developed and improved upon by a large community of software developers in collaboration. It is based on the UNIX operating system and has roots in the hacker culture perpetuated by the Free Software Foundation.

- Because Linux is published under the GNU Public License, it is referred to as Open Source Software (OSS). Most additional software that is run on Linux is also OSS.

- Companies find Linux a stable, low-risk, and flexible alternative to other operating systems; it can be installed on several hardware platforms to meet business needs and results in a lower TCO.

- Linux is available in various distributions, all of which have a common kernel but are packaged with different OSS applications.

- A wide variety of documentation and resources for Linux exists in the form of websites, HOWTOs, FAQs, newsgroups, and LUGs.

- Linux is an extremely versatile operating system that can provide a wide range of workstation and server services to meet most computing needs of companies and individuals.

Key Terms

AIX
Android
application (app)
Arch
artistic license
asymmetric encryption
authentication
Beowulf clustering
BSD (Berkeley Software Distribution)
certificate
Certification Authority (CA)
closed source software
cloud
cloud platform
cloud provider
cluster
clustering
container
cracker
cybersecurity
database
Database Management System (DBMS)
Debian
developmental kernel
device driver
digital signature
distribution
distribution kernel
Domain Name Space (DNS)
Dynamic Host Configuration Protocol (DHCP)
flavor
Free Software Foundation (FSF)
freeware
frequently asked questions (FAQs)
fully qualified domain name (FQDN)

Gentoo
GNU
GNU General Public License (GPL)
GNU Network Object Model Environment (GNOME)
GNU Project
graphical user interface (GUI)
GUI environment
hacker
hardware
hardware platform
hot fix
HOWTO
HP-UX
Infrastructure as a Service (IaaS)
Internet Protocol (IP) address
iOS
K Desktop Environment (KDE)
Kerberos
kernel
key
Linus Torvalds
Linux
Linux Documentation Project (LDP)
Linux Mint
Linux User Group (LUG)
load balancing
macOS
Mail Delivery Agent (MDA)
Mail Transfer Agent (MTA)
Mail User Agent (MUA)
major number
Message Passing Interface (MPI)
MINIX
minor number

Multiplexed Information and Computing Service (MULTICS)
multitasking
multiuser
Network Time Protocol (NTP)
newsgroup
Next Generation Firewall (NGFW)
Open Source Software (OSS)
openSUSE
operating system (OS)
package manager
penetration test
Platform as a Service (PaaS)
private cloud
private key
process
production kernel
program
programming language
proxy server
public key
Public Key Infrastructure (PKI)
Red Hat
revision number
router
scalability
search engine
security appliance
server
server services
shareware
software
Software as a Service (SaaS)
source code
symmetric encryption
system service
tarball

total cost of ownership (TCO)	UNIX	workstation
Ubuntu	user	workstation services
Unified Threat Management (UTM)	user interface	X Windows
	vulnerability assessment	

Review Questions

1. Every computer consists of physical components and non-physical components. The non-physical components of a computer that understand how to work with the physical components are referred to as _____.
   a. hardware
   b. records
   c. software
   d. processors

2. The operating system software is necessary for a computer to function. True or False?

3. Linux is a _____ and _____ operating system.
   a. production, stable
   b. multiuser, multitasking
   c. processing, closed source
   d. large, useful

4. The core component of the Linux operating system is the Linux kernel. If you were a Linux systems administrator for a company, when would you need to upgrade your Linux kernel? (Choose all that apply.)
   a. when you need support in Linux for new hardware
   b. when you need another user interface
   c. when you need to increase the stability of Linux
   d. when you need to use kernel modules

5. Which of the following kernels are developmental kernels? (Choose all that apply.)
   a. 2.3.4
   b. 3.5.5
   c. 4.1-rc5
   d. 4.4.4

6. Many types of software are available today. Which type of software does Linux represent?
   a. open source software
   b. closed source software
   c. freeware
   d. shareware

7. Which of the following are characteristics of Open Source Software? (Choose all that apply.)
   a. The value of the software is directly related to its price.
   b. The software is developed collaboratively.
   c. The source code for software is available for a small fee.
   d. Any bugs are fixed quickly.

8. To which license does Linux adhere?
   a. open license
   b. artistic license
   c. GNU General Public License
   d. free source license

9. What are some good reasons for using Linux in a corporate environment? (Choose all that apply.)
   a. Linux software is unlikely to be abandoned by its developers.
   b. Linux is secure and has a lower total cost of ownership than other operating systems.
   c. Linux is widely available for many platforms and supports many programming languages.
   d. Most Linux software is closed source.

10. Which of the following are common methods for gaining support for Linux?
   a. HOWTO documents at *www.tldp.org*
   b. a local Linux User Group
   c. Internet newsgroups
   d. all the above

11. Which two people are credited with creating the UNIX operating system? (Choose two answers.)
   a. Dennis Ritchie
   b. Richard Stallman
   c. Linus Torvalds
   d. Ken Thompson

12. Who formed the Free Software Foundation to promote open development?
   a. Dennis Ritchie
   b. Richard Stallman
   c. Linus Torvalds
   d. Ken Thompson

13. Which culture embraced the term "GNU" (GNU's Not UNIX) and laid the free software groundwork for Linux?
   a. the hacker culture
   b. the MIT culture
   c. the cracker culture
   d. the Artificial Intelligence culture

14. Linux was developed by _____ to resemble the _____ operating system.
   a. Linus Torvalds, MINIX
   b. Linus Torvalds, GNU
   c. Richard Stallman, GNU
   d. Richard Stallman, MINIX

15. When the core components of the Linux operating system are packaged together with other Open Source Software, it is called a _____.
   a. new kernel
   b. new platform
   c. Linux distribution
   d. GNU Project

16. Which common GUI environments are available in most Linux distributions? (Choose all that apply.)
   a. GNOME
   b. CDE
   c. KDE
   d. RPM

17. Which of the following are factors that determine which Linux distribution a user will use? (Choose all that apply.)
   a. package manager support
   b. hardware platform
   c. kernel features
   d. language support

18. What is the most common open source Web server available for Linux?
   a. Samba
   b. Apache
   c. Squid
   d. OpenStack

19. Which of the following can be used on Linux to provide file and print services?

a. Samba

b. Apache

c. Squid

d. OpenStack

20. Which of the following Linux distributions is likely to be used by a cybersecurity worker?

a. Fedora

b. Ubuntu

c. Kali

d. Gentoo

Discovery Exercises

1. You work for a large manufacturing company which is considering Linux as a solution for some or all servers in its IT Department. The company hosts an Oracle database on UNIX, and the UNIX servers that host this database contain several small programs that were custom made. Furthermore, Windows 10 is currently used on desktops throughout the company, and users store their data on Windows Server 2016 file servers. What considerations must you keep in mind before migrating your company's servers to Linux? Which distribution(s) and Open Source Software would you choose to accomplish this? If you need to create a report detailing the benefits of moving to an open source solution using Linux, what benefits would you list in the report to persuade others in the company that Linux lowers the total cost of ownership?

2. At a local Linux User Group (LUG) meeting, some people who are unfamiliar with Linux ask you to explain what the GPL is and how it relates to OSS. These people also don't understand how OSS generates profit and are under the impression that the quality of OSS is poor compared to commercial software. They suggest that the potential for OSS in the future might be limited. How do you reply? Include examples to demonstrate your points. To which websites can you direct them for further information?

3. As a software developer working for a large clothing store chain, you are responsible for creating software used to connect retail store computers to a central database at the head office. Recently, some friends of yours suggested that you publish your software under the GPL. What are some direct benefits to publishing your software under the GPL? To publish software made for a company under the GPL, you need the company's permission because the company owns any software that it pays developers to create. When you approach people in your company regarding OSS and explain how companies benefit from releasing software as open source, you are asked what benefits the company will receive from funding an open source project over time. Your company also wants to know what the procedure is for releasing and maintaining OSS. What benefits will you offer them? Where could you send them to gain more information on procedures involved in the open source community?

4. You are a network administrator who is in charge of a medium-sized Linux network. The company you work for asks you to implement routing in the network, a topic with which you are unfamiliar. Where could you go to learn what you must obtain to enable routing on your Linux network? Provided that you have a functional Web browser and an Internet connection, explore this topic on the Internet and list the websites that you used to obtain the information required. This information might range from broad descriptions of what you need to do to accomplish a certain task to detailed guides and instructions on putting your plan into action. From these sources of information, devise a report outlining the major steps necessary to implement routing on your network.

5. At a company function, a top executive corners you and complains that your department is wasting too much money. The executive demands to know why the company must spend so much money on computers and software, especially operating systems and related licenses (for closed source programs and operating systems). Write a report that defends your department by explaining the nature of hardware, software, and operating systems. In the report, be sure to explain how OSS and the Linux operating system can be used to reduce these costs in the long term.

6. You are contacted by a project organizer for a university computer science fair. The project organizer asks you to hold a forum that discusses the origins of the Linux operating system, including how it has evolved and continues to develop. The main focus of this forum is to encourage university students toward participating in the open source community; therefore, it should detail the philosophy, major features, and methods of the hacker culture. Prepare a bulleted list of the major topics that you will discuss and write some sample questions that you anticipate from the participants as well as your responses.

7. Research three different distributions of Linux on the Internet. Record where you went to obtain your information. Compare and contrast the distributions with regard to their strengths and the packages available for each. After you finish, locate and visit two Linux newsgroups. How did you locate them and where did you obtain the information? What are the topics specific to each? Find two questions per newsgroup posted by a user in need of a solution to a problem, and follow the thread of responses suggested by others to solve that problem.

## CHAPTER 2

LINUX INSTALLATION AND USAGE

After completing this chapter, you will be able to:

Prepare for and install Fedora Linux using good practices

Outline the structure of the Linux interface

Enter basic shell commands and find command documentation

Properly shut down the Linux operating system

This chapter explores the concepts and procedures needed to install a Fedora Linux system. The latter half of the chapter presents an overview of the various components that you will use when interacting with the operating system, as well as how to enter basic shell commands, obtain help, and properly shut down the Linux system.

Installing Linux

Installing Linux requires careful planning as well as configuring parts of the Linux operating system via an installation program.

Preparing for Installation

An operating system is merely a series of software programs that interact with and control the computer hardware. Thus, all operating systems have a certain minimum set of computer hardware requirements to function properly. Although most up-to-date hardware is sufficient to run the Linux operating system, it is, nonetheless, important to ensure that a computer meets the minimum hardware requirements before performing an installation.

These minimum installation requirements can be obtained from several sources. If you obtained the operating system on DVD, a printed manual or file on the DVD might specify these requirements. You can also find the minimum hardware requirements for most operating systems on the vendor's website. For the Fedora 28 Linux operating system, you can find the minimum hardware requirements at *docs.fedoraproject.org* or in Table 2-1.

Table 2-1	Fedora 28 recommended minimum hardware requirements
Type of hardware	**Requirement**
Central processing unit (CPU)	1GHz or faster Intel x64 CPU
Random access memory (RAM)	1GB
Free disk space (permanent storage)	10GB free space
Additional drives	DVD drive (for DVD-based installation)
Peripheral devices	Fedora-compliant peripheral devices (e.g., video cards, sound cards, network cards)

Furthermore, each operating system supports only particular types of hardware components. While modern Linux distributions support nearly all hardware components available on the market, it's good practice to check a hardware vendor's website to see whether uncommon components are compatible with Linux. Additionally, many Linux distribution websites and computer manufacturer websites have a Linux **Hardware Compatibility List (HCL)** that identifies whether the computer and hardware have Linux driver support.

Note

You can visit *linux-drivers.org* to locate hardware and distribution-specific HCLs.

Understanding Installation Media

Before performing a Linux installation, you must choose the source of the Linux packages and the installation program itself. The most common source of these packages is DVD media.

To install from DVD, you place the Linux DVD in the DVD drive and turn on the computer. Most computers automatically search for a startup program on the DVD immediately after being turned on; the computer can then use the DVD to start the Linux installation. Alternatively, most modern computers allow you to manually select the boot device using a special manufacturer-specific key, such as F12, during the startup sequence.

> **Note** 📎
>
> Turning on a computer to load an operating system is commonly referred to as booting a computer. Because the Linux installation program on DVD can be loaded when you first turn on the computer, it is referred to as a bootable DVD.

Nearly all Linux distributions provide a website from which you can download DVD images (called **ISO images**) that have an .iso file extension. These ISO images can be written to a blank writable DVD using disc burning software on a Windows, Linux, or Macintosh computer and then used to boot your computer to start the Linux installation.

In addition to a standard Linux installation DVD image, many Linux distribution websites allow you to download a bootable **live media** DVD image. If you write a live media DVD image to a blank DVD and boot your computer with it, a fully functional graphical Linux operating system that you can use will be loaded into RAM. This allows you to test the operating system on your computer to ensure that all hardware drivers were detected properly before installing it to permanent storage, such as hard disk or **solid-state drive (SSD)**. After you are satisfied with the functionality of your Linux system loaded from live media, you can select the appropriate icon on the desktop to start the installation program that will install the Linux system to permanent storage.

> **Note** 📎
>
> To obtain a standard DVD image or live media DVD image of Fedora 28, you can visit *getfedora.org*.

If your computer does not have a DVD drive, you can still install Linux by imaging the standard DVD or live media DVD ISO image to a USB flash drive, provided that your computer supports booting from USB flash drive media. To make this process easier, many distributions provide a program and instructions that can be used to perform the imaging process. For Fedora Linux, you can download and install the Fedora Media

Writer tool on a Windows or Macintosh system, as shown in Figure 2-1. If you click Custom image, the Fedora Media Writer tool allows you to download the latest version of Fedora Workstation or Fedora Server as well as image an already downloaded DVD ISO image of Fedora to a USB flash drive. After clicking Custom image, you select the appropriate DVD ISO image and target USB flash drive, and then click Write to disk to start the imaging process.

Note 📎

You can download the Fedora Media Writer tool from *getfedora.org/workstation/download/*.

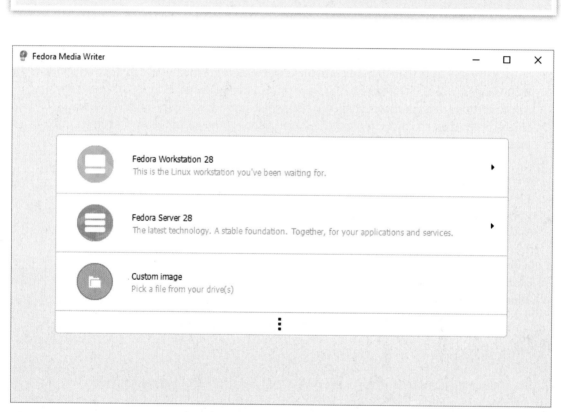

Figure 2-1 The Fedora Media Writer tool

After the imaging process is complete, you can insert your USB flash drive into a free USB slot, turn on your computer, use the appropriate key for your computer to select the target boot device (e.g., F12), and then choose the option to boot from your USB flash drive.

Many server and workstation computers today can run multiple operating systems concurrently using virtualization software. Several virtualization software products are available on the market today, including:

- Microsoft Hyper-V
- VMWare
- Oracle VM VirtualBox

Each operating system that is run within virtualization software is called a virtual machine, and the underlying operating system running the virtualization software is called the virtual machine host. Figure 2-2 shows a Fedora Linux virtual machine running on the Windows 10 operating system using the Microsoft Hyper-V virtualization software.

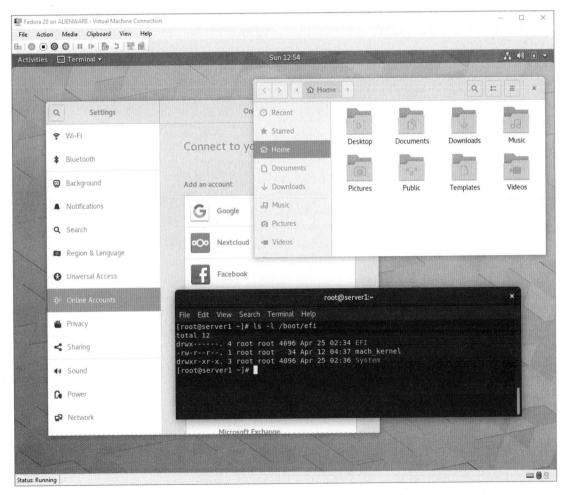

Figure 2-2   Fedora Linux running as a virtual machine on the Windows 10 operating system

Note

Most enterprise environments today take advantage of virtualization software to run multiple server operating systems concurrently on the same computer hardware. This allows organizations to better utilize their server hardware and reduce costs. Chapter 6 discusses this use of virtualization.

To install Linux as a virtual machine, you need to download the standard DVD or live media DVD ISO image to a directory on your virtual machine host (e.g., Windows). When you open the virtualization software and choose to create a new virtual machine, you can specify the file location of the appropriate ISO image, and the virtualization software will boot from the ISO image directly, without requiring you to

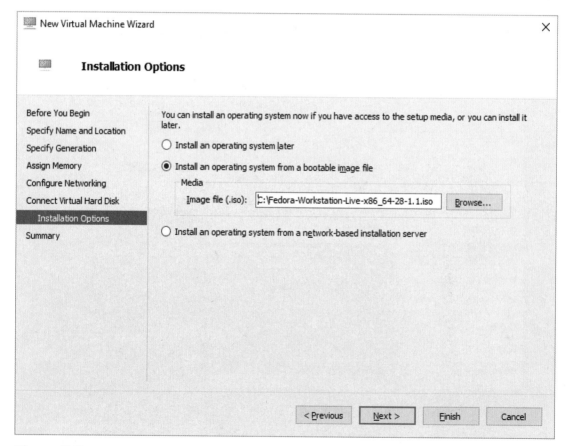

Figure 2-3   Selecting installation media within the Hyper-V New Virtual Machine Wizardv

write the ISO image to a DVD or a USB flash drive. Figure 2-3 shows the section of the Hyper-V New Virtual Machine Wizard that allows you to specify the location of an ISO image containing the Fedora 28 installation media.

Performing the Installation

Installing the Linux operating system involves interacting with an installation program, which prompts you for information regarding the nature of the Linux system being installed. More specifically, the installation program for Fedora 28 Linux involves the following general stages:

- Starting the installation
- Choosing an installation language, localization, and system options
- Configuring disk partitions and filesystems
- Configuring user accounts

Starting the Installation

As mentioned earlier, to perform an installation of Fedora Linux, you can boot your computer using Fedora installation media. If you are booting your system from standard Fedora installation media, you will be prompted to start the installation or perform troubleshooting actions. However, if you boot your system from Fedora live media, you will instead be prompted to start a live Fedora system (which later allows you to install Fedora), test your installation media, and start a live Fedora system or perform troubleshooting actions, as shown in Figure 2-4.

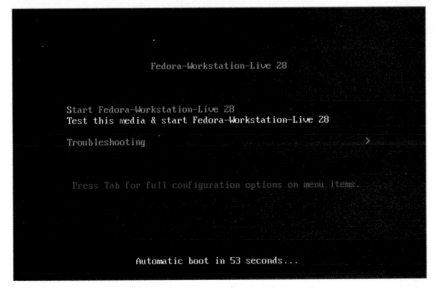

Figure 2-4   Beginning a Fedora installation

If you select the *Troubleshooting* option shown in Figure 2-4, you will be presented with four additional options, as shown in Figure 2-5.

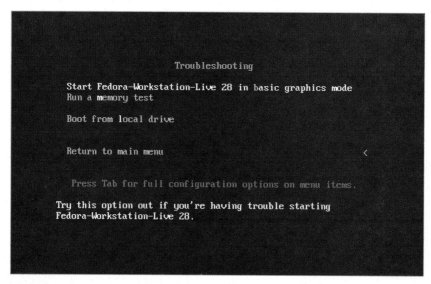

Figure 2-5   Fedora installation troubleshooting options

Selecting *Start Fedora-Workstation-Live 28 in basic graphics mode* shown in Figure 2-5 will start the Fedora system with generic video drivers and low resolution, which is useful if the live Fedora system doesn't detect the correct driver for your video card and cannot display a graphical desktop as a result.

Defective RAM is a common cause of a failed Linux installation. If you select *Run a memory test* shown in Figure 2-5, the **memtest86** utility will start and perform a thorough check of your RAM for hardware errors, as shown in Figure 2-6.

The *Boot from local drive* option shown in Figure 2-5 is useful if you forget to remove your Fedora installation media after the installation has completed and your

```
   Memtest86  5.01          | Intel(R) Xeon(R) CPU E5-1650 v2 @ 3.50GHz
CLK: 3500 MHz  (X64 Mode)    | Pass  0%
L1 Cache:   32K 140007 MB/s | Test 30% ###########
L2 Cache:  256K  57380 MB/s | Test #3  [Moving inversions, 1s & 0s Parallel]
L3 Cache:   12M  39774 MB/s | Testing: 1024K - 2048M   2047M of 4096M
Memory :  4096M  16279 MB/s | Pattern:   00000000            | Time:   0:00:04

Core#:  0 (SMP: Disabled)                | RAM: 1550MHz (DDR3-3100) - BCLK: 100
State: | Running...                      | Timings: CAS 19-15-15-31 @ 192-bit Mode
Cores:  1 Active / 1 Total (Run: All) | Pass:      0        Errors:      0


                            S  S
(ESC)exit  (c)configuration  (SP)scroll_lock  (CR)scroll_unlock          Locked
```

Figure 2-6   The memtest86 utility

system is configured to boot an operating system from your DVD or USB drive before searching for an operating system on permanent storage.

In most cases, the troubleshooting options shown in Figure 2-5 aren't necessary when installing Fedora Linux. As a result, you can choose *Start Fedora-Workstation-Live 28* shown in Figure 2-4 to start a live Fedora system. After the live Fedora system has loaded, you will be presented with a welcome screen that prompts you to install Fedora Linux on permanent storage or continue using the live Fedora system loaded from your installation media, as shown in Figure 2-7.

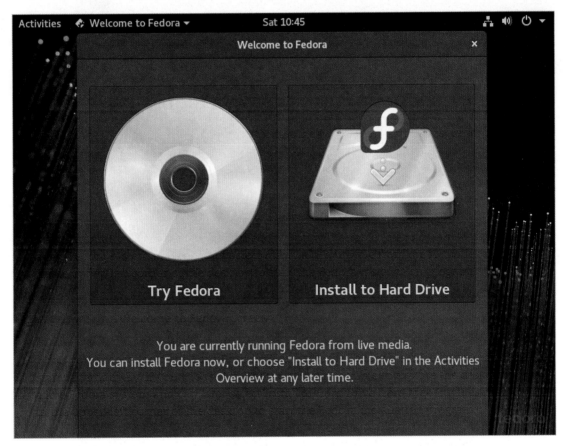

Figure 2-7   The Welcome to Fedora screen

If you choose *Install to Hard Drive* in Figure 2-7, the Fedora installation program will start. Alternatively, if you choose *Try Fedora*, you will be able to explore the desktop of a live Fedora system and can later select *Install to Hard Drive* from the Activities menu in the upper-left corner of the desktop to start the Fedora installation program.

Choosing an Installation Language, Localization, and System Options

After you start a Fedora installation, you will be prompted to select a language that is used during the installation program, as shown in Figure 2-8. If you click *Continue*, you will be prompted to configure the date and time, keyboard layout, and installation destination (e.g., hard disk, SSD) as shown in Figure 2-9.

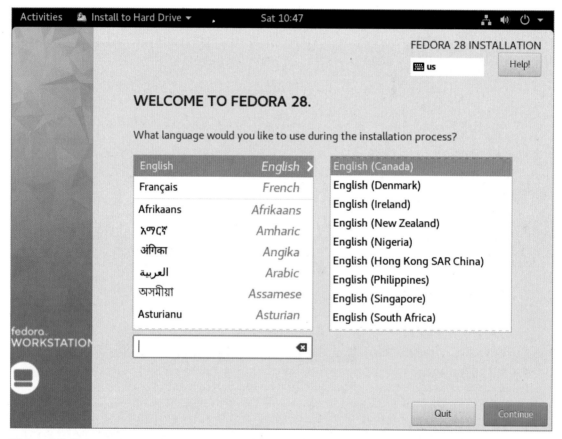

Figure 2-8   Selecting an installation language

You can click each of the localization and system option icons in Figure 2-9 to modify the configuration. By default, your keyboard layout is automatically detected, your network interface is set to obtain network configuration using the DHCP protocol, and the date and time are obtained from the Internet if your network has Internet connectivity. However, you must manually review the installation destination settings before the installation can continue (hence the warning shown in Figure 2-9). The installation destination is a permanent storage device that will contain the Linux operating system; it is often a hard disk or an SSD.

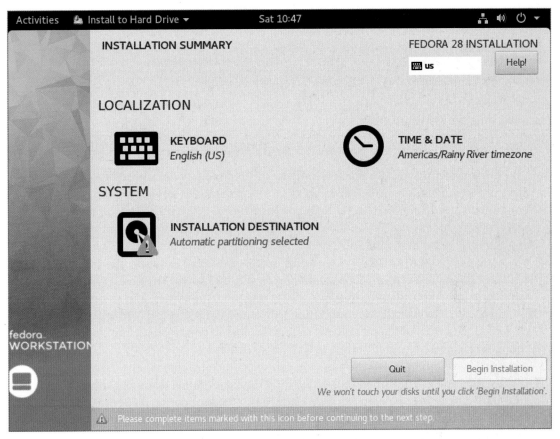

Figure 2-9 Configuring localization and system options

Older systems often use **Parallel Advanced Technology Attachment (PATA)** hard disks that physically connect to the computer in one of four configurations. As shown in Table 2-2, Linux refers to each of these disks according to its configuration on your computer.

 Note

In the past, PATA hard disks were referred to as **Integrated Drive Electronics (IDE)** or **Advanced Technology Attachment (ATA)** hard disks.

 Note

You can verify your PATA disk configuration by accessing your computer's **Basic Input/Output System (BIOS)** *configuration*. You can access your BIOS configuration by pressing the appropriate manufacturer-specific key, such as F10, during system startup.

Table 2-2	PATA hard disk configurations	
Description	**Linux name**
Primary master PATA hard disk	hda
Primary slave PATA hard disk	hdb
Secondary master PATA hard disk	hdc
Secondary slave PATA hard disk	hdd

Newer systems typically use **Serial Advanced Technology Attachment (SATA)** hard disks or SSDs or **Non-Volatile Memory Express (NVMe)** SSDs. Server systems have traditionally used **Small Computer Systems Interface (SCSI)** hard disks, and many server systems today use **Serial Attached SCSI (SAS)** hard disks or SSDs. Unlike PATA, you can have more than four SATA, NVMe, SCSI, and SAS hard disks or SSDs within a system. The first SATA/SCSI/SAS hard disk or SSD is referred to as sda, the second SATA/SCSI/SAS hard disk or SSD is referred to as sdb, and so on. The first NVMe SSD is referred to as nvme0, the second NVMe SSD is referred to as nvme1, and so on.

If you click the installation destination icon shown in Figure 2-9, you will be presented with a list of the permanent storage devices in your system. The system shown in Figure 2-10 contains a single SATA hard disk (sda).

If you have multiple disk devices, you can select the disk that will be used to contain the Fedora Linux operating system and then click *Done*. Normally, this is a local hard disk or SSD, but you can also install Linux on an external iSCSI or FCoE Storage Area Network (SAN), Direct Access Storage Device (DASD), Multipath IO (MPIO), or firmware **Redundant Array of Inexpensive Disks (RAID)** device if you select *Add a disk* shown in Figure 2-10 and supply the appropriate configuration information.

Configuring Disk Partitions and Filesystems

Regardless of type, each hard disk or SSD is divided into sections called **partitions**. Before you can store files in a partition, you must format it with a filesystem. A **filesystem** is a structure that specifies how data should reside on the hard disk or SSD itself.

> **Note** 🔗
>
> In the Windows operating system, each drive letter (e.g., C:, D:, E:) can correspond to a separate filesystem that resides on a partition on your hard disk or SSD.

There are limits to the number and types of partitions into which a hard disk or an SSD can be divided. By default, you can create a maximum of four major partitions (called **primary partitions**). To overcome this limitation, you can optionally label one

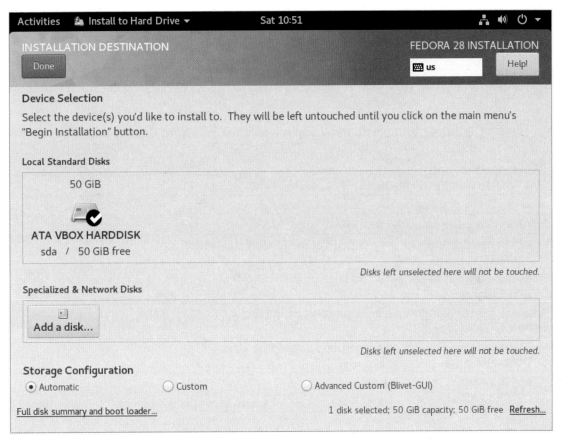

Figure 2-10   Configuring an installation destination

of these primary partitions as "extended"; this **extended partition** can then contain an unlimited number of smaller partitions called **logical drives**. Each logical drive within the extended partition and all other primary partitions can contain a filesystem and be used to store data. The table of all partition information for a certain hard disk or an SSD is stored in the first readable sector outside all partitions; it is called the **Master Boot Record (MBR)**. The MBR is limited to devices that are less than 2TB in size. Newer devices and devices larger than 2TB use a **GUID Partition Table (GPT)** instead of an MBR.

Note

The MBR and GPT are functionally equivalent.

Recall that, in Linux, the first SATA/SCSI/SAS device in your system is referred to as sda, the first primary partition on this device is labeled sda1, the second sda2, and so on. Because only four primary partitions are allowed on an MBR disk, logical drives inside the extended partition are labeled sda5, sda6, and so on. An example of this partition strategy is listed in Table 2-3.

Table 2-3   **Example MBR partitioning scheme for the first SATA/SCSI/SAS device**

Description	Linux name	Windows name
First primary partition on the first SATA/SCSI/SAS device	sda1	C:
Second primary partition on the first SATA/SCSI/SAS device	sda2	D:
Third primary partition on the first SATA/SCSI/SAS device	sda3	E:
Fourth primary partition on the first SATA/SCSI/SAS device (EXTENDED)	sda4	F:
First logical drive in the extended partition on the first SATA/SCSI/SAS device	sda5	G:
Second logical drive in the extended partition on the first SATA/SCSI/SAS device	sda6	H:
Third logical drive in the extended partition on the first SATA/SCSI/SAS device	sda7	I:

Note 📎

For the primary master PATA device, replace sda with hda in Table 2-3. NVMe devices can use **namespace** divisions in addition to partitions. As a result, the first NVMe partition (p1) within the first namespace (n1) on the first NVMe SSD (nvme0) would be called nvme0n1p1.

Note 📎

For devices that use a GPT instead of an MBR, there is no primary partition limitation, and hence no need for extended partitions or logical drives. The sda1 through sda7 partitions shown in Table 2-3 would refer to the first through seventh partitions on a GPT device.

Partitioning divides a hard disk into sections, each of which can contain a separate filesystem used to store data. Each of these filesystems can then be accessed by Linux if it is attached (or mounted) to a certain directory. When data is stored in that particular directory, it is physically stored on the respective filesystem on the hard disk.

The Fedora installation program can automatically create partitions based on common configurations; however, it is generally good practice to manually partition to suit the needs of the specific Linux system.

At minimum, Linux typically requires only two partitions to be created: a partition that is mounted to the root directory in Linux (/) and that can contain all of the files used by the operating system, applications, and users, and a partition used for **virtual memory** (also known as **swap memory**). Virtual memory consists of an area on the hard disk or SSD that can be used to store information that would normally reside in physical memory (RAM) if the physical memory was being used excessively. When programs are executed that require a great deal of resources on the computer, information is continuously swapped from physical memory to virtual memory, and vice versa. Traditionally, Linux swap partitions were made to be at least the size of the physical RAM in the computer; however, they can be much larger if the Linux system is intended to run large applications. A swap partition does not contain a filesystem and is never mounted to a directory because the Linux operating system is ultimately responsible for swapping information.

Although you might choose to create only root and swap partitions, extra partitions make Linux more robust against filesystem errors. For example, if the filesystem on one partition encounters an error, only data on one part of the system is affected and not the entire system (i.e., other filesystems). Because some common directories in Linux are used vigorously and as a result are more prone to failure, it is good practice to mount these directories to their own filesystems. Additionally, having a /boot partition allows your system to be recovered easily in the event of a boot-related issue, and is often a requirement if your / partition uses a particular technology that is not directly bootable, such as Logical Volume Manager (LVM) or B-tree Filesystem (BTRFS). Consequently, most Linux installation programs will create a /boot partition if you select the option to automatically have partitions created for you. Table 2-4 lists directories that are commonly mounted to separate partitions as well as their recommended sizes.

Each of these filesystems can be of different types. The most common types used today are the **ext2**, **ext3**, **ext4**, **VFAT**, and **XFS** filesystems, although Linux can support upward of 50 filesystems. Each filesystem essentially performs the same function, which is to store files on a partition; however, each filesystem offers different features and is specialized for different uses. The ext2 filesystem is the traditional filesystem, and the Virtual File Allocation Table (VFAT) filesystem is compatible with the FAT and FAT32 filesystems in Windows. The ext3, ext4, and XFS filesystems, however, are much more robust than the ext2 and VFAT filesystems, as they perform a function called journaling. A **journaling** filesystem uses a journal to keep track of the information written to the hard disk. If you copy a file on the hard disk from one directory to another, that file must pass into RAM and then be written to the new location on the hard disk. If the power to the computer is turned off during this process, information might not be transmitted as expected and data might be lost or corrupted.

Table 2-4	Common Linux filesystems and sizes	
Directory	**Description**	**Recommended size**
/	Contains all directories not present on other filesystems	Depends on the size and number of other filesystems present, but is typically 20GB or more
/boot	Contains the Linux kernel and boot files	1GB
/home	Default location for user home directories	500MB per user
/usr	System commands and utilities	Depends on the packages installed—typically 30GB or more
/usr/local	Location for most additional programs	Depends on the packages installed—typically 30GB or more
/opt	An alternate location for additional programs	Depends on the packages installed—typically 30GB or more
/var	Contains log files and spools	Depends on whether the Linux system is used as a print server (which contains a large spool). For print servers, 10GB or more is typical. For other systems, 2GB or more is usually sufficient.
/tmp	Holds temporary files created by programs	1GB

With a journaling filesystem, each step required to copy the file to the new location is first written to a journal; this means the system can retrace the steps the system took prior to a power outage and complete the file copy. These filesystems also host a variety of additional improvements compared to ext2 and VFAT, including faster data transfer and indexing, which makes them common choices for Linux servers today.

After you have selected the appropriate hard disk or SSD as an installation destination during the Fedora Linux installation shown in Figure 2-10, you must also choose whether the installation program should create partitions for you (*Automatic*), or whether you want to configure partitions manually (*Custom*) or manually using an advanced interface (*Advanced Custom*). If you choose *Custom* shown in Figure 2-10 and click *Done*, you will be prompted to choose the partitioning scheme, and optionally create a default partition layout that you can modify to suit your needs. If you choose a Standard partitioning scheme, this default partition layout will consist of a /boot and a / partition with an ext4 filesystem (not encrypted), as well as a swap partition that is the same size as the RAM in your computer, as shown in Figure 2-11.

In addition to the standard partitions that we have discussed already, you can instead choose a partition scheme that creates logical volumes for your Linux filesystems using the **Logical Volume Manager (LVM)** or partitions that support the new **B-tree Filesystem (BTRFS)**. LVM and BTRFS are discussed in Chapters 5 and 6.

To allow for easier system recovery, it is good form to choose a standard partition scheme and ensure that contents of disk partitions are not encrypted.

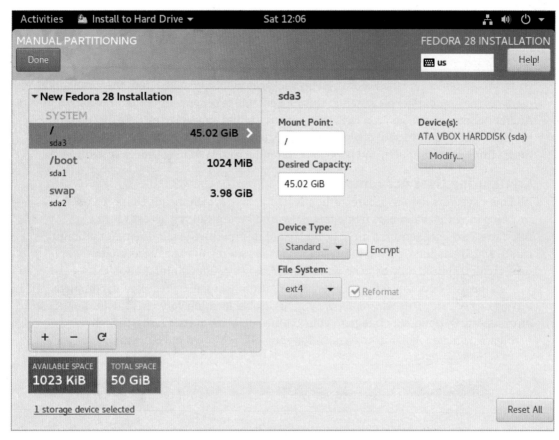

Figure 2-11   Configuring disk partitions and filesystems

Note

If your system has a **Unified Extensible Firmware Interface (UEFI)** BIOS on the motherboard, the installation program will also create a small **UEFI System Partition** to store boot-related information.

Note

If your system has a hard disk or an SSD that uses a GPT instead of an MBR and does not contain a UEFI BIOS on the motherboard, the installation program will also create a small **BIOS Boot partition** to store boot-related information.

After you are satisfied with your partition and filesystem configuration, you can click *Done* shown in Figure 2-11, confirm your changes in the dialog box that appears, and return to the localization and system options configuration screen shown in Figure 2-9. If you click the *Begin Installation* button in Figure 2-9, partition changes will be written to your storage device and the Fedora system packages will be installed from the installation media to the appropriate filesystems. This process will take some time to complete. After it has completed, you can click the *Quit* button that appears to exit the installation program. Next, you can shut down your live Fedora system, remove the installation media from your computer, and boot your computer into your new Fedora system.

Configuring User Accounts

All Linux systems require secure authenticated access, which means that each user must log in with a valid user name and password before gaining access to a user interface. Two user accounts must be created at minimum: the administrator account (root), which has full rights to the system, as well as a regular user account; the root user account should only be used when performing system administration tasks.

On the first boot following a Fedora installation, you will be required to complete a Welcome wizard. This wizard allows you to disable location services and automatic error reporting, optionally integrate your online social media accounts, as well as configure a single regular user account for yourself, as shown in Figure 2-12. You can

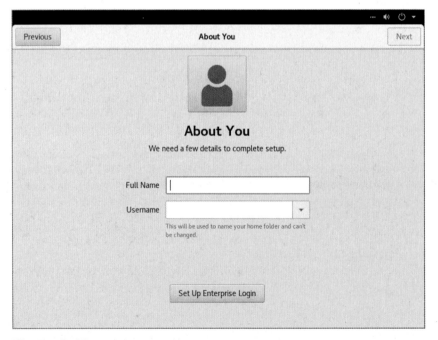

Figure 2-12   Choosing a regular user account username during the Welcome wizard

optionally click Set Up Enterprise Login in Figure 2-12 to join your Linux system to an Active Directory or Kerberos domain. After you click *Next* in Figure 2-12, you will be prompted to supply a password for your newly created user account and the Welcome wizard will then continue to boot into your system.

By default, a root user is created during the installation process but not assigned a valid password. The regular user account that you create during the Welcome wizard is given special rights that allow you set a valid password for the root user using the `sudo password root` command following installation.

Basic Linux Usage

After the Linux operating system has been installed, you must log in to the system with a valid user name and password and interact with the user interface to perform tasks. To do this, it is essential to understand the Linux user interfaces, as well as basic tasks, such as command execution, obtaining online help, and shutting down the Linux system.

Shells, Terminals, and the Kernel

Recall that an operating system is merely a collection of software that allows you to use your computer hardware in a meaningful fashion. Every operating system has a core component, which loads all other components and serves to centrally control the activities of the computer. This component is known as the kernel, and in Linux it is simply a file, usually called vmlinuz, that is located on the hard disk and loaded when you first turn on your computer.

When you interact with a computer, you are ultimately interacting with the kernel of the computer's operating system. However, this interaction cannot happen directly; it must have a channel through which it can access the kernel as well as a user interface that passes user input to the kernel for processing. The channel that allows you to log in is called a **terminal**. Linux can have many terminals that allow you to log in to the computer locally or across a network. After you log in to a terminal, you receive a user interface called a **shell**, which then accepts your input and passes it to the kernel for processing. The shell that is used by default in Linux is the **BASH shell** (short for Bourne Again Shell), which is an improved version of the Bourne shell from AT&T and is the shell that is used throughout this book. The whole process looks similar to what is shown in Figure 2-13.

As mentioned earlier, Linux is a multiuser and multitasking operating system and, as such, can allow for thousands of terminals. Each terminal could represent a separate logged-in user that has its own shell. The four different "channels" shown in Figure 2-13 could be different users logged in to the same Linux computer. Two users could be logged in locally to the server (seated at the server itself), and the other two could be logged in across a network, such as the Internet.

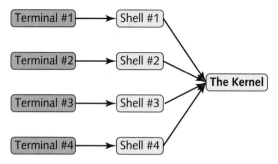

Figure 2-13   Shells, terminals, and the kernel

By default, when you log in to a terminal, you receive a command-line shell (BASH shell), which prompts you to type commands to tell the Linux kernel what to do. However, in this computing age, most people prefer to use a graphical interface in which they can use a pointing device such as a mouse to navigate and start tasks. In this case, you can choose to start a graphical user interface (GUI) environment on top of your BASH shell after you are logged in to a command-line terminal, or you can switch to a graphical terminal, which allows users to log in and immediately receive a GUI environment. A typical command-line terminal login prompt looks like the following:

```
Fedora 28 (Workstation Edition)
Kernel 4.16.3-301.fc28.x86_64 on an x86_64 (tty2)

server1 login:
```

A typical graphical terminal login for Fedora Linux (called the GNOME Display Manager or gdm) is shown in Figure 2-14.

Figure 2-14   The GNOME display manager (gdm)

To access a terminal device at the local server, you can press a combination of keys, such as Ctrl+Alt+F2, to change to a separate terminal. If you are logging in across the network, you can use a variety of programs that connect to a terminal on the Linux computer. A list of local Linux terminals, along with their names and types, is shown in Table 2-5.

Table 2-5   Common Linux terminals

Terminal name	Key combination	Login type
tty1	Ctrl+Alt+F1	graphical (gdm)
tty2	Ctrl+Alt+F2	command-line
tty3	Ctrl+Alt+F3	command-line
tty4	Ctrl+Alt+F4	command-line
tty5	Ctrl+Alt+F5	command-line
tty6	Ctrl+Alt+F6	command-line

After you are logged in to a command-line terminal, you receive a prompt at which you can enter commands. The following example shows the user logging in as the root (administrator) user. As you can see in this example, after you log in as the root user, you see a # prompt:

```
Fedora 28 (Workstation Edition)
Kernel 4.16.3-301.fc28.x86_64 on an x86_64 (tty2)

server1 login: root
Password:
Last login: Mon Aug 16 09:45:42 from tty2
[root@server1 ~]#_
```

However, if you log in as a regular user to a command-line terminal (e.g., user1), you see a $ prompt, as follows:

```
Fedora 28 (Workstation Edition)
Kernel 4.16.3-301.fc28.x86_64 on an x86_64 (tty2)

server1 login: user1
Password:
Last login: Mon Aug 16 09:45:42 from tty2
[user1@server1 ~]$_
```

When you log in to a graphical terminal, the GUI environment of your choice is started; the default GUI environment in Fedora Linux is GNOME on Wayland, but you can instead select GNOME on X.org from the settings icon next to the Sign In button within the gdm. On most legacy Linux systems, the GUI environment replaces the gdm on tty1. However, on modern Linux systems such as Fedora 28, the GUI environment is typically loaded on tty2, and the gdm remains available on tty1 to allow for additional graphical logins for different users. Each additional graphical login results in an additional GUI environment loaded on the next available terminal (tty3, tty4, and so on).

After the GUI environment starts, you can access a command-line terminal window by accessing the Activities menu in the upper left of the desktop and navigating to Show Applications, Utilities, Terminal. This will start a command-line terminal window within your GNOME desktop, as shown in Figure 2-15. You can open multiple, separate command-line terminal windows within a single GUI environment. Similarly, you can access several different BASH windows within a single command-line terminal (e.g., tty3) using an interactive terminal program such as `screen` or `tmux`. A sample `tmux` session with three BASH windows on tty3 is shown in Figure 2-16.

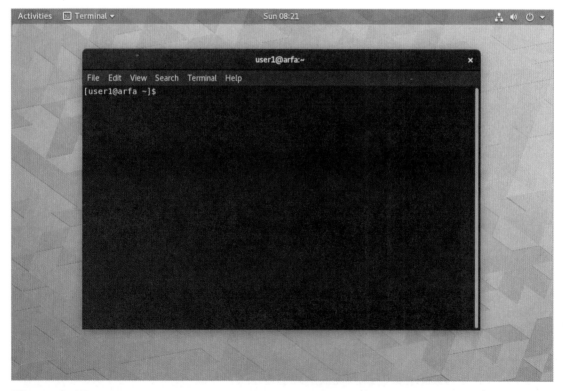

Figure 2-15 Using a command-line terminal within the GNOME desktop

Figure 2-16   Accessing multiple BASH windows within a single command-line terminal using tmux

Note 🔗

By default, Fedora 28 does not allow the root user to log in to a GUI environment from the gdm for security reasons, as several graphical programs are not designed to be run as the root user. Instead, you should log in to a GUI environment as a regular user. When you run a graphical administrative utility as a regular user, the GUI environment prompts you for the root user password in order to continue.

Basic Shell Commands

When using a command-line terminal, the shell ultimately interprets all information you enter into the command line. This information includes the command itself, as well as options and arguments. **Commands** indicate the name of the program to execute and are case sensitive. **Options** are specific letters that start with a dash (-) and appear after the command name to alter the way the command works. Options are specific to the command in question; the persons who developed the command determined which options to allow for that command.

Note 🔗

Some options start with two dashes (--); these options are referred to as POSIX options and are usually composed of a whole word, not just a letter.

Arguments also appear after the command name, yet they do not start with a dash. They specify the parameters that tailor the command to your particular needs. Suppose, for example, that you want to list all of the files in the /etc/rpm directory on the hard disk. You could use the ls command with the –a option (which tells the ls command to list all files, including hidden files) and the /etc/rpm argument (which tells ls to look in the /etc/rpm directory), as shown in the following example:

```
[root@server1 root]# ls -a /etc/rpm
.       macros.color  macros.fjava    macros.imgcreate
..      macros.dist   macros.gconf2   macros.jpackage
[root@server1 root]#_
```

After you type the command and press Enter in the preceding output, the ls command shows that there are six files in the /etc/rpm directory (macros.color, macros. fjava, and so on). The command prompt then reappears, so that you can enter another command.

> **Note** 📎
>
> Commands, options, and arguments are case sensitive; an uppercase letter (A), for instance, is treated differently than a lowercase letter (a).

> **Note** 📎
>
> Always put a space between the command name, options, and arguments; otherwise, the shell does not understand that they are separate, and your command might not work as expected.

Although you can pass options and arguments to commands, not all commands need to have arguments or options to work properly. The date command, which simply prints the current date and time, is an example:

```
[root@server1 root]# date
Sun Aug 19 08:46:57 EDT 2019
[root@server1 root]#_
```

Table 2-6 lists some common commands that you can use without specifying any options or arguments.

If the output of a certain command is too large to fit on the terminal screen, press the Shift+Page Up keys simultaneously to view previous screens of information. Press Shift+Page Down simultaneously to navigate in the opposite direction.

Table 2-6	Some common Linux commands
Command	**Description**
clear	Clears the terminal screen
reset	Resets your terminal to use default terminal settings
who	Displays currently logged-in users
w	Displays currently logged-in users and their tasks
whoami	Displays your login name
id	Displays the numbers associated with your user account name and group names; these are commonly referred to as User IDs (UIDs) and Group IDs (GIDs)
date	Displays the current date and time
cal	Displays the calendar for the current month
uname -a	Displays system information
ls	Lists files
exit	Exits out of your current shell

You can recall commands previously entered in the BASH shell using the keyboard arrow keys (the up, down, right, and left arrow keys). Thus, if you want to enter the same command again, cycle through the list of available commands with the keyboard up and down arrow keys and press Enter to re-execute that command.

As a Linux administrator, you will regularly run commands that only the root user can run to perform system configuration. Even if you are logged in to the system as a regular user account, you can easily switch to the root user to perform any administrative tasks using the su (switch user) command. To switch to the root user and load the root user's environment variables, you can run the su command with the – option and supply the root user's password when prompted:

```
[user1@server1 ~]$ su - root
Password:
Last login: Mon Aug 16 09:45:42 EDT 2019 from tty2
[root@server1 root]#_
```

Alternatively, to run a single command as the root only, you can run su -c "command" root and specify the root user's password when prompted.

If you do not specify the user name when using the su command, the root user is assumed. Additionally, the root user can use the su command to switch to any other user account without specifying a password:

```
[root@server1 root]# su - user1
Last login: Mon Aug 16 10:22:21 EDT 2019 from tty2
[user1@server1 ~]$_
```

Shell Metacharacters

Another important part of the shell are shell **metacharacters**, which are keyboard characters that have special meaning. One of the most commonly used metacharacters is the $ character, which tells the shell that the following text refers to a variable. A variable is a piece of information that is stored in memory; variable names are typically uppercase words, and most variables are set by the Linux system when you log in. An example of how you might use the $ metacharacter to refer to a variable is by using the echo command (which prints text to the terminal screen):

```
[root@server1 root]# echo Hi There!
Hi There!
[root@server1 root]# echo My shell is $SHELL
My Shell is /bin/bash
[root@server1 root]#_
```

Notice from the preceding output that $SHELL was translated into its appropriate value from memory (/bin/bash, the BASH shell). The shell recognized SHELL as a variable because it was prefixed by the $ metacharacter. Table 2-7 presents a list of common BASH shell metacharacters that are discussed throughout this book.

Table 2-7   Common BASH shell metacharacters

Metacharacter(s)	Description
$	Shell variable
~	Special home directory variable
#	Shell script comment
&	Background command execution
;	Command termination
< << > >>	Input/Output redirection
|	Command piping
* ? [ ]	Shell wildcards
' " \	Metacharacter quotes
`	Command substitution
( ) { }	Command grouping

It is good practice to avoid metacharacters when typing commands unless you need to take advantage of their special functionality, as the shell readily interprets them, which might lead to unexpected results.

> **Note** 📎
>
> If you accidentally use one of these characters and your shell does not return you to the normal command prompt, press the Ctrl+c keys to cancel your current command and return to the normal command prompt.

In some circumstances, you might need to use a metacharacter in a command and prevent the shell from interpreting its special meaning. To do this, enclose the metacharacters in single quotation marks ´ ´. Single quotation marks protect those metacharacters from being interpreted specially by the shell (i.e., a $ is interpreted as a $ character and not a variable identifier). You can also use double quotation marks (" ") to perform the same task; however, double quotation marks do not protect $, \, and ` characters. If only one character needs to be protected from shell interpretation, you can precede that character by a slash \ rather than enclosing it within quotation marks. An example of this type of quoting follows:

```
[root@server1 root]# echo My Shell is $SHELL
My Shell is /bin/bash
[root@server1 root]# echo 'My Shell is $SHELL'
My Shell is $SHELL
[root@server1 root]# echo "My Shell is $SHELL"
My Shell is /bin/bash
[root@server1 root]# echo My Shell is \$SHELL
My Shell is $SHELL
[root@server1 root]#_
```

As shown in Table 2-7, not all quotation characters protect characters from the shell. The back quotation characters ` ` can be used to perform command substitution; anything between back quotes is treated as another command by the shell, and its output is substituted in place of the back quotes. Take the expression `date` as an example:

```
[root@server1 root]# echo Today is `date`
Today is Tue Mar 29 09:28:11 EST 2019
[root@server1 root]#_
```

Getting Command Help

Most distributions of Linux contain more than 1000 Linux commands in their standard configurations, and thus it is impractical to memorize the syntax and use of each command. Fortunately, Linux stores documentation for each command in central locations so that it can be accessed easily. The most common form of documentation for Linux commands is **manual pages** (commonly referred to as **man pages**). Type the man command followed by a command name to display extensive page-by-page information about that Linux command on the terminal screen. This information includes a description of the command and its syntax, as well as available options, related files, and related commands. For example, to receive information on the format and usage of the whoami command, you can use the following command:

```
[root@server1 root]# man whoami
```

The manual page is then displayed page-by-page on the terminal screen. You can use the arrow keys on the keyboard to scroll through the information or press q to quit. The manual page for whoami is similar to the following:

```
WHOAMI(1)                      User Commands                      WHOAMI(1)


NAME
       whoami - print effective userid

SYNOPSIS
       whoami [OPTION]...

DESCRIPTION
       Print the user name associated with the current effective
       user id. Same as id -un.
       --help display this help and exit
       --version
            output version information and exit

AUTHOR
       Written by Richard Mlynarik.

REPORTING BUGS
       GNU coreutils home page:<https://www.gnu.org/software/coreutils/>
       Report translation bugs to <https://translationproject.org/team>

COPYRIGHT
       Copyright©2017 Free Software Foundation, Inc. License GPLv3+: GNU
       GPL version 3 or later <https://gnu.org/licenses/gpl.html>.
       This is free software: you are free to change and redistribute it.
       There is NO WARRANTY, to the extent permitted by law.
```

```
SEE ALSO
      Full documentation:<https://www.gnu.org/software/coreutils/whoami>
      or available locally via: info coreutils 'whoami invocation'

GNU coreutils 8.29                                        December 2017
[root@server1 root]#_
```

Notice that the whoami command is displayed as WHOAMI(1) at the top of the preceding manual page output. The (1) denotes a section of the manual pages; section (1) means that whoami is a command that can be executed by any user. All manual pages contain certain section numbers that describe the category of the command in the manual page database; Table 2-8 lists the manual page section numbers.

Table 2-8   Manual page section numbers

Manual page section	Description
1	Commands that any user can execute
2	Linux system calls
3	Library routines
4	Special device files
5	File formats
6	Games
7	Miscellaneous
8	Commands that only the root user can execute
9	Linux kernel routines
n	New commands not categorized yet

Sometimes, more than one command, library routine, or file has the same name. If you run the man command with that name as an argument, Linux returns the manual page with the lowest section number. For example, if there is a file called whoami as well as a command named whoami and you type man whoami, the manual page for the whoami command (section 1 of the manual pages) is displayed. To display the manual page for the whoami file format instead, you type man 5 whoami to display the whoami file format (section 5 of the manual pages).

Recall that many commands are available to the Linux user; thus, it might be cumbersome to find the command that you need to perform a certain task without using a Linux command dictionary. Fortunately, you can search the manual pages by keyword. To find all of the commands that have the word "usb" in their names or descriptions, type the following:

```
[root@server1 root] # man -k usb
```

This command produces the following output:

```
lsusb (8)                           - list USB devices
sane-canon630u (5)                  - SANE backend for the Canon 630u USB
sane-cardscan (5)                   - SANE backend for Corex CardScan usb
sane-epjitsu (5)                    - SANE backend for Epson-based Fujitsu USB
sane-find-scanner (1)               - find SCSI and USB scanners and their
sane-genesys (5)                    - SANE backend for GL646, GL841, GL843,
sane-gt68xx (5)                     - SANE backend for GT-68XX based USB
sane-kvs1025 (5)                    - SANE backend for Panasonic KV-S102xC USB
sane-kvs20xx (5)                    - SANE backend for Panasonic KV-S20xxC USB/
sane-kvs40xx (5)                    - SANE backend for Panasonic KV-S40xxC USB/
sane-ma1509 (5)                     - SANE backend for Mustek BearPaw 1200F USB
sane-mustek_usb (5)                 - SANE backend for Mustek USB flatbed
sane-mustek_usb2 (5)                - SANE backend for SQ113 based USB flatbed
sane-pieusb (5)                     - SANE backend for USB-connected PIE
sane-plustek (5)                    - SANE backend for LM983[1/2/3] based USB
sane-sm3600 (5)                     - SANE backend for Microtek scanners with
sane-sm3840 (5)                     - SANE backend for Microtek scanners with
sane-u12 (5)                        - SANE backend for Plustek USB flatbed
sane-usb (5)                        - USB configuration tips for SANE
usb-devices (1)                     - print USB device details
usb_modeswitch (1)                  - control the mode of 'multi-state' USB
usb_modeswitch_dispatcher (1)       - Linux wrapper for usb_modeswitch (not
usbhid-dump (8)                     - dump USB HID device report descriptors/
usbmuxd (1)                         - Expose a socket to multiplex connections
```

After you find the command needed, you can run the man command on that command without the -k option to find out detailed information about the command.

Note 🖉

You can also use the `apropos usb` command to perform the same function as the `man -k usb` command. Both commands yield the exact same output on the terminal screen.

Note 🖉

If you do not see any output from the `man -k` or `apropos` command following a Linux installation, you might need to run the `mandb` command to index the manual page database.

Note 🖉

If you want to only view a short description of a command (e.g., to see what the command does), you can use the `whatis` command. For example, the `whatis whoami` command will only display the name and description from the `whoami` manual page.

Another utility, originally intended to replace the `man` command in Linux, is the GNU **info pages**. You can access this utility by typing the `info` command followed by the name of the command in question. The `info` command returns an easy-to-read description of each command and contains links to other information pages (called hyperlinks). Today, however, both the info pages and the manual pages are used to find documentation because manual pages have been used in Linux since its conception, and for over two decades in the UNIX operating system. An example of using the info utility to find information about the `whoami` command follows:

```
[root@server1 root]# info whoami
```

The info page is then displayed interactively:

```
Next: groups invocation,  Prev: logname invocation, Up: User
information
```

```
20.3 'whoami': Print effective user ID
======================================


'whoami' prints the user name associated with the current
effective user ID. It is equivalent to the command 'id -un'.

   The only options are '--help' and '--version'. *Note Common
options::.

   An exit status of zero indicates success, and a nonzero value
indicates failure

-----Info: (coreutils)whoami invocation, 14 lines -All----------
Welcome to Info version 6.5. Type H for help, h for tutorial.
[root@server1 root]#_
```

> **Note** 📎
>
> While in the info utility, press the H key to display a help screen that describes the usage of
> info. As with the man command, you can use the q key to quit.

Some commands do not have manual pages or info pages. These commands are
usually functions that are built into the BASH shell itself. To find help on these
commands, you must use the help command, as follows:

```
[root@server1 root]# help echo
echo: echo [-neE] [arg ...]
    Write arguments to the standard output.

    Display the ARGs, separated by a single space character and
    followed by a newline, on the standard output.

    Options:
      -n    do not append a newline
      -e    enable interpretation of the following backslash escapes
      -E    explicitly suppress interpretation of backslash escapes

     'echo' interprets the following backslash-escaped characters:
      \a    alert (bell)
      \b    backspace
```

```
        \c   suppress further output
        \e   escape character
        \E   escape character
        \f   form feed
        \n   new line
        \r   carriage return
        \t   horizontal tab
        \v   vertical tab
        \\   backslash
        \0nnn the character whose ASCII code is NNN (octal).  NNN can be
             0 to 3 octal digits
        \xHH  the eight-bit character whose value is HH (hexadecimal). HH
              can be one or two hex digits


     Exit Status:
     Returns success unless a write error occurs.
[root@server1 root]#_
```

Shutting Down the Linux System

Because the operating system handles writing data from computer memory to the disk drives in a computer, turning off the power to the computer might result in damaged user and system files. Thus, it is important to prepare the operating system for shutdown before turning off the power to the hardware components of the computer. To do this, you can issue the shutdown command, which can power off or reboot (restart) your computer after a certain period of time. To power off your system in 15 minutes, for example, you could type:

```
[root@server1 root] # shutdown -P +15
```

This produces output similar to the following:

```
Shutdown scheduled for Wed 2019-09-17 15:51:48 EDT, use 'shutdown
-c' to cancel.
```

Before scheduling a system shutdown, it is good form to advise users who are currently logged in to the system such that they can save their work and log off beforehand. You can do this using the wall (warn all) command followed by the message to send to users on the system:

```
[root@server1 root] # wall The system is shutting down in 15 min
- ensure that you save your work and log off before then.
```

To power off your system now, you could type:

```
[root@server1 root] # poweroff
```

Other examples of the `shutdown` command and their descriptions are shown in Table 2-9.

Table 2-9   Commands to halt and reboot the Linux operating system

Command	Description
`shutdown -P +4`	Powers off your system in four minutes
`shutdown -H +4`	Halts the operating system from executing in four minutes, but does not invoke the ACPI function in your BIOS to turn off power to your computer
`shutdown -r +4`	Reboots your system in four minutes
`shutdown -P now`	Powers off your system immediately
`shutdown -r now`	Reboots your system immediately
`shutdown -c`	Cancels a scheduled shutdown
`halt`	Halts your system immediately, but does not power it off
`poweroff`	Powers off your system immediately
`reboot`	Reboots your system immediately

Chapter Summary

- Prior to installation, you should verify hardware requirements and compatibility.

- You can obtain Linux installation media by downloading an ISO image from the Internet that can be written to a DVD or a USB flash drive or can be used directly by virtualization software.

- A typical Linux installation prompts the user for information such as language, date, time zone, keyboard layout, user account configuration, and permanent storage configuration.

- Users must log in to a terminal and receive a shell before they can interact with the Linux system and kernel. A single user can log in several times simultaneously to different terminals locally or across a network.

- Regardless of the type of terminal that you use (graphical or command-line), you can enter commands, options, and arguments at a shell prompt to perform system tasks, obtain command help, or shut down the Linux system. The shell is case sensitive and understands a variety of special characters called shell metacharacters, which should be protected if their special meaning is not required.

Key Terms

Advanced Technology
  Attachment (ATA)
arguments
B-tree Filesystem (BTRFS)
BASH shell
Basic Input/Output System
  (BIOS)
BIOS Boot Partition
command
ext2
ext3
ext4
extended partition
filesystem
GUID Partition Table (GPT)
Hardware Compatibility List
  (HCL)
info pages
Integrated Drive Electronics
  (IDE)
ISO image

journaling
live media
logical drives
Logical Volume Manager
  (LVM)
man pages
manual pages
Master Boot Record (MBR)
memtest86
metacharacters
namespace
Non-Volatile Memory
  Express (NVMe)
options
Parallel Advanced
  Technology Attachment
  (PATA)
partitions
primary partitions
Redundant Array of
  Inexpensive Disks (RAID)

Serial Advanced Technology
  Attachment (SATA)
Serial Attached SCSI (SAS)
shell
Small Computer Systems
  Interface (SCSI)
solid-state drive (SSD)
swap memory
terminal
UEFI System Partition
Unified Extensible
  Firmware Interface (UEFI)
VFAT (Virtual File Allocation
  Table)
virtual machine
virtual machine host
virtual memory
virtualization software
XFS

Review Questions

1. What is the default shell in Linux called?
   a. SH
   b. BSH
   c. CSH
   d. BASH

2. What equivalent to the man command generally provides an easier-to-read description of the queried command and contains links to other related information?
   a. who
   b. man help
   c. man -descriptive
   d. info

3. What command can you use to safely shut down the Linux system immediately?
   a. shutdown -c
   b. shutdown -r
   c. down
   d. halt

4. What command is equivalent to the man -k *keyword* command?
   a. find *keyword*
   b. man *keyword*
   c. apropos *keyword*
   d. appaloosa *keyword*

5. Which of the following is *not* a piece of information that the Fedora installation program prompts you for?
   a. time zone
   b. installation destination
   c. firewall settings
   d. installation language

6. Linux commands entered via the command line are not case sensitive. True or False?

7. Which command blanks the terminal screen, erasing previously displayed output?
   a. `erase`
   b. `clean`
   c. `blank`
   d. `clear`

8. When sitting at a computer running Linux, what key combination do you press to open the graphical terminal?
   a. Ctrl+Alt+G
   b. Ctrl+Alt+F4
   c. Ctrl+Alt+F1
   d. Ctrl+7

9. To install Linux within a virtual machine, you can specify the path to an ISO image that contains the Linux installation media within virtualization software without having to first write the ISO image to a DVD or a USB flash drive. True or False?

10. After you log in to a terminal, you receive a user interface called a

    _____.
    a. GUID
    b. shell
    c. text box
    d. command screen

11. Users enter commands directly to the kernel of the Linux operating system. True or False?

12. How can you protect a metacharacter (such as the $ character) from shell interpretation?
    a. Precede it with a /.
    b. Follow it with a \.
    c. Precede it with a $.
    d. It cannot be done because metacharacters are essential.
    e. Precede it with a \.

13. You know a Linux command will perform a desired function for you, but you cannot remember the full name of the command. You do remember it will flush a variable from your system. Which command typed at a command prompt displays a list of commands that would likely contain the command you desire?
    a. `man –k flush`
    b. `man –k find all`
    c. `man flush`
    d. `man –key flush`

14. Which command displays the users who are currently logged in to the Linux system?
    a. `finger`
    b. `who`
    c. `id`
    d. `date`

15. Which prompt does the root user receive when logged in to the system?
    a. $
    b. @
    c. #
    d. !

16. Which prompt do regular users receive when logged in to the system?
    a. $
    b. @
    c. #
    d. !

17. Which of the following refers to the third primary partition on the second SAS hard disk within Linux?
    a. hdb2
    b. sda3
    c. hdb3
    d. sdb3

18. Which two partitions do you typically create at minimum during a Fedora Linux installation? (Choose two answers.)
    a. /
    b. /boot
    c. swap
    d. /home

19. If you boot your computer from Linux live media, you will be able to use a fully functional Linux system prior to installing Linux on permanent storage. True or False?

20. Which of the following is *not* an example of virtualization software that can be used to install Linux within another operating system?
    a. Oracle VirtualBox
    b. Microsoft Hyper-V
    c. Spiceworks
    d. VMWare

Hands-On Projects

These projects should be completed in the order given and should take a total of three hours to complete. The software and hardware requirements for these projects include the following:

- A 64-bit computer with at least 8GB of RAM, 120GB of permanent disk storage, and a DVD drive
- A Windows operating system that contains a virtualization software product, a Web browser, and an Internet connection
- The ISO image for Fedora 28 live media (Fedora-Workstation-Live-x86_64-28-1.1.iso)

Project 2-1

In this hands-on project, you install Fedora 28 Linux within a virtual machine on a Windows computer.

1. In your virtualization software, create a new virtual machine called **Fedora Linux** that has the following characteristics:
    - 4GB of memory
    - An Internet connection via your PC's network card (preferably using an external virtual switch or bridged mode)
    - A 50GB SATA/SCSI/SAS virtual hard disk (dynamically allocated)
    - The virtual machine DVD drive attached to the ISO file for Fedora 28 live media (Fedora-Workstation-Live-x86_64-28-1.1.iso)

2. Start and then connect to your Fedora Linux virtual machine using your virtualization software.

3. At the Fedora-Workstation-Live 28 welcome screen, press **Enter** to test your installation media and boot Fedora Live.

4. After the graphical desktop and Welcome to Fedora screen has loaded, select the option **Install to Hard Drive** to start the Fedora installation program.

5. At the Welcome to Fedora 28 screen, select **English (United States)** and click **Continue**.

6. On the Installation Summary page, click **Time & Date**, select your time zone (and time if necessary), and press **Done**.

7. On the Installation Summary page, click **Installation Destination**. You should see that your 50GB virtual disk is already selected and called sda. Select **Custom** under Storage Configuration and click **Done** when finished.

8. At the Manual Partitioning screen, choose a partition scheme of **Standard Partition** from the list box and select the link **Click here to create them automatically**. This will create several partitions.

   a. Highlight the **/ (sda3)** partition, reduce the Desired Capacity to 35GB (**35GiB**), and click **Update Settings**. This will leave some free unpartitioned space on your first disk for a later exercise.

   b. Click **Done** and then click **Accept Changes** when prompted.

9. At the Installation Summary page, click **Begin Installation**.

10. When the installation has finished, click **Quit**. This will return you to your Fedora live desktop.

11. Click the power icon in the upper-right corner, select the power icon that appears, and click **Power Off** to shut down your Fedora Live installation image.

12. In the Settings for your virtual machine in your virtualization software, ensure that the DVD drive is no longer attached to the Fedora ISO image.

13. Finally, start your Fedora Linux virtual machine using your virtualization software to boot into your new Fedora Linux OS.

14. At the Welcome wizard, press **Next**.

    a. At the Privacy page, disable Location Services and Automatic Problem Reporting using the sliders and press **Next**.

    b. At the Online Accounts page, press **Skip**.

    c. On the About You page, supply your full name in the Full Name text box, the name **user1** in the Username text box, and then click **Next**.

    d. At the Password page, supply a password of **LINUXrocks!** and click **Next** and then click **Start Using Fedora**.

Project 2-2

In this hands-on project, you set a password for the root user, explore some command-line terminals on a Linux system and enter some basic commands into the BASH shell.

1. After your Linux system has been loaded following installation and the completion of the Welcome wizard, you are placed at a graphical terminal (tty1). Instead of logging

in to this graphical terminal, press **Ctrl+Alt+F3** to switch to a command-line terminal (tty3) and then log in to the terminal using the user name of **user1** and the password of **LINUXrocks!**. Which prompt did you receive and why?

2. At the command prompt, type `sudo passwd root` and press **Enter** to set the root user password. When prompted, enter your password **LINUXrocks!**, and then enter the desired root password of **LINUXrocks!** twice to set the root user password to LINUXrocks!

3. At the command prompt, type `date` and press **Enter** to view the current date and time. Now, type `Date` and press **Enter**. Why did you receive an error message? Can you tell which shell gave you the error message?

4. Switch to a different command-line terminal (tty5) by pressing **Ctrl+Alt+F5** and log in to the terminal using the user name of **root** and the password of **LINUXrocks!**. Which prompt did you receive and why?

5. At the command prompt, type `who` and press **Enter** to view the users logged in to the system. Who is logged in and on which terminal?

6. Switch back to the terminal tty3 by pressing **Ctrl+Alt+F3**. Did you need to log in? Are the outputs from the `date` and `Date` commands still visible?

7. Try typing each command listed in Table 2-6 in order (pressing **Enter** after each) and observe the output. What did the last command (`exit`) do?

8. Switch to the terminal tty5 by pressing **Ctrl+Alt+F5** and type **exit** to log out of your shell.

Project 2-3

In this hands-on project, you log in to a graphical terminal in Fedora Linux and interact with the GNOME and KDE desktops.

1. Switch to the graphical terminal (tty1) by pressing **Ctrl+Alt+F1**, click your name (which is simply the display name for the user account named user1), supply the password of **LINUXrocks!**, and click **Sign In**. Close the Getting Started window. Which GUI environment is started and why?

2. Observe the GNOME desktop. Use your mouse to select the **Activities** menu in the upper-left corner of your screen, select the **Show Applications** icon (at the bottom of the application panel), and then navigate to **Utilities**, **Terminal** to open a BASH shell prompt. What prompt do you receive and why?

3. At the command prompt, type `who` and press **Enter** to view the users logged in to the system. Note that you are currently logged into tty2.

4. Switch to the terminal tty1 by pressing **Ctrl+Alt+F1**. Is the gdm still available? Switch back to your GNOME desktop on tty2 by pressing **Ctrl+Alt+F2**.

5. At the command prompt, type `su -` and press **Enter** to switch to the root user. Supply the root user password **LINUXrocks!** when prompted.

6. By default, the KDE desktop is not installed in Fedora 28. To download and install the KDE desktop (the latest edition is called Plasma Workspaces), type `dnf groupinstall`

"KDE Plasma Workspaces" and press **Enter** when finished. Press **y** when prompted to download and install the required packages from the Internet, which could take several minutes, depending on your Internet speed. The dnf command will be discussed in more detail in Chapter 11.

7. Type **reboot** to restart Fedora Linux. After the system has rebooted, click your name at the gdm screen and then click the settings (cog wheel) icon next to the Sign In button. Select **Plasma**, supply your password (**LINUXrocks!**), and click **Sign In**.

8. Click the Fedora start button in the lower-left of the desktop and navigate to **Applications**, **System**, **Terminal** to start a command-line shell. How does application navigation in the KDE desktop differ from the GNOME desktop?

9. At the command prompt, type **who** and press **Enter**. While your GUI environment is still loaded on tty2, the who command lists port 0 (:0) as your terminal. This is because the KDE desktop on Fedora 28 uses **X.org** instead of Wayland when creating the GUI environment. Additionally, any command-line BASH shells that you open within a GUI environment on **X.org** are started as pseudo terminal sessions (pts); the first pseudo terminal session is called pts/0, the second pseudo terminal session is called pts/1, and so on.

10. Click the **File** menu in your Konsole terminal window and select **New Window**. At the command prompt in this new window, type **who** and press **Enter**. Do you see an additional pseudo terminal session?

11. Click the Fedora start button, navigate to **Leave**, **Log out**, and click **Log out** to exit the KDE desktop.

Project 2-4

In this hands-on project, you work with multiple BASH windows within a single terminal using the screen and tmux tools.

1. Switch to a command-line terminal (tty5) by pressing **Ctrl+Alt+F5** and log in to the terminal using the user name of **root** and the password of **LINUXrocks!**.

2. At the command prompt, type **screen** and press **Enter**. When prompted to install the command, press **y** (twice). Next, type **screen** and press **Enter** to open a new window within the screen tool.

3. At the command prompt in this new window, type **who** and press **Enter**. Note that the screen tool turns your tty5 terminal into a pseudo terminal session in order to provide additional BASH windows.

4. Press the **Ctrl+a** keys and then immediately press **c** to create a new BASH window. At the command prompt in this new window, type **who** and press **Enter**. Note that you see an additional pseudo terminal session for the current window.

5. Press the **Ctrl+a** keys again and then immediately press **c** to create a third BASH window. At the command prompt in this new window, type **who** and press **Enter**. You should now see three pseudo terminal sessions within the tty5 terminal.

6. Press the **Ctrl+a** keys and then immediately press **p** to switch to the previous BASH window. Next, press the **Ctrl+a** keys and then immediately press **n** to switch to the next BASH window.

7. Type **exit** and press **Enter** to log out of your current BASH window.

8. Repeat Step 7 twice more to log out of the remaining two BASH windows and the screen tool. Type **who** and press **Enter** to verify that you are within your original tty5 terminal.

9. At the command prompt, type **tmux** and press **Enter** to start the **tmux** tool. Next, type **who** and press **Enter**. Does the **tmux** tool turn your tty5 terminal into a pseudo terminal session?

10. Press the **Ctrl+b** keys and then immediately press **%** (percent) to create a new BASH window split horizontally. Next, press the **Ctrl+b** keys again and then immediately press **"** (double quote) to create a third BASH window split vertically.

11. Press the **Ctrl+b** keys and then use a keyboard arrow key (**up**, **down**, **left**, **right**) of your choice to navigate between the windows. Repeat this to navigate among all three BASH windows within your tty5 terminal.

12. Type **exit** and press **Enter** to log out of your current BASH window.

13. Repeat Step 7 twice more to log out of the remaining two BASH windows and the tmux tool. Finally, type **exit** and press **Enter** to log out of your shell.

Project 2-5

In this hands-on project, you use and protect shell metacharacters.

1. Switch to a command-line terminal (tty5) by pressing **Ctrl+Alt+F5** and log in to the terminal using the user name of **root** and the password of **LINUXrocks!**.

2. At the command prompt, type **date;who** and press **Enter** to run the date command immediately followed by the who command. Use the information in Table 2-7 to describe the purpose of the ; metacharacter.

3. At the command prompt, type **echo This is OK** and press **Enter** to display a message on the terminal screen.

4. At the command prompt, type **echo Don't do this** and press **Enter**. Which character needs to be protected in the previous command? Press the **Ctrl+c** keys to cancel your command and return to a BASH shell prompt.

5. At the command prompt, type **echo "Don't do this"** and press **Enter**. What is displayed on the terminal screen?

6. At the command prompt, type **echo Don\'t do this** and press **Enter**. What is displayed on the terminal screen?

7. At the command prompt, type **echo $SHELL** and press **Enter** to view the expansion of a variable using a shell metacharacter. What is displayed on the terminal screen? Next, type **echo $TEST** and press **Enter** to find out what happens when a variable that does not exist is used in a command. What is displayed?

8. At the command prompt, type **echo You have $4.50** and press **Enter**. What is displayed? Why? Which character needs to be protected in the previous command? What are two different ways that you can protect this character from interpretation by the shell?

9. At the command prompt, type echo `You have $4.50` and press **Enter**. What is displayed on the terminal screen? Did the single quotation marks protect this metacharacter from shell interpretation?

10. At the command prompt, type echo "You have $4.50" and press **Enter**. What is displayed on the terminal screen? Did the double quotation marks protect this metacharacter from shell interpretation?

11. At the command prompt, type echo You have \$4.50 and press **Enter**. What is displayed on the terminal screen? Did the backslash protect this metacharacter from shell interpretation?

12. At the command prompt, type echo My name is `whoami` and press **Enter**. What function do back quotes perform?

13. Type exit and press **Enter** to log out of your shell.

Project 2-6

In this hands-on project, you find information about commands using help utilities.

1. Press **Ctrl+Alt+F5** to switch to a command-line terminal (tty5), and then log in to the terminal using the user name of **root** and the password of **LINUXrocks!**.

2. At the command prompt, type man -k cron and press **Enter** to view a list of manual pages that have the word "cron" in the name or description. Use Table 2-8 to determine what type of manual pages are displayed. How many manual pages are there for crontab? Are they different types of manual pages?

Note 📎

> If you do not see any output from the man -k command, run the mandb command to generate the manual pages index.

3. At the command prompt, type man crontab and press **Enter** to view the manual page for the crontab command. Observe the syntax of the crontab command and press **q** when finished to quit the manual page and return to your command prompt.

4. At the command prompt, type man 5 crontab and press **Enter** to view the manual page for the crontab file format. Observe the syntax of the crontab file format and press **q** when finished to quit the manual page and return to your command prompt.

5. At the command prompt, type info and press **Enter** to view a list of available GNU info pages. When finished, press **q** to quit the info utility.

6. At the command prompt, type info date and press **Enter** to view syntax information regarding the date command, and press **q** to quit the info utility when finished.

7. At the command prompt, type help to view a list of BASH shell functions that have documentation. If the list is too long for your terminal, press the **Shift+Page Up** keys to shift one page up to view the top of the list. Then press the **Shift+Page Down** keys to shift one page down to view your command prompt again.

8. At the command prompt, type **help exit** to view information on the exit command, a function of your BASH shell.
9. Type exit and press **Enter** to log out of your shell.

Project 2-7

In this hands-on project, you properly shut down your Linux system.

1. Press **Ctrl+Alt+F5** to switch to a command-line terminal (tty5), and then log in to the terminal using the user name of **root** and the password of **LINUXrocks!**.
2. At the command prompt, type **poweroff** to shut down your Linux system immediately. Which commands from Table 2-9 can also be used to shut down your Linux system?

Discovery Exercises

1. You are the network administrator for Slimjim, a peripheral device company. The network uses Linux, and you need information on some commands to perform your job. Open the manual pages and find all the commands that have the word "copy" in their name or description. What command did you use to accomplish this task? Are there any commands in this list that only a root user can execute? How are they indicated? Select any two of them and compare their info and manual pages. Access and read the manual pages on three other commands that interest you either by using the command name or by searching for them by related keyword (try using apropos).

2. Identify the errors with the following commands and indicate possible solutions. (*Hint:* Try typing them at a shell prompt to view the error message.)

```
Echo "This command does not
    work properly"
date -z
apropos man -k
help date
shutdown -c now
echo "I would like lots of
    $$$"
man 8 date
```

## CHAPTER 3

EXPLORING LINUX FILESYSTEMS

After completing this chapter, you will be able to:

Understand and navigate the Linux directory structure using relative and absolute pathnames

Describe the various types of Linux files

View filenames and file types

Use shell wildcards to specify multiple filenames

Display the contents of text files and binary files

Search text files for regular expressions using `grep`

Use the vi editor to manipulate text files

Identify common alternatives to the vi text editor used today

An understanding of the structure and commands surrounding the Linux filesystem is essential for effectively using Linux to manipulate data. In the first part of this chapter, you explore the Linux filesystem hierarchy by changing your position in the filesystem tree and listing filenames of various types. Next, you examine the shell wildcard metacharacters used to specify multiple filenames as well as view the contents of files using standard Linux commands. You then learn about the regular expression metacharacters used when searching for text within files and are introduced to the vi text editor and its equivalents.

The Linux Directory Structure

Fundamental to using the Linux operating system is an understanding of how Linux stores files on the filesystem. Typical Linux systems could have thousands of data and program files; thus, a structure that organizes those files is necessary to make it easier to find and manipulate data and run programs. Recall from the previous chapter that Linux uses a logical directory tree to organize files into directories (also known as folders). When a user stores files in a certain **directory**, the files are physically stored in the filesystem of a certain partition on a hard disk or SSD inside the computer. Most people are familiar with the Windows operating system directory tree structure as shown in Figure 3-1; each filesystem on a hard drive partition is referred to by a drive letter (such as C: or D:) and has a root directory (indicated by the \ character) containing subdirectories that together form a hierarchical tree.

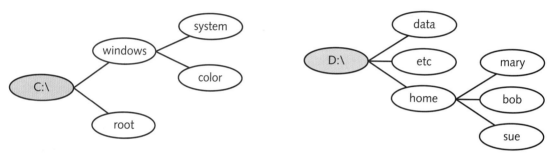

Figure 3-1   The Windows filesystem structure

It is important to describe directories in the directory tree properly; the **absolute pathname** to a file or directory is the full pathname of a certain file or directory starting from the root directory. In Figure 3-1, the absolute pathname for the color directory is C:\windows\color and the absolute pathname for the sue directory is D:\home\sue. In other words, you refer to C:\windows\color as the color directory below the windows directory below the root of C drive. Similarly, you refer to D:\home\sue as the sue directory below the home directory below the root of D drive.

Linux uses a similar directory structure, but with no drive letters. The structure contains a single root (referred to using the / character), with different filesystems on hard drive partitions mounted (or attached) to different directories on this directory tree. The directory that each filesystem is mounted to is transparent to the user. An example of a sample Linux directory tree equivalent to the Windows sample directory tree shown in Figure 3-1 is shown in Figure 3-2. Note that the subdirectory named "root" in Figure 3-2 is different from the root (/) directory. You'll learn more about the root subdirectory in the next section.

In Figure 3-2, the absolute pathname for the color directory is /windows/color and the absolute pathname for the sue directory is /home/sue. In other words, you refer to the /windows/color directory as the color directory below the windows directory below the root of the system (the / character). Similarly, you refer to the /home/sue directory as the sue directory below the home directory below the root of the system.

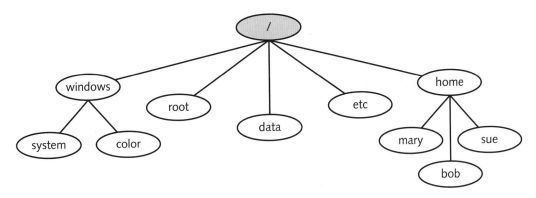

Figure 3-2   The Linux filesystem structure

Changing Directories

When you log into a Linux system, you are placed in your **home directory**, which is a place unique to your user account for storing personal files. Regular users usually have a home directory named after their user account under the /home directory, as in /home/sue. The root user, however, has a home directory called root under the root directory of the system (/root), as shown in Figure 3-2. Regardless of your user name, you can always refer to your own home directory using the ~ **metacharacter**.

To confirm the system directory that you are currently in, simply observe the name at the end of the shell prompt or run the pwd **(print working directory) command** at a command-line prompt. If you are logged in as the root user, the following output is displayed on the terminal screen:

```
[root@server1 ~]# pwd
/root
[root@server1 ~]#_
```

However, if you are logged in as the user sue, you see the following output:

```
[sue@server1 ~]$ pwd
/home/sue
[sue@server1 ~]$_
```

To change directories, you can issue the cd **(change directory) command** with an argument specifying the destination directory. If you do not specify a destination directory, the cd command returns you to your home directory:

```
[root@server1 ~]# cd /home/mary
[root@server1 mary]# pwd
/home/mary
[root@server1 mary]# cd /etc
[root@server1 etc]# pwd
```

```
/etc
[root@server1 etc]# cd
[root@server1 ~]# pwd
/root
[root@server1 ~]#_
```

You can also use the ~ metacharacter to refer to another user's home directory by appending a user name at the end:

```
[root@server1 ~]# cd ~mary
[root@server1 mary]# pwd
/home/mary
[root@server1 mary]# cd ~
[root@server1 ~]# pwd
/root
[root@server1 ~]#_
```

In many of the examples discussed earlier, the argument specified after the cd command is an absolute pathname to a directory, meaning that the system has all the information it needs to find the destination directory because the pathname starts from the root (/) of the system. However, in most Linux commands, you can also use a relative pathname in place of an absolute pathname to reduce typing. A **relative pathname** is the pathname of a target file or directory relative to your current directory in the tree. To specify a directory below your current directory, refer to that directory by name (do not start the pathname with a / character). To refer to a directory one step closer to the root of the tree (also known as a **parent directory**), use two dots (..). An example of using relative pathnames to move around the directory tree is shown next:

```
[root@server1 ~]# cd /home/mary
[root@server1 mary]# pwd
/home/mary
[root@server1 mary]# cd ..
[root@server1 home]# pwd
/home
[root@server1 home]# cd mary
[root@server1 mary]# pwd
/home/mary
[root@server1 mary]#_
```

The preceding example used ".." to move up one parent directory and then used the word "mary" to specify the mary **subdirectory** relative to the current location in the tree; however, you can also move more than one level up or down the directory tree:

```
[root@server1 ~]# cd /home/mary
[root@server1 mary]# pwd
/home/mary
```

```
[root@server1 mary]# cd ../..
[root@server1 /]# pwd
/
[root@server1 /]# cd home/mary
[root@server1 mary]# pwd
/home/mary
[root@server1 mary]#_
```

> **Note**
>
> You can also use one dot (.) to refer to the current directory. Although this is not useful when using the cd command, you do use one dot later in this book.

Although absolute pathnames are straightforward to use as arguments to commands when specifying the location of a certain file or directory, relative pathnames can save you a great deal of typing and reduce the potential for error if your current directory is far away from the root directory. Suppose, for example, that the current directory is /home/sue/projects/acme/plans and you need to change to the /home/sue/projects/acme directory. Using an absolute pathname, you would type cd /home/sue/projects/acme; however, using a relative pathname, you only need to type cd .. to perform the same task because the /home/sue/projects/acme directory is one parent directory above the current location in the directory tree.

An alternate method for saving time when typing pathnames as arguments to commands is to use the **Tab-completion feature** of the BASH shell. To do this, type enough unique letters of a directory and press the Tab key to allow the BASH shell to find the intended file or directory being specified and fill in the appropriate information. If there is more than one possible match, the Tab-completion feature alerts you with a beep; pressing the Tab key again after this beep presents you with a list of possible files or directories.

Observe the directory structure in Figure 3-2. To use the Tab-completion feature to change the current directory to /home/sue, you type cd /h and then press the Tab key. This changes the previous characters on the terminal screen to display cd /home/ (the BASH shell was able to fill in the appropriate information because the /home directory is the only directory under the / directory that starts with the letter "h"). Then, you could add an s character to the command, so that the command line displays cd /home/s, and press the Tab key once again to allow the shell to fill in the remaining letters. This results in the command cd /home/sue/ being displayed on the terminal screen (the sue directory is the only directory that begins with the s character under the /home directory). At this point, you can press Enter to execute the command and change the current directory to /home/sue.

Viewing Files and Directories

The point of a directory structure is to organize files into an easy-to-use format. In order to locate the file you need to execute, view, or edit, you need to be able to display a list of the contents of a particular directory. You'll learn how to do that shortly, but first you need to learn about the various types of files and filenames, as well as the different commands used to select filenames for viewing.

File Types

Fundamental to viewing files and directories is a solid understanding of the various types of files present on most Linux systems. A Linux system can have several types of files; the most common include the following:

- Text files
- Binary data files
- Executable program files
- Directory files
- Linked files
- Special device files
- Named pipes and sockets

Most files on a Linux system that contain configuration information are **text files**. Another type of file is a program that exists on the hard drive before it is executed in memory to become processes. A program is typically associated with several supporting **binary data files** that store information such as common functions and graphics. In addition, directories themselves are actually files; they are special files that serve as placeholders to organize other files. When you create a directory, a file is placed on the hard drive to represent that directory.

Linked files are files that have an association with one another; they can represent the same data or they can point to another file (also known as a shortcut file). **Special device files** are less common than the other file types that have been mentioned, yet they are important for systems administrators because they represent different devices on the system, such as hard disks and serial ports. These device files are used in conjunction with commands that manipulate devices on the system; special device files are typically found only in the /dev directory and are discussed in later chapters of this book. As with special device files, **named pipe files** are uncommon and used primarily by administrators. Named pipes identify channels that pass information from one process in memory to another, and in some cases they can be mediated by files on the hard drive. Writes to the file are processed while another process reads from it to achieve this passing of information. Another variant of a named pipe file is a **socket file**, which allows a process on another computer to write to a file on the local computer while another process reads from that file.

Filenames

Files are recognized by their **filenames**, which can include up to 255 characters, yet are rarely longer than 20 characters on most Linux systems. Filenames are typically composed of alphanumeric characters, the underscore (_) character, the dash (-) character, and the period (.) character.

> **Note**
>
> It is important to avoid using the shell metacharacters discussed in the previous chapter when naming files. Using a filename that contains a shell metacharacter as an argument to a Linux command might produce unexpected results.

> **Note**
>
> Filenames that start with a period (.) are referred to as hidden files. You need to use a special command to display them in a file list. This command is discussed later in this chapter.

Filenames used by the Windows operating system typically end with a period and three characters that identify the file type—for example, document.txt (a text file) and server.exe (an **executable program** file). However, most files on the hard drive of a Linux system do not follow this pattern, although some files on the Linux filesystem do contain characters at the end of the filename that indicate the file type. These characters are commonly referred to as **filename extensions**. Table 3-1 lists common examples of filename extensions and their associated file types.

Table 3-1   Common filename extensions

Metacharacter	Description
.bin	Binary executable program files (similar to .exe files within Windows)
.c	C programming language source code files
.cc, .cpp	C++ programming language source code files
.html, .htm	HTML (Hypertext Markup Language) files

(continues)

Table 3-1   Common filename extensions *(continued)*

Metacharacter	Description
.ps	Files formatted for printing with postscript
.txt	Text files
.tar	Archived files (contain other files within)
.gz, .bz2, .xz, .Z	Compressed files
.tar.gz, .tgz, .tar.bz2, .tar.xz, .tar.Z	Compressed archived files
.conf, .cfg	Configuration files (contain text)
.so	Shared object (programming library) files
.o, .ko	Compiled object files
.pl	PERL (Practical Extraction and Report Language) programs
.tcl	Tcl (Tool Command Language) programs
.jpg, .jpeg, .png, .tiff, .xpm, .gif	Binary files that contain graphical images
.sh	Shell scripts (contain text that is executed by the shell)

Listing Files

Linux hosts a variety of commands that can be used to display files and their types
in various directories on hard drive partitions. By far, the most common method for
displaying files is to use the **ls command**. Following is an example of a file listing in
the root user's home directory:

```
[root@server1 ~]# pwd
/root
[root@server1 ~]# ls
current myprogram project project12 project2 project4
Desktop myscript project1 project13 project3 project5
[root@server1 ~]#_
```

Note 📎

The files listed previously and discussed throughout this chapter are for example purposes
only. The Hands-On Projects use different files.

The ls command displays all the files in the current directory in columnar format;
however, you can also pass an argument to the ls command indicating the directory
to list if the current directory listing is not required. In the following example, the files
are listed under the /home/bob directory without changing the current directory.

```
[root@server1 ~]# pwd
/root
```

```
[root@server1 ~]# ls /home/bob
assignment1 file1 letter letter2 project1
[root@server1 ~]#_
```

> **Note**
>
> When running the `ls` command, you will notice that files of different types are often represented as different colors; however, the specific colors used to represent files of certain types might vary from terminal to terminal and distribution to distribution. As a result, do not assume color alone indicates the file type.

> **Note**
>
> Windows uses the `dir` command to list files and directories; to simplify the learning of Linux for Windows users, there is a `dir` command in Linux, which is simply a copy of, or shortcut to, the `ls` command.

Recall from the previous chapter that you can use switches to alter the behavior of commands. To view a list of files and their type, use the `-F` switch to the `ls` command:

```
[root@server1 ~]# pwd
/root
[root@server1 ~]# ls -F
current@  myprogram*  project    project12  project2  project4
Desktop/ myscript*    project1   project13  project3  project5
[root@server1 ~]#_
```

The `ls -F` command appends a special character at the end of each filename displayed to indicate the type of file. In the preceding output, note that the filenames current, Desktop, myprogram, and myscript have special characters appended to their names. The @ symbol indicates a linked file, the * symbol indicates an executable file, the / indicates a subdirectory, the = character indicates a socket, and the | character indicates a named pipe. Other file types do not have a special character appended to them and could be text files, binary data files, or special device files.

> **Note**
>
> It is a common convention to name directories starting with an uppercase letter, such as the D in the Desktop directory shown in the preceding output. This allows you to quickly determine which names refer to directories when running the `ls` command without any options that specify file type.

Although the `ls -F` command is a quick way of getting file type information in an easy-to-read format, at times you need to obtain more detailed information about each file. The `ls -l` command can be used to provide a long listing for each file in a certain directory.

```
[root@server1 ~]# pwd
/root
[root@server1 ~]# ls -l
total 548
lrwxrwxrwx    1 root    root              9 Apr  7 09:56 current ->
project12
drwx------    3 root    root           4096 Mar 29 10:01 Desktop
-rwxr-xr-x    1 root    root         519964 Apr  7 09:59 myprogram
-rwxr-xr-x    1 root    root             20 Apr  7 09:58 myscript
-rw-r--r--    1 root    root             71 Apr  7 09:58 project
-rw-r--r--    1 root    root             71 Apr  7 09:59 project1
-rw-r--r--    1 root    root             71 Apr  7 09:59 project12
-rw-r--r--    1 root    root              0 Apr  7 09:56 project13
-rw-r--r--    1 root    root             71 Apr  7 09:59 project2
-rw-r--r--    1 root    root             90 Apr  7 10:01 project3
-rw-r--r--    1 root    root             99 Apr  7 10:01 project4
-rw-r--r--    1 root    root            108 Apr  7 10:01 project5
[root@server1 ~]#_
```

Each file listed in the preceding example has eight components of information listed in columns from left to right:

1. A file type character:
   - The d character represents a directory.
   - The l character represents a symbolically linked file (discussed in Chapter 4).
   - The b or c characters represent special device files (discussed in Chapter 5).
   - The n character represents a named pipe.
   - The s character represents a socket.
   - The – character represents all other file types (text files, binary data files).
2. A list of permissions on the file (also called the mode of the file).
3. A hard link count (discussed in Chapter 4).
4. The owner of the file (discussed in Chapter 4).
5. The group owner of the file (discussed in Chapter 4).
6. The file size.
7. The most recent modification time of the file (or creation time if the file was not modified following creation).
8. The filename. Some files are shortcuts or pointers to other files and indicated with an arrow ->, as with the file called "current" in the preceding output; these are known as symbolic links and are discussed in Chapter 4.

For the file named "project" in the previous example, you can see that this file is a regular file because its long listing begins with a – character, the permissions on the file are rw-r--r--, the hard link count is 1, the owner of the file is the root user, the group owner of the file is the root group, the size of the file is 71 bytes, and the file was modified last on April 7 at 9:58 a.m.

Note 📎

If SELinux is enabled on your system, you may also notice a period (.) immediately following the permissions on a file or directory that is managed by SELinux. SELinux will be discussed in Chapter 14.

Note 📎

On most Linux systems, a shortcut to the ls command can be used to display the same columns of information as the ls -l command. Some users prefer to use this shortcut, commonly known as an alias, which is invoked when a user types ll at a command prompt. This is known as the **ll command**.

The ls -F and ls -l commands are valuable to a user who wants to display file types; however, neither of these commands can display all file types using special characters. To display the file type of any file, you can use the **file command**; you give the file command an argument specifying what file to analyze. You can also pass multiple files as arguments or use the * metacharacter to refer to all files in the current directory. An example of using the file command in the root user's home directory is as follows:

```
[root@server1 ~]# pwd
/root
[root@server1 ~]# ls
current   myprogram  project   project12  project2  project4
Desktop   myscript   project1  project13  project3  project5
[root@server1 ~]# file Desktop
Desktop:    directory
[root@server1 ~]# file project Desktop
project:    ASCII text
Desktop:    directory
[root@server1 ~]# file *
Desktop:    directory
current:    symbolic link to project12
myprogram: ELF 32-bit LSB executable, Intel 80386, version 1,
dynamically linked (uses shared libs), stripped
```

```
myscript:  Bourne-Again shell script text executable
project:   ASCII text
project1:  ASCII text
project12: ASCII text
project13: empty
project2:  ASCII text
project3:  ASCII text
project4:  ASCII text
project5:  ASCII text
[root@server1 ~]#_
```

As shown in the preceding example, the `file` command can also identify the differences between types of executable files. The myscript file is a text file that contains executable commands (also known as a **shell script**), whereas the myprogram file is a 32-bit executable compiled program. The `file` command also identifies empty files such as project13 in the previous example.

Some filenames inside each user's home directory represent important configuration files or program directories. Because these files are rarely edited by the user and can clutter the listing of files, they are normally hidden from view when using the `ls` and `file` commands. Recall that filenames for hidden files start with a period character (.). To view them, pass the –a option to the `ls` command. Some hidden files that are commonly seen in the root user's home directory are shown next:

```
[root@server1 ~]# ls
myprogram  project    project12  project2   project4
myscript   project1   project13  project3   project5
[root@server1 ~]# ls -a
.                .bash_profile  .cshrc      project    project2   .pki
..               .bashrc        .esd_auth   project1   project3
.tcshrc
.bash_history    .cache         myprogram   project12  project4
.bash_logout     .config        myscript    project13  project5
[root@server1 ~]#_
```

As discussed earlier, the (.) character refers to the current working directory and the (..) character refers to the parent directory relative to your current location in the directory tree. Each of these pointers is seen as a special (or fictitious) file when using the `ls -a` command, as each starts with a period.

You can also specify several options simultaneously for most commands on the command line and receive the combined functionality of all the options. For example, to view all hidden files and their file types, you could type:

```
[root@server1 ~]# ls -aF
.                .bash_profile  .cshrc      project    project2
.pki/
```

```
  ..              .bashrc        .esd_auth  project1   project3
.tcshrc
.bash_history   .cache/        myprogram  project12  project4
.bash_logout    .config/       myscript   project13  project5
[root@server1 ~]#_
```

The aforementioned options to the ls command (-l, -F, -a) are the most common options you would use when navigating the Linux directory tree; however, many options are available in the ls command that alter the listing of files on the filesystem. Table 3-2 lists the most common of these options and their descriptions.

Table 3-2   Common options to the ls command

Option	Description
-a --all	Lists all filenames
-A --almost-all	Lists most filenames (excludes the . and .. special files)
-C	Lists filenames in column format
--color=n	Lists filenames without color
-d --directory	Lists directory names instead of their contents
-f	Lists all filenames without sorting
-F --classify	Lists filenames classified by file type
--full-time	Lists filenames in long format and displays the full modification time
-l	Lists filenames in long format
-lh -l --human-readable	Lists filenames in long format with human-readable (easy-to-read) file sizes
-lG -l --no-group-o	Lists filenames in long format but omits the group information
-r --reverse	Lists filenames reverse sorted
-R --recursive	Lists filenames in the specified directory and all subdirectories
-s	Lists filenames and their associated sizes in kilobytes (KB)
-S	Lists filenames sorted by file size (largest first)
-t	Lists filenames sorted by modification time (newest first)
-U	Lists filenames without sorting
-x	Lists filenames in rows rather than in columns

Wildcard Metacharacters

In the previous section, you saw that the * metacharacter stands for all the files in the current directory, much like a wildcard stands for, or matches, certain cards in a card game. As a result, the * metacharacter is called a **wildcard metacharacter**. Wildcard metacharacters can simplify commands that specify more than one filename on the command line, as you saw with the file command earlier. They match certain portions of filenames or the entire filename itself. Because they are interpreted by the shell, they can be used with most common Linux filesystem commands, including a few that have already been mentioned (ls, file, and cd). Table 3-3 displays a list of wildcard metacharacters and their descriptions.

Table 3-3   Wildcard metacharacters

Metacharacter	Description
*	Matches 0 or more characters in a filename
?	Matches 1 character in a filename
[aegh]	Matches 1 character in a filename—provided this character is either an a, e, g, or h
[a-e]	Matches 1 character in a filename—provided this character is either an a, b, c, d, or e
[!a-e]	Matches 1 character in a filename—provided this character is NOT an a, b, c, d, or e

Wildcards can be demonstrated using the ls command. Examples of using wildcard metacharacters to narrow the listing produced by the ls command are shown next.

```
[root@server1 ~]# ls
current     myprogram  project   project12  project2  project4
document1   myscript   project1  project13  project3  project5
[root@server1 ~]# ls project*
project  project1  project12  project13  project2  project3
project4  project5
[root@server1 ~]# ls project?
project1  project2  project3  project4  project5
[root@server1 ~]# ls project??
project12  project13
[root@server1 ~]# ls project[135]
project1  project3  project5
[root@server1 ~]# ls project[!135]
project2  project4
[root@server1 ~]# _
```

Note

Using wildcards to match multiple files or directories within a command is often called **file globbing**.

Displaying the Contents of Text Files

So far, this chapter has discussed commands that can be used to navigate the Linux directory structure and view filenames and file types; it is usual now to display the contents of these files. By far, the most common file type that users display is text files. These files are usually small and contain configuration information or instructions that the shell interprets (called a shell script) but can also contain other forms of text, as in email messages. To view an entire text file on the terminal screen (also referred to as concatenation), you can use the `cat` **command**. The following is an example of using the `cat` command to display the contents of an email message (in the fictitious file project4):

```
[root@server1 ~]# ls
current     myprogram  project    project12  project2  project4
document1  myscript   project1   project13  project3  project5
[root@server1 ~]# cat project4
Hi there, I hope this day finds you well.

Unfortunately, we were not able to make it to your dining
room this year while vacationing in Algonquin Park - I
especially wished to see the model of the Highland Inn
and the train station in the dining room.

I have been reading on the history of Algonquin Park but
nowhere could I find a description of where the Highland
Inn was originally located on Cache Lake.

If it is no trouble, could you kindly let me know such that
I need not wait until next year when I visit your lodge?

Regards,
Mackenzie Elizabeth
[root@server1 ~]#_
```

You can also use the `cat` command to display the line number of each line in the file in addition to the contents by passing the –n option to the `cat` command. In the following example, the number of each line in the project4 file is displayed:

```
[root@server1 ~]# cat -n project4
     1  Hi there, I hope this day finds you well.
     2
     3  Unfortunately, we were not able to make it to your dining
     4  room this year while vacationing in Algonquin Park - I
     5  especially wished to see the model of the Highland Inn
     6  and the train station in the dining room.
     7
     8  I have been reading on the history of Algonquin Park but
     9  nowhere could I find a description of where the Highland
    10  Inn was originally located on Cache Lake.
    11
    12  If it is no trouble, could you kindly let me know such
        that
    13  I need not wait until next year when I visit your lodge?
    14
    15  Regards,
    16  Mackenzie Elizabeth
[root@server1 ~]#_
```

In some cases, you might want to display the contents of a certain text file in reverse order, which is useful when displaying files that have text appended to them continuously by system services. These files, also known as **log files**, contain the most recent entries at the bottom of the file. To display a file in reverse order, use the `tac` **command** (tac is cat spelled backwards), as shown next with the file project4:

```
[root@server1 ~]# tac project4
Mackenzie Elizabeth
Regards,

I need not wait until next year when I visit your lodge?
If it is no trouble, could you kindly let me know such that

Inn was originally located on Cache Lake.
nowhere could I find a description of where the Highland
I have been reading on the history of Algonquin Park but

and the train station in the dining room.
especially wished to see the model of the Highland Inn
room this year while vacationing in Algonquin Park - I
Unfortunately, we were not able to make it to your dining
```

```
Hi there, I hope this day finds you well.
[root@server1 ~]#_
```

If the file displayed is very large and you only want to view the first few lines of it, you can use the **head command**. The head command displays the first 10 lines (including blank lines) of a text file to the terminal screen but can also take a numeric option specifying a different number of lines to display. The following shows an example of using the head command to view the top of the project4 file:

```
[root@server1 ~]# head project4
Hi there, I hope this day finds you well.

Unfortunately, we were not able to make it to your dining
room this year while vacationing in Algonquin Park - I
especially wished to see the model of the Highland Inn
and the train station in the dining room.

I have been reading on the history of Algonquin Park but
nowhere could I find a description of where the Highland
Inn was originally located on Cache Lake.
[root@server1 ~]# head -3 project4
Hi there, I hope this day finds you well.

Unfortunately, we were not able to make it to your dining
[root@server1 ~]#_
```

Just as the head command displays the beginning of text files, the **tail command** can be used to display the end of text files. By default, the tail command displays the final 10 lines of a file, but it can also take a numeric option specifying the number of lines to display on the terminal screen, as shown in the following example with the project4 file:

```
[root@server1 ~]# tail project4

I have been reading on the history of Algonquin Park but
nowhere could I find a description of where the Highland
Inn was originally located on Cache Lake.

If it is no trouble, could you kindly let me know such that
I need not wait until next year when I visit your lodge?

Regards,
Mackenzie Elizabeth
[root@server1 ~]# tail -2 project4
```

```
Regards,
Mackenzie Elizabeth
[root@server1 ~]#_
```

Although some text files are small enough to be displayed completely on the terminal screen, you might encounter text files that are too large to fit in a single screen. In this case, the cat command sends the entire file contents to the terminal screen; however, the screen only displays as much of the text as it has room for. To display a large text file in a page-by-page fashion, you need to use the more and less commands.

The more command gets its name from the pg command once used on UNIX systems. The pg command displayed a text file page-by-page on the terminal screen, starting at the beginning of the file; pressing the spacebar or Enter key displays the next page, and so on. The more command does more than pg did, because it displays the next complete page of a text file if you press the spacebar, but displays only the next line of a text file if you press Enter. In that way, you can browse the contents of a text file page-by-page or line-by-line. The fictitious file project5 is an excerpt from Shakespeare's tragedy *Macbeth* and is too large to be displayed fully on the terminal screen using the cat command. Using the more command to view its contents results in the following output:

```
[root@server1 ~]# more project5
Go bid thy mistress, when my drink is ready,
She strike upon the bell. Get thee to bed.
Is this a dagger which I see before me,
The handle toward my hand? Come, let me clutch thee.
I have thee not, and yet I see thee still.
Art thou not, fatal vision, sensible
To feeling as to sight? or art thou but
A dagger of the mind, a false creation,
Proceeding from the heat-oppressed brain?
I see thee yet, in form as palpable
As this which now I draw.
Thou marshall'st me the way that I was going;
And such an instrument I was to use.
Mine eyes are made the fools o' the other senses,
Or else worth all the rest; I see thee still,
And on thy blade and dudgeon gouts of blood,
Which was not so before. There's no such thing:
It is the bloody business which informs
Thus to mine eyes. Now o'er the one halfworld
Nature seems dead, and wicked dreams abuse
```

The curtain'd sleep; witchcraft celebrates
Pale Hecate's offerings, and wither'd murder,
Alarum'd by his sentinel, the wolf,
--More--(71%)

As you can see in the preceding output, the more command displays the first page without returning you to the shell prompt. Instead, the more command displays a prompt at the bottom of the terminal screen that indicates how much of the file is displayed on the screen as a percentage of the total file size. In the preceding example, 71 percent of the project5 file is displayed. At this prompt, you can press the spacebar to advance one whole page, or you can press the Enter key to advance to the next line. In addition, the more command allows other user interactions at this prompt. Pressing the h character at the prompt displays a help screen, which is shown in the following output, and pressing the q character quits the more command completely without viewing the remainder of the file.

```
--More--(71%)
Most commands optionally preceded by integer argument k. Defaults
in brackets. Star (*) indicates argument becomes new default.
-------------------------------------------------------------------
<space>                 Display next k lines of text
z                       Display next k lines of text
<return>                Display next k lines of text [1]
d or ctrl-D             Scroll k lines [current scroll size,
                        initially 11]
q or Q or <interrupt>   Exit from more
s                       Skip forward k lines of text [1]
f                       Skip forward k screenfuls of text [1]
b or ctrl-B             Skip backward k screenfuls of text [1]
'                       Go to place where previous search started
=                       Display current line number
/<regular expression>   Search for kth occurrence of expression [1]
n                       Search for kth occurrence of last r.e [1]
!<cmd> or :!<cmd>       Execute <cmd> in a subshell
v                       Start up /usr/bin/vi at current line
ctrl-L                  Redraw screen
:n                      Go to kth next file [1]
:p                      Go to kth previous file [1]
:f                      Display current filename and line number
                        Repeat previous command
-------------------------------------------------------------------
--More—(71%)
```

Just as the `more` command was named as a result of allowing more user functionality, the `less` command is named for doing more than the `more` command (remember that "less is more," more or less). Like the `more` command, the `less` command can browse the contents of a text file page-by-page by pressing the spacebar and line-by-line by pressing the Enter key; however, you can also use the arrow keys on the keyboard to scroll up and down the contents of the file. The output of the `less` command, when used to view the project5 file, is as follows:

```
[root@server1 ~]# less project5
Go bid thy mistress, when my drink is ready,
She strike upon the bell. Get thee to bed.
Is this a dagger which I see before me,
The handle toward my hand? Come, let me clutch thee.
I have thee not, and yet I see thee still.
Art thou not, fatal vision, sensible
To feeling as to sight? or art thou but
A dagger of the mind, a false creation,
Proceeding from the heat-oppressed brain?
I see thee yet, in form as palpable
As this which now I draw.
Thou marshall'st me the way that I was going;
And such an instrument I was to use.
Mine eyes are made the fools o' the other senses,
Or else worth all the rest; I see thee still,
And on thy blade and dudgeon gouts of blood,
Which was not so before. There's no such thing:
It is the bloody business which informs
Thus to mine eyes. Now o'er the one halfworld
Nature seems dead, and wicked dreams abuse
The curtain'd sleep; witchcraft celebrates
Pale Hecate's offerings, and wither'd murder,
Alarum'd by his sentinel, the wolf,
Whose howl's his watch, thus with his stealthy pace.
project5
```

Like the `more` command, the `less` command displays a prompt at the bottom of the file using the : character or the filename of the file being viewed (project5 in our example), yet the `less` command contains more keyboard shortcuts for searching out text within files. At the prompt, you can press the h key to obtain a help screen or the q key to quit. The first help screen for the `less` command is shown next:

```
                    SUMMARY OF LESS COMMANDS

Commands marked with * may be preceded by a number, N.
```

Notes in parentheses indicate the behavior if N is given.
A key preceded by a caret indicates the Ctrl key; thus ^K is
ctrl-K.


```
h  H                     Display this help.
q  :q  Q  :Q  ZZ         Exit.
```

                         MOVING


```
e   ^E  j   ^N  CR   *  Forward one line(or N lines).
y   ^Y  k   ^K  ^P   *  Backward one line (or N lines).
f   ^F  ^V  SPACE    *  Forward one window (or N lines).
b   ^B  ESC-v        *  Backward one window (or N lines).
z                    *  Forward one window (and set window to N).
w                    *  Backward one window (and set window to N).
ESC-SPACE            *  Forward one window, but don't stop at
                          end-of-file.
d   ^D               *  Forward one half-window(and set half-window
                          to N)
u   ^U               *  Backward one half-window(and set half window
                          to N)
ESC-(  RightArrow    *  Left  8 character positions (or N positions).
ESC-)  LeftArrow     *  Right 8 character positions (or N positions).
F                       Forward forever; like "tail -f".
```

HELP -- Press RETURN for more, or q when done

The more and less commands can also be used in conjunction with the output of
commands if that output is too large to fit on the terminal screen. To do this, use the |
metacharacter after the command, followed by either the more or less command, as
follows:

```
[root@server1 ~]# cd /etc
[root@server1 etc]# ls -l | more
total 3688
-rw-r--r--   1 root     root     15276 Mar 22 12:20 a2ps.cfg
-rw-r--r--   1 root     root      2562 Mar 22 12:20 a2ps-site.cfg
drwxr-xr-x   4 root     root      4096 Jun 11 08:45 acpi
-rw-r--r--   1 root     root        46 Jun 16 16:42 adjtime
drwxr-xr-x   2 root     root      4096 Jun 11 08:47 aep
-rw-r--r--   1 root     root       688 Feb 17 00:35 aep.conf
-rw-r--r--   1 root     root       703 Feb 17 00:35 aeplog.conf
```

```
drwxr-xr-x   4 root     root       4096 Jun 11 08:47 alchemist
-rw-r--r--   1 root     root       1419 Jan 26 10:14 aliases
-rw-r-----   1 root     smmsp     12288 Jun 17 13:17 aliases.db
drwxr-xr-x   2 root     root       4096 Jun 11 11:11 alternatives
drwxr-xr-x   3 amanda   disk       4096 Jun 11 10:16 amanda
-rw-r--r--   1 amanda   disk          0 Mar 22 12:28 amandates
-rw-------   1 root     root        688 Mar  4 22:34 amd.conf
-rw-r-----   1 root     root        105 Mar  4 22:34 amd.net
-rw-r--r--   1 root     root        317 Feb 15 14:33 anacrontab
-rw-r--r--   1 root     root        331 May  5 08:07 ant.conf
-rw-r--r--   1 root     root       6200 Jun 16 16:42 asound.state
drwxr-xr-x   3 root     root       4096 Jun 11 10:37 atalk
-rw-------   1 root     root          1 May  5 13:39 at.deny
-rw-r--r--   1 root     root        325 Apr 14 13:39 auto.master
-rw-r--r--   1 root     root        581 Apr 14 13:39 auto.misc
--More--
```

In the preceding example, the output of the `ls -l` command was redirected to the `more` command, which displays the first page of output on the terminal. You can then advance through the output page-by-page or line-by-line. This type of redirection is discussed in Chapter 7.

Note

You can also use the **diff command** to identify the content differences between two text files, which is often useful when comparing revisions of configuration files on a Linux system. For example, the `diff file1 file2` command would list the lines that are different between file1 and file2.

Displaying the Contents of Binary Files

It is important to employ text file commands, such as `cat`, `tac`, `head`, `tail`, `more`, and `less`, only on files that contain text; otherwise, you might find yourself with random output on the terminal screen or even a dysfunctional terminal. To view the contents of binary files, you typically use the program that was used to create the file. However, some commands can be used to safely display the contents of most binary files. The **strings command** searches for text characters in a binary file and outputs them to the screen. In many cases, these text characters might indicate what the binary file is used for. For example, to find the text characters inside the /bin/echo binary executable program page-by-page, you could use the following command:

```
[root@server1 ~]# strings /bin/echo | more
/lib/ld-linux.so.2
PTRh|
<nt7<e
|[^_]
[^_]
[^_]
Try '%s --help' for more information.
Usage: %s [OPTION]... [STRING]...
Echo the STRING(s) to standard output.
  -n              do not output the trailing newline
  -e              enable interpretation of the
backslash-escapedcharacters
                      listed below
  -E              disable interpretation of those sequences in
STRINGs
      --help     display this help and exit
      --version  output version information and exit
Without -E, the following sequences are recognized and
interpolated:
  \NNN   the character whose ASCII code is NNN (octal)
  \\     backslash
  \a     alert (BEL)
  \b     backspace
  \c     suppress trailing newline
  \f     form feed
  \n     new line
--More--
```

Although this output might not be easy to read, it does contain portions of text that can point a user in the right direction to find out more about the /bin/echo command. Another command that is safe to use on binary files and text files is the od **command**, which displays the contents of the file in octal format (numeric base 8 format). An example of using the od command to display the first five lines of the file project4 is shown in the following example:

```
[root@server1 ~]# od project4 | head -5
0000000 064510 072040 062550 062562 020054 020111 067550 062560
0000020 072040 064550 020163 060544 020171 064546 062156 020163
0000040 067571 020165 062567 066154 006456 006412 052412 063156
```

```
0000060 071157 072564 060556 062564 074554 073440 020145 062567
0000100 062562 067040 072157 060440 066142 020145 067564 066440
[root@server1 ~]#_
```

> **Note**
>
> You can use the -x option to the od command to display a file in hexadecimal format (numeric base 16 format).

Searching for Text Within Files

Recall that Linux was modeled after the UNIX operating system. The UNIX operating system is often referred to as the "grandfather" of all operating systems because it is over 40 years old and has formed the basis for most advances in computing technology. The major use of the UNIX operating system in the past 40 years involved simplifying business and scientific management through database applications. As a result, many commands (referred to as **text tools**) were developed for the UNIX operating system that could search for and manipulate text, such as database information, in many advantageous ways. A set of text wildcards was also developed to ease the searching of specific text information. These text wildcards are called **regular expressions (regexp)** and are recognized by several text tools and programming languages, including, but not limited to, the following:

- grep
- awk
- sed
- vi
- Emacs
- ex
- ed
- C++
- PERL
- Python

Because Linux is a close relative of the UNIX operating system, these text tools and regular expressions are available to Linux as well. By combining text tools, a typical Linux system can search for and manipulate data in almost every way possible (as you will see later). As a result, regular expressions and the text tools that use them are commonly used in business today.

Regular Expressions

As mentioned earlier, regular expressions allow you to specify a certain pattern of text within a text document. They work similarly to wildcard metacharacters in that they are used to match characters, yet they have many differences:

- Wildcard metacharacters are interpreted by the shell, whereas regular expressions are interpreted by a text tool program.
- Wildcard metacharacters match characters in filenames (or directory names) on a Linux filesystem, whereas regular expressions match characters *within* text files on a Linux filesystem.
- Wildcard metacharacters typically have different definitions than regular expression metacharacters.
- More regular expression metacharacters are available than wildcard metacharacters.

In addition, regular expression metacharacters are divided into two categories: common (basic) regular expressions and extended regular expressions. Common regular expressions are available to most text tools; however, extended regular expressions are less common and available in only certain text tools. Table 3-4 shows definitions and examples of some common and extended regular expressions.

Table 3-4 Regular expressions

Regular expression	Description	Example	Type
*	Matches 0 or more occurrences of the previous character	letter* matches lette, letter, letterr, letterrrr, letterrrrr, and so on	Common
?	Matches 0 or 1 occurrences of the previous character	letter? matches lette, letter	Extended
+	Matches 1 or more occurrences of the previous character	letter+ matches letter, letterr, letterrrr, letterrrrr, and so on	Extended
. (period)	Matches 1 character of any type	letter. matches lettera, letterb, letterc, letter1, letter2, letter3, and so on	Common
[...]	Matches one character from the range specified within the braces	letter[1238] matches letter1, letter2, letter3, and letter8; letter[a-c] matches lettera, letterb, and letterc	Common
[^...]	Matches one character NOT from the range specified within the braces	letter[^1238] matches letter4, letter5, letter6, lettera, letterb, and so on (any character except 1, 2, 3, or 8)	Common
{ }	Matches a specific number or range of the previous character	letter{3} matches letterrr letter, whereas letter {2,4} matches letterr, letterrr, and letterrrr	Extended

(continues)

Table 3-4 Regular expressions *(continued)*

Regular expression	Description	Example	Type
^	Matches the following characters if they are the first characters on the line	^letter matches letter if letter is the first set of characters in the line	Common
$	Matches the previous characters if they are the last characters on the line	letter$ matches letter if letter is the last set of characters in the line	Common
(... | ...)	Matches either of two sets of characters	(mother|father) matches the word "mother" or "father"	Extended

The grep Command

The most common way to search for information using regular expressions is the grep command. The **grep command** (the command name is short for global regular expression print) is used to display lines in a text file that match a certain common regular expression. To display lines of text that match extended regular expressions, you must use the **egrep command** (or the -E option to the grep command). In addition, the **fgrep command** (or the -F option to the grep command) does not interpret any regular expressions and consequently returns results much faster. Take, for example, the project4 file shown earlier:

```
[root@server1 ~]# cat project4
Hi there, I hope this day finds you well.

Unfortunately, we were not able to make it to your dining
room this year while vacationing in Algonquin Park - I
especially wished to see the model of the Highland Inn
and the train station in the dining room.

I have been reading on the history of Algonquin Park but
nowhere could I find a description of where the Highland
Inn was originally located on Cache Lake.

If it is no trouble, could you kindly let me know such that
I need not wait until next year when I visit your lodge?

Regards,
Mackenzie Elizabeth
[root@server1 ~]#_
```

The grep command requires two arguments at minimum, the first argument specifies which text to search for, and the remaining arguments specify the files to search. If a pattern of text is matched, the grep command displays the entire line on the terminal screen. For example, to list only those lines in the file project4 that contain the words "Algonquin Park," enter the following command:

```
[root@server1 ~]# grep "Algonquin Park" project4
room this year while vacationing in Algonquin Park - I
I have been reading on the history of Algonquin Park but
[root@server1 ~]#_
```

To return the lines that do not contain the text "Algonquin Park," you can use the −v option of the grep command to reverse the meaning of the previous command:

```
[root@server1 ~]# grep -v "Algonquin Park" project4
Hi there, I hope this day finds you well.

Unfortunately, we were not able to make it to your dining
especially wished to see the model of the Highland Inn
and the train station in the dining room.

nowhere could I find a description of where the Highland
Inn was originally located on Cache Lake.

If it is no trouble, could you kindly let me know such that
I need not wait until next year when I visit your lodge?

Regards,
Mackenzie Elizabeth
[root@server1 ~]#_
```

Keep in mind that the text being searched is case sensitive; to perform a case-insensitive search, use the −i option to the grep command:

```
[root@server1 ~]# grep "algonquin park" project4
[root@server1 ~]#_
[root@server1 ~]# grep -i "algonquin park" project4
room this year while vacationing in Algonquin Park - I
I have been reading on the history of Algonquin Park but
[root@server1 ~]#_
```

Another important note to keep in mind regarding text tools such as grep is that they match only patterns of text; they are unable to discern words or phrases unless they are specified. For example, if you want to search for the lines that contain the word "we," you can use the following grep command:

```
[root@server1 ~]# grep "we" project4
Hi there, I hope this day finds you well.
Unfortunately, we were not able to make it to your dining
[root@server1 ~]#_
```

However, notice from the preceding output that the first line displayed does not contain the word "we"; the word "well" contains the text pattern "we" and is displayed as a result. To display only lines that contain the word "we," you can type the following to match the letters "we" surrounded by space characters:

```
[root@server1 ~]# grep " we " project4
Unfortunately, we were not able to make it to your dining
[root@server1 ~]#_
```

All of the previous grep examples did not use regular expression metacharacters to search for text in the project4 file. Some examples of using regular expressions (see Table 3-4) when searching this file are shown throughout the remainder of this section.

To view lines that contain the word "toe" or "the" or "tie," you can enter the following command:

```
[root@server1 ~]# grep " t.e " project4
especially wished to see the model of the Highland Inn
and the train station in the dining room.
I have been reading on the history of Algonquin Park but
nowhere could I find a description of where the Highland
[root@server1 ~]#_
```

To view lines that start with the word "I," you can enter the following command:

```
[root@server1 ~]# grep "^I " project4
I have been reading on the history of Algonquin Park but
I need not wait until next year when I visit your lodge?
[root@server1 ~]#_
```

To view lines that contain the text "lodge" or "Lake," you need to use an extended regular expression and the egrep command, as follows:

```
[root@server1 ~]# egrep "(lodge|Lake)" project4
Inn was originally located on Cache Lake.
I need not wait until next year when I visit your lodge?
[root@server1 ~]#_
```

Editing Text Files

Recall that text files are the most common type of file modified by Linux users and administrators. Most system configuration is stored in text files, as is commonly accessed information such as email and program source code. Consequently, most Linux distributions come with an assortment of text editors, and many more are available for Linux systems via the Internet. Text editors come in two varieties: editors that can be used on the command line, including vi (vim), nano, and Emacs, and editors that can be used in a GUI environment, including Emacs (graphical version) and gedit.

The vi Editor

The **vi editor** (pronounced "vee eye") is one of the oldest and most popular visual text editors available for UNIX operating systems. Its Linux equivalent (known as vim, which is short for "vi improved") is, therefore, standard on almost every Linux distribution. Although the vi editor is not the easiest of the editors to use when editing text files, it has the advantage of portability. A Fedora Linux user who is proficient in using the vi editor will find editing files on all other UNIX and Linux systems easy because the interface and features of the vi editor are nearly identical across Linux and UNIX systems. In addition, the vi editor supports regular expressions and can perform over 1,000 different functions for the user.

To open an existing text file for editing, you can type vi filename (or vim filename), where *filename* specifies the file to be edited. To open a new file for editing, type vi or vim at the command line:

[root@server1 ~]# **vi**

The vi editor then runs interactively and replaces the command-line interface with the following output:

```
~
~
~
~
~
~                       VIM - Vi IMproved
~
~                        version 8.0.1704
~                      by Bram Moolenaar et al.
~                   Modified by <bugzilla@redhat.com>
~               Vim is open source and freely distributable
~
~                      Become a registered Vim user!
~            type  :help register<Enter>     for information
~
~            type  :q<Enter>                 to exit
~            type  :help<Enter>  or  <F1>  for on-line help
~            type  :help version7<Enter>    for version info
~
~
~
~
```

```
~
~
~
```

The tilde (~) characters on the left indicate the end of the file; they are pushed further down the screen as you enter text. The vi editor is called a bimodal editor because it functions in one of two modes: **command mode** and **insert mode**. The vi editor opens command mode, in which you must use the keyboard to perform functions, such as deleting text, copying text, saving changes to a file, and exiting the vi editor. To insert text into the document, you must enter insert mode by typing one of the characters listed in Table 3-5. One such method to enter insert mode is to type the i key while in command mode; the vi editor then displays -- INSERT -- at the bottom of the screen and allows the user to enter a sentence such as the following:

```
This is a sample sentence.
~
~
~
~
~
~
~
~
~
-- INSERT --
```

Table 3-5 Common keyboard keys used to change to and from insert mode

Key	Description
i	Changes to insert mode and places the cursor before the current character for entering text
a	Changes to insert mode and places the cursor after the current character for entering text
o	Changes to insert mode and opens a new line below the current line for entering text
I	Changes to insert mode and places the cursor at the beginning of the current line for entering text
A	Changes to insert mode and places the cursor at the end of the current line for entering text
O	Changes to insert mode and opens a new line above the current line for entering text
Esc	Changes back to command mode while in insert mode

When in insert mode, you can use the keyboard to type text as required, but when finished you must press the Esc key to return to command mode to perform other functions via keys on the keyboard. Table 3-6 provides a list of keys useful in command mode and their associated functions.

Table 3-6   Key combinations commonly used in command mode

Key	Description
w, W	Moves the cursor forward one word to the beginning of the next word
e, E	Moves the cursor forward one word to the end of the next word
b, B	Moves the cursor backward one word
53G	Moves the cursor to line 53
G	Moves the cursor to the last line in the document
0, ^	Moves the cursor to the beginning of the line
$	Moves the cursor to the end of the line
X	Deletes the character the cursor is on
3x	Deletes three characters starting from the character the cursor is on
dw	Deletes one word starting from the character the cursor is on
d3w, 3dw	Deletes three words starting from the character the cursor is on
dd	Deletes one whole line starting from the line the cursor is on
d3d, 3dd	Deletes three whole lines starting from the line the cursor is on
d$	Deletes from the cursor character to the end of the current line
d^, d0	Deletes from the cursor character to the beginning of the current line
yw	Copies one word (starting from the character the cursor is on) into a temporary buffer in memory for later use
y3w, 3yw	Copies three words (starting from the character the cursor is on) into a temporary buffer in memory for later use
yy	Copies the current line into a temporary buffer in memory for later use
y3y, 3yy	Copies three lines (starting from the current line) into a temporary buffer in memory for later use
y$	Copies the current line from the cursor to the end of the line into a temporary buffer in memory for later use
y^, y0	Copies the current line from the cursor to the beginning of the line into a temporary buffer in memory for later use
p	Pastes the contents of the temporary memory buffer underneath the current line
P	Pastes the contents of the temporary memory buffer above the current line
J	Joins the line below the current line to the current line
Ctrl+g	Displays current line statistics
u	Undoes the last function (undo)
.	Repeats the last function (repeat)
/pattern	Searches for the first occurrence of pattern in the forward direction
?pattern	Searches for the first occurrence of pattern in the reverse direction
n	Repeats the previous search in the forward direction
N	Repeats the previous search in the reverse direction

After you are in command mode, to save the text in a file called samplefile in the current directory, you need to type the : (colon) character (by pressing the Shift and ; keys simultaneously) to reach a : prompt where you can enter a command to save the contents of the current document to a file, as shown in the following example and in Table 3-7.

```
This is a sample sentence.
~
~
~
~
~
~
~
~
~
:w samplefile
```

Table 3-7 Key combinations commonly used at the command mode : prompt

Function	Description
:q	Quits from the vi editor if no changes were made
:q!	Quits from the vi editor and does not save any changes
:wq	Saves any changes to the file and quits from the vi editor
:w filename	Saves the current document to a file called filename
:!date	Executes the `date` command using a BASH shell
:r !date	Reads the output of the `date` command into the document under the current line
:r filename	Reads the contents of the text file called filename into the document under the current line
:set all	Displays all vi environment settings
:set	Sets a vi environment setting to a certain value
:s/the/THE/g	Searches for the regular expression "the" and replaces each occurrence globally throughout the current line with the word "THE"
:1,$ s/the/THE/g	Searches for the regular expression "the" and replaces each occurrence globally from line 1 to the end of the document with the word "THE"

As shown in Table 3-7, you can quit the vi editor by typing the : character and entering q!, which then returns the user to the shell prompt:

```
This is a sample sentence.
~
```

```
~
~
~
~
~
~
~
~
:q!
[root@server1 ~]# _
```

The vi editor also offers some advanced features to Linux users, as explained in Table 3-7. Examples of some of these features are discussed next, using the project4 file shown earlier in this chapter. To edit the project4 file, type `vi project4` and view the following screen:

```
Hi there, I hope this day finds you well.

Unfortunately, we were not able to make it to your dining
room this year while vacationing in Algonquin Park - I
especially wished to see the model of the Highland Inn
and the train station in the dining room.

I have been reading on the history of Algonquin Park but
nowhere could I find a description of where the Highland
Inn was originally located on Cache Lake.

If it is no trouble, could you kindly let me know such that
I need not wait until next year when I visit your lodge?

Regards,
Mackenzie Elizabeth
~
~
~
~
~
~
~
"project4" 17L, 583C
```

Note that the name of the file as well as the number of lines and characters in total are displayed at the bottom of the screen (project4 has 17 lines and 583 characters in this example). To insert the current date and time at the bottom of the file, you can move the cursor to the final line in the file and type the following at the : prompt while in command mode:

```
Hi there, I hope this day finds you well.

Unfortunately, we were not able to make it to your dining
room this year while vacationing in Algonquin Park - I
especially wished to see the model of the Highland Inn
and the train station in the dining room.

I have been reading on the history of Algonquin Park but
nowhere could I find a description of where the Highland
Inn was originally located on Cache Lake.

If it is no trouble, could you kindly let me know such that
I need not wait until next year when I visit your lodge?

Regards,
Mackenzie Elizabeth
~
~
~
~
~
~
~
~
:r !date
```

When you press Enter, the output of the date command is inserted below the current line:

```
Hi there, I hope this day finds you well.

Unfortunately, we were not able to make it to your dining
room this year while vacationing in Algonquin Park - I
especially wished to see the model of the Highland Inn
and the train station in the dining room.

I have been reading on the history of Algonquin Park but
nowhere could I find a description of where the Highland
Inn was originally located on Cache Lake.

If it is no trouble, could you kindly let me know such that
I need not wait until next year when I visit your lodge?
```

```
Regards,
Mackenzie Elizabeth
Sat Aug 7 18:33:10 EDT 2019
~

~

~

~

~

~
```

To change all occurrences of the word "Algonquin" to "ALGONQUIN," you can type the following at the : prompt while in command mode:

```
Hi there, I hope this day finds you well.

Unfortunately, we were not able to make it to your dining
room this year while vacationing in Algonquin Park - I
especially wished to see the model of the Highland Inn
and the train station in the dining room.

I have been reading on the history of Algonquin Park but
nowhere could I find a description of where the Highland
Inn was originally located on Cache Lake.

If it is no trouble, could you kindly let me know such that
I need not wait until next year when I visit your lodge?

Regards,
Mackenzie Elizabeth
Sat Aug 7 18:33:10 EDT 2019
~

~

~

~

~

~
```

:1,$ s/Algonquin/ALGONQUIN/g

The output changes to the following:

```
Hi there, I hope this day finds you well.

Unfortunately, we were not able to make it to your dining
room this year while vacationing in ALGONQUIN Park - I
especially wished to see the model of the Highland Inn
and the train station in the dining room.
```

I have been reading on the history of ALGONQUIN Park but
nowhere could I find a description of where the Highland
Inn was originally located on Cache Lake.

If it is no trouble, could you kindly let me know such that
I need not wait until next year when I visit your lodge?

Regards,
Mackenzie Elizabeth
Sat Aug 7 18:33:10 EDT 2019
~
~
~
~
~
~
~

Another attractive feature of the vi editor is its ability to customize the user
environment through settings that can be altered at the : prompt while in command
mode. Type set all at this prompt to observe the list of available settings and their
current values:

```
:set all
--- Options ---
  aleph=224            fileencoding=       menuitems=25
swapsync=fsync
noarabic               fileformat=unix    modeline             switchbuf=
  arabicshape          filetype=          modelines=5          syntax=
noallowrevins      nofkmap               modifiable           tabstop=8
noaltkeymap            foldclose=         modified             tagbsearch
  ambiwidth=single   foldcolumn=0         more
taglength=0
noautoindent           foldenable         mouse=
tagrelative
noautoread             foldexpr=0         mousemodel=extend   tagstack
noautowrite            foldignore=#        mousetime=500        term=xterm
noautowriteall         foldlevel=0        nonumber             notermbidi
-- More --
```

Note in the preceding output that, although some settings have a configured
value (e.g., fileformat=unix), most settings are set to either on or off; those that are

turned off are prefixed with a "no." In the preceding example, line numbering is turned off (nonumber in the preceding output); however, you can turn it on by typing set number at the : prompt while in command mode. This results in the following output in vi:

```
 1 Hi there, I hope this day finds you well.
 2
 3 Unfortunately, we were not able to make it to your dining
 4 room this year while vacationing in ALGONQUIN Park - I
 5 especially wished to see the model of the Highland Inn
 6 and the train station in the dining room.
 7
 8 I have been reading on the history of ALGONQUIN Park but
 9 nowhere could I find a description of where the Highland
10 Inn was originally located on Cache Lake.
11
12 If it is no trouble, could you kindly let me know such that
13 I need not wait until next year when I visit your lodge?
14
15 Regards,
16 Mackenzie Elizabeth
17 Sat Aug 7 18:33:10 EDT 2019
18
~
~
~
~
~
~
:set number
```

Conversely, to turn off line numbering, you could type set nonumber at the : prompt while in command mode.

Other Common Text Editors

Although the vi editor is the most common text editor used on Linux and UNIX systems, some other text editors are easier to use.

An alternative to the vi editor that offers an equal set of functionalities is the GNU **Emacs (Editor MACroS) editor.** Emacs is not installed by default in Fedora 28. To install it, you can run the command dnf install emacs at a command prompt to obtain

Emacs from a free software repository on the Internet. Next, to open the project4 file in the Emacs editor in a command-line terminal, type `emacs project4` and the following is displayed on the terminal screen:

```
File   Edit   Options   Buffers   Tools   Conf Help
Hi there, I hope this day finds you well.

Unfortunately, we were not able to make it to your dining
room this year while vacationing in Algonquin Park - I
especially wished to see the model of the Highland Inn
and the train station in the dining room.

I have been reading on the history of Algonquin Park but
nowhere could I find a description of where the Highland
Inn was originally located on Cache Lake.

If it is no trouble, could you kindly let me know such that
I need not wait until next year when I visit your lodge?

Regards,
Mackenzie Elizabeth




-UU-:----F1   project4      Top L1      (Conf[Space])------------------
For information about GNU Emacs and the GNU system, type C-h C-a.
```

The Emacs editor uses the Ctrl key in combination with certain letters to perform special functions, can be used with the LISP (LISt Processing) artificial intelligence programming language, and supports hundreds of keyboard functions, similar to the vi editor. Table 3-8 shows a list of some common keyboard functions used in the Emacs editor.

Table 3-8   Keyboard functions commonly used in the GNU Emacs editor

Key	Description
Ctrl+a	Moves the cursor to the beginning of the line
Ctrl+e	Moves the cursor to the end of the line
Ctrl+h	Displays Emacs documentation
Ctrl+d	Deletes the current character
Ctrl+k	Deletes all characters between the cursor and the end of the line

Table 3-8   Keyboard functions commonly used in the GNU Emacs editor (*continued*)

Key	Description
Esc+d	Deletes the current word
Ctrl+x + Ctrl+c	Exits the Emacs editor
Ctrl+x + Ctrl+s	Saves the current document
Ctrl+x + Ctrl+w	Saves the current document as a new filename
Ctrl+x + u	Undoes the last change

Another text editor that uses Ctrl key combinations for performing functions is the **nano editor** (based on the Pine UNIX editor). Unlike vi or Emacs, nano is a very basic and easy-to-use editor that many Linux administrators use to quickly modify configuration files if they don't need advanced functionality. As a result, nano is often installed by default on most modern Linux distributions. If you type nano project4, you will see the following displayed on the terminal screen:

```
GNU nano 2.9.5                        project4.txt
Hi there, I hope this day finds you well.

Unfortunately, we were not able to make it to your dining
room this year while vacationing in Algonquin Park - I
especially wished to see the model of the Highland Inn
and the train station in the dining room.

I have been reading on the history of Algonquin Park but
nowhere could I find a description of where the Highland
Inn was originally located on Cache Lake.

If it is no trouble, could you kindly let me know such that
I need not wait until next year when I visit your lodge?

Regards,
Mackenzie Elizabeth



                        [ Read 16 lines ]
^G Get Help ^O WriteOut   ^W Where Is ^K Cut Text    ^J Justify ^C CurPos
^X Exit       ^R Read File ^\ Replace   ^U UnCut Text ^T Spell    ^_ Go To
```

The bottom of the screen lists all the Ctrl key combinations. The ^ symbol represents the Ctrl key. This means that, to exit nano, you can press Ctrl+X (^X = Ctrl+X).

If you are using a GUI environment, there is often a graphical editor built into your desktop environment. For GNOME, you can use the **gedit editor** to quickly edit text files. Although the gedit editor does not have the advanced functionality that vi or Emacs has, it is the easiest editor to use as it is functionally analogous to the Windows Wordpad and Notepad editors. If you type `gedit project4` within GNOME, you will be able to edit the project4 file content graphically, as well as access any gedit functionality from the drop-down menu shown in Figure 3-3.

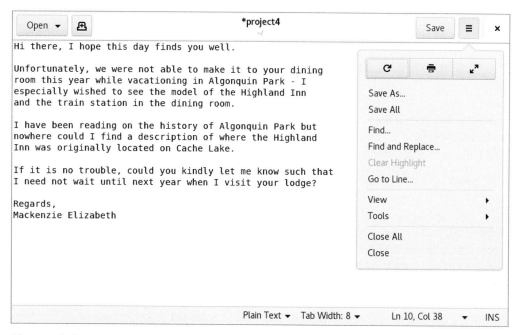

Figure 3-3 **The gedit text editor**

Chapter Summary

- The Linux filesystem is arranged hierarchically using a series of directories to store files. The location of these directories and files can be described using a relative or absolute pathname. The Linux filesystem can contain many types of files, such as text files, binary data, executable programs, directories, linked files, and special device files.

- The `ls` command can be used to view filenames and offers a wide range of options to modify this view.

- Wildcard metacharacters are special keyboard characters. They can be used to simplify the selection of several files when using common Linux file commands.

- Text files are the most common file type whose contents can be viewed by several utilities, such as `head`, `tail`, `cat`, `tac`, `more`, and `less`.
- Regular expression metacharacters can be used to specify certain patterns of text when used with certain programming languages and text tool utilities, such as `grep`.
- Although many command-line and graphical text editors exist, vi (vim) is a powerful, bimodal text editor that is standard on most UNIX and Linux systems.

Key Terms

~ metacharacter
absolute pathname
binary data file
`cat` command
`cd (change directory)` command
command mode
concatenation
`diff` command
directory
`egrep` command
Emacs (Editor MACroS) editor
executable program
`fgrep` command
`file` command
file globbing

filename
filename extension
gedit editor
`grep` command
`head` command
home directory
insert mode
`less` command
linked file
`ll` command
log file
`ls` command
`more` command
named pipe file
nano editor
`od` command
parent directory

pwd (print working directory) command
regular expressions (regexp)
relative pathname
shell script
socket file
special device file
`strings` command
subdirectory
Tab-completion feature
`tac` command
`tail` command
text file
text tools
vi editor
wildcard metacharacters

Review Questions

1. A directory is a type of file. True or False?
2. Which command would a user type on the command line to find out the current directory in the directory tree?
   a. pd
   b. cd
   c. where
   d. pwd
3. Which of the following is an absolute pathname? (Choose all that apply.)
   a. Home/resume
   b. C:\myfolder\resume
   c. resume
   d. /home/resume
   e. C:home/resume
4. A special device file is used to _____.
   a. enable proprietary custom-built devices to work with Linux
   b. represent hardware devices such as hard disk drives and ports
   c. keep a list of device settings specific to each individual user
   d. do nothing in Linux

5. If a user's current directory is /home/mary/project1, which command could she use to move to the etc directory directly under the root?
   a. `cd ..`
   b. `cd /home/mary/etc`
   c. `cd etc`
   d. `cd /etc`
   e. `cd \etc`

6. After typing the `ls -a` command, you notice a file whose filename begins with a dot (.). What does this mean?
   a. It is a binary file.
   b. It is a system file.
   c. It is a file in the current directory.
   d. It is a hidden file.

7. After typing the `ls -F` command, you notice a filename that ends with an * (asterisk) character. What does this mean?
   a. It is a hidden file.
   b. It is a linked file.
   c. It is a special device file.
   d. It is an executable file.

8. The vi editor can function in which two of the following modes? (Choose both that apply.)
   a. text
   b. command
   c. input
   d. interactive
   e. insert

9. The `less` command offers less functionality than the `more` command. True or False?

10. Which command searches for and displays any text contents of a binary file?
    a. `text`
    b. `strings`
    c. `od`
    d. `less`

11. How can a user switch from insert mode to command mode when using the vi editor?
    a. Press the Ctrl+Alt+Del keys simultaneously.
    b. Press the Del key.
    c. Type a : character.
    d. Press the Esc key.

12. If "resume" is the name of a file in the home directory off the root of the filesystem and your present working directory is home, what is the relative name for the file named resume?
    a. /home/resume
    b. /resume
    c. resume
    d. \home\resume

13. What will the following wildcard regular expression return: `file[a-c]`?
    a. `filea-c`
    b. `filea, filec`
    c. `filea, fileb, filec`
    d. `fileabc`

14. What will typing `q!` at the : prompt in command mode do when using the vi editor?
    a. quit as no changes were made
    b. quit after saving any changes
    c. nothing because the ! is a metacharacter
    d. quit without saving any changes

15. A user types the command `head /poems/mary`. What will be displayed on the terminal screen?
    a. the first line of the file mary
    b. the header for the file mary
    c. the first 20 lines of the file mary
    d. the last 10 lines of the file mary
    e. the first 10 lines of the file mary

16. The `tac` command _____.
    a. is not a valid Linux command
    b. displays the contents of hidden files

   c. displays the contents of a file in reverse order, last word on the line first and first word on the line last

   d. displays the contents of a file in reverse order, last line first and first line last

17. How can you specify a text pattern that must be at the beginning of a line of text using a regular expression?

   a. Precede the string with a /.

   b. Follow the string with a \.

   c. Precede the string with a $.

   d. Precede the string with a ^.

18. Linux has only one root directory per directory tree. True or False?

19. Using wildcard metacharacters, how can you indicate a character that is *not* an a or b or c or d?

   a. `[^abcd]`

   b. `not [a-d]`

   c. `[!a-d]`

   d. `!a-d`

20. A user typed the command `pwd` and saw the output: /home/jim/sales/pending. How could that user navigate to the /home/jim directory?

   a. `cd ..`

   b. `cd /jim`

   c. `cd ../..`

   d. `cd ./.`

Hands-On Projects

These projects should be completed in the order given. The hands-on projects presented in this chapter should take a total of three hours to complete. The requirements for this lab include:

- A computer with Fedora Linux installed according to Hands-On Project 2-1.

Project 3-1

In this hands-on project, you log in to the computer and navigate the file structure.

1. Boot your Fedora Linux virtual machine. After your Linux system has been loaded, switch to a command-line terminal (tty5) by pressing **Ctrl+Alt+F5** and log in to the terminal using the user name of **root** and the password of **LINUXrocks!**.

2. At the command prompt, type **pwd** and press **Enter** to view the current working directory. What is your current working directory?

3. At the command prompt, type **cd** and press **Enter**. At the command prompt, type **pwd** and press **Enter** to view the current working directory. Did your current working directory change? Why or why not?

4. At the command prompt, type **cd .** and press **Enter**. At the command prompt, type **pwd** and press **Enter** to view the current working directory. Did your current working directory change? Why or why not?

5. At the command prompt, type **cd ..** and press **Enter**. At the command prompt, type **pwd** and press **Enter** to view the current working directory. Did your current working directory change? Why or why not?

6. At the command prompt, type **cd root** and press **Enter**. At the command prompt, type **pwd** and press **Enter** to view the current working directory. Did your current working directory change? Where are you now? Did you specify a relative or absolute pathname to your home directory when you used the **cd root** command?

7. At the command prompt, type **cd etc** and press **Enter**. What error message did you receive and why?

8. At the command prompt, type **cd /etc** and press **Enter**. At the command prompt, type **pwd** and press **Enter** to view the current working directory. Did your current working directory change? Did you specify a relative or absolute pathname to the /etc directory when you used the **cd /etc** command?

9. At the command prompt, type **cd /** and press **Enter**. At the command prompt, type **pwd** and press **Enter** to view the current working directory. Did your current working directory change? Did you specify a relative or absolute pathname to the / directory when you used the **cd /** command?

10. At the command prompt, type **cd ~user1** and then press **Enter**. At the command prompt, type **pwd** and press **Enter** to view the current working directory. Did your current working directory change? Which command discussed earlier performs the same function as the **cd ~** command?

11. At the command prompt, type **cd Desktop** and press **Enter** (be certain to use a capital D). At the command prompt, type **pwd** and press **Enter** to view the current working directory. Did your current working directory change? Where are you now? What kind of pathname did you use here (absolute or relative)?

12. Currently, you are in a subdirectory of user1's home folder, three levels below the root. To go up three parent directories to the / directory, type **cd ../../..** and press **Enter** at the command prompt. Next, type **pwd** and press **Enter** to ensure that you are in the / directory.

13. At the command prompt, type **cd /etc/samba** and press **Enter** to change the current working directory using an absolute pathname. Next, type **pwd** and press **Enter** at the command prompt to ensure that you have changed to the /etc/samba directory. Now, type the command **cd ../sysconfig** at the command prompt and press **Enter**. Type **pwd** and press **Enter** to view your current location. Explain how the relative pathname seen in the **cd ../sysconfig** command specified your current working directory.

14. At the command prompt, type **cd ../../home/user1/Desktop** and press **Enter** to change your current working directory to the Desktop directory under user1's home directory. Verify that you are in the target directory by typing the **pwd** command at a command prompt and press **Enter**. Would it have been more advantageous to use an absolute pathname to change to this directory instead of the relative pathname that you used?

15. Type **exit** and press **Enter** to log out of your shell.

Project 3-2

In this hands-on project, you navigate the Linux filesystem using the Tab-completion feature of the BASH shell.

1. Switch to a command-line terminal (tty5) by pressing **Ctrl**+**Alt**+**F5** and log in to the terminal using the user name of **root** and the password of **LINUXrocks!**.
2. At the command prompt, type `cd /` and press **Enter**.
3. Next, type `cd ro` at the command prompt and press **Tab**. What is displayed on the screen and why? How many subdirectories under the root begin with "ro"?
4. Press the **Ctrl**+**c** keys to cancel the command and return to an empty command prompt.
5. At the command prompt, type `cd b` and press **Tab**. Did the display change?
6. Press the **Tab** key again. How many subdirectories under the root begin with "b"?
7. Type the letter **i**. Notice that the command now reads "cd bi." Press the **Tab** key again. Which directory did it expand to? Why? Press the **Ctrl**+**c** keys to cancel the command and return to an empty command prompt.
8. At the command prompt, type `cd m` and press **Tab**. Press **Tab** once again after hearing the beep. How many subdirectories under the root begin with "m"?
9. Type the letter **e**. Notice that the command now reads "cd me." Press **Tab**.
10. Press **Enter** to execute the command at the command prompt. Next, type the `pwd` command and press **Enter** to verify that you are in the /media directory.
11. Type `exit` and press **Enter** to log out of your shell.

Project 3-3

In this hands-on project, you examine files and file types using the `ls` and `file` commands.

1. Switch to a command-line terminal (tty5) by pressing **Ctrl**+**Alt**+**F5** and log in to the terminal using the user name of **root** and the password of **LINUXrocks!**.
2. At the command prompt, type `cd /etc` and press **Enter**. Verify that you are in the /etc directory by typing `pwd` at the command prompt and press **Enter**.
3. At the command prompt, type `ls` and press **Enter**. What do you see listed in the four columns? Do any of the files have extensions? What is the most common extension you see and what does it indicate? Is the list you are viewing on the screen the entire contents of /etc?
4. At the command prompt, type `ls | more` and then press **Enter** (the | symbol is usually near the Enter key on the keyboard and is obtained by pressing the Shift and \ keys in combination). What does the display show? Notice the highlighted --More-- prompt at the bottom of the screen. Press **Enter**. Press **Enter** again. Press **Enter** once more. Notice that each time you press Enter, you advance one line further into the file. Now, press the **spacebar**. Press the **spacebar** again. Notice that with each press of the

spacebar, you advance one full page into the displayed directory contents. Press the **h** key to get a help screen. Examine the command options.

5. Press the **q** key to quit the `more` command and return to an empty command prompt.

6. At the command prompt, type `ls | less` and then press **Enter**. What does the display show? Notice the : at the bottom of the screen. Press **Enter**. Press **Enter** again. Press **Enter** once more. Notice that each time you press Enter, you advance one line further into the file. Now press the **spacebar**. Press the **spacebar** again. Notice that with each press of the spacebar, you advance one full page into the displayed directory contents. Press the **h** key to get a help screen. Examine the command options, and then press **q** to return to the command output.

7. Press the ↑ (up arrow) key. Press ↑ again. Press ↑ once more. Notice that each time you press the ↑ key, you go up one line in the file display toward the beginning of the file. Now, press the ↓ (down arrow) key. Press ↓ again. Press ↓ once more. Notice that each time you press the ↓ key, you move forward into the file display.

8. Press the **q** key to quit the `less` command and return to a shell command prompt.

9. At the command prompt, type `cd` and press **Enter**. At the command prompt, type `pwd` and press **Enter**. What is your current working directory? At the command prompt, type `ls` and press **Enter**.

10. At the command prompt, type `ls /etc` and press **Enter**. How does this output compare with what you saw in Step 9? Has your current directory changed? Verify your answer by typing `pwd` at the command prompt and press **Enter**. Notice that you were able to list the contents of another directory by giving the absolute name of it as an argument to the `ls` command without leaving the directory in which you are currently located.

11. At the command prompt, type `ls /etc/skel` and press **Enter**. Did you see a listing of any files? At the command prompt, type `ls -a /etc/skel` and press **Enter**. What is special about these files? What do the first two entries in the list (. and ..) represent?

12. At the command prompt, type `ls -aF /etc/skel` and press **Enter**. Which file types are available in the /etc/skel directory?

13. At the command prompt, type `ls /bin` and press **Enter**. Did you see a listing of any files? At the command prompt, type `ls -F /bin/*` and press **Enter**. What file types are present in the /bin directory?

14. At the command prompt, type `ls /boot` and press **Enter**. Next, type `ls -l /boot` and press **Enter**. What additional information is available on the screen? What types of files are available in the /boot directory? At the command prompt, type `ll /boot` and press **Enter**. Is the output any different from that of the `ls -l /boot` command you just entered? Why or why not?

15. At the command prompt, type `file /etc` and press **Enter**. What kind of file is etc?

16. At the command prompt, type `file /etc/inittab` and press **Enter**. What type of file is /etc/inittab?

17. At the command prompt, type `file /boot/*` to see the types of files in the /boot directory. Is this information more specific than the information you gathered in Step 14?

18. Type `exit` and press **Enter** to log out of your shell.

Project 3-4

In this hands-on project, you display file contents using the `cat`, `tac`, `head`, `tail`, `strings`, and `od` commands.

1. Switch to a command-line terminal (tty5) by pressing **Ctrl+Alt+F5**, and then log in to the terminal using the user name of **root** and the password of **LINUXrocks!**.

2. At the command prompt, type `cat /etc/hosts` and press **Enter** to view the contents of the file hosts, which reside in the directory /etc. Next, type `cat -n /etc/hosts` and press **Enter**. How many lines does the file have? At the command prompt, type `tac /etc/hosts` and press **Enter** to view the same file in reverse order. The output of both commands should be visible on the same screen. Compare them.

3. To see the contents of the same file in octal format instead of ASCII text, type `od /etc/hosts` at the command prompt and press **Enter**.

4. At the command prompt, type `cat /etc/inittab` and press **Enter**.

5. At the command prompt, type `head /etc/inittab` and press **Enter**. What is displayed on the screen? How many lines are displayed, which ones are they, and why?

6. At the command prompt, type `head -5 /etc/inittab` and press **Enter**. How many lines are displayed and why? Next, type `head -3 /etc/inittab` and press **Enter**. How many lines are displayed and why?

7. At the command prompt, type `tail /etc/inittab` and press **Enter**. What is displayed on the screen? How many lines are displayed; which ones are they and why?

8. At the command prompt, type `tail -5 /etc/inittab` and press **Enter**. How many lines are displayed and why? Type the `cat -n /etc/inittab` command at a command prompt and press **Enter** to justify your answer.

9. At the command prompt, type `file /bin/nice` and press **Enter**. What type of file is it? Should you use a text tool command on this file?

10. At the command prompt, type `strings /bin/nice` and press **Enter**. Notice that you can see some text within this binary file. Next, type `strings /bin/nice | more` to view the same content page-by-page. When finished, press **q** to quit the more command.

11. Type `exit` and press **Enter** to log out of your shell.

Project 3-5

In this hands-on project, you create and edit text files using the vi editor.

1. Switch to a command-line terminal (tty5) by pressing **Ctrl+Alt+F5** and log in to the terminal using the user name of **root** and the password of **LINUXrocks!**.

2. At the command prompt, type `pwd`, press **Enter**, and ensure that /root is displayed, showing that you are in the root user's home folder. At the command prompt, type

`vi sample1` and press **Enter** to open the vi editor and create a new text file called sample1. Notice that this name appears at the bottom of the screen along with the indication that it is a new file.

3. At the command prompt, type `My letter` and press **Enter**. Why was nothing displayed on the screen? To switch from command mode to insert mode so you can type text, press **i**. Notice that the word Insert appears at the bottom of the screen. Next, type `My letter` and notice that this text is displayed on the screen. What types of tasks can be accomplished in insert mode?

4. Press **Esc**. Did the cursor move? What mode are you in now? Press ← two times until the cursor is under the last t in letter. Press the **x** key. What happened? Next, type **i** to enter insert mode, then type the letter "**h**." Was the letter "h" inserted before or after the cursor?

5. Press **Esc** to switch back to command mode and then move your cursor to the end of the line. Next, type the letter "**o**" to open a line underneath the current line and enter insert mode.

6. Type the following:

   `It might look like I am doing nothing, but at the cellular level I can assure you that I am quite busy. And to a typical cell, it may seem like they are doing all the work!`

   Notice that the line wraps to the next line partway through the sentence. Though displayed over two lines on the screen, this sentence is treated as one continuous line of text in vi. Press **Esc** to return to command mode, and then press ↑. Where does the cursor move? Use the cursor keys to navigate to the letter "l" at the beginning of the word "level," and then press the **i** key to enter insert mode. Press the **Enter** key while in insert mode. Next, press **Esc** to return to command mode, and then press ↑. Where does the cursor move?

7. Type **dd** three times to delete all lines in the file.

8. Type **i** to enter insert mode, and then type:

   `Hi there, I hope this day finds you well.`

   and press **Enter**. Press **Enter** again. Type:

   `Unfortunately, we were not able to make it to your dining`

   and press **Enter**. Type:

   `room this year while vacationing in Algonquin Park - I`

   and press **Enter**. Type:

   `especially wished to see the model of the Highland Inn`

   and press **Enter**. Type:

   `and the train station in the dining room.`

   and press **Enter**. Press **Enter** again. Type:

   `I have been reading on the history of Algonquin Park but`

   and press **Enter**. Type:

   `nowhere could I find a description of where the Highland`

   and press **Enter**. Type:

   `Inn was originally located on Cache Lake.`

and press **Enter**. Press **Enter** again. Type:

`If it is no trouble, could you kindly let me know such that`

and press **Enter**. Type:

`I need not wait until next year when I visit your lodge?`

and press **Enter**. Press **Enter** again. Type:

`Regards,`

and press **Enter**. Type:

`Mackenzie Elizabeth`

and press **Enter**. You should now have the sample letter used in this chapter on your screen. It should resemble the letter in Figure 3-3.

9. Press **Esc** to switch to command mode. Next press the **Shift**+**;** keys to open the **:** prompt at the bottom of the screen. At this prompt, type **w** and press **Enter** to save the changes you have made to the file. What is displayed at the bottom of the file when you are finished?

10. Press the **Shift**+**;** keys to open the **:** prompt at the bottom of the screen again, type **q**, and then press **Enter** to exit the vi editor.

11. At the command prompt, type `ls` and press **Enter** to view the contents of your current directory. Notice that there is now a file called sample1 listed.

12. Next, type `file sample1` and press **Enter**. What type of file is sample1? At the command prompt, type `cat sample1` and press **Enter**.

13. At the command prompt, type `vi sample1` and press **Enter** to open the letter again in the vi editor. What is displayed at the bottom of the screen? How does this compare with Step 9?

14. Use the cursor keys to navigate to the bottom of the document. Press the **Shift**+**;** keys to open the **:** prompt at the bottom of the screen again, type `!date` and press **Enter**. The current system date and time appear at the bottom of the screen. As indicated, press **Enter** to return to the document.

15. Press the **Shift**+**;** keys again to open the **:** prompt at the bottom of the screen again, type `r !date` and press **Enter**. What happened and why?

16. Use the cursor keys to position your cursor on the line in the document that displays the current date and time, and type **yy** to copy it to the buffer in memory. Next, use the cursor keys to position your cursor on the first line in the document, and type **P** (capitalized) to paste the contents of the memory buffer above your current line. Does the original line remain at the bottom of the document?

17. Use the cursor keys to position your cursor on the line at the end of the document that displays the current date and time, and type **dd** to delete it.

18. Use the cursor keys to position your cursor on the **t** in the word "there" on the second line of the file that reads **Hi there, I hope this day finds you well.**, and press **dw** to delete the word. Next, type **i** to enter insert mode, type the word **Bob**, and then press **Esc** to switch back to command mode.

19. Press the **Shift**+**;** keys to open the **:** prompt at the bottom of the screen again, type `w sample2` and press **Enter**. What happened and why?

20. Press **i** to enter insert mode, and type the word **test**. Next, press **Esc** to switch to command mode. Press the **Shift**+**;** keys to open the **:** prompt at the bottom of the screen again, type **q**, and press **Enter** to quit the vi editor. Were you able to quit? Why not?

21. Press the **Shift**+**;** keys to open the **:** prompt at the bottom of the screen again, type **q!**, and press **Enter** to quit the vi editor and discard any changes since the last save.

22. At the command prompt, type **ls** and press **Enter** to view the contents of your current directory. Notice it now includes a file called sample2, which was created in Step 19. Type **diff sample1 sample2** and press **Enter** to view the difference in content between the two files you created.

23. At the command prompt, type **vi sample2** and press **Enter** to open the letter again in the vi editor.

24. Use the cursor keys to position your cursor on the line that reads **Hi Bob, I hope this day finds you well.**

25. Press the **Shift**+**;** simultaneously to open the **:** prompt at the bottom of the screen, type **s/Bob/Barb/g**, and press **Enter** to change all occurrences of "Bob" to "Barb" on the current line.

26. Press the **Shift**+**;** keys to open the **:** prompt at the bottom of the screen again, type **1,$ s/to/TO/g**, and press **Enter** to change all occurrences of the word "to" to "TO" for the entire file.

27. Press the **u** key to undo the last function performed. What happened and why?

28. Press the **Shift**+**;** keys to open the **:** prompt at the bottom of the screen again, type **wq**, and press **Enter** to save your document and quit the vi editor.

29. At the command prompt, type **vi sample3** and press **Enter** to open a new file called sample3 in the vi editor. Type **i** to enter insert mode. Next, type **P.S. How were the flies this year?** Press the **Esc** key when finished.

30. Press the **Shift**+**;** keys to open the **:** prompt at the bottom of the screen, type **wq**, and press **Enter** to save your document and quit the vi editor.

31. At the command prompt, type **vi sample1**, press **Enter** to open the file sample1 again, and use the cursor keys to position your cursor on the line that reads "Mackenzie Elizabeth."

32. Press the **Shift**+**;** keys to open the **:** prompt at the bottom of the screen again, type **r sample3**, and press **Enter** to insert the contents of the file sample3 below your current line.

33. Press the **Shift**+**;** keys to open the **:** prompt at the bottom of the screen, type **s/flies/ flies and bears/g** and press **Enter**. What happened and why?

34. Press the **Shift**+**;** keys to open the **:** prompt at the bottom of the screen again, type **set number**, and press **Enter** to turn on line numbering.

35. Press the **Shift**+**;** keys to open the **:** prompt at the bottom of the screen again, type **set nonumber**, and press **Enter** to turn off line numbering.

36. Press the **Shift**+**;** keys to open the **:** prompt at the bottom of the screen again, type **set all**, and press **Enter** to view all vi parameters. Press **Enter** to advance through the list, and press **q** when finished to return to the vi editor.

37. Press the **Shift**+; keys to open the : prompt at the bottom of the screen again, type **wq**, and press **Enter** to save your document and quit the vi editor.
38. Type **exit** and press **Enter** to log out of your shell.

Project 3-6

In this hands-on project, you use the `ls` command alongside wildcard metacharacters in your shell to explore the contents of your home directory.

1. Switch to a command-line terminal (tty5) by pressing **Ctrl**+**Alt**+**F5** and log in to the terminal using the user name of **root** and the password of **LINUXrocks!**.
2. At the command prompt, type **pwd**, press **Enter**, and ensure /root is displayed showing that you are in the root user's home folder. At the command prompt, type `ls`. How many files with a name beginning with the word "sample" exist in **/root**?
3. At the command prompt, type `ls *` and press **Enter**. What is listed and why?
4. At the command prompt, type `ls sample*` and press **Enter**. What is listed and why?
5. At the command prompt, type `ls sample?` and press **Enter**. What is listed and why?
6. At the command prompt, type `ls sample??` and press **Enter**. What is listed and why?
7. At the command prompt, type `ls sample[13]` and press **Enter**. What is listed and why?
8. At the command prompt, type `ls sample[!13]` and press **Enter**. What is listed and why? How does this compare to the results from Step 7?
9. At the command prompt, type `ls sample[1-3]` and press **Enter**. What is listed and why?
10. At the command prompt, type `ls sample[!1-3]` and press **Enter**. What is listed and why? How does this compare to the results from Step 9?
11. Type **exit** and press **Enter** to log out of your shell.

Project 3-7

In this hands-on project, you use the `grep` and `egrep` commands alongside regular expression metacharacters to explore the contents of text files.

1. Switch to a command-line terminal (tty5) by pressing **Ctrl**+**Alt**+**F5** and log in to the terminal using the user name of **root** and the password of **LINUXrocks!**.
2. At the command prompt, type **grep** "Inn" **sample1** and press **Enter**. What is displayed and why?
3. At the command prompt, type **grep** -v "Inn" **sample1** and press **Enter**. What is displayed and why? How does this compare to the results from Step 2?
4. At the command prompt, type **grep** "inn" **sample1** and press **Enter**. What is displayed and why?
5. At the command prompt, type **grep** -i "inn" **sample1** and press **Enter**. What is displayed and why? How does this compare to the results from Steps 2 and 4?
6. At the command prompt, type **grep** "I" **sample1** and press **Enter**. What is displayed and why?

7. At the command prompt, type `grep " I " sample1` and press **Enter**. What is displayed and why?

8. At the command prompt, type `grep "t.e" sample1` and press **Enter**. What is displayed and why?

9. At the command prompt, type `grep "w...e" sample1` and press **Enter**. What is displayed and why?

10. At the command prompt, type `grep "^I" sample1` and press **Enter**. What is displayed and why?

11. At the command prompt, type `grep "^I " sample1` and press **Enter**. What is displayed and why?

12. At the command prompt, type `grep "(we|next)" sample1` and press **Enter**. What is displayed? Why?

13. At the command prompt, type `egrep "(we|next)" sample1` and press **Enter**. What is displayed and why?

14. At the command prompt, type `grep "Inn$" sample1` and press **Enter**. What is displayed and why?

15. At the command prompt, type `grep "?$" sample1` and press **Enter**. What is displayed and why? Does the ? metacharacter have special meaning here? Why?

16. At the command prompt, type `grep "^$" sample1` and press **Enter**. Is anything displayed? (*Hint:* Be certain to look closely!) Can you explain the output?

17. Type `exit` and press **Enter** to log out of your shell.

Discovery Exercises

1. You are the systems administrator for a scientific research company that employs over 100 scientists who write and run Linux programs to analyze their work. All of these programs are stored in each scientist's home directory on the Linux system. One scientist has left the company, and you are instructed to retrieve any work from that scientist's home directory. When you enter the home directory for that user, you notice that there are very few files and only two directories (one named Projects and one named Lab). List the commands that you would use to navigate through this user's home directory and view filenames and file types. If there are any text files, what commands could you use to view their contents?

2. When you type the `pwd` command, you notice that your current location on the Linux filesystem is the /usr/local directory. Answer the following questions, assuming that your current directory is /usr/local for each question.

   a. Which command could you use to change to the /usr directory using an absolute pathname?

   b. Which command could you use to change to the /usr directory using a relative pathname?

c. Which command could you use to change to the /usr/local/share/info directory using an absolute pathname?

d. Which command could you use to change to the /usr/local/share/info directory using a relative pathname?

e. Which command could you use to change to the /etc directory using an absolute pathname?

f. Which command could you use to change to the /etc directory using a relative pathname?

3. Using wildcard metacharacters and options to the `ls` command, view the following:

a. All the files that end with .cfg under the /etc directory

b. All hidden files in the /home/user1 directory

c. The directory names that exist under the /var directory

d. All the files that start with the letter "a" under the /bin directory

e. All the files that have exactly three letters in their filename in the /bin directory

f. All files that have exactly three letters in their filename and end with either the letter "t" or the letter "h" in the /bin directory

4. Explore the manual pages for the `ls`, `grep`, `cat`, `od`, `tac`, `head`, `tail`, `diff`, `pwd`, `cd`, `strings`, and `vi` commands. Experiment with what you learn using the file sample1 that you created earlier.

5. The famous quote from Shakespeare's Hamlet "To be or not to be" can be represented by the following regular expression:

(2b|[^b]{2})

If you used this expression when searching a text file using the `egrep` command (`egrep "(2b|[^b]{2})" filename`), what would be displayed? Try this command on a file that you have created. Why does it display what it does? That is the question.

6. By default, a minimal version of the vi editor is installed on Fedora 28. Run the command **dnf update vim-minimal** to update this editor to the latest version from software repositories on the Internet and then type **dnf install vim** to install the full vi editor package. The full vi editor package comes with a short 30-minute tutorial on its usage. Start this tutorial by typing **vimtutor** at a command prompt and then follow the directions. Provided you have a functional Web browser and an Internet connection, explore the resources available at *www.vim.org*.

7. Enter the following text into a new document called question7 using the vi editor. Next, use the vi editor to fix the mistakes in the file using the information in Table 3-5, Table 3-6, and Table 3-7 as well as the examples provided in this chapter.

```
Hi there,
Unfortunately, we were not
able to make it to your
dining room
Unfortunately, we were not
able to make it to your
dining room
this year while vacationing
in Algonuin Park - I
especially wished
```

```
to see the model of the
highland inn and the train
station in the
dining rooms.

I have been readng on the
history of Algonuin Park
but
no where could I find a
description of where the
Highland Inn was
originally located on Cache
lake.

If it is not trouble, could
you kindly let me that I
need
not wait until next year
when we visit Lodge?

I hope this day finds you
well.
Regard
Elizabeth Mackenzie
```

8. The knowledge gained from using the vi editor can be transferred easily to the Emacs editor. Perform Question 7 using the Emacs editor instead of the vi editor.

9. When you use the vi editor and change environment settings at the : prompt, such as `:set number` to enable line numbering, those changes are lost when you exit the vi editor. To continuously apply the same environment settings, you can choose to put the `set` commands in a special hidden file in their home directory called .exrc; this .exrc file is then applied each time you open the vi editor. Enter the vi editor and find three environment settings that you want to change in addition to line numbering. Then create a new file called .exrc in your home directory and enter the four lines changing these vi environment settings (do not start each line with a : character, just enter the `set` command—e.g., set number). When finished, open the vi editor to edit a new file and test to see whether the settings were applied automatically.

## CHAPTER 4

LINUX FILESYSTEM MANAGEMENT

After completing this chapter, you will be able to:

Find files and directories on the filesystem

Understand and create linked files

Explain the function of the Filesystem Hierarchy Standard

Use standard Linux commands to manage files and directories

Modify file and directory ownership

Define and change Linux file and directory permissions

Identify the default permissions created on files and directories

Apply special file and directory permissions

Modify the default access control list (ACL)

View and set filesystem attributes

In the previous chapter, you learned about navigating the Linux filesystem as well as viewing and editing files. This chapter focuses on the organization of files on the Linux filesystem as well as their linking and security. First, you explore standard Linux directories using the Filesystem Hierarchy Standard. Next, you explore common commands used to manage files and directories as well as learn methods that are used to find files and directories on the filesystems. Finally, you learn about file and directory linking, permissions, special permissions, and attributes.

The Filesystem Hierarchy Standard

The many thousands of files on a typical Linux system are organized into directories in the Linux directory tree. It's a complex system, made even more complex in the past by the fact that different Linux distributions were free to place files in different locations. This meant that you could waste a great deal of time searching for a configuration file on a Linux system with which you were unfamiliar. To simplify the task of finding specific files, the **Filesystem Hierarchy Standard (FHS)** was created.

FHS defines a standard set of directories for use by all Linux and UNIX systems as well as the file and subdirectory contents of each directory. This ensures that, because the filename and location follow a standard convention, a Fedora Linux user will find the correct configuration file on an openSUSE Linux or Hewlett-Packard UNIX computer with little difficulty. The FHS also gives Linux software developers the ability to locate files on a Linux system regardless of the distribution, allowing them to create software that is not distribution-specific.

A comprehensive understanding of the standard types of directories found on Linux systems is valuable when locating and managing files and directories; some standard UNIX and Linux directories defined by FHS and their descriptions are listed in Table 4-1. These directories are discussed throughout this chapter and subsequent chapters.

Table 4-1 Linux directories defined by the Filesystem Hierarchy Standard

Directory	Description
/bin	Contains binary commands for use by all users (on most Linux systems, this directory is a shortcut to /usr/bin)
/boot	Contains the Linux kernel and files used by the boot loader
/dev	Contains device files
/etc	Contains system-specific configuration files
/home	Is the default location for user home directories
/lib	Contains shared program libraries (used by the commands in /bin and /sbin) as well as kernel modules
/media	A directory that contains subdirectories used for accessing (mounting) filesystems on removable media devices such as floppy disks, DVDs, and USB flash drives
/mnt	An empty directory used for temporarily accessing filesystems on removable media devices
/opt	Stores additional software programs
/proc	Contains process and kernel information
/root	Is the root user's home directory
/sbin	Contains system binary commands (used for administration)

Table 4-1   Linux directories defined by the Filesystem Hierarchy Standard *(continued)*

Directory	Description
/sys	Contains configuration information for hardware devices on the system
/tmp	Holds temporary files created by programs
/usr	Contains most system commands and utilities—contains the following directories:
	/usr/bin—User binary commands
	/usr/games—Educational programs and games
	/usr/include—C program header files
	/usr/lib—Libraries/usr/local—Local programs
	/usr/sbin—System binary commands
	/usr/share—Files that are architecture independent
	/usr/src—Source code
	/usr/X11R6—The X Window system (sometimes replaced by /etc/X11)
/usr/local	Is the location for most additional programs
/var	Contains log files and spools

Note

To read the complete Filesystem Hierarchy Standard definition, go to *www.pathname.com/fhs*.

Managing Files and Directories

As mentioned earlier, using a Linux system involves navigating several directories and manipulating the files inside them. Thus, an efficient Linux user must understand how to create directories as needed, copy or move files from one directory to another, and delete files and directories. These tasks are commonly referred to as file management tasks.

Following is an example of a directory listing displayed by a user who is logged in as the root user:

```
[root@server1 ~]# pwd
/root
[root@server1 ~]# ls -F
myprogram*  project      project12  project2  project4
myscript*   project1     project13  project3  project5
[root@server1 ~]#_
```

As shown in the preceding output, two executable files (myprogram and myscript), and several project-related files (project*) exist on this example system.

Although this directory structure is not cluttered and appears in an easy-to-read format on the terminal screen, typical home directories on a Linux system contain many more files; typical Linux users might have over 100 files in their home directories. As a result, it is good practice to organize these files into subdirectories based on file purpose. Because several project files are in the root user's home directory in the preceding output, you could create a subdirectory called proj_files to contain the project-related files and decrease the size of the directory listing. To do this, you use the mkdir (make directory) command, which takes arguments specifying the absolute or relative pathnames of the directories to create. To create a proj_files directory under the current directory, you can use the mkdir command with a relative pathname:

```
[root@server1 ~]# mkdir proj_files
[root@server1 ~]# ls -F
myprogram* project   project12   project2   project4    proj_files/
myscript*   project1 project13   project3   project5
[root@server1 ~]#_
```

Now, you can move the project files into the proj_files subdirectory by using the mv (move) command. The mv command requires two arguments at minimum: the source file/directory and the target file/directory. For example, to move the /etc/sample1 file to the /root directory, you could use the command mv /etc/sample1 /root.

If you want to move several files, you include one source argument for each file you want to move and then include the target directory as the last argument. For example, to move the /etc/sample1 and /etc/sample2 files to the /root directory, you could use the command mv /etc/sample1 /etc/sample2 /root.

Note that both the source (or sources) and the destination can be absolute or relative pathnames and the source can contain wildcards if several files are to be moved. For example, to move all of the project files to the proj_files directory, you could type mv with the source argument project* (to match all files starting with the letters "project") and the target argument proj_files (relative pathname to the destination directory), as shown in the following output:

```
[root@server1 ~]# mv project* proj_files
[root@server1 ~]# ls -F
myprogram*  myscript*  proj_files/
[root@server1 ~]# ls -F proj_files
project   project12   project2   project4
project1 project13   project3   project5
[root@server1 ~]#_
```

In the preceding output, the current directory listing does not show the project files anymore, yet the listing of the proj_files subdirectory indicates that they were moved successfully.

> **Note** 🖇️
>
> If the target is the name of a directory, the mv command moves those files to that directory. If the target is a filename of an existing file in a certain directory and there is one source file, the mv command overwrites the target with the source. If the target is a filename of a nonexistent file in a certain directory, the mv command creates a new file with that filename in the target directory and moves the source file to that file.

Another important use of the mv command is to rename files, which is simply moving a file to the same directory but with a different filename. To rename the myscript file from earlier examples to myscript2, you can use the following mv command:

```
[root@server1 ~]# ls -F
myprogram*  myscript*  proj_files/
[root@server1 ~]# mv myscript myscript2
[root@server1 ~]# ls -F
myprogram*  myscript2*  proj_files/
[root@server1 ~]#_
```

Similarly, the mv command can rename directories. If the source is the name of an existing directory, it is renamed to whatever directory name is specified as the target.

The mv command works similarly to a cut-and-paste operation in which the file is copied to a new directory and deleted from the source directory. In some cases, however, you might want to keep the file in the source directory and instead insert a copy of the file in the target directory. You can do this using the cp **(copy) command**. Much like the mv command, the cp command takes two arguments at minimum. The first argument specifies the source file/directory to be copied and the second argument specifies the target file/directory. If several files need to be copied to a destination directory, specify several source arguments, with the final argument on the command line serving as the target directory. Each argument can be an absolute or relative pathname and can contain wildcards or the special metacharacters "." (which specifies the current directory) and ".." (which specifies the parent directory). For example, to make a copy of the file /etc/hosts in the current directory (/root), you can specify the absolute pathname to the /etc/hosts file (/etc/hosts) and the relative pathname indicating the current directory (.):

```
[root@server1 ~]# cp /etc/hosts .
[root@server1 ~]# ls -F
hosts  myprogram*  myscript2*  proj_files/
[root@server1 ~]#_
```

You can also make copies of files in the same directory. To make a copy of the hosts file called hosts2 in the current directory and view the results, type the following commands:

```
[root@server1 ~]# cp hosts hosts2
[root@server1 ~]# ls -F
hosts hosts2 myprogram* myscript2* proj_files/
[root@server1 ~]#_
```

Despite their similarities, the mv and cp commands work on directories differently. The mv command renames a directory, whereas the cp command creates a whole new copy of the directory and its contents. To copy a directory full of files in Linux, you must tell the cp command that the copy will be **recursive** (involve files and subdirectories too) by using the -r option. The following example demonstrates copying the proj_files directory and all of its contents to the /home/user1 directory without and with the -r option:

```
[root@server1 ~]# ls -F
hosts  myprogram*  myscript2*  proj_files/
[root@server1 ~]# ls -F /home/user1
Desktop/
[root@server1 ~]# cp proj_files /home/user1
cp: -r not specified; omitting directory 'proj_files'
[root@server1 ~]# ls -F /home/user1
Desktop/
[root@server1 ~]# cp -r proj_files /home/user1
[root@server1 ~]# ls -F /home/user1
Desktop/  proj_files/
[root@server1 ~]#_
```

If the target is a file that exists, both the mv and cp commands warn the user that the target file will be overwritten and will ask whether to continue. This is not a feature of the command as normally invoked, but it is a feature of the default configuration in Fedora Linux because the BASH shell in Fedora Linux contains aliases to the cp and mv commands.

Note

Aliases are special variables in memory that point to commands; they are fully discussed in Chapter 7.

When you type mv, you are actually running the mv command with the −i option without realizing it. If the target file already exists, both the mv command and the mv command with the −i option interactively prompt the user to choose whether to overwrite the existing file. Similarly, when you type the cp command, the cp −i command is actually run to prevent the accidental overwriting of files. To see the aliases in your current shell, type alias, as shown in the following output:

```
[root@server1 ~]# alias
alias   cp='cp -i'
alias   egrep='egrep --color=auto'
alias   fgrep='fgrep --color=auto'
alias   grep='grep --color=auto'
alias   l.='ls -d .* --color=auto'
alias   ll='ls -l --color=auto'
alias   ls='ls --color=auto'
alias   mv='mv -i'
alias   rm='rm -i'
alias   which=' (alias; declare -f) | /usr/bin/which --tty-only --read-
alias   --read-functions --show-tilde --show-dot'
alias   xzegrep='xzegrep --color=auto'
alias   xzfgrep='xzfgrep --color=auto'
alias   xzgrep='xzgrep --color=auto'
alias   zegrep='zegrep --color=auto'
alias   zfgrep='zfgrep --color=auto'
alias   zgrep='zgrep --color=auto'
[root@server1 ~]#_
```

If you want to override this interactive option, which is known as **interactive mode,** use the −f (force) option to override the choice, as shown in the following example. In this example, the root user tries to rename the hosts file using the name "hosts2," a name already assigned to an existing file. The example shows the user attempting this task both without and with the −f option to the mv command:

```
[root@server1 ~]# ls -F
hosts  hosts2  myprogram*  myscript2*  proj_files/
[root@server1 ~]# mv hosts hosts2
mv: overwrite 'hosts2'? n
[root@server1 ~]# mv -f hosts hosts2
[root@server1 ~]# ls -F
hosts2  myprogram*  myscript2*  proj_files/
[root@server1 ~]#_
```

Creating directories, copying, and moving files are file management tasks that preserve or create data on the hard disk. To remove files or directories, you must use either the rm command or the rmdir command.

The rm **(remove) command** takes a list of arguments specifying the absolute or relative pathnames of files to remove. As with most commands, wildcards can be used to simplify the process of removing multiple files. After a file has been removed from the filesystem, it cannot be recovered. As a result, the rm command is aliased in Fedora Linux to the rm command with the -i option, which interactively prompts the user to choose whether to continue with the deletion. Like the cp and mv commands, the rm command accepts the -f option to override this choice and immediately delete the file. An example demonstrating the use of the rm and rm -f commands to remove the current and hosts2 files is shown here:

```
[root@server1 ~]# ls -F
hosts2  myprogram*  myscript2*  proj_files/
[root@server1 ~]# rm myprogram
rm: remove regular file 'myprogram'? y
[root@server1 ~]# rm -f hosts2
[root@server1 ~]# ls -F
myscript2*  proj_files/
[root@server1 ~]#_
```

To remove a directory, you can use the rmdir **(remove directory) command**; however, the rmdir command only removes a directory if it contains no files. To remove a directory and the files inside, you must use the rm command and specify that a directory full of files should be removed. As explained earlier in this chapter, you need to use the recursive option (-r) with the cp command to copy directories; to remove a directory full of files, you can also use a recursive option (-r) with the rm command. If, for example, the root user wants to remove the proj_files subdirectory and all of the files within it without being prompted to confirm each file deletion, they could use the command rm -rf proj_files, as shown in the following example:

```
[root@server1 ~]# ls -F
myscript2*  proj_files/
[root@server1 ~]# rmdir proj_files
rmdir: failed to remove 'proj_files': Directory not empty
[root@server1 ~]# rm -rf proj_files
[root@server1 ~]# ls -F
myscript2*
[root@server1 ~]#_
```

> **Note** 📎
>
> In many commands, such as rm and cp, both the –r and the –R options have the same meaning (recursive).
>
> The recursive (–r or –R) option to the rm command is dangerous if you are not certain which files exist in the directory to be deleted recursively. As a result, this option to the rm command is commonly referred to as the -résumé option; if you use it incorrectly in a production server environment, you might need to prepare your résumé, as there is no Linux command to restore deleted files.
>
> An alternative to the rm command is the unlink **command**. However, the unlink command can be used to remove files only (not directories).

The aforementioned file management commands are commonly used by Linux users, developers, and administrators alike. Table 4-2 shows a summary of these common file management commands.

Table 4-2   **Common Linux file management commands**

Command	Description
mkdir	Creates directories
rmdir	Removes empty directories
mv	Moves/renames files and directories
cp	Copies files and directories full of files (with the –r or –R option)
alias	Displays BASH shell aliases
rm	Removes files and directories full of files (with the –r or –R option)
unlink	Removes files

Finding Files

Before using the file management commands mentioned in the preceding section, you must know the locations of the files involved. The fastest method to search for files in the Linux directory tree is to use the locate **command**. For example, to view all of the files under the root directory with the text "inittab" or with "inittab" as part of the filename, you can type locate inittab at a command prompt, which produces the following output:

```
[root@server1 ~]# locate inittab
/etc/inittab
/usr/share/Augeas/lenses/dist/inittab.aug
/usr/share/vim/vim81/syntax/inittab.vim
[root@server1 ~]#_
```

The locate command looks in a premade database that contains a list of all the files on the system. This database is indexed much like a textbook for fast searching, yet can become outdated as files are added and removed from the system, which happens on a regular basis. As a result, the database used for the locate command (/var/lib/mlocate/mlocate.db) is updated each day automatically and can be updated manually by running the updatedb command at a command prompt. You can also exclude specific directories, file extensions, and whole filesystems from being indexed by the updatedb command by adding them to the /etc/updatedb.conf file; this is called **pruning**. For example, to exclude the /etc directory from being indexed by the updatedb command, add etc as an argument to the PRUNEPATHS = line within /etc/updatedb.conf.

As the locate command searches all files on the filesystem, it often returns too much information to display on the screen. To make the output easier to read, you can use the more (or less) command to pause the output; if the locate inittab command produced too many results, you could run the command locate inittab | more. To prevent the problem entirely, you can do more specific searches.

A slower, yet more versatile, method for locating files on the filesystem is to use the find **command**. The find command does not use a premade index of files; instead, it searches the directory tree recursively, starting from a certain directory, for files that meet a certain criterion. The format of the find command is as follows:

```
find <start directory> -criteria <what to find>
```

For example, to find any files named "inittab" under the /etc directory, you can use the command find /etc –name inittab and receive the following output:

```
[root@server1 ~]# find /etc -name inittab
/etc/inittab
[root@server1 ~]#_
```

You can also use wildcard metacharacters with the find command; however, these wildcards must be protected from shell interpretation, as they must only be interpreted by the find command. To do this, ensure that any wildcard metacharacters are enclosed within quote characters. An example of using the find command with wildcard metacharacters to find all files that start with the letters "host" underneath the /etc directory is shown in the following output:

```
[root@server1 ~]# find /etc -name "host*"
/etc/hosts.allow
/etc/hostname
/etc/host.atm
/etc/avahi/hosts
/etc/hosts
/etc/host.conf
/etc/hosts.deny
[root@server1 ~]#_
```

Although searching by name is the most common criterion used with the find command, many other criteria can be used with the find command as well. To find all files starting from the /var directory that have a size greater than 4096K (kilobytes), you can use the following command:

```
[root@server1 ~]# find /var -size +4096k
/var/lib/rpm/Packages
/var/lib/rpm/Basenames
/var/lib/PackageKit/system.package-list
/var/log/journal/034ec8ccdf4642f7a2493195e11d7df6/user-1000.journal
/var/log/journal/034ec8ccdf4642f7a2493195e11d7df6/user-42.journal
/var/log/journal/034ec8ccdf4642f7a2493195e11d7df6/system.journal
/var/cache/yum/x86_64/28/updates/gen/prestodelta.xml
/var/cache/yum/x86_64/28/updates/gen/primary_db.sqlite
/var/cache/yum/x86_64/28/updates/gen/filelists_db.sqlite
/var/cache/yum/x86_64/28/updates/gen/updateinfo.xml
/var/cache/yum/x86_64/28/updates/gen/other_db.sqlite
/var/cache/dnf/x86_64/28/fedora-filenames.solvx
/var/cache/dnf/x86_64/28/fedora.solv
/var/cache/dnf/x86_64/28/updates-filenames.solvx
/var/tmp/kdecache-user1/plasma_theme_internal-system-colors.kcache
/var/tmp/kdecache-user1/plasma_theme_Heisenbug_v19.90.2.kcache
/var/tmp/kdecache-user1/icon-cache.kcache
[root@server1 ~]#
```

As well, if you want to find all the directories only under the /boot directory, you can type the following command:

```
[root@server1 ~]# find /boot -type d
/boot
/boot/loader
/boot/loader/entries
/boot/efi
/boot/efi/System
/boot/efi/System/Library
/boot/efi/System/Library/CoreServices
/boot/efi/EFI
/boot/efi/EFI/BOOT
/boot/efi/EFI/fedora
/boot/efi/EFI/fedora/fw
/boot/efi/EFI/fedora/loader
/boot/efi/EFI/fedora/loader/entries
/boot/efi/EFI/fedora/fonts
/boot/extlinux
/boot/lost+found
```

```
/boot/grub2
/boot/grub2/fonts
/boot/grub2/locale
/boot/grub2/i386-pc
/boot/grub2/themes
/boot/grub2/themes/system
[root@server1 ~]#_
```

Table 4-3 provides a list of some common criteria used with the `find` command.

Table 4-3   Common criteria used with the `find` command

Criteria	Description
`-amin -x`	Searches for files that were accessed less than x minutes ago
`-amin +x`	Searches for files that were accessed more than x minutes ago
`-atime -x`	Searches for files that were accessed less than x days ago
`-atime +x`	Searches for files that were accessed more than x days ago
`-empty`	Searches for empty files or directories
`-fstype x`	Searches for files if they are on a certain filesystem x (where n could be ext2, ext3, and so on)
`-group x`	Searches for files that are owned by a certain group or GID (x)
`-inum x`	Searches for files that have an inode number of x
`-mmin -x`	Searches for files that were modified less than x minutes ago
`-mmin +x`	Searches for files that were modified more than x minutes ago
`-mtime -x`	Searches for files that were modified less than x days ago
`-mtime +x`	Searches for files that were modified more than x days ago
`-name x`	Searches for a certain filename x (x can contain wildcards)
`-regex x`	Searches for certain filenames using regular expressions instead of wildcard metacharacters
`-size -x`	Searches for files with a size less than x
`-size x`	Searches for files with a size of x
`-size +x`	Searches for files with a size greater than x
`-type x`	Searches for files of type x where x is: b for block files c for character files d for directory files p for named pipes f for regular files l for symbolic links (shortcuts) s for sockets
`-user x`	Searches for files owned by a certain user or UID (x)

Although the `find` command can be used to search for files based on many criteria, it might take several minutes to complete the search if the number of directories and files being searched is large. To reduce the time needed to search, narrow the directories searched by specifying a subdirectory when possible. It takes less time to search the /usr/local/bin directory and its subdirectories, compared to searching the /usr directory and all of its subdirectories. As well, if the filename that you are searching for is an executable file, that file can likely be found in less time using the `which` command. The `which` command only searches directories that are listed in a special variable called the **PATH variable** in the current BASH shell. Before exploring the `which` command, you must understand the usage of PATH.

Executable files can be stored in directories scattered around the directory tree. Recall from FHS that most executable files are stored in directories named bin or sbin, yet there are over 20 bin and sbin directories scattered around the directory tree after a typical Fedora Linux installation. To ensure that users do not need to specify the full pathname to commands such as `ls` (which is the executable file /usr/bin/ls), a special variable called PATH is placed into memory each time a user logs in to the Linux system. Recall that you can see the contents of a certain variable in memory by using the $ metacharacter with the `echo` command:

```
[root@server1 ~]# echo $PATH
/usr/share/Modules/bin:/usr/local/sbin:/usr/local/bin:/usr/sbin:/
usr/bin:/root/bin
[root@server1 ~]#_
```

The PATH variable lists directories that are searched for executable files if a relative or absolute pathname was not specified when executing a command on the command line. Assuming the PATH variable in the preceding output, if a user types the `ls` command on the command line and presses Enter, the system recognizes that the command was not an absolute pathname (e.g., /usr/bin/ls) or relative pathname (e.g., ../../usr/bin/ls) and then proceeds to look for the ls executable file in the /usr/share/Modules/bin directory, then the /usr/local/sbin directory, then the /usr/local/bin directory, then the /usr/sbin directory, and so on. If all the directories in the PATH variable are searched and no ls command is found, the shell gives an error message to the user stating that the command was not found. In the preceding output, the /usr/bin directory is in the PATH variable and, thus, the `ls` command is found and executed, but not until the previous directories in the PATH variable are searched first.

To search the directories in the PATH variable for the file called "grep," you could use the word "grep" as an argument for the `which` command and receive the following output:

```
[root@server1 ~]# which grep
alias grep='grep --color=auto'
        /usr/bin/grep
[root@server1 ~]#_
```

As shown in the previous output, the `which` command will also list any command aliases for a particular command. In this example, the `grep` command has the path /usr/bin/grep, but it also has an alias that ensures that each time the user runs the `grep` command, it runs it using the `--color=auto` option.

If the file being searched does not exist in the PATH variable directories, the `which` command lets you know in which directories it was not found, as shown in the following output:

```
[root@server1 ~]# which grepper
/usr/bin/which: no grepper in (/usr/share/Modules/bin:/usr/local/
sbin: /usr/local/bin:/usr/sbin:/usr/bin:/root/bin)
[root@server1 ~]#_
```

There are two alternatives to the `which` command: the `type` command displays only the first result normally outputted by the `which` command, and the `whereis` command displays the location of the command as well as any associated man and info pages, as shown in the following output:

```
[root@server1 ~]# type grep
grep is aliased to 'grep --color=auto'
[root@server1 ~]# whereis grep
grep: /usr/bin/grep /usr/share/man/man1p/grep.1p.gz
/usr/share/man/man1/grep.1.gz /usr/share/info/grep.info.gz
[root@server1 ~]#_
```

Linking Files

Files can be linked to one another in two ways. In a **symbolic link**, or symlink, one file is a pointer, or shortcut, to another file. In a **hard link**, two files share the same data.

To better understand how files are linked, you must understand how files are stored on a filesystem. On a structural level, a filesystem has three main sections:

- Superblock
- Inode table
- Data blocks

The **superblock** is the section that contains information about the filesystem in general, such as the number of inodes and data blocks, as well as how much data a data block stores, in kilobytes. The **inode table** consists of several **inodes** (information nodes); each inode describes one file or directory on the filesystem, and contains a unique inode number for identification. What is more important, the inode stores information such as the file size, data block locations, last date modified, permissions, and ownership. When a file is deleted, only its inode (which serves as a pointer to the actual data) is deleted. The data that makes up the contents of the file as well as the filename are stored in **data blocks**, which are referenced by the inode. In filesystem-neutral terminology, blocks are known as allocation units because they are the unit by which disk space is allocated for storage.

> **Note** 🔗
>
> Each file and directory must have an inode. All files except for special device files also have data blocks associated with the inode. Special device files are discussed in Chapter 5.

> **Note** 🔗
>
> Recall that directories are simply files that are used to organize other files; they too have an inode and data blocks, but their data blocks contain a list of filenames that are located within the directory.

Hard-linked files share the same inode and inode number. As a result, they share the same inode number and data blocks, but the data blocks allow for multiple filenames. Thus, when one hard-linked file is modified, the other hard-linked files are updated as well. This relationship between hard-linked files is shown in Figure 4-1. You can hard-link a file an unlimited number of times; however, the hard-linked files must reside on the same filesystem.

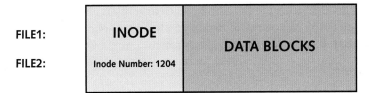

Figure 4-1   The structure of hard-linked files

To create a hard link, you must use the `ln` **(link) command** and specify two arguments: the existing file to hard-link and the target file that will be created as a hard link to the existing file. Each argument can be the absolute or relative pathname to a file. Take, for example, the following contents of the root user's home directory:

```
[root@server1 ~]# ls -l
total 520
drwx------    3 root      root         4096 Apr  8  07:12  Desktop
-rwxr-xr-x    1 root      root       519964 Apr  7  09:59  file1
-rwxr-xr-x    1 root      root         1244 Apr 27  18:17  file3
[root@server1 ~]#_
```

Suppose you want to make a hard link to file1 and call the new hard link file2, as shown in Figure 4-1. To accomplish this, you issue the command `ln file1 file2` at the command prompt; a file called file2 is created and hard-linked to file1. To view the hard-linked filenames after creation, you can use the `ls -1` command:

```
[root@server1 ~]# ln file1 file2
[root@server1 ~]# ls -1
total 1032
drwx------   3 root      root          4096  Apr   8  07:12  Desktop
-rwxr-xr-x   2 root      root        519964  Apr   7  09:59  file1
-rwxr-xr-x   2 root      root        519964  Apr   7  09:59  file2
-rwxr-xr-x   1 root      root          1244  Apr  27  18:17  file3
[root@server1 ~]#_
```

Notice from the preceding long listing that file1 and file2 share the same inode and data section, as they have the same size, permissions, ownership, modification date, and so on. Also note that the link count (the number after the permission set) for file1 has increased from the number one to the number two in the preceding output. A link count of one indicates that only one inode number is shared by the file. A file that is hard-linked to another file shares the same inode number twice and, thus, has a link count of two. Similarly, a file that is hard-linked to three other files shares the same inode number four times and, thus, has a link count of four.

Although hard links share the same inode and data section, deleting a hard-linked file does not delete all the other hard-linked files; it simply removes one filename reference. Removing a hard link can be achieved by removing one of the files, which then lowers the link count.

To view the inode number of hard-linked files to verify that they are identical, you can use the `-i` option to the `ls` command in addition to any other options. The inode number is placed on the left of the directory listing on each line, as shown in the following output:

```
[root@server1 ~]# ls -li
total 1032
  37595 drwx------   3 root   root     4096  Apr   8 07:12 Desktop
   1204 -rwxr-xr-x   2 root   root   519964  Apr   7 09:59 file1
   1204 -rwxr-xr-x   2 root   root   519964  Apr   7 09:59 file2
  17440 -rwxr-xr-x   1 root   root     1244  Apr  27 18:17 file3
[root@server1 ~]#_
```

Note 📎

Directory files are not normally hard-linked, as the result would consist of two directories that contain the same contents. However, the root user has the ability to hard-link directories in some cases, using the –F or –d option to the `ln` command. Only directories that have files regularly added and need to maintain identical file contents are typically hard-linked. For example, on Fedora 28, the /etc/init.d directory is hard linked to the /etc/rc.d/init.d directory.

Symbolic links (shown in Figure 4-2) are different from hard links because they do not share the same inode and data blocks with their target file; one is merely a pointer to the other, thus both files have different sizes. The data blocks in a symbolically linked file contain only the pathname to the target file. When a user edits a symbolically linked file, she is actually editing the target file. Thus, if the target file is deleted, the symbolic link serves no function, as it points to a nonexistent file.

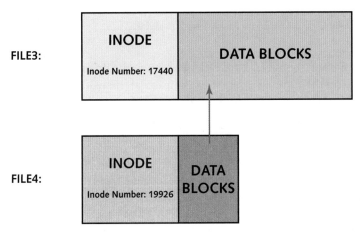

Figure 4-2   The structure of symbolically linked files

Note

Symbolic links are sometimes referred to as "soft links" or "symlinks."

To create a symbolic link, you use the −s option to the ln command. To create a symbolic link to file3 called file4, as in Figure 4-2, you can type ln −s file3 file4 at the command prompt. As with hard links, the arguments specified can be absolute or relative pathnames. To view the symbolically linked filenames after creation, you can use the ls −l command, as shown in the following example:

```
[root@server1 ~]# ln -s file3 file4
[root@server1 ~]# ls -l
total 1032
drwx------     3 root      root          4096  Apr  8 07:12 Desktop
-rwxr-xr-x     2 root      root        519964  Apr  7 09:59 file1
-rwxr-xr-x     2 root      root        519964  Apr  7 09:59 file2
-rwxr-xr-x     1 root      root          1244  Apr 27 18:17 file3
lrwxrwxrwx     1 root      root             5  Apr 27 19:05 file4 -> file3
[root@server1 ~]#_
```

Notice from the preceding output that file4 does not share the same inode, because the permissions, size, and modification date are different from file3. In addition, symbolic links are easier to identify than hard links; the file type character (before the permissions) is l, which indicates a symbolic link, and the filename points to the target using an arrow. The `ls -F` command also indicates symbolic links by appending an @ symbol, as shown in the following output:

```
[root@server1 ~]# ls -F
Desktop/  file1*  file2*  file3*  file4@
[root@server1 ~]#_
```

Another difference between hard links and symbolic links is that symbolic links need not reside on the same filesystem as their target. Instead, they point to the target filename and do not require the same inode, as shown in the following output:

```
[root@server1 ~]# ls -li
total 1032
37595 drwx------    3 root    root      4096 Apr  8 07:12 Desktop
 1204 -rwxr-xr-x    2 root    root    519964 Apr  7 09:59 file1
 1204 -rwxr-xr-x    2 root    root    519964 Apr  7 09:59 file2
17440 -rwxr-xr-x    1 root    root      1244 Apr 27 18:17 file3
19926 lrwxrwxrwx    1 root    root         5 Apr 27 19:05 file4 -> file3
[root@server1 ~]#_
```

Note

Unlike hard links, symbolic links are commonly made to directories to simplify navigating the filesystem tree. Also, symbolic links made to directories are typically used to maintain compatibility with other UNIX and Linux systems. For example, on Fedora 28, the /usr/tmp directory is symbolically linked to the /var/tmp directory for this reason.

File and Directory Permissions

Recall that all users must log in with a user name and password to gain access to a Linux system. After logging in, a user is identified by her user name and group memberships; all access to resources depends on whether the user name and group memberships have the required **permissions**. Thus, a firm understanding of ownership and permissions is necessary to operate a Linux system in a secure manner and to prevent unauthorized users from having access to sensitive files, directories, and commands.

File and Directory Ownership

When a user creates a file or directory, that user's name and **primary group** becomes the owner and group owner of the file, respectively. This affects the permission structure, as you see in the next section; however, it also determines who has the ability to modify file and directory permissions and ownership. Only two users on a Linux system can modify permissions on a file or directory or change its ownership: the owner of the file or directory and the root user.

To view your current user name, you can use the whoami command. To view your group memberships and primary group, you can use the groups command. An example of these two commands when logged in as the root user is shown in the following output:

```
[root@server1 ~]# whoami
root
[root@server1 ~]# groups
root bin daemon sys adm disk wheel
[root@server1 ~]#_
```

Notice from the preceding output that the root user is a member of seven groups, yet the root user's primary group is also called "root," as it is the first group mentioned in the output of the group's command.

> **Note** @
>
> On Fedora 28, the root user is only a member of one group by default (the "root" group).

If the root user creates a file, the owner is "root" and the group owner is also "root." To quickly create an empty file, you can use the touch command:

```
[root@server1 ~]# touch file1
[root@server1 ~]# ls -l
total 4
drwx------      3 root        root        4096 Apr  8 07:12 Desktop
-rw-r--r--      1 root        root           0 Apr 29 15:40 file1
[root@server1 ~]#_
```

> **Note** @
>
> Although the main purpose of the touch command is to update the modification date on an existing file to the current time, it will create a new empty file if the file specified as an argument does not exist.

Notice from the preceding output that the owner of file1 is "root" and the group owner is the "root" group. To change the ownership of a file or directory, you can use the `chown` **(change owner) command**, which takes two arguments at minimum: the new owner and the files or directories to change. Both arguments can be absolute or relative pathnames, and you can also change permissions recursively throughout the directory tree using the `-R` option to the `chown` command. To change the ownership of file1 to the user user1 and the ownership of the directory Desktop and all of its contents to user1 as well, you can enter the following commands:

```
[root@server1 ~]# chown user1 file1
[root@server1 ~]# chown -R user1 Desktop
[root@server1 ~]# ls -l
total 4
drwx------    3 user1    root       4096 Apr  8 07:12 Desktop
-rw-r--r--    1 user1    root          0 Apr 29 15:40 file1
[root@server1 ~]# ls -l Desktop
total 16
-rw-------    1 user1    root        163 Mar 29 09:58 Work
-rw-r--r--    1 user1    root       3578 Mar 29 09:58 Home
-rw-r--r--    1 user1    root       1791 Mar 29 09:58 Start Here
drwx------    2 user1    root       4096 Mar 29 09:58 Trash
[root@server1 ~]#_
```

Recall that the owner of a file or directory and the root user can change ownership of a particular file or directory. If a regular user changes the ownership of a file or directory that she owns, that user cannot gain back the ownership. Instead, the new owner of that file or directory must change it to the original user. However, the root user always has the ability to regain the ownership:

```
[root@server1 ~]# chown root file1
[root@server1 ~]# chown -R root Desktop
[root@server1 ~]# ls -l
total 4
drwx------    3 root     root       4096 Apr  8 07:12 Desktop
-rw-r--r--    1 root     root          0 Apr 29 15:40 file1
[root@server1 ~]# ls -l Desktop
total 16
-rw-------    1 root     root        163 Mar 29 09:58 Work
-rw-r--r--    1 root     root       3578 Mar 29 09:58 Home
-rw-r--r--    1 root     root       1791 Mar 29 09:58 Start Here
drwx------    2 root     root       4096 Mar 29 09:58 Trash
[root@server1 ~]#_
```

Just as the `chown` (change owner) command can be used to change the owner of a file or directory, you can use the `chgrp` **(change group) command** to change the group owner of a file or directory. The chgrp command takes two arguments at minimum: the new group owner and the files or directories to change. As with the chown command, the chgrp command also accepts the -R option to change group ownership recursively throughout the directory tree. To change the group owner of file1 and the Desktop directory recursively throughout the directory tree, you can execute the following commands:

```
[root@server1 ~]# chgrp sys file1
[root@server1 ~]# chgrp -R sys Desktop
[root@server1 ~]# ls -l
total 4
drwx------    3 root      sys       4096 Apr  8 07:12 Desktop
-rw-r--r--    1 root      sys          0 Apr 29 15:40 file1
[root@server1 ~]# ls -l Desktop
total 16
-rw-------    1 root      sys        163 Mar 29 09:58 Work
-rw-r--r--    1 root      sys       3578 Mar 29 09:58 Home
-rw-r--r--    1 root      sys       1791 Mar 29 09:58 Start Here
drwx------    2 root      sys       4096 Mar 29 09:58 Trash
[root@server1 ~]#_
```

Note

Regular users can change the group of a file or directory only to a group to which they belong.

Normally, you change both the ownership and the group ownership on a file when that file needs to be maintained by someone else. As a result, you can change both the owner and the group owner at the same time using the chown command. To change the owner to user1 and the group owner to root for file1 and the directory Desktop recursively, you can enter the following commands:

```
[root@server1 ~]# chown user1.root file1
[root@server1 ~]# chown -R user1.root Desktop
[root@server1 ~]# ls -l
total 4
drwx------    3 user1     root      4096 Apr  8 07:12 Desktop
-rw-r--r--    1 user1     root         0 Apr 29 15:40 file1
[root@server1 ~]# ls -l Desktop
total 16
-rw-------    1 user1     root       163 Mar 29 09:58 Work
-rw-r--r--    1 user1     root      3578 Mar 29 09:58 Home
```

```
-rw-r--r--     1 user1     root       1791 Mar 29 09:58 Start Here
drwx------     2 user1     root       4096 Mar 29 09:58 Trash
[root@server1 ~]#_
```

Note that there must be no spaces before and after the . character in the chown commands shown in the preceding output.

Note 📎

You can also use the : character instead of the . character in the chown command to change both the owner and group ownership (e.g., chown -R user1:root Desktop).

To protect your system's security, you should ensure that most files residing in a user's home directory are owned by that user; some files in a user's home directory (especially the hidden files and directories) require this to function properly. To change the ownership back to the root user for file1 and the Desktop directory to avoid future problems, you can type the following:

```
[root@server1 ~]# chown root.root file1
[root@server1 ~]# chown -R root.root Desktop
[root@server1 ~]# ls -l
total 4
drwx------     3 root      root       4096 Apr  8 07:12 Desktop
-rw-r--r--     1 root      root          0 Apr 29 15:40 file1
[root@server1 root]# ls -l Desktop
total 16
-rw-------     1 root      root        163 Mar 29 09:58 Work
-rw-r--r--     1 root      root       3578 Mar 29 09:58 Home
-rw-r--r--     1 root      root       1791 Mar 29 09:58 Start Here
drwx------     2 root      root       4096 Mar 29 09:58 Trash
[root@server1 ~]#_
```

Note 📎

You can override who is allowed to change ownership and permissions using a system setting. Many Linux distributions, including Fedora 28 Linux, use this system setting by default to restrict regular (non-root) users from changing the ownership and group ownership of files and directories. This prevents these users from bypassing disk quota restrictions, which rely on the ownership of files and directories to function properly. Disk quotas are discussed in Chapter 5.

Managing File and Directory Permissions

Every file and directory file on a Linux filesystem contains information regarding permissions in its inode. The section of the inode that stores permissions is called the mode of the file and is divided into three sections based on the user(s) who receive(s) the permissions to that file or directory:

- User (owner) permissions
- Group (group owner) permissions
- Other (everyone else on the Linux system) permissions

Furthermore, you can assign to each of these users the following regular permissions:

- Read
- Write
- Execute

Interpreting the Mode

Recall that the three sections of the mode and the permissions that you can assign to each section are viewed when you perform an ls -l command; a detailed depiction of this is shown in Figure 4-3. Note that the root user supersedes all file and directory permissions; in other words, the root user has all permissions to every file and directory regardless of what the mode of the file or directory indicates.

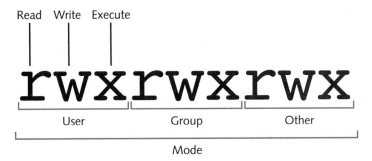

Figure 4-3   The Structure of a mode

Consider the root user's home directory listing shown in the following example:

```
[root@server1 ~]# ls -l
total 28
drwx------    3 root      root        4096 Apr  8 07:12 Desktop
-r---w---x    1 bob       proj         282 Apr 29 22:06 file1
-------rwx    1 root      root         282 Apr 29 22:06 file2
-rwxrwxrwx    1 root      root         282 Apr 29 22:06 file3
----------    1 root      root         282 Apr 29 22:06 file4
-rw-r--r--    1 root      root         282 Apr 29 22:06 file5
-rw-r--r--    1 user1     sys          282 Apr 29 22:06 file6
[root@server1 ~]#_
```

Note from the preceding output that all permissions (as shown in Figure 4-3) need not be on a file or directory; if the permission is unavailable, a dash (the hyphen character on your keyboard, -) replaces its position in the mode. Be certain not to confuse the character to the left of the mode (which determines the file type) with the mode, as it is unrelated to the permissions on the file or directory. From the preceding output, the Desktop directory gives the **user** or **owner** of the directory (the root user) read, write, and execute permission, yet members of the **group** (the root group) do not receive any permissions to the directory. Note that **other** (everyone on the system) does not receive permissions to this directory either.

Permissions are not additive; the system assigns the first set of permissions that are matched in the mode order: user, group, other. Let us assume that the bob user is a member of the proj group. In this case, the file called file1 in the preceding output gives the user or owner of the file (the bob user) read permission, gives members of the group (the proj group) write permission, and gives other (everyone else on the system) execute permission only. Because permissions are not additive, the bob user will only receive read permission to file1 from the system.

Linux permissions should not be assigned to other only. Although file2 in our example does not give the user or group any permissions, all other users receive read, write, and execute permission via the other category. Thus, file2 should not contain sensitive data because many users have full access to it. For the same reason, it is bad form to assign all permissions to a file that contains sensitive data, as shown with file3 in the preceding example.

On the contrary, it is also possible to have a file that has no permissions assigned to it, as shown in the preceding example with respect to file4. In this case, the only user who has permissions to the file is the root user.

The permission structure that you choose for a file or directory might result in too few or too many permissions. You can follow some general guidelines to avoid these situations. The owner of a file or directory is typically the person who maintains it; members of the group are typically users in the same company department and must have limited access to the file or directory. As a result, most files and directories that you find on a Linux filesystem have more permissions assigned to the user of the file/directory than to the group of the file/directory, and the other category has either the same permissions or less than the group of the file/directory, depending on how private that file or directory is. The file file5 in the previous output depicts this common permission structure. In addition, files in a user's home directory are typically owned by that user; however, you might occasionally find files that are not. For these files, their permission definition changes, as shown in the previous example with respect to file1 and file6. The user or owner of file6 is user1, who has read and write permissions to the file. The group owner of file6 is the sys group; thus, any members of the sys group have read permission to the file. Finally, everyone on the system receives read permission to the file via the other category. Regardless of the mode, the root user receives all permissions to this file.

Interpreting Permissions

After you understand how to identify the permissions that are applied to user, group, and other on a certain file or directory, you can then interpret the function of those permissions. Permissions for files are interpreted differently than those for directories. Also, if a user has a certain permission on a directory, that user does not have the same permission for all files or subdirectories within that directory; file and directory permissions are treated separately by the Linux system. Table 4-4 shows a summary of the different permissions and their definitions.

Table 4-4   Linux permissions

Permission	Definition for files	Definition for directories
Read	Allows a user to open and read the contents of a file	Allows a user to list the contents of the directory (if the user has also been given execute permission)
Write	Allows a user to open, read, and edit the contents of a file	Allows a user to add or remove files to and from the directory (if the user has also been given execute permission)
Execute	Allows a user to execute the file in memory (if it is a program file or script)	Allows a user to enter the directory and work with directory contents

The implications of the permission definitions described in Table 4-4 are important to understand. If a user has the read permission to a text file, that user can use, among others, the `cat`, `more`, `head`, `tail`, `less`, `strings`, and `od` commands to view its contents. That same user can also open that file with a text editor such as vi; however, the user does not have the ability to save any changes to the document unless that user has the write permission to the file as well.

Recall from earlier that some text files contain instructions for the shell to execute and are called shell scripts. Shell scripts can be executed in much the same way that binary compiled programs are; the user who executes the shell script must then have execute permission to that file to execute it as a program.

> **Note** 📎
>
> Avoid giving execute permission to files that are not programs or shell scripts. This ensures that these files will not be executed accidentally, causing the shell to interpret the contents.

Remember that directories are simply special files that have an inode and a data section, but what the data section contains is a list of that directory's contents. If you want to read that list (using the `ls` command, for example), then you require the read permission to the directory. To modify that list by adding or removing files, you require the write permission to the directory. Thus, if you want to create a new file in a directory with a text editor such as vi, you must have the write permission to that directory. Similarly, when a source file is copied to a target directory with the `cp` command, a new file is created in the target directory. You must have the write permission to the target directory for the copy to be successful. Conversely, to delete a certain file, you must have the write permission to the directory that contains that file. A user who has the write permission to a directory can delete all files and subdirectories within it.

The execute permission on a directory is sometimes referred to as the search permission, and it works similarly to a light switch. When a light switch is turned on, you can navigate a room and use the objects within it. However, when a light switch is turned off, you cannot see the objects in the room, nor can you walk around and view them. A user who does not have the execute permission to a directory is prevented from listing the directory's contents, adding and removing files, and working with files and subdirectories inside that directory, regardless of what permissions the user has to them. In short, a quick way to deny a user from accessing a directory and all of its contents in Linux is to take away the execute permission on that directory. Because the execute permission on a directory is crucial for user access, it is commonly given to all users via the other category, unless the directory must be private.

Changing Permissions

To change the permissions for a certain file or directory, you can use the `chmod` (change mode) command. The `chmod` command takes two arguments at minimum; the first argument specifies the criteria used to change the permissions (see Table 4-5), and the remaining arguments indicate the filenames to change.

Table 4-5   Criteria used within the `chmod` command

Category	Operation	Permission
u (user)	+ (adds a permission)	r (read)
g (group)	- (removes a permission)	w (write)
o (other)	= (makes a permission equal to)	x (execute)
a (all categories)		

Take, for example, the directory list used earlier:

```
[root@server1 ~]# ls -l
total 28
drwx------    3 root      root          4096 Apr  8 07:12 Desktop
-r---w---x    1 bob       proj           282 Apr 29 22:06 file1
-------rwx    1 root      root           282 Apr 29 22:06 file2
-rwxrwxrwx    1 root      root           282 Apr 29 22:06 file3
----------    1 root      root           282 Apr 29 22:06 file4
-rw-r--r--    1 root      root           282 Apr 29 22:06 file5
-rw-r--r--    1 user1     sys            282 Apr 29 22:06 file6
[root@server1 ~]#_
```

To change the mode of file1 to rw-r--r--, you must add the write permission to the user of the file, add the read permission and take away the write permission for the group of the file, and add the read permission and take away the execute permission for other.

From the information listed in Table 4-5, you can use the following command:

```
[root@server1 ~]# chmod u+w,g+r-w,o+r-x file1
[root@server1 ~]# ls -l
total 28
drwx------    3 root      root          4096 Apr  8 07:12 Desktop
-rw-r--r--    1 bob       proj           282 Apr 29 22:06 file1
----r--rwx    1 root      root           282 Apr 29 22:06 file2
-rwxrwxrwx    1 root      root           282 Apr 29 22:06 file3
----------    1 root      root           282 Apr 29 22:06 file4
-rw-r--r--    1 root      root           282 Apr 29 22:06 file5
-rw-r--r--    1 user1     sys            282 Apr 29 22:06 file6
[root@server1 ~]#_
```

Note

You should ensure that there are no spaces between any criteria used in the chmod command because all criteria make up the first argument only.

You can also use the = criteria from Table 4-5 to specify the exact permissions to change. To change the mode on file2 in the preceding output to the same as file1 (rw-r--r--), you can use the following chmod command:

```
[root@server1 ~]# chmod u=rw,g=r,o=r file2
[root@server1 ~]# ls -l
```

```
total 28
drwx------    3 root       root         4096 Apr  8 07:12 Desktop
-rw-r--r--    1 bob        proj          282 Apr 29 22:06 file1
-rw-r--r--    1 root       root          282 Apr 29 22:06 file2
-rwxrwxrwx    1 root       root          282 Apr 29 22:06 file3
----------    1 root       root          282 Apr 29 22:06 file4
-rw-r--r--    1 root       root          282 Apr 29 22:06 file5
-rw-r--r--    1 user1      sys           282 Apr 29 22:06 file6
[root@server1 ~]#_
```

If the permissions to change are identical for the user, group, and other categories, you can use the "a" character to refer to all categories, as shown in Table 4-5 and in the following example, when adding the execute permission to user, group, and other for file1:

```
[root@server1 ~]# chmod a+x file1
[root@server1 ~]# ls -l
total 28
drwx------    3 root       root         4096 Apr  8 07:12 Desktop
-rwxr-xr-x    1 bob        proj          282 Apr 29 22:06 file1
-rw-r--r--    1 root       root          282 Apr 29 22:06 file2
-rwxrwxrwx    1 root       root          282 Apr 29 22:06 file3
----------    1 root       root          282 Apr 29 22:06 file4
-rw-r--r--    1 root       root          282 Apr 29 22:06 file5
-rw-r--r--    1 user1      sys           282 Apr 29 22:06 file6
[root@server1 ~]#_
```

However, if there is no character specifying the category of user to affect, all users are assumed, as shown in the following example when adding the execute permission to user, group, and other for file2:

```
[root@server1 ~]# chmod +x file2
[root@server1 ~]# ls -l
total 28
drwx------    3 root       root         4096 Apr  8 07:12 Desktop
-rwxr-xr-x    1 bob        proj          282 Apr 29 22:06 file1
-rwxr-xr-x    1 root       root          282 Apr 29 22:06 file2
-rwxrwxrwx    1 root       root          282 Apr 29 22:06 file3
----------    1 root       root          282 Apr 29 22:06 file4
-rw-r--r--    1 root       root          282 Apr 29 22:06 file5
-rw-r--r--    1 user1      sys           282 Apr 29 22:06 file6
[root@server1 ~]#_
```

All of the aforementioned chmod examples use the symbols listed in Table 4-5 as the criteria for changing the permissions on a file or directory. You might instead choose to use numeric criteria with the chmod command to change permissions. All permissions are stored in the inode of a file or directory as binary powers of two:

- read $= 2^2 = 4$
- write $= 2^1 = 2$
- execute $= 2^0 = 1$

Thus, the mode of a file or directory can be represented using the numbers 421421421 instead of rwxrwxrwx. Because permissions are grouped into the categories user, group, and other, you can then simplify this further by using only three numbers, one for each category that represents the sum of the permissions, as shown in Figure 4-4.

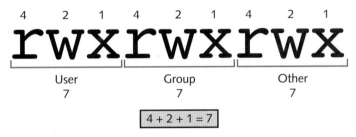

Figure 4-4   Numeric representation of the mode

Similarly, to represent the mode rw-r--r--, you can use the numbers 644 because user has read and write $(4 + 2 = 6)$, group has read (4), and other has read (4). The mode rwxr-x--- can also be represented by 750 because user has read, write, and execute $(4 + 2 + 1 = 7)$, group has read and execute $(4 + 1 = 5)$, and other has nothing (0). Table 4-6 provides a list of the different permissions and their corresponding numbers.

Table 4-6   Numeric representations of the permissions in a mode

Mode (one section only)	Corresponding number
rwx	$4 + 2 + 1 = 7$
rw-	$4 + 2 = 6$
r-x	$4 + 1 = 5$
r--	4
-wx	$2 + 1 = 3$
-w-	2
--x	1
---	0

To change the mode of the file1 file used earlier to r-xr-----, you can use the command chmod 540 file1, as shown in the following example:

```
[root@server1 ~]# chmod 540 file1
[root@server1 ~]# ls -l
total 28
drwx------    3 root     root           4096 Apr  8 07:12 Desktop
-r-xr-----    1 bob      proj            282 Apr 29 22:06 file1
-rwxr-xr-x    1 root     root            282 Apr 29 22:06 file2
-rwxrwxrwx    1 root     root            282 Apr 29 22:06 file3
----------    1 root     root            282 Apr 29 22:06 file4
-rw-r--r--    1 root     root            282 Apr 29 22:06 file5
-rw-r--r--    1 user1    sys             282 Apr 29 22:06 file6
[root@server1 ~]#_
```

Similarly, to change the mode of all files in the directory that start with the word "file" to 644 (which is common permissions for files), you can use the following command:

```
[root@server1 ~]# chmod 644 file*
[root@server1 ~]# ls -l
total 28
drwx------    3 root     root           4096 Apr  8 07:12 Desktop
-rw-r--r--    1 bob      proj            282 Apr 29 22:06 file1
-rw-r--r--    1 root     root            282 Apr 29 22:06 file2
-rw-r--r--    1 root     root            282 Apr 29 22:06 file3
-rw-r--r--    1 root     root            282 Apr 29 22:06 file4
-rw-r--r--    1 root     root            282 Apr 29 22:06 file5
-rw-r--r--    1 user1    sys             282 Apr 29 22:06 file6
[root@server1 ~]#_
```

Like the chown and chgrp commands, the chmod command can be used to change the permission on a directory and all of its contents recursively by using the -R option, as shown in the following example when changing the mode of the Desktop directory:

```
[root@server1 ~]# chmod -R 755 Desktop
[root@server1 ~]# ls -l
total 28
drwxr-xr-x    3 root     root           4096 Apr  8 07:12 Desktop
-rw-r--r--    1 bob      proj            282 Apr 29 22:06 file1
-rw-r--r--    1 root     root            282 Apr 29 22:06 file2
-rw-r--r--    1 root     root            282 Apr 29 22:06 file3
```

```
-rw-r--r--    1 root     root          282 Apr 29 22:06 file4
-rw-r--r--    1 root     root          282 Apr 29 22:06 file5
-rw-r--r--    1 user1    sys           282 Apr 29 22:06 file6
[root@server1 ~]# ls -l Desktop
total 16
-rwxr-xr-x    1 root     root          163 Mar 29 09:58 Work
-rwxr-xr-x    1 root     root         3578 Mar 29 09:58 Home
-rwxr-xr-x    1 root     root         1791 Mar 29 09:58 Start Here
drwxr-xr-x    2 root     root         4096 Mar 29 09:58 Trash
[root@server1 ~]#_
```

Default Permissions

Recall that permissions provide security for files and directories by allowing only certain users access, and that there are common guidelines for setting permissions on files and directories, so that permissions are not too strict or too permissive. Also important to maintaining security are the permissions that are given to new files and directories after they are created. New files are given rw-rw-rw- by the system when they are created (because execute should not be given unless necessary), and new directories are given rwxrwxrwx by the system when they are created (because execute needs to exist on a directory for other directory permissions to work). These default permissions are too permissive for most files, as they allow other full access to directories and nearly full access to files. Hence, a special variable on the system called the **umask** (user mask) takes away permissions on new files and directories immediately after they are created. The most common umask that you will find is 022, which specifies that nothing (0) is taken away from the user, write permission (2) is taken away from members of the group, and write permission (2) is taken away from other on new files and directories when they are first created and given permissions by the system.

> **Note** 🖉
>
> Keep in mind that the umask applies only to newly created files and directories; it is never used to modify the permissions of existing files and directories. You must use the chmod command to modify existing permissions.

An example of how a umask of 022 can be used to alter the permissions of a new file or directory after creation is shown in Figure 4-5.

To verify the umask used, you can use the umask **command** and note the final three digits in the output. To ensure that the umask functions as shown in Figure 4-5,

	New Files	New Directories
Permissions assigned by system	rw-rw-rw-	rwxrwxrwx
- umask	0 2 2	0 2 2
= resulting permissions	rw-r--r--	rwxr-xr-x

Figure 4-5   Performing a umask 022 calculation

create a new file using the `touch` command and a new directory using the `mkdir` command, as shown in the following output:

```
[root@server1 ~]# ls -l
total 28
drwx------      3 root       root         4096 Apr  8 07:12 Desktop
[root@server1 ~]# umask
0022
[root@server1 ~]# mkdir dir1
[root@server1 ~]# touch file1
[root@server1 ~]# ls -l
total 8
drwx------      3 root       root         4096 Apr  8 07:12 Desktop
drwxr-xr-x      2 root       root         4096 May  3 21:39 dir1
-rw-r--r--      1 root       root            0 May  3 21:40 file1
[root@server1 ~]#_
```

Because the umask is a variable stored in memory, it can be changed. To change the current umask, you can specify the new umask as an argument to the `umask` command. Suppose, for example, you want to change the umask to 007; the resulting permissions on new files and directories is calculated in Figure 4-6.

	New Files	New Directories
Permissions assigned by system	rw-rw-rw-	rwxrwxrwx
- umask	0 0 7	0 0 7
= resulting permissions	rw-rw----	rwxrwx---

Figure 4-6   Performing a umask 007 calculation

To change the umask to 007 and view its effect, you can type the following commands on the command line:

```
[root@server1 ~]# ls -l
total 8
drwx------       3 root       root           4096 Apr  8 07:12 Desktop
drwxr-xr-x       2 root       root           4096 May  3 21:39 dir1
-rw-r--r--       1 root       root              0 May  3 21:40 file1
[root@server1 ~]# umask 007
[root@server1 ~]# umask
0007
[root@server1 ~]# mkdir dir2
[root@server1 ~]# touch file2
[root@server1 ~]# ls -l
total 12
drwx------       3 root       root           4096 Apr  8 07:12 Desktop
drwxr-xr-x       2 root       root           4096 May  3 21:39 dir1
drwxrwx---       2 root       root           4096 May  3 21:41 dir2
-rw-r--r--       1 root       root              0 May  3 21:40 file1
-rw-rw----       1 root       root              0 May  3 21:41 file2
[root@server1 ~]#_
```

Special Permissions

Read, write, and execute are the regular file permissions that you would use to assign security to files; however, you can optionally use three more special permissions on files and directories:

- SUID (Set User ID)
- SGID (Set Group ID)
- Sticky bit

Defining Special Permissions

The SUID has no special function when set on a directory; however, if the SUID is set on a file and that file is executed, the person who executed the file temporarily becomes the owner of the file while it is executing. Many commands on a typical Linux system have this special permission set; the `passwd` command (/usr/bin/passwd) that is used to change your password is one such file. Because this file is owned by the root user, when a regular user executes the `passwd` command to change his own password, that user temporarily becomes the root user while the `passwd` command is executing in memory. This ensures that any user can change her own password because the default setting on Linux systems only allows the root user to change passwords. Furthermore, the SUID can only be applied to binary compiled programs. The Linux kernel does not let you apply the SUID to an executable text file, such as a shell script, because text files are easy to edit and, thus, pose a security hazard to the system.

Contrary to the SUID, the SGID has a function when applied to both files and directories. Just as the SUID allows regular users to execute a binary compiled program and become the owner of the file for the duration of execution, the SGID allows regular users to execute a binary compiled program and become a member of the group that is attached to the file. Thus, if a file is owned by the group "sys" and also has the SGID permission, any user who executes that file will be a member of the group "sys" during execution. If a command or file requires the user executing it to have the same permissions applied to the sys group, setting the SGID on the file simplifies assigning rights to the file for user execution.

The SGID also has a special function when placed on a directory. When a user creates a file, recall that that user's name and primary group become the owner and group owner of the file, respectively. However, if a user creates a file in a directory that has the SGID permission set, that user's name becomes the owner of the file and the directory's group becomes the group owner of the file.

Finally, the sticky bit was used on files in the past to lock them in memory; however, today the sticky bit performs a useful function only on directories. As explained earlier in this chapter, the write permission applied to a directory allows you to add and remove any file to and from that directory. Thus, if you have the write permission to a certain directory but no permission to files within it, you could delete all of those files. Consider a company that requires a common directory that gives all employees the ability to add files; this directory must give everyone the write permission. Unfortunately, the write permission also gives all employees the ability to delete all files and directories within, including the ones that others have added to the directory. If the sticky bit is applied to this common directory in addition to the write permission, employees can add files to the directory but only delete those files that they have added and not others.

Note 📎

Note that all special permissions also require the execute permission to work properly; the SUID and SGID work on executable files, and the SGID and sticky bit work on directories (which must have execute permission for access).

Setting Special Permissions

The mode of a file that is displayed using the `ls -l` command does not have a section for special permissions. However, because special permissions require execute, they mask the execute permission when displayed using the `ls -l` command, as shown in Figure 4-7.

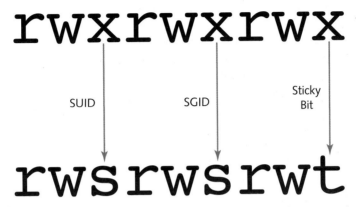

Figure 4-7   Representing special permissions in the mode

The system allows you to set special permissions even if the file or directory does not have execute permission. However, the special permissions will not perform their function. If the special permissions are set on a file or directory without execute permissions, then the ineffective special permissions are capitalized as shown in Figure 4-8.

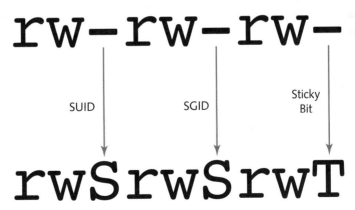

Figure 4-8   Representing special permission in the absence of the execute permission

To set the special permissions, you can visualize them to the left of the mode, as shown in Figure 4-9.

Figure 4-9 Numeric representation of regular and special permissions

Thus, to set all of the special permissions on a certain file or directory, you can use the command chmod 7777 name, as indicated from Figure 4-9. However, the SUID and SGID bits are typically set on files. To change the permissions on the file1 file used earlier such that other can view and execute the file as the owner and a member of the group, you can use the command chmod 6755 file1, as shown in the following example:

```
[root@server1 ~]# ls -l
total 12
drwx------    3 root      root        4096 Apr  8 07:12 Desktop
drwxr-xr-x    2 root      root        4096 May  3 21:39 dir1
drwx------    2 root      root        4096 May  3 21:41 dir2
-rw-r--r--    1 root      root           0 May  3 21:40 file1
-rw-------    1 root      root           0 May  3 21:41 file2
[root@server1 ~]# chmod 6755 file1
[root@server1 ~]# ls -l
total 12
drwx------    3 root      root        4096 Apr  8 07:12 Desktop
drwxr-xr-x    2 root      root        4096 May  3 21:39 dir1
drwx------    2 root      root        4096 May  3 21:41 dir2
-rwsr-sr-x    1 root      root           0 May  3 21:40 file1
-rw-------    1 root      root           0 May  3 21:41 file2
[root@server1 ~]#_
```

Similarly, to set the sticky bit permission on the directory dir1 used earlier, you can use the command chmod 1777 dir1, which allows all users (including other) to add files to the dir1 directory. This is because you gave the write permission; however, users can only delete the files that they own in dir1 because you set the sticky bit. This is shown in the following example:

```
[root@server1 ~]# ls -l
total 12
drwx------    3 root      root        4096 Apr  8 07:12 Desktop
drwxr-xr-x    2 root      root        4096 May  3 21:39 dir1
```

```
drwx------         2 root        root         4096 May  3 21:41 dir2
-rwsr-sr-x         1 root        root            0 May  3 21:40 file1
-rw-------         1 root        root            0 May  3 21:41 file2
[root@server1 ~]# chmod 1777 dir1
[root@server1 ~]# ls -l
total 12
drwx------         3 root        root         4096 Apr  8 07:12 Desktop
drwxrwxrwt         2 root        root         4096 May  3 21:39 dir1
drwx------         2 root        root         4096 May  3 21:41 dir2
-rwsr-sr-x         1 root        root            0 May  3 21:40 file1
-rw-------         1 root        root            0 May  3 21:41 file2
[root@server1 ~]#_
```

Also, remember that assigning special permissions without execute renders those permissions useless. For example, you may forget to give execute permission to user, group, or other, and the long listing covers the execute permission with a special permission. In that case, the special permission is capitalized, as shown in the following example when dir2 is not given execute underneath the position in the mode that indicates the sticky bit (t):

```
[root@server1 ~]# ls -l
total 12
drwx------         3 root        root         4096 Apr  8 07:12 Desktop
drwxrwxrwt         2 root        root         4096 May  3 21:39 dir1
drwx------         2 root        root         4096 May  3 21:41 dir2
-rwsr-sr-x         1 root        root            0 May  3 21:40 file1
-rw-------         1 root        root            0 May  3 21:41 file2
[root@server1 ~]# chmod 1770 dir2
[root@server1 ~]# ls -l
total 12
drwx------         3 root        root         4096 Apr  8 07:12 Desktop
drwxrwxrwt         2 root        root         4096 May  3 21:39 dir1
drwxrwx--T         2 root        root         4096 May  3 21:41 dir2
-rwsr-sr-x         1 root        root            0 May  3 21:40 file1
-rw-------         1 root        root            0 May  3 21:41 file2
[root@server1 ~]#_
```

> **Note** 📎
>
> You can also use symbols to set special permissions on a file or directory. For example, the chmod u+s,g+s file1 command can be used to add the SUID and SGID to file1, and the chmod o+t dir1 command can be used to add the sticky bit to dir1.

Setting Custom Permissions in the Access Control List (ACL)

An **access control list (ACL)** is a list of users or groups that you can assign permissions to. As discussed earlier, the default ACL used in Linux consists of three entities: user, group, and other. However, there may be situations where you need to assign a specific set of permissions on a file or directory to an individual user or group.

Take, for example, the file doc1:

```
[root@server1 ~]# ls -l doc1
-rw-rw----    1 user1      acctg            0 May  2 22:01 doc1
[root@server1 ~]#_
```

The owner of the file (user1) has read and write permission, the group (acctg) has read and write permission, and everyone else has no access to the file.

Now imagine that you need to give read permission to the bob user without giving permissions to anyone else. The solution to this problem is to modify the ACL on the doc1 file and add a special entry for bob only. This can be accomplished by using the following `setfacl` **(set file ACL)** command:

```
[root@server1 ~]# setfacl -m u:bob:r-- doc1
[root@server1 ~]#_
```

The –m option in the command above modifies the ACL, You can use g instead of u to add a group to the ACL.

Now, when you perform a long listing of the file doc1, you will see a + symbol next to the mode to indicate that there are additional entries in the ACL for this file. To see these additional members, use the `getfacl` **(get file ACL) command**:

```
[root@server1 ~]# ls -l doc1
-rw-rw----+   1 user1      acctg            0 May  2 22:01 doc1
  [root@server1 ~]# getfacl doc1
# file: doc1
# owner: user1
# group: acctg
user::rw-
user:bob:r--
group::rw-
mask::rw-
other::---
[root@server1 ~]#_
```

After running the `getfacl` command, you will notice an extra node in the output: the mask. The mask is compared to all additional user and group permissions in the ACL. If the mask is more restrictive, it takes precedence when it comes to permissions. For example, if the mask is set to r-- and the user bob has rw-, then the user bob actually gets r-- to the file. When you run the `setfacl` command, the mask is always made equal to the least restrictive permission assigned so that it does not affect additional ACL entries. The mask was created as a mechanism that could easily revoke permissions on a file that had several additional users and groups added to the ACL.

To remove all extra ACL assignments on the doc1 file, use the –b option to the setfacl command:

```
[root@server1 ~]# setfacl –b doc1
[root@server1 ~]# ls –l doc1
-rw-rw----    1 user1      acctg           0 May  2 22:01 doc1
[root@server1 ~]#_
```

Managing Filesystem Attributes

As with the Windows operating system, Linux has file attributes that can be set, if necessary. These attributes work outside Linux permissions and are filesystem-specific. This section examines attributes for the ext4 filesystem that you configured earlier during Lab 2.1. Filesystem types will be discussed in more depth in Chapter 5.

To see the filesystem attributes that are currently assigned to a file, you can use the lsattr (**list attributes**) **command**, as shown here for the doc1 file:

```
[root@server1 ~]# lsattr doc1
--------------e---- doc1
[root@server1 ~]#_
```

By default, all files have the e attribute, which writes to the file in "extent" blocks (rather than immediately in a byte-by-byte fashion). If you would like to add or remove attributes, you can use the chattr (**change attributes**) **command**. The following example assigns the immutable attribute (i) to the doc1 file and displays the results:

```
[root@server1 ~]# chattr +i doc1
[root@server1 ~]# lsattr doc1
----i---------e---- doc1
[root@server1 ~]#_
```

The immutable attribute is the most commonly used filesystem attribute and prevents the file from being modified in any way. Because attributes are applied at a filesystem level, not even the root user can modify a file that has the immutable attribute set.

> **Note** 📎
>
> Most filesystem attributes are rarely set, as they provide for low-level filesystem functionality. To view a full listing of filesystem attributes, visit the manual page for the chattr command.

Similarly, to remove an attribute, use the `chattr` command with the – option, as shown here with the doc1 file:

```
[root@server1 ~]# chattr -i doc1
[root@server1 ~]# lsattr doc1
-------------e---- doc1
[root@server1 ~]#_
```

Chapter Summary

- The Linux directory tree obeys the Filesystem Hierarchy Standard, which allows Linux users and developers to locate system files in standard directories.

- Many file management commands are designed to create, change the location of, or remove files and directories. The most common of these include `cp`, `mv`, `rm`, `rmdir`, and `mkdir`.

- You can find files on the filesystem using a preindexed database (the `locate` command) or by searching the directories listed in the PATH variable (the `which` command). However, the most versatile command used to find files is the `find` command, which searches for files based on a wide range of criteria.

- Files can be linked two ways. In a symbolic link, one file serves as a pointer to another file. In a hard link, one file is a linked duplicate of another file.

- Each file and directory has an owner and a group owner. In the absence of system restrictions, the owner of the file or directory can change permissions and give ownership to others.

- Permissions can be set on the user or owner of a file, members of the group of the file, as well as everyone on the system (other).

- There are three regular file and directory permissions (read, write, and execute) and three special file and directory permissions (SUID, SGID, and sticky bit). The definitions of these permissions are different for files and directories.

- Permissions can be changed using the `chmod` command by specifying symbols or numbers to represent the changed permissions.

- To ensure security, new files and directories receive default permissions from the system, less the value of the umask variable.

- The root user has all permissions to all files and directories on the Linux filesystem. Similarly, the root user can change the ownership of any file or directory on the Linux filesystem.

- The default ACL on a file or directory can be modified to include additional users or groups.

- Filesystem attributes can be set on Linux files to provide low-level functionality such as immutability.

Key Terms

access control list (ACL)

chattr (change attributes) command

chgrp (change group) command

chmod (change mode) command

chown (change owner) command

cp (copy) command

data blocks

Filesystem Hierarchy Standard (FHS)

find command

getfacl (get file ACL) command

group

hard link

inode

inode table

interactive mode

ln (link) command

locate command

lsattr (list attributes) command

mkdir (make directory) command

mode

mv (move) command

other

owner

passwd command

PATH variable

permissions

primary group

pruning

recursive

rm (remove) command

rmdir (remove directory) command

setfacl (set file ACL) command

source file/directory

superblock

symbolic link

target file/directory

touch command

type command

umask

umask command

unlink command

user

whereis command

which command

Review Questions

1. A symbolic link is also known as a soft link and is depicted by an @ symbol appearing at the beginning of the filename when viewed using the ls -l command. True or False?

2. What was created to define a standard directory structure and common file location for Linux?
   a. FSH
   b. X.500
   c. FHS
   d. root directory

3. There is no real difference between the "S" and "s" special permissions when displayed using the ls -l command. One just means it is on a file, and the other means that it is on a directory. True or False?

4. The default permissions given by the system prior to analyzing the umask are _____ for directories and _____ for files.
   a. rw-rw-rw- and rw-rw-rw-
   b. rw-rw-rw- and r--r--r--
   c. rw-rw-rw- and rwxrwxrwx
   d. rwxrwxrwx and rw-rw-rw-
   e. rwxrw-rw- and rwx-rw-rw-

5. What must a user do to run cp or mv interactively and be asked whether to overwrite an existing file?
   a. There is no choice because the new file will overwrite the old one by default.
   b. Type interactive cp or interactive mv.
   c. Type cp -i or mv -i.

d. Type `cp –interactive` or `mv –interactive`.

e. Just type `cp` or `mv` because they run in interactive mode by default.

6. The root user utilizes the `chgrp` command to give ownership of a file to another user. What must the root user do to regain ownership of the file?

  a. Run `chgrp` again listing the root user as the new owner.

  b. Nothing, because this is a one-way, one-time action.

  c. Have the new owner run `chgrp`, and list the root user as the new owner.

  d. Run `chown` and list the root user as the new owner.

7. After typing the `ls –F` command, you see the following line in the output:

   -rw-r-xr--   1 user1   root   0 Apr 29 15:40 file1

   What does this mean?

  a. User1 has read and write, members of the root group have read and execute, and all others have read permissions to the file.

  b. Members of the root group have read and write, user1 has read and execute, and all others have read permissions to the file.

  c. All users have read and write, members of the root group have read and execute, and user1 has read permissions to the file.

  d. User1 has read and write, all others have read and execute, and members of the root group have read permissions to the file.

8. After typing the command `umask 731`, the permissions on all subsequently created files and directories will be affected. In this case, what will be the permissions on all new files?

  a. rw-rw-rw-

  b. rwxrw-r--

  c. ---r--rw-

  d. ----wx--x

9. You noticed a file in your home directory that has a + symbol appended to the mode. What does this indicate?

  a. Special permissions have been set on the file.

  b. The file has one or more files on the filesystem that are hard-linked to it.

  c. The sticky bit directory permission has been set on the file and will remain inactive as a result.

  d. Additional entries exist within the ACL of the file that can be viewed using the `getfacl` command.

10. When you change the data in a file that is hard-linked to three others, _____.

  a. only the data in the file you modified is affected

  b. only the data in the file you modified and any hard-linked files in the same directory are affected

  c. the data in the file you modified and the data in all hard-linked files are modified because they have different inodes

  d. the data in the file you modified as well as the data in all hard-linked files are modified because they share the same data and all have the same inode and file size

11. The command `chmod 317 file1` would produce which of the following lines in the `ls` command?

  a. --w-r--rwx 1 user1 root 0 Apr 29 15:40 file1

  b. --wx--xrwx 1 user1 root 0 Apr 29 15:40 file1

c. -rwxrw-r-x 1 user1 root 0 Apr 29 15:40 file1

d. --w-rw-r-e 1 user1 root 0 Apr 29 15:40 file1

12. Which of the following commands will change the user ownership and group ownership of *file1* to user1 and root, respectively?

   a. `chown user1:root file1`

   b. `chown user1 : root file1`

   c. This cannot be done because user and group ownership properties of a file must be modified separately.

   d. `chown root:user1 file1`

   e. `chown root : user1 file1`

13. What does the /var directory contain?

   a. various additional programs

   b. spools and log files

   c. temporary files

   d. files that are architecture-independent

   e. local variance devices

14. What does the mv command do? (Choose all that apply.)

   a. It makes a volume.

   b. It makes a directory.

   c. It moves a directory.

   d. It moves a file.

15. A file has the following permissions: *r--- -x-w-*. The command `chmod 143` would have the same effect as the command _____. (Choose all that apply.)

   a. `chmod u+x-r,g+r-x,o+w file1`

   b. `chmod u=w,g=rw,o=rx file1`

   c. `chmod u-r-w,g+r-w,o+r-x file1`

   d. `chmod u=x,g=r,o=wx file1`

   e. `chmod u+w,g+r-w,o+r-x file1`

   f. `chmod u=rw,g=r,o=r file1`

16. The which command _____.

   a. can only be used to search for executables

   b. searches for a file in all directories, starting from the root

   c. is not a valid Linux command

   d. searches for a file only in directories that are in the PATH variable

17. Hard links need to reside on the same filesystem as the target, whereas symbolic links need not be on the same filesystem as the target. True or False?

18. When applied to a directory, the SGID special permission _____.

   a. causes all new files created in the directory to have the same group membership as the directory, and not the entity that created them

   b. cannot be used, because it is applied only to files

   c. allows users the ability to use more than two groups for files that they create within the directory

   d. causes users to have their permissions checked before they are allowed to access files in the directory

19. Which command do you use to rename files and directories?

   a. `cp`

   b. `mv`

   c. `rn`

   d. `rename`

20. What are the three standard Linux permissions?

   a. full control, read-execute, write

   b. read, write, modify

   c. execute, read, write

   d. read, write, examine

21. Given the following output from the `ls` command, how many files are linked with file1?

```
drwxr-xr-x    3 root      root      4096 Apr  8 07:12 Desktop
-rw-r--r--    3 root      root       282 Apr 29 22:06 file1
-rw-r--r--    1 root      root       282 Apr 29 22:06 file2
-rw-r--r--    4 root      root       282 Apr 29 22:06 file3
-rw-r--r--    2 root      root       282 Apr 29 22:06 file4
-rw-r--r--    1 root      root       282 Apr 29 22:06 file5
-rw-r--r--    1 user1     sys        282 Apr 29 22:06 file6
```

   a. one
   b. two
   c. three
   d. four

22. Only the root user can modify a file that has the immutable attribute set. True or False?

Hands-On Projects

These projects should be completed in the order given. The hands-on projects presented in this chapter should take a total of three hours to complete. The requirements for this lab include:

- A computer with Fedora 28 installed according to Hands-On Project 2-1
- Completion of all Hands-On Projects in Chapter 3

Project 4-1

In this hands-on project, you log in to the computer and create new directories.

1. Boot your Fedora Linux virtual machine. After your Linux system has loaded, switch to a command-line terminal (tty5) by pressing **Ctrl+Alt+F5**. Log in to the terminal using the user name of **root** and the password of **LINUXrocks!**.
2. At the command prompt, type `ls -F` and press **Enter**. Note the contents of your home folder.
3. At the command prompt, type `mkdir mysamples` and press **Enter**. Next type `ls -F` at the command prompt, and press **Enter** to verify the creation of the subdirectory.
4. At the command prompt, type `cd mysamples` and press **Enter**. Next, type `ls -F` at the command prompt and press **Enter**. What are the contents of the subdirectory mysamples?
5. At the command prompt, type `mkdir undermysamples` and press **Enter**. Next, type `ls -F` at the command prompt and press **Enter**. What are the contents of the subdirectory mysamples?

6. At the command prompt, type `mkdir todelete` and press **Enter**. Next, type `ls -F` at the command prompt and press **Enter**. Does the subdirectory todelete you just created appear listed in the display?

7. At the command prompt, type `cd ..` and press **Enter**. Next, type `ls -R` and press **Enter**. Notice that the subdirectory mysamples and its subdirectory undermysamples are both displayed.

8. At the command prompt, type `cd ..` and press **Enter**. At the command prompt, type `pwd` and press **Enter**. What is your current directory?

9. At the command prompt, type `mkdir foruser1` and press **Enter**. At the command prompt, type `ls -F` and press **Enter**. Does the subdirectory you just created appear listed in the display?

10. Type `exit` and press **Enter** to log out of your shell.

Project 4-2

In this hands-on project, you copy files using the `cp` command.

1. Switch to a command-line terminal (tty5) by pressing **Ctrl+Alt+F5** and log in to the terminal using the user name of **root** and the password of **LINUXrocks!**.

2. Next, type `ls -F` at the command prompt and press **Enter**. Note the contents of your home folder.

3. At the command prompt, type `cp sample1` and press **Enter**. What error message was displayed and why?

4. At the command prompt, type `cp sample1 sample1A` and press **Enter**. Next, type `ls -F` at the command prompt and press **Enter**. How many files are there and what are their names? Why?

5. At the command prompt, type `cp sample1 mysamples/sample1B` and press **Enter**. Next, type `ls -F` at the command prompt and press **Enter**. How many files are there and what are their names? Why?

6. At the command prompt, type `cd mysamples` and press **Enter**. Next, type `ls -F` at the command prompt and press **Enter**. Was sample1B copied successfully?

7. At the command prompt, type `cp /root/sample2 .` and press **Enter**. Next, type `ls -F` at the command prompt and press **Enter**. How many files are there and what are their names? Why?

8. At the command prompt, type `cp sample1B ..` and press **Enter**. Next, type `cd ..` at the command prompt and press **Enter**. At the command prompt, type `ls -F` and press **Enter**. Was the sample1B file copied successfully?

9. At the command prompt, type `cp sample1 sample2 sample3 mysamples` and press **Enter**. What message do you get and why? Choose **y** and press **Enter**. Next, type `cd mysamples` at the command prompt and press **Enter**. At the command prompt, type `ls -F` and press **Enter**. How many files are there and what are their names? Why?

10. At the command prompt, type `cd ..` and press **Enter**. Next, type `cp mysamples mysamples2` at the command prompt and press **Enter**. What error message did you receive? Why?

11. At the command prompt, type `cp -R mysamples mysamples2` and press **Enter**. Next, type `ls -F` at the command prompt, and press **Enter**. Was the directory copied successfully? Type `ls -F mysamples2` at the command prompt and press **Enter**. Were the contents of mysamples successfully copied to mysamples2?

12. Type `exit` and press **Enter** to log out of your shell.

Project 4-3

In this hands-on project, you use the `mv` command to rename files and directories.

1. Switch to a command-line terminal (tty5) by pressing **Ctrl+Alt+F5** and log in to the terminal using the user name of **root** and the password of **LINUXrocks!**.

2. Next, type `ls -F` at the command prompt and press **Enter**. Note the contents of your home folder.

3. At the command prompt, type `mv sample1` and press **Enter**. What error message was displayed and why?

4. At the command prompt, type `mv sample1 sample4` and press **Enter**. Next, type `ls -F` at the command prompt and press **Enter**. How many files are listed and what are their names? What happened to sample1?

5. At the command prompt, type `mv sample4 mysamples` and press **Enter**. Next, type `ls -F` at the command prompt and press **Enter**. How many files are there and what are their names? Where did sample4 go?

6. At the command prompt, type `cd mysamples` and press **Enter**. Next, type `ls -F` at the command prompt and press **Enter**. Notice that the sample4 file you moved in Step 5 was moved here.

7. At the command prompt, type `mv sample4 ..` and press **Enter**. Next, type `ls -F` at the command prompt and press **Enter**. How many files are there and what are their names? Where did the sample4 file go?

8. At the command prompt, type `cd ..` and press **Enter**. Next, type `ls -F` at the command prompt and press **Enter** to view the new location of sample4.

9. At the command prompt, type `mv sample4 mysamples/sample2` and press **Enter**. What message appeared on the screen and why?

10. Type `y` and press **Enter** to confirm you want to overwrite the file in the destination folder.

11. At the command prompt, type `mv sample? mysamples` and press **Enter**. Type `y` and press **Enter** to confirm you want to overwrite the file sample3 in the destination folder.

12. At the command prompt, type `ls -F` and press **Enter**. How many files are there and why?

13. At the command prompt, type `mv sample1* mysamples` and press **Enter**. Type `y` and press **Enter** to confirm you want to overwrite the file sample1B in the destination directory.

14. At the command prompt, type `ls -F` and press **Enter**. Notice that there are no sample files in the /root directory.

15. At the command prompt, type `cd mysamples` and press **Enter**. Next, type `ls -F` at the command prompt and press **Enter**. Notice that all files originally in /root have been moved to this directory.

16. At the command prompt, type `cd ..` and press **Enter**. Next, type `ls -F` at the command prompt and press **Enter**. Type `mv mysamples samples` and press **Enter**. Next, type `ls -F` at the command prompt and press **Enter**. Why did you not need to specify the recursive option to the `mv` command to rename the mysamples directory to samples?

17. Type `exit` and press **Enter** to log out of your shell.

Project 4-4

In this hands-on project, you make and view links to files and directories.

1. Switch to a command-line terminal (tty5) by pressing **Ctrl+Alt+F5** and log in to the terminal using the user name of **root** and the password of **LINUXrocks!**.

2. At the command prompt, type `cd samples` and press **Enter**. Next, type `ls -F` at the command prompt and press **Enter**. What files do you see? Next, type `ls -l` at the command prompt and press **Enter**. What is the link count for the sample1 file?

3. At the command prompt, type `ln sample1 hardlinksample` and press **Enter**. Next, type `ls -F` at the command prompt and press **Enter**. Does anything in the terminal output indicate that sample1 and hardlinksample are hard-linked? Next, type `ls -l` at the command prompt and press **Enter**. Does anything in the terminal output indicate that sample1 and hardlinksample are hard-linked? What is the link count for sample1 and hardlinksample? Next, type `ls -li` at the command prompt and press **Enter** to view the inode numbers of each file. Do the two hard-linked files have the same inode number?

4. At the command prompt, type `ln sample1 hardlinksample2` and press **Enter**. Next, type `ls -l` at the command prompt and press **Enter**. What is the link count for the files sample1, hardlinksample, and hardlinksample2? Why?

5. At the command prompt, type `vi sample1` and press **Enter**. Enter a sentence of your choice into the vi editor, and then save your document and quit the vi editor.

6. At the command prompt, type `cat sample1` and press **Enter**. Next, type `cat hardlinksample` at the command prompt and press **Enter**. Next, type `cat hardlinksample2` at the command prompt and press **Enter**. Are the contents of each file the same? Why?

7. At the command prompt, type `ln -s sample2 symlinksample` and press **Enter**. Next, type `ls -F` at the command prompt and press **Enter**. Does anything in the terminal output indicate that sample2 and symlinksample are symbolically linked? Which file is the target file? Next, type `ls -l` at the command prompt and press **Enter**. Does anything in the terminal output indicate that sample2 and symlinksample are symbolically linked? Next, type `ls -li` at the command prompt and press **Enter** to

view the inode numbers of each file. Do the two symbolically linked files have the same inode number?

8. At the command prompt, type `vi symlinksample` and press **Enter**. Enter a sentence of your choice into the vi editor, and then save your document and quit the vi editor.

9. At the command prompt, type `ls -l` and press **Enter**. What is the size of the symlinksample file compared to sample2? Why? Next, type `cat sample2` at the command prompt and press **Enter**. What are the contents and why?

10. At the command prompt, type `ln -s /etc/sysconfig/network-scripts netscripts` and press **Enter**. Next, type `ls -F` at the command prompt and press **Enter**. What file type is indicated for netscripts? Next, type `cd netscripts` at the command prompt and press **Enter**. Type `pwd` at the command prompt and press **Enter** to view your current directory. What is your current directory? Next, type `ls -F` at the command prompt and press **Enter**. What files are listed? Next, type `ls -F /etc/sysconfig/network-scripts` at the command prompt and press **Enter**. Note that your netscripts directory is merely a pointer to the /etc/sysconfig/network-scripts directory. How can this type of linking be useful?

11. Type `exit` and press **Enter** to log out of your shell.

Project 4-5

In this hands-on project, you find files on the filesystem using the `find`, `locate`, `which`, `type`, and `whereis` commands.

1. Switch to a command-line terminal (tty5) by pressing **Ctrl+Alt+F5** and log in to the terminal using the user name of **root** and the password of **LINUXrocks!**.

2. At the command prompt, type `touch newfile` and press **Enter**. Next, type `locate newfile` at the command prompt and press **Enter**. Did the `locate` command find the file you just created? Why?

3. At the command prompt, type `updatedb` and press **Enter**. When the command is finished, type `locate newfile` at the command prompt and press **Enter**. Did the `locate` command find the file? If so, how quickly did it find it? Why?

4. At the command prompt, type `find / -name "newfile"` and press **Enter**. Did the `find` command find the file? If so, how quickly did it find it? Why?

5. At the command prompt, type `find /root -name "newfile"` and press **Enter**. Did the `find` command find the file? How quickly did it find it? Why?

6. At the command prompt, type `which newfile` and press **Enter**. Did the `which` command find the file? Why? Type `echo $PATH` at the command prompt and press **Enter**. Is the /root directory listed in the PATH variable? Is the /usr/bin directory listed in the PATH variable?

7. At the command prompt, type `which grep` and press **Enter**. Did the `which` command find the file? Why?

8. At the command prompt, type `type grep` and press **Enter**. Next, type `whereis grep` and press **Enter**. Do these commands return less or more than the which command did in the previous step? Why?

9. At the command prompt, type `find /root -name "sample"` and press **Enter**. What files are listed? Why?

10. At the command prompt, type `find /root -type l` and press **Enter**. What files are listed? Why?

11. At the command prompt, type `find /root -size 0` and press **Enter**. What types of files are listed? Type `find / -size 0 | more` to see all of the files of this type on the system.

12. Type `exit` and press **Enter** to log out of your shell.

Project 4-6

In this hands-on project, you delete files and directories using the `rmdir` and `rm` commands.

1. Switch to a command-line terminal (tty5) by pressing **Ctrl+Alt+F5** and log in to the terminal using the user name of **root** and the password of **LINUXrocks!**.

2. At the command prompt, type `cd samples` and press **Enter**. At the command prompt, type `ls -R` and press **Enter**. Note the two empty directories todelete and undermysamples.

3. At the command prompt, type `rmdir undermysamples todelete` and press **Enter**. Did the command work? Why? Next, type `ls -F` at the command prompt and press **Enter**. Were both directories deleted successfully?

4. At the command prompt, type `rm sample1*` and press **Enter**. What message is displayed? Answer **n** to all three questions.

5. At the command prompt, type `rm -f sample1*` and press **Enter**. Why were you not prompted to continue? Next, type `ls -F` at the command prompt and press **Enter**. Were all three files deleted successfully? What other command may be used to delete a file within Linux?

6. At the command prompt, type `cd ..` and press **Enter**. Next, type `rmdir samples` at the command prompt and press **Enter**. What error message do you receive and why?

7. At the command prompt, type `rm -rf samples` and press **Enter**. Next, type `ls -F` at the command prompt and press **Enter**. Was the samples directory and all files within it deleted successfully?

8. Type `exit` and press **Enter** to log out of your shell.

Project 4-7

In this hands-on project, you apply and modify access permissions on files and directories and test their effects.

1. Switch to a command-line terminal (tty5) by pressing **Ctrl+Alt+F5** and log in to the terminal using the user name of **root** and the password of **LINUXrocks!**.

2. At the command prompt, type `touch permsample` and press **Enter**. Next, type `chmod 777 permsample` at the command prompt and press **Enter**.

3. At the command prompt, type `ls -l` and press **Enter**. Who has permissions to this file?

4. At the command prompt, type `chmod 000 permsample` and press **Enter**. Next, type `ls -l` at the command prompt and press **Enter**. Who has permissions to this file?

5. At the command prompt, type `rm -f permsample` and press **Enter**. Were you able to delete this file? Why?

6. At the command prompt, type `cd /` and press **Enter**. Next, type `pwd` at the command prompt and press **Enter**. What directory are you in? Type `ls -F` at the command prompt and press **Enter**. What directories do you see?

7. At the command prompt, type `ls -l` and press **Enter** to view the owner, group owner, and permissions on the foruser1 directory created in Hands-On Project 4-1. Who is the owner and group owner? If you were logged in as the user user1, in which category would you be placed (user, group, other)? What permissions do you have as this category (read, write, execute)?

8. At the command prompt, type `cd /foruser1` and press **Enter** to enter the foruser1 directory. Next, type `ls -F` at the command prompt and press **Enter**. Are there any files in this directory? Type `cp /etc/hosts .` at the command prompt and press **Enter**. Next, type `ls -F` at the command prompt and press **Enter** to ensure that a copy of the hosts file was made in your current directory.

9. Switch to a different command-line terminal (tty3) by pressing **Ctrl+Alt+F3** and log in to the terminal using the user name of **user1** and the password of **LINUXrocks!**.

10. At the command prompt, type `cd /foruser1` and press **Enter**. Were you successful? Why? Next, type `ls -F` at the command prompt and press **Enter**. Were you able to see the contents of the directory? Why? Next, type `rm -f hosts` at the command prompt and press **Enter**. What error message did you see? Why?

11. Switch back to your previous command-line terminal (tty5) by pressing **Ctrl+Alt+F5**. Note that you are logged in as the root user on this terminal and within the /foruser1 directory.

12. At the command prompt, type `chmod o+w /foruser1` and press **Enter**. Were you able to change the permissions on the /foruser1 directory successfully? Why?

13. Switch back to your previous command-line terminal (tty3) by pressing **Ctrl+Alt+F3**. Note that you are logged in as the user1 user on this terminal and within the /foruser1 directory.

14. At the command prompt, type `rm -f hosts` at the command prompt and press **Enter**. Were you successful now? Why?

15. Switch back to your previous command-line terminal (tty5) by pressing **Ctrl+Alt+F5**. Note that you are logged in as the root user on this terminal.

16. At the command prompt, type `cp /etc/hosts .` at the command prompt and press **Enter** to place another copy of the hosts file in your current directory (/foruser1).

17. At the command prompt, type `ls -l` and press **Enter**. Who is the owner and group owner of this file? If you were logged in as the user user1, in which category would you be placed (user, group, other)? What permissions do you have as this category (read, write, execute)?

18. Switch back to your previous command-line terminal (tty3) by pressing **Ctrl+Alt+F3**. Note that you are logged in as the user1 user on this terminal and in the /foruser1 directory.

19. At the command prompt, type `cat hosts` at the command prompt and press **Enter**. Were you successful? Why? Next, type `vi hosts` at the command prompt to open the hosts file in the vi editor. Delete the first line of this file and save your changes. Were you successful? Why? Exit the vi editor and discard your changes.

20. Switch back to your previous command-line terminal (tty5) by pressing **Ctrl+Alt+F5**. Note that you are logged in as the root user on this terminal and in the /foruser1 directory.

21. At the command prompt, type `chmod o+w hosts` and press **Enter**.

22. Switch back to your previous command-line terminal (tty3) by pressing **Ctrl+Alt+F3**. Note that you are logged in as the user1 user on this terminal and in the /foruser1 directory.

23. At the command prompt, type `vi hosts` at the command prompt to open the hosts file in the vi editor. Delete the first line of this file and save your changes. Why were you successful this time? Exit the vi editor.

24. At the command prompt, type `ls -l` and press **Enter**. Do you have permission to execute the hosts file? Should you make this file executable? Why? Next, type `ls -l /usr/bin` at the command prompt and press **Enter**. Note how many of these files to which you have execute permission. Type `file /usr/bin/* | more` at the command prompt and press **Enter** to view the file types of the files in the /bin directory. Should these files have the execute permission?

25. Type `exit` and press **Enter** to log out of your shell.

26. Switch back to your previous command-line terminal (tty5) by pressing **Ctrl+Alt+F5**. Note that you are logged in as the root user on this terminal.

27. Type `exit` and press **Enter** to log out of your shell.

Project 4-8

In this hands-on project, you view and manipulate the default file and directory permissions using the umask variable.

1. Switch to a command-line terminal (tty5) by pressing **Ctrl+Alt+F5** and log in to the terminal using the user name of **user1** and the password of **LINUXrocks!**.

2. At the command prompt, type `umask` and press **Enter**. What is the default umask variable?

3. At the command prompt, type `touch utest1` and press **Enter**. Next, type `ls -l` at the command prompt and press **Enter**. What are the permissions on the utest1 file? Do these agree with the calculation in Figure 4-4? Create a new directory by typing the command `mkdir udir1` at the command prompt and pressing **Enter**. Next, type `ls -l` at the command prompt and press **Enter**. What are the permissions on the udir1 directory? Do these agree with the calculation in Figure 4-4?

4. At the command prompt, type **umask 007** and press **Enter**. Next, type **umask** at the command prompt and press **Enter** to verify that your umask variable has been changed to 007.

5. At the command prompt, type **touch utest2** and press **Enter**. Next, type **ls -l** at the command prompt and press **Enter**. What are the permissions on the utest2 file? Do these agree with the calculation in Figure 4-5? Create a new directory by typing the command **mkdir udir2** at the command prompt and pressing **Enter**. Next, type **ls -l** at the command prompt and press **Enter**. What are the permissions on the udir2 directory? Do these agree with the calculation in Figure 4-5?

6. Type **exit** and press **Enter** to log out of your shell.

Project 4-9

In this hands-on project, you view and change file and directory ownership using the chown and chgrp commands.

1. Switch to a command-line terminal (tty5) by pressing **Ctrl+Alt+F5** and log in to the terminal using the user name of **root** and the password of **LINUXrocks!**.

2. At the command prompt, type **touch ownersample** and press **Enter**. Next, type **mkdir ownerdir** at the command prompt and press **Enter**. Next, type **ls -l** at the command prompt and press **Enter** to verify that the file ownersample and directory ownerdir were created and that root is the owner and group owner of each.

3. At the command prompt, type **chgrp sys owner*** and press **Enter** to change the group ownership to the sys group for both ownersample and ownerdir. Why were you successful?

4. At the command prompt, type **chown user1 owner*** and press **Enter** to change the ownership to the user1 user for both ownersample and ownerdir. Why were you successful?

5. At the command prompt, type **chown root.root owner*** and press **Enter** to change the ownership and group ownership back to the root user for both ownersample and ownerdir. Although you are not the current owner of these files, why did you not receive an error message?

6. At the command prompt, type **mv ownersample ownerdir** and press **Enter**. Next, type **ls -1R** at the command prompt and press **Enter** to note that the ownersample file now exists within the ownerdir directory and that both are owned by root.

7. At the command prompt, type **chown -R user1 ownerdir** and press **Enter**. Next, type **ls -1R** at the command prompt and press **Enter**. Who owns the ownerdir directory and ownersample file? Why?

8. At the command prompt, type **rm -Rf ownerdir** and press **Enter**. Why were you able to delete this directory without being the owner of it?

9. Type **exit** and press **Enter** to log out of your shell.

Project 4-10

In this hands-on project, you view and set special permissions on files and directories as well as modify the default ACL on a file.

1. Switch to a command-line terminal (tty3) by pressing **Ctrl+Alt+F3** and log in to the terminal using the user name of **user1** and the password of **LINUXrocks!**.

2. At the command prompt, type `touch specialfile` and press **Enter**. Next, type `ls -l` at the command prompt and press **Enter** to verify that specialfile was created successfully. Who is the owner and group owner of specialfile?

3. At the command prompt, type `chmod 4777 specialfile` and press **Enter**. Next, type `ls -l` at the command prompt and press **Enter**. Which special permission is set on this file? If this file were executed by another user, who would that user be during execution?

4. At the command prompt, type `chmod 6777 specialfile` and press **Enter**. Next, type `ls -l` at the command prompt and press **Enter**. Which special permissions are set on this file? If this file were executed by another user, who would that user be during execution and which group would that user be a member of?

5. At the command prompt, type `chmod 6444 specialfile` and press **Enter**. Next, type `ls -l` at the command prompt and press **Enter**. Can you tell if execute is not given underneath the special permission listings? Would the special permissions retain their meaning in this case?

6. Switch to a command-line terminal (tty5) by pressing **Ctrl+Alt+F5** and log in to the terminal using the user name of **root** and the password of **LINUXrocks!**.

7. At the command prompt, type `mkdir /public` and press **Enter**. Next, type `chmod 1777 /public` at the command prompt and press **Enter**. Which special permission is set on this directory? Who can add or remove files to and from this directory?

8. At the command prompt, type `touch /public/rootfile` and press **Enter**.

9. Type `exit` and press **Enter** to log out of your shell.

10. Switch back to your previous command-line terminal (tty3) by pressing **Ctrl+Alt+F3**. Note that you are logged in as the user1 user on this terminal.

11. At the command prompt, type `touch /public/user1file` and press **Enter**. Next, type `ls -l /public` at the command prompt and press **Enter**. What files exist in this directory and who are the owners?

12. At the command prompt, type `rm /public/user1file` and press **Enter**. Were you prompted to confirm the deletion of the file?

13. At the command prompt, type `rm /public/rootfile` and press **Enter**. Note the error message that you receive because of the sticky bit.

14. Type `exit` and press **Enter** to log out of your shell.

15. Switch to a command-line terminal (tty5) by pressing **Ctrl+Alt+F5** and log in to the terminal using the user name of **root** and the password of **LINUXrocks!**.

16. At the command prompt, type **touch aclfile** and press **Enter**. Next, type **getfacl aclfile** at the command prompt and press **Enter**. Are there any additional entries beyond user, group, and other?

17. At the command prompt, type **setfacl -m u:user1:r-- aclfile** and press **Enter**. Next, type **ls -l aclfile** at the command prompt and press **Enter**. Is there a + symbol following the mode? Next, type **getfacl aclfile** at the command prompt and press **Enter**. Explain the permissions. When would this permission set be useful?

18. At the command prompt, type **setfacl -b aclfile** and press **Enter**. Next, type **ls -l aclfile** at the command prompt and press **Enter**. Is there a + symbol following the mode?

19. Type **exit** and press **Enter** to log out of your shell.

Project 4-11

In this hands-on project, you configure and research filesystem attributes.

1. Switch to a command-line terminal (tty5) by pressing **Ctrl+Alt+F5** and log in to the terminal using the user name of **root** and the password of **LINUXrocks!**.

2. At the command prompt, type **touch toughfile** and press **Enter**. Next, type **lsattr toughfile** at the command prompt and press **Enter**. What filesystem attributes are set on toughfile by default?

3. At the command prompt, type **chattr +i toughfile** and press **Enter**. Next, type **lsattr toughfile** at the command prompt and press **Enter**. Is the immutable attribute set on toughfile?

4. At the command prompt, type **vi toughfile** and press **Enter**. Does the vi editor warn you that the file is read-only? Add a line of text of your choice in the vi editor and attempt to save your changes using **w!** at the **:** prompt. Were you successful? Quit the vi editor using **q!** at the **:** prompt.

5. At the command prompt, type **rm -f toughfile** and press **Enter**. Were you successful? Why?

6. At the command prompt, type **chattr -i toughfile** and press **Enter**. Next, type **rm -f toughfile** and press **Enter**. Were you successful this time? Why?

7. At the command prompt, type **man chattr** and press **Enter**. Search the manual page for other filesystem attributes. Which attribute tells the Linux kernel to automatically compress/decompress the file as it is written and read from the filesystem? Which attribute causes the data blocks of a file to be immediately overwritten once the file has been deleted? Type **q** and press **Enter** to quit out of the manual page when finished.

8. Type **exit** and press **Enter** to log out of your shell.

Discovery Exercises

1. Use the `ls` command with the `-F` option to explore directories described in the Filesystem Hierarchy Standard starting with /bin. Do you recognize any of the commands in /bin? Explore several other FHS directories and note their contents. Refer to Table 4-1 for a list of directories to explore. Further, visit *www.pathname.com/fhs* and read about the Filesystem Hierarchy Standard. What benefits does it offer Linux?

2. Write the commands required for the following tasks. Try out each command on your system to ensure that it is correct:
   a. Make a hierarchical directory structure under /root that consists of one directory containing three subdirectories.
   b. Copy two files into each of the subdirectories.
   c. Create one more directory with three subdirectories beneath it and move files from the subdirectories containing them to the counterparts you just created.
   d. Hard-link three of the files. Examine their inodes.
   e. Symbolically link two of the files and examine their link count and inode information.
   f. Make symbolic links from your home directory to two directories in this structure and examine the results.
   g. Delete the symbolic links in your home directory and the directory structure you created under /root.

3. Write the command that can be used to answer the following questions. (*Hint:* Try each out on the system to check your results.)
   a. Find all files on the system that have the word "test" as part of their filename.
   b. Search the PATH variable for the pathname to the `awk` command.
   c. Find all files in the /usr directory and subdirectories that are larger than 50 kilobytes in size.
   d. Find all files in the /usr directory and subdirectories that are less than 70 kilobytes in size.
   e. Find all files in the / directory and subdirectories that are symbolic links.
   f. Find all files in the /var directory and subdirectories that were accessed less than 60 minutes ago.
   g. Find all files in the /var directory and subdirectories that were accessed less than six days ago.
   h. Find all files in the /home directory and subdirectories that are empty.
   i. Find all files in the /etc directory and subdirectories that are owned by the group bin.

4. For each of the following modes, write the numeric equivalent (e.g., 777):
   a. rw-r--r--
   b. r--r--r--
   c. ---rwxrw-
   d. -wxr-xrw-
   e. rw-rw-rwx
   f. -w-r-----

5. Fill in the permissions in Table 4-7 with checkmarks, assuming that all four files are in the directory /public, which has a mode of rwxr-xr-x.

Table 4-7 Permissions table for Discovery Exercise 5

Filename	Mode		Read	Edit	Execute	List	Delete
sample1	rw-rw-rw-	**User**					
		Group					
		Other					
sample2	r--r-----	**User**					
		Group					
		Other					
sample3	rwxr-x---	**User**					
		Group					
		Other					
sample4	r-x------	**User**					
		Group					
		Other					

6. Fill in the permissions in Table 4-8 with checkmarks, assuming that all four files are in the directory /public, which has a mode of rwx--x---.

Table 4-8 Permissions table for Discovery Exercise 6

Filename	Mode		Read	Edit	Execute	List	Delete
sample1	rwxr--r--	**User**					
		Group					
		Other					
sample2	r-xr--rw-	**User**					
		Group					
		Other					
sample3	--xr-x---	**User**					
		Group					
		Other					
sample4	r-xr--r--	**User**					
		Group					
		Other					

7. For each of the following umasks, calculate the default permissions given to new files and new directories:
   a. 017
   b. 272
   c. 777
   d. 000
   e. 077
   f. 027

8. For each of the umasks in Question 7, list the umasks that are reasonable to use to increase security on your Linux system and explain why.

9. Starting from the Linux default permissions for file and directories, what umask would you use to ensure that for all new_____?
   a. directories, the owner would have read, write, and execute; members of the group would have read and execute; and others would have read
   b. files, the owner would have read and execute; the group would have read, write, and execute; and others would have execute
   c. files, the owner would have write; the group would have read, write, and execute; and others would have read and write
   d. directories, the owner would have read, write, and execute; the group would have read, write, and execute; and others would have read, write, and execute
   e. directories, the owner would have execute; the group would have read, write, and execute; and others would have no permissions

   f. files, the owner would have read and write; the group would have no permissions; and others would have write
   g. directories, the owner would have read, write, and execute; the group would have read; and others would have read and execute
   h. directories, the owner would have write; the group would have read, write, and execute; and others would have read, write, and execute
   i. files, the owner would have no permissions; the group would have no permissions; and others would have no permissions

10. What chmod command would you use to impose the following permissions?
    a. on a directory such that: the owner would have read, write, and execute; the group would have read and execute; and others would have read
    b. on a file such that: the owner would have read and write; the group would have no permissions; and others would have write
    c. on a file such that: the owner would have write; the group would have read, write, and execute; and others would have read and write
    d. on a file such that: the owner would have read and execute; the group would have read, write, and execute; and others would have execute
    e. on a directory such that: the owner would have execute; the group would have read, write, and execute; and others would have no permissions

f. on a directory such that: the owner would have write; the group would have read, write, and execute; and others would have read, write, and execute

g. on a directory such that: the owner would have read, write, and execute; the group would have read; and others would have read and execute

h. on a directory such that: the owner would have read, write, and execute; the group would have read, write, and execute; and others would have read, write, and execute

i. on a file such that: the owner would have no permissions; the group would have no permissions; and others would have no permissions

## CHAPTER 5

LINUX FILESYSTEM ADMINISTRATION

After completing this chapter, you will be able to:

Identify the structure and types of device files in the /dev directory

Understand common filesystem types and their features

Mount and unmount filesystems to and from the Linux directory tree

Create and manage filesystems on hard disks, SSDs, and removable media storage devices

Create and use ISO images

Use the LVM to create and manage logical volumes

Monitor free space on mounted filesystems

Check filesystems for errors

Use disk quotas to limit user space usage

Navigating the Linux directory tree and manipulating files are common tasks that are performed on a daily basis by all users. However, administrators must provide this directory tree for users, as well as manage and fix the storage devices that support it. In this chapter, you learn about the various device files that represent storage devices and the different filesystems that can be placed on those devices. Next, you learn how to create and manage filesystems on a wide variety of different storage devices, as well as learn standard disk partitioning, LVM configuration, and filesystem management. The chapter concludes with a discussion of disk usage, filesystem errors, and restricting the ability of users to store files.

The /dev Directory

Fundamental to administering the disks used to store information is an understanding of how these disks are specified by the Linux operating system. Most devices on a Linux system (such as disks, terminals, and serial ports) are represented by a file on the hard disk called a **device file**. There is one file per device, and these files are typically found in the **/dev directory**. This allows you to specify devices on the system using the pathname to the file that represents it in the /dev directory.

Recall from Chapter 2 that the first partition on the first SATA/SCSI/SAS hard disk or SSD is identified by the installation program as sda1. When working with Linux utilities, you can specify the pathname to the file /dev/sda1 to refer to this hard disk or SSD.

Furthermore, each device file specifies how data should be transferred to and from the device. There are two methods for transferring data to and from a device. The first method involves transferring information character-by-character to and from the device. Devices that transfer data in this fashion are referred to as **character devices**. The second method transfers chunks or blocks of information at a time by using physical memory to buffer the transfer. Devices that use this method of transfer are called **block devices**; they can transfer information much faster than character devices. Device files that represent disks, such as CDs, DVDs, USB flash drives, hard disks, and SSDs, are typically block device files because they are formatted with a filesystem that organizes the available storage into discrete blocks that can be written to. Tape drives and most other devices, however, are typically represented by character device files.

To see whether a particular device transfers data character-by-character or block-by-block, recall that the ls -l command displays a c or b character in the type column indicating the type of device file. To view the type of the file /dev/sda1, you can use the following command:

```
[root@server1 ~]# ls -l /dev/sda1
brw-rw----    1 root       disk       8,    1 Feb 23 16:02 /dev/sda1
[root@server1 ~]#_
```

From the leftmost character in the preceding output, you can see that the /dev/sda1 file is a block device file. Table 5-1 lists common device files that you may find on your Linux system and their types.

Table 5-1 Common device files

Device file	Description	Block or character
/dev/hda1	First partition on the first PATA hard disk or SSD (primary master)	Block
/dev/hdb1	First partition on the second PATA hard disk or SSD (primary slave)	Block

Table 5-1   Common device files *(continued)*

Device file	Description	Block or character
/dev/hdc1	First partition on the third PATA hard disk or SSD (secondary master)	Block
/dev/hdd1	First partition on the fourth PATA hard disk or SSD (secondary slave)	Block
/dev/sda1	First partition on the first SATA/SCSI/SAS hard disk or SSD	Block
/dev/sdb1	First partition on the second SATA/SCSI/SAS hard disk or SSD	Block
/dev/nvme0n1p1	First partition in the first namespace on the first NVMe SSD	Block
/dev/nvme1n1p1	First partition in the first namespace on the second NVMe SSD	Block
/dev/sr0	First writeable SATA CD or DVD device in the system	Block
/dev/loop0	First loopback interface	Block
/dev/tty1	First local terminal on the system (Ctrl+Alt+F1)	Character
/dev/tty2	Second local terminal on the system (Ctrl+Alt+F2)	Character
/dev/ttyS0	First serial port on the system (COM1)	Character
/dev/ttyS1	Second serial port on the system (COM2)	Character
/dev/psaux	PS/2 mouse port	Character
/dev/lp0	First parallel port on the system (LPT1)	Character
/dev/null	Device file that represents nothing; any data sent to this device is discarded	Character
/dev/st0	First SCSI tape device in the system	Character
/dev/bus/usb/*	USB device files	Block or Character

Note 📎

If a device file is not present on your system, the underlying hardware was not detected by the **udev daemon**, which is responsible for automatically creating device files as necessary.

After a typical Fedora Linux installation, you will find several hundred different device files in the /dev directory that represent devices on the system. This large number of device files on a Linux system does not require much disk space because all device files consist of inodes and no data blocks; as a result, the entire contents of the /dev directory is 0 kilobytes in size unless other regular files are stored within it.

When using the `ls -l` command to view device files, the portion of the listing describing the file size in kilobytes is replaced by two numbers: the major number and the minor number. The **major number** of a device file points to the device driver for the device in the Linux kernel; several devices can share the same major number if they are of the same general type (i.e., two different SATA devices might share the same major number as they use the same driver in the Linux kernel). The **minor number** indicates the particular device itself; in the case of hard disk and SSD devices, different minor numbers are used to represent different partitions as shown in the following output:

```
[root@server1 ~]# ls -l /dev/sda /dev/sda1 /dev/sda2 /dev/sda3
brw-rw----   1 root     disk      8,   0 Feb 23 16:02 /dev/sda
brw-rw----   1 root     disk      8,   1 Feb 23 16:02 /dev/sda1
brw-rw----   1 root     disk      8,   2 Feb 23 16:02 /dev/sda2
brw-rw----   1 root     disk      8,   3 Feb 23 16:02 /dev/sda3
[root@server1 ~]# ls -l /dev/sdb /dev/sdb1 /dev/sdb2 /dev/sdb3
brw-rw----   1 root     disk      8,  16 Feb 23 16:02 /dev/sdb
brw-rw----   1 root     disk      8,  17 Feb 23 16:02 /dev/sdb1
brw-rw----   1 root     disk      8,  18 Feb 23 16:02 /dev/sdb2
brw-rw----   1 root     disk      8,  19 Feb 23 16:02 /dev/sdb3
[root@server1 ~]#_
```

> **Note**
>
> In the previous output, note that /dev/sdb* shares the same major number as /dev/sda* because they use the same driver in the Linux kernel. Because it is rare to create more than 15 partitions on a single device, Linux starts minor numbers for additional devices of the same type in increments of 16; thus the minor number for /dev/sdb is 16, and the minor number for /dev/sdc is 32, and so on. If you create more than 15 partitions on a single device, this minor numbering scheme is automatically adjusted by the udev daemon.

Together, the device file type (block or character), the major number (device driver), and the minor number (specific device) make up the unique characteristics of each device file. To create a device file, you need to know these three pieces of information.

If a device file becomes corrupted, it is usually listed as a regular file instead of a block or character special file. Recall from Chapter 4 that you can use the `find /dev -type f` command to search for regular files under the /dev directory to identify whether corruption has taken place. If you find a corrupted device file or accidentally delete a device file, the `mknod` command can be used to re-create the device file if you know the type and major and minor numbers. An example of re-creating the /dev/sda1 block device file used earlier with a major number of 8 and a minor number of 1 is shown in the following example:

```
[root@server1 ~]# mknod /dev/sda1 b 8 1
[root@server1 ~]# ls -l /dev/sda1
brw-rw----   1 root     disk     8,   1 May 8 16:02 /dev/sda1
[root@server1 ~]#_
```

To see a list of block and character devices that are currently used on the system and their major numbers, you can view the contents of the **/proc/devices** file. To view the block devices on the system, you can view the contents of the /sys/block directory, and to view detailed information for these block devices (including their major and minor numbers) you can use the `lsblk` command as shown below:

```
[root@server1 ~]# cat /proc/devices
Character devices:
  1 mem
  4 /dev/vc/0
  4 tty
  4 ttyS
  5 /dev/tty
  5 /dev/console
  5 /dev/ptmx
  7 vcs
 10 misc
 13 input
 14 sound
 21 sg
 29 fb
116 alsa
128 ptm
136 pts
162 raw
180 usb
188 ttyUSB
189 usb_device
202 cpu/msr
203 cpu/cpuid
245 hidraw
246 usbmon
```

```
Block devices:
   8 sd
   9 md
  11 sr
  65 sd
  66 sd
 128 sd
 129 sd
 130 sd
 253 device-mapper
 254 mdp
 259 blkext
[root@server1 ~]#_
[root@server1 ~]# ls /sys/block
sda   sdb   sr0
[root@server1 ~]# lsblk
NAME    MAJ:MIN RM   SIZE RO TYPE MOUNTPOINT
sda        8:0    0    50G  0 disk
├─sda1     8:1    0     1G  0 part /boot
├─sda2     8:2    0     4G  0 part [SWAP]
└─sda3     8:3    0    35G  0 part /
sdb        8:16   0     8G  0 disk
├─sdb1     8:17   0   1.9G  0 part /var
├─sdb2     8:18   0   1.9G  0 part /var/spool
└─sdb3     8:19   0   4.3G  0 part /var/log
sr0       11:0    1  1024M  0 rom
[root@server1 ~]#_
```

Filesystems

Recall from Chapter 2 that files must be stored on the hard disk in a defined format called a **filesystem** so that the operating system can work with them. The type of filesystem used determines how files are managed on the physical hard disk. Each filesystem can have different methods for storing files and features that make the filesystem robust against errors. Although many types of filesystems are available, all filesystems share three common components, as discussed in Chapter 4: the superblock, the inode table, and the data blocks. On a structural level, these three components work together to organize files and allow rapid access to, and retrieval of, data. Some filesystems contain a fourth component called a journal that keeps track of changes that are to be written to the filesystem; as a result, these filesystems are called **journaling** filesystems. In the event of a power outage, the filesystem can check the journal to complete any changes that were not performed to prevent filesystem errors related to the power outage. All storage media, such as hard disks, SSDs, USB flash drives, and DVDs, need to contain a filesystem before they can be used.

Note

Creating a filesystem on a device is commonly referred to as **formatting**.

Filesystem Types

As mentioned, many filesystems are available for use in the Linux operating system. Each has its own strengths and weaknesses; thus, some are better suited to some tasks and not as well suited to others. One benefit of Linux is that you need not use only one type of filesystem on the system; you can use several devices formatted with different filesystems under the same directory tree. In addition, files and directories appear the same throughout the directory tree regardless of whether there is one filesystem or 20 filesystems in use by the Linux system. Table 5-2 lists some common filesystems available for use in Linux.

Table 5-2   Common Linux filesystems

Filesystem	Description
btrfs	B-tree File System—A new filesystem for Linux systems that includes many features that are geared toward large-scale storage, including compression, subvolumes, quotas, snapshots, and the ability to span multiple devices. While relatively new and still in development, it is envisioned to be a replacement for the ext4 filesystem in the long term. Its name is commonly pronounced as "Butter F S." You will learn how to configure btrfs in Chapter 6.
exFAT	Extended FAT filesystem—An improved version of the FAT32 filesystem with large file support. It is the most common filesystem used on removable storage devices such as USB flash drives and portable USB hard drives, as it has full support on modern Linux, macOS, and Windows operating systems.
ext2	Second extended filesystem—The traditional filesystem used on Linux, it supports access control lists (individual user permissions). In addition, it retains its name from being the new version of the original extended filesystem, based on the Minix filesystem.
ext3	Third extended filesystem—A variation on ext2 that allows for journaling and, thus, has a faster startup and recovery time.

(continues)

Table 5-2 Common Linux filesystems (*continued*)

Filesystem	Description
ext4	Fourth extended filesystem—A variation on ext3 that has larger filesystem support and speed enhancements.
iso9660	ISO 9660 filesystem—A filesystem that originated from the International Standards Organization recommendation 9660 and is used to access data stored on CDs and DVDs.
msdos, fat	DOS FAT filesystem. It can use a 12, 16, or 32-bit table to store file locations.
ntfs	New Technology File System (NTFS)—A Microsoft proprietary filesystem developed for its Windows operating systems.
reiserfs	Reiser filesystem—A journaling filesystem similar to ext3, and more suited for use with databases.
squashfs	Squash filesystem—A read-only filesystem typically used on embedded Linux systems to host system files in a small amount of storage space.
udf	Universal Disk Format (UDF) filesystem—A filesystem used by software programs that write to a CD-RW or DVD-RW drive.
vfat	DOS FAT filesystem with long filename support.
vxfs	Veritas File System (VXFS)—A journaling filesystem that supports large files and access control lists (individual user permissions) and is commonly used by many UNIX flavors.
xfs	X File System (XFS)—A very high-performance filesystem created by Silicon Graphics for use on their IRIX UNIX systems. Many Linux administrators prefer to use xfs on systems that need to quickly write large numbers of files to the hard disk.
zfs	Zettabyte File System (ZFS)—A very high-performance filesystem and volume manager originally created by Sun Microsystems that protects against data corruption and has features that support very large distributed storage systems. Many large-scale Linux server systems in industry use the zfs filesystem to store and manage large amounts of data. You will learn how to configure zfs in Chapter 6.

Note

Filesystem support is typically built into the Linux kernel or added as a package on most distributions.

Mounting

The term **mounting** originated in the 1960s when information was stored on large tape reels that had to be mounted on computers to make the data available. Today, mounting still refers to making data available. More specifically, it refers to the process whereby a device is made accessible to users via the logical directory tree. This device is attached to a certain directory on the directory tree called a **mount point**. Users can then create files and subdirectories in this mount point directory, which are then stored on the filesystem that was mounted to that particular directory.

Remember that directories are merely files that do not contain data; instead, they contain a list of files and subdirectories organized within them. Thus, it is easy for the Linux system to cover up directories to prevent user access to that data. This is essentially what happens when a device is mounted to a certain directory; the mount point directory is temporarily covered up by that device while the device remains mounted. Any file contents that were present in the mount point directory prior to mounting are not lost; when the device is unmounted, the mount point directory is uncovered, and the previous file contents are revealed. Suppose, for example, that you mount a USB flash memory drive that contains a filesystem to the /mnt directory. The /mnt directory is an empty directory that is commonly used as a temporary mount point for mounting removable media devices. Before mounting, the directory structure would resemble that depicted in Figure 5-1. After the USB flash memory drive is mounted to the /mnt directory, the contents of the /mnt directory would be covered up by the filesystem on the USB flash memory drive, as illustrated in Figure 5-2.

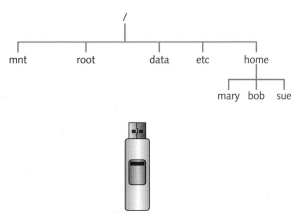

Figure 5-1   The directory structure prior to mounting

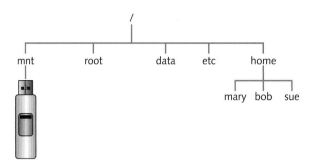

Figure 5-2   The directory structure after mounting a USB flash memory drive

If a user then stores a file in the /mnt directory, as shown in Figure 5-2, that file will be stored on the USB flash memory drive. Similarly, if a user creates a subdirectory under the /mnt directory depicted in Figure 5-2, that subdirectory will be made on the USB flash memory drive.

Any existing directory can be used as a mount point. If a user mounts a USB flash memory drive to the /bin directory, all files in the /bin directory are covered up during the time the drive is mounted, including the command used to unmount the drive. Thus, it is safe practice to create empty directories used specifically for mounting devices to avoid making existing files inaccessible to users.

Note

Most systems today have several removable media devices such as CDs, DVDs, USB flash memory drives, and USB hard drives that may be connected to your PC for long periods of time. As a result, it is considered good form to create subdirectories under the /media directory on your Linux system to mount these removable media devices and only use the /mnt directory to temporarily mount devices. For example, you could mount your USB flash memory drive to the /media/USBdrive directory and your DVD to the /media/DVD directory. You can then access the files on your USB flash memory drive by navigating to the /media/USBdrive directory, as well as access the files on your DVD by navigating to the /media/DVD directory.

When the Linux system is first turned on, a filesystem on the hard drive is mounted to the **/** directory. This is referred to as the **root filesystem** and contains most of the operating system files. Other filesystems on hard disks inside the computer can also be mounted to various mount point directories under the **/** directory at boot time, as well as via entries in the filesystem table (**/etc/fstab**) discussed in the following sections.

The `mount` **command** is used to mount devices to mount point directories, and the `umount` **command** is used to unmount devices from mount point directories; both of these commands are discussed throughout the remainder of this chapter.

Working with USB Flash Memory Drives

The most common type of removable media used to store small files, such as spreadsheets documents, that need to be transferred from computer to computer are USB flash memory drives. USB flash memory drives are recognized as SCSI drives by operating systems, and often ship with a single partition formatted with the DOS FAT or exFAT filesystem. However, you can reformat the filesystem on this partition with a different filesystem of your choice after determining the appropriate device file. If your system has a single hard disk (/dev/sda), the first USB flash memory drive inserted into your system will be recognized as /dev/sdb, and the partition on it can be represented by /dev/sdb1. To verify that your USB flash memory drive model (e.g., Kingston DataTraveler) was recognized by the system after inserting it, you can use the `lsusb` **command**:

```
Bus 001 Device 003: ID 0930:6545 Toshiba Corp. Kingston DataTraveler
Bus 001 Device 002: ID 80ee:0021 VirtualBox USB Tablet
Bus 001 Device 001: ID 1d6b:0001 Linux Foundation 1.1 root hub
[root@server1 ~]#_
```

To verify the device file used to represent the partition on your USB flash memory drive, you can use the `lsblk` command; a number 1 in the RM column indicates that the device is removable storage. The `lsblk` output shown below indicates that the first partition on the first removable storage device is /dev/sdb1, and that it is not currently mounted to a directory:

```
[root@server1 ~]# lsblk
NAME     MAJ:MIN RM   SIZE RO TYPE MOUNTPOINT
sda        8:0    0    50G  0 disk
├─sda1     8:1    0     1G  0 part /boot
├─sda2     8:2    0     4G  0 part [SWAP]
└─sda3     8:3    0    35G  0 part /
sdb        8:16   1   7.5G  0 disk
├─sdb1     8:17   1   7.5G  0 part
sr0       11:0    1  1024M  0 rom
[root@server1 ~]#_
```

To create a new filesystem on a USB flash memory drive, you can use the `mkfs` **(make filesystem) command** and specify the filesystem type using the -t switch and the device file representing the partition. Thus, to format /dev/sdb1 with the ext2 filesystem, you can type the following command:

```
[root@server1 ~]# mkfs -t ext2 /dev/sdb1
mke2fs 1.43.8 (1-Jan-2018)
Creating filesystem with 1952512 4k blocks and 488640 inodes
Filesystem UUID: 95b7fdcd-8baa-4e3f-ad6b-1ff5b5ba1f2f
Superblock backups stored on blocks:
     32768, 98304, 163840, 229376, 294912, 819200, 884736, 1605632

Allocating group tables: done
Writing inode tables: done
Writing superblocks and filesystem accounting information: done
[root@server1 ~]#_
```

Note 📎

Note from the previous output that each newly formatted Linux filesystem is given a **Universally Unique Identifier (UUID)** that can be used to identify the filesystem. This UUID can be used to identify filesystems that need to be mounted at boot time, as discussed later in this chapter.

Alternatively, you can specify a different filesystem after the -t option, such as the DOS FAT filesystem with long filename support (vfat). This results in output different from the mkfs command, as shown in the following example:

```
[root@server1 ~]# mkfs -t vfat /dev/sdb1
mkfs.fat 4.1 (2017-01-24)
[root@server1 ~]#_
```

If you do not specify the filesystem using the mkfs command, the default filesystem assumed is the ext2 filesystem as shown below:

```
[root@server1 ~]# mkfs /dev/sdb1
mke2fs 1.43.8 (1-Jan-202018)
Creating filesystem with 1952512 4k blocks and 488640 inodes
Filesystem UUID: 95b7fdcd-8baa-4e3f-ad6b-1ff5b5ba1f2f
Superblock backups stored on blocks:
     32768, 98304, 163840, 229376, 294912, 819200, 884736, 1605632
```

```
Allocating group tables: done
Writing inode tables: done
Writing superblocks and filesystem accounting information: done
[root@server1 ~]#_
```

If your Linux distribution doesn't support the filesystem that you'd like to use, you can install the appropriate filesystem tools afterward. For example, to install support for exFAT on Fedora 28 as the root user and use it to format /dev/sdb1, you can run the `dnf install https://download1.rpmfusion.org/free/fedora/rpmfusion-free-release-$(rpm -E %fedora).noarch.rpm https://download1.rpmfusion.org/nonfree/fedora/rpmfusion-nonfree-release-$(rpm -E %fedora).noarch.rpm` command to add the RPM Fusion Internet repository, followed by the `dnf install exfat-utils fuse-exfat` command to install the exFAT filesystem tools. Finally, you can run the following command to format the /dev/sdb1 device with the exFAT filesystem:

```
[root@server1 ~]# mkfs -t exfat /dev/sdb1
mkexfatfs 1.2.8
Creating... done.
Flushing... done.
File system created successfully.
[root@server1 ~]#_
```

Although the most common command to create filesystems is the `mkfs` command, you can use other variants and shortcuts to the `mkfs` command. For example, to create an ext2 filesystem, you could type `mke2fs /dev/sdb1` on the command line. Other alternatives to the `mkfs` command are listed in Table 5-3.

Table 5-3   Commands used to create filesystems

Command	Filesystem It creates
mkfs	Filesystems of most types
mkdosfs mkfs.msdos mkfs.fat mkfs.vfat	DOS FAT (12, 16, or 32-bit, depending on the size of the filesystem)
mkfs.ext2 mke2fs	ext2
mkfs.ext3 mke2fs -t ext3	ext3

(continues)

Table 5-3   Commands used to create filesystems *(continued)*

Command	Filesystem It creates
`mkfs.ext4` `mke2fs -t ext4`	ext4
`mkisofs`	ISO 9660
`mkreiserfs` `mkfs.reiserfs`	reiser
`mkfs.xfs`	XFS
`mkudffs` `mkfs.udf`	UDF
`mkntfs` `mkfs.ntfs`	NTFS
`mkexfatfs` `mkfs.exfat`	exFAT

After a USB flash memory drive has been formatted with a filesystem, it must be mounted on the directory tree before it can be used. A list of currently mounted filesystems can be obtained using the mount command with no options or arguments, which reads the information listed in the **/etc/mtab** (mount table) file. On modern systems, the output of this command is quite lengthy as it contains many special filesystems and filesystem parameters. Consequently, it is much easier to see a list of currently mounted filesystems using the df **(disk free space) command**. The -T option to the df command will also print the filesystem type as shown in the following sample output:

```
[root@server1 ~]# df -T
Filesystem    Type       1K-blocks      Used   Available Use% Mounted on
devtmpfs      devtmpfs     2006860          0     2006860   0% /dev
tmpfs         tmpfs        2019492          0     2019492   0% /dev/shm
tmpfs         tmpfs        2019492       1200     2018292   1% /run
tmpfs         tmpfs        2019492          0     2019492   0% /sys/fs/cgroup
/dev/sda3     ext4        35862048    8844932    25165724  27% /
tmpfs         tmpfs        2019492         72     2019420   1% /tmp
/dev/sda1     ext4          999320     151300      779208  17% /boot
tmpfs         tmpfs         403896         28      403868   1% /run/user/42
tmpfs         tmpfs         403896          4      403892   1% /run/user/0
[root@server1 ~]#_
```

From the preceding example output, you can see that the ext4 filesystem on /dev/sda3 is mounted on the **/** directory, and that the ext4 filesystem on /dev/sda1 is mounted on the /boot directory. The other filesystems listed are special filesystems that are used by the system; these filesystems are called **virtual filesystems** or **pseudo filesystems** and are discussed later in this book.

To mount a device on the directory tree, you can use the `mount` command with options and arguments to specify the filesystem type, the device to mount, and the directory on which to mount the device (mount point). It is important to ensure that no user is currently using the mount point directory; otherwise, the system gives you an error message and the device is not mounted. To check whether the /media/USBdrive directory is being used by any users, you can use the `fuser` **command** with the -u option, as shown in the following output:

```
[root@server1 ~]# fuser -u /media/USBdrive
[root@server1 ~]#_
```

The preceding output indicates the /media/USBdrive directory is not being used by any user processes; to mount a USB flash memory drive (/dev/sdb1) formatted with the ext2 filesystem to this directory, you could run the following command:

```
[root@server1 ~]# mount -t ext2 /dev/sdb1 /media/USBdrive
[root@server1 ~]# df -T
Filesystem     Type        1K-blocks      Used Available Use% Mounted on
devtmpfs       devtmpfs     2006860          0   2006860   0% /dev
tmpfs          tmpfs        2019492          0   2019492   0% /dev/shm
tmpfs          tmpfs        2019492       1208   2018284   1% /run
tmpfs          tmpfs        2019492          0   2019492   0% /sys/fs/cgroup
/dev/sda3      ext4        35862048    8845052  25165604  27% /
tmpfs          tmpfs        2019492      18720   2000772   1% /tmp
/dev/sda1      ext4          999320     151300    779208  17% /boot
tmpfs          tmpfs         403896         28    403868   1% /run/user/42
tmpfs          tmpfs         403896          4    403892   1% /run/user/0
/dev/sdb1      ext2         7687336      17160   7279676   1% /media/USBdrive
[root@server1 ~]#_
```

Note

If you omit the -t option to the `mount` command, it attempts to automatically detect the filesystem on the device. Thus, the command `mount /dev/sdb1 /media/USBdrive` will perform the same action as the `mount` command shown in the preceding output.

Notice that /dev/sdb1 appears mounted to the /media/USBdrive directory in the preceding output of the `mount` command. To access and store files on the USB flash memory drive, you can now treat the /media/USBdrive directory as the root of the

USB flash memory drive. When an ext2, ext3, or ext4 filesystem is created on a device, one directory called lost+found is created by default and used by the `fsck` command discussed later in this chapter. To explore the recently mounted filesystem, you can use the following commands:

```
[root@server1 ~]# cd /media/USBdrive
[root@server1 USBdrive]# pwd
/media/USBdrive
[root@server1 USBdrive]# ls -F
lost+found/
[root@server1 USBdrive]#_
```

To copy files to the USB flash memory drive, specify the /media/USBdrive directory as the target for the `cp` command, as follows:

```
[root@server1 USBdrive]# cd /etc
[root@server1 etc]# cat issue
\s
Kernel \r on an \m (\l)
[root@server1 etc]# cp issue /media/USBdrive
[root@server1 etc]# cd /media/USBdrive
[root@server1 USBdrive]# ls -F
issue   lost+found/
[root@server1 USBdrive]# cat issue
\s
Kernel \r on an \m (\l)
[root@server1 USBdrive]#_
```

Similarly, you can also create subdirectories under the USB flash memory drive to store files; these subdirectories are referenced under the mount point directory. To make a directory called workfiles on the USB flash memory drive mounted in the previous example and copy the /etc/inittab file to it, you can use the following commands:

```
[root@server1 USBdrive]# pwd
/media/USBdrive
[root@server1 USBdrive]# ls -F
issue   lost+found/
[root@server1 USBdrive]# mkdir workfiles
[root@server1 USBdrive]# ls -F
issue   lost+found/   workfiles
[root@server1 USBdrive]# cd workfiles
[root@server1 workfiles]# pwd
/media/USBdrive/workfiles
[root@server1 workfiles]# cp /etc/inittab .
```

```
[root@server1 workfiles]# ls
inittab
[root@server1 workfiles]#_
```

Even though you can remove a USB flash memory drive without permission from the system, doing so is likely to cause error messages to appear on the terminal screen. Before a USB flash memory drive is removed, it must be properly unmounted using the umount command. The umount command can take the name of the device to unmount or the mount point directory as an argument. Similar to mounting a device, unmounting a device requires that the mount point directory has no users using it. If you try to unmount the USB flash memory drive mounted to the /media/USBdrive directory while it is being used, you receive an error message similar to the one in the following example:

```
[root@server1 USBdrive]# pwd
/media/USBdrive
[root@server1 USBdrive]# umount /media/USBdrive
umount: /media/USBdrive: target is busy.
[root@server1 USBdrive]# fuser -u /media/USBdrive
/media/USBdrive:        17368c(root)
[root@server1 USBdrive]# cd /root
[root@server1 ~]# umount /media/USBdrive
[root@server1 ~]# df -T
Filesystem     Type      1K-blocks     Used  Available Use% Mounted on
devtmpfs       devtmpfs    2006860        0    2006860   0% /dev
tmpfs          tmpfs       2019492        0    2019492   0% /dev/shm
tmpfs          tmpfs       2019492     1208    2018284   1% /run
tmpfs          tmpfs       2019492        0    2019492   0% /sys/fs/cgroup
/dev/sda3      ext4       35862048  8845052   25165604  27% /
tmpfs          tmpfs       2019492    18720    2000772   1% /tmp
/dev/sda1      ext4         999320   151300     779208  17% /boot
tmpfs          tmpfs        403896       28     403868   1% /run/user/42
tmpfs          tmpfs        403896        4     403892   1% /run/user/0
[root@server1 ~]#_
```

Notice from the preceding output that you were still using the /media/USBdrive directory because it was the current working directory. The fuser command also indicated that the root user had a process using the directory. After the current working directory was changed, the umount command was able to unmount the USB flash memory drive from the /media/USBdrive directory, and the output of the mount command indicated that it was no longer mounted.

Recall that mounting simply attaches a disk device to the Linux directory tree so that you can treat the device like a directory full of files and subdirectories. A device can be mounted to any existing directory. However, if the directory contains files, those files are inaccessible until the device is unmounted. Suppose, for example, that you create a directory called /USBdrive for mounting USB flash memory drives and a file inside called samplefile, as shown in the following output:

```
[root@server1 ~]# mkdir /USBdrive
[root@server1 ~]# touch /USBdrive/samplefile
[root@server1 ~]# ls /USBdrive
samplefile
[root@server1 ~]#_
```

If the USB flash memory drive used earlier is mounted to the /USBdrive directory, a user who uses the /USBdrive directory will be using the USB flash memory drive; however, when nothing is mounted to the /USBdrive directory, the previous contents are available for use:

```
[root@server1 ~]# mount /dev/sdb1 /USBdrive
[root@server1 ~]# df -T
Filesystem     Type      1K-blocks     Used Available Use% Mounted on
devtmpfs       devtmpfs    2006860        0   2006860   0% /dev
tmpfs          tmpfs       2019492        0   2019492   0% /dev/shm
tmpfs          tmpfs       2019492     1208   2018284   1% /run
tmpfs          tmpfs       2019492        0   2019492   0% /sys/fs/cgroup
/dev/sda3      ext4       35862048  8845052  25165604  27% /
tmpfs          tmpfs       2019492    18720   2000772   1% /tmp
/dev/sda1      ext4         999320   151300    779208  17% /boot
tmpfs          tmpfs        403896       28    403868   1% /run/user/42
tmpfs          tmpfs        403896        4    403892   1% /run/user/0
/dev/sdb1      ext2        7687336    17168   7279668   1% /USBdrive
[root@server1 ~]# ls -F /USBdrive
issue   lost+found/   workfiles
[root@server1 ~]# umount /USBdrive
[root@server1 ~]# ls /USBdrive
samplefile
[root@server1 ~]#_
```

The mount command used in the preceding output specifies the filesystem type, the device to mount, and the mount point directory. To save time typing on the command line, you can alternatively specify one argument and allow the system to look up the remaining information in the /etc/fstab (filesystem table) file. The /etc/fstab file has a dual purpose; it is used to mount devices at boot time and is consulted when a user does not specify enough arguments on the command line when using the mount command.

The /etc/fstab file has six fields:

<device to mount> <mount point> <type> <mount options> <dump#> <fsck#>

The device to mount can be the path to a device file (e.g., /dev/sda1), the filesystem UUID (e.g., UUID=db545f1d-c1ee-4b70-acbe-3dc61b41db20), the GPT partition UUID (e.g., PARTUUID=ed835873-01), or the filesystem label (e.g., LABEL=BackupDisk). The mount point specifies where to mount the device. The type can be a specific value (such as ext4) or can be automatically detected. The mount options are additional options that the mount command accepts when mounting the volume (such as read only, or "ro"). Any filesystems with the mount option "noauto" are not automatically mounted at boot time; a complete list of options that the mount command accepts can be found by viewing the manual page for the mount command.

The dump# is used by the dump command (discussed in Chapter 11) when backing up filesystems; a 1 in this field indicates that the filesystem should be backed up, whereas a 0 indicates that no backup is necessary. The fsck# is used by the fsck command discussed later in this chapter when checking filesystems at boot time for errors; any filesystems with a 1 in this field are checked before any filesystems with a number 2, and filesystems with a number 0 are not checked.

> ## Note 📎
>
> You can use the blkid **command** to display the filesystem and partition UUIDs on your system. You can also use the lsblk --fs command to display filesystem UUIDs and labels.
>
> Filesystem labels are optional; to set a label on a filesystem, you must use a command for the filesystem type. For example, the e2label **command** can be used to set a label on an ext2/ext3/ext4 filesystem, the fatlabel **command** can be used to set a label on a FAT filesystem, the exfatlabel **command** can be used to set a label on an exFAT filesystem, and the xfs_admin **command** can be used to set a label on an XFS filesystem.
>
> To easily associate filesystem UUIDs and labels with their device files, the udev daemon creates symbolic links for each UUID and label under the /dev/disk subdirectory that point to the correct device file (e.g., /dev/sdb1); /dev/disk/by-uuid/ stores symbolic links by filesystem UUID, /dev/disk/by-partuuid/ stores symbolic links by GPT partition UUID, and /dev/disk/by-label/ stores symbolic links by filesystem label. You can also find symbolic links for each disk by Linux kernel identifier under /dev/disk/by-id/ and by PCI bus identifier under /dev/disk/by-path/.
>
> To mount all filesystems in the /etc/fstab file that are intended to mount at boot time, you can type the mount -a command.

The following output displays the contents of a sample /etc/fstab file:

```
[root@server1 ~]# cat /etc/fstab
#
# /etc/fstab
# Accessible filesystems by reference are maintained under /dev/disk
```

```
# See man pages fstab(5), findfs(8), mount(8) and/or blkid(8)
#
UUID=9ff25add-035b-4d26-a9d0a6fa3   /          ext4   defaults   1 1
UUID=8789961a-fbca-4411-195f13719   /boot      ext4   defaults   1 2
UUID=4837de7b-d96e-4edc-56d17ca62   swap       swap   defaults   0 0
/dev/sdb1                           /USBdrive  auto   noauto     0 0
[root@server1 ~]#_
```

Thus, to mount the first USB flash memory drive (/dev/sdb1) to the /USBdrive directory and automatically detect the type of filesystem on the device, specify enough information for the mount command to find the appropriate line in the /etc/fstab file:

```
[root@server1 ~]# mount /dev/sdb1
[root@server1 ~]# df -T
Filesystem   Type       1K-blocks      Used  Available Use% Mounted on
devtmpfs     devtmpfs     2006860         0    2006860   0% /dev
tmpfs        tmpfs        2019492         0    2019492   0% /dev/shm
tmpfs        tmpfs        2019492      1208    2018284   1% /run
tmpfs        tmpfs        2019492         0    2019492   0% /sys/fs/cgroup
/dev/sda3    ext4        35862048   8845052   25165604  27% /
tmpfs        tmpfs        2019492     18720    2000772   1% /tmp
/dev/sda1    ext4          999320    151300     779208  17% /boot
tmpfs        tmpfs         403896        28     403868   1% /run/user/42
tmpfs        tmpfs         403896         4     403892   1% /run/user/0
/dev/sdb1    ext2         7687336     17168    7279668   1% /USBdrive
[root@server1 ~]# umount /dev/sdb1
[root@server1 ~]#_
```

The mount command in the preceding output succeeded because a line in /etc/fstab described the mounting of the /dev/sdb1 device.

Alternatively, you could specify the mount point as an argument to the mount command to mount the same device via the correct entry in /etc/fstab:

```
[root@server1 ~]# mount /USBdrive
[root@server1 ~]# df -T
Filesystem   Type       1K-blocks      Used  Available Use% Mounted on
devtmpfs     devtmpfs     2006860         0    2006860   0% /dev
tmpfs        tmpfs        2019492         0    2019492   0% /dev/shm
tmpfs        tmpfs        2019492      1208    2018284   1% /run
tmpfs        tmpfs        2019492         0    2019492   0% /sys/fs/cgroup
/dev/sda3    ext4        35862048   8845052   25165604  27% /
tmpfs        tmpfs        2019492     18720    2000772   1% /tmp
/dev/sda1    ext4          999320    151300     779208  17% /boot
tmpfs        tmpfs         403896        28     403868   1% /run/user/42
```

```
tmpfs          tmpfs        403896         4      403892    1% /run/user/0
/dev/sdb1      ext2        7687336     17168    7279668    1% /USBdrive
[root@server1 ~]# umount /USBdrive
[root@server1 ~]#_
```

Table 5-4 lists commands that are useful when mounting and unmounting USB flash memory drives.

Table 5-4	Useful commands when mounting and unmounting filesystem
Command	**Description**
`mount` `df -T`	Displays mounted filesystems and their type
`mount -t <type> <device> <mount point>`	Mounts a `<device>` of a certain `<type>` to a `<mount point>` directory
`fuser -u <directory>`	Displays the users using a particular directory
`umount <mount point>` or `umount <device>`	Unmounts a `<device>` from its `<mount point>` directory

Working with CDs, DVDs, and ISO Images

Most software that is not downloaded from the Internet is packaged on CDs and DVDs. Like USB flash memory drives, CDs and DVDs can be mounted with the `mount` command and unmounted with the `umount` command, as shown in Table 5-4; however, the device file used with these commands is different. The device files used by CD and DVD depend on the technology used by the drive itself. If your computer has a PATA CD or DVD drive, you can refer to it using one of the following four standard PATA hard drive configurations (discussed in Chapter 2):

- Primary master (/dev/hda)
- Primary slave (/dev/hdb)
- Secondary master (/dev/hdc)
- Secondary slave (/dev/hdd)

However, if you have a SATA or SCSI CD or DVD drive, Linux may use different names, depending on your actual CD or DVD drive:

- First SATA/SCSI drive (/dev/sda, /dev/scd0, /dev/sr0, and /dev/sg0)
- Second SATA/SCSI drive (/dev/sdb, /dev/scd1, /dev/sr1, and /dev/sg1)
- Third SATA/SCSI drive (/dev/sdc, /dev/scd2, /dev/sr2, and /dev/sg2)
- And so on

To make the identification of your CD or DVD drive easier, Fedora Linux creates a file called /dev/cdrom, which is merely a symbolic link to the correct device file for your first CD or DVD drive. For example, if your system contains a writable SATA CD/DVD drive, a long listing of /dev/cdrom may show the following:

```
[root@server1 ~]# ls -l /dev/cdrom
lrwxrwxrwx. 1 root root 3 Jul 19 07:51 /dev/cdrom -> sr0
[root@server1 ~]#_
```

In this case, you could use /dev/cdrom or /dev/sro to mount CDs or DVDs. To write to a CD or DVD in this same drive, however, you must use disc-burning software that knows how to write data to /dev/cdrom or /dev/sro.

Note 📎

Nearly all DVD-ROM and DVD-RW drives can also work with CDs.

Many OSS disc-burning software applications are available for Linux. One example is the graphical Brasero Disc Burner program that you can install by running the command `dnf install brasero` as the root user.

In addition, CDs and DVDs typically use either the ISO 9660 or UDF filesystem type and are read-only when accessed using Linux (recall that you must use disc-burning software to record to a CD or DVD). Thus, to mount a CD or DVD to a directory, you should use the -r (read-only) option to the mount command to avoid warnings. To mount a sample CD to the /media/cd directory and view its contents, you could use the following commands:

```
[root@server1 ~]# mount -r /dev/cdrom /media/cd
[root@server1 ~]# df -T
Filesystem      Type       1K-blocks      Used Available Use% Mounted on
devtmpfs        devtmpfs    2006860          0   2006860   0% /dev
tmpfs           tmpfs       2019492          0   2019492   0% /dev/shm
tmpfs           tmpfs       2019492       1188   2018304   1% /run
tmpfs           tmpfs       2019492          0   2019492   0% /sys/fs/cgroup
/dev/sda3       ext4       35862048    8846076  25164580  27% /
tmpfs           tmpfs       2019492         72   2019420   1% /tmp
/dev/sda1       ext4         999320     151300    779208  17% /boot
tmpfs           tmpfs        403896         28    403868   1% /run/user/42
tmpfs           tmpfs        403896          4    403892   1% /run/user/0
/dev/sr0        iso9660     1745024    1745024         0 100% /media/cd
[root@server1 ~]# ls -l /media/cd
autorun.inf*    install*   graphics/   jungle/    jungle.txt*
joystick/
[root@server1 ~]# umount /media/cd
[root@server1 ~]#_
```

Note

The /media/cd directory must exist for the mount command to succeed in the previous example.

As with USB flash memory drives, you can modify the /etc/fstab file such that you can specify only a single argument to the mount command to mount a CD or DVD. Also remember that the mount point directory must not be in use to successfully mount or unmount CDs and DVDs; the fuser command can be used to verify this.

Unlike USB flash memory drives, CDs and DVDs cannot be ejected from the drive until they are properly unmounted, because the mount command locks the CD/DVD drive as a precaution. Alternatively, you can use the eject **command**, which unmounts the filesystem and forces the CD or DVD drive to physically eject the disc.

The ISO 9660 filesystem type is not limited to CDs and DVDs. You can also create image files, called ISO images, that contain other files. Recall from Chapter 2 that most operating system softwares available for download from the Internet, such as Linux distributions, are available as ISO image files. Once downloaded, ISO images can be easily written to a CD or DVD using disc-burning software or mounted and accessed by your Linux system. If you download an ISO image called sample.iso, you can mount it to the /mnt directory as a read-only loopback device, which allows your system to access the contents of the sample.iso file, using the following command:

```
[root@server1 ~]# mount -o loop -r -t iso9660 sample.iso /mnt
[root@server1 ~]# df -T
Filesystem      Type       1K-blocks     Used Available Use% Mounted on
devtmpfs        devtmpfs    2006860         0   2006860   0% /dev
tmpfs           tmpfs       2019492         0   2019492   0% /dev/shm
tmpfs           tmpfs       2019492      1192   2018300   1% /run
tmpfs           tmpfs       2019492         0   2019492   0% /sys/fs/cgroup
/dev/sda3       ext4       35862048   8846440  25164216  27% /
tmpfs           tmpfs       2019492        72   2019420   1% /tmp
/dev/sda1       ext4         999320    151300    779208  17% /boot
tmpfs           tmpfs        403896        28    403868   1% /run/user/42
tmpfs           tmpfs        403896         4    403892   1% /run/user/0
/dev/loop0      iso9660         364       364         0 100% /mnt
[root@server1 ~]# ls /mnt
setup.exe    tools        binaries
[root@server1 ~]#_
```

You can then view or execute files within the /mnt directory, or copy files from the /mnt directory to another directory to extract the contents of the ISO image file.

To create a new ISO image from a directory of files, simply use the `mkisofs` command. The following command creates an ISO image called newimage.iso from all the information in the /data directory with additional support for the Rock Ridge (-R) and Joliet (-J) standards:

```
[root@server1 ~]# mkisofs -RJ -o newimage.iso /data
I: -input-charset not specified, using utf-8 (detected in locale
settings)
Total translation table size: 0
Total rockridge attributes bytes: 537
Total directory bytes: 0
Path table size(bytes): 10
Max brk space used 0
182 extents written (0MB)
[root@server1 ~]#_
```

Working with Removable Media Within a GUI Environment

Because of their large capacity and portability, removable storage devices often store copies of data, pictures, music, movies, programs, and documents that users regularly use within a GUI environment. When working within a GUI environment, a process automatically mounts removable media to a directory so that you can work with it immediately, much like on a Windows or macOS computer. When you insert a USB flash memory drive, CD, or DVD while in a GUI environment, it is automatically mounted by the system to a directory under the /run/media/*username* directory (where *username* is the name of the user logged into the GUI environment) that is named for the filesystem label on the CD or DVD (specified in the disc-burning software). For example, if you insert a DVD with a label of "Fedora-WS-Live-28-1-1" into your system while logged into a GUI environment as user1, the system will automatically create a /run/media/user1/Fedora-WS-Live-28-1-1 directory and mount the DVD to this directory. Similarly, if you insert a USB flash memory drive with a label of "Kingston" into your system while logged into a GUI environment as user1, the system will automatically create a /run/media/user1/Kingston directory and mount the USB flash memory drive to this directory. This is shown in the following output:

```
[root@server1 ~]#df -T
Filesystem      Type       1K-blocks      Used Available Use% Mounted on
devtmpfs        devtmpfs   2006860           0   2006860   0% /dev
tmpfs           tmpfs      2019492           0   2019492   0% /dev/shm
tmpfs           tmpfs      2019492        1612   2017880   1% /run
tmpfs           tmpfs      2019492           0   2019492   0% /sys/fs/cgroup
/dev/sda3       ext4      35862048     8923916  25086740  27% /
```

```
tmpfs             tmpfs       2019492      160   2019332    1% /tmp
/dev/sda1         ext4         999320   151300    779208   17% /boot
/dev/sr0          iso9660    1745024  1745024         0  100% /run/
media/ user1/Fedora-WS-Live-28-1-1
/dev/sdc1         ext2        7687336    17168   7279668    1% /run/
media/ user1/Kingston
[root@server1 ~]#_
```

In addition, the system will also place filesystem label shortcuts to the /run/media/ user1/Fedora-WS-Live-28-1-1 and /run/media/user1/Kingston directories in the Files application within the GUI environment so that you can easily access the contents of your removable media, as shown in Figure 5-3.

Figure 5-3   Accessing removable media within the GNOME desktop

When you are finished accessing the files on the removable media, you can click the eject icon next to the filesystem label shortcuts shown in Figure 5-3 to unmount the removable media device, and, in the case of a CD or DVD, eject the physical disk as well.

Removable media is not limited to USB flash memory drives, CDs, and DVDs; you can use many other types of removable media devices on Linux, including:

- External hard drives
- Digital cameras (that contain flash memory cards)
- Media players (such as Apple iPods)
- Smartphones
- Tablets

Nearly all removable storage device manufacturers emulate the SCSI protocol in the firmware of the device itself, much like a USB flash memory drive. Consequently, if a GUI environment is loaded, Fedora 28 will automatically mount the filesystem on these devices to a new directory under the /run/media/*username* directory named for the label on the device, and place a filesystem label shortcut within the Files application.

Since it is common to work with removable media devices within a GUI environment, understanding the device names and mount point directories used by the devices themselves is often irrelevant. You can work with the files on removable media devices by accessing the appropriate icons in the Files application that represent the devices in the GUI environment. However, if you are working in a command-line terminal (perhaps on a Linux server that does not have a GUI environment), you need to keep track of when a removable storage device is plugged into the computer in order to understand which device file the Linux operating system will assign to it.

Working with Hard Disks and SSDs

Hard disks typically come in three flavors: PATA, SATA, and SCSI/SAS. PATA hard disks must be set to one of four configurations, each of which has a different device file:

- Primary master (/dev/hda)
- Primary slave (/dev/hdb)
- Secondary master (/dev/hdc)
- Secondary slave (/dev/hdd)

SATA and SCSI/SAS hard disks typically have faster data transfer speeds than PATA hard disks, and most systems allow for the connection of more than four SATA or SCSI/SAS hard disks. As a result of these benefits, both SATA and SCSI/SAS hard disks are well suited to Linux servers that require a great deal of storage space for programs and user files. However, SATA and SCSI/SAS hard disks have different device files associated with them:

- First SCSI hard disk drive (/dev/sda)
- Second SCSI hard disk drive (/dev/sdb)
- Third SCSI hard disk drive (/dev/sdc)
- Fourth SCSI hard disk drive (/dev/sdd)

- Fifth SCSI hard disk drive (/dev/sde)
- Sixth SCSI hard disk drive (/dev/sdf)
- And so on

SSDs are a newer technology that use much faster NAND flash storage. PATA, SATA, and SCSI/SAS SSDs provide a hard disk compatible interface so that they can function as a drop-in replacement for hard disks. Most SSDs of this type on the market are SATA or SAS; as a result, /dev/sda could refer to the first hard disk or the first SSD, /dev/sdb could refer to the second hard disk or second SSD, and so on. NVMe SSDs are often faster than SATA and SAS SSDs as they provide an SSD-only architecture that directly connects to the PCIe bus on a computer. As a result, NVMe SSDs use different device files; /dev/nvmeo is the first NVMe SSD, /dev/nvme1 is the second NVMe SSD, and so on. Unlike other SSDs or hard disks, NVMe SSDs can be divided into namespaces, and each namespace can then be further subdivided into partitions that contain a filesystem. The device files for NVMe SSDs reflect this; the first partition on the first namespace on the first NVMe SSD is /dev/nvmeon1p1, the second partition on the first namespace on the first NVMe SSD is /dev/nvmeon1p2, and so on.

Note

For simplicity, this book will refer primarily to hard disk drives when discussing permanent storage from now on. However, all of the concepts related to hard disk drives apply equally to SSDs.

Standard Hard Disk Partitioning

Recall that hard disks have the largest storage capacity of any device that you use to store information on a regular basis. As helpful as this storage capacity can be, it also poses some problems; as the size of a disk increases, organization becomes more difficult and the chance of error increases. To solve these problems, Linux administrators typically divide a hard disk into smaller, more usable sections called **partitions**. Each partition can contain a separate filesystem and can be mounted to different mount point directories. Recall from Chapter 2 that Linux requires two partitions at minimum: a partition that is mounted to the root directory (the root partition) and a partition used to hold virtual memory (the swap partition). The swap partition does not require a filesystem, because it is written to, and maintained by, the operating system alone. It is good practice, however, to use more than just two partitions on a Linux system. This division allows you to do the following:

- Segregate different types of data—for example, home directory data is stored on a separate partition mounted to /home.
- Allow for the use of more than one type of filesystem on one hard disk drive— for example, some filesystems are tuned for database use.

- Reduce the chance that filesystem corruption will render a system unusable; if the partition that is mounted to the /home directory becomes corrupted, it does not affect the system because operating system files are stored on a separate partition mounted to the / directory.
- Speed up access to stored data by keeping filesystems as small as possible.
- Allow for certain operating system features—for example, a /boot partition is required to boot systems that use the LVM discussed later in this chapter.

Segregation of data into physically separate areas of the hard disk drive can be exceptionally useful from an organizational standpoint. Keeping different types of data on different partitions lets you manipulate one type of data without affecting the rest of the system. This also reduces the likelihood that filesystem corruption will affect all files in the directory tree. Access speed is improved because a smaller area needs to be searched in a hard disk drive to locate data. This process is similar to searching for a penny in a 20,000-square-foot warehouse. It takes much less time to find the penny if that warehouse is divided into four separate departments of 5,000 square feet each and you know in which department the penny is located. Searching and maneuvering is much quicker and easier in a smaller, defined space than in a larger one.

On a physical level, hard disks are circular metal platters that spin at a fast speed. Data is read off these disks in concentric circles called **tracks**; each track is divided into **sectors** of information, and sectors are combined into more usable **blocks** of data, as shown in Figure 5-4. Most hard disk drives contain several platters organized on top of each other such that they can be written to simultaneously to speed up data transfer. A series consisting of the same concentric track on all of the metal platters inside a hard disk drive is known as a **cylinder**.

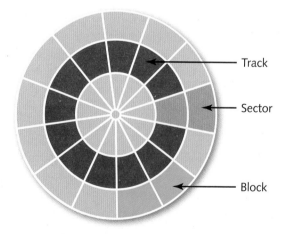

Figure 5-4 The physical areas of a hard disk

> **Note** 📎
>
> SSDs use circuitry within the drive itself to map data to logical tracks, sectors, blocks, and cylinders to ensure that the OS can work with SSDs like any hard disk. This allows you to create partitions and filesystems on an SSD in the same way that you would with a hard disk. Because SSDs are much faster at reading and writing data compared to hard disks, they are typically used on production Linux servers today.

Partition definitions are stored in the first readable sector of the hard disk known as the Master Boot Record (MBR) or master boot block (MBB). Large hard disks (>2TB) and many newer hard disks use a GUID Partition Table (GPT) in place of an MBR to allow for the additional addressing of sectors. If the MBR or GPT area of the hard disk becomes corrupted, the entire contents of the hard disk might be lost.

> **Note** 📎
>
> It is common for Linux servers to have several hard disks. In these situations, it is also common to configure one partition on each hard disk and mount each partition to different directories on the directory tree. Thus, if one partition fails, an entire hard disk can be replaced with a new one and the data retrieved from a back-up source.

Recall from Chapter 2 that hard disks with an MBR normally contain up to four primary partitions; to overcome this limitation, you can use an extended partition in place of one of these primary partitions. An extended partition can then contain many more subpartitions called logical drives. Because it is on these partitions that you place a filesystem, you can have device files that refer to the various types of partitions on a hard disk. These device files start with the name of the hard disk (/dev/hda, /dev/hdb, /dev/sda, /dev/sdb, and so on) and append a number indicating the partition on that hard disk. The first primary partition is given the number 1, the second primary partition is given the number 2, the third primary partition is given the number 3, and the fourth primary partition is given the number 4. If any one of these primary partitions is labeled as an extended partition, the logical drives within are named starting with number 5. Unlike hard disks that use an MBR, GPT hard disks don't need to adhere to the limitation of four primary partitions. Instead, you can create as many as 128 primary partitions (/dev/sda1 to /dev/sda128). Consequently, a hard disk that uses a GPT has no need for extended partitions or logical drives. Table 5-5 lists some common hard disk partition names.

Table 5-5 Common MBR hard disk partition device files for /dev/hda and /dev/sda

MBR partition	GPT partition	PATA device name (assuming /dev/hda)	SATA/SCSI/SAS device name (assuming /dev/sda)
1st primary partition	1st partition	/dev/hda1	/dev/sda1
2nd primary partition	2nd partition	/dev/hda2	/dev/sda2
3rd primary partition	3rd partition	/dev/hda3	/dev/sda3
4th primary partition	4th partition	/dev/hda4	/dev/sda4
1st logical drive in the extended partition	5th partition	/dev/hda5	/dev/sda5
2nd logical drive in the extended partition	6th partition	/dev/hda6	/dev/sda6
3rd logical drive in the extended partition	7th partition	/dev/hda7	/dev/sda7
4th logical drive in the extended partition	8th partition	/dev/hda8	/dev/sda8
5th logical drive in the extended partition	9th partition	/dev/hda9	/dev/sda9
nth logical drive in the extended partition	**n**th partition	/dev/hda**n**	/dev/sda**n**

Note from Table 5-5 that any one of the MBR primary partitions can be labeled as an extended partition. Also, for disk drives other than those listed in Table 5-5 (e.g., /dev/sdc), the partition numbers remain the same (e.g., /dev/sdc1, /dev/sdc2, and so on).

Hard disk partitions can be created specific to a certain filesystem. To create a partition that will later be formatted with a native Linux filesystem (such as ext2, ex3, or ext4), you should create a Linux partition (also known as type 83). Similarly, you should create a Linux swap partition (also known as type 82) if that partition is intended for use as virtual memory. This explicit choice of partition type allows for partitions that better suit the needs of a filesystem.

An example Linux MBR hard disk structure for the first SATA/SCSI/SAS hard disk (/dev/sda) can contain a partition for the /boot filesystem (/dev/sda1), a partition for the / filesystem (/dev/sda2), as well as an extended partition (/dev/sda3) that further contains a swap partition (/dev/sda5), a /home filesystem partition, and some free space, as shown in Figure 5-5.

A more complicated example Linux GPT hard disk structure for the first SATA/SCSI/SAS hard disk might involve preserving the Windows operating system partition, allowing a user to boot into and use the Linux operating system or boot into and use the Windows operating system. This is known as dual booting and is discussed in Chapter 6. Recall from Chapter 2 that systems that have a UEFI BIOS create a small UEFI System Partition; this partition is formatted with the FAT filesystem and used to store boot-related information for one or more operating systems. If Windows has created this partition, Linux will modify and use it to store the information needed to dual boot both operating systems.

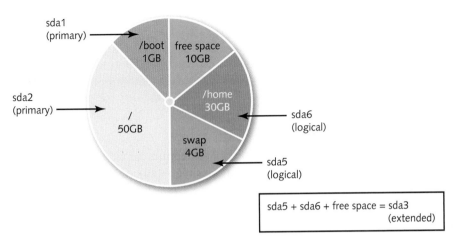

Figure 5-5   A sample MBR partitioning strategy

In Figure 5-6, a UEFI System Partition was created as /dev/sda1 because the system had a UEFI BIOS, and the Windows partition was created as /dev/sda2. Linux mounted the UEFI System Partition to the /boot/efi directory and created a separate partition for the /boot filesystem (/dev/sda3), the / filesystem (/dev/sda4), and the /home filesystem (/dev/sda5).

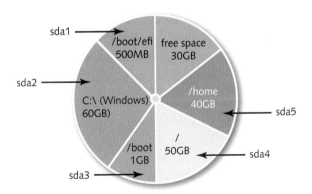

Figure 5-6   A sample dual-boot GPT partitioning strategy

Working with Standard Hard Disk Partitions

Recall that you can create partitions at installation using the graphical installation program. To create partitions after installation, you can use the `fdisk` **command** to create partitions that will be stored in an MBR on the hard disk. To use the `fdisk` command, specify the hard disk to partition as an argument. An example of using fdisk to work with the first SATA hard disk (/dev/sda) is shown in the following output:

```
[root@server1 ~]# fdisk /dev/sda
Welcome to fdisk (util-linux 2.32).
Changes will remain in memory only, until you decide to write them.
Be careful before using the write command.
Command (m for help):
```

Note from the preceding output that the fdisk command displays a prompt for the user to accept fdisk commands; a list of possible fdisk commands can be seen if the user presses the m key at this prompt, as shown in the following example:

```
Command (m for help): m
Help:

  DOS (MBR)
    a    toggle a bootable flag
    b    edit nested BSD disklabel
    c    toggle the dos compatibility flag

  Generic
    d    delete a partition
    F    list free unpartitioned space
    l    list known partition types
    n    add a new partition
    p    print the partition table
    t    change a partition type
    v    verify the partition table
    i    print information about a partition

  Misc
    m    print this menu
    u    change display/entry units
    x    extra functionality (experts only)

  Script
    I    load disk layout from sfdisk script file
    O    dump disk layout to sfdisk script file

  Save & Exit
    w    write table to disk and exit
    q    quit without saving changes
```

```
Create a new label
   g    create a new empty GPT partition table
   G    create a new empty SGI (IRIX) partition table
   o    create a new empty DOS partition table
   s    create a new empty Sun partition table
Command (m for help):_
```

To print a list of the partitions currently set on /dev/sda, you could press the p key at the fdisk prompt:

```
Command (m for help): p
Disk /dev/sda: 50 GiB, 53687091200 bytes, 104857600 sectors
Units: sectors of 1 * 512 = 512 bytes
Sector size (logical/physical): 512 bytes / 512 bytes
I/O size (minimum/optimal): 512 bytes / 512 bytes
Disklabel type: dos
Disk identifier: 0x1ac21808


Device      Boot     Start       End   Sectors Size Id Type
/dev/sda1   *         2048   2099199   2097152  1G 83 Linux
/dev/sda2          2099200  10440703   8341504  4G 82 Linux swap/Solaris
/dev/sda3         10440704  83841023  73400320 35G 83 Linux
/dev/sda4         83841024 104857599  21016576 10G 83 Linux
Command (m for help):_
```

Notice that the device names appear on the left side of the preceding output, including the partition that is booted to (/dev/sda1), the start and end location of partitions on the physical hard disk (start and end cylinders), the number of total blocks for storing information in the partition, as well as the partition type and description (83 is a Linux partition, 82 is a Linux swap partition). A Linux partition can contain a Linux filesystem—for example, ext4.

To remove the /dev/sda4 partition and all the data contained on the filesystem within, you could use the d key noted earlier:

```
Command (m for help): d
Partition number (1-4, default 4): 4
Partition 4 has been deleted.

Command (m for help): p
Disk /dev/sda: 50 GiB, 53687091200 bytes, 104857600 sectors
Units: sectors of 1 * 512 = 512 bytes
Sector size (logical/physical): 512 bytes / 512 bytes
I/O size (minimum/optimal): 512 bytes / 512 bytes
Disklabel type: dos
Disk identifier: 0x1ac21808
```

```
Device     Boot    Start      End  Sectors Size Id Type
/dev/sda1  *        2048  2099199  2097152  1G 83 Linux
/dev/sda2        2099200 10440703  8341504  4G 82 Linux swap/Solaris
/dev/sda3       10440704 83841023 73400320 35G 83 Linux
Command (m for help):_
```

To create an extended partition using the fourth primary partition (/dev/sda4) with two logical drives (/dev/sda5 and /dev/sda6), you could use the n key noted earlier and specify the partition to create, the starting cylinder on the hard disk, and the size in blocks (+5G makes a 5GB partition):

```
Command (m for help): n
Partition type
   p   primary (3 primary, 0 extended, 1 free)
   e   extended (container for logical partitions)
Select (default e): e

Selected partition 4
First sector (83841024-104857599, default 83841024): 83841024
Last sector, +sectors or +size{K,M,G,T,P} (83841024-104857599, default
104857599): +5G

Created a new partition 4 of type 'Extended' and of size 5 GiB.
Command (m for help): p
Disk /dev/sda: 50 GiB, 53687091200 bytes, 104857600 sectors
Units: sectors of 1 * 512 = 512 bytes
Sector size (logical/physical): 512 bytes / 512 bytes
I/O size (minimum/optimal): 512 bytes / 512 bytes
Disklabel type: dos
Disk identifier: 0x1ac21808

Device     Boot    Start      End  Sectors Size Id Type
/dev/sda1  *        2048  2099199  2097152  1G 83 Linux
/dev/sda2        2099200 10440703  8341504  4G 82 Linux swap/Solaris
/dev/sda3       10440704 83841023 73400320 35G 83 Linux
/dev/sda4       83841024 94326783 10485760  5G  5 Extended

Command (m for help): n
All primary partitions are in use.
Adding logical partition 5
First sector (83843072-94326783, default 83843072): 83843072
```

```
Last sector, +sectors or +size{K,M,G,T,P} (83843072-94326783, default
94326783): +3GB

Created a new partition 5 of type 'Linux' and of size 2.8 GiB.

Command (m for help): n
All primary partitions are in use.
Adding logical partition 6
First sector (89704448-94326783, default 89704448): 89704448
Last sector, +sectors or +size{K,M,G,T,P} (89704448-94326783,
default 94326783): 94326783

Created a new partition 6 of type 'Linux' and of size 2.2 GiB.

Command (m for help): p

Disk /dev/sda: 50 GiB, 53687091200 bytes, 104857600 sectors
Units: sectors of 1 * 512 = 512 bytes
Sector size (logical/physical): 512 bytes / 512 bytes
I/O size (minimum/optimal): 512 bytes / 512 bytes
Disklabel type: dos
Disk identifier: 0x1ac21808

Device     Boot  Start      End  Sectors  Size Id Type
/dev/sda1  *      2048  2099199  2097152   1G 83 Linux
/dev/sda2       2099200 10440703 8341504   4G 82 Linux swap / Solaris
/dev/sda3      10440704 83841023 73400320  35G 83 Linux
/dev/sda4      83841024 94326783 10485760   5G  5 Extended
/dev/sda5      83843072 89702399 5859328  2.8G 83 Linux
/dev/sda6      89704448 94326783 4622336  2.2G 83 Linux

Command (m for help):_
```

Note

Instead of entering the first available sector for a new partition in the examples above, you can press Enter to accept the default value of the next available sector; for example, when creating the extended partition in the above example, pressing Enter would have chosen the default value of 83841024.

Notice from the preceding output that the default type for new partitions created with fdisk is 83 (Linux); to change this, you can press the t key at the fdisk prompt. To change the /dev/sda6 partition to type 82 (Linux swap), you can do the following at the fdisk prompt:

```
Command (m for help): t
Partition number (1-6, default 6): 6
Hex code (type L to list all codes): L
```

0	Empty	24	NEC DOS	81	Minix / old Lin	bf	Solaris
1	FAT12	27	Hidden NTFS Win	82	Linux swap / So	c1	DRDOS/sec (FAT-
2	XENIX root	39	Plan 9	83	Linux	c4	DRDOS/sec (FAT-
3	XENIX usr	3c	PartitionMagic	84	OS/2 hidden or	c6	DRDOS/sec (FAT-
4	FAT16 <32M	40	Venix 80286	85	Linux extended	c7	Syrinx
5	Extended	41	PPC PReP Boot	86	NTFS volume set	da	Non-FS data
6	FAT16	42	SFS	87	NTFS volume set	db	CP/M / CTOS / .
7	HPFS/NTFS/exFAT	4d	QNX4.x	88	Linux plaintext	de	Dell Utility
8	AIX	4e	QNX4.x 2nd part	8e	Linux LVM	df	BootIt
9	AIX bootable	4f	QNX4.x 3rd part	93	Amoeba	e1	DOS access
a	OS/2 Boot Manag	50	OnTrack DM	94	Amoeba BBT	e3	DOS R/O
b	W95 FAT32	51	OnTrack DM6 Aux	9f	BSD/OS	e4	SpeedStor
c	W95 FAT32 (LBA)	52	CP/M	a0	IBM Thinkpad hi	ea	Rufus alignment
e	W95 FAT16 (LBA)	53	OnTrack DM6 Aux	a5	FreeBSD	eb	BeOS fs
f	W95 Ext'd (LBA)	54	OnTrackDM6	a6	OpenBSD	ee	GPT
10	OPUS	55	EZ-Drive	a7	NeXTSTEP	ef	EFI (FAT-12/16/
11	Hidden FAT12	56	Golden Bow	a8	Darwin UFS	f0	Linux/PA-RISC b
12	Compaq diagnost	5c	Priam Edisk	a9	NetBSD	f1	SpeedStor
14	Hidden FAT16 <3	61	SpeedStor	ab	Darwin boot	f4	SpeedStor
16	Hidden FAT16	63	GNU HURD or Sys	af	HFS / HFS+	f2	DOS secondary
17	Hidden HPFS/NTF	64	Novell Netware	b7	BSDI fs	fb	VMware VMFS
18	AST SmartSleep	65	Novell Netware	b8	BSDI swap	fc	VMware VMKCORE
1b	Hidden W95 FAT3	70	DiskSecure Mult	bb	Boot Wizard hid	fd	Linux raid auto
1c	Hidden W95 FAT3	75	PC/IX	bc	Acronis FAT32 L	fe	LANstep
1e	Hidden W95 FAT1	80	Old Minix	be	Solaris boot	ff	BBT

```
Hex code (type L to list all codes): 82

Changed type of partition 'Linux' to 'Linux swap / Solaris'.

Command (m for help): p
Disk /dev/sda: 50 GiB, 53687091200 bytes, 104857600 sectors
Units: sectors of 1 * 512 = 512 bytes
Sector size (logical/physical): 512 bytes / 512 bytes
```

```
I/O size (minimum/optimal): 512 bytes / 512 bytes
Disklabel type: dos
Disk identifier: 0x1ac21808

Device     Boot    Start       End   Sectors  Size Id Type
/dev/sda1  *        2048   2099199   2097152   1G 83 Linux
/dev/sda2        2099200  10440703   8341504    4G 82 Linux swap/Solaris
/dev/sda3       10440704  83841023  73400320   35G 83 Linux
/dev/sda4       83841024  94326783  10485760    5G  5 Extended
/dev/sda5       83843072  89702399   5859328  2.8G 83 Linux
/dev/sda6       89704448  94326783   4622336  2.2G 82 Linux swap/Solaris

Command (m for help):_
```

Finally, to save partition changes to the hard disk and attempt to reload the new partition information back into memory, use the w key at the fdisk prompt:

```
Command (m for help): w
The partition table has been altered.
Failed to add partition 5 to system: Device or resource busy
Failed to add partition 6 to system: Device or resource busy

The kernel still uses the old partitions. The new table will be
used at the next reboot.
Syncing disks.
[root@server1 ~]#_
```

If the fdisk command indicates that the new partition information must be reloaded manually because you modified the hard disk that also hosts the operating system (as in the preceding example), you can either run the partprobe command or reboot your system. However, rebooting your system is the most reliable way to ensure that the MBR is reloaded into memory successfully.

An easier alternative to fdisk is the cfdisk command. If you run the cfdisk /dev/sda command following the creation of the partitions you examined earlier, you will see the interactive graphical utility shown in Figure 5-7. You can use this utility to quickly create, manipulate, and delete partitions using choices at the bottom of the screen that you can navigate using your cursor keys. As with fdisk, after making changes within the cfdisk utility, you should reboot your system to ensure that the MBR is reloaded into memory successfully.

```
                              Disk: /dev/sda
            Size: 50 GiB, 53687091200 bytes, 104857600 sectors
                     Label: dos, identifier: 0x1ac21808

     Device      Boot      Start        End    Sectors   Size  Id Type
>> /dev/sda1      *         2048    2099199    2097152    1G  83 Linux
   /dev/sda2             2099200   10440703    8341504    4G  82 Linux swap / Solaris
   /dev/sda3            10440704   83841023   73400320   35G  83 Linux
   /dev/sda4            83841024   94326783   10485760    5G   5 Extended
   ├─/dev/sda5          83843072   89702399    5859328  2.8G  83 Linux
   └─/dev/sda6          89704448   94326783    4622336  2.2G  82 Linux swap / Solaris
   Free space           94326784  104857599   10530816    5G

┌──────────────────────────────────────────────────────────────────────────────┐
│Partition type: Linux (83)                                                      │
│     Attributes: 80                                                             │
│Filesystem UUID: 8789961a-fbca-4411-a300-195556f13719                           │
│     Filesystem: ext4                                                           │
│     Mountpoint: /boot (mounted)                                                │
└──────────────────────────────────────────────────────────────────────────────┘

  [Bootable]  [ Delete ]  [ Resize ]  [  Quit  ]  [ Type ]  [ Help ]  [ Write ]  [ Dump ]

                    Quit program without writing changes
```

Figure 5-7   The cfdisk utility

After your computer has rebooted, you can use the `mkfs`, `mount`, and `umount` commands discussed earlier, specifying the partition device file as an argument. To create an ext4 filesystem on the /dev/sda5 partition created earlier, you can use the following command:

```
[root@server1 ~]# mkfs -t ext4 /dev/sda5
mke2fs 1.43.8 (1-Jan-2020)
Creating filesystem with 732416 4k blocks and 183264 inodes
Filesystem UUID: c5ce0e70-8eaf-4b1c-8a5f-606d66d56717
Superblock backups stored on blocks:
        32768, 98304, 163840, 229376, 294912

Allocating group tables: done
Writing inode tables: done
Creating journal (16384 blocks): done
```

```
Writing superblocks and filesystem accounting information: done
[root@server1 ~]#_
```

To mount this ext4 filesystem to a new mount point directory called /data and view the contents, you can use the following commands:

```
[root@server1 ~]# mkdir /data
[root@server1 ~]# mount /dev/sda5 /data
[root@server1 ~]# df -T
Filesystem      Type       1K-blocks      Used Available Use% Mounted on
devtmpfs        devtmpfs    2006860          0   2006860   0% /dev
tmpfs           tmpfs       2019492          0   2019492   0% /dev/shm
tmpfs           tmpfs       2019492       1200   2018292   1% /run
tmpfs           tmpfs       2019492          0   2019492   0% /sys/fs/cgroup
/dev/sda3       ext4       35862048    8881300  25129356  27% /
tmpfs           tmpfs       2019492         72   2019420   1% /tmp
/dev/sda1       ext4         999320     151300    779208  17% /boot
tmpfs           tmpfs        403896         28    403868   1% /run/user/42
tmpfs           tmpfs        403896          4    403892   1% /run/user/0
/dev/sda5       ext4        2818080       8592   2646624   1% /data
[root@server1 ~]# ls -F /data
lost+found/
[root@server1 ~]#_
```

To allow the system to mount this filesystem automatically at every boot, simply edit the /etc/fstab file such that it has the following entry for /dev/sda5:

```
[root@server1 ~]# cat /etc/fstab
#
# /etc/fstab
# Accessible filesystems by reference are maintained under /dev/disk
# See man pages fstab(5), findfs(8), mount(8) and/or blkid(8)
#
UUID=9ff25add-035b-4d26-a9d0a6fa3    /           ext4   defaults   1 1
UUID=8789961a-fbca-4411-195f13719    /boot       ext4   defaults   1 2
UUID=4837de7b-d96e-4edc-56d17ca62    swap        swap   defaults   0 0
/dev/sdb1                            /USBdrive   auto   noauto     0 0
/dev/sda5                            /data       ext4   defaults   0 0
[root@server1 ~]#_
```

Although swap partitions do not contain a filesystem, you must still prepare swap partitions and activate them for use on the Linux system. To do this, you can use the `mkswap` command to prepare the swap partition and the `swapon` command to activate it. To prepare and activate the /dev/sda6 partition created earlier as virtual memory, you can use the following commands:

```
[root@server1 ~]# mkswap /dev/sda6
Setting up swapspace version 1, size = 2.2 GiB (2366631936 bytes)
no label, UUID=6a18eb09-caa5-42e9-b329-0f56d2a42db9
[root@server1 ~]# swapon /dev/sda6
[root@server1 ~]#_
```

Note

You can also use the `swapoff` command to deactivate a swap partition.

Next, you can edit the /etc/fstab file to ensure that the new /dev/sda6 partition is activated as virtual memory, as shown here:

```
[root@server1 ~]# cat /etc/fstab
#
# /etc/fstab
# Accessible filesystems by reference are maintained under /dev/disk
# See man pages fstab(5), findfs(8), mount(8) and/or blkid(8)
#
UUID=9ff25add-035b-4d26-a9d0a6fa3  /          ext4   defaults   1 1
UUID=8789961a-fbca-4411-195f13719  /boot      ext4   defaults   1 2
UUID=4837de7b-d96e-4edc-56d17ca62  swap       swap   defaults   0 0
/dev/sdb1                          /USBdrive  auto   noauto     0 0
/dev/sda5                          /data      ext4   defaults   0 0
/dev/sda6                          swap       swap   defaults   0 0
[root@server1 ~]#_
```

If your hard disk uses a GPT instead of an MBR, you can also use the `fdisk` or `cfdisk` commands to create or modify GPT partitions before you format them with a filesystem or prepare them for use as Linux swap memory. Alternatively, you can use the `gdisk` **(GPT fdisk) command** to create and work with GPT partitions using an interface that is nearly identical to `fdisk`. If your hard disk has an MBR, `gdisk` will first prompt you to convert the MBR to a GPT, which will destroy all existing MBR partitions on the disk.

Many Linux distributions also contain the `parted` (GNU Parted) command, which can be used to create and modify partitions on both MBR and GPT hard disks. Run the `parted` command with the device file as an argument. Once in the GNU Parted utility, you can type `help` to obtain a list of valid commands, or type `print` to print the existing partitions, as shown here:

```
[root@server1 ~]# parted /dev/sdb
GNU Parted 3.2
Using /dev/sdb
Welcome to GNU Parted! Type 'help' to view a list of commands.
(parted) print
Model: ATA INTEL SSDSA2CW08 (scsi)
Disk /dev/sdb: 80.0GB
Sector size (logical/physical): 512B/512B
Partition Table: gpt
Disk Flags:

Number  Start   End     Size    File system  Name  Flags
 1      1049kB  2001MB  2000MB  xfs
(parted)_
```

Note from the previous output that the Intel SSD uses a GPT partition table and contains a single 2001MB partition (/dev/sdb1) that contains the XFS filesystem. In the following example, two additional partitions are created using the free space on the hard disk within the GNU parted utility: a 3GB partition with the label "data" (/dev/sdb2) and a 2GB partition with the label "logs" (/dev/sdb3). During the creation process, you are prompted for the filesystem type. If you plan on formatting the partition with a Linux filesystem afterward, choosing the default partition type of `ext2` will suffice. However, if you plan on using the partition for swap, you should specify `linux-swap` when prompted for the filesystem type.

```
(parted) mkpart
Partition name?  []? data
File system type?  [ext2]? ext4
Start? 2GB
End? 5GB
(parted) mkpart
Partition name?  []? logs
File system type?  [ext2]? ext2
Start? 5GB
End? 7GB
(parted) print
Model: ATA INTEL SSDSA2CW08 (scsi)
Disk /dev/sdb: 80.0GB
```

```
Sector size (logical/physical): 512B/512B
Partition Table: gpt
Disk Flags:

Number  Start    End     Size    File system  Name  Flags
  1     1049kB   2001MB  2000MB  xfs
  2     2001MB   5000MB  2999MB  ext4               data
  3     5000MB   7000MB  2001MB  ext2               logs

(parted) quit
Information: You may need to update /etc/fstab.
[root@server1 ~]#_
```

After creating GPT partitions that should contain a filesystem, you can proceed to formatting those partitions with a filesystem using `mkfs`, mounting them to the directory tree with the `mount` command, like you did earlier after creating partitions with `fdisk`. Alternatively, if you've created a Linux swap partition on a GPT hard disk, you can proceed to preparing that partition using `mkswap` and activating it using the `swapon` command. Finally, you can update the /etc/fstab file to mount new filesystems and activate new swap partitions automatically at boot time.

> **Note** 📎
>
> Recall that `parted` can also work with disks that contain an MBR. If you create partitions on an MBR hard disk, `parted` will additionally prompt you for the partition type (primary/extended/logical).

To remove the two GPT partitions that were added in the previous example, you can use the `rm` command within the parted utility and specify the partition number:

```
[root@server1 ~]# parted /dev/sdb
GNU Parted 3.2
Using /dev/sdb
Welcome to GNU Parted! Type 'help' to view a list of commands.
(parted) print
Model: ATA INTEL SSDSA2CW08 (scsi)
Disk /dev/sdb: 80.0GB
Sector size (logical/physical): 512B/512B
Partition Table: gpt
Disk Flags:
```

```
Number   Start    End      Size     File system   Name   Flags
 1       1049kB   2001MB   2000MB   xfs
 2       2001MB   5000MB   2999MB   ext4                  data
 3       5000MB   7000MB   2001MB   ext2                  logs

(parted) rm 3
(parted) rm 2
(parted) print
Model: ATA INTEL SSDSA2CW08 (scsi)
Disk /dev/sdb: 80.0GB
Sector size (logical/physical): 512B/512B
Partition Table: gpt
Disk Flags:

Number   Start    End      Size     File system   Name   Flags
 1       1049kB   2001MB   2000MB   xfs

(parted) quit
Information: You may need to update /etc/fstab.
[root@server1 ~]#_
```

Working with the LVM

In the previous section, you learned how to create standard hard disk partitions on an MBR or GPT hard disk. You also learned how to create filesystems on those partitions and mount the filesystems to a directory within the Linux filesystem hierarchy.

Instead of creating and mounting filesystems that reside on standard partitions, you can use the **Logical Volume Manager (LVM)** to create logical volumes that can be mounted to directories within the Linux filesystem hierarchy. Using volumes to host filesystems is far more flexible than using standard partitions because it allows you to select free space from unused partitions across multiple hard disks in your computer. This free space is then pooled together into a single group from which volumes can be created. These volumes can be formatted with a filesystem and mounted to a directory on the Linux filesystem hierarchy. Furthermore, additional hard disks can easily be added to the LVM, where existing volumes can take advantage of the additional storage space.

The LVM consists of several different components:

- **Physical Volumes (PVs)** are unused partitions on hard disks that the LVM can use to store information.
- **Volume Groups (VGs)** contain one or more PVs. They represent the pools of hard disk storage space that are available to the LVM for creating logical volumes. Additional PVs can easily be added to a VG after creation.

- **Logical Volumes (LVs)** are the usable volumes that are created by the LVM from the available storage space within a VG. LVs contain a filesystem and are mounted to a directory in the Linux filesystem hierarchy. In addition, LVs can be resized easily by the LVM to use more or less storage space.

The LVM subsystem in Linux manages the storage of all data that is saved to LVs. The physical location of the data is transparent to the user. Furthermore, the LVM has error correction abilities that minimize the chance that data will become corrupted or lost. Figure 5-8 illustrates the relationships among LVM components in a sample LVM configuration that creates four PVs from the standard partitions on three hard disks. These PVs are added to a VG divided into three LVs that are each mounted to a directory on the Linux filesystem hierarchy (/directory1, /directory2, and /directory3).

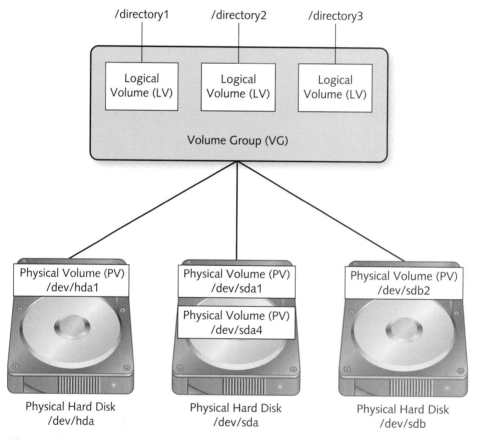

Figure 5-8   A sample LVM configuration

To configure the LVM, you must first create one or more PVs that reference an unused partition on a hard disk in your computer. Say, for example, that you recently created a new partition called /dev/sda4. Rather than placing a filesystem on /dev/sda4,

you could instead allow the LVM to use the /dev/sda4 partition using the `pvcreate`
command, as shown here:

```
[root@server1 ~]# pvcreate /dev/sda4
Physical volume "/dev/sda4" successfully created
[root@server1 ~]#_
```

> **Note** 📎
>
> You should use the `pvcreate` command to create PVs for each unused partition that you
> want the LVM to use. For simplicity in code output, this section shows how to create a single
> PV to demonstrate the configuration of LVM.

The `pvdisplay` **command** can be used to display detailed information about each PV.
The following `pvdisplay` command indicates that /dev/sda4 has 10GB of available space:

```
[root@server1 ~]# pvdisplay
  "/dev/sda4" is a new physical volume of "10.02 GiB"
  --- NEW Physical volume ---
  PV Name                /dev/sda4
  VG Name
  PV Size                10.02 GiB
  Allocatable            NO
  PE Size                0
  Total PE               0
  Free PE                0
  Allocated PE           0
  PV UUID                CzFqSO-9pNX-igfF-7t7N-Cgi0-Qcl8-dkh9C0

[root@server1 ~]#_
```

After you have created PVs, you can create a VG that uses the space in the PVs by
using the `vgcreate` **command.** For example, to create a VG called vg00 that uses the
/dev/sda4 PV, you could use the following `vgcreate` command:

```
[root@server1 ~]# vgcreate vg00 /dev/sda4
Volume group "vg00" successfully created
[root@server1 ~]#_
```

To create a VG that uses multiple PVs, add multiple device arguments to the
`vgcreate` command. For example, the `vgcreate vg00 /dev/sda5 /dev/sdb1`
`/dev/sdc3` command would create a VG called vg00 that uses three PVs (/dev/sda5,
/dev/sdb1, and /dev/sdc3).

When creating a VG, it is important to choose the block size for saving data as it cannot be safely changed later. This is called the **physical extent (PE) size** of the VG. A large PE size results in larger write operations and a larger maximum filesystem size for LVs. For example, a PE size of 32MB will allow for a maximum LV size of 2TB.

By default, the vgcreate command chooses an appropriate PE size according to the current sizes of the PVs that are associated with the VG, but you can use the -s or --physicalextentsize options with the vgcreate command to select a different PE size during VG creation.

The vgdisplay **command** can be used to display detailed information about each VG. The following vgdisplay command indicates that vg00 has just under 10GB of available space:

```
[root@server1 ~]#  vgdisplay
  --- Volume group ---
  VG Name                vg00
  System ID
  Format                 lvm2
  Metadata Areas         1
  Metadata Sequence No   1
  VG Access              read/write
  VG Status              resizable
  MAX LV                 0
  Cur LV                 0
  Open LV                0
  Max PV                 0
  Cur PV                 1
  Act PV                 1
  VG Size                <10.02 GiB
  PE Size                4.00 MiB
  Total PE               2565
  Alloc PE / Size        0 / 0
  Free  PE / Size        2565 / <10.02 GiB
  VG UUID                Mdta42-3L0A-YNGW-z1zc-oLAc-95P1-KGSM9K
[root@server1 ~]#_
```

Next, you can create LVs from the available space in your VG using the lvcreate **command** and view your results using the lvdisplay **command**. The following commands create an LV called "data1" that uses 5GB of space from vg00 as well as an LV called "data2" that uses 3GB of space from vg00, and it displays the results.

```
[root@server1 ~]# lvcreate -L 5GB -n data1 vg00
  Logical volume "data1" created
[root@server1 ~]# lvcreate -L 3GB -n data2 vg00
  Logical volume "data2" created
```

```
[root@server1 ~]# lvdisplay
  --- Logical volume ---
  LV Path                /dev/vg00/data1
  LV Name                data1
  VG Name                vg00
  LV UUID                MHGr8z-Oukh-xSMw-wb4n-V9Jw-M5eu-mWoXQQ
  LV Write Access        read/write
  LV Creation host, time server1, 2019-07-21 21:15:02 -0400
  LV Status              available
  # open                 0
  LV Size                5.00 GiB
  Current LE             1280
  Segments               1
  Allocation             inherit
  Read ahead sectors     auto
  - currently set to     256
  Block device           253:0

  --- Logical volume ---
  LV Path                /dev/vg00/data2
  LV Name                data2
  VG Name                vg00
  LV UUID                Po2yZh-Lx63-tiG4-6sdx-AfCe-PvR1-wpFp7N
  LV Write Access        read/write
  LV Creation host, time server1, 2019-07-21 21:15:22 -0400
  LV Status              available
  # open                 0
  LV Size                3.00 GiB
  Current LE             768
  Segments               1
  Allocation             inherit
  Read ahead sectors     auto
  - currently set to     256
  Block device           253:1

[root@server1 ~]#_
```

Notice from the preceding output that the new VGs can be accessed using the device files /dev/vgoo/data and /dev/vgoo/extras. You can also refer to your new VGs using the device files /dev/mapper/vgoo-data and /dev/mapper/vgoo-extras, which are typically used by the system when accessing the filesystems on your VGs. These device files are created by the device mapper framework within the Linux kernel, which maps physical block devices such as /dev/sda4 to logical devices within the LVM; as a result, these device files are merely shortcuts to device mapper device files (/dev/dm-*), as shown below:

```
[root@server1 ~]# ll /dev/vg00/
total 0
lrwxrwxrwx. 1 root root 7 Jul 21 21:15 data1 -> ../dm-0
lrwxrwxrwx. 1 root root 7 Jul 21 21:15 data2 -> ../dm-1
[root@server1 ~]# ll /dev/mapper/
total 0
crw-------. 1 root root 10, 236 Jul 21 20:55 control
lrwxrwxrwx. 1 root root         7 Jul 21 21:15 vg00-data1 -> ../dm-0
lrwxrwxrwx. 1 root root         7 Jul 21 21:15 vg00-data2 -> ../dm-1
[root@server1 ~]#_
```

Note 📎

The device mapper files shown in the previous output reflect the identifiers that the Linux kernel uses when working with LVs, as the kernel stores configuration for each LV within the associated /sys/block/dm-*/ directory. However, Linux administrators need only reference to VG and LV names (such as vg00 and data1) when working with LVM commands, as these names are automatically mapped to the appropriate device mapper file.

You can work with these device files as you would normally work with any other hard disk partition device file. For example, to create an ext4 filesystem on these devices and mount them to the appropriate directories on the filesystem, you could use the following commands:

```
[root@server1 ~]# mke2fs -t ext4 /dev/vg00/data1
mke2fs 1.43.8 (1-Jan-2018)
Creating filesystem with 1310720 4k blocks and 327680 inodes
Filesystem UUID: 11b43aec-a3f8-44e3-a6bf-3df54e24b9cc
Superblock backups stored on blocks:
        32768, 98304, 163840, 229376, 294912, 819200, 884736

Allocating group tables: done
Writing inode tables: done
Creating journal (16384 blocks): done
Writing superblocks and filesystem accounting information: done
```

```
[root@server1 ~]# mke2fs -t ext4 /dev/vg00/data2
mke2fs 1.43.8 (1-Jan-2018)
Creating filesystem with 786432 4k blocks and 196608 inodes
Filesystem UUID: 87ffa5be-25e6-4d9c-8326-ac2f9890f54e
Superblock backups stored on blocks:
        32768, 98304, 163840, 229376, 294912

Allocating group tables: done
Writing inode tables: done
Creating journal (16384 blocks): done
Writing superblocks and filesystem accounting information: done

[root@server1 ~]# mkdir /data1
[root@server1 ~]# mkdir /data2
[root@server1 ~]# mount /dev/vg00/data1 /data1
[root@server1 ~]# mount /dev/vg00/data2 /data2
[root@server1 ~]# df -T
Filesystem              Type      1K-blocks      Used Available Use% Mounted
devtmpfs                devtmpfs    2006860         0   2006860   0% /dev
tmpfs                   tmpfs       2019492         0   2019492   0% /dev/shm
tmpfs                   tmpfs       2019492      1192   2018300   1% /run
/dev/sda3               ext4       35862048   8881660  25128996  27% /
tmpfs                   tmpfs       2019492        72   2019420   1% /tmp
/dev/sda1               ext4         999320    151300    779208  17% /boot
/dev/mapper/vg00-data1 ext4        5095040     20472   4796040   1% /data1
/dev/mapper/vg00-data2 ext4        3030800      9216   2847916   1% /data2
[root@server1 ~]# lsblk
NAME             MAJ:MIN RM  SIZE RO TYPE MOUNTPOINT
sda                  8:0  0   50G  0 disk
├─sda1               8:1  0    1G  0 part /boot
├─sda2               8:2  0    4G  0 part [SWAP]
├─sda3               8:3  0   35G  0 part /
└─sda4               8:4  0   10G  0 part
  ├─vg00-data1 253:0  0    5G  0 lvm  /data1
  └─vg00-data2 253:1  0    3G  0 lvm  /data2
sr0                 11:0  1 1024M  0 rom
[root@server1 ~]#_
```

Next, you can edit the /etc/fstab file to ensure that your new logical volumes are automatically mounted at system startup, as shown here:

```
[root@server1 ~]# cat /etc/fstab
#
```

```
# /etc/fstab
# Accessible filesystems by reference are maintained under /dev/disk
# See man pages fstab(5), findfs(8), mount(8) and/or blkid(8)
#
UUID=9ff25add-035b-4d26-a9d0a6fa3    /          ext4   defaults   1 1
UUID=8789961a-fbca-4411-195f13719    /boot      ext4   defaults   1 2
UUID=4837de7b-d96e-4edc-56d17ca62    swap       swap   defaults   0 0
/dev/vg00/data1                      /data1     ext4   defaults   0 0
/dev/vg00/data2                      /data2     ext4   defaults   0 0
[root@server1 ~]#_
```

Three other useful commands that can display information about the PVs, VGs, and LVs that are configured on your system are the `pvscan` command, the `vgscan` command, and `lvscan` command, respectively.

You can also add storage space to your LVs after configuration. More specifically, you can add another PV using the `pvcreate` command, add this PV to your existing VG using the `vgextend` command, and then increase the size of your LVs to use the additional space using the `lvextend` command. Say, for example, that you added a new hard drive to your computer that was recognized as /dev/sdb; you could create a /dev/sdb1 partition that spans that entire hard drive using the `fdisk /dev/sdb` command, and then create a PV for that partition using the `pvcreate /dev/sdb1` command. Next, you could use the `vgextend vg00 /dev/sdb1` command to add the PV to the existing VG called vg00. Finally, you could create other LVs from the additional available space in the VG, or extend existing LVs to use the additional space. To extend the existing data2 LV by 50GB and resize the existing filesystem on it accordingly, you could use the `lvextend -L +50GB -r /dev/vg00/data2` command. All of these commands can be performed while the existing LVs are mounted on the system and accessible by users.

Note 📎

If you don't use the `-r` option to the `lvextend` command to resize the existing filesystem when extending an LV, your filesystem will not be able to use the additional space. In this case, you can use a command to resize your filesystem after extending your LV. For example, to extend an ext2/ext3/ext4 filesystem, you can use the `resize2fs` command, and to extend an XFS filesystem, you can use either the `xfs_info` command or `xfs_growfs` command.

Monitoring Filesystems

After filesystems are created on devices and those devices are mounted to the directory tree, they should be checked periodically for errors, disk space usage, and inode usage. This minimizes the problems that can occur as a result of a damaged filesystem and reduces the likelihood that a file cannot be saved due to insufficient disk space.

Disk Usage

Several filesystems can be mounted to the directory tree. As mentioned earlier, the more filesystems that are used, the less likely a corrupted filesystem will interfere with normal system operations. Conversely, more filesystems typically result in less hard disk space per filesystem and might result in system errors if certain filesystems fill up with data. Many Linux administrators create filesystems for the /boot, /, /home, /usr, and /var directories during installation. The /home directory stores user home directories, which could grow depending on how much data users store. The /usr directory contains most utilities and installed programs on a Linux system, and it should have enough space for future software installations. The /var directory grows in size continuously as it stores log files. Old log files should be removed periodically to leave room for new ones. The **/** filesystem is the most vital of these; it should always contain a great deal of free space used as working space for the operating system. As a result, the **/** filesystem should be monitored frequently. If free space on the **/** filesystem falls below 10 percent, the system might suffer from poorer performance or cease to operate.

The easiest method for monitoring free space by mounted filesystems is to use the df command discussed earlier; the -h option prints results in a more user-friendly (or human-readable) format using commonly used units (G = gigabyte, M = megabyte):

```
[root@server1 ~]# df -h
Filesystem               Size  Used Avail Use% Mounted on
devtmpfs                 2.0G     0  2.0G   0% /dev
tmpfs                    2.0G     0  2.0G   0% /dev/shm
tmpfs                    2.0G  1.2M  2.0G   1% /run
tmpfs                    2.0G     0  2.0G   0% /sys/fs/cgroup
/dev/sda3                 35G  8.5G   24G  27% /
tmpfs                    2.0G   72K  2.0G   1% /tmp
/dev/sda1                976M  148M  761M  17% /boot
tmpfs                    395M   28K  395M   1% /run/user/42
tmpfs                    395M  4.0K  395M   1% /run/user/0
/dev/mapper/vg00-data1   4.9G   20M  4.6G   1% /data1
/dev/mapper/vg00-data2   2.9G   14M  2.5G   1% /data2
[root@server1 ~]#_
```

From the preceding output, the only filesystems used are the /boot, /, /data1, and /data2 filesystems; the /home, /usr, and /var directories are simply directories on the / filesystem, which increases the importance of monitoring the **/** filesystem. Because the **/** filesystem is 27 percent used in the preceding output, there is no immediate concern. However, log files and software installed in the future will increase this number and might warrant the purchase of an additional hard disk for data to reside on.

The df command only views mounted filesystems; thus, to get disk free space statistics for a USB flash memory drive filesystem, you should mount it prior to viewing the output of the df command:

```
[root@server1 ~]# mount /dev/sdb1 /media/USBdrive
[root@server1 ~]# df -h
Filesystem               Size  Used Avail Use% Mounted on
devtmpfs                 2.0G     0  2.0G   0% /dev
tmpfs                    2.0G     0  2.0G   0% /dev/shm
tmpfs                    2.0G  1.2M  2.0G   1% /run
tmpfs                    2.0G     0  2.0G   0% /sys/fs/cgroup
/dev/sda3                 35G  8.5G   24G  27% /
tmpfs                    2.0G   72K  2.0G   1% /tmp
/dev/sda1                976M  148M  761M  17% /boot
tmpfs                    395M   28K  395M   1% /run/user/42
tmpfs                    395M  4.0K  395M   1% /run/user/0
/dev/mapper/vg00-data1   4.9G   20M  4.6G   1% /data1
/dev/mapper/vg00-data2   2.9G   14M  2.5G   1% /data2
/dev/sdb1                7.5G    2M  7.5G   1% /media/USBdrive
[root@server1 ~]# umount /dev/sdb1
[root@server1 ~]# df -h
Filesystem               Size  Used Avail Use% Mounted on
devtmpfs                 2.0G     0  2.0G   0% /dev
tmpfs                    2.0G     0  2.0G   0% /dev/shm
tmpfs                    2.0G  1.2M  2.0G   1% /run
tmpfs                    2.0G     0  2.0G   0% /sys/fs/cgroup
/dev/sda3                 35G  8.5G   24G  27% /
tmpfs                    2.0G   72K  2.0G   1% /tmp
/dev/sda1                976M  148M  761M  17% /boot
tmpfs                    395M   28K  395M   1% /run/user/42
tmpfs                    395M  4.0K  395M   1% /run/user/0
/dev/mapper/vg00-data1   4.9G   20M  4.6G   1% /data1
/dev/mapper/vg00-data2   2.9G   14M  2.5G   1% /data2
[root@server1 ~]#_
```

If a filesystem is approaching full capacity, it might be useful to examine which directories on that filesystem are taking up the most disk space. You can then remove or move files from that directory to another filesystem that has sufficient space. To view the size of a directory and its contents in kilobytes, you can use the du **(directory usage) command**. If the directory is large, you should use either the more or less command to view the output page-by-page, as shown with the following /usr directory:

```
[root@server1 ~]# du /usr | more
4       /usr/share/backgrounds/images
7832    /usr/share/backgrounds/f28/default/tv-wide
10580   /usr/share/backgrounds/f28/default/normalish
10748   /usr/share/backgrounds/f28/default/wide
11092   /usr/share/backgrounds/f28/default/standard
40260   /usr/share/backgrounds/f28/default
40264   /usr/share/backgrounds/f28
2008    /usr/share/backgrounds/gnome
42280   /usr/share/backgrounds
268     /usr/share/kf5/sonnet
44      /usr/share/kf5/widgets/pics
48      /usr/share/kf5/widgets
8       /usr/share/kf5/knewstuff/pics
12      /usr/share/kf5/knewstuff
4       /usr/share/kf5/kssl
168     /usr/share/kf5/kjava
--More--
```

To view only a summary of the total size of a directory, use the -s switch to the du command, as shown in the following example with the /usr directory:

```
[root@server1 ~]# du -s /usr
6643532       /usr
[root@server1 ~]#_
```

As with the df command, the du command also accepts the -h option to make the view more human readable; the following indicates that the total size of the /usr directory is 6.4GB:

```
[root@server1 ~]# du -hs /usr
6.4G    /usr
[root@server1 ~]#_
```

Recall that every filesystem has an inode table that contains the inodes for the files and directories on the filesystem; this inode table is made during filesystem creation and is usually proportionate to the size of the filesystem. Each file and directory uses one inode; thus, a filesystem with several small files might use up all of the inodes in the inode table and prevent new files from being created on the filesystem. To view the total number of inodes and free inodes for an ext2, ext3, or ext4 filesystem, you can use the dumpe2fs command with the –h switch, as shown in the following output:

```
[root@server1 ~]# dumpe2fs -h /dev/sda1
dumpe2fs 1.43.8 (1-Jan-2018)
Filesystem volume name:    <none>
Last mounted on:           /
Filesystem UUID:           9ff25add-035b-4d26-9129-a9da6d0a6fa3
Filesystem magic number:   0xEF53
Filesystem revision #:     1 (dynamic)
Filesystem features:       has_journal ext_attr resize_inode dir_index
filetype needs_recovery extent 64bit flex_bg sparse_super large_file
huge_file uninit_bg dir_nlink extra_isize
Filesystem flags:          signed_directory_hash
Default mount options:     user_xattr acl
Filesystem state:          clean
Errors behavior:           Continue
Filesystem OS type:        Linux
Inode count:               2293760
Block count:               9175040
Reserved block count:      458752
Free blocks:               6745094
Free inodes:               2036064
First block:               0
Block size:                4096
Fragment size:             4096
Group descriptor size:     64
Reserved GDT blocks:       1024
Blocks per group:          32768
Fragments per group:       32768
Inodes per group:          8192
Inode blocks per group:    512
Flex block group size:     16
Filesystem created:        Sun Jul  8 20:07:15 2019
Last mount time:           Sat Jul 21 22:15:39 2019
Last write time:           Sat Jul 21 22:15:38 2019
Mount count:               24
Maximum mount count:       -1
Last checked:              Sun Jul  8 20:07:15 2019
Check interval:            0 (<none>)
Lifetime writes:           15GB
Reserved blocks uid:       0 (user root)
Reserved blocks gid:       0 (group root)
```

```
First inode:              11
Inode size:               256
Required extra isize:     32
Desired extra isize:      32
Journal inode:            8
First orphan inode:       660730
Default directory hash:   half_md4
Directory Hash Seed:      d86beb5a-c679-4bbe-9321-18e9cd379d1f
Journal backup:           inode blocks
Journal features:         journal_incompat_revoke journal_64bit
Journal size:             256M
Journal length:           65536
Journal sequence:         0x00001c3a
Journal start:            1
[root@server1 ~]#_
```

The preceding output shows that the inode table has 2293760 inodes and 2036064 of them are free to use when creating new files and directories.

Note

To monitor the available inodes on an XFS filesystem, you can use the `xfs_info` command.

Checking Filesystems for Errors

Filesystems themselves can accumulate errors over time. These errors are often referred to as **filesystem corruption** and are common on most filesystems. Those filesystems that are accessed frequently are more prone to corruption than those that are not. As a result, such filesystems should be checked regularly for errors.

The most common filesystem corruption occurs because a system was not shut down properly using the `shutdown`, `poweroff`, `halt`, or `reboot` commands. Data is stored in memory for a short period of time before it is written to a file on the hard disk. This process of saving data to the hard disk is called **syncing**. If the computer's power is turned off, data in memory might not be synced properly to the hard disk, causing corruption.

Filesystem corruption can also occur if the hard disks are used frequently for time-intensive tasks such as database access. As the usage of any system increases, so does the possibility for operating system errors when writing to the hard disks. Along the same lines, the physical hard disks themselves are mechanical in nature and can wear during time. Some areas of the hard disk platter might become unusable if they cannot hold a magnetic charge; these areas are known as **bad blocks**. When the operating system finds a bad block, it puts a reference to the block in the bad blocks table on the filesystem. Any entries in the bad blocks table are not used for any future disk storage.

To check a filesystem for errors, you can use the `fsck` **(filesystem check) command**, which can check filesystems of many different types. The `fsck` command takes an option specifying the filesystem type and an argument specifying the device to check; if the filesystem type is not specified, the filesystem is automatically detected. The filesystem being checked must be unmounted beforehand for the `fsck` command to work properly, as shown next:

```
[root@server1 ~]# fsck /dev/vg00/data1
fsck from util-linux 2.32
e2fsck 1.43.8 (1-Jan-2018)
/dev/mapper/vg00-data1 is mounted.
e2fsck: Cannot continue, aborting.
[root@server1 ~]# umount /dev/vg00/data1
[root@server1 ~]# fsck /dev/vg00/data1
e2fsck 1.43.8 (1-Jan-2020)
/dev/mapper/vg00-data1: clean, 11/327680 files, 42078/1310720
blocks [root@server1 ~]#_
```

> **Note** 🖉
>
> Because the / filesystem cannot be unmounted, you should only run the `fsck` command on the / filesystem from single-user mode (discussed in Chapter 8) or from live installation media (discussed in Chapter 6).

Notice from the preceding output that the `fsck` command does not display lengthy output when checking the filesystem; this is because the `fsck` command only performs a quick check for errors unless the `-f` option is used to perform a full check, as shown in the following example:

```
[root@server1 ~]# fsck -f /dev/vg00/data1
fsck from util-linux 2.32
e2fsck 1.43.8 (1-Jan-2018)
Pass 1: Checking inodes, blocks, and sizes
Pass 2: Checking directory structure
Pass 3: Checking directory connectivity
Pass 4: Checking reference counts
Pass 5: Checking group summary information
```

```
/dev/mapper/vg00-data1: 11/327680 files (0.0% non-contiguous),
42078/1310720 blocks
[root@server1 ~]#_
```

Table 5-6 displays a list of common options used with the `fsck` command.

Table 5-6   Common options to the `fsck` command

Option	Description
-f	Performs a full filesystem check
-y	Allows `fsck` to automatically repair any errors (if not run in interactive mode)
-A	Checks all filesystems in /etc/fstab that have a 1 or 2 in the sixth field
-Cf	Performs a full filesystem check and displays a progress line
-AR	Checks all filesystems in /etc/fstab that have a 1 or 2 in the sixth field but skips the / filesystem
-V	Displays verbose output

If the `fsck` command finds a corrupted file, it displays a message to the user asking whether to fix the error; to avoid these messages, you may use the `-y` option listed in Table 5-6 to specify that the `fsck` command should automatically repair any corruption. If the `fsck` command finds files it cannot repair, it places them in the lost+found directory on that filesystem and renames the file to the inode number.

To view the contents of the lost+found directory, mount the device and view the contents of the lost+found directory immediately under the mount point. Because it is difficult to identify lost files by their inode number, most users delete the contents of this directory periodically. Recall that the lost+found directory is automatically created when an ext2, ext3, or ext4 filesystem is created.

Just as you can use the `mke2fs` command to make an ext2, ext3, or ext4 filesystem, you can use the `e2fsck` command to check an ext2, ext3, or ext4 filesystem. The `e2fsck` command accepts more options and can check a filesytem more thoroughly than `fsck`. For example, using the `-c` option to the `e2fsck` command, you can check for bad blocks on the hard disk and add them to a bad block table on the filesystem so that they are not used in the future, as shown in the following example:

```
[root@server1 ~]# e2fsck -c /dev/vg00/data
e2fsck 1.43.8 (1-Jan-2018)
Checking for bad blocks (read-only test): done
/dev/vg00/data1: Updating bad block inode.
Pass 1: Checking inodes, blocks, and sizes
Pass 2: Checking directory structure
```

```
Pass 3: Checking directory connectivity
Pass 4: Checking reference counts
Pass 5: Checking group summary information

/dev/vg00/data1: ***** FILE SYSTEM WAS MODIFIED *****
/dev/vg00/data1: 11/327680 files (0.0% non-contiguous),
42078/1310720 blocks
[root@server1 ~]#_
```

> **Note** 📎
>
> The `badblocks` command can be used to perform the same function as the `e2fsck` command with the `-c` option.
>
> You cannot use the `fsck` command to check and repair an XFS filesystem. Instead, you can use the **`xfs_db` command** to examine an XFS filesystem for corruption, the **`xfs_repair` command** to check and repair an XFS filesystem, as well as the **`xfs_fsr` command** to optimize an XFS filesystem and minimize the chance of future corruption.

Recall from earlier in this chapter that the `fsck` command is run at boot time when filesystems are mounted from entries in the /etc/fstab file. Any entries in /etc/fstab that have a 1 in the sixth field are checked first, followed by entries that have a 2 in the sixth field. However, on many Linux systems, a full filesystem check is forced periodically each time an ext2, ext3, or ext4 filesystem is mounted. This might delay booting for several minutes or even hours, depending on the size of the filesystems being checked. To change this interval to a longer interval, such as 20 days, you can use the `-i` option to the **`tune2fs` command**, as shown next:

```
[root@server1 ~]# tune2fs -i 20d /dev/vg00/data
tune2fs 1.43.8 (1-Jan-2020)
Setting interval between checks to 1728000 seconds
[root@server1 ~]#_
```

The `tune2fs` command can be used to change or "tune" filesystem parameters after a filesystem has been created. Changing the interval between automatic filesystem checks to 0 disables filesystem checks altogether.

Disk Quotas

If there are several users on a Linux system, the system must have enough hard disk space to support the files that each user expects to store on the hard disk. However, if hard disk space is limited or company policy limits disk usage, you should impose limits on filesystem usage. These restrictions, called **disk quotas**, can be applied to users or groups of users. Furthermore, **quotas** can restrict how many files and directories a user can create (i.e., restrict the number of inodes created) on a particular filesystem or the total size of all files that a user can own on a filesystem. Two types of quota limits are available: soft limits and hard limits. **Soft limits** are disk quotas that the user can exceed for a certain period of time with warnings (seven days by default), whereas **hard limits** are rigid quotas that the user cannot exceed. Quotas are typically enabled at boot time if there are quota entries in /etc/fstab, but they can also be turned on and off afterward using the quotaon **command** and quotaoff **command**, respectively.

To set up quotas for the /data filesystem and restrict the user user1, you can perform the following steps:

1. Edit the /etc/fstab file to add the usrquota and grpquota mount options for the /data1 filesystem. The resulting line in /etc/fstab file should look like the following:

   ```
   [root@server1 ~]# grep data1 /etc/fstab
   /dev/vg00/data1    /data1  ext4    defaults,usrquota,grpquota  0 0
   [root@server1 ~]#_
   ```

Note 📎

You can also use journaled quotas on modern Linux kernels, which protects quota data during an unexpected shutdown. To use journaled quotas, replace the mount options of defaults,usrquota,grpquota in Step 1 with: defaults,usrjquota=aquota. user,grpjquota=aquota.group,jqfmt=vfsv0.

---

2. Remount the /data filesystem as read-write to update the system with the new options from /etc/fstab, as follows:

   ```
   [root@server1 ~]# mount /data1 -o remount,rw
   [root@server1 ~]#_
   ```

3. Run the quotacheck -mavugf -F vfsv0 command, which looks on the system for file ownership and creates the quota database (-f) using the default quota format (-F vfsv0) for all filesystems with quota options listed in /etc/fstab (-a), giving verbose output (-v) for all users and groups (-u and -g) even if the filesystem is used by other processes (-m). This creates and places

information in the /data/aquota.user and /data/aquota.group files. Sample output from the `quotacheck` command is shown here:

```
[root@server1 ~]# quotacheck -mavugf -F vfsv0
quotacheck: Your kernel probably supports journaled quota but
you are not using it. Consider switching to journaled quota
to avoid running quotacheck after an unclean shutdown.
quotacheck: Scanning /dev/mapper/vg00-data1 [/data1] done
quotacheck: Checked 4 directories and 17 files
[root@server1 ~]#_
```

> **Note** 📎
>
> If you receive any warnings at the beginning of the `quotacheck` output at this stage, you can safely ignore them because they are the result of newly created aquota.user and aquota.group files that have not been used yet.

4. Turn user and group quotas on for all filesystems that have quotas configured using the `quotaon -avug` command:

```
[root@server1 ~]# quotaon -avug
/dev/mapper/vg00-data1 [/data1]: group quotas turned on
/dev/mapper/vg00-data1 [/data1]: user quotas turned on
[root@server1 ~]#_
```

> **Note** 📎
>
> You can also enable and disable quotas for individual filesystems. For example, you can use the `quotaon /data1` command to enable quotas for the /data1 filesystem and the `quotaoff /data1` command to disable them.

5. Edit the quotas for certain users using the `edquota` command as follows: edquota -u <username>. This brings up the vi editor and allows you to set soft and hard quotas for the number of blocks a user can own on the filesystem (typically, 1 block = 1 kilobyte) and the total number of inodes (files and directories) that a user can own on the filesystem. A soft limit and hard limit of zero (0) indicates that there is no limit. To set a hard limit of 20MB (=20480KB) and 1000

inodes, as well as a soft limit of 18MB (=18432KB) and 900 inodes, you can do the following:

```
[root@server1 ~]# edquota -u user1
Disk quotas for user user1 (uid 1000):
  Filesystem                 blocks    soft    hard    inodes    soft    hard
, /dev/mapper/vg001-data1    1188         0       0       326         0       0
~
~
~
~
"/tmp//EdP.aclpslv" 3L, 216C
```

Next, place the appropriate values in the columns provided and then save and quit the vi editor:

```
Disk quotas for user user1 (uid 1000):
  Filesystem                 blocks    soft    hard    inodes    soft    hard
  /dev/mapper/vg00-data1     1188     18432   20480       326      900    1000
~
~
~
~
~
:wq
"/tmp/EdP.aclpslv" 3L, 216C written
[root@server1 ~]#_
```

6. Edit the time limit for which users can go beyond soft quotas using the edquota -u -t command. The default time limit for soft quotas is seven days, but it can be changed as follows:

```
[root@server1 ~]# edquota -u -t
Grace period before enforcing soft limits for users:
Time units may be: days, hours, minutes, or seconds
  Filesystem                Block grace period      Inode grace period
  /dev/mapper/vg00-data1         7days                    7days
~
~
~
"/tmp//EdP.alvzfSy" 4L, 233C
```

7. Ensure that quotas were updated properly by gathering a report for quotas by user on the /data filesystem using the repquota command, as shown in the following output:

```
[root@server1 ~]# repquota /data1
*** Report for user quotas on device /dev/mapper/vg00-data1
```

```
Block grace time: 7days; Inode grace time: 7days
                        Block limits             File limits
User            used    soft    hard  grace   used  soft  hard  grace
---------------------------------------------------------------------
root      --     573       0       0           20     0     0
user1     --    1188   18432   20480          326   900  1000
[root@server1 ~]#_
```

The aforementioned commands are only available to the root user; however, regular users can view their own quota using the `quota` **command**. The root user can also use the `quota` command but can also use it to view quotas of other users:

```
[root@server1 ~]# quota
Disk quotas for user root (uid 0): none
[root@server1 ~]# quota -u user1
Disk quotas for user user1 (uid 500):
Filesystem        blocks  quota  limit  grace  files  quota  limit grace
/dev/mapper/vg00-data1
                    1188  18432  20480           326    900   1000
[root@server1 ~]#_
```

Note

To configure and manage quotas for an XFS filesystem, you must use the `xfs_quota` **command**.

Chapter Summary

- Disk devices are represented by device files that reside in the /dev directory. These device files specify the type of data transfer, the major number of the device driver in the Linux kernel, and the minor number of the specific device.

- Each disk device must contain a filesystem, which is then mounted to the Linux directory tree for usage with the `mount`

command. The filesystem can later be unmounted using the `umount` command. The directory used to mount the device must not be in use by any logged-in users for mounting and unmounting to take place.

- Hard disks must be partitioned into distinct sections before filesystems are created on those partitions. To partition a hard disk with an MBR or GPT, you can use a wide variety of tools including `fdisk`, `cfdisk`, `gdisk`, and `parted`.

- Many filesystems are available to Linux; each filesystem is specialized for a certain purpose, and several filesystems can be mounted to different mount points on the directory tree. You can create a filesystem on a device using the `mkfs` command and its variants.

- The LVM can be used to create logical volumes from the free space within multiple partitions on the various hard disks within your system. Like standard hard disk partitions, logical volumes can contain a filesystem and be mounted to the Linux directory tree. They allow for the easy expansion and reconfiguration of storage.

- Most removable media devices are recognized as SCSI disks by the Linux system and are automounted by GUI environments.

- It is important to monitor disk usage using the `df`, `du`, and `dumpe2fs` commands to avoid running out of storage space. Similarly, it is important to check disks for errors using the `fsck` command and its variants.

- If hard disk space is limited, you can use disk quotas to limit the space that each user has on filesystems.

Key Terms

/dev directory	filesystem corruption	`mount` command
/etc/fstab	formatting	mount point
/etc/mtab	`fsck` (filesystem check)	mounting
/proc/devices	command	`parted` (GNU Parted)
bad blocks	`fuser` command	command
`blkid` command	`gdisk` (GPT fdisk) command	partition
block	hard limit	`partprobe` command
block devices	journaling	physical extent (PE) size
`cfdisk` command	Logical Volume (LV)	Physical Volumes (PVs)
character devices	Logical Volume Manager	pseudo filesystem
cylinder	(LVM)	`pvcreate` command
device file	`lsblk` command	`pvdisplay` command
`df` (disk free space)	`lsusb` command	`pvscan` command
command	`lvcreate` command	`quota` command
disk quotas	`lvdisplay` command	`quotaoff` command
`du` (directory usage)	`lvextend` command	`quotaon` command
command	`lvscan` command	quotas
`e2label` command	major number	`repquota` command
`edquota` command	minor number	`resize2fs` command
`eject` command	`mkfs` (make filesystem)	root filesystem
`exfatlabel` command	command	sector
`fatlabel` command	`mkisofs` command	soft limit
`fdisk` command	`mknod` command	`swapoff` command
filesystem	`mkswap` command	`swapon` command

syncing	vgcreate command	xfs_db command
track	vgdisplay command	xfs_fsr command
tune2fs command	vgextend command	xfs_growfs command
udev daemon	vgscan command	xfs_info command
umount command	virtual filesystem	xfs_quota command
Universally Unique	Volume Group (VG)	xfs_repair command
Identifier (UUID)	xfs_admin command	

Review Questions

1. Which of the following commands can only be used to create partitions on a GPT hard disk?
   a. gdisk
   b. cfdisk
   c. fdisk
   d. parted

2. After a partition on a hard disk is formatted with a filesystem, all partitions on that hard disk drive must use the same filesystem. True or False?

3. You want to see the filesystems that are in use on the system. What command could you use? (Choose all that apply.)
   a. cat /etc/fstab
   b. df -T
   c. cat /etc/mtab
   d. ls /sys/block

4. Jim has just installed two new SAS SSDs in his system. He properly installs the hardware in his machine. Before he can use them for data storage and retrieval, what must he do? (Choose all that apply.)
   a. Mount the two SSDs so they are accessible by the operating system.
   b. Mount a filesystem to each of SSDs.
   c. Create one or more partitions on each of the SSDs.
   d. Use the vi editor to edit /etc/mtab and create an entry for the SSDs.
   e. Mount any partitions created on the two SSDs such that they are accessible by the operating system.
   f. Format any partitions created on the SSDs with a valid filesystem recognized by Linux.

5. Given the following output from /etc/fstab, which filesystems will be automatically checked on boot by the fsck command?

/dev/sda1	/	ext4	defaults	1 1
none	/dev/pts	devpts	gid=5,mode=620	1 0
none	/proc	proc	defaults	0 1
none	/dev/shm	tmpfs	defaults	1 0
/dev/sdc2	swap	swap	defaults	0 1
/dev/dvd	/media/dvd	iso9660	noauto,ro	0 0

   a. none, as fsck must be run manually for each filesystem
   b. /, /dev/pts, and /dev/shm
   c. /, /proc, and swap
   d. all of them, as fsck is run automatically at boot for all filesystems

6. A user mounts a device to a mount point directory and realizes afterward she needs files previously found within the mount point directory. What should this user do?
   a. Nothing; the files are lost and cannot ever be accessed.
   b. Nothing; the files could not have been there because you can only mount to empty directories.
   c. Unmount the device from the directory.
   d. Run the `fsck` command to recover the file.
   e. Look in the lost+found directory for the file.

7. Which command is used to display the amount of free space that exists on a filesystem?
   a. `fsck`
   b. `quota`
   c. `du`
   d. `df`

8. What must you do to successfully run the `fsck` command on a filesystem?
   a. Run the `fsck` command with the `-u` option to automatically unmount the filesystem first.
   b. Choose yes when warned that running `fsck` on a mounted filesystem can cause damage.
   c. Unmount the filesystem.
   d. Ensure that the filesystem is mounted.

9. Character devices typically transfer data more quickly than block devices. True or False?

10. What does the `du -s /var` command do?
    a. shows the users connected to the /var directory
    b. shows the size of all directories within the /var directory
    c. dumps the /var directory
    d. displays the total size of the /var directory

11. What does the command `dumpe2fs -h` do?
    a. backs up an ext2 filesystem
    b. displays the number of used and available inodes for an ext2/ext3/ext4 filesystem
    c. dumps an ext2 filesystem
    d. nothing; it is not a valid command

12. Which command can be used to repair an XFS filesystem?
    a. `fsck -t xfs /dev/sdb1`
    b. `e2fsck /dev/sdb1`
    c. `fsck.xfs /dev/sdb1`
    d. `xfs_repair /dev/sdb1`

13. Which of the following statements are true? (Choose all that apply.)
    a. Quotas can only limit user space.
    b. Quotas can only limit the number of files a user can own.
    c. Quotas can limit both user space and the number of files a user can own.
    d. Hard limits can never be exceeded.
    e. Hard limits allow a user to exceed them for a certain period of time.
    f. Soft limits can never be exceeded.
    g. Soft limits allow a user to exceed them for a certain period of time.
    h. Either a hard limit or a soft limit can be set, but not both concurrently.

14. A device file _____. (Choose all that apply.)
    a. has no inode section
    b. has no data section
    c. displays a major and minor number in place of a file size
    d. has a fixed size of 300 kilobytes

15. Which of the following statements regarding LVM structure is correct?
    a. PVs are collections of VGs.
    b. LVs are created from the free space available within PVs.
    c. VGs are comprised of one or more PVs.
    d. PVs use the space within LVs to create VGs.

16. The `lvextend` command can be used to add unused space within a volume group to an existing logical volume. True or False?

17. You plug a USB flash memory drive into a system that has two SATA hard disks. How will the partition on this USB flash memory drive be identified by Linux?
    a. /dev/sda1
    b. /dev/sda2
    c. /dev/sdb1
    d. /dev/sdc1

18. Which command mounts all existing filesystems in /etc/fstab?
    a. `mount -f`
    b. `mount -a`
    c. `mount /etc/fstab`
    d. `mount /etc/mtab`

19. A user runs the `fsck` command with the `-f` option on an ext4 filesystem that is showing signs of corruption. How would that user locate any files the system was unable to repair?
    a. Look in the root of the filesystem.
    b. The system prompts the user for a target location when it comes across a file it cannot repair.
    c. Mount the filesystem and check the lost+found directory underneath the mount point.
    d. View the contents of the directory /lost+found.

20. Which command is used to format a partition on a hard disk drive with the ext4 filesystem?
    a. `format_ext4` *device*
    b. `ext4mkfs` *device*
    c. `e2mkfs -t ext4` *device*
    d. `makeext4FS` *device*

Hands-On Projects

These projects should be completed in the order given. The hands-on projects presented in this chapter should take a total of three hours to complete. The requirements for this lab include:

- A computer with Fedora 28 installed according to Hands-On Project 2-1

Project 5-1

In this hands-on project, you view and create device files.

1. Boot your Fedora Linux virtual machine. After your Linux system has loaded, switch to a command-line terminal (tty5) by pressing **Ctrl+Alt+F5**. Log in to the terminal using the user name of **root** and the password of **LINUXrocks!**.

2. At the command prompt, type `ls -l /dev/tty6` and press **Enter**. What device does /dev/tty6 represent? Is this file a block or character device file? Why? What are the major and minor numbers for this file?

3. At the command prompt, type `rm -f /dev/tty6` and press **Enter**. Next, type `ls -l /dev/tty6` at the command prompt and press **Enter**. Was the file removed successfully?

4. Switch to tty6 by pressing **Ctrl+Alt+F6** and attempt to log in to the terminal using the user name of **root** and the password of **LINUXrocks!**. Were you successful?

5. Switch back to tty5 by pressing **Ctrl+Alt+F5**, type the command `mknod /dev/tty6 c 4 6` at the command prompt, and press **Enter**. What did this command do? Next, type `ls -l /dev/tty6` at the command prompt and press **Enter**. Was the file re-created successfully?

6. Switch back to tty6 by pressing **Ctrl+Alt+F6** and log in to the terminal using the user name of **root** and the password of **LINUXrocks!**. Why were you successful?

7. At the command prompt, type `ls -l /dev/tty?` and press **Enter**. What is similar about all of these files? Is the major number different for each file? Is the minor number different for each file? Why?

8. At the command prompt, type `find /dev` and press **Enter** to list all of the filenames under the /dev directory. Are there many files? Next, type `du -s /dev` at the command prompt and press **Enter**. How large in kilobytes are all files within the /dev directory? Why?

9. At the command prompt, type `less /proc/devices` and press **Enter**. Which devices and major numbers are present on your system? What character devices have a major number of 4? How does this compare with what you observed in Step 2? Press **q** to exit the less utility when finished.

10. Type `exit` and press **Enter** to log out of your shell.

Project 5-2

In this hands-on project, you practice mounting and viewing removable DVD media.

1. Switch to the graphical terminal (tty1) by pressing **Ctrl+Alt+F1** and log in to the GNOME desktop using your user account and the password of **LINUXrocks!**.

2. In your virtualization software, attach the DVD ISO image for Fedora Linux (Fedora-Workstation-Live-x86_64-28-1.1.iso) to the DVD drive for the virtual machine. After you have completed this action, view your Files application. Is there an icon that represents your Fedora Live Desktop DVD in the left pane? Place your mouse over this icon to view the mount point directory. Which directory was your DVD automatically mounted to? Take a few moments to explore the contents of the DVD within the Files application. When finished, close the Files application.

3. Switch to a command-line terminal (tty5) by pressing **Ctrl+Alt+F5**. Log in to the terminal using the user name of **root** and the password of **LINUXrocks!**.

4. At the command prompt, type `du -hT` and press **Enter**. Is your Fedora DVD still mounted? What filesystem type is used? What device file is used? Next, type `ls -l /dev/cdrom` and press **Enter**. Is /dev/cdrom a symbolic link to this device file?

5. At the command prompt, type `umount /dev/cdrom` and press **Enter** to unmount your Fedora DVD. Next, type `du -hT` and press **Enter** to verify that it is no longer mounted.

6. At the command prompt, type `cp /etc/hosts /mnt` and press **Enter**. Next, type `ls /mnt` and press **Enter** to verify that the /etc/hosts file was successfully copied to the /mnt directory.

7. At the command prompt, type `mount /dev/cdrom /mnt` and press **Enter**. What warning did you receive? Next, type `du -hT` and press **Enter** to verify that your Fedora DVD is mounted to the /mnt directory.

8. At the command prompt, type `mount` and press **Enter** and view the output. Next, type `cat /etc/mtab` and press **Enter**. Is the output shown by these commands more verbose than in Step 7?

9. At the command prompt, type `cd /mnt` and press **Enter**. Next, type `ls -F` and press **Enter**. Are the contents of the DVD the same as Step 2?

10. At the command prompt, type `umount /mnt` and press **Enter**. What error did you receive? Next, type `fuser -u /mnt` and press **Enter**. Note that you are currently using the /mnt directory, which prevents unmounting.

11. At the command prompt, type `cd` and press **Enter** to return to your home directory and then type `umount /mnt` and press **Enter** to unmount your Fedora DVD.

12. At the command prompt, type `ls /mnt` and press **Enter**. Is the copy of /etc/hosts available again after the Fedora DVD was unmounted?

13. Type `exit` and press **Enter** to log out of your shell.

Project 5-3

In this hands-on project, you work with standard hard disk partitions. You will first create a hard disk partition using the fdisk utility. Next, you create an ext4 filesystem on the partition and mount it to the directory tree. Finally, you use the /etc/fstab file to automatically mount the partition at boot time.

1. Switch to a command-line terminal (tty5) by pressing **Ctrl+Alt+F5** and log in to the terminal using the user name of **root** and the password of **LINUXrocks!**.

2. At the command prompt, type `lsblk` and press **Enter**. What block device holds the partitions that you created during Fedora installation? Also note that you have three partitions under this block device: the first partition is mounted to the /boot directory, the second partition is used as Linux swap and the third partition is mounted to the / directory.

3. At the command prompt, type `fdisk /dev/sda` and press **Enter**. At the `fdisk` prompt, type `m` and press **Enter** to view the various `fdisk` commands.

4. At the `fdisk` prompt, type `p` and press **Enter** to view the partition table on your hard disk. Do the partitions match the output from Step 2?

5. At the `fdisk` prompt, type `n` and press **Enter** to create a new partition. Next, type `e` to select an extended partition and press **Enter**. When prompted for the start sector, observe the valid range within the brackets and press **Enter** to select the default (the first available sector). When prompted for the end cylinder, observe the valid range within the brackets and press **Enter** to select the default (the last available sector).

6. At the `fdisk` prompt, type **p** and press **Enter** to view the partition table on your hard disk. How many partitions are present? What type of partition is /dev/sda4?

7. At the `fdisk` prompt, type **n** and press **Enter** to create a new partition. Note that logical drive is automatically selected as the partition type because all available primary partitions have been used and there is already an extended partition. When prompted for the start sector, observe the valid range within the brackets and press **Enter** to select the default (the first available sector). When prompted for the end cylinder, type **+1GB** and press **Enter**.

8. At the `fdisk` prompt, type **p** and press **Enter** to view the partition table on your hard disk. How many partitions are present? What type of partition is /dev/sda5?

9. At the `fdisk` prompt, type **l** and press **Enter** to view the different partition types. What type is used for Linux swap? Which character would you type at the fdisk prompt to change the type of partition?

10. At the `fdisk` prompt, type **w** and press **Enter** to save the changes to the hard disk and exit the fdisk utility.

11. At the command prompt, type **reboot** and press **Enter** to reboot your machine and ensure that the partition table was read into memory correctly. After your Linux system has been loaded, switch to a command-line terminal (tty5) by pressing **Ctrl+Alt+F5** and log in to the terminal using the user name of **root** and the password of **LINUXrocks!**.

12. At the command prompt, type **mkfs -t ext4 /dev/sda5** and press **Enter** to format the first logical drive on your first hard disk with the ext4 filesystem.

13. At the command prompt, type **mkdir /newmount** and press **Enter** to create a mount point directory under the / directory for mounting the third partition on your first hard disk.

14. At the command prompt, type **mount -t ext4 /dev/sda5 /newmount** and press **Enter** to mount the filesystem on your first logical drive in the extended partition to the /newmount directory. Next, type the **df -hT** command and press **Enter** to verify that the filesystem was mounted correctly.

15. At the command prompt, type **ls -F /newmount** and press **Enter**. Is the lost+found directory present? Next, type **cp /etc/hosts /newmount** at the command prompt and press **Enter** to copy the hosts file to the new partition. Verify that the copy was successful by typing the **ls -F /newmount** command at the command prompt again, and press **Enter**.

16. At the command prompt, type **umount /newmount** and press **Enter**. Next, type the **df -hT** command and press **Enter** to verify that the filesystem was unmounted correctly.

17. At the command prompt, type **vi /etc/fstab** and press **Enter**. Observe the contents of the file. Add a line to the bottom of the file as shown below:

```
/dev/sda5 /newmount ext4 defaults 0 0
```

18. Save your changes and quit the vi editor.

19. At the command prompt, type `reboot` and press **Enter**. After your Linux system has been loaded, switch to a command-line terminal (tty5) by pressing **Ctrl+Alt+F5** and log in to the terminal using the user name of **root** and the password of **LINUXrocks!**.

20. At the command prompt, type `mount` and press **Enter**. Is your new filesystem mounted? Why?

21. At the command prompt, type `umount /newmount` and press **Enter**. Next, type the `df -hT` command to verify that the filesystem was unmounted correctly.

22. At the command prompt, type `mount -a` and press **Enter**. Next, type the `df -hT` command and press **Enter**. Is the third partition on your hard disk mounted? Why?

23. Type `exit` and press **Enter** to log out of your shell.

Project 5-4

In this hands-on project, you create two new partitions using the GNU Parted utility, and configure the LVM to host an LV using the space within. During this process, you will learn how to create PVs, VGs, and LVs, as well as add storage to extend a VG and LV. Finally, you will edit the /etc/fstab file to ensure that your LV is mounted at boot time.

1. Switch to a command-line terminal (tty5) by pressing **Ctrl+Alt+F5** and log in to the terminal using the user name of **root** and the password of **LINUXrocks!**.

2. At the command prompt, type `parted /dev/sda` and press **Enter**. At the parted prompt, type `help` and press **Enter** to view the available commands.

3. At the parted prompt, type `print` and press **Enter**. Write down the End value for your first logical drive (/dev/sda5): _____ (A). Next, write down the End value for your extended partition (/dev/sda4): _____ (B). These two values represent the start and end of the remainder of the free space on your virtual hard disk.

4. At the parted prompt, type `mkpart` and press **Enter** to accept the default of logical drive. Press **Enter** again to accept the default partition type (Linux ext2). When prompted for the Start of the new partition, enter the (A) value you recorded in Step 3 and press **Enter**. When prompted for the End of the new partition, enter the (A) value you recorded in Step 3 plus 1GB and press **Enter** to create a 1GB partition.

5. At the parted prompt, type `p` and press **Enter** to view the partition table on your hard disk. What type of partition is /dev/sda6? Write down the End value for your second logical drive (/dev/sda6): _____ (C).

6. At the parted prompt, type `mkpart` and press **Enter** to accept the default of logical drive. Press **Enter** again to accept the default partition type (Linux ext2). When prompted for the Start of the new partition, enter the (C) value you recorded in Step 5 and press **Enter**. When prompted for the End of the new partition, enter the (C) value you recorded in Step 5 plus 1GB and press **Enter** to create another 1GB partition.

7. At the parted prompt, type `quit` and press **Enter** to save the changes to the hard disk and exit the GNU Parted utility.

8. At the command prompt, type `reboot` and press **Enter** to reboot your machine and ensure that the partition table was read into memory correctly. After your Linux system

has been loaded, switch to a command-line terminal (tty5) by pressing **Ctrl+Alt+F5** and log in to the terminal using the user name of **root** and the password of **LINUXrocks!**.

9. At the command prompt, type `pvcreate /dev/sda6` and press **Enter**. Next, type `pvscan` and press **Enter** to verify the creation of your PV. Following this, type `pvdisplay` and press **Enter** to view the PE size chosen as well as the total size of the PV.

10. At the command prompt, type `vgcreate vg00 /dev/sda6` and press **Enter**. Next, type `vgscan` and press **Enter** to verify the creation of your vg00 VG. Following this, type `vgdisplay` and press **Enter** to view the PE size chosen as well as the total size of your VG.

11. At the command prompt, type `lvcreate -L 0.9GB -n newdata vg00` and press **Enter** to create a 0.9GB LV called newdata from the vg00 VG. Why couldn't you specify a 1GB size for your LV? Next, type `lvscan` and press **Enter** to verify the creation of your LV. Following this, type `lvdisplay` and press **Enter** to view the path to the LV device file as well as the total size of your LV.

12. At the command prompt, type `mkfs -t ext4 /dev/vg00/newdata` and press **Enter** to format the newdata LV using the ext4 filesystem. Next, type `mkdir /newdata` and press **Enter** to create a mount point for the newdata LV. Following this, type `mount /dev/vg00/newdata /newdata` and press **Enter** to mount the newdata LV to the /newdata directory.

13. At the command prompt, type `df -hT` and press **Enter** to verify that your LV is mounted via the device mapper. Next, type `ls -l /dev/vg00/newdata` and press **Enter**, noting it is a symbolic link to a device mapper device file. Following this, type `lsblk` and press **Enter** to note the relationship between your LV and your PV (/dev/sda6).

14. At the command prompt, type `ls -F /newdata` and press **Enter**. Is there a lost+found directory available? Why?

15. At the command prompt, type `pvcreate /dev/sda7` and press **Enter**. Next, type `pvscan` and press **Enter** to verify the creation of your PV. Following this, type `pvdisplay` and press **Enter** to view the PE size chosen as well as the total size of the PV.

16. At the command prompt, type `vgextend vg00 /dev/sda7` and press **Enter**. Next, type `vgdisplay` and press **Enter** to view the PE size chosen as well as note that the total size of your VG reflects both PVs.

17. At the command prompt, type `lvextend -L +0.9GB -r /dev/vg00/newdata` and press **Enter** to extend your newdata LV by another 0.9GB. Next, type `lvdisplay` and press **Enter**, noting the size has doubled. Following this, type `df -hT` and press **Enter**, noting the ext4 filesystem was automatically resized to match the new LV capacity.

18. At the command prompt, type `lsblk` and press **Enter** to note the relationship between your LV and your two PVs (/dev/sda6 and /dev/sda7).

19. At the command prompt, type `vi /etc/fstab` and press **Enter**. Add the following line to the bottom of the file to ensure that the newdata LV is mounted at boot time:

```
/dev/vg00/newdata /newdata ext4 defaults 0 0
```

20. Save your changes and quit the vi editor.

21. At the command prompt, type `reboot` and press **Enter**. After your Linux system has been loaded, switch to a command-line terminal (tty5) by pressing **Ctrl+Alt+F5** and log in to the terminal using the user name of **root** and the password of **LINUXrocks!**.

22. At the command prompt, type `df -hT` and press **Enter** to verify that your LV was automatically mounted at boot time.

23. Type `exit` and press **Enter** to log out of your shell.

Project 5-5

In this hands-on project, you view disk usage and check filesystems for errors.

1. Switch to a command-line terminal (tty5) by pressing **Ctrl+Alt+F5** and log in to the terminal using the user name of **root** and the password of **LINUXrocks!**.

2. At the command prompt, type `df -hT` and press **Enter**. What nonvirtual filesystems are displayed? Can you see the swap partition? Why?

3. At the command prompt, type `dumpe2fs -h /dev/vg00/newdata | more` and press **Enter**. How many inodes are available to this filesystem? How many inodes are free to be used? Why?

4. At the command prompt, type `fsck /dev/vg00/newdata` and press **Enter**. What error message do you receive and why?

5. At the command prompt, type `umount /newdata` and press **Enter**. Next, type `fsck /dev/vg00/newdata` and press **Enter**. How long did the filesystem check take and why?

6. At the command prompt, type `fsck -f /dev/vg00/newdata` and press **Enter**. How long did the filesystem check take and why?

7. At the command prompt, type `e2fsck -c /dev/vg00/newdata` and press **Enter**. What does this command do?

8. At the command prompt, type `tune2fs -i 0 /dev/vg00/newdata` and press **Enter** to change the interval for forced checks such that they are avoided. Is this a good idea for the ext4 filesystem? Why?

9. At the command prompt, type `mount /dev/vg00/newdata` and press **Enter**. Next, type the `df -hT` command and press **Enter** to verify that the filesystem was mounted correctly. Why did the `mount` command work even though you didn't specify the mount point directory?

10. Type **exit** and press **Enter** to log out of your shell.

Project 5-6

In this hands-on project, you enable, set, and view disk quotas for the /newmount filesystem created earlier in Project 5-3.

1. Switch to a command-line terminal (tty5) by pressing **Ctrl+Alt+F5** and log in to the terminal using the user name of **root** and the password of **LINUXrocks!**.

2. At the command prompt, type `chmod 777 /newmount` to give all users the ability to create files within the /newmount directory.
3. Switch to tty6 by pressing **Ctrl**+**Alt**+**F6** and log in to the terminal using the user name of **user1** and the password of **LINUXrocks!**.
4. At the command prompt, type `touch /newmount/samplefile` and press **Enter** to create a file in /newmount that is owned by the user user1.
5. Type `exit` and press **Enter** to log out of your shell.
6. Switch back to tty5 by pressing **Ctrl**+**Alt**+**F5** and note that you are still logged in as the root user on this terminal.
7. At the command prompt, type `vi /etc/fstab` and press **Enter**. Observe the options for the /newmount filesystem. Change the line that mounts /dev/sda5 to the following:

    ```
    /dev/sda5    /newmount    ext4    defaults,usrquota,grpquota    0 0
    ```

8. Save your changes and quit the vi editor.
9. Remount the filesystem as read-write by typing the command `mount /newmount -o remount,rw` and press **Enter**.
10. At the command prompt, type `quotacheck -mavugf -F vfsv0` and press **Enter**. Ignore any warnings that appear. What does this command do? Next, type `ls -l /newmount` and press **Enter**. What are the sizes of the aquota.user and aquota.group files? What are these files used for?
11. At the command prompt, type `quotaon -avug` and press **Enter** to activate quotas for all partitions that have quota options defined within /etc/fstab.
12. At the command prompt, type `edquota -u user1` and press **Enter**. Are there any quota limits applied to the user user1 by default? Change the value of the soft quota for blocks to `50000` and the value of the hard quota for blocks to `60000`. Similarly, change the value of the soft quota for inodes to `300` and the value of the hard quota for inodes to `400`. How many files and directories can user1 create on this partition? How much space can user1 use in total on this partition?
13. Save your changes and quit the vi editor.
14. At the command prompt, type `edquota -u -t` and press **Enter**. Change the time limit for users who extend the soft limit to `5 days` for both inodes and blocks.
15. Save your changes and quit the vi editor.
16. At the command prompt, type `repquota /newmount` and press **Enter**. Are the quota changes you made for the user user1 visible? How many files has user1 stored on this volume so far? What is the total size of those files (in 1KB blocks) and why?
17. At the command prompt, type `quota -u user1` and press **Enter**. How do the values compare with those from the previous step?
18. Type `exit` and press **Enter** to log out of your shell.

Project 5-7

In this hands-on project, you create a new partition using the `cfdisk` utility, format and check an XFS filesystem on that partition, as well as mount the filesystem using a GUID at boot time.

1. Switch to a command-line terminal (tty5) by pressing **Ctrl+Alt+F5** and log in to the terminal using the user name of **root** and the password of **LINUXrocks!**.
2. At the command prompt, type `cfdisk /dev/sda` and press **Enter**. Highlight the **Free space** within the `cfdisk` utility and select **New**. Specify a partition size of 2G and press **Enter**. Note that `cfdisk` creates the next logical drive (/dev/sda8) of type Linux (83).
3. Select **Write** to save your changes; type **yes** and press **Enter** when prompted to confirm. Next, select **Quit** to save your changes and exit the `cfdisk` utility.
4. At the command prompt, type `reboot` and press **Enter** to reboot your machine and ensure that the partition table was read into memory correctly. After your Linux system has been loaded, switch to a command-line terminal (tty5) by pressing **Ctrl+Alt+F5** and log in to the terminal using the user name of **root** and the password of **LINUXrocks!**.
5. At the command prompt, type `mkfs -t xfs /dev/sda8` and press **Enter**. Next, type `mkdir /xfsmount` and press **Enter** to create a mount point directory for your filesystem. Following this, type `mount /dev/sda8 /xfsmount` and press **Enter**.
6. At the command prompt, type `df -hT` and press **Enter** to verify that your XFS filesystem was mounted successfully. Next, type `ls /xfsmount` and press **Enter**. Why is there no lost+found directory?
7. At the command prompt, type `umount /xfsmount` and press **Enter**. Next, type `fsck -f /dev/sda8` and press **Enter**. Why did you receive an error? Following this, type `xfs_repair /dev/sda8` and press **Enter**.
8. At the command prompt, type `blkid` and press **Enter**. Record the UUID of your XFS filesystem (/dev/sda8): _____.
9. At the command prompt, type `vi /etc/fstab` and press **Enter**. Add the following line to the bottom of the file, where `filesystemUUID` is the UUID that you recorded in the previous step:

   ```
   UUID="filesystemUUID" /xfsmount xfs defaults 0 0
   ```

10. Save your changes and quit the vi editor.
11. At the command prompt, type `reboot` and press **Enter** to reboot your machine and ensure that the partition table was read into memory correctly. After your Linux system has been loaded, switch to a command-line terminal (tty5) by pressing **Ctrl+Alt+F5** and log in to the terminal using the user name of **root** and the password of **LINUXrocks!**.
12. At the command prompt, type `df -hT` and press **Enter**. Is your XFS filesystem mounted?
13. Type `exit` and press **Enter** to log out of your shell.

Discovery Exercises

1. Answer the following questions regarding your system using the commands listed in this chapter. For each question, write the command you used to obtain the answer. If there are multiple commands that can be used to obtain the answer, list all of the commands available.

    a. What are the total number of inodes in the root filesystem? How many are currently utilized? How many are available for use?

    b. What filesystems are currently mounted on your system?

    c. What filesystems are available to be mounted on your system?

    d. What filesystems will be automatically mounted at boot time?

2. Power off your virtual machine. Next, use your virtualization software to add a second 8GB hard disk to your virtual machine that will be recognized as /dev/sdb. Create two 4GB partitions on this device.

    a. For the first partition, use the appropriate commands to add the available space to the vg00 VG that you created in Project 5-4, and extend your newdata LV to use the additional space.

    b. For the second partition, create an exFAT filesystem and mount it to the /exFATdata directory. Modify the /etc/fstab file to mount the filesystem automatically at boot time by label. Finally, perform a filesystem check on your new exFAT filesystem.

3. Provided that your virtualization software allows for USB device pass-through, connect a USB flash memory drive to your system. Use the appropriate commands to locate the device file used by the device, mount the filesystem to a directory of your choice, and check the filesystem for errors. Finally, add a line to /etc/fstab to ensure that the filesystem can be easily mounted in the future (this line should not automount the filesystem at boot time).

4. Provided that your virtualization software supports the creation of NVMe SSDs, attach an NVMe controller and SSD to your virtual machine and create a partition within the first namespace that is formatted using XFS. Next, create a mount point directory for it called /SSD and mount your new filesystem to this directory, ensuring that it is mounted automatically by UUID at boot time from the appropriate entry within /etc/fstab. Note that Oracle VirtualBox requires that you first download and install the Oracle VirtualBox Extension Pack in order to obtain NVMe support.

5. Use the Internet to gather information on four filesystems compatible with Linux. For each filesystem, list the situations for which the filesystem was designed and the key features that the filesystem provides.

6. You have a Linux system that has a 1000GB SSD, which has a 90GB partition containing an ext4 filesystem mounted to the / directory and a 4GB swap partition. Currently, this Linux system is only used by a few users for storing small files; however, the department manager wants to upgrade this system and use it to run a database application that will be used by 100 users. The

database application and the associated data will take up over 200GB of hard disk space. In addition, these 100 users will store their personal files on the hard disk of the system. Each user must have a maximum of 5GB of storage space. The department manager has made it very clear that this system must not exhibit any downtime as a result of hard disk errors. How much hard disk space will you require, and what partitions would you need to ensure that the system will perform as needed? Where would these partitions be mounted? What quotas would you implement? What commands would you need to run and what entries to /etc/fstab would you need to create? Justify your answers.

7. You have several filesystems on your hard disk that are mounted to separate directories on the Linux directory tree. The /dev/sdc6 filesystem was unable to be mounted at boot time. What could have caused this? What commands could you use to find more information about the nature of the problem?

## CHAPTER 6

LINUX SERVER DEPLOYMENT

After completing this chapter, you will be able to:

Identify the types of hardware present in most server systems

Describe the configuration of SCSI devices and SANs

Explain the different levels of RAID and types of RAID configurations

Configure the ZFS and BTRFS filesystems

Install a Linux server distribution

Troubleshoot the Linux server installation process

Identify and resolve issues related to hardware device driver support

Access an installed system using system rescue

In Chapter 2, you examined a standard Linux installation process using common hardware components and practices. This chapter examines the specialized hardware and software configurations that affect your choices as you install a Linux server distribution. In addition, you install the Ubuntu Server Linux distribution (modern and legacy) and learn how to deal with common installation problems. Finally, this chapter discusses how to access and use system rescue.

Understanding Server Hardware

Recall from Chapter 2 that the minimum hardware requirements for Fedora Linux include a meager 1GHz CPU, 1GB of RAM, and 10GB of disk space, which is far lower than most modern operating systems. However, Linux is incredibly scalable and often configured to work with far more hardware to perform a specialized set of tasks. For example, a Linux computer used as a desktop workstation usually requires enough RAM to run GNOME and desktop applications smoothly, as well as a modern CPU and plenty of disk space to store files, pictures, movies, and so on. An Intel Core i5 system with 16GB of RAM and a 500GB SSD is typical hardware for a Linux desktop workstation. If the workstation is for personal use or gaming, expect to add a high-end graphics card supported by game platforms, such as Steam. For server computers, the amount of hardware should adequately support its intended use. A Linux Web server that handles e-commerce and a database engine may require 128GB of RAM, multiple CPUs, and high-capacity SSDs to host the operating system, Web server software, and database engine.

Nearly all standard server hardware is supported by Linux. If you have recently purchased modern server hardware, most likely your Linux distribution has all of the drivers that you need. However, if your system has specialized hardware (e.g., a specific Fibre Channel controller), first verify with the hardware vendor that it has an adequate driver included for your Linux distribution (or available for download).

The form factor for server hardware is different from other computers. Nearly all servers within an organization are housed within a rackmount case mounted alongside other servers on a vertical server storage rack. Consequently, these servers are called **rackmount servers**.

Note

Rackmount servers are sometimes called **blade servers**.

Each rackmount server may contain a different operating system (or multiple operating systems if virtualization software is used) and connect to a shared monitor/keyboard/mouse. The shared monitor/keyboard/mouse often folds into the rack for storage, and is used for initial configuration tasks such as server installation. All other server administration is performed remotely using the remote administration methods discussed in Chapter 12.

Most racks also contain one or more **Storage Area Network (SAN)** devices that provide a large amount of hard disk or SSD storage for the servers within the rack. They also include one or more **uninterruptible power supply (UPS)** devices to provide backup battery power to servers and SANs within the rack in the event of a power loss.

The minimum height of a rackmount server is 1.75 inches; this is called a **1U server**. Most 1U servers have up to two hard drives (or SSDs) and up to two CPUs. Other rackmount servers take up more than one spot on the rack. Their height is a multiple of a 1U server. For example, a 2U server is twice as high as a 1U server and often contains up to four CPUs and eight hard disks (or SSDs). Rackmount servers rarely exceed 4U, but SAN devices are often 4U or more.

Figure 6-1 shows a sample server rack configuration that hosts three 1U servers (Web server, file server, and firewall server), two 2U servers (database server and email server), a 2U UPS, a 4U SAN, and a management station with a shared monitor/keyboard/mouse.

Figure 6-1   A sample server rack

Note 📎

If NVMe SSDs are used, then the number of SSDs within a rackmount server or SAN may be substantially higher due to the small physical size of NVMe devices.

Understanding Server Virtualization

Virtualization is the process of running more than one operating system at the same time on a single computer, and has been used in various capacities since the dawn of computing in the 1960s. To perform virtualization, you must use software that allows the hardware to host multiple operating systems. This software is called a **hypervisor**, and serves to efficiently handle simultaneous requests for underlying hardware.

Type 2 hypervisors are designed to run on an existing workstation operating system (referred to as the **host operating system**). All additional operating systems (called guest operating systems or virtual machines) must access the hardware through the hypervisor and the underlying host operating system. Type 2 hypervisors are common today for software testing and development. For example, a software developer can test a specific application or Web app on a variety of operating systems without requiring separate computers. Many college technology courses also take advantage of Type 2 hypervisors to run multiple operating systems within a classroom or lab environment.

Note

Common Type 2 hypervisors include VMWare Workstation, Oracle VirtualBox, and Hyper-V (early versions).

By the mid-2000s, a typical server closet or data center contained many individual rackmount servers. To maintain security and stability, each rackmount server contained a single or a small number of separate server software applications. Often, one rackmount server hosted Web server software, while another hosted file sharing services, and so on. Unfortunately, most of these server software applications used only a small fraction of the actual rackmount server hardware. Supplying power and cooling the rackmount servers was expensive. To solve these problems, many IT administrators turned to server virtualization, but with a **Type 1 hypervisor** to ensure that each virtual machine would run as efficiently as possible. A Type 1 hypervisor interacts with the hardware directly and contains a small operating system to manage the hypervisor configuration and virtual machines. Figure 6-2 shows the difference between Type 1 and Type 2 hypervisors.

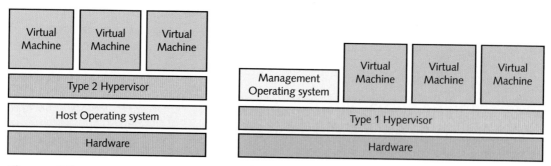

Figure 6-2 **Comparing Type 1 and Type 2 hypervisors**

Note 📎

Common Type 1 hypervisors include VMWare ESX/ESXi, Microsoft Hyper-V (later versions), and Linux KVM. Each of these hypervisors can also be used alongside IaaS cloud technologies like OpenStack (discussed in Chapter 1) to provide access to thousands of different virtual machines within a datacenter across the Internet.

Nearly all hypervisors today require that your CPU supports hypervisor acceleration; this is called Intel-VT (for Intel CPUs) and AMD-V (for AMD CPUs).

The Linux kernel has built-in hypervisor functionality called **Kernel Virtual Machine (KVM)**. KVM works with another Linux software package called **Quick Emulator (Qemu)** to provide near native speed for virtual machines using a process called binary translation. You can use KVM and Qemu to run virtual machines of other Linux and non-Linux operating systems on a Linux desktop workstation similar to how Type 2 hypervisors are used today. Alternatively, you can run a Linux system that only provides KVM and Qemu functionality to run several server virtual machines faster; in this configuration, KVM and Qemu work as a Type 1 hypervisor, and the Linux system is merely used to manage the hypervisor functionality.

Regardless of the hypervisor used, all virtual machines store their configuration in a small configuration file specific to the hypervisor. They store the actual operating system data for the virtual machine in a virtual hard disk file. When you create a virtual machine, you must choose the size of this virtual hard disk file. You must also specify whether the space allocated for the virtual hard disk file is set to a fixed size during creation (called **thick provisioning**) or dynamically allocated as the virtual machine uses the space (called **thin provisioning**). For example, if you create a 250GB fixed sized virtual disk, then 250GB is reserved on the storage device immediately; however, if you create a disk with thin provisioning, it uses a small virtual disk file that can grow up to 250GB as the virtual machine stores more data. Thin provisioning is often preferred for server virtualization as it conserves space on the underlying server storage hardware.

Note 📎

Hyper-V virtual hard disk files have a `.vhdx` extension, VMWare virtual hard disk files have a `.vmdk` extension, Oracle VirtualBox virtual hard disk files have a `.vdi` extension, and KVM/Qemu virtual hard disk files have either a `.qcow2` extension or omit the extension altogether.

> **Note** 📎
>
> Many hypervisors support virtual machine **snapshots**. If you take a snapshot of a virtual machine, it creates a second virtual hard disk file that stores any changes to the operating system after the time the snapshot was taken. This is useful before testing a risky software configuration; if the software configuration fails, the snapshot can be used to roll back the operating system to the state it was at before the software configuration was applied.

To create and manage KVM/Qemu virtual machines, a Linux system must have virtualization libraries (libvirt) installed as well as a program that can use these libraries to perform virtualization functions. In Fedora 28, KVM and Qemu can be easily configured and managed using a program called **Boxes** within the GNOME desktop, but you can also install other graphical and command-line virtual machine creation and management tools, such as `virsh`, `virt-install`, and `virt-manager`.

You can use Boxes to manage multiple KVM/Qemu virtual machines hosted on the local computer or on other computers across the network using the graphical **Virtual Network Computing (VNC)** protocol, or the faster **Simple Protocol for Independent Computing Environments (SPICE)** protocol and related QXL graphical driver framework, which is the default in Fedora 28. Figure 6-3 shows a SPICE connection to a Windows Server 2016 virtual machine.

Figure 6-3 Managing a Windows Server virtual machine using Boxes

Source: Used with permissions from Microsoft

Note

While most Linux guest operating systems already contain SPICE and QXL support, you should install the guest tools from *https://spice-space.org* on other guest operating systems, such as Windows, in order to obtain full remote management functionality within Boxes.

To configure and manage virtual machines, you can navigate to Activities, Show Applications, Boxes to open the Boxes interface shown in Figure 6-4. Click the New button shown in Figure 6-4 to choose the installation source files and the amount of memory and disk space to allocate to the virtual machine. By default, Boxes stores virtual machine configuration information in the ~/.config/libvirt/qemu/ directory and virtual hard disk files in the ~/.local/share/gnome-boxes/ directory. Virtual hard disk files created by Boxes are thin provisioned by default.

Figure 6-4   The Boxes application

Configuring Server Storage

During the Fedora installation process, described in Chapter 2, one of the most important configuration tasks involves configuring the permanent storage devices that will host the Linux operating system. This task involves selecting the storage devices and creating partitions and filesystems. The storage that you configure during installation depends on your specific storage technologies and the space needs of your Linux system. In this section, you examine the configuration of advanced storage technologies commonly used on Linux servers, including SCSI, RAID, SAN storage, ZFS, and BTRFS.

Note

You can choose from different advanced storage technologies. However, because many of these technologies involve proprietary hardware and are used primarily on specialized systems, the discussion is limited to the general-use technologies discussed in this section. To learn more about configuring other advanced storage technologies during a Linux server installation, consult the installation guide available on the Linux distribution's website.

SCSI Configuration

The Small Computer System Interface (SCSI) was designed as a way to connect multiple peripherals to the system in a scalable, high-speed manner. In most systems, a SCSI device is connected to a controller card, which, in turn, connects all devices attached to it to the system.

Legacy SCSI Configuration

SCSI technology dates back to 1986 and originally relied on ribbon cables to transmit information between a SCSI hard disk and SCSI controller in a parallel fashion; this type of SCSI is called **parallel SCSI**. Parallel SCSI hard disks are often connected to a single SCSI controller via a single cable in a daisy-chain fashion. To prevent signals from bouncing back and forth on the cable, each end of the cable contains a **terminator** device that stops signals from being perpetuated.

Each SCSI controller and hard disk has a unique ID number known as a **SCSI ID** or **target ID**. SCSI controllers typically support up to 15 devices for a total of 16 SCSI IDs (0–15). This SCSI ID also gives priority to the device. The highest priority device is given the number 7, followed by 6, 5, 4, 3, 2, 1, 0, 15, 14, 13, 12, 11, 10, 9, and 8. Moreover, some SCSI devices act as a gateway to other devices; in this case, each device is associated with a unique **Logical Unit Number (LUN)**.

SCSI controllers often add a second SCSI BIOS to your system that is started after the system BIOS. To configure SCSI IDs and LUNs, you could enter the SCSI BIOS configuration tool by pressing a vendor-specific key combination at boot time.

While parallel SCSI technology has evolved dramatically over the past several decades, it is rarely found on Linux servers today due to the proliferation of SAS. The last version of parallel SCSI is called SCSI-3 (Ultra640); it was released in 2003 and boasted speeds of up to 640MB/s.

 Note

Regardless of type, all SCSI hard disks and SSDs use the device files /dev/sda, /dev/sdb, and so on.

SAS Configuration

Serial Attached SCSI (SAS) is a newer SCSI technology designed in 2005 to replace parallel SCSI that can transfer data at up to 22.5Gb/s. Up to 65,535 SAS hard disks or SSDs can be connected to a single SCSI controller via serial cables with small serial connectors; many types of SAS connectors are available, including one that is compatible with SATA devices.

Before you install Linux on a system that includes SAS devices, you must first connect them to the SCSI controller via the correct serial cable. Then, you must ensure that the hard disks are detected properly by the system or SCSI BIOS. All other SAS configuration (SCSI ID, LUN, etc.) is performed automatically by the SCSI controller but can be changed manually if you access the SCSI BIOS.

RAID Configuration

Recall that you typically create several partitions during installation to decrease the likelihood that the failure of a filesystem on one partition will affect the rest of the system. These partitions can be spread across several hard disks to minimize the impact of a hard disk failure; if one hard disk fails, the data on the other hard disks is unaffected.

If a hard disk failure occurs, you must power down the computer, replace the failed hard disk drive, power on the computer, and restore the data that was originally on the hard disk drive from a backup copy. The whole process can take several hours. However, for many server systems, no amount of downtime is acceptable. For these systems, you can use a **fault tolerant** hard disk configuration, which has traditionally been implemented by a **Redundant Array of Independent Disks (RAID)**. Note that RAID has other uses besides creating a fault tolerant system. It can be used to speed up access to hard disks or combine multiple hard disks into a single volume.

> **Note** 📎
>
> Most SAN devices use RAID internally to provide for data fault tolerance.

Seven basic RAID configurations, ranging from level 0 to level 6, are available. RAID level 0 configurations are not fault tolerant. One type of RAID level 0, known as **spanning** or **Just a Bunch of Disks (JBOD)**, consists of two or more hard disks that the system sees as one large volume. Using this technology, you could, for example, combine two 1TB hard disks into a single 2TB volume. Spanning is useful when you need a large amount of storage space in a single volume without fault tolerance.

In another type of RAID level 0, called **disk striping**, an individual file is divided into sections and saved concurrently on two or more hard disks, one section per disk. For example, suppose you have a disk striping configuration made up of three hard disks. In that case, when you save a file, it is divided into three sections, with each section written to separate hard disk devices concurrently, in a third of the amount of time it would take to save the entire file on one hard disk device. Note that the system can also read the same file in one-third the time it would take if the file were stored on a single hard drive. Disk striping is useful when you need to speed up disk access, but it is not fault tolerant. If one hard disk fails in a RAID level 0 configuration, all data is lost.

RAID level 1, often referred to as **disk mirroring**, provides fault tolerance in the case of a hard disk failure. In this RAID configuration, the same data is written to two separate hard disks at the same time. This results in two hard disks with identical information. If one fails, the copy can replace the failed hard disk in a short period of time. The only drawback to RAID level 1 is the cost, because you need to purchase twice the hard disk space needed for a given computer.

RAID level 2 is no longer used and was a variant of RAID 0 that allowed for error and integrity checking on hard disk drives. Modern hard disk drives do this intrinsically.

RAID level 3 is disk striping with a parity bit, or marker, which indicates what data is where. It requires a minimum of three hard disk drives to function, with one of the hard disks used to store the parity information. Should one of the hard disks containing data fail, you can replace the hard disk drive and regenerate the data using the parity information stored on the parity disk. If the parity disk fails, the system must be restored from a backup device.

RAID level 4 is only a slight variant on RAID level 3. RAID level 4 offers greater access speed than RAID level 3, because it can store data in blocks and, thus, does not need to access all disks in the array at once to read data.

RAID level 5 replaces RAID levels 3 and 4; it is the most common RAID configuration used today and is called **disk striping with parity**. As with RAID levels 3 and 4, it requires a minimum of three hard disks; however, the parity information is not stored on a separate drive, but is intermixed with data on the drives that make up the set. This offers better performance and fault tolerance; if any drive in the RAID configuration fails, the information on the other drives can be used to regenerate the lost information such that users can still access their data. After the failed hard disk has been replaced, the data can automatically be rebuilt on the new hard drive, returning the RAID configuration to its original state. However, if two hard disks fail at the same time, the data must be restored from a backup copy. Figure 6-5 shows how data can be calculated on a RAID level 5 using parity information. The parity bits shown in the figure are a sum of the information on the other two disks ($22 + 12 = 34$). If the third hard disk fails, the information can be regenerated because only one element is missing from each equation:

$$22 + 12 = 34$$
$$68 - 65 = 3$$
$$13 - 9 = 4$$

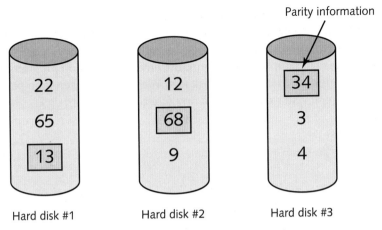

Parity information

Figure 6-5   Organization of data on RAID level 5

RAID level 6 is basically the same as RAID level 5, but it adds a second set of parity bits for added fault tolerance and allows up to two simultaneous hard disk drive failures while remaining fault tolerant. As a result, RAID level 6 requires a minimum of four hard disks.

Note

RAID levels are often combined; for example, RAID level 10 refers to a stripe set (RAID level 0) that is mirrored (RAID level 1) to another stripe set. Similarly, RAID level 15 refers to a stripe set with parity (RAID level 5) that is mirrored (RAID level 1) to another stripe set with parity.

RAID configurations can be handled by software running on an operating system (called **software RAID**) but are more commonly handled by the hardware contained within a SCSI/SAS/SATA hard disk controller (called **hardware RAID**), or by the system BIOS (called **firmware RAID**).

Note

Most firmware RAID devices only support RAID level 0 and 1.

To configure and manage hardware RAID, you must use the RAID setup utility for your specific SCSI/SAS/SATA hard disk controller. You can access this setup utility by entering the system or SCSI BIOS at system startup, or by using a manufacturer-supplied program. After you have configured a hardware RAID volume within the setup utility, it will automatically appear as a single hard disk to the Linux operating system or Linux installation program if you are installing Linux to a RAID volume. For example, if you configure three hard disks in a RAID level 5 volume using the RAID setup utility prior to installing the Linux operating system, the Linux installation program will see the RAID level 5 volume as a single hard disk (e.g., /dev/sda). You can then partition and place filesystems on /dev/sda as you would any other physical hard disk.

Note

While firmware RAID functions identically to hardware RAID, you must configure and manage firmware RAID using the RAID setup utility within the system BIOS.

Unlike hardware or firmware RAID, software RAID is performed entirely by the Linux operating system; as a result, it can be configured within the Linux installation program during a Linux installation, or afterwards using the appropriate utilities. Your first RAID volume will use a multiple disk (md) device file called /dev/mdo that uses multiple disk files for the RAID level chosen. For example, /dev/mdo can be used to refer to a RAID 5 volume that spans the /dev/sdb, /dev/sdc, /dev/sdd, and /dev/sde devices as shown in the contents of the /proc/mdstat file below:

```
[root@server1 ~]# cat /proc/mdstat
Personalities : [raid6] [raid5] [raid4] [linear] [multipath]
[raid0] [raid1] [raid10]

md0 : active raid5 sde[4] sdd[2] sdc[1] sdb[0]
        3139584 blocks super 1.2 level 5, 512k chunk, algorithm 2 [4/3]

unused devices: <none>
[root@server1 ~]#_
```

You can create a filesystem on /dev/mdo and mount it to a directory as you would any other device. The output of the lsblk command below indicates that the RAID 5 volume shown earlier was mounted to the /data directory:

```
[root@server1 ~]# lsblk
NAME                         MAJ:MIN RM  SIZE RO TYPE  MOUNTPOINT
sda                              8:0   0   50G  0 disk
├─sda1                           8:1   0    1M  0 part
├─sda2                           8:2   0    1G  0 part  /boot
└─sda3                           8:3   0   49G  0 part
  ├─fedora-root                253:0   0   44G  0 lvm   /
  └─fedora-swap                253:1   0    4G  0 lvm   [SWAP]
```

```
sdb                          8:16    0    1G   0 disk
└─md0                        9:0     0    3G   0 raid5 /data
sdc                          8:32    0    1G   0 disk
└─md0                        9:0     0    3G   0 raid5 /data
sdd                          8:48    0    1G   0 disk
└─md0                        9:0     0    3G   0 raid5 /data
sde                          8:64    0    1G   0 disk
└─md0                        9:0     0    3G   0 raid5 /data
sr0                          1:0     1 1024M   0 rom
[root@server1 ~]#_
```

The specific structure of software RAID volumes is autodetected at boot time, but can be written to /etc/mdadm/mdadm.conf to ensure correctness. Additionally, RAID filesystems can be mounted at boot time via entries within /etc/fstab; however, you should list the filesystem UUID instead of the /dev/mdo device file within /etc/fstab to avoid problems should the system rename the /dev/mdo device file.

To create and manage software RAID configuration after installation, you can use the mdadm **command.** For example, you can use the command mdadm --create /dev/md0 --level=5 --raid-devices=4 /dev/sdb /dev/sdc /dev/sdd /dev/sde to create a RAID level 5 called /dev/mdo from the /dev/sdb, /dev/sdc, /dev /sdd and /dev/sde devices. Next, you can view detailed information about the RAID volume using the following command:

```
[root@server1 ~]# mdadm --detail /dev/md0
/dev/md0:
              Version : 1.2
        Creation Time : Sat Jul 28 16:59:43 2019
           Raid Level : raid5
           Array Size : 3139584 (2.99 GiB 3.21GB)
        Used Dev Size : 1046528 (1022.00 MiB 1071.64MB)
         Raid Devices : 4
        Total Devices : 4
          Persistence : Superblock is persistent

          Update Time : Sat Jul 28 17:03:28 2019
                State : clean
       Active Devices : 4
      Working Devices : 4
       Failed Devices : 0
        Spare Devices : 0

               Layout : left-symmetric
           Chunk Size : 512K

   Consistency Policy : resync
```

```
        Name : ubuntu18:0   (local to host fedora)
        UUID : 74a89dce:ffffcce8:8d09726d:ada816f5
      Events : 18

  Number    Major    Minor    RaidDevice State
     0        8        16          0        active sync   /dev/sdb
     1        8        32          1        active sync   /dev/sdc
     2        8        48          2        active sync   /dev/sdd
     4        8        64          3        active sync   /dev/sde
[root@server1 ~]#_
```

SAN Storage Configuration

Many rackmount servers today contain only enough storage to host the Linux
operating system and associated server programs. All other data files, databases, Web
content, virtual hard disk files, and so on are stored on an external SAN device on the
server rack that is connected to the Linux operating system using a SAN protocol. The
two most common SAN protocols today include iSCSI and Fibre Channel. You can also
use DM-MPIO to provide multiple connections to one or more SANs.

iSCSI Configuration

Internet SCSI (iSCSI) is a technology that uses Ethernet network cables to transfer data
to and from a SAN device, either on the local network or across the Internet, using
the SCSI protocol. The software component within the operating system that connects
to the SAN device via iSCSI is referred to as an iSCSI initiator, and the storage that is
made available to iSCSI initiator on the SAN is called the iSCSI target. A single iSCSI
target typically contains multiple hard disks or SSDs that are combined using
fault-tolerant hardware RAID (e.g., RAID 5) on the SAN device itself. As a result, the
iSCSI initiator and Linux operating system will see the iSCSI target as a single device
file (e.g., /dev/sdb).

> **Note** 📎
>
> iSCSI is simply a transfer protocol used between a server and a SAN device. The SAN device
> itself can use different storage technologies to physically store the data, including NVMe
> SSDs, or SATA/SAS hard disks or SSDs.
>
>   SAN is considered a high-capacity storage device that is located on a server rack. A single
> iSCSI SAN device can host multiple iSCSI targets that are accessed by the iSCSI initiators on
> several servers on the same rack; each of these servers that access the iSCSI SAN device are
> said to be part of a "storage area network."

To connect a Linux server to an iSCSI SAN, you must first ensure that the appropriate iSCSI targets have been configured via the configuration tools provided by the iSCSI SAN device manufacturer. Next, you must connect an iSCSI-compatible Ethernet cable from an iSCSI-compliant network interface on your Linux server to an Ethernet port on your iSCSI SAN device. Finally, you must configure the iSCSI initiator on your Linux server using the `iscsiadm` command. For example, to configure the iSCSI initiator to connect to a target available on the SAN device with the IP address 192.168.1.1, you could use the following commands (and optionally specifying the iSCSI target password, if one was configured on the SAN device):

```
[root@server1 ~]# iscsiadm -m discovery -t st -p 192.168.1.1
192.168.1.1:3260,1 iqn.2001-05.com.equallogic:0-8a0120425dbe
[root@server1 ~]# iscsiadm -m node --login
Enter password: **********
[root@server1 ~]#_
```

Following this, the iSCSI target should be identified by the Linux system as the next available SCSI device (e.g., /dev/sdb). You can partition and format it as you would any other SCSI hard drive, as well as mount any filesystems on it to a mount point directory and update the /etc/fstab to ensure that the filesystems are mounted automatically at boot time. Additionally, you must ensure that you add or uncomment the `node.startup = automatic` line within the /etc/iscsi/iscsid.conf file to ensure that the iSCSI initiator software is loaded at boot time; otherwise the filesystems on the SAN device will not be accessible.

You can also configure an iSCSI initiator during a Linux installation. For example, to configure an iSCSI initiator during a Fedora 28 installation, select Add a disk shown in Figure 2-10. This will allow you to select advanced storage options, as shown in Figure 6-6. You can then click the Add iSCSI Target button shown in Figure 6-6 and supply the IP address and password for your iSCSI SAN device.

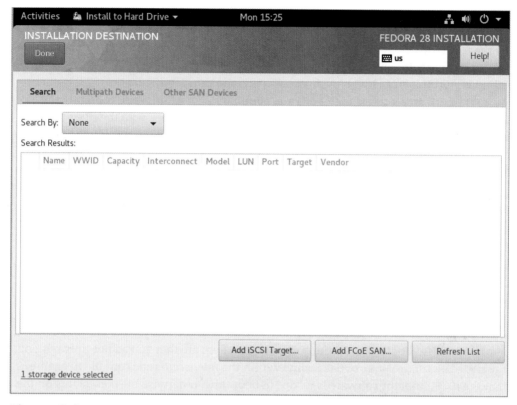

Figure 6-6 Configuring advanced storage options during a Fedora 28 installation

Fibre Channel Configuration

Fibre Channel (FC) is a technology that can be used to transport SCSI data to local FC-capable hard disks or SSDs or to a remote FC SAN device, across an Ethernet or a fiber-optic cable at speeds of up to 128Gb/s. A server typically uses a FC controller called a FC **Host Bus Adapter (HBA)** that connects to one or more local FC-capable storage devices (hard disks or SSDs), or to a FC SAN that contains many FC-capable storage devices connected via a FC switch. All FC-capable storage devices must have a **World Wide Name (WWN)** identifier that is normally assigned by the FC HBA in order to function with the FC protocol.

Note

WWN identifiers are not specific to FC; they are storage-specific identifiers that can optionally be given to SATA and SAS devices.

A FC HBA can also be a FC-capable 10Gb Ethernet network interface if the FC SAN uses FC over Ethernet (FCoE).

Most FC HBAs contain proprietary firmware that cannot be bundled within a Linux distribution due to GPL license incompatibility. As a result, to configure FC devices on a Linux system, you must first obtain and install the firmware package for your FC HBA from the manufacturer. Manufacturers often make their firmware available for installation from a private software repository and list instructions needed to install it on different Linux distributions. After installing the appropriate firmware package, you should see your FC HBA listed in the output of the `lspci` command, as shown below:

```
[root@server1 ~]# lspci
0000:00:01.0 SCSI storage controller: LSI Logic / Symbios Logic
53c875 (rev 04)
0001:00:01.0 Ethernet controller: Oracle Corporation GEM
10/100/1000 Ethernet [ge] (rev 01)
0001:00:02.0 SCSI storage controller: QLogic Corp. QLA2200 64-bit
Fibre Channel Adapter (rev 05)
0003:01:04.0 SCSI storage controller: QLogic Corp. QLA2200 64-bit
Fibre Channel Adapter (rev 05)
0003:01:05.0 SCSI storage controller: QLogic Corp. QLA2200 64-bit
Fibre Channel Adapter (rev 05)
0003:02:04.0 SCSI storage controller: QLogic Corp. QLA2200 64-bit
Fibre Channel Adapter (rev 05)
0003:02:05.0 SCSI storage controller: QLogic Corp. QLA2200 64-bit
Fibre Channel Adapter (rev 05)
[root@server1 ~]#_
```

The FC HBA provides the same functionality as an iSCSI initiator; if connected properly, the FC HBA should detect and make any FC storage devices available to the Linux system. The /dev/disk/by-id/ directory should contain an entry for each FC SCSI device, as well as a matching WWN entry as shown in the output below. Each of these entries is a symbolic link to the appropriate device file (/dev/sdb, /dev/sdc, and so on) that you can use to create partitions and filesystems. You can then mount these filesystems and modify the /etc/fstab to mount them at boot time like any other disk device.

```
[root@server1 ~]# ls /dev/disk/by-id/
lrwxrwxrwx 1 root root  9 Jul 24 scsi-320000004cf4cfb8f -> ../../sdb
lrwxrwxrwx 1 root root  9 Jul 24 scsi-32000000c507aa387 -> ../../sde
lrwxrwxrwx 1 root root  9 Jul 24 scsi-32000000c507aa421 -> ../../sdd
lrwxrwxrwx 1 root root  9 Jul 24 scsi-32000000c507aa43c -> ../../sdg
lrwxrwxrwx 1 root root  9 Jul 24 scsi-32000000c507aa50b -> ../../sdc
lrwxrwxrwx 1 root root  9 Jul 24 scsi-32000000c507aa5c0 -> ../../sdf
lrwxrwxrwx 1 root root  9 Jul 24 wwn-0x20000004cf4cfb8f -> ../../sdb
lrwxrwxrwx 1 root root  9 Jul 24 wwn-0x2000000c507aa387 -> ../../sde
lrwxrwxrwx 1 root root  9 Jul 24 wwn-0x2000000c507aa421 -> ../../sdd
```

```
lrwxrwxrwx 1 root root  9 Jul 24 wwn-0x2000000c507aa43c -> ../../sdg
lrwxrwxrwx 1 root root  9 Jul 24 wwn-0x2000000c507aa50b -> ../../sdc
lrwxrwxrwx 1 root root  9 Jul 24 wwn-0x2000000c507aa5c0 -> ../../sdf
[root@server1 ~]# _
```

> **Note** 📎
>
> Like iSCSI SAN devices, FC SAN devices often use hardware RAID to create fault-tolerant volumes; in this case, each SCSI (and associated WWN) identifier shown in the previous output may refer to a different RAID volume on the FC SAN itself.
>
> Most storage devices that support FC are either SCSI or SAS hard disks or SSDs. However, FC can also be used to transport data to and from NVMe devices that do not use the SCSI protocol; in this case, the /dev/disk/by-id/ directory will list both nvme and wwn identifiers.
>
> You can also configure FC HBAs during a Linux installation. For example, to configure a FCoE SAN during a Fedora 28 installation, click the Add FCoE SAN button shown in Figure 6-6 and select the appropriate FC-capable network interface. To configure a different FC HBA, select Other SAN Devices shown in Figure 6-6, choose the associated FC HBA, and supply the firmware, if necessary.

Configuring DM-MPIO

Data center server environments often have several iSCSI or FC SAN devices. Additionally, each server within a data center can have multiple connections to a single SAN for fault tolerance in case a single connection becomes unavailable, or to load balance requests across multiple connections for greater speed. Larger data centers often have multiple SANs that host the same information; in this case, servers can have multiple connections to different SANs to provide fault tolerance in case a single SAN becomes unavailable, or to load balance requests across multiple SANs for greater speed.

This configuration is called **Multipath Input Output (MPIO)**. On Linux systems it is implemented by the same device mapper used to map LVM logical volumes to physical devices; as a result, Linux often refers to this configuration as **Device Mapper MPIO (DM-MPIO)**.

Before you configure DM-MPIO, each server must have multiple iSCSI targets or FC HBAs configured, and the associated SAN volumes represented by a device file (/dev/sdb, /dev/sdc, and so on). Following this, you can configure DM-MPIO using the `mpathconf` **command**, which autodetects your SAN configuration, creates the appropriate configuration entries within the /etc/multipath.conf file and starts the multipath daemon. An example of this command that scans for available SANs and configures them for DM-MPIO fault tolerance is shown below:

```
[root@server1 ~]# mpathconf --enable --with_multipathd y
[root@server1 ~]#_
```

After DM-MPIO has been configured, the device mapper will create a device mapping file that refers to two or more device files; for example, the /dev/mapper/ mpath1 device mapping file may refer to the /dev/sdb and /dev/sdc iSCSI targets. You can then use this device mapping file when mounting and accessing your SAN filesystems.

> **Note** 🖉
>
> You can also configure DM-MPIO during a Linux installation. For example, if you add multiple iSCSI targets or FB HBAs during a Fedora 28 installation, you can configure them to use DM-MPIO by selecting the Multipath Devices tab shown in Figure 6-6.

ZFS Configuration

The **Zettabyte File System (ZFS)** is a high-performance filesystem and volume management software that was designed for large-scale Linux systems that need to store data on multiple disks, SANs, and remote systems. You can create RAID-like ZFS volumes that span thousands of local and network storage devices, such as local hard disks, local SSDs, SANs, and remote file shares, as well as resize volumes, while the filesystem is mounted. Moreover, the ZFS filesystem detects and repairs data errors automatically as data is read and written, as well as protects against problems that are commonly seen on systems that write large amounts of data to a non-ZFS filesystem, including:

- Silent data corruption
- Bit rot
- Disk firmware bugs
- Phantom writes
- Misdirected writes
- Driver and kernel buffer errors
- Accidental driver overwrites

ZFS caches frequently accessed information in RAM and on faster storage devices such as SSDs to provide ultra-fast performance. ZFS also supports advanced filesystem features, including deduplication (storing one copy of a file that is located in multiple directories until one of the files change), snapshots, cloning, compression, encryption, NFSv4, volume management, and more.

> **Note** @
>
> ZFS was initially created by Sun Microsystems in 2001 and is often used by the largest Linux and UNIX systems in the world. It is available for Solaris UNIX, Mac OSX, Linux, FreeBSD, FreeNAS, and more. Because ZFS does not currently have a GPL-compatible license, it cannot be bundled within a Linux distribution, but it can be easily added afterwards. On Linux, ZFS support is maintained by *zfsonlinux.org*.

Although ZFS is primarily used on large Linux systems that may have hundreds or thousands of storage devices, it is also used within small and medium-sized organizations that require flexible volume management for data that is easy to configure.

ZFS pools are groups of physical disks that ZFS can manage (local disks, SANs, shared devices, large raw files, remote shares, etc.), and **ZFS volumes** are simply ZFS-managed filesystems that are created from ZFS pools.

Take, for example, a system that hosts several hard disks, with the Linux OS installed on /dev/sda. To create a simple ZFS pool called datastorage1 from the second SATA/SCSI/SAS hard disk, you could use the following `zpool` **command**:

```
[root@server1 ~]# zpool create datastorage1 /dev/sdb
[root@server1 ~]#_
```

This will also create a new ZFS volume called datastorage1 and mount it to /datastorage1, as shown here in the last line of the `mount` command output:

```
[root@server1 ~]# df -hT
Filesystem                 Type    Size   Used  Avail  Use%  Mounted on
/dev/mapper/fedora-root    ext4    44G    1.6G   40G    4%   /
/dev/sda2                  ext4    976M    75M   835M   9%   /boot
tmpfs                      tmpfs   200M      0   200M   0%   /run/user/0
tmpfs                      tmpfs   200M      0   200M   0%   /run/user/1000
datastorage1                zfs    880M      0   880M   0%   /datastorage1
[root@server1 ~]#_
```

You can also use the `zpool` command to view the details for your datastorage1 volume:

```
[root@server1 ~]# zpool list
NAME           SIZE   ALLOC   FREE EXPANDSZ FRAG CAP DEDUP  HEALTH ALTROOT
datastorage1 1008M    272K 1008M        -   0%  0% 1.00x ONLINE -
[root@server1 ~]#_
```

> **Note**
>
> You can remove a ZFS volume using the `zpool` command. For example, `zpool destroy datastorage1` would remove the ZFS volume and pool created in the previous output.

If you specify multiple devices when creating a simple ZFS volume, then those devices are automatically added to the ZFS pool and a ZFS volume is created from their contents. For example, if you run the following command, the /dev/sdc and /dev/sdd hard disks would be added to the datastorage2 pool, and a ZFS volume called datastorage2 would be created (with a capacity of both hard disks combined) and mounted to the /datastorage2 directory. This would act as the equivalent of a RAID 0 volume, but with the file corruption prevention benefits of ZFS.

```
[root@server1 ~]# zpool create datastorage2 /dev/sdc /dev/sdd
[root@server1 ~]#_
```

To create a ZFS pool and mirrored ZFS volume called datastorage3 from the /dev/sde and /dev/sdf hard disks and mount the volume to /datastorage3, you specify the `mirror` keyword during creation, as shown here:

```
[root@server1 ~]# zpool create datastorage3 mirror /dev/sde /dev/sdf
[root@server1 ~]#_
```

The datastorage3 volume is the equivalent of RAID 1 but resizeable under ZFS, and the total size of the volume is identical to the size of one of the hard disks.

> **Note**
>
> To create a ZFS mirrored volume, you need to specify a minimum of two hard disk devices to protect against a single disk failure.

To view the status of the disks that are part of the datastorage3 pool, you can use the following command:

```
[root@server1 ~]# zpool status datastorage3
  pool: datastorage3
 state: DEGRADED
status: One or more devices could not be used because the label is
        missing or invalid. Sufficient replicas exist for the pool
        to continue functioning in a degraded state.
action: Replace the device using 'zpool replace'.
   see: http://zfsonlinux.org/msg/ZFS-8000-4J
  scan: scrub repaired 0 in 0h0m with 0 errors
config:

        NAME            STATE       READ WRITE CKSUM
        datastorage3    DEGRADED       0     0     0
          mirror-0      DEGRADED       0     0     0
            /dev/sde    UNAVAIL        0     0     0  corrupted data
            /dev/sdf    ONLINE         0     0     0

errors: No known data errors
[root@server1 ~]#
```

Notice from the preceding example that one of the disks in the mirror has failed (/dev/sde). In this case, you should detach the device from the pool using the `zpool detach datastorage3 /dev/sde` command, replace the failed hard disk, and reattach the disk to the mirror using the `zpool attach datastorage3 /dev/sdf /dev/sde` command. During this process, the filesystem is still available to users for reading and writing data. After reattaching the new hard disk, the output of the `zpool status datastorage3` command should resemble the following output:

```
[root@server1 ~]# zpool status datastorage3
  pool: datastorage3
 state: ONLINE
  scan: none requested
config:

        NAME            STATE       READ WRITE CKSUM
        datastorage3    ONLINE         0     0     0
          mirror-0      ONLINE         0     0     0
            /dev/sde    ONLINE         0     0     0
            /dev/sdf    ONLINE         0     0     0
```

```
errors: No known data errors
[root@server1 ~]#_
```

To create a ZFS pool and **RAID-Z** volume (the equivalent of a RAID-5 volume with a variable-sized stripe) called datastorage4 from the /dev/sdg, /dev/sdh, and /dev/sdi hard disks and mount it to /datastorage4, specify the `raidz` keyword during creation, as shown here:

```
[root@server1 ~]# zpool create datastorage4 raidz /dev/sdg /dev/
sdh /dev/sdi
[root@server1 ~]#_
```

> **Note** 🖉
>
> A RAID-Z volume needs a minimum of three hard disks to protect against a single disk failure, and a minimum of seven hard disks to protect against a multi-disk failure.
>
> You can also use `raidz2` (double parity like RAID-6) and `raidz3` (triple parity) in place of `raidz` in the previous command. You need a minimum of four devices for `raidz2` and a minimum of five devices for `raidz3`.
>
> Because ZFS writes parity info with a variable-sized stripe, performance is maximized, and there is virtually no chance of the infamous "RAID 5 Hole" (data loss in the event of a power failure) that plagues traditional RAID systems.

Following this, you can view the state and performance of the RAID-Z volume using the `zpool status` and `zpool iostat -v` commands:

```
[root@server1 ~]# zpool status datastorage4
  pool: datastorage4
 state: ONLINE
  scan: none requested
config:

        NAME            STATE     READ WRITE CKSUM
        datastorage4    ONLINE       0     0     0
          raidz1-0      ONLINE       0     0     0
            /dev/sdg    ONLINE       0     0     0
            /dev/sdh    ONLINE       0     0     0
            /dev/sdi    ONLINE       0     0     0
```

```
errors: No known data errors
root@server1:~# zpool iostat -v datastorage4
                   capacity        operations       bandwidth
pool             alloc   free    read   write     read   write
----------       -----   -----   -----  -----     -----  -----
datastorage4     220K    970M       0      11      701   10.5K
  raidz1         220K    970M       0      11      701   10.5K
    /dev/sdg       -       -        0      10     25.2K  83.6K
    /dev/sdh       -       -        0      10     25.1K  83.6K
    /dev/sdi       -       -        0      10     1.48K  83.6K
----------       -----   -----   -----  -----     -----  -----

[root@server1 ~]#_
```

For more granular management of ZFS, you can use the `zfs` **command** to manage the specific features of the ZFS filesystem stored within ZFS volumes. The `zfs` command allows you to set a wide variety of ZFS-specific functionality, including directory size quotas, automatic compression, as well as many more file- and directory-specific features and performance options. Moreover, you can identify specific subdirectories on a ZFS filesystem to tag for ZFS management; these subdirectories are often called **ZFS subfilesystems**. For example, if you create a directory under /datastorage4 called research, you can run the following command to specify that the research subdirectory should be treated as a ZFS subfilesystem:

```
[root@server1 ~]# zfs create datastorage4/research
[root@server1 ~]#_
```

To see a list of ZFS filesystems and subfilesystems that are available for ZFS management, you can run the `zfs list` command:

```
[root@server1 ~]# zfs list
NAME                     USED   AVAIL  REFER  MOUNTPOINT
datastorage4             286K   970M   42.6K  /datastorage4
datastorage4/research    38.6K  970M   38.6K  /datastorage4/research
[root@server1 ~]# _
```

To list the specific configuration parameters that you can modify for the research subfilesystem, you can use the `zfs get all` command:

```
[root@server1 ~]# zfs get all datastorage4/research | less
NAME                        PROPERTY    VALUE               SOURCE
datastorage4/research       type        filesystem          -
datastorage4/research       creation    Tue Sep 30 13:41 2019    -
```

```
datastorage4/research used            38.6K                          -
datastorage4/research available       214M                           -
datastorage4/research referenced      38.6K                          -
datastorage4/research compressratio   1.00x                          -
datastorage4/research mounted         yes                            -
datastorage4/research quota           none                    default
datastorage4/research reservation     none                    default
datastorage4/research recordsize      128K                    default
datastorage4/research mountpoint      /datastorage4/research  default
datastorage4/research sharenfs        off                     default
datastorage4/research checksum        on                      default
datastorage4/research compression     off                     default
datastorage4/research atime           on                      default
datastorage4/research devices         on                      default
datastorage4/research exec            on                      default
datastorage4/research setuid          on                      default
datastorage4/research readonly        off                     default
:
```

You can modify the settings for the research subfilesystem to suit your needs. For example, to limit the total size of files within the research subfilesystem to 5GB, you could use the `zfs set quota=5G datastorage4/research` command, or to ensure that the contents of the research subfilesystem are read-only, you could run the `zfs set readonly=on datastorage4/research` command.

ZFS volumes store their configuration within the volume itself and are mounted by the ZFS system software and not via entries within the /etc/fstab file. By default, the ZFS system software searches for and mounts all ZFS volumes on the system, but this can be disabled by modifying the `ZFS_MOUNT='yes'` line within the /etc/default/zfs file; in this case, you will need to run the `zfs mount datastorage1` command to manually mount the datastorage1 ZFS filesystem, or the `zfs mount -a` command to manually mount all ZFS filesystems after boot time.

BTRFS Configuration

The **B-tree File System (BTRFS)** has many features that are similar to those found in ZFS, and is currently being developed to become a replacement for ext4. Currently, BTRFS isn't as fast or robust as ZFS; it does not detect and repair data errors automatically as data is read and written. However, it can be used to create volumes that span multiple storage devices using RAID 0, RAID 1, RAID 10, RAID 5, and RAID 6. It also supports some of the enterprise features available in ZFS, including compression, deduplication, snapshots, resizing, quotas, and subfilesystems (called **BTRFS subvolumes**).

Note

BTRFS is still in development; as a result, many features of BTRFS, including RAID 5/6 and quotas, are not recommended for production use at the time of this writing.

BTRFS uses three terms to refer to its filesystem structure: **data** refers to the blocks available for data storage, **metadata** refers to the inode table, and **system** refers to the superblock. All BTRFS metadata is stored in B-tree structures for fast access. In addition, you can specify whether the data and metadata can be fault tolerant when creating a BTRFS filesystem that spans multiple storage devices; for example, to create a BTRFS filesystem that spans /dev/sdb and /dev/sdc, as well as uses RAID 1 for the system and metadata (-m) and data (-d), you could use the following mkfs.btrfs **command**:

```
[root@server1 ~]# mkfs.btrfs -m raid1 -d raid1 /dev/sdb /dev/sdc
btrfs-progs v4.15.1
See http://btrfs.wiki.kernel.org for more information.

Label:                  (null)
UUID:                   d24b970b-86f1-4245-a382-d2a3da02b18f
Node size:              16384
Sector size:            4096
Filesystem size:        2.00GiB
Block group profiles:
  Data:                 RAID1              102.38MiB
  Metadata:             RAID1              102.38MiB
  System:               RAID1                8.00MiB
SSD detected:           no
Incompat features:      extref, skinny-metadata
Number of devices:      2
Devices:
   ID         SIZE    PATH
    1      1.00GiB    /dev/sdb
    2      1.00GiB    /dev/sdc

[root@server1 ~]#_
```

Note

If you omit the -m and -d options to the mkfs.btrfs command, the default is to use RAID 0 for the data and RAID 1 for the metadata.

You can then mount the filesystem to a mount point directory by using any device file within the filesystem; in this example, you could use either the `mount /dev/sdb /storage` command or the `mount /dev/sdc /storage` command to mount the BTRFS filesystem to the /storage directory. Similarly, you could add either the `/dev /sdb /storage btrfs defaults 0 0` line or the `/dev/sdc /storage btrfs defaults 0 0` line to /etc/fstab to ensure that the BTRFS filesystem is mounted at boot time.

BRFS filesystem compression is enabled using a mount option. For example, the `mount -o compress=lzo /dev/sdb /storage` command would mount the BTRFS filesystem in our example using LZO compression, and the `/dev/sdb /storage btrfs defaults,compress=lzo 0 0` line in /etc/fstab would ensure that it is mounted with LZO compression at boot time.

> **Note** 📎
>
> While both ZFS and BTRFS support multiple compression algorithms, Lempel–Ziv–Oberhumer (LZO) is the preferred one for automatic filesystem compression within production environments due to its speed.

After a BRFS filesystem has been created, it can be managed using the `btrfs` command. Because BTRFS does not have the automatic repair functionality that ZFS has, you can check the unmounted BTRFS filesystem in the previous example and automatically repair any errors using the following command:

```
[root@server1 ~]# btrfs check /dev/sdb
Checking filesystem on /dev/sdb
UUID: d24b970b-86f1-4245-a382-d2a3da02b18f
checking extents
checking free space cache
checking fs roots
checking csums
checking root refs
found 114688 bytes used, no error found
total csum bytes: 0
total tree bytes: 114688
total fs tree bytes: 32768
total extent tree bytes: 16384
btree space waste bytes: 109243
file data blocks allocated: 0
 referenced 0
[root@server1 ~]#_
```

Note

The `btrfsck` **command** can be used instead of the `btrs check` command. For example, `btrfsck /dev/sdb` performs the same check as the `btrfs` command in the previous example.

The `btrfs` command can also be used to display BTRFS configuration and usage. For example, the `btrfs filesystem show /dev/sdb` command can be used to show the configuration of the BTRFS filesystem that includes the /dev/sdb device, while the `btrfs filesystem df /storage` command will show usage information for the BTRFS filesystem mounted to the /storage directory.

BTRFS subvolumes function similar to ZFS subfilesystems, and can be mounted separately to their own mount point directory with different options. To create a subvolume called backup on the BTRFS filesystem mounted to the storage directory, you could use the `btrfs subvolume create /storage/backup` command, and to mount it to the /backup directory using compression, you could use the `mount -o subvol=backup,compress=lzo /dev/sdb /backup` command, if one of the devices in the BTRFS filesystem is /dev/sdb.

You can also add devices and extend BTRFS filesystems while the BTRFS filesystem is mounted and online. For example, to add the /dev/sdd and /dev/sde devices to the RAID 1 BTRFS filesystem created earlier and mounted to /storage, as well as view the resulting configuration, you can use the following commands:

```
[root@server1 ~]# btrfs device add /dev/sdd /dev/sde /storage
[root@server1 ~]# btrfs filesystem balance /storage
WARNING:
        Full balance without filters requested. This operation is very
        intense and takes potentially very long. It is recommended to
        use the balance filters to narrow down the scope of balance.
        Use 'btrfs balance start --full-balance' option to skip this
        warning. The operation will start in 10 seconds.
        Use Ctrl-C to stop it.
10 9 8 7 6 5 4 3 2 1
Starting balance without any filters.
Done, had to relocate 3 out of 3 chunks
[root@server1 ~]# btrfs filesystem show /dev/sdb
Label: none   uuid: d24b970b-86f1-4245-a382-d2a3da02b18f
        Total     devices 4    FS bytes used 256.00KiB
        devid         1 size    1.00GiB used 288.00MiB path /dev/sdb
        devid         2 size    1.00GiB used 288.00MiB path /dev/sdc
        devid         3 size    1.00GiB used 416.00MiB path /dev/sdd
        devid         4 size    1.00GiB used 416.00MiB path /dev/sde
[root@server1 ~]#_
```

Server Storage Configuration Scenarios

For a Linux workstation, fault tolerance for storage is rarely configured; however, for a Linux server, keeping the operating system, applications, and data fault tolerance is key to ensuring that the server can continue to provide services on the network. On most servers, two fault-tolerant storage approaches are used simultaneously; one to protect the operating system and applications, and another to protect the data that is used by the applications. Consequently, most rackmount servers on the market today come standard with two hard disk or SSDs for hosting the operating system and applications in a RAID 1 configuration. The administrator must choose whether to add local storage or an iSCSI-capable network interface or FC HBA for connection to a SAN.

Although the specific storage configuration of a rackmount server varies widely depending on the intended use of the server, some common fault-tolerant storage configurations for the operating system and applications include the following:

- Two hard disks or SSDs in a hardware RAID 1 configuration
- Two hard disks or SSDs in a firmware RAID 1 configuration
- Two hard disks or SSDs in a software RAID 1 configuration (configured during Linux installation)
- Two hard disks or SSDs in a BTRFS RAID 1 configuration (configured during Linux installation)

Additionally, some common fault-tolerant storage configurations used to host application data and virtual hard disk files include the following:

- Multiple hard disks or SSDs in a hardware RAID 5, 6, 10, or 15 configuration
- Multiple hard disks or SSDs in a software RAID 5, 6, 10, or 15 configuration
- A connection to an iSCSI or FC SAN (which uses fault-tolerant hardware RAID 5, 6, 10, or 15 on the SAN device)
- Multiple hard disks, SSDs, or SANs in a ZFS raidz, raidz2, or raidz3 configuration
- Multiple hard disks or SSDs in a BTRFS RAID 5, 6, or 10 configuration

Note

Of the fault-tolerant storage configurations for data listed, SAN and ZFS configurations are the most commonly implemented today.

Installing a Linux Server Distribution

Any Linux distribution can be used as a server if the necessary packages are installed that provide for server services on the network. However, many Linux distributions also provide a version that is geared for Linux servers. These **Linux server distributions** do not have a GUI environment installed by default, because administration of Linux installed on a rackmount server is often performed using commands within a BASH terminal on a remote computer across the network.

Although most Linux software is normally obtained from Internet software repositories, many Linux server distributions ship with a set of server software packages that you can optionally select during the installation process.

Note

Remote administration methods are discussed in Chapter 12.

Note

The configuration of common server software packages is covered in Chapter 13.

The installation process for a Linux server distribution differs from a standard or live Linux installation process. No GUI environment is loaded during the installation process, and the installation program often prompts you for additional information that is necessary for a server, so that you don't need to configure that same information afterwards, including:

- *The host name and IP configuration of the server*—For a desktop system, the default hostname (localhost) will often suffice. However, for a server system, the host name is often used by the configuration of server services and should match the name that other computers on the network will use when contacting the server. Additionally, many Linux administrators prefer to configure a static IP address on server systems rather than obtain an IP address automatically. This ensures that the IP address of the server cannot change over time.
- *Whether to allow for automatic updating*—Most Linux systems are configured by default to download important OS and application updates periodically. However, for a Linux server, an update could potentially cause problems with software that is currently running on the server. As a result, most Linux administrators prefer to manually update software after testing the update on a non-production computer that contains the same software as the server. Application updates will be discussed in more depth in Chapter 11.
- *Package selection*—While most Linux workstation distributions automatically install a predefined set of software packages during installation without user input, Linux server distributions often prompt you to select the specific software packages that will be needed on the Linux server. This prevents unnecessary packages from being installed and space from being wasted on the server filesystems.
- *Server service configuration*—Some server service packages that are installed require additional configuration in order to provide functionality. The installation

program for a Linux server distribution may prompt you for that information during the installation so that you don't need to configure it afterwards.

- *Boot loader configuration*—During the Fedora installation program, you are not prompted to supply information regarding the boot loader that will be used to boot the Linux kernel. However, some Linux server distributions prompt you for the location of the Linux boot loader during the installation. **GRUB (GRand Unified Boot loader)** is the standard boot loader used on Linux systems. On systems that have a UEFI BIOS, the first part of GRUB is typically installed on the UEFI System Partition that is created by the Linux installation program or previously by another operating system. On systems that have a regular BIOS, most Linux distributions install the first part of GRUB on the MBR/GPT (e.g., /dev/sda). However, you can also choose to install the first part of GRUB on the first sector of the Linux partition that holds the kernel (e.g., /dev/sda1). Boot loaders will be discussed in more depth in Chapter 8.

Note

In Hands-On Project 6-1, you install the Ubuntu Server 18.04 Linux distribution, and in Hands-On Project 6-7, you install the legacy Ubuntu Server 14.04 Linux distribution. In addition to providing the opportunity to apply concepts in later chapters to more than one Linux distribution, these projects allow you to configure both modern and legacy Linux components that are not found in Fedora Linux, such as the Debian Package Manager, the SysV initialization system, and the system log daemon.

Because servers provide a critical role within the organization, it is important to verify that the installation process has completed successfully and that all hardware components are working properly with the OS after installation.

Dealing with Problems during Installation

Most problems that occur during a Linux installation are related to faulty hardware or an incorrect device driver for a hardware component. In both cases, the installation may end abnormally and a "fatal signal 11" error message may appear on the screen. This indicates an error, known as a **segmentation fault**, in which a program accesses an unassigned area of RAM. If a segmentation fault occurs when you are installing Linux, first check the RAM for errors by running the memtest86 utility shown in Figure 2-6. The memtest86 utility is included on nearly all Linux installation media and can be run from the welcome screen that first appears when you boot the computer from the installation media.

If you experience a segmentation fault during installation and the memtest86 utility finds no RAM errors, check with the hardware manufacturer of the system (as well as the hardware manufacturer of any additional hardware devices added to the system prior to installation) to determine if an updated chipset or storage controller driver is available for your distribution of Linux. If one is available that is needed during the installation process, the manufacturer will often provide instructions that allow you to specify the new driver during the installation process. This often involves switching to another terminal during installation (e.g., tty5), mounting a USB flash memory drive that contains the drivers, and running a manufacturer-provided driver installation script.

You can also experience a segmentation fault during installation if your CPU is overclocked or some hardware component is faulty. Zeroing in on the right piece of hardware can be tricky, and most often it is CPU, RAM, or storage-related. Some segmentation faults can be fixed by turning off the CPU cache memory, disabling power management functionality, or by increasing the number of memory wait states in the BIOS/UEFI. Segmentation faults caused by storage device failures can sometimes be solved by disabling the associated storage controller in the BIOS/UEFI.

> **Note** 🖉
>
> An **overclocked** CPU is a CPU that is faster than the speed for which the processor was designed. Although this might lead to increased performance, it also makes the processor hotter and can result in intermittent computer crashes.

> **Note** 🖉
>
> If the installation fails with an error other than fatal signal 11, consult the support documentation for your distribution of Linux, or check the associated Internet forums.

Dealing with Problems after Installation

Even after a successful Linux installation, problems might arise if an installation task, such as an application installation or configuration task, failed to execute during installation or a system process failed to load successfully at boot time. Additionally, hardware components may not be recognized or function properly when used by applications if the system does not have the correct Linux device drivers configured for each hardware device within the system.

Viewing Installation Logs

To see whether all installation tasks performed successfully, you should check the **installation log files** immediately following installation; these are created by the installation program, and record the events that occurred during installation, including errors. For Fedora Linux, these log files are stored in the /var/log/anaconda/ directory; and for Ubuntu Server Linux, these log files are stored in the /var/log/installer/ directory. To search these files for errors and warnings, you should use the grep command, as their contents are often quite lengthy. For example, the egrep -i "(error|warn)" /var/log/anaconda/* command can be used to search for any errors or warnings within the log files in the /var/log/anaconda directory.

Understanding Linux Device Drivers

In order for the Linux kernel to work with any hardware device, it must have the correct device driver software for the device. After the Linux kernel is loaded into memory at the beginning of the boot process, it detects the hardware devices within the system. For hardware devices that are essential at the beginning of the boot process, such as storage devices, the associated device drivers are often compiled into the Linux kernel and referenced by a device file in the /dev directory, as discussed earlier in Chapter 5. Other devices (such as video cards, motherboard chipsets, network interface cards, FC HBAs, and so on) typically have a device driver loaded into the Linux kernel as a **module**.

Modules end with the .ko (kernel object) extension and are typically stored within subdirectories under the /lib/modules/*kernelversion*/ or /usr/lib/modules/*kernelversion*/ directory. They can be manually loaded into the Linux kernel using the insmod command or the modprobe **command**. To see a list of modules that are currently loaded into the Linux kernel, you can use the lsmod **command**. You can also view detailed information about a particular module using the modinfo **command**, or remove a module from the Linux kernel using the rmmod **command**.

Note

Some Linux distributions, such as Fedora, compress kernel modules; as a result, these modules will end with a longer *extension*, such as .ko.xz. Compression is discussed in Chapter 11.

As the Linux kernel detects each hardware component at boot time, it loads the associated module. However, for some hardware devices, the Linux kernel cannot detect them at all; for others, it cannot detect them properly. In these cases, the system can load the module manually at boot time via entries in a configuration file. Legacy Linux distributions list modules to load manually within the /etc/modprobe.conf, /etc/modules.conf, or /etc/modules text files, depending on the distribution. Modern Linux distributions list modules to load manually at boot time within text files located in the /etc/modprobe.d/, /etc/modules-load.d/, or /usr/lib/modules-load.d/ directories. Software packages often add files to these directories when they are installed if they require a module to be loaded into the Linux kernel manually.

Note

Not all modules are used to provide device drivers for hardware; many software components, such as ZFS, are implemented by modules that are loaded manually into the Linux kernel at boot time.

Hardware components are also detected as part of the Linux installation process. If the Linux installation program finds that a particular piece of hardware is not automatically detectable by the Linux kernel, it will modify the appropriate file to ensure that the module is loaded manually at boot time. However, if no module is available for the hardware device, or the Linux installation program cannot successfully detect the hardware, you need to identify the hardware component that requires the device driver after installation, and then search for and install the associated module. Most hardware vendors provide a Linux software package with device drivers for their products. Installing this software package adds the module to a subfolder under the /lib/modules/*kernelversion*/ or /usr/lib/modules/*kernelversion*/ directory as well as add a file within the /etc/modprobe.d/, /etc/modules-load.d/, or /usr/lib/modules-load.d /directory to ensure that the module is loaded manually at boot time.

Note

Vendor websites list the instructions necessary to install Linux device drivers for their hardware. Software installation will be discussed in depth within Chapter 11.

Note

Some modules depend on other modules. After installing a new module by adding a Linux device driver package to the system, you should run the `depmod` **command** to update the module dependency database.

If you are running Linux as a guest operating system within virtualization software, it needs the appropriate modules loaded to interact with the virtualized hardware provided by the hypervisor. Most modern Linux distributions ship with the modules needed to interact with most mainstream hypervisors used within server environments, including Hyper-V, VMWare, and KVM. For example, if you run Linux as a guest operating system within Hyper-V, you will see several modules that start with either hv_ or hyperv_ in the output of the lsmod command. These modules provide the necessary support for the virtualized hardware provided by Hyper-V. Similarly, lsmod will list several modules that start with vmw on a VMWare hypervisor, or several modules that start with virtio on a KVM hypervisor. If you do not see these modules running on your Linux distribution, you can download and install the appropriate guest driver package for your Linux distribution from the hypervisor vendor's website.

Verifying Hardware Configuration

After a Linux installation, you should ensure that all of your hardware has been detected and is functioning properly; if it is not, you may need to make configuration changes to your system or install the appropriate device driver software as described in the previous section. You can use many methods to view and verify your hardware configuration, including the /proc directory, the /sys directory, hardware commands, and startup logs.

The /proc directory is mounted to a pseudo filesystem (procfs) contained within RAM that lists system information made available by the Linux kernel. The following sample listing of the /proc directory shows many file and subdirectory contents:

```
[root@server1 ~]# ls -F /proc
1/      1171/   171/    3/      415/    48/     801/            kallsyms        softirqs
10/     12/     172/    300/    417/    484/    9/              kcore           stat
1018/   1224/   173/    334/    418/    485/    acpi/           keys            swaps
1020/   1239/   174/    361/    419/    49/     buddyinfo       key-users       sys/
1024/   1257/   175/    362/    422/    5/      bus/            kmsg            sysrq
1028/   1266/   176/    364/    424/    548/    cgroups         kpagecount      sysvipc/
1038/   1282/   177/    365/    425/    550/    cmdline         kpageflags      timer
1068/   1284/   178/    367/    426/    58/     consoles        loadavg         timer_s
1074/   1288/   179/    368/    428/    59/     cpuinfo         locks           tty/
1077/   13/     18/     369/    434/    6/      crypto          mdstat          uptime
1084/   1317/   180/    371/    436/    60/     devices         meminfo         version
1090/   14/     187/    372/    437/    62/     diskstats       misc            vmallocin
11/     15/     188/    373/    449/    624/    dma             modules         vmstat
1106/   16/     19/     383/    45/     64/     driver/         mounts@         zoneinfo
1109/   163/    190/    384/    455/    7/      execdomains     mtrr
1112/   165/    2/      385/    456/    72/     fb              net@
1117/   166/    20/     392/    459/    748/    filesystems     pagetypeinfo
1137/   167/    203/    393/    46/     751/    fs/             partitions
1141/   168/    204/    394/    460/    752/    interrupts      sched_debug
1159/   169/    205/    399/    462/    755/    iomem           scsi/
1165/   17/     287/    410/    47/     758/    ioports         self@
1168/   170/    297/    413/    478/    8/      irq/            slabinfo
[root@server1 ~]#
```

The subdirectories that start with a number in the preceding output are used to display process information; other directories can contain kernel parameters. The files listed in the preceding output are text representations of various parts of the Linux system; they are updated continuously by the Linux kernel and can be viewed using standard text commands, such as `cat` or `less`. For example, you could view the output of the `less /proc/cpuinfo` command to see the information Linux has detected regarding the CPUs in the system, or you could view the output of the `less /proc/meminfo` command to see the information Linux has detected regarding the RAM in the system. If this information is incorrect because Linux failed to detect the processor or RAM information properly, you might need to change a setting in the BIOS/UEFI or install the correct device driver for your motherboard chipset.

The /proc directory contains many more files that you will find useful when examining a system after installation; Table 6-1 describes the most common of these files.

Table 6-1   Files commonly found in the /proc directory

Filename	Contents
cmdline	The command used to load the current Linux kernel
cpuinfo	Information regarding the processors in the computer
devices	List of the character and block devices that are currently in use by the Linux kernel
execdomains	List of execution domains for processes on the system; execution domains allow a process to execute in a specific manner
fb	List of framebuffer devices in use on the Linux system; typically, these include video adapter card devices
filesystems	List of filesystems supported by the Linux kernel
interrupts	List of IRQs in use on the system
iomem	List of memory addresses currently used
ioports	List of memory address ranges reserved for device use
kcore	A representation of the physical memory inside the computer; this file should not be viewed
kmsg	Temporary storage location for messages from the kernel
loadavg	Statistics on the performance of the processor
locks	List of files currently locked by the kernel
mdstat	Configuration of RAID volumes
meminfo	Information regarding physical and virtual memory on the Linux system
misc	List of miscellaneous devices and their minor numbers (major number = 10)
modules	List of currently loaded modules in the Linux kernel
mounts	List of currently mounted filesystems
partitions	Information regarding partition tables loaded in memory on the system
swaps	Information on virtual memory utilization
version	Version information for the Linux kernel and libraries

Like the /proc directory, the /sys directory is also mounted to a special filesystem (sysfs) contained within RAM. However, it primarily lists the detailed configuration of different types of devices on the system for use by commands and other software. The following output shows the major subdirectories under /sys, the block devices that were detected on the system, as well as the detailed configuration (including partition names) for sda:

```
[root@server1 ~]# ls -F /sys
block/   class/   devices/    fs/            kernel/   power/
bus/     dev/     firmware/   hypervisor/    module/
[root@server1 ~]# ls /sys/block
dm-0  nvme0n1  sda  sdb  sdc  sr0
[root@server1 ~]# ls /sys/block/sda
alignment_offset   events             inflight    ro      sda6    subsys
bdi                events_async       integrity   sda1    sda7    trace
capability         events_poll_msecs  power       sda2    sda8    uevent
dev                ext_range          queue       sda3    size
device             hidden             range       sda4    slaves
discard_alignment  holders            removable   sda5    stat
[root@server1 ~]#_
```

While the /proc and /sys directories contain the most detailed hardware information, it is often difficult to interpret easily. However, you can use many Linux commands to display key hardware information as shown in Table 6-2.

Table 6-2	Linux commands that display hardware information
Command	**Description**
lscpu	Displays system CPU information
lsmem	Displays system RAM information
lsdev	Displays interrupts, IO ports, and DMA channels used by hardware devices on the system
lspci	Displays information about connected PCI controllers and devices on the system
lsusb	Displays information about connected USB controllers and devices on the system
lsscsi	Displays information about connected SCSI controllers and devices on the system
lsblk	Displays information about connected block storage devices on the system
lshw	Displays general hardware information for the entire system

The lshw **command** shown in Table 6-2 is the most versatile; it can display hardware information regarding the motherboard, firmware, RAM, CPU, storage, network, video, PCI, and USB hardware devices within your system in an easy-to-read format. When run without options, it displays all information, but you can specify a class (type) of hardware; for example, the `lshw -class video` command would only list installed video display adapter hardware, and the `lshw -class network` command would only list installed network hardware. If the output from these commands does not list the correct video display adapter or network hardware in your system, you will need to install the appropriate device driver software.

You can also view the hardware detected by the Linux kernel during boot time using the **dmesg** command after system startup, as shown in the following output:

```
[root@server1 ~]# dmesg | less
[0.000000] Initializing cgroup subsys cpuset
[0.000000] Initializing cgroup subsys cpu
[0.000000] Initializing cgroup subsys cpuacct
[0.000000] Linux version 3.11.10-301.fc20.x86_64
(mockbuild@bkernel01.phx2.fedoraproject.org) (gcc version 4.8.2
20131017 (Red Hat 4.8.2-1) (GCC) ) #1 SMP Thu Dec 5 14:01:17 UTC 2013
[0.000000] Command line: BOOT_IMAGE=/vmlinuz-3.11.10-301.fc20.x86_64
root=/dev/sda3 ro vconsole.font=latarcyrheb-sun16 rhgb quiet
LANG=en_US.UTF-8
[0.000000] e820: BIOS-provided physical RAM map:
[0.000000] BIOS-e820: [mem 0x000000000000-0x000000000009fbff] usable
[0.000000] BIOS-e820: [mem 0x00000009fc00-0x000000009ffff] reserved
[0.000000] BIOS-e820: [mem 0x0000000e0000-0x0000000fffff] reserved
[0.000000] BIOS-e820: [mem 0x000000100000-0x000000007ffefff] usable
[0.000000] BIOS-e820: [mem 0x00007fff0000-0x000000007fffefff] ACPI data
[0.000000] BIOS-e820: [mem 0x00007ffff000-0x000000007fffffff] ACPI NVS
[0.000000] NX (Execute Disable) protection: active
[0.000000] SMBIOS 2.3 present.
[0.000000] DMI: Microsoft Corporation Virtual Machine/Virtual Machine, BIOS
090006   05/23/2012
[0.000000] Hypervisor detected: Microsoft HyperV
[0.000000] HyperV: features 0xe7f, hints 0x2c
[0.000000] e820: update [mem 0x00000000-0x00000fff] usable ==> reserved
[0.000000] e820: remove [mem 0x000a0000-0x000fffff] usable
:
```

Note

Modern Linux systems that include Systemd use a database system called **journald** to store system events; to view these events, you can use the `journalctl` **command**. On these systems, the `journalctl -k` command will display the same information shown by the dmesg command. Systemd is discussed in Chapter 8.

If `dmesg` reports that the hardware device was detected at boot time, but other hardware commands do not list the hardware device, then the device driver for that hardware was not available on the system and must be installed. Alternatively, `dmesg` may report that a particular hardware device is unavailable for other reasons. For example, if `dmesg` reports that a Wi-Fi network interface was detected but not loaded due to a chipset restriction, the Wi-Fi functionality may have been disabled by a keyboard combination, which is common on laptop computers.

Verifying System Processes

After installing a Linux system, several system processes will be loaded during each boot process. If a software component is missing or misconfigured, one or more of these system processes may fail during the boot process. You can view the system processes that started successfully or unsuccessfully during boot time by viewing the contents of the /var/log/boot.log, /var/log/messages, or /var/log/syslog file on most Linux distributions. A sample boot.log file from the Fedora system that indicates the Virtualization daemon failed to load is shown in the following output:

```
root@server1:~# tail /var/log/boot.log
[  OK  ] Starting Network Manager Script Dispatcher Service...
[  OK  ] Started Permit User Sessions.
[  OK  ] Starting GNOME Display Manager...
[  OK  ] Started Job spooling tools.
[  OK  ] Started Command Scheduler.
[FAILED] Starting Virtualization daemon...
[  OK  ] Started Network Manager Script Dispatcher Service.
[  OK  ] Started Disk Manager.
[  OK  ] Started GNOME Display Manager.
[  OK  ] Started Virtualization daemon.root@server1:~# _
```

On modern Linux systems that include Systemd, you can instead use the `journalctl -b` command to display the system process that started or failed to start at boot time. Because the `journalctl` command will display entries for multiple system boots, it is important to narrow down the time frame. The following command only displays boot information from the current day:

```
[root@server1 ~]# journalctl -b --since=today | less
-- Logs begin at Sun 2019-07-08 20:15:49 EDT, end at Wed 2019-08-01
20:45:24 EDT. -
Aug 01 20:44:12 server1 systemd[1]: Starting Virtual Machine and
Container Registration Service...
Aug 01 20:44:12 server1 systemd[1]: Starting Avahi mDNS/DNS-SD Stack...
Aug 01 20:44:12 server1 systemd[1]: Starting Login Service...
Aug 01 20:44:12 server1 systemd[1]: Starting Disk Manager...
Aug 01 20:44:12 server1 systemd[1]: Started D-Bus System Message Bus.
```

```
Aug 01 20:44:12 server1 ModemManager[639]: <info> ModemManager
(version 1.6.12-3.fc28) starting in system bus...
Aug 01 20:44:12 server1 systemd[1]: Starting firewalld...
Aug 01 20:44:12 server1 systemd[1]: Starting GSSAPI Proxy Daemon...
Aug 01 20:44:12 server1 systemd-logind[647]: New seat seat0.
Aug 01 20:44:12 server1 systemd[1]: Started Switcheroo Control Proxy.
:
```

If a system process fails to load, it may be because it has misconfigured settings that are specific to the service, or that it was not installed properly during the Linux installation; in this case, you can often remove and reinstall the process to remedy the problem.

System Rescue

Booting to a live Linux OS from live installation media offers several benefits to Linux administrators when repairing a damaged Linux system. The live OS contains a small bootable Linux kernel and virtual filesystem that are loaded into RAM and have access to the filesystems on the underlying hard disk. As a result, you can use the utilities on the live OS to fix problems within a Linux installation on the hard disk that are preventing the Linux installation from booting, such as:

- Boot loader problems
- Filesystem/partition problems
- Configuration file problems
- Driver problems

All live OS systems contain several utilities for fixing system problems, including fdisk, parted, e2mkfs, fsck, and several more that will be introduced in later chapters. Recall from the previous chapter that the `fsck` command can only be run on an unmounted filesystem. If the / (root) filesystem becomes corrupted, you can boot your system using the live installation media for your Linux distribution and use the `fsck` command in the live OS to check the / (root) filesystem on the hard disk as it is not mounted by the live OS by default.

> **Note** 📎
>
> The process of using a live OS to repair problems on another Linux system installed on the hard disk is commonly called **system rescue**.

You can also configure the Linux kernel loaded by the live OS to use the / (root) filesystem on the hard disk. To do this, mount the / (root) filesystem on your local disk under an empty directory in the live OS (e.g., /mnt) and then type `chroot /mnt` at the command prompt. The `chroot` **command** will then change the root of the live OS to the /mnt directory, which is actually the / (root) filesystem on the local disk. From this point, you will have root user access to any commands on your / (root) filesystem, as you normally would if you had booted your Linux system on the hard disk. For example, if you run the `passwd` command (used for changing user passwords), you'll actually be changing the password for the root user on the Linux system installed on the hard drive. This is often used to recover a locally accessible Linux system if the root password has been lost or forgotten.

This feature is not limited to live installation media. If you install Linux from standard installation media, the welcome screen often provides a system rescue option for booting a small live Linux system that does not contain a GUI environment. This small live Linux system contains the same recovery utilities (fdisk, parted, e2mkfs, fsck, etc.) and will allow you to mount the / (root) filesystem on your hard disk as well as run the `chroot` command to switch your live Linux system to it.

Chapter Summary

- Linux servers typically use far more hardware than desktop systems. This hardware is installed in a rack using a rackmount form factor.
- SCSI storage (specifically SAS) is common on Linux servers, as are connections to SAN storage devices using the iSCSI or Fibre Channel protocols. DM-MPIO can be optionally used to provide multiple redundant connections to one or more SANs.
- RAID is often used within Linux servers to combine several hard disks into a single volume for speed or fault tolerance. It can be implemented by software that runs within the OS, hardware on a hard disk controller card, or by the system firmware.
- ZFS is a high-performance, fault-tolerant filesystem that is commonly installed on Linux servers. ZFS provides much of the

same functionality as RAID, using storage space that spans a wide range of storage devices, including local disks, SANs, shared devices, large raw files, and remote shares.

- Although it is still being developed, BTRFS is designed to be a replacement for the ext4 filesystem that offers some of the volume and RAID features of ZFS.
- Linux server distributions do not contain a GUI environment and are often administered remotely. They have an installation process that prompts for additional information compared to other Linux distributions.
- Unsupported or defective hardware is the most common cause of a failed Linux installation. Improper or missing device drivers are the most common cause of issues immediately following a Linux installation.

- Following a Linux installation, you should check installation logs, examine the files within the /proc and /sys directories, view the output of hardware-related commands, as well as view system logs created during boot time.

- You can use the bootable OS found on standard and live Linux installation media to access and repair a damaged Linux installation.

Key Terms

1U server
blade server
Boxes
B-tree File System (BTRFS)
btrfs command
BTRFS subvolume
btrfsck command
chroot command
data
depmod command
Device Mapper MPIO (DM-MPIO)
disk mirroring
disk striping
disk striping with parity
dmesg command
fault tolerant
Fibre Channel (FC)
firmware RAID
GRUB (GRand Unified Boot loader)
guest operating system
hardware RAID
Host Bus Adapter (HBA)
host operating system
hypervisor
insmod command
installation log files
Internet SCSI (iSCSI)
iSCSI initiator

iSCSI target
iscsiadm command
journalctl command
journald
Just a Bunch of Disks (JBOD)
Kernel Virtual Machine (KVM)
Linux server distribution
Logical Unit Number (LUN)
lshw command
lsmod command
mdadm command
metadata
mkfs.btrfs command
modinfo command
modprobe command
module
mpathconf command
Multipath Input Output (MPIO)
overclocked
parallel SCSI
Quick Emulator (Qemu)
rackmount server
RAID-Z
Redundant Array of Independent Disks (RAID)
rmmod command
SCSI ID

segmentation fault
Serial Attached SCSI (SAS)
Simple Protocol for Independent Computing Environments (SPICE)
snapshot
software RAID
spanning
Storage Area Network (SAN)
system
system rescue
target ID
terminator
thick provisioning
thin provisioning
Type 1 hypervisor
Type 2 hypervisor
uninterruptible power supply (UPS)
virtual machine
Virtual Network Computing (VNC)
virtualization
World Wide Name (WWN)
Zettabyte File System (ZFS)
zfs command
ZFS pool
ZFS subfilesystem
ZFS volume
zpool command

Review Questions

1. BTRFS filesystems do not need to be checked for errors as they are resilient to data corruption. True or False?

2. Which of the following describes a computer that is used to access an iSCSI hard disk across the network?
   a. iSCSI target
   b. iSCSI requestor
   c. iSCSI initiator
   d. iSCSI terminator

3. You want to view log files to get information about a problem that occurred during a Linux installation. In which directory will you likely find the log files?
   a. /root/log
   b. /sys/log
   c. /var/log
   d. /etc/log

4. Which of the following RAID levels is not fault tolerant?
   a. RAID 0
   b. RAID 1
   c. RAID 4
   d. RAID 5

5. Which command can you use during a system rescue to switch from the root of the live OS to the root of the Linux system installed on the hard disk?
   a. `mount`
   b. `sysimage`
   c. `chroot`
   d. `rescue`

6. Which of the following is not a type of RAID?
   a. hardware RAID
   b. software RAID
   c. firmware RAID
   d. serial RAID

7. Where is the /proc filesystem stored?
   a. in RAM
   b. on the hard disk drive in the / directory
   c. on the hard disk drive in the /etc directory
   d. on the hard disk drive in the /var directory

8. When configuring a virtual hard disk file, which term refers to the feature that allows the virtual hard disk file to expand dynamically as space is requested by the guest operating system?
   a. thick provisioning
   b. Type 1
   c. thin provisioning
   d. Type 2

9. DM-MPIO can be configured to provide multiple, redundant connections to data stored on a SAN. True or False?

10. What component of a Linux server is used to connect to a Fibre Channel SAN?
    a. FC initiator
    b. FC target
    c. FC HBA
    d. WWPN

11. Which type of RAID can be entirely configured during the Linux installation process?
    a. hardware RAID
    b. software RAID
    c. firmware RAID
    d. serial RAID

12. What command can be used to create a ZFS volume called test from the space on /dev/sdb and /dev/sdc that functions like RAID level 1?
    a. `zpool create test /dev/sdb /dev/sdc`
    b. `zpool create test mirror /dev/sdb /dev/sdc`
    c. `zpool create test raidz /dev /sdb /dev/sdc`
    d. `zpool create test raidz2 /dev/sdb /dev/sdc`

13. To which directory will the test ZFS volume from the previous question be mounted by the ZFS system?
    a. /mnt/test
    b. /media/test
    c. /zfs/test
    d. /test

14. Linux servers are typically installed in a rack using rackmount server hardware. Which of the following describes the minimum height of a rackmount server?
    a. 1U
    b. Series A
    c. Type A
    d. Level 5

15. Which of the following commands can quickly determine whether your network hardware was detected properly following a Linux installation?
    a. `cat /proc/modules/network`
    b. `lspci`
    c. `lshw -class network`
    d. `dmesg`

16. ZFS volumes are mounted at boot time from entries within /etc/fstab by default. True or False?

17. Which of the following could result in a segmentation fault (fatal signal 11) during a Fedora installation?
    a. RAM problems
    b. overclocked CPU
    c. faulty hardware components
    d. all of the above

18. When viewing the output of the lsmod command, you notice several modules that start with vmw. What does this indicate?
    a. Linux is running as a guest operating system.
    b. Device drivers need to be installed on your system.
    c. There is no virtual memory in your system.
    d. The system is running the KVM hypervisor.

19. What type of redundant storage configuration is most common for hosting the operating system and applications on a server?
    a. RAID 5
    b. ZFS
    c. RAID 1
    d. SAN + DM-MPIO

20. Which of the following commands can be used on a modern Linux system to view hardware information that was captured at the beginning of the boot process?
    a. `less /var/log/boot.log`
    b. `less /var/log/messages`
    c. `less /var/log/syslog`
    d. `journalctl -k`

Hands-On Projects

These projects should be completed in the order given. The hands-on projects presented in this chapter should take a total of three hours to complete. The requirements for this lab include:

- A computer with Fedora 28 installed according to Hands-On Project 2-1
- The ISO image for Ubuntu Server 18.04 installation media (ubuntu-18.04.1-live-server-amd64.iso)
- The ISO image for Ubuntu Server 14.04 LTS installation media (ubuntu-14.04.5-server-amd64.iso)

Project 6-1

In this hands-on project, you install Ubuntu Server 18.04 Linux within a virtual machine on a Windows computer and examine the LVM partition configuration afterwards.

1. In your virtualization software, create a new virtual machine called **Ubuntu Server 18** that has the following characteristics:
   a. 2GB of memory
   b. An Internet connection via your PC's network card (preferably using an external virtual switch or bridged mode)
   c. A 50GB SATA/SCSI/SAS virtual hard disk (dynamically allocated)
   d. The virtual machine DVD drive attached to the ISO file for the Ubuntu Server 18.04 installation media (ubuntu-18.04.1-live-server-amd64.iso)
2. Start and then connect to your Ubuntu Server Linux virtual machine using your virtualization software.

Note

The Ubuntu Server Linux installation program does not use a graphical desktop. As a result, you must switch between buttons shown on the screen using the Tab key and then press Enter to make your selections.

3. At the Welcome screen, ensure that **English** is selected and press **Enter**.
4. At the Keyboard configuration screen, select the correct keyboard layout and select **Done**. For most keyboards this layout will be English (US).
5. At the Ubuntu 18.04 welcome screen, examine the options. Note that Ubuntu allows you the option to install in a small footprint Type 1 hypervisor configuration designed to host virtual machines within a cloud environment that they've called Metal as a Service (MaaS); you will install a full Ubuntu Server installation instead. Ensure that **Install Ubuntu** is selected and press **Enter**.

6. At the Network connections screen, note that your network interface is set to obtain an IP address from a DHCP server by default and select **Done**.

7. At the Configure proxy screen, optionally supply the URL address of your classroom proxy (if your classroom uses one), and select **Done**.

8. At the Configure Ubuntu archive mirror screen, select **Done**.

9. At the Filesystem setup screen, select **Use Entire Disk And Set Up LVM**, and then select your 50GB virtual hard disk. Note that the installation program will create a partition for the /boot filesystem (as well as a GPT BIOS boot partition, or partition for the /boot/efi filesystem, if applicable), as well as an LVM PV for the remainder of the hard drive that is part of the ubuntu-vg VG. Also note that there is a single 4GB ubuntu-lv LV created for the / filesystem.

   a. Navigate to the ubuntu-lv LV, press **Enter**, and select **Edit**. Change the name of this LV to **ubuntu-lv-root** and the size to **44.000G**, and then select **Save**.

   b. Navigate to the ubuntu-vg VG, press **Enter**, and select **Create Logical Volume**. Change the name of this LV to **ubuntu-lv-swap** and the size to **4.000G**. Select a format of **swap** and then select **Create**.

   c. Select **Done** and then select **Continue** when prompted to complete the disk configuration.

10. At the Profile setup screen, supply the following information and select **Done** when finished:

    a. Your name = supply your real name

    b. Your server's name = **ubuntu18**

    c. Username = **user1**

    d. Password = **LINUXrocks!**

11. At the Featured Server Snaps screen, select **Done**.

12. At the Install complete screen, select **Reboot Now**. When prompted to remove your installation medium, use your virtualization software to disconnect your Ubuntu Server 18 ISO (ubuntu-18.04.1-live-server-amd64.iso) from the virtual DVD drive and press **Enter**.

13. After the system has booted, note that a graphical login is not available. Log into tty1 as **user1** with the password **LINUXrocks!**.

14. At the command prompt, type `sudo passwd root` and press **Enter** to set the root user password. When prompted, enter your password (**LINUXrocks!**), and then enter the desired root password of **LINUXrocks!** twice to set the root user password to LINUXrocks!.

15. At the command prompt, type `su -` and press **Enter** to switch to the root user. Supply the root user password (**LINUXrocks!**) when prompted.

16. At the command prompt, type the following commands in turn and press **Enter**. Examine the output of each one:

    a. `df -hT`

    b. `fdisk -l`

    c. `lvdisplay`

    d. `lsblk`

    e. `blkid`

    f. `ls -l /dev/disk/by-uuid`

    g. `ls -l /dev/disk/by-partuuid`

    h. `ls -l /dev/disk/by-id`

    i. `ls -l /dev/disk/by-path`

    j. `cat /etc/fstab`

17. Type `exit` and press **Enter** to log out of your shell.

Project 6-2

In this hands-on project, you add hard disks to your Ubuntu Server 18 virtual machine, configure a software RAID 5 volume, and simulate a hard disk failure and recovery. At the end of this project, you will remove your RAID configuration.

1. On your Ubuntu Server 18 virtual machine, log into the command-line terminal (tty1) using the user name of **root** and the password of **LINUXrocks!**.

2. At the command prompt, type `poweroff` and press **Enter** to power down your virtual machine. In your virtualization software, add four new 1GB dynamically allocated SATA/SAS virtual hard disks to your virtual machine configuration. When finished, boot your Ubuntu Server 18 virtual machine.

3. After your Ubuntu Server 18 virtual machine has booted, log into the command-line terminal (tty1) using the user name of **root** and the password of **LINUXrocks!**.

4. At the command prompt, type `lsblk` and press **Enter**. Note that the names of the additional disk devices are sdb, sdc, sdd, and sde.

5. At the command prompt, type `mdadm --create /dev/md0 --level=5 --raid-devices=4 /dev/sdb /dev/sdc /dev/sdd /dev/sdd --verbose` and press **Enter**.

6. At the command prompt, type `cat /proc/mdstat` and press **Enter**. Was your RAID 5 volume created successfully?

7. At the command prompt, type `cat /etc/mdadm/mdadm.conf` and press **Enter**. Is your RAID 5 volume listed within this configuration file by default?

8. At the command prompt, type `mdadm --detail --scan --verbose >/etc/mdadm/mdadm.conf` and press **Enter**. Next, type `cat /etc/mdadm/mdadm.conf` and press **Enter** and view your startup configuration.

9. At the command prompt, type `mkfs -t ext4 /dev/md0` and press **Enter** to format your RAID 5 volume with the ext4 filesystem.

10. At the command prompt, type `mkdir /data` and press **Enter** to create a mount point for your RAID 5 volume, and then type `mount /dev/md0 /data` and press **Enter** to mount your RAID 5 volume to it.

11. At the command prompt, type `cp /etc/hosts /data` and press **Enter**. Next, type `ls -F /data` and press **Enter** to verify that the hosts file was copied to your filesystem. What other directory was created on this filesystem and why?

12. At the command prompt, type `df -hT` and press **Enter**. What is the total size of your RAID 5 volume? Why is it not 4GB (4 x 1GB disks)?

13. At the command prompt, type `lsblk` and press **Enter**. Note the md0 device associations for each of your disks. Next, type `blkid` and press **Enter**. Does /dev/md0 have a filesystem UUID that can be used within /etc/fstab to automount the RAID volume at boot time?

14. At the command prompt, type `mdadm --detail /dev/md0` and press **Enter**. Are all of your four devices within the RAID volume active and working?

15. At the command prompt, type `mdadm --manage --set-faulty /dev/md0 /dev/sdc` and press **Enter** to simulate disk corruption on /dev/sdc. Next, type `mdadm --detail /dev/md0` and press **Enter** to view the failed device. Also note that the state of the RAID volume is listed as *clean* (working) and *degraded* (not fully functional).

16. Type `ls -F /data` and press **Enter**. Are your files still available and accessible? Why?

17. At the command prompt, type `mdadm --manage /dev/md0 -r /dev/sdc` and press **Enter** to remove the /dev/sdc device from the RAID volume. In a production environment, this is when you would physically remove the hard disk from the server and replace it with a working one.

18. At the command prompt, type `mdadm --manage /dev/md0 -a /dev/sdc` and press **Enter** to add the /dev/sdc device to the RAID volume again. Next, type `mdadm --detail /dev/md0` and press **Enter**. Note that the state of the drive is listed as *spare rebuilding* as the RAID volume is rebuilding the data on this drive. After a few minutes, rerun your previous command. The state should list *active sync*, which indicates that the newly added device is now fully functional and part of your RAID volume.

19. At the command prompt, type `umount /data` and press **Enter** to unmount your RAID volume. Next, type `mdadm --stop /dev/md0` and press **Enter** to remove your RAID volume.

20. At the command prompt, type `fdisk /dev/sdb` and press **Enter**. Next, type `w` and press **Enter** to save your changes, which will remove the existing RAID signature from the /dev/sdc device file. Repeat this step three more times for /dev/sdc, /dev/sdd, and /dev/sde.

21. Finally, type `rm -f /etc/mdadm/mdadm.conf` to remove the RAID configuration file.

22. Type `exit` and press **Enter** to log out of your shell.

Project 6-3

In this hands-on project, you install and configure the ZFS filesystem on your Ubuntu Server 18 virtual machine. At the end of this project, you will remove your ZFS configuration.

1. On your Ubuntu Server 18 virtual machine, log into the command-line terminal (tty1) using the user name of **root** and the password of **LINUXrocks!**.

2. At the command prompt, type the following commands (in order) to add software repositories and install ZFS support on your Ubuntu system:

   a. `apt-get update`

   b. `add-apt-repository main`

   c. `add-apt-repository restricted`

   d. `add-apt-repository universe`

   e. `add-apt-repository multiverse`

   f. `apt-get install zfsutils-linux`

> **Note** 🔗
>
> Ubuntu Server Linux uses a different package manager than Fedora Linux. The `apt-get` command is functionally equivalent to the `dnf` command that you used in previous chapters to download and install software from Internet repositories. Both `apt-get` and `dnf` are discussed in Chapter 11.

3. At the command prompt, type `zpool create data /dev/sdb -f` and press **Enter** to create a simple ZFS volume called data from the space on /dev/sdb (the `-f` option is necessary because /dev/sdb still has a RAID signature from Project 6-2). Next, type `zpool list` at the command prompt and press **Enter** to view your configuration.

4. At the command prompt, type `df -hT` and press **Enter**. Note that the data ZFS volume was mounted to /data automatically. Next, type `lsblk` at the command prompt and press **Enter**. Note that ZFS created a single partition for the data (/dev/sdb1) as well as a partition for the ZFS configuration (/dev/sdb9).

5. At the command prompt, type `cp /etc/hosts /data` and press **Enter** to copy the /etc/hosts file to the new ZFS filesystem. Next, type `ls -F /data` to verify that the hosts file was copied successfully.

6. At the command prompt, type `zpool destroy data` and press **Enter** to remove the data volume.

7. At the command prompt, type `zpool create data mirror /dev/sdb /dev/sdc -f` and press **Enter** to create a mirrored ZFS volume called data from the space on /dev/sdb and /dev/sdc that is mounted to the /data directory. Next, type `zpool list` at the command prompt and press **Enter** to view your configuration. Following this, type `zpool status data` at the command prompt and press **Enter**. Does your mirror have any problems listed?

8. At the command prompt, type `lsblk` at the command prompt and press **Enter**. Note that ZFS created partitions for the data on each hard disk (/dev/sdb1 and /dev/sdc1) as well as partitions for the ZFS configuration (/dev/sdb9 and /dev/sdc9).

9. At the command prompt, type `dd if=/dev/zero of=/dev/sdb1 count=100` and press **Enter** to overwrite a portion of /dev/sdb1 using the dd command, simulating disk corruption. Next, type `zpool scrub data` at the command prompt and press **Enter**

to update the status of the ZFS filesystem, and then type `zpool status data` at the command prompt and press **Enter**. Does your mirror have any problems listed?

10. At the command prompt, type `zpool detach data /dev/sdb` and press **Enter** to remove the bad disk (/dev/sdb) from the mirror. Type `zpool status data` at the command prompt and press **Enter** to verify that it is no longer listed.

11. At the command prompt, type `zpool attach data /dev/sdc /dev/sdd -f` and press **Enter** to mirror the data on /dev/sdc to a new disk (/dev/sdd), and then type `zpool status data` at the command prompt and press **Enter**. Is the mirror fully functional using /dev/sdc and /dev/sdd?

12. At the command prompt, type `zpool iostat -v data` and press **Enter** to view the input and output statistics for your mirror. Next, type `zpool destroy data` and press **Enter** to remove the data mirror.

13. At the command prompt, type `zpool create data raidz /dev/sdb /dev/sdc /dev/sdd /dev/sde -f` and press **Enter** to create a RAID-Z volume called data using /dev/sdb, /dev/sdc, /dev/sdd, and /dev/sde, and then type `zpool status data` at the command prompt and press **Enter** to verify the results. Next, type `zpool iostat -v data` and press **Enter** to view the input and output statistics for your RAID-Z volume.

14. At the command prompt, type each of the following commands in turn and press **Enter** to create three subdirectories under /data:

    ```
    mkdir /data/webstorage
    mkdir /data/databases
    mkdir /data/filestorage
    ```

15. At the command prompt, type `zfs list` and press **Enter**. Are the webstorage, databases, and filestorage directories listed? Why? Next, type each of the following commands in turn and press **Enter** to create three subfilesystems for each of these directories:

    ```
    zfs create data/webstorage
    zfs create data/databases
    zfs create data/filestorage
    ```

16. At the command prompt, type `zfs list` and press **Enter**. Are the webstorage, databases, and filestorage directories listed? Why?

17. At the command prompt, type `zfs get all data/webstorage` and press **Enter** to view the available options for the webstorage subfilesystem. Next, type `zfs set quota=1G data/webstorage` at the command prompt and press **Enter** to set a quota of 1GB for the subfilesystem. Next, type `zfs set compression=lz4 data /webstorage` at the command prompt and press **Enter** to enable automatic lz4 compression for files stored within the subfilesystem. Finally, type `zfs get all data/webstorage` and press **Enter** to verify that your settings were changed.

18. At the command prompt, type `zpool destroy data` and press **Enter** to remove the data volume.

19. At the command prompt, type `fdisk /dev/sdb` and press **Enter**. Next, type `d` and press **Enter** and **Enter** again to delete the ZFS configuration partition. Next, type `d` and

press **Enter** to delete the ZFS data partition. Finally, type **w** and press **Enter** to save your changes. Repeat this step three more times for /dev/sdc, /dev/sdd, and /dev/sde.

20. Type **exit** and press **Enter** to log out of your shell.

Project 6-4

In this hands-on project, you configure the BTRFS filesystem on your Ubuntu Server 18 virtual machine. At the end of this project, you will remove your BTRFS configuration.

1. On your Ubuntu Server 18 virtual machine, log into the command-line terminal (tty1) using the user name of **root** and the password of **LINUXrocks!**.

2. At the command prompt, type `mkfs.btrfs -m raid0 -d raid0 /dev/sdb /dev/sdc /dev/sdd -f` and press **Enter** to create a RAID 0 BTRFS volume that spans the three disks (the `-f` option is necessary because /dev/sdb, /dev/sdc, and /dev /sdd still have a ZFS signature from Project 6-3). Note from the output that the system configuration, data, and filesystem metadata are not fault tolerant (RAID 0). Next, type `btrfs filesystem show /dev/sdb` and press **Enter**. Note the output.

3. At the command prompt, type `mount /dev/sdb /data` and press **Enter** to mount your new BTRFS volume to the /data directory.

4. At the command prompt, type `df -hT` and press **Enter**. Note that the volume size is 3GB. Next, type `lsblk` and press **Enter**. Note that, while the BTRFS filesystem spans the three 1GB sdb, sdc, and sdd devices, only sdb is shown to be mounted to the / data directory. Finally, type `btrfs filesystem df /data` and press **Enter**. Note the output.

5. At the command prompt, type `btrfs device add -f /dev/sde /data` and press **Enter** to add /dev/sde to your BTRFS volume. Next, type `btrfs filesystem balance /data` and press **Enter** to extend the existing data, system and metadata structures to the new device.

6. At the command prompt, type `df -hT` and press **Enter**. Note that the volume size is 4GB. Next, type `btrfs filesystem df /data` and press **Enter**. Note the output.

7. At the command prompt, type `btrfs subvolume list /data` and press **Enter**. Are any subvolumes listed? Next, type `btrfs subvolume create /data/archive` and press **Enter** to create a subvolume and subdirectory under /data called archive. Finally, type `btrfs subvolume list /data` and press **Enter** to view your new subvolume.

8. At the command prompt, type `cp /etc/hosts /data/archive` and press **Enter** to create a copy of the hosts file within the archive subvolume.

9. At the command prompt, type `mkdir /archive` and press **Enter**. Next, type `mount -o subvol=archive,compress=lzo /dev/sdb /archive` and press **Enter** to mount your archive subvolume to the /archive directory with automatic compression enabled.

10. At the command prompt, type `df -hT` and press **Enter**. Next, type `ls -F /archive` and press **Enter**. Is your hosts file listed?

11. Next, type `umount /archive ; umount /data` and press **Enter** to unmount your BTRFS subvolume and volume.

12. At the command prompt, type `mkfs.btrfs -m raid1 -d raid1 /dev/sdb /dev/sdc /dev/sdd /dev/sde -f` and press **Enter** to create a RAID 1 BTRFS volume that spans the four disks. Note from the output that the system configuration, data, and filesystem metadata are fault tolerant (RAID 1). Next, type `btrfs filesystem show /dev/sdb` and press **Enter**. Note the output.

13. At the command prompt, type `mount /dev/sdb /data` and press **Enter** to mount your new BTRFS volume to the /data directory.

14. At the command prompt, type the following commands in turn and press **Enter**. Compare the output to the output you saw earlier in Step 4:

    a. `df -hT`

    b. `lsblk`

    c. `btrfs filesystem df /data`

15. Next, type `umount /data` and press **Enter** to unmount your BTRFS volume.

16. At the command prompt, type `mkfs.btrfs -m raid5 -d raid5 /dev/sdb /dev/sdc /dev/sdd /dev/sde -f` and press **Enter** to create a RAID 5 BTRFS volume that spans the four disks. Note from the output that the system configuration, data, and filesystem metadata are fault tolerant (RAID 5). Next, type `btrfs filesystem show /dev/sdb` and press **Enter**. Note the output.

17. At the command prompt, type `mount /dev/sdb /data` and press **Enter** to mount your new BTRFS volume to the /data directory.

18. At the command prompt, type the following commands in turn and press **Enter**. Compare the output to the output you saw earlier in Step 4:

    a. `df -hT`

    b. `lsblk`

    c. `btrfs filesystem df /data`

19. Next, type `umount /data` and press **Enter** to unmount your BTRFS volume.

20. At the command prompt, type `btrfs check /dev/sdb` and press **Enter** to check your BTRFS filesystem for errors. What other command can be used to perform the same check?

21. Type `exit` and press **Enter** to log out of your shell.

Project 6-5

In this hands-on project, you examine installation log files and system information on your Ubuntu Server 18 virtual machine.

1. On your Ubuntu Server 18 virtual machine, log into the command-line terminal (tty1) using the user name of **root** and the password of **LINUXrocks!**.

2. At the command prompt, type `ls /var/log/installer` and press **Enter**. Note the different log files in this directory. Next, type `less /var/log/installer/installer-journal.txt` and press **Enter**. Briefly examine the entries within this file to see each action taken during the installation process, and then type **q** to quit the less utility. Finally, type `egrep -i "(error|warn)" /var/log/installer`

`/installer-journal.txt` and press **Enter**. View any warnings or errors that the installation program generated during your installation.

3. At the command prompt, type `ls -F /proc` and press **Enter** to view the file and directory contents of the proc filesystem.

4. At the command prompt, type `less /proc/cpuinfo` and press **Enter**. Did the installation detect your CPU correctly? Type `q` to quit the less utility. Use the less command to examine some of the other files within the /proc directory listed in Table 6-1.

5. At the command prompt, type `lshw | less` and press **Enter**. Examine the entries for your system hardware and type `q` to quit the less utility when finished. Next, execute some of the other hardware commands listed in Table 6-2 (for the `lsscsi` command, you will first be prompted to install the associated package using the `apt install lsscsi` command).

6. At the command prompt, type `lsmod | less` and press **Enter**. Spend a few moments to examine the modules that are loaded into your kernel in depth, Googling their names, if necessary. Can you match them to the hardware devices you saw in the previous step? Do you see modules that are used to interact with virtualized hardware? Do you see modules that are used to provide software feature or filesystem support? Type `q` to quit the less utility when finished.

7. At the command prompt, type `modinfo dummy` and press **Enter** to view the information about the dummy module.

8. At the command prompt, type `modprobe dummy` and press **Enter** to insert the dummy module into your Linux kernel. Next, type `lsmod | less` and press **Enter**. Is the dummy module listed? Type `q` to quit the less utility, and then type `rmmod dummy` and press **Enter** to remove the dummy module from the Linux kernel.

9. At the command prompt, type `ls /etc/modprobe.d` and press **Enter**. Next, type `ls /etc/modules-load.d` and press **Enter**. Observe the entries. What are the files within these directories used for?

10. At the command prompt, type `vi /etc/modules-load.d/modules.conf` and press **Enter**. Add the line `dummy` to the end of this file, save your changes, and quit the vi editor. Next, type `reboot` and press **Enter** to reboot your virtual machine.

11. After Ubuntu Server 18 has booted, log into the command-line terminal (tty1) using the user name of **root** and the password of **LINUXrocks!**. At the command prompt, type `lsmod | less` and press **Enter**. Is the dummy module listed? Type `q` to quit the less utility.

12. At the command prompt, type `dmesg | less` and press **Enter**. Observe the entries. How do they correspond with the hardware information that you saw within this project? Type `q` to quit the less utility.

13. At the command prompt, type `journalctl -k | less` and press **Enter**. How does the information compare to the previous step? Type `q` to quit the less utility.

14. At the command prompt, type `less /var/log/syslog` and press **Enter**. What does each entry represent? Type `q` to quit the less utility.

15. At the command prompt, type `journalctl -b | less` and press **Enter**. How does the information compare to the previous step? Type `q` to quit the less utility.

16. Type `poweroff` and press **Enter** to power off your Ubuntu Server 18 virtual machine.

Project 6-6

In this hands-on project, you use system rescue on your Fedora Linux virtual machine using your live installation media to check your root filesystem for errors and change the root user's password.

1. In your virtualization software, ensure that the DVD for your **Fedora Linux** virtual machine is attached to the ISO image for Fedora 28 Live (Fedora-Workstation-Live-x86_64-28-1.1.iso). Next, start and then connect to your Fedora Linux virtual machine using your virtualization software.

2. At the Fedora Live welcome screen, select **Start Fedora-Workstation-Live 28** and press **Enter**.

3. After the graphical desktop and Welcome to Fedora screen have loaded, select the option **Try Fedora** and click **Close** when prompted.

4. Navigate to **Activities**, **Show Applications**, **Terminal** within the GNOME desktop to open a BASH terminal.

5. At the command prompt, type `su - root` and press **Enter** to switch to the root user.

6. At the command prompt, type `df` and press **Enter** to view the mounted filesystems. Is the root filesystem on your hard disk mounted?

7. At the command prompt, type `fsck -f /dev/sda3` and press **Enter** to check your (/) root filesystem for errors.

8. At the command prompt, type `mount /dev/sda3 /mnt` and press **Enter** to mount the (/) root filesystem on your hard disk to the /mnt directory on the Fedora live system. Next, type `mount /dev/sda1 /mnt/boot` and press **Enter** to mount the /boot filesystem on your hard disk to the /mnt/boot directory on the Fedora live system.

9. At the command prompt, type `mount -t proc proc /proc` and press **Enter** to mount the /proc filesystem.

10. At the command prompt, type `chroot /mnt` and press **Enter** to switch from the root filesystem on your Live Fedora system to the root filesystem on your hard disk (ignore any warnings). Next, type `ls /root` and press **Enter**. Do you recognize the files?

11. At the command prompt, type `passwd root` and press **Enter**. Supply a new root user password of `Secret123` and press **Enter** when prompted (twice). What warning did you receive regarding the Secret123 password?

12. Click the power icon in the upper-right corner, select the power icon that appears, and click **Power Off** to shut down your Fedora Live installation image.

13. In the Settings for your virtual machine in your virtualization software, ensure that the DVD drive is no longer attached to the Fedora ISO image.

14. Finally, start your Fedora Linux virtual machine using your virtualization software. After the system has loaded, switch to a command-line terminal (tty5) by pressing **Ctrl+Alt+F5** and log in to the terminal using the user name of **root** and the password of **Secret123**. Were you successful?

15. At the command prompt, type **passwd root** and press **Enter**. Supply a new root user password of **LINUXrocks!** and press **Enter** when prompted (twice).

16. At the command prompt, type **poweroff** and press **Enter** to shut down your Fedora Linux virtual machine.

Project 6-7

In this hands-on project, you install Ubuntu Server 14.04 LTS Linux within a virtual machine on a Windows computer and examine the LVM partition configuration afterwards.

1. In your virtualization software, create a new virtual machine called **Ubuntu Server 14** that has the following characteristics:

   a. 2GB of memory

   b. An Internet connection via your PC's network card (preferably using an external virtual switch or bridged mode)

   c. A 50GB SATA/SCSI/SAS virtual hard disk (dynamically allocated)

   d. The virtual machine DVD drive attached to the ISO file for the Ubuntu Server 14.04 installation media (ubuntu-14.04.5-server-amd64.iso)

2. Start and then connect to your Ubuntu Server 14 virtual machine using your virtualization software.

3. At the Language screen, ensure that **English** is selected and press **Enter**.

4. At the Ubuntu welcome screen, examine the options. Ensure that **Install Ubuntu Server** is selected and press **Enter**.

5. At the Select a language page, ensure that **English** is selected and press **Enter**.

6. At the Select your location screen, ensure that **United States** is selected and press **Enter**.

7. At the Configure the keyboard screen, select **Yes** and press **Enter**. Follow the prompts to complete the detection. When the detection process finds a "us" keyboard layout, select **Continue** and press **Enter**.

8. At the Configure the network screen, type a hostname of **Ubuntu14**, select **Continue**, and press **Enter**.

9. At the Set up users and passwords page, type **user1** as the full user name, select **Continue**, and press **Enter**. When prompted for the simple user name, ensure that **user1** is displayed, select **Continue**, and press **Enter**. When prompted for a password for user1, type **LINUXrocks!**, select **Continue**, and press **Enter**. When prompted to repeat the password, enter **LINUXrocks!** again, select **Continue**, and press **Enter**. When prompted to encrypt user1's home directory, ensure that **No** is selected and press **Enter**.

10. At the Configure the clock screen, ensure that the correct time zone is displayed, select **Yes**, and press **Enter**. Alternatively, if an incorrect time zone is displayed, select **No**, press **Enter**, select your time zone, and press **Enter**.

11. At the Partition disks screen, note that the default selection is **Guided – use entire disk and set up LVM** and press **Enter**. Press **Enter** again to select your disk (sda), and then select **Yes** and press **Enter** to write your partition changes to the disk. Note that the full size is used for the volume group, select **Continue**, and press **Enter**.

12. At the summary screen, note that Ubuntu will create an LV for the root filesystem with an ext4 filesystem and an LV for swap as well. Select **Yes** and press **Enter** to write the changes to the disk and start the installation of the core system packages.

13. At the Configure the package manager screen, optionally supply the URL address of your classroom proxy (if your classroom uses one), select **Continue**, and press **Enter**.

14. At the Configuring tasksel screen, ensure that **No automatic updates** is selected and press **Enter**.

15. At the Software selection screen, use the spacebar to individually choose all packages (except for Manual package selection), select **Continue**, and press **Enter**.

16. At the Configuring mysql-server-5.5 screen, supply a password of `LINUXrocks!`, select **Continue**, and press **Enter**. When prompted to confirm the password, type `LINUXrocks!`, select **Continue**, and press **Enter**.

17. At the Postfix Configuration screen, ensure that **Internet Site** is selected and press **Enter**. When prompted for a system mail name, ensure that **Ubuntu14** is listed, select **Continue**, and press **Enter**.

18. At the configuring dovecot-core screen, ensure that **Yes** is selected and press **Enter** to create an SSL encryption certificate. When prompted for the host name used in the certificate, type `Ubuntu14` in place of localhost, select **Continue**, and press **Enter**.

19. At the Install the GRUB boot loader on a hard disk screen, ensure that **Yes** is selected and press **Enter**.

20. At the Finish the installation screen, ensure that **Continue** is selected and press **Enter** to reboot into the new system.

21. After the system has booted, log into tty1 as **user1** with the password **LINUXrocks!**. At the command prompt, type `who` and press **Enter**.

22. At the command prompt, type `sudo passwd root` and press **Enter**. Supply user1's password of `LINUXrocks!` when prompted and press **Enter**. Supply a password of `LINUXrocks!` for the root user when prompted and press **Enter**. Confirm the root user password by typing `LINUXrocks!` and press **Enter**.

23. At the command prompt, type `su - root` and supply a password of `LINUXrocks!` to switch to the root user.

24. At the command prompt, type `lsblk` and press **Enter**. Examine the output. Why was a /boot partition created on your hard disk? Is the / (root) filesystem a volume managed by the LVM?

25. At the command prompt, type `fdisk -l` and press **Enter**. Note that the remainder of the drive is an extended partition (/dev/sda2) that contains a single logical drive (/dev/sda5) used exclusively by the LVM.

26. At the command prompt, type `lvdisplay` and press **Enter**. Note the logical volumes created for the root filesystem and swap partition within the Ubuntu14-vg volume group.

27. At the command prompt, type `poweroff` and press **Enter** to shut down your Ubuntu Server 14 virtual machine.

Discovery Exercises

1. Project 6-5 was performed on your Ubuntu Server 18 virtual machine. Perform the same project using your Fedora Linux virtual machine, as well as your Ubuntu Server 14 virtual machine and note any differences.

2. Modern Linux distributions often allow you to create fault-tolerant BTRFS volumes during installation to host the Linux operating system and applications. Provided that you have adequate storage space on your host operating system, create a new virtual machine called Fedora BTRFS that has the following characteristics:

   a. 4GB of memory

   b. Two 50GB SATA/SCSI/SAS virtual hard disks (both dynamically allocated)

   c. The virtual machine DVD drive attached to the ISO file for Fedora 28 live media (Fedora-Workstation-Live-x86_64-28-1.1.iso)

   Next, perform an installation of Fedora Linux that contains a / (root) filesystem that uses BTRFS RAID 1 fault tolerance for both data and metadata from space on both virtual hard disks. In order to configure this during the Fedora installation program, you will need to choose the Advanced Custom (Blivet-GUI) option on the Installation Destination screen. Also note that the /boot filesystem cannot use BTRFS. Following the installation, verify your BTRFS configuration using the appropriate commands. When finished, remove your virtual machine and both virtual hard disk files.

3. An alternative to BTRFS RAID 1 for operating system and application fault tolerance is software RAID 1. Perform Discovery Exercise 2 again, but instead of using a BTRFS RAID 1 volume for the / (root) filesystem, select the appropriate options to create a software RAID 1 volume formatted with ext4.

4. The LVM can also be used to provide RAID for logical volumes, provided that the underlying volume group consists of multiple physical volumes. View the lvmraid manual page to learn how to implement LVM RAID 0, 1, and 5 using the lvcreate command. Next, add three 10GB SATA/SCSI/SAS virtual hard disks (dynamically expanding) to your Fedora Linux virtual machine, and configure them as a single LVM RAID 5 logical volume.

5. Search the Internet for information about five Linux installation problems that are different from those described in this chapter. How have other people solved these problems? If you had similar difficulties during installation, how could you get help?

6. Linux servers are typically stored in a locked server closet to prevent physical access by unauthorized persons. Given the steps that you performed in Project 6-6, describe why these physical restrictions are warranted.

## CHAPTER 7

WORKING WITH THE BASH SHELL

After completing this chapter, you will be able to:

Redirect the input and output of a command

Identify and manipulate common shell environment variables

Create and export new shell variables

Edit environment files to create variables upon shell startup

Describe the purpose and nature of shell scripts

Create and execute basic shell scripts

Effectively use constructs, special variables, and functions in shell scripts

Use Git to perform version control for shell scripts

A solid understanding of shell features is vital to both administrators and users who must interact with the shell on a daily basis. The first part of this chapter describes how the shell can manipulate command input and output using redirection and pipe shell metacharacters. Next, you explore the different types of variables present in a BASH shell after login, as well as their purpose and usage. Following this, you learn how to create and execute BASH shell scripts. Finally, this chapter ends with an introduction to using Git to provide version control for files on the system that are modified over time, such as shell scripts.

Command Input and Output

The BASH shell is responsible for providing a user interface and interpreting commands entered on the command line. In addition, the BASH shell can manipulate command input and output, provided the user specifies certain shell metacharacters on the command line alongside the command. Command input and output are represented by labels known as file descriptors. For each command that can be manipulated by the BASH shell, there are three file descriptors:

- Standard Input (stdin)
- Standard Output (stdout)
- Standard Error (stderr)

Standard Input (stdin) refers to the information processed by the command during execution; this often takes the form of user input typed on the keyboard. Standard Output (stdout) refers to the normal output of a command, whereas Standard Error (stderr) refers to any error messages generated by the command. Both stdin and stderr are displayed on the terminal screen by default. All three components are depicted in Figure 7-1.

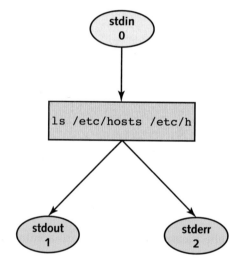

Figure 7-1 The three common file descriptors

As shown in Figure 7-1, each file descriptor is represented by a number, with stdin represented by the number 0, stdout represented by the number 1, and stderr represented by the number 2.

Although all three descriptors are available to any command, not all commands use every descriptor. The ls /etc/hosts /etc/h command used in Figure 7-1 gives stdout (the listing of the /etc/hosts file) and stderr (an error message indicating that the /etc/h file does not exist) to the terminal screen, as shown in the following output:

```
[root@server1 ~]# ls /etc/hosts /etc/h
ls: cannot access /etc/h: No such file or directory
/etc/hosts
[root@server1 ~]#
```

Redirection

You can use the BASH shell to redirect stdout and stderr from the terminal screen to a file on the filesystem. To do this, include the > shell metacharacter followed by the absolute or relative pathname of the file. For example, to redirect only the stdout to a file called goodoutput for the command used in Figure 7-1, you append the number of the file descriptor (1) followed by the **redirection** symbol > and the file to redirect the stdout to (goodoutput), as shown in the following output:

```
[root@server1 ~]# ls /etc/hosts /etc/h   1>goodoutput
ls: cannot access /etc/h: No such file or directory
[root@server1 ~]#_
```

Note

You can include a space character after the > metacharacter, but it is not necessary.

In the preceding output, the stderr is still displayed to the terminal screen because it was not redirected to a file. The listing of /etc/hosts was not displayed, however; instead, it was redirected to a file called goodoutput in the current directory. If the goodoutput file did not exist prior to running the command in the preceding output, Linux creates it automatically. However, if the goodoutput file did exist prior to the redirection, the BASH shell clears its contents before executing the command. To see that the stdout was redirected to the goodoutput file, you can run the following commands:

```
[root@server1 ~]# ls -F
Desktop/    goodoutput
[root@server1 ~]# cat goodoutput
/etc/hosts
[root@server1 ~]#_
```

Similarly, you can redirect the stderr of a command to a file by specifying file descriptor number 2, as shown in the following output:

```
[root@server1 ~]# ls /etc/hosts /etc/h   2>badoutput
/etc/hosts
[root@server1 ~]# cat badoutput
ls: cannot access /etc/h: No such file or directory
[root@server1 ~]#_
```

In the preceding output, only the stderr was redirected to a file called badoutput. The stdout (a listing of /etc/hosts) was displayed on the terminal screen.

Because redirecting the stdout to a file for later use is more common than redirecting the stderr to a file, the BASH shell assumes stdout in the absence of a numeric file descriptor:

```
[root@server1 ~]# ls /etc/hosts /etc/h  >goodoutput
ls: cannot access /etc/h: No such file or directory
[root@server1 ~]# cat goodoutput
/etc/hosts
[root@server1 ~]#_
```

In addition, you can redirect both stdout and stderr to separate files at the same time, as shown in the following output:

```
[root@server1 ~]# ls /etc/hosts /etc/h  >goodoutput  2>badoutput
[root@server1 ~]# cat goodoutput
/etc/hosts
[root@server1 ~]# cat badoutput
ls: cannot access /etc/h: No such file or directory
[root@server1 ~]#_
```

Note

The order of redirection on the command line does not matter; the command `ls /etc/hosts /etc/h >goodoutput 2>badoutput` is the same as `ls /etc/hosts /etc/h 2>badoutput >goodoutput`.

It is important to use separate filenames to hold the contents of stdout and stderr. Using the same filename for both results in a loss of data because the system attempts to write both contents to the file at the same time:

```
[root@server1 ~]#ls /etc/hosts /etc/h  >goodoutput  2>goodoutput
[root@server1 ~]# cat goodoutput
/etc/hosts
access /etc/h: No such file or directory
[root@server1 ~]#_
```

To redirect both stdout and stderr to the same file without any loss of data, you must use special notation. To send stdout to the file goodoutput and stderr to the same place as stdout, you can do the following:

```
[root@server1 ~]# ls /etc/hosts /etc/h  >goodoutput  2>&1
[root@server1 ~]# cat goodoutput
ls: cannot access /etc/h: No such file or directory
/etc/hosts
[root@server1 ~]#_
```

Alternatively, you can send stderr to the file badoutput and stdout to the same place as stderr:

```
[root@server1 ~]# ls /etc/hosts /etc/h  2>badoutput  >&2
[root@server1 ~]# cat badoutput
ls: cannot access /etc/h: No such file or directory
/etc/hosts
[root@server1 ~]#_
```

An easier alternative is to use the &> special notation. For example, to redirect both stdout and stderr to the alloutput file, you could use the following command:

```
[root@server1 ~]# ls /etc/hosts /etc/h  &>alloutput
[root@server1 ~]# cat alloutput
ls: cannot access /etc/h: No such file or directory
/etc/hosts
[root@server1 ~]#_
```

Note

To remove errors from command output, you can redirect the stderr to /dev/null to discard them. For example, the command `find / -name httpd.conf >/dev/null` would only display the locations of the httpd.conf file; any errors resulting from attempting to search protected filesystems (such as /proc) would be omitted from the search results.

In all of the examples used earlier, the contents of the files used to store the output from commands were cleared prior to use by the BASH shell. Another example of this is shown in the following output when redirecting the stdout of the `date` command to the file dateoutput:

```
[root@server1 ~]# date >dateoutput
[root@server1 ~]# cat dateoutput
Fri Aug 20 07:54:00 EDT 2019
[root@server1 ~]# date >dateoutput
[root@server1 ~]# cat dateoutput
Fri Aug 20 07:54:41 EDT 2019
[root@server1 ~]#_
```

To prevent the file from being cleared by the BASH shell and append output to the existing output, you can specify two > metacharacters alongside the file descriptor, as shown in the following output:

```
[root@server1 ~]# date >dateoutput
[root@server1 ~]# cat dateoutput
Fri Aug 20 07:55:32 EDT 2019
```

```
[root@server1 ~]# date >>dateoutput
[root@server1 ~]# cat dateoutput
Fri Aug 20 07:55:32 EDT 2019
Fri Aug 20 07:55:48 EDT 2019
[root@server1 ~]#_
```

You can also redirect a file to the stdin of a command using the < metacharacter. Because input has only one file descriptor, you do not need to specify the number 0 before the < metacharacter to indicate stdin, as shown next:

```
[root@server1 ~]# cat </etc/issue
\S
Kernel \r on an \m (\l)

[root@server1 ~]#_
```

In the preceding output, the BASH shell located and sent the /etc/issue file to the cat command as stdin. Because the cat command normally takes the filename to display as an argument on the command line (e.g., cat /etc/issue), you do not need to use stdin redirection with the cat command as in the previous example. However, some commands only accept files that the shell passes through stdin. The tr **command** is one such command that can be used to replace characters in a file sent via stdin. To replace all of the lowercase r characters in the /etc/issue file to uppercase R characters, you can run the following command:

```
[root@server1 ~]# tr r R </etc/issue
\S
KeRnel \R on an \m (\l)
[root@server1 ~]#_
```

The preceding command does not modify the /etc/issue file; it simply takes a copy of the /etc/issue file, manipulates it, and then sends the stdout to the terminal screen. To save a copy of the stdout for later use, you can use both stdin and stdout redirection together:

```
[root@server1 ~]# tr r R </etc/issue >newissue
[root@server1 ~]# cat newissue
\S
KeRnel \R on an \m (\l)

[root@server1 ~]#_
```

As with redirecting stdout and stderr in the same command, you should use different filenames when redirecting stdin and stdout. In this case, the BASH shell clears a file that already exists before performing the redirection. An example is shown in the following output:

```
[root@server1 ~]# sort <newissue >newissue
[root@server1 ~]# cat newissue
[root@server1 ~]#_
```

The newissue file has no contents when displayed in the preceding output. The BASH shell saw that output redirection was indicated on the command line, cleared the contents of the file newissue, then sorted the blank file and saved the output (nothing in our example) into the file newissue. Because of this feature of shell redirection, Linux administrators commonly use the command `>filename` at the command prompt to clear the contents of a file.

> **Note** 📎
>
> The contents of log files are typically cleared periodically using the command `>/path/to/logfile`.

You can also use two < metacharacters to redirect multiple lines of stdin from the keyboard into a command. This is often called a **here document** and requires a special delimiter that indicates the last line, such as the letters EOF (which is a common delimiter that stands for End Of File). For example, to redirect the three lines of input into the `cat` command, you can run the following command, supply the three lines when prompted (pressing Enter after each one), followed by a single line with the delimiter (in our example, EOF) to indicate the end of the input:

```
[root@server1 ~]# cat << EOF
>This is line one.
>This is line two.
>This is line three.
>EOF
This is line one.
This is line two.
This is line three.
[root@server1 ~]#_
```

The BASH shell in the preceding output accepts each line of input, and when the line of input matches the delimiter, it sends the multiline stdin to the `cat` command, which displays the three lines on the screen.

Table 7-1 summarizes the different types of redirection discussed in this section.

Pipes

Note from Table 7-1 that redirection only occurs between a command and a file and vice versa. However, you can send the stdout of one command to another command as stdin. To do this, you use the pipe | shell metacharacter and specify commands on either side. The shell sends the stdout of the command on the left to the command on the right, which interprets the information as stdin. This process is shown in Figure 7-2.

Table 7-1   Common redirection examples

Command	Description
`command 1>file` `command >file`	The Standard Output of the command is sent to a file instead of to the terminal screen.
`command 2>file`	The Standard Error of the command is sent to a file instead of to the terminal screen.
`command 1>fileA 2>fileB` `command >fileA 2>fileB`	The Standard Output of the command is sent to fileA instead of to the terminal screen, and the Standard Error of the command is sent to fileB instead of to the terminal screen.

`command 1>file 2>&1`
`command >file 2>&1`
`command 1>&2 2>file`
`command >&2 2>file`
`command &>file`
	Both the Standard Output and the Standard Error are sent to the same file instead of to the terminal screen.

`command 1>>file` `command >>file`	The Standard Output of the command is appended to a file instead of being sent to the terminal screen.
`command 2>>file`	The Standard Error of the command is appended to a file instead of being sent to the terminal screen.
`command 0<file` `command <file`	The Standard Input of a command is taken from a file.
`command <<delimiter`	The Standard Input of a command is taken from multiple lines of input that end with a specified delimiter. Often called a here document.

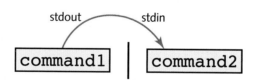

Figure 7-2   Piping information from one command to another

For example, the Standard Output of the `ls -1 /etc` command is too large to fit on one terminal screen. To send the Standard Output of this command to the `less` command, which views Standard Input page by page, you can use the following command:

```
[root@server1 ~]# ls -l /etc | less
total 2196
drwxr-xr-x.  3 root root      4096 Apr 25 02:35  abrt
-rw-r--r--.  1 root root        16 Jul  8 20:13  adjtime
-rw-r--r--.  1 root root      1518 Feb 22 11:56  aliases
drwxr-xr-x.  3 root root      4096 Apr 25 02:36  alsa
drwxr-xr-x.  2 root root      4096 Jul 11 15:01  alternatives
-rw-r--r--.  1 root root       541 Feb  7 00:58  anacrontab
-rw-r--r--.  1 root root       769 Apr  4 11:53  appstream.conf
-rw-r--r--.  1 root root        55 Apr  4 05:05  asound.conf
-rw-r--r--.  1 root root         1 Feb 25 05:54  at.deny
-rw-r--r--.  1 root root       186 Feb  8 05:02  atmsigd.conf
drwxr-x---.  3 root root      4096 Apr 25 02:36  audisp
drwxr-x---.  3 root root      4096 Jul  8 20:15  audit
drwxr-xr-x.  3 root root      4096 Apr 25 02:38  authselect
drwxr-xr-x.  4 root root      4096 Apr 25 02:35  avahi
drwxr-xr-x.  2 root root      4096 Jul  9 13:59  bash_completion.d
-rw-r--r--.  1 root root      3001 Feb 22 11:56  bashrc
drwxr-xr-x.  2 root root      4096 Apr 18 18:00  binfmt.d
drwxr-xr-x.  2 root root      4096 Apr 25 02:34  bluetooth
-rw-r-----.  1 root brlapi      33 Apr 25 02:35  brlapi.key
drwxr-xr-x.  7 root root      4096 Apr 25 02:35  brltty
-rw-r--r--.  1 root root     25696 Mar  6 09:47  brltty.conf
-rw-r--r--.  1 root root       520 Feb  6 23:29  cagibid.conf
:
```

You do not need spaces around the | metacharacter. The commands `ls -l /etc|less` and `ls -l /etc | less` are equivalent.

A common use of piping is to reduce the amount of information displayed on the terminal screen from commands that display too much information. For example, by showing all mounted filesystems, including special filesystems, the mount command normally displays too much information for a Linux administrator. To view only those lines regarding ext4 or xfs filesystems, you could send the stdout of the mount command to the `egrep` command as stdin, which can then print only the results that match the appropriate extended regular expression as shown in the following output:

```
[root@server1 ~]# mount | egrep "(ext4|xfs)"
/dev/sda3 on / type ext4 (rw,relatime,seclabel,data=ordered)
selinuxfs on /sys/fs/selinux type selinuxfs (rw,relatime)
```

```
/dev/sda5 on /newmount type ext4 (rw,relatime,seclabel,data=ordered)
/dev/mapper/vg00-data1 on /data type ext4 (rw,relatime,data=ordered)
/dev/sda1 on /boot type ext4 (rw,relatime,seclabel,data=ordered)
/dev/sda8 on /data2 type xfs (rw,relatime,attr2,inode64,noquota)
[root@server1 ~]#_
```

The egrep command in the preceding output receives the full output from the mount command and then displays only those lines that have ext4 or xfs in them. The egrep command normally takes two arguments; the first specifies the text to search for and the second specifies the filename(s) to search within. The egrep command used in the preceding output requires no second argument because the material to search comes from stdin (the mount command) instead of from a file.

Furthermore, you can use more than one pipe | metacharacter on the command line to pipe information from one command to another command, similar to an assembly line in a factory. Typically, an assembly line goes through several departments, each of which performs a specialized task. For example, one department might assemble the product, another might paint the product, and another might package the product. Every product must pass through each department to be complete.

You can use Linux commands that manipulate data in the same way, connecting them into an assembly line via piping. One command manipulates information, and then that manipulated information is sent to another command, which manipulates it further. The process continues until the information attains the form required by the user.

Recall from the previous output that the special selinuxfs filesystem was also shown in the output because it contains the letters "xfs" and was matched by the egrep command as a result. To omit these results, you could send the stdout of the previous command to the grep -v selinuxfs command which can show all lines except those that contain selinuxfs as shown in the following output:

```
[root@server1 ~]# mount | egrep "(ext4|xfs)" | grep -v selinuxfs
/dev/sda3 on / type ext4 (rw,relatime,seclabel,data=ordered)
/dev/sda5 on /newmount type ext4 (rw,relatime,seclabel,data=ordered)
/dev/mapper/vg00-data1 on /data type ext4 (rw,relatime,data=ordered)
/dev/sda1 on /boot type ext4 (rw,relatime,seclabel,data=ordered)
/dev/sda8 on /data2 type xfs (rw,relatime,attr2,inode64,noquota)
[root@server1 ~]#_
```

The pipe in the preceding output uses three commands; the mount command sends its stdout to the egrep command, which then sends its stdout to the grep command. The piping process is depicted in Figure 7-3.

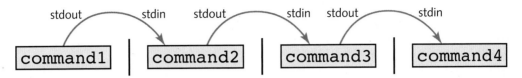

Figure 7-3   Piping several commands

Any command that can take stdin and transform it into stdout is called a **filter**. However, commands such as ls and mount are not filter commands because they do not accept stdin from other commands, but instead find information from the system and display it to the user. As a result, these commands must be at the beginning of a pipe. Other commands, such as vi, are interactive and cannot appear between two pipe symbols because they cannot take from stdin and give to stdout.

Several hundred filter commands are available to Linux users. Table 7-2 lists some common ones that are useful within pipes.

Table 7-2   Common pipe-related commands

Command	Description
sort	Sorts lines in a file alphanumerically
sort -r	Reverse-sorts lines in a file alphanumerically
wc	Counts the number of lines, words, and characters
wc -l	Counts the number of lines
wc -w	Counts the number of words
wc -c	Counts the number of characters
pr	Formats a file for printing, with several options available; it places a date and page number at the top of each page
pr -d	Formats a file double-spaced
uniq	Omits duplicate results
cut	Displays specific columns of delimited data
paste	Combines lines together from two separate sources
tr	Replaces characters in the text of a file
tee filename	Sends stdin to a specified filename as well as stdout; the contents of the file are overwritten unless the -a (append) option is specified
xargs command	Converts stdin to command line arguments that are executed by a specified command

(continues)

Table 7-2	Common pipe-related commands (continued)
Command	**Description**
split	Splits the contents of a file into smaller sections for easier processing by pipes; for example, split -n 400 bigfile would save the first 400 lines of bigfile to xaa, the second 400 lines of bigfile to xab, and so on
grep	Displays lines in a file that match a regular expression
egrep	Displays lines in a file that match an extended or basic regular expression
nl	Numbers lines
awk	Extracts, manipulates, and formats text using pattern-action statements
sed	Manipulates text using search-and-replace expressions

Take, for example, the prologue from Shakespeare's *Romeo and Juliet*:

```
[root@server1 ~]# cat prologue
Two households, both alike in dignity,
In fair Verona, where we lay our scene,
From ancient grudge break to new mutiny,
Where civil blood makes civil hands unclean.
From forth the fatal loins of these two foes
A pair of star-cross'd lovers take their life;
Whole misadventured piteous overthrows
Do with their death bury their parents' strife.
The fearful passage of their death-mark'd love,
And the continuance of their parents' rage,
Which, but their children's end, nought could remove,
Is now the two hours' traffic of our stage;
The which if you with patient ears attend,
What here shall miss, our toil shall strive to mend.
[root@server1 ~]#_
```

Now suppose you want to replace all lowercase "a" characters with uppercase "A" characters in the preceding file, sort the contents by the first character on each line, double-space the output, and view the results page-by-page. To accomplish these tasks, you can use the following pipe:

```
[root@server1 ~]# cat prologue | tr a A | sort | pr -d | less
```

```
2019-08-20 08:06                                    Page 1


And the continuAnce of their pArents' rAge,


A pAir of stAr-cross'd lovers tAke their life;
```

Do with their deAth bury their pArents' strife.

From Ancient grudge breAk to new mutiny,

From forth the fAtAl loins of these two foes

In fAir VeronA, where we lAy our scene,

Is now the two hours' trAffic of our stAge;

The feArful pAssAge of their deAth-mArk'd love,

The which if you with pAtient eArs Attend,

Two households, both Alike in dignity,

WhAt here shAll miss, our toil shAll strive to mend.

Where civil blood mAkes civil hAnds uncleAn.

Which, but their children's end, nought could remove,

Whole misAdventured piteous overthrows

:

The command used in the preceding example displays the final stdout to the terminal screen via the `less` command. In many cases, you might want to display the results of the pipe while saving a copy in a file on the hard disk using the `tee` command, which takes information from stdin and sends that information to a file, as well as to stdout.

To save a copy of the manipulated prologue before displaying it to the terminal screen with the `less` command, you can use the following command:

```
[root@server1 ~]# cat prologue|tr a A|sort|pr -d|tee newfile|less
```

2019-08-20 08:06   Page 1

And the continuAnce of their pArents' rAge,

A pAir of stAr-cross'd lovers tAke their life;

Do with their deAth bury their pArents' strife.

From Ancient grudge breAk to new mutiny,

From forth the fAtAl loins of these two foes

In fAir VeronA, where we lAy our scene,

Is now the two hours' trAffic of our stAge;

The feArful pAssAge of their deAth-mArk'd love,

The which if you with pAtient eArs Attend,

Two households, both Alike in dignity,

WhAt here shAll miss, our toil shAll strive to mend.

Where civil blood mAkes civil hAnds uncleAn.

Which, but their children's end, nought could remove,

Whole misAdventured piteous overthrows

```
:q
[root@server1 ~]#_
[root@server1 ~]# cat newfile
```

2019-08-20 08:06   Page 1

And the continuAnce of their pArents' rAge,

A pAir of stAr-cross'd lovers tAke their life;

Do with their deAth bury their pArentsv strife.

From Ancient grudge breAk to new mutiny,

From forth the fAtAl loins of these two foes

In fAir VeronA, where we lAy our scene,

Is now the two hours' trAffic of our stAge;

```
The feArful pAssAge of their deAth-mArk'd love,

The which if you with pAtient eArs Attend,

Two households, both Alike in dignity,

WhAt here shAll miss, our toil shAll strive to mend.

Where civil blood mAkes civil hAnds uncleAn.

Which, but their children's end, nought could remove,

Whole misAdventured piteous overthrows

[root@server1 ~]#_
```

You can also combine redirection and piping, as long as input redirection occurs at the beginning of the pipe and output redirection occurs at the end of the pipe. An example of this is shown in the following output, which replaces all lowercase a characters with uppercase A characters in the prologue file used in the previous example, then sorts the file, numbers each line, and saves the output to a file called newprologue instead of sending the output to the terminal screen.

```
[root@server1 ~]# tr a A <prologue | sort | nl >newprologue
[root@server1 ~]# cat newprologue
     1  And the continuAnce of their pArents' rAge,
     2  A pAir of stAr-cross'd lovers tAke their life;
     3  Do with their deAth bury their pArents' strife.
     4  From Ancient grudge breAk to new mutiny,
     5  From forth the fAtAl loins of these two foes
     6  In fAir VeronA, where we lAy our scene,
     7  Is now the two hoursv trAffic of our stAge;
     8  The feArful pAssAge of their deAth-mArk'd love,
     9  The which if you with pAtient eArs Attend,
    10  Two households, both Alike in dignity,
    11  WhAt here shAll miss, our toil shAll strive to mend.
    12  Where civil blood mAkes civil hAnds uncleAn.
    13  Which, but their children's end, nought could remove,
    14  Whole misAdventured piteous overthrows
[root@server1 ~]#_
```

Many Linux commands can provide large amounts of useful text information. As a result, Linux administrators often use the sed and awk filter commands with pipes to manipulate text information that these commands produce.

The sed command is typically used to search for a certain string of text, and replaces that text string with another text string using the syntax s/search/replace/. For example, the following output demonstrates how to use sed to search for the string "the" and replace it with the string "THE" in the prologue file used earlier:

```
[root@server1 ~]# cat prologue | sed s/the/THE/
Two households, both alike in dignity,
In fair Verona, where we lay our scene,
From ancient grudge break to new mutiny,
Where civil blood makes civil hands unclean.
From forth THE fatal loins of these two foes
A pair of star-cross'd lovers take THEir life;
Whole misadventured piteous overthrows
Do with THEir death bury their parents' strife.
The fearful passage of THEir death-mark'd love,
And THE continuance of their parents' rage,
Which, but THEir children's end, nought could remove,
Is now THE two hours' traffic of our stage;
The which if you with patient ears attend,
What here shall miss, our toil shall strive to mend.
[root@server1 ~]#_
```

Notice from the preceding output that sed only searched for and replaced the first occurrence of the string "the" in each line. To have sed globally replace all occurrences of the string "the" in each line, append a g to the search-and-replace expression:

```
[root@server1 ~]# cat prologue | sed s/the/THE/g

Two households, both alike in dignity,
In fair Verona, where we lay our scene,
From ancient grudge break to new mutiny,
Where civil blood makes civil hands unclean.
From forth THE fatal loins of THEse two foes
A pair of star-cross'd lovers take THEir life;
Whole misadventured piteous overthrows
Do with THEir death bury THEir parents' strife.
The fearful passage of THEir death-mark'd love,
And THE continuance of THEir parents' rage,
Which, but THEir children's end, nought could remove,
Is now THE two hours' traffic of our stage;
The which if you with patient ears attend,
```

```
What here shall miss, our toil shall strive to mend.
[root@server1 ~]#_
```

You can also tell sed the specific lines to search by prefixing the search-and-replace expression. For example, to force sed to replace the string "the" with "THE" globally on lines that contain the string "love," you can use the following command:

```
[root@server1 ~]# cat prologue | sed /love/s/the/THE/g
Two households, both alike in dignity,
In fair Verona, where we lay our scene,
From ancient grudge break to new mutiny,
Where civil blood makes civil hands unclean.
From forth the fatal loins of these two foes
A pair of star-cross'd lovers take THEir life;
Whole misadventured piteous overthrows
Do with their death bury their parents' strife.
The fearful passage of THEir death-mark'd love,
And the continuance of their parents' rage,
Which, but their children's end, nought could remove,
Is now the two hours' traffic of our stage;
The which if you with patient ears attend,
What here shall miss, our toil shall strive to mend.
[root@server1 ~]#_
```

You can also force sed to perform a search-and-replace on certain lines only. To replace the string "the" with "THE" globally on lines 5 to 8 only, you can use the following command:

```
[root@server1 ~]# cat prologue | sed 5,8s/the/THE/g
Two households, both alike in dignity,
In fair Verona, where we lay our scene,
From ancient grudge break to new mutiny,
Where civil blood makes civil hands unclean.
From forth THE fatal loins of THEse two foes
A pair of star-cross'd lovers take THEir life;
Whole misadventured piteous overthrows
Do with THEir death bury THEir parents' strife.
The fearful passage of their death-mark'd love,
And the continuance of their parents' rage,
Which, but their children's end, nought could remove,
Is now the two hours' traffic of our stage;
The which if you with patient ears attend,
What here shall miss, our toil shall strive to mend.
[root@server1 ~]#_
```

You can also use sed to remove unwanted lines of text. To delete all the lines that contain the word "the," you can use the following command:

```
[root@server1 ~]# cat prologue | sed /the/d
Two households, both alike in dignity,
In fair Verona, where we lay our scene,
From ancient grudge break to new mutiny,
Where civil blood makes civil hands unclean.
Whole misadventured piteous overthrows
The which if you with patient ears attend,
What here shall miss, our toil shall strive to mend.
[root@server1 ~]#_
```

Like sed, the awk command searches for patterns of text and performs some action on the text it finds. However, the awk command treats each line of text as a record in a database, and each word in a line as a database field. For example, the line "Hello, how are you?" has four fields: "Hello," "how," "are," and "you?." These fields can be referenced in the awk command using $1, $2, $3, and $4. For example, to display only the first and fourth words on lines of the prologue file that contain the word "the," you can use the following command:

```
[root@server1 ~]# cat prologue | awk '/the/ {print $1, $4}'
From fatal
A star-cross'd
Do death
The of
And of
Which, children's
Is two
[root@server1 ~]#_
```

By default, the awk command uses space or tab characters as delimiters for each field in a line. Most configuration files on Linux systems, however, are delimited using colon (:) characters. To change the delimiter that awk uses, you can specify the –F option to the command. For example, the following example lists the last 10 lines of the colon-delimited file /etc/passwd and views only the sixth and seventh fields for lines that contain the word "bob" in the last 10 lines of the file:

```
[root@server1 ~]# tail /etc/passwd
news:x:9:13:News server user:/etc/news:/sbin/nologin
smolt:x:490:474:Smolt:/usr/share/smolt:/sbin/nologin
backuppc:x:489:473::/var/lib/BackupPC:/sbin/nologin
pulse:x:488:472:PulseAudio System Daemon:/var/run/pulse:/sbin/nologin
```

```
gdm:x:42:468::/var/lib/gdm:/sbin/nologin
hsqldb:x:96:96::/var/lib/hsqldb:/sbin/nologin
jetty:x:487:467::/usr/share/jetty:/bin/sh
bozo:x:500:500:bozo the clown:/home/bozo:/bin/bash
bob:x:501:501:Bob Smith:/home/bob:/bin/bash
user1:x:502:502:sample user one:/home/user1:/bin/bash
[root@server1 ~]# tail /etc/passwd | awk -F : '/bob/ {print $6, $7}'
/home/bob /bin/bash
[root@server1 ~]#_
```

Note

Both awk and sed allow you to specify regular expressions in the search pattern.

Because Linux systems have a rich set of utilities that can be used within a pipe, you can often use more than one way to obtain the same results. For example, the following pipe would also display the sixth and seventh field from the colon-delimited /etc/passwd file for the user bob, using the grep and cut commands:

```
[root@server1 ~]# grep bob /etc/passwd | cut -d: -f6,7
/home/bob:/bin/bash
[root@server1 ~]#_
```

However, note from the output above that the : character was included by the cut command when multiple lines were cut. To remove this colon, you could extend the pipe to use the tr command to replace colon characters with space characters:

```
[root@server1 ~]# grep bob /etc/passwd | cut -d: -f6,7 | tr ":" " "
/home/bob /bin/bash
[root@server1 ~]#_
```

Alternatively, you could use a combination of piped and non-piped commands together. For example, you could use pipes to save the output of each column to a file and then combine those files afterwards using the paste command, which will separate the contents of the two files using a space delimiter:

```
[root@server1 ~]# grep lala /etc/passwd | cut -d: -f6 >file1
[root@server1 ~]# grep lala /etc/passwd | cut -d: -f6 >file1
[root@server1 ~]# paste -d " " file1 file2
/home/bob /bin/bash
[root@server1 ~]#_
```

Shell Variables

A BASH shell has several **variables** in memory at any one time. Recall that a variable is simply a reserved portion of memory containing information that might be accessed. Most variables in the shell are referred to as **environment variables** because they are typically set by the system and contain information that the system and programs access regularly. Users can also create their own custom variables. These variables are called **user-defined variables**. In addition to these two types of variables, special variables are available that are useful when executing commands and creating new files and directories.

Environment Variables

Many environment variables are set by default in the BASH shell. To see a list of these variables and their current values, you can use the `set` **command**, as shown in the following output:

```
[root@server1 ~]# set | less
BASH=/bin/bash
BASHOPTS=checkwinsize:cmdhist:complete_fullquote:expand_aliases:
extglob:extquote:force_fignore:histappend:interactive_comments:
login_shell:progcomp:promptvars:sourcepath
BASHRCSOURCED=Y
BASH_ALIASES=()
BASH_ARGC=()
BASH_ARGV=()
BASH_CMDS=()
BASH_COMPLETION_VERSINFO=([0]="2" [1]="7")
BASH_ENV=/usr/share/Modules/init/bash
BASH_LINENO=()
BASH_REMATCH=([0]=":/usr/share/man:")
BASH_SOURCE=()
BASH_VERSINFO=([0]="4" [1]="4" [2]="19" [3]="1" [4]="release"
[5]="x86_64-redhat-linux-gnu")
BASH_VERSION='4.4.19(1)-release'
COLUMNS=80
DBUS_SESSION_BUS_ADDRESS=unix:path=/run/user/0/bus
DIRSTACK=()
ENV=/usr/share/Modules/init/profile.sh
EUID=0
:
```

Some environment variables are used by programs that require information about the system; the OSTYPE (Operating System TYPE) and SHELL (Pathname to shell) variables are examples of these. Other variables are used to set the user's working environment; the most common of these include the following:

- PS1—The default shell prompt
- HOME—The absolute pathname to the user's home directory
- PWD—The present working directory in the directory tree
- PATH—A list of directories to search for executable programs
- HISTSIZE—The number of previously executed commands to store in memory
- HISTFILESIZE—The number of previously executed commands to save to a file upon shell exit
- HISTFILE—The file that contains previously executed commands

The PS1 variable represents the BASH shell prompt. To view the contents of this variable only, you can use the echo **command** and specify the variable name prefixed by the $ shell metacharacter, as shown in the following output:

```
[root@server1 ~]# echo $PS1
[\u@\h \W]\$
[root@server1 ~]#_
```

Note that a special notation is used to define the prompt in the preceding output: \u indicates the user name, \h indicates the host name, and \W indicates the name of the current directory. A list of BASH notations can be found by navigating the manual page for the BASH shell.

To change the value of a variable, you specify the variable name followed immediately by an equal sign (=) and the new value. The following output demonstrates how you can change the value of the PS1 variable. The new prompt takes effect immediately and allows the user to type commands.

```
[root@server1 ~]# PS1="This is the new prompt: #"
This is the new prompt: # _
This is the new prompt: # date
Fri Aug 20 08:16:59 EDT 2019
This is the new prompt: # _
This is the new prompt: # who
root      tty5          2019-08-07 13:31
root      tty6          2019-08-07 13:31
This is the new prompt: # _
This is the new prompt: # PS1="[\u@\h \W]#"
[root@server1 ~#_
```

The HOME variable is used by programs that require the pathname to the current user's home directory to store or search for files; therefore, it should not be changed. If the root user logs in to the system, the HOME variable is set to /root; alternatively, the HOME variable is set to /home/user1 if the user named user1 logs in to the system.

Recall that the tilde ~ metacharacter represents the current user's home directory; this metacharacter is a pointer to the HOME variable, as shown here:

```
[root@server1 ~]# echo $HOME
/root
[root@server1 ~]# echo ~
/root
[root@server1 ~]# HOME=/etc
[root@server1 root]# echo $HOME
/etc
[root@server1 root]# echo ~
/etc
[root@server1 root]# _
```

Like the HOME variable, the PWD (Print Working Directory) variable is vital to the user's environment and should not be changed. PWD stores the current user's location in the directory tree. It is affected by the cd command and used by other commands such as pwd when the current directory needs to be identified. The following output demonstrates how this variable works:

```
[root@server1 ~]# pwd
/root
[root@server1 ~]# echo $PWD
/root
[root@server1 ~]# cd /etc
[root@server1 etc]# pwd
/etc
[root@server1 ~]# echo $PWD
/etc
[root@server1 ~]#_
```

The PATH variable is one of the most important variables in the BASH shell, as it allows users to execute commands by typing the command name alone. Recall that most commands are represented by an executable file on the hard drive. These executables are typically stored in directories named bin or sbin in various locations throughout the Linux directory tree. To execute the ls command, you could either type the absolute or relative pathname to the file (that is, /usr/bin/ls or ../usr/bin/ls) or simply type the letters "ls" and allow the system to search the directories listed in the PATH variable for a command named ls. Sample contents of the PATH variable are shown in the following output:

```
[root@server1 ~]# echo $PATH
/usr/local/sbin:/usr/local/bin:/usr/sbin:/usr/bin:/root/bin
[root@server1 ~]#_
```

In this example, if the user had typed the command ls at the command prompt and pressed Enter, the shell would have noticed the lack of a / character in the pathname and proceeded to search for the file ls in the /usr/local/sbin directory, then the /usr/local/bin directory, the /usr/sbin directory, and then the /usr/bin directory before finding the ls executable file. If no ls file is found in any directory in the PATH variable, the shell returns an error message, as shown here with a misspelled command and any similar command suggestions:

```
[root@server1 ~]# lss
bash: lss: command not found...
Similar command is: 'ls'
[root@server1 ~]#_
```

Thus, if a command is located within a directory that is listed in the PATH variable, you can simply type the name of the command on the command line to execute it. The shell will then find the appropriate executable file on the filesystem. All of the commands used in this book so far have been located in directories listed in the PATH variable. However, if the executable file is not in a directory listed in the PATH variable, the user must specify either the absolute or relative pathname to the executable file. The following example uses the myprogram file in the /root directory (a directory that is not listed in the PATH variable):

```
[root@server1 ~]# pwd
/root
[root@server1 ~]# ls -F
Desktop/  myprogram*
[root@server1 ~]# myprogram
bash: myprogram: command not found...
[root@server1 ~]# /root/myprogram
This is a sample program.
[root@server1 ~]# ./myprogram
This is a sample program.
[root@server1 ~]# cp myprogram /usr/bin
[root@server1 ~]# myprogram
This is a sample program.
[root@server1 ~]#_
```

After the myprogram executable file was copied to the /usr/bin directory in the preceding output, the user was able to execute it by typing its name, because the /usr/bin directory is listed in the PATH variable.

Another important feature of your BASH shell is the ability to recall and execute previous commands; you can cycle through previously executed commands using the up and down cursor keys on your keyboard. Alternatively, you can use the history command to view a list of previously executed commands; for example, to view the last five commands that you entered in the BASH shell, you could run the following command:

```
[root@server1 ~]# history 5
 102   ls -l /etc
 103   cp /etc/hosts ~
 104   cat hosts
 105   ls -l hosts
 106   history 5
[root@server1 ~]#_
```

To recall and execute the command 105 from the previous output, you could enter !105 on the command line as shown below:

```
[root@server1 ~]# !105
ls -l hosts
-rw-r--r--. 1 root root 158 Aug  8 09:51 hosts.
[root@server1 ~]#_
```

Variables within your BASH shell provide the functionality needed to recall previous commands, as well as use the history and ! commands. The HISTSIZE variable determines the maximum number of commands that will be stored in shell memory before the oldest ones are removed. The HISTFILESIZE variable determines how many of these commands will be saved to the file listed within the HISTFILE variable when you exit your BASH shell, such that they are available for recall when you start a new BASH shell.

Table 7-3 provides a list of environment variables used in most BASH shells.

Table 7-3   Common bash environment variables

Variable	Description
BASH	The full path to the BASH shell
BASH_VERSION	The version of the current BASH shell
DISPLAY	The variable used to redirect the output of X Windows to another computer or device
EDITOR	The default text editor used by commands on the system (usually vi or nano)
ENV	The location of the BASH run-time configuration file
EUID	The effective UID (User ID) of the current user
HISTFILE	The filename used to store previously entered commands in the BASH shell (usually ~/.bash_history)
HISTFILESIZE	The number of previously entered commands that can be stored in the HISTFILE upon logout for use during the next login; it is typically 1000 commands

Table 7-3	Common bash environment variables *(continued)*

Variable	Description
HISTSIZE	The number of previously entered commands that will be stored in memory during the current login session; it is typically 1000 commands
HOME	The absolute pathname of the current user's home directory
HOSTNAME	The host name of the Linux system
LOGNAME	The user name of the current user used when logging in to the shell
MAIL	The location of the mailbox file (where e-mail is stored)
OSTYPE	The current operating system
PATH	The directories to search for executable program files in the absence of an absolute or relative pathname containing a / character
PS1	The current shell prompt
PWD	The current working directory
RANDOM	The variable that creates a random number when accessed
SHELL	The absolute pathname of the current shell
TERM	The variable used to determine the terminal settings; it is typically set to "linux" or "xterm" on newer Linux systems and "console" on older Linux systems
TERMCAP	The variable used to determine the terminal settings on Linux systems that use a TERMCAP database (/etc/termcap)

User-Defined Variables

You can set your own variables using the same method discussed earlier to change the contents of existing environment variables. To do so, you specify the name of the variable (known as the **variable identifier**) immediately followed by the equal sign (=) and the new contents. When creating new variables, it is important to note the following features of variable identifiers:

- They can contain alphanumeric characters (0–9, A–Z, a–z), the dash (-) character, or the underscore (_) character.
- They must not start with a number.
- They are typically capitalized to follow convention (e.g., HOME, PATH).

To create a variable called MYVAR with the contents "This is a sample variable" and display its contents, you can use the following commands:

```
[root@server1 ~]# MYVAR="This is a sample variable"
[root@server1 ~]# echo $MYVAR
This is a sample variable
[root@server1 ~]#_
```

The preceding command created a variable that is available to the current shell. Most commands that are run by the shell are run in a separate **subshell**, which is created by the current shell. Any variables created in the current shell are not available to those subshells and the commands running within them. Thus, if a user creates a variable to be used within a certain program such as a database editor, that variable should be exported to all subshells using the `export` **command** to ensure that all programs started by the current shell can access the variable.

As explained earlier in this chapter, all environment variables in the BASH shell can be listed using the `set` command; user-defined variables are also indicated in this list. Similarly, to see a list of all exported environment and user-defined variables in the shell, you can use the `env` **command**. Because the outputs of `set` and `env` are typically large, you would commonly redirect the stdout of these commands to the `grep` command to display certain lines only.

To see the difference between the `set` and `env` commands as well as export the MYVAR variable created earlier, you can perform the following commands:

```
[root@server1 ~]# set | grep MYVAR
MYVAR='This is a sample variable'
[root@server1 ~]# env | grep MYVAR
[root@server1 ~]#
[root@server1 ~]# export MYVAR
[root@server1 ~]# env | grep MYVAR
MYVAR=This is a sample variable
[root@server1 ~]#
```

Note

You can also use the `printenv` **command** to view the exported variables in your shell.

Not all environment variables are exported; the PS1 variable is an example of a variable that does not need to be available to subshells and is not exported as a result. However, it is good form to export user-defined variables because they will likely be used by processes that run in subshells. This means, to create and export a user-defined variable called MYVAR2, you can use the `export` command alone, as shown in the following output:

```
[root@server1 ~]# export MYVAR2="This is another sample variable"
[root@server1 ~]# set | grep MYVAR2
MYVAR2='This is another sample variable'
_=MYVAR2
[root@server1 ~]# env | grep MYVAR2
MYVAR2=This is another sample variable
[root@server1 ~]#
```

Note

You can also use the `unset` **command** to remove a variable from shell memory.

Other Variables

Other variables are not displayed by the `set` or `env` commands; these variables perform specialized functions in the shell.

The UMASK variable used earlier in this textbook is an example of a special variable that performs a special function in the BASH shell and must be set by the `umask` command. Also recall that when you type the `cp` command, you are actually running an alias to the `cp -i` command. Aliases are shortcuts to commands stored in special variables that can be created and viewed using the `alias` **command**. To create an alias to the command `mount /dev/cdrom /mnt` called mdisc and view it, you can use the following commands:

```
[root@server1 ~]# alias mdisc="mount /dev/cdrom /mnt"
[root@server1 ~]# alias
alias cp='cp -i'
alias egrep='egrep --color=auto'
alias fgrep='fgrep --color=auto'
alias grep='grep --color=auto'
alias l.='ls -d .* --color=auto'
alias ll='ls -l --color=auto'
alias ls='ls --color=auto'
alias mdisc='mount /dev/cdrom /mnt'
alias mv='mv -i'
alias rm='rm -i'
alias which='(alias; declare -f) | /usr/bin/which --tty-only
--read-alias --read-functions --show-tilde --show-dot'
alias xzegrep='xzegrep --color=auto'
alias xzfgrep='xzfgrep --color=auto'
alias xzgrep='xzgrep --color=auto'
alias zegrep='zegrep --color=auto'
alias zfgrep='zfgrep --color=auto'
alias zgrep='zgrep --color=auto'
[root@server1 ~]#_
```

Now, you can run the `mdisc` command to mount a CD or DVD to the /mnt directory, as shown in the following output:

```
[root@server1 ~]# mdisc
[root@server1 ~]# mount | grep mnt
```

```
/dev/sr0 on /mnt type iso9660 (ro,relatime,nojoliet,blocksize=2048)
[root@server1 ~]#_
```

You can also create aliases to multiple commands, provided they are separated by the ; metacharacter introduced in Chapter 2. To create and test an alias called dw that runs the date command followed by the who command, you can do the following:

```
[root@server1 ~]# alias dw="date;who"
[root@server1 ~]# alias | grep dw
alias dw='date;who'
[root@server1 ~]# dw
Tue Aug   7 13:54:43 EDT 2019
root       tty5            2019-08-07 13:31
root       pts/0           2019-08-07 13:38
[root@server1 ~]#_
```

Environment Files

Recall that variables are stored in memory. When a user exits the BASH shell, all variables stored in memory are destroyed along with the shell itself. To ensure that variables are accessible to a shell at all times, you must place variables in a file that is executed each time a user logs in and starts a BASH shell. These files are called **environment files**. Common BASH shell environment files and the order in which they are typically executed are as follows:

```
/etc/profile
/etc/profile.d/*
/etc/bashrc
~/.bashrc
~/.bash_profile
~/.bash_login
~/.profile
```

The BASH runtime configuration files (/etc/bashrc and ~/.bashrc) are typically used to set aliases and variables that must be present in the BASH shell. They are executed immediately after a new login as well as when a new BASH shell is created after login.

The /etc/bashrc file contains aliases and variables for all users on the system, whereas the ~/.bashrc file contains aliases and variables for a specific user.

The other environment files are only executed after a new login. The /etc/profile file and all files under the /etc/profile.d/ directory are executed after login for all users on the system; they set most aliases and environment variables. After they finish executing, the home directory of the user is searched for the hidden environment files .bash_profile, .bash_login, and .profile. If these files exist, the first one found is executed; as a result, only one of these files is typically used. These hidden environment files allow a user to set customized variables independent of BASH shells used by other users on the system; any values assigned to variables in these files override those set in /etc/profile, /etc/profile.d/*, /etc/bashrc, and ~/.bashrc due to the order of execution.

To add a variable to any of these files, you add a line that has the same format as the command used on the command line. To add the MYVAR2 variable used previously to the .bash_profile file, edit the file using a text editor such as vi and add the line `export MYVAR2="This is another sample variable"` to the file.

Variables are not the only type of information that can be entered into an environment file; any command that can be executed on the command line can also be placed inside any environment file. If you want to set the UMASK to 077, display the date after each login, and create an alias, you can add the following lines to one of the hidden environment files in your home directory:

```
umask 077
date
alias dw="date;who"
```

Also, you might want to execute cleanup tasks upon exiting the shell; to do this, add those cleanup commands to the .bash_logout file in your home directory.

Shell Scripts

> *Talk is cheap. Show me the code.*
>
> —*Linus Torvalds*

In the previous section, you learned that the BASH shell can execute commands that exist within environment files. The BASH shell also has the ability to execute other text files containing commands and special constructs. These files are referred to as shell scripts and are typically used to create custom programs that perform administrative tasks on Linux systems. Throughout the remainder of this book, we'll introduce administrative commands that can be used within a shell script, as well as sample shell scripts that can be used to automate key system administration tasks. In this section, we'll examine the structure and methods used to write and execute shell scripts.

Any command that can be entered on the command line in Linux can be entered into a shell script because it is a BASH shell that interprets the contents of the shell script itself. The most basic shell script is one that contains a list of commands, one per line, for the shell to execute in order, as shown here in the text file called myscript:

```
[root@server1 ~]# cat myscript
#!/bin/bash
#this is a comment
date
who
ls -F /
[root@server1 ~]#_
```

The first line in the preceding shell script (#!/bin/bash) is called the **hashpling** or **shebang** line; it specifies the pathname to the shell that interprets the contents of the shell script. Different shells can use different constructs in their shell scripts. Thus, it is important to identify which shell was used to create a particular shell script. The hashpling allows C shell a user to use a BASH shell when executing the myscript shell script shown previously. The second line of the shell script is referred to as a comment because it begins with a # character and is ignored by the shell; the only exception to this is the hashpling on the first line of a shell script. The remainder of the shell script shown in the preceding output consists of three commands that will be executed by the shell in order: date, who, and ls.

> **Note** 🔗
>
> Like other Linux files, shell scripts don't need to have a file extension, but many Linux administrators add the .sh file extension (e.g., myscript.sh) for ease in identifying shell scripts.

If you have read permission to a shell script, you can execute the shell script by starting another BASH shell and specifying the shell script as an argument. To execute the myscript shell script shown earlier, you can use the following command:

```
[root@server1 ~]# bash myscript
Fri Aug 20 11:36:18 EDT 2019
user1    tty1      2019-08-20 07:47
root     tty2      2019-08-20 11:36
bin/     dev/      home/        media/   proc/    sbin/     sys/    var/
boot/    etc/      lib/         mnt/     public/  selinux/  tmp/
data/    extras/   lost+found/  opt/     root/    srv/      usr/
[root@server1 ~]#_
```

Alternatively, if you have read and execute permission to a shell script, you can execute the shell script like any other executable program on the system, as shown here using the myscript shell script:

```
[root@server1 ~]# chmod a+x myscript
[root@server1 ~]# ./myscript
Fri Aug 20 11:36:58 EDT 2019
user1     tty1        2019-08-20 07:47
root      tty2        2019-08-20 11:36
bin/      dev/        home/          media/    proc/      sbin/       sys/     var/
boot/     etc/        lib/           mnt/      public/    selinux/    tmp/
data/     extras/     lost+found/    opt/      root/      srv/        usr/
[root@server1 ~]#_
```

The preceding output is difficult to read because the output from each command is not separated by blank lines or identified by a label. Using the echo command results in a more user-friendly myscript, as shown here:

```
[root@server1 ~]# cat myscript
#!/bin/bash
echo "Today's date is:"
date
echo ""
echo "The people logged into the system include:"
who
echo ""
echo "The contents of the / directory are:"
ls -F /
[root@server1 ~]# ./myscript
Today's date is:
Fri Aug 20 11:37:24 EDT 2019

The people logged into the system include:
user1     tty1        2019-08-20 07:47
root      tty2        2019-08-20 11:36

The contents of the / directory are:
bin/      dev/        home/          media/    proc/      sbin/       sys/     var/
boot/     etc/        lib/           mnt/      public/    selinux/    tmp/
data/     extras/     lost+found/    opt/      root/      srv/        usr/
[root@server1 ~]#_
```

Shell scripts are executed within subshells like most other commands on a Linux system. As a result, if your shell script needs to access environment or user variables in your current BASH shell, those variables need to be exported. Alternatively, you could use the `source` **command** or **dot (.) command** to prevent your shell script from executing within a subshell; for example, the `source ./myscript` command (or `. ./myscript` command) would execute the myscript shell script in the previous example within the current BASH shell.

> **Note**
>
> You can also use the `-xv` options with the `bash` command when executing a shell script to display each command and argument executed within the shell script. This is often useful when troubleshooting shell scripts that do not function as expected. For example, you could use the `bash -xv myscript` command to troubleshoot myscript.

Escape Sequences

In the previous example, you used the `echo` command to manipulate data that appeared on the screen. The `echo` command also supports several special notations called **escape sequences**. You can use escape sequences to further manipulate the way text is displayed to the terminal screen, provided the –e option is specified to the `echo` command. Table 7-4 provides a list of these echo escape sequences.

Table 7-4   Common echo escape sequences

Escape sequence	Description
\0???	Inserts an ASCII character represented by a three-digit octal number (???)
\x??	Inserts an ASCII character represented by a two-digit hexadecimal number (??)
\\	Backslash
\a	ASCII beep
\b	Backspace
\c	Prevents a new line following the command
\f	Form feed
\n	Starts a new line
\r	Carriage return
\t	Horizontal tab
\v	Vertical tab

The escape sequences listed in Table 7-4 can be used to further manipulate the output of the myscript shell script used earlier, as shown in the following example:

```
[root@server1 ~]# cat myscript
#!/bin/bash
```

```
echo -e "Today's date is: \c"
date
echo -e "\nThe people logged into the system include:"
who
echo -e "\nThe contents of the / directory are:"
ls -F /
[root@server1 ~]# ./myscript
Today's date is: Fri Aug 20 11:44:24 EDT 2019

The people logged into the system include:
user1    tty1       2019-08-20 07:47
root     tty2       2019-08-20 11:36

The contents of the / directory are:
bin/     dev/      home/        media/    proc/     sbin/      sys/   var/
boot/    etc/      lib/         mnt/      public/   selinux/   tmp/
data/    extras/   lost+found/  opt/      root/     srv/       usr/
[root@server1 ~]#_
```

Notice from preceding output that the \c escape sequence prevented the newline character at the end of the output "Today's date is:" when myscript was executed. Similarly, newline characters (\n) were inserted prior to displaying "The people logged into the system include:" and "The contents of the / directory are:" to create blank lines between command outputs. This eliminated the need for using the echo "" command shown earlier.

Reading Standard Input

At times, a shell script might need input from the user executing the program; this input can then be stored in a variable for later use. The **read command** takes user input from Standard Input and places it in a variable specified by an argument to the read command. After the input has been read into a variable, the contents of that variable can then be used, as shown in the following shell script:

```
[root@server1 ~]# cat newscript
#!/bin/bash
echo -e "What is your name? -->\c"
read USERNAME
echo "Hello $USERNAME"
[root@server1 ~]# chmod a+x newscript
[root@server1 ~]# ./newscript
What is your name? --> Fred
Hello Fred
[root@server1 ~]#_
```

Note from the preceding output that the echo command used to pose a question to the user ends with - -> to simulate an arrow prompt on the screen and the \c escape sequence to place the cursor after the arrow prompt; this is common among Linux administrators when writing shell scripts that require user input.

Decision Constructs

Decision constructs are the most common type of construct used in shell scripts. They alter the flow of a program based on whether a command in the program completed successfully or based on a decision that the user makes in response to a question posed by the program. Figures 7-4 and 7-5 illustrate some decision constructs.

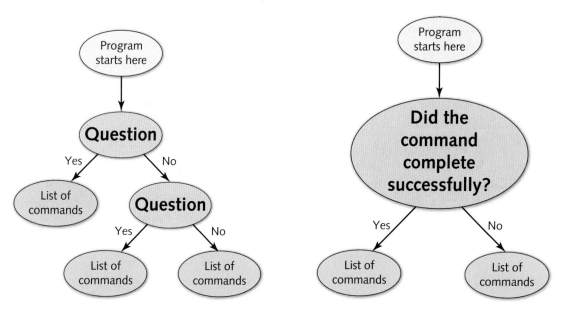

Figure 7-4   A two-question decision construct

Figure 7-5   A command-based decision construct

The if Construct

The most common type of decision construct, the if construct, has the following syntax:

```
if this is true
then
do these commands
elif this is true
then
do these commands
else
do these commands
fi
```

Some common rules govern `if` constructs:

1. elif (else if) and else statements are optional.
2. You can have an unlimited number of elif statements.
3. The *do these commands* section can consist of multiple commands, one per line.
4. The *do these commands* section is typically indented from the left side of the text file for readability but does not need to be.
5. The end of the statement must be a backward "if" (`fi`).
6. The *this is true* part of the if syntax shown earlier can be a command or a **test statement**:
   - Commands return true if they perform their function properly.
   - Test statements are enclosed within square brackets [ ] or prefixed by the word "test" and used to test certain conditions on the system.

In the following example, a basic `if` construct is used to ensure that the /etc/hosts file is only copied to the /etc/sample directory if that directory could be created successfully:

```
[root@server1 ~]# cat testmkdir
#!/bin/bash
if mkdir /etc/sample
then
cp /etc/hosts /etc/sample
echo "The hosts file was successfully copied to /etc/sample"
else
echo "The /etc/sample directory could not be created."
fi
[root@server1 ~]# chmod a+x testmkdir
[root@server1 ~]# ./testmkdir
The hosts file was successfully copied to /etc/sample
[root@server1 ~]#_
```

In the preceding output, the `mkdir /etc/sample` command is always run. If it runs successfully, the shell script proceeds to the `cp /etc/hosts /etc/sample` and `echo "The hosts file was successfully copied to /etc/sample"` commands. If the `mkdir /etc/sample` command is unsuccessful, the shell script skips ahead and executes the `echo "The /etc/sample directory could not be created."` command. If there were more lines of text following the `fi` in the preceding shell script, they would be executed after the `if` construct, regardless of its outcome.

Note

For a decision construct to work, there must be a condition that returns true or false. True and false are represented by an **exit status** number within Linux systems; an exit status of 0 is true, whereas an exit status of 1-255 is false. When a command (such as `mkdir /etc/sample` in the previous example) finishes successfully, it returns a 0 exit status. If a command fails to execute successfully, it will return an exit status between 1 and 255, depending on how the program was written. Because all Linux commands return a true or false exit status, they can be easily used to provide the decision within a decision construct.

Often, it is useful to use the `if` construct to alter the flow of the program given input from the user. Recall the myscript shell script used earlier:

```
[root@server1 ~]# cat myscript
#!/bin/bash
echo -e "Today's date is: \c"
date
echo -e "\nThe people logged into the system include:"
who
echo -e "\nThe contents of the / directory are:"
ls -F /
[root@server1 ~]#_
```

To ask the user whether to display the contents of the / directory, you could use the following `if` construct in the myscript file:

```
[root@server1 ~]# cat myscript
#!/bin/bash
echo -e "Today's date is: \c"
date
echo -e "\nThe people logged into the system include:"
who
echo -e "\nWould you like to see the contents of /?(y/n)-->\c"
read ANSWER
if [ $ANSWER = "y" ]
then
echo -e "\nThe contents of the / directory are:"
ls -F /
fi
[root@server1 ~]# ./myscript
Today's date is: Fri Aug 20 11:47:14 EDT 2019
```

```
The people logged into the system include:
user1      tty1           2019-08-20 07:47
root       tty2           2019-08-20 11:36

Would you like to see the contents of /?(y/n)--> y

The contents of the / directory are:
bin/    dev/      home/           media/   proc/      sbin/      sys/    var/
boot/   etc/      lib/            mnt/     public/    selinux/   tmp/
data/   extras/   lost+found/     opt/     root/      srv/       usr/
[root@server1 ~]#_
```

In the preceding output, the test statement [$ANSWER = "y"] is used to test whether the contents of the ANSWER variable are equal to the letter "y." Any other character in this variable causes this test statement to return false, and the directory listing is then skipped altogether. The type of comparison used previously is called a string comparison because two values are compared for strings of characters; it is indicated by the operator of the test statement, which is the equal sign (=) in this example. Table 7-5 shows a list of common operators used in test statements and their definitions.

Note 📎

The test statement [$ANSWER = "y"] is equivalent to the test statement test $ANSWER = "y".

It is important to include a space character after the beginning square bracket and before the ending square bracket; otherwise, the test statement produces an error.

Table 7-5   Common test statements

Test statement	Returns true if:
[A = B]	String A is equal to String B.
[A != B]	String A is not equal to String B.
[A -eq B]	A is numerically equal to B.
[A -ne B]	A is numerically not equal to B.
[A -lt B]	A is numerically less than B.
[A -gt B]	A is numerically greater than B.
[A -le B]	A is numerically less than or equal to B.

(continues)

Table 7-5 Common test statements *(continued)*

Test statement	Returns true if:
[A –ge B]	A is numerically greater than or equal to B.
[-r A]	A is a file/directory that exists and is readable (r permission).
[-w A]	A is a file/directory that exists and is writable (w permission).
[-x A]	A is a file/directory that exists and is executable (x permission).
[-f A]	A is a file that exists.
[-d A]	A is a directory that exists.

You can combine any test statement with another test statement using the comparison operators –o (OR) and -a (AND). To reverse the meaning of a test statement, you can use the ! (NOT) operator. Table 7-6 provides some examples of using these operators in test statements.

Note

One test statement can contain several –o, -a, and ! operators.

Table 7-6 Special operators in test statements

Test statement	Returns true if:
[A = B –o C = D]	String A is equal to String B OR String C is equal to String D.
[A = B –a C = D]	String A is equal to String B AND String C is equal to String D.
[! A = B]	String A is NOT equal to String B.

By modifying the myscript shell script in the previous output, you can proceed with the directory listing if the user enters "y" or "Y," as shown in the following example:

```
[root@server1 ~]# cat myscript
#!/bin/bash
echo -e "Today's date is: \c"
date
echo -e "\nThe people logged into the system include:"
who
echo -e "\nWould you like to see the contents of /? (y/n)-->\c"
read ANSWER
if [ $ANSWER = "y" -o $ANSWER = "Y" ]
then
echo -e "\nThe contents of the / directory are:"
```

```
ls -F /
fi
[root@server1 ~]# ./myscript
Today's date is: Fri Aug 20 12:01:22 EDT 2019

The people logged into the system include:
user1    tty1         2019-08-20 07:47
root     tty2         2019-08-20 11:36

Would you like to see the contents of /?(y/n)--> Y

The contents of the / directory are:
bin/    dev/      home/           media/   proc/     sbin/      sys/  var/
boot/   etc/      lib/            mnt/     public/   selinux/   tmp/
data/   extras/   lost+found/     opt/     root/     srv/       usr/
[root@server1 ~]#_
```

The case Construct

The if construct used earlier is well suited for a limited number of choices. In the following example, which uses the myscript example presented earlier, several elif statements perform tasks based on user input:

```
[root@server1 ~]# cat myscript
#!/bin/bash
echo -e "What would you like to see?
Today's date (d)
Currently logged in users (u)
The contents of the / directory (r)

Enter your choice(d/u/r)-->\c"
read ANSWER
if [ $ANSWER = "d" -o $ANSWER = "D" ]
then
echo -e "Today's date is: \c"
date
elif [ $ANSWER = "u" -o $ANSWER = "U" ]
then
echo -e "\nThe people logged into the system include:"
who
elif [ $ANSWER = "r" -o $ANSWER = "R" ]
then
echo -e "\nThe contents of the / directory are:"
ls -F /
```

```
fi
[root@server1 ~]#_
```

```
[root@server1 ~]# ./myscript
What would you like to see?
Today's date (d)
Currently logged in users (u)
The contents of the / directory (r)

Enter your choice(d/u/r)--> d
Today's date is: Fri Aug 20 12:13:12 EDT 2019
[root@server1 ~]#_
```

The preceding shell script becomes increasingly difficult to read as the number of choices available increases. Thus, when presenting several choices, it is commonplace to use a case construct. The syntax of the case construct is as follows:

```
case variable in
pattern1  )   do this
                ;;
pattern2  )   do this
                ;;
pattern3  )   do this
                ;;
esac
```

The case statement compares the value of a variable with several patterns of text or numbers. When a match occurs, the commands to the right of the pattern are executed (*do this* in the preceding syntax). As with the if construct, the case construct must be ended by a backward "case" (esac).

An example that simplifies the previous myscript example by using the case construct is shown in the following output:

```
[root@server1 ~]# cat myscript
#!/bin/bash
echo -e "What would you like to see?
Today's date (d)
Currently logged in users (u)
The contents of the / directory (r)

Enter your choice(d/u/r)-->\c"
read ANSWER

case $ANSWER in
d | D ) echo -e "\nToday's date is: \c"
```

```
date
                ;;
u | U ) echo -e "\nThe people logged into the system include:"
who
                ;;
r | R ) echo -e "\nThe contents of the / directory are:"
ls -F /
                ;;
*) echo -e "Invalid choice! \a"
                ;;
esac
[root@server1 ~]# ./myscript
What would you like to see?
Today's date (d)
Currently logged in users (u)
The contents of the / directory (r)

Enter your choice(d/u/r)--> d
Today's date is: Fri Aug 20 12:33:08 EDT 2019
[root@server1 ~]#_
```

The preceding example prompts the user with a menu and allows the user to select an item that is then placed into the ANSWER variable. If the ANSWER variable is equal to the letter "d" or "D," the date command is executed; however, if the ANSWER variable is equal to the letter "u" or "U," the who command is executed, and if the ANSWER variable is equal to the letter "r" or "R," the ls command is executed. If the ANSWER variable contains something other than the aforementioned letters, the * wildcard metacharacter matches it and prints an error message to the screen. As with if constructs, any statements present in the shell script following the case construct are executed after the case construct.

The && and || Constructs

Although the if and case constructs are versatile, when only one decision needs to be made during the execution of a program, it's faster to use the && and || constructs. The syntax of these constructs is listed as follows:

```
command   &&   command
command   ||   command
```

For the preceding && syntax, the command on the right of the && construct is executed only if the command on the left of the && construct completed successfully. The opposite is true for the || syntax; the command on the right of the || construct is executed only if the command on the left of the || construct did not complete successfully.

Consider the testmkdir example presented earlier in this chapter:

```
[root@server1 ~]# cat testmkdir
#!/bin/bash
if mkdir /etc/sample
then
cp /etc/hosts /etc/sample
echo "The hosts file was successfully copied to /etc/sample"
else
echo "The /etc/sample directory could not be created!"
fi
[root@server1 ~]#_
```

You can rewrite the preceding shell script using the && construct as follows:

```
[root@server1 ~]# cat testmkdir
#!/bin/bash
mkdir /etc/sample && cp /etc/hosts /etc/sample
[root@server1 ~]#_
```

The preceding shell script creates the directory /etc/sample and only copies the /etc/hosts file to it if the mkdir /etc/sample command was successful. You can instead use the || construct to generate error messages if one of the commands fails to execute properly:

```
[root@server1 ~]# cat testmkdir
#!/bin/bash
mkdir /etc/sample || echo "Could not create /etc/sample"
cp /etc/hosts /etc/sample || echo "Could not copy /etc/hosts"
[root@server1 ~]#_
```

Loop Constructs

To execute commands repetitively, you can write shell scripts that contain loop constructs. Like decision constructs, loop constructs alter the flow of a program based on the result of a particular statement. But unlike decision constructs, which run different parts of a program depending on the results of the test statement, a loop construct simply repeats the entire program. Although several loop constructs are available within the BASH shell, the most common are for, while, and until.

The for Construct

The for construct is the most useful looping construct for Linux administrators because it can be used to process a list of objects, such as files, directories, users, printers, and so on. The syntax of the for construct is as follows:

```
for var_name in string1  string2  string3  ... ...
do
these commands
done
```

When a `for` construct is executed, it creates a variable (var_name), sets its value equal to `string1`, and executes the commands between do and done, which can access the var_name variable. Next, the `for` construct sets the value of var_name to `string2` and executes the commands between do and done again. Following this, the `for` construct sets the value of var_name to `string3` and executes the commands between do and done again. This process repeats as long as there are strings to process. Thus, if there are three strings, the `for` construct will execute three times. If there are 20 strings, the `for` construct will execute 20 times.

The following example uses the `for` construct to email a list of users with a new schedule:

```
[root@server1 ~]# cat emailusers
#!/bin/bash
for NAME in bob sue mary jane frank lisa jason
do
mail -s "Your new project schedule" < newschedule $NAME
echo "$NAME was emailed successfully"
done
[root@server1 ~]#_
[root@server1 ~]# chmod a+x emailusers
[root@server1 ~]# ./emailusers
bob was emailed successfully
sue was emailed successfully
mary was emailed successfully
jane was emailed successfully
frank was emailed successfully
lisa was emailed successfully
jason was emailed successfully
[root@server1 ~]#_
```

When the `for` construct in the preceding example is executed, it creates a NAME variable and sets its value to bob. Then it executes the `mail` command to email bob the contents of the newschedule file with a subject line of Your new project schedule. Next, it sets the NAME variable to sue and executes the `mail` command to send sue the same email. This process is repeated until the last person receives the email.

A more common use of the `for` construct within shell scripts is to process several files. The following example renames each file within a specified directory to include a .txt extension.

```
[root@server1 ~]# ls stuff
file1   file2   file3   file4   file5   file6   file7   file8
[root@server1 ~]#
[root@server1 ~]# cat multiplerename
#!/bin/bash
```

```
echo -e "What directory has the files that you would like to
rename? -->\c"
read DIR
for NAME in $DIR/*
do
mv $NAME $NAME.txt
done
[root@server1 ~]#_
[root@server1 ~]# chmod a+x multiplerename
[root@server1 ~]# ./multiplerename
What directory has the files that you would like to rename? --> stuff
[root@server1 ~]# ls stuff
file1.txt   file2.txt   file3.txt   file4.txt   file5.txt   file6.txt
file7.txt   file8.txt
[root@server1 ~]#_
```

When the `for` construct in the previous example is executed, it sets the list of strings to stuff/* (which expands to file1 file2 file3 file4 file5 file6 file7 file8). It then creates a NAME variable, sets its value to file1, and executes the `mv` command to rename file1 to file1.txt. Next, the `for` construct sets the value of the NAME variable to file2 and executes the `mv` command to rename file2 to file2.txt. This is repeated until all of the files have been processed.

You can also specify that the `for` construct should run a specific number of times by generating a list of strings using a command. The `seq` **command** is often used for this purpose; it generates a list of incremented integer numbers. For example, the shell script in the following output displays a message five times using a `for` loop:

```
[root@server1 ~]# seq 5
1
2
3
4
5
[root@server1 ~]#_
[root@server1 ~]# cat echorepeat
#!/bin/bash
for NUM in `seq 5`
do
      echo "All work and no play makes Jack a dull boy"
done
[root@server1 ~]# chmod a+x echorepeat
[root@server1 ~]# ./echorepeat
```

```
All work and no play makes Jack a dull boy
All work and no play makes Jack a dull boy
All work and no play makes Jack a dull boy
All work and no play makes Jack a dull boy
All work and no play makes Jack a dull boy
[root@server1 ~]#_
```

The seq command within the echorepeat shell script in the previous example is executed using backquotes (command substitution) and serves simply to generate a list of strings that the for construct will process. Also note that in the previous example, the NUM variable is not processed at all within the body of the loop.

The while Construct

The while construct is another common loop construct used within shell scripts. Unlike the for construct, the while construct begins with a test statement. As long as (or while) the test statement returns true, the commands within the loop construct are executed. When the test statement returns false, the commands within the while construct stop executing. A while construct typically contains a variable, called a **counter variable**, whose value changes each time through the loop. For the while construct to work properly, it must be set up so that, when the counter variable reaches a certain value, the test statement returns false. This prevents the loop from executing indefinitely.

The syntax of the while construct is as follows:

```
while this returns true
do
these commands
done
```

The following example illustrates the general use of the while construct.

```
[root@server1 ~]# cat echorepeat
#!/bin/bash
COUNTER=0
while [ $COUNTER -lt 7 ]
do
        echo "All work and no play makes Jack a dull boy" >> /tmp/redrum
        COUNTER=`expr $COUNTER + 1`
done
[root@server1 ~]#_
[root@server1 ~]# ./echorepeat
[root@server1 ~]# cat /tmp/redrum
All work and no play makes Jack a dull boy
All work and no play makes Jack a dull boy
```

```
All work and no play makes Jack a dull boy
All work and no play makes Jack a dull boy
All work and no play makes Jack a dull boy
All work and no play makes Jack a dull boy
All work and no play makes Jack a dull boy
[root@server1 ~]#_
```

The echorepeat shell script shown above creates a counter variable called COUNTER and sets its value to 0. Next, the `while` construct uses a test statement to determine whether the value of the COUNTER variable is less than 7 before executing the commands within the loop. Because the initial value of COUNTER variable is 0, it appends the text `All work and no play makes Jack a dull boy` to the /tmp/redrum file and increments the value of the COUNTER variable to 1. Note the backquotes surrounding the `expr` command, which are required to numerically add 1 to the COUNTER variable (0 + 1 = 1). Because the value of the COUNTER variable at this stage (1) is still less than 7, the `while` construct executes the commands again. This process repeats until the value of the COUNTER variable is equal to 8.

Note

You can use `true` or `:` in place of a test statement to create a `while` construct that executes indefinitely.

The `until` Construct

The `until` construct is simply the opposite of the `while` construct; it begins with a test statement, and the commands within the loop construct are executed until the test statement returns true. As a result, the `until` construct typically contains a counter variable and has nearly the same syntax as the `while` construct:

```
until this returns true
do
these commands
done
```

For example, the following `until` construct would be equivalent to the `while` construct in the previous example:

```
[root@server1 ~]# cat echorepeat
#!/bin/bash
COUNTER=0
until [ $COUNTER -eq 7 ]
do
        echo "All work and no play makes Jack a dull boy" >> /tmp/redrum
```

```
          COUNTER='expr $COUNTER + 1'
done
[root@server1 ~]#_
```

Special Variables

As shown in previous examples, variables are often used within shell scripts to hold information for processing by commands and constructs. However, there are some special variables that are useful specifically for shell scripts, including shell expansion variables, positional parameters, and built-in variables.

Shell Expansion Variables

Normally, the $ metacharacter is used to expand the results of a user or environment variable in shell memory. However, you can also use the $ metacharacter alongside regular braces to perform command substitution using the $ (command) syntax. While this functionality is identical to using backquotes, it is more common to see shell expansion variable syntax for performing command substitution within a shell script as it is easier to read. Take, for example, the shell script used in the previous example:

```
[root@server1 ~]# cat echorepeat
#!/bin/bash
COUNTER=0
until [ $COUNTER -eq 7 ]
do
        echo "All work and no play makes Jack a dull boy" >> /tmp/redrum
        COUNTER='expr $COUNTER + 1'
done
[root@server1 ~]#_
```

The expr $COUNTER + 1 command is performed using backquote command substitution. The following example is the same shell script written using a shell expansion variable:

```
[root@server1 ~]# cat echorepeat
#!/bin/bash
COUNTER=0
until [ $COUNTER -eq 7 ]
do
        echo "All work and no play makes Jack a dull boy" >> /tmp/redrum
        COUNTER=$(expr $COUNTER + 1)
done
[root@server1 ~]#_
```

You can also use shell expansion to perform variable substitution; simply use curly braces instead of regular braces. For example, to return variable names in memory that match a certain pattern, you could use the ${!pattern} syntax. The following example returns any variable names that start with HOST:

```
[root@server1 ~]# echo ${!HOST*}
HOSTNAME HOSTTYPE
[root@server1 ~]#_
```

Alternatively, you could use the ${VAR:=value} syntax to create a variable as well as return its value as shown in the example below:

```
[root@server1 ~]# echo ${MYVAR:="This is a sample variable"}
This is a sample variable
[root@server1 ~]#_
```

Positional Parameters

A shell script can take arguments when it is executed on the command line; these arguments are called **positional parameters** and may be referenced using special variables within the shell script itself. The special variable $1 refers to the contents of the first argument, $2 refers to the contents of the second argument, $3 refers to the contents of the third argument, and so on. If there are more than nine arguments, then you can use curly braces to indicate the appropriate positional parameter; for example, ${10} refers to the contents of the tenth argument. The special variable $0 refers to the command itself.

The following example illustrates the use of positional parameters:

```
[root@server1 ~]# cat pptest
#!/bin/bash
echo The command you typed was: $0
echo The first argument you typed was: $1
echo The second argument you typed was: $2
echo The third argument you typed was: $3
[root@server1 ~]# chmod a+x pptest
[root@server1 ~]# ./pptest
The command you typed was: ./pptest
The first argument you typed was:
The second argument you typed was:
The third argument you typed was:
[root@server1 ~]# ./pptest one two three
The command you typed was: ./pptest
The first argument you typed was: one
The second argument you typed was: two
The third argument you typed was: three
[root@server1 ~]#_
```

Using positional parameters is an efficient alternative to prompting the user for input. For example, you could modify the testmkdir shell script described earlier in this chapter to instead use two positional parameters that specify the source file and target directory. Each time the script is run, different arguments can be specified to perform different actions, as shown in the following output:

```
[root@server1 ~]# cat testmkdir
#!/bin/bash
#This script requires two arguments: <file> and <target directory>
if mkdir $2
then
cp $1 $2
echo "The $1 file was successfully copied to $2"
else
echo "The $2 directory could not be created."
fi
[root@server1 ~]#_
[root@server1 ~]# ./testmkdir /etc/hosts /etc/sample
The /etc/hosts file was successfully copied to /etc/sample
[root@server1 ~]# ./testmkdir /etc/issue /var
mkdir: cannot create directory '/var': File exists
The /var directory could not be created.
[root@server1 ~]# ./testmkdir /etc/issue /var/backup
The /etc/issue file was successfully copied to /var/backup
[root@server1 ~]#_
```

Built-in Variables

Many built-in special shell variables are useful within shell scripts; the most common are shown in Table 7-7. To demonstrate the use of some of these built-in variables, let's examine the following output of the addtxt shell script that accepts filename arguments, renames each filename to end with .txt, and displays the results:

Table 7-7 Special built-in shell variables

Variable	Return value
$#	The number of positional parameters
$*	All positional parameter values
$?	Exit status of the last foreground process
$$	Process ID (PID) of the current shell
$!	Process ID (PID) of the last background process
$-	Flags set in the current shell

```
[root@server1 ~]# ls
addtxt file1   file2   file3   file4   file5
[root@server1 ~]#_
[root@server1 ~]# cat addtxt
#!/bin/bash
if  [ $# -eq 0 ]
then
echo You must enter at least one filename to rename as an argument.
exit 255
fi

for NAME in $@
do
mv $NAME $NAME.txt
echo $NAME was successfully renamed $NAME.txt >>/tmp/$$.tmp
done

cat /tmp/$$
rm -f /tmp/$$
[root@server1 ~]#_
[root@server1 ~]# chmod a+x addtxt
[root@server1 ~]# ./addtxt
You must enter at least one filename to rename as an argument.
[root@server1 ~]# echo $?
255
[root@server1 ~]# ./addtxt file1 file2 file3
file1 was successfully renamed file1.txt
file2 was successfully renamed file2.txt
file3 was successfully renamed file3.txt
[root@server1 ~]# echo $?
0
[root@server1 ~]# ls
addtxt file1.txt   file2.txt   file3.txt   file4   file5
[root@server1 ~]#_
```

The if decision construct at the beginning of the shell script checks to see if the number of positional parameters ($#) is equal to 0; if it is, then a message is printed indicating the proper use of the shell script and the shell script stops executing, returning a false exit status (exit 255). If the decision construct evaluates as false, then a for loop construct processes the list of filenames specified as arguments ($@) and renames each filename to end with .txt. It also appends a line to a file in the /tmp directory named for the process ID of the current BASH shell ($$), which is likely to be unique within the /tmp directory. Finally, the shell script displays the contents of the /tmp/$$ file to indicate which files were renamed, and then the shell script completes successfully, returning a true exit status.

Functions

Some shell scripts contain specific commands and constructs that are used in various places throughout the shell script. To save time typing these commands and constructs each time they are needed, you can create a shell function that contains the appropriate commands and constructs at the beginning of the shell script. Each time you need to perform these commands and constructs throughout the shell script, you can execute the shell function with a single command. Much like aliases, a shell function is simply a special variable that contains one or more commands that are executed when you execute (or call) the shell function. However, functions can also accept positional parameters that refer to the arguments specified when the function is executed (or called). The BASH shell has several shell functions built into it that you have used throughout the book, including cd, exit, and help.

The shell script in the following output uses a function called createdir that creates a directory after checking whether it exists:

```
[root@server1 ~]# ls -F
functionscript
[root@server1 ~]# cat functionscript
#!/bin/bash

function createdir(){
  if  [ ! -d $1 ]
  then
    mkdir $1
  else
    echo Directory $1 already exists. Exiting script.
    exit 255
  fi
}

createdir dir1
createdir dir2
createdir dir3
[root@server1 ~]# ls
Functionscript  dir1/  dir2/  dir3/
[root@server1 ~]#_
```

> **Note**
>
> You can omit the word `function` in the example above and the resulting function would still be created.

In the previous example, the `createdir` function was called three times, each with a different, single argument that was associated with the first positional parameter within the function ($1).

Functions are special variables that are stored in memory; to view the functions in your shell, you can use the `set` command. To make a function available to subshells you can use the `export -f` *functionname* command, and view exported functions using the `env` command. To remove a function from your shell, use the `unset -f` *functionname* command.

As you create more shell scripts, you may find yourself using the same functions again and again. To save time, add these functions to a single shell script that contains functions only; this shell script is commonly called a **function library**. You can then use the `source` or dot (.) command to execute this function library at the beginning of each shell script that you create in order to re-create all of the functions within the function library within the BASH shell, executing your shell script as shown below:

```
[root@server1 ~]# cat /etc/functionlibrary
#!/bin/bash
function createdir(){
   if  [ ! -d $1 ]
   then
     mkdir $1
   else
     echo Directory $1 already exists. Exiting script.
     exit 255
   fi
}
function helloworld(){
   echo Hello World
}
[root@server1 ~]# cat newscript
#!/bin/bash
source /etc/functionlibrary

createdir lala
createdir music
```

```
createdir notes
helloworld
[root@server1 ~]#_
```

Version Control using Git

Version control is a system that keeps track of the changes that you make to files that you create, such as shell scripts, by tracking changes made to the files over time. If you create changes that you later find undesirable, it allows you to revert a file to a previous state easily, and if you work collaboratively on files with others, it allows you to see who made changes at different times.

Git is the most common open source version control system used today; it was originally designed in 2005 by Linus Torvalds to aid in making changes to the Linux kernel source code, and is primarily used to provide version control for software development projects on Linux, macOS, and Windows computers. Git performs version control by taking snapshots of what your files look like at different points in time. Each snapshot is called a **commit**, and includes the changes made to the files since the previous commit to allow you to undo or compare changes made to your files over time.

While Git can perform version control for files on your local computer, it also allows you to maintain version control for files that you work on collaboratively with others. Moreover, Git does not require constant Internet access for collaboration; each user downloads an original copy of the files (a process called **cloning**), and then creates commits periodically after making key changes to the files. These commits can then be pushed back to the original location, where they can be merged into the original copy or pulled to other cloned copies that others are working on.

The files and the associated commits that are managed by Git are stored in a directory called a **Git repository** (or **Git repo**). Any computer running Git can host Git repos that can be cloned to other computers running Git across the Internet. Many servers on the Internet provide free Git repo hosting, including GitHub.com.

By default, any changes you make to an original or cloned Git repo are said to be made to the **master branch**. To make collaboration easier, each user that clones a Git repo can create a separate **branch** to store just the changes that they are experimenting with; they would make all of their commits within this branch instead of the master branch. This branch (and the related commits) can then be pushed back to the original repo and merged into the master branch, or pulled down to other computers that are also working on the same branch.

Nearly all Git management is performed using the `git` **command**. Before you use Git to provide version control for your files, you must first provide information about yourself that Git will use when tracking changes made to the files themselves; this configuration will be stored in the ~/.gitconfig file. At minimum, you must provide an email address and name as shown in the following output:

```
[root@server1 ~]# git config --global user.email "jason@lala.com"
[root@server1 ~]# git config --global user.name "Jason Eckert"
[root@server1 ~]# cat ~/.gitconfig
[user]
        email = jason@lala.com
        name = Jason Eckert
[root@server1 ~]#_
```

Next, you must ensure that the files you want Git to provide version control for are within a directory, and that the directory is labelled as a Git repo using the `git init` command. This creates a hidden .git/ subdirectory that stores all information about the Git repo, including future commits. In the following output, a Git repo is created from the /scripts directory, which contains three shell scripts:

```
[root@server1 ~]# ls -aF /scripts
./   ../   script1.sh   script2.sh   script3.sh
[root@server1 ~]# cd /scripts
[root@server1 scripts]# git init
Initialized empty Git repository in /scripts/.git/
[root@server1 scripts]# ls -aF
./   ../   .git/   script1.sh   script2.sh   script3.sh
[root@server1 scripts]# git status
On branch master

No commits yet

Untracked files:
  (use "git add <file>..." to include in what will be committed)

        script1.sh
        script2.sh
        script3.sh

nothing added to commit but untracked files present (use "git add"
to track)
[root@server1 scripts]# _
```

Note from the previous output that the git status command indicates that the three shell scripts are not currently being tracked by Git for version control; this is because Git does not assume that all files in the directory should be automatically added to the version control. Instead, you must specify which files should be version tracked by adding those files to a Git index using the `git add` command (this process is called staging). After the necessary files have been staged, you can use the `git commit` command to create a snapshot of them with a description of My first commit, as shown in the following output:

```
[root@server1 scripts]# git add *
[root@server1 scripts]# git status
On branch master

No commits yet

Changes to be committed:
  (use "git rm --cached <file>..." to unstage)

      new file:   script1.sh
      new file:   script2.sh
      new file:   script3.sh
[root@server1 scripts]# git commit -m "My first commit"
3 files changed, 38 insertions(+)
 create mode 100644 script1.sh
 create mode 100644 script2.sh
 create mode 100644 script3.sh
[root@server1 scripts]# _
```

Note

To exclude files within your Git repo from being staged, add their filenames (or wildcard matches) to a .gitignore file; this allows you to safely use the `git add *` command shown in the previous output without inadvertently adding any unnecessary files.

Now, you can modify one or more of the scripts, stage the modified scripts, and create a snapshot of them. The following output demonstrates this process with script3.sh:

```
[root@server1 scripts]# vi script3.sh
[root@server1 scripts]# git status
On branch master
Changes not staged for commit:
  (use "git add <file>..." to update what will be committed)
  (use "git checkout -- <file>..." to discard changes in working
directory)

      modified:   script3.sh
```

```
no changes added to commit (use "git add" and/or "git commit -a")
[root@server1 scripts]# git add script3.sh
[root@server1 scripts]# git commit -m "Added comment to script3.sh"
[master dd148af] Added comment to script3.sh
 1 file changed, 1 insertion(+)
[root@server1 scripts]# _
```

To see a list of all modifications to files within your Git repo, you can use the `git log` command; the word HEAD is used to refer to the most recent commit in the output. To revert to a previous version of files within a commit, you can use the `git reset --hard` command alongside the commit number as shown below:

```
[root@server1 scripts]# git log
commit dd148af2d4bc769af054ce (HEAD -> master)
Author: Jason Eckert <jason@lala.com>
Date:   Sat Aug 11 15:53:55 2019 -0400

    Added comment to script3.sh


commit f991c87b4b9a3a9ffedb38
Author: Jason Eckert <jason@lala.com>
Date:   Sat Aug 11 15:45:01 2019 -0400

    My first commit
[root@server1 scripts]# git reset --hard f991c87b4b9a3a9ffedb38
[root@server1 scripts]# git log
commit f991c87b4b9a3a9ffedb38 (HEAD -> master)
Author: Jason Eckert <jason@lala.com>
Date:   Sat Aug 11 15:45:01 2019 -0400

    My first commit
[root@server1 scripts]# _
```

You can also use Git to perform version control for other users that need to modify on the scripts in the /scripts directory. Say, for example, that a user named Bob on the same system needs to modify the scripts within the /scripts directory. Bob can simply run the `git clone` command to download a copy of the /scripts repo to his current directory as shown in the following output:

```
[Bob@server1 ~]$ git clone /scripts
Cloning into 'scripts'...
done.
[Bob@server1 scripts]$ cd scripts
[Bob@server1 scripts]$ pwd
```

```
/home/Bob/scripts
[Bob@server1 scripts]$ ls -aF
./  ../  .git/  script1.sh  script2.sh  script3.sh
[Bob@server1 scripts]$ _
```

> **Note** 📎
>
> To download a Git repo from a remote computer, you must additionally supply the hostname of the remote computer, and a username with access to the Git repo on that computer. For example, `git clone root@server1:/scripts` could be used to download the /scripts repo from server1 as the root user (you will be prompted for root's password).
>
> After a repo has been cloned, the location of the original repo is referred to as origin from that point onwards within Git commands.

Bob can then create a new branch to perform and test his modifications without affecting the original cloned scripts within the master branch. For example, to create and switch to a new branch called AddErrorChecks, and then view the results, Bob could run the following commands:

```
[Bob@server1 ~]$ git checkout -b AddErrorChecks
Switched to a new branch 'AddErrorChecks'
[Bob@server1 scripts]$ git branch
* AddErrorChecks
  master
[Bob@server1 scripts]$ _
```

The * character next to AddErrorChecks in the previous output of the `git branch` command indicates that it is the current branch being used. Next, Bob can modify script2.sh in the AddErrorChecks branch, and test the results. Once Bob is satisfied that the modifications work as expected, he could stage and commit script2.sh within the AddErrorChecks branch as shown below:

```
[Bob@server1 ~]$ git add script2.sh
[Bob@server1 ~]$ git status
On branch AddErrorChecks
Changes to be committed:
  (use "git reset HEAD <file>..." to unstage)

    modified:   script2.sh

[Bob@server1 scripts]$ git commit -m "Added error checks to script2.sh"
[AddErrorChecks 6ed6551] Added error checks to script2.sh
```

```
1 file changed, 1 insertion(+), 1 deletion(-)
[Bob@server1 scripts]$ _
```

If Bob switched to the master branch at this point using the `git checkout master` command and then viewed the contents of script2.sh, he would not see his modifications, as they were performed only within the AddErrorChecks branch. By creating and using a separate branch called AddErrorChecks, Bob separated his modifications from the master branch. The AddErrorChecks branch can then easily be pushed back to the original repo (/scripts) as shown below:

```
[Bob@server1 scripts]$ git push origin AddErrorChecks
Counting objects: 3, done.
Compressing objects: 100% (3/3), done.
Writing objects: 100% (3/3), 355 bytes | 355.00 KiB/s, done.
Total 3 (delta 1), reused 0 (delta 0)
To /scripts/
 * [new branch]        AddErrorChecks -> AddErrorChecks
[Bob@server1 scripts]$ _
```

The user that manages the original /scripts repo (in our example, root) can then view the branch and merge it into the original repo's master branch using the following commands:

```
[root@server1 scripts]# git branch
  AddErrorChecks
* master
[root@server1 scripts]# git merge AddErrorChecks
Updating f991c87..6ed6551
Fast-forward
 script2.sh | 2 +-
 1 file changed, 1 insertion(+), 1 deletion(-)
[root@server1 scripts]# _
```

At this point, other users with a cloned repo can pull the updated copy of the master branch from the original repo; for example, Bob can pull the updated copy of the master branch from the original repo using the following command:

```
[Bob@server1 scripts]$ git pull origin master
From /scripts
 * branch              master      -> FETCH_HEAD
   f991c87..6ed6551  master      -> origin/master
[Bob@server1 scripts]$ _
```

Following this, Bob can repeat this process by creating additional branches to experiment with script modifications, pushing them to the original repo where they can be merged into the master branch, and then pulling updated copies of the original master branch.

Table 7-8 lists common git commands for use in Git version control.

Table 7-8   Common git commands

Command	Description
`git config`	Sets general Git parameters
`git init`	Creates a Git repo within the current directory
`git clone /path`	Clones a local Git repo to the current directory
`git clone username@hostname:/path`	Clones a remote Git repo to the current directory
`git add filenames`	Adds files to a Git index
`git rm filenames`	Removes files from a Git index
`git commit -m description`	Creates a commit with the specified description from the files listed in the Git index
`git status`	Views repo status
`git log`	Views commit history for the current branch
`git checkout -b branchname`	Creates a new branch and switches to it
`git checkout branchname`	Switches to a different branch
`git branch`	Views branches in the repo
`git branch -d branchname`	Deletes a branch
`git push origin branchname`	Pushes a branch to the original repo location
`git pull origin branchname`	Pulls a branch from the original repo location
`git reset --hard commitidentifier`	Reverts files within a repo to a previous commit

Chapter Summary

- Three components are available to commands: Standard Input (stdin), Standard Output (stdout), and Standard Error (stderr). Not all commands use every component.

- Standard Input is typically user input taken from the keyboard, whereas Standard Output and Standard Error are sent to the terminal screen by default.

- You can redirect the Standard Output and Standard Error of a command to a file using redirection symbols. Similarly, you can use redirection symbols to redirect a file to the Standard Input of a command.

- To redirect the Standard Output from one command to the Standard Input of another, you must use the pipe symbol (|).

- Most variables available to the BASH shell are environment variables that are loaded into memory after login from environment files.

- You can create your own variables in the BASH shell and export them to programs started by the shell. These variables can also be placed in environment files, so that they are loaded into memory on every shell login.
- The UMASK variable and command aliases are special variables that must be set using a certain command.
- Shell scripts can be used to execute several Linux commands.
- Decision constructs can be used within shell scripts to execute certain Linux commands based on user input or the results of a certain command.
- Loop constructs can be used within shell scripts to execute a series of commands repetitively.
- Special variables can be used within shell scripts to access built-in shell information, access positional parameters, and to expand commands and variables.

- Functions can be created within a shell script to store commands and constructs for later execution. Function libraries are shell scripts that only contain functions; they can be run at the beginning of other shell scripts to provide a rich set of functions.
- Git can be used to provide version control for files on your system that are modified over time, including shell scripts. These files are stored as a master branch within a Git repository that can be cloned to other computers for collaboration. Git users can create additional branches to test file modifications before merging them into the master branch.
- After changes are made to files within a Git repo, they are normally staged and added to a commit that provides a snapshot of the files at that time. You can revert files to a previous state by referencing the associated commit.

Key Terms

|	file descriptors	seq command
<	filter	set command
>	function	shebang
alias command	function library	shell scripts
branch	Git	source command
cloning	git command	staging
commit	Git repo	Standard Error (stderr)
counter variable	Git repository	Standard Input (stdin)
decision construct	hashpling	Standard Output (stdout)
dot (.) command	here document	subshell
echo command	history command	test statement
env command	loop construct	tr command
environment files	master branch	unalias command
environment variables	pipe	unset command
escape sequences	positional parameter	user-defined variables
exit status	printenv command	variable
export command	read command	variable identifier
expr command	redirection	version control

Review Questions

1. Because stderr and stdout represent the results of a command and stdin represents the input required for a command, only stderr and stdout can be redirected to/from a file. True or False?

2. Before a user-defined variable can be used by processes that run in subshells, that variable must be _____.
   a. imported
   b. validated by running the env command
   c. exported
   d. redirected to the BASH shell

3. Both aliases and functions can be used to store commands that can be executed, but functions can also accept positional parameters. True or False?

4. Which of the following files is always executed immediately after any user logs in to a Linux system and receives a BASH shell?
   a. /etc/profile
   b. ~/.bash_profile
   c. ~/.bash_login
   d. ~/.profile

5. Which command could you use to see a list of all environment and user-defined shell variables as well as their current values?
   a. ls /var
   b. env
   c. set
   d. echo

6. Every if construct begins with if and must be terminated with _____.
   a. end
   b. endif
   c. stop
   d. fi

7. Which of the following will display the message welcome home if the cd /home/user1 command is successfully executed?
   a. cd /home/user1 && echo "welcome home"
   b. cat "welcome home" || cd /home/user1
   c. cd /home/user1 || cat "welcome home"
   d. echo "welcome home" && cd /home/user1

8. The current value for the HOME variable is displayed by which of the following commands? (Choose all that apply.)
   a. echo HOME=
   b. echo ~
   c. echo $HOME
   d. echo ls HOME

9. Which of the following variables could access the value "/etc" within the sample shell script, if the sample shell script was executed using the bash sample /var /etc /bin command?
   a. $0
   b. $1
   c. $2
   d. $3

10. Which of the following operators reverses the meaning of a test statement?
   a. #!
   b. -o
   c. -a
   d. !

11. What would be the effect of using the alias command to make an alias for the date command named cat in honor of your favorite pet?
   a. It cannot be done because there already is an environment variable cat associated with the cat command.

b. It cannot be done because there already is a command `cat` on the system.

c. When you use the `cat` command at the command prompt with the intention of viewing a text file, the date appears instead.

d. There is no effect until the alias is imported because it is a user-declared variable.

12. How do you indicate a comment line in a shell script?

a. There are no comment lines in a shell script.

b. Begin the line with `#!`.

c. Begin the line with `!`.

d. Begin the line with `#`.

13. You have redirected stderr to a file called Errors. You view the contents of this file afterward and notice that there are six error messages. After repeating the procedure, you notice that there are only two error messages in this file. Why?

a. After you open the file and view the contents, the contents are lost.

b. The system generated different stdout.

c. You did not append the stderr to the Error file, and, as a result, it was overwritten when the command was run a second time.

d. You must specify a new file each time you redirect because the system creates the specified file by default.

14. The `sed` and `awk` commands are filter commands commonly used to format data within a pipe. True or False?

15. You attempt to perform the `git commit -m "Added listdir function"` but the command fails. What are possible reasons for the failure? (Choose all that apply.)

a. The user performing the commit has not set their Git user information.

b. No files were added to the Git index beforehand.

c. The user performing the commit is not running the command from within the Git repo directory.

d. The master branch was not specified within the command itself.

16. Which of the following lines can be used to perform command substitution within a shell script? (Choose all that apply.)

a. `` `command` ``

b. `${command}`

c. `${!command}`

d. `$(command)`

17. Which construct can be used in a shell script to read stdin and place it in a variable?

a. `read`

b. `sum`

c. `verify`

d. `test`

18. A `for` construct is a loop construct that processes a specified list of objects. As a result, it is executed as long as there are remaining objects to process. True or False?

19. What does `&>` accomplish when entered on the command line after a command?

a. It redirects both stderr and stdout to the same location.

b. It does not accomplish anything.

c. It redirects stderr and stdin to the same location.

d. It appends stdout to a file.

20. Consider the following shell script:

```
echo -e "What is your
favorite color?--> \c"
read REPLY
```

```
if [ "$REPLY" = "red"  -o
"$REPLY" = "blue" ]
then
echo "The answer is red or
blue."
else
echo "The answer is not red
nor blue."
fi
```

What would be displayed if a user executes this shell script and answers Blue when prompted?

a. The answer is red or blue.
b. The answer is not red nor blue.
c. The code would cause an error.
d. The answer is red or blue. The answer is not red nor blue.

Hands-On Projects

These projects should be completed in the order given. The hands-on projects presented in this chapter should take a total of three hours to complete. The requirements for this lab include:

- A computer with Fedora Linux installed according to Hands-On Project 2-1.

Project 7-1

In this hands-on project, you use the shell to redirect the stdout and stderr to a file and take stdin from a file.

1. Boot your Fedora Linux virtual machine. After your Linux system has been loaded, switch to a command-line terminal (tty5) by pressing **Ctrl+Alt+F5** and log in to the terminal using the user name of **root** and the password of **LINUXrocks!**.

2. At the command prompt, type **touch sample1 sample2** and press **Enter** to create two new files named sample1 and sample2 in your home directory. Verify their creation by typing **ls -F** at the command prompt, and press **Enter**.

3. At the command prompt, type **ls -l sample1 sample2 sample3** and press **Enter**. Is there any stdout displayed on the terminal screen? Is there any stderr displayed on the terminal screen? Why?

4. At the command prompt, type **ls -l sample1 sample2 sample3 > file** and press **Enter**. Is there any stdout displayed on the terminal screen? Is there any stderr displayed on the terminal screen? Why?

5. At the command prompt, type **cat file** and press **Enter**. What are the contents of the file and why?

6. At the command prompt, type **ls -l sample1 sample2 sample3 2> file** and press **Enter**. Is there any stdout displayed on the terminal screen? Is there any stderr displayed on the terminal screen? Why?

7. At the command prompt, type **cat file** and press **Enter**. What are the contents of the file and why? Were the previous contents retained? Why?

8. At the command prompt, type `ls -l sample1 sample2 sample3 > file 2>file2` and press **Enter**. Is there any stdout displayed on the terminal screen? Is there any stderr displayed on the terminal screen? Why?

9. At the command prompt, type `cat file` and press **Enter**. What are the contents of the file and why?

10. At the command prompt, type `cat file2` and press **Enter**. What are the contents of the file2 and why?

11. At the command prompt, type `ls -l sample1 sample2 sample3 > file 2>&1` and press **Enter**. Is there any stdout displayed on the terminal screen? Is there any stderr displayed on the terminal screen? Why?

12. At the command prompt, type `cat file` and press **Enter**. What are the contents of the file and why?

13. At the command prompt, type `ls -l sample1 sample2 sample3 >&2 2>file2` and press **Enter**. Is there any stdout displayed on the terminal screen? Is there any stderr displayed on the terminal screen? Why?

14. At the command prompt, type `cat file2` and press **Enter**. What are the contents of file2 and why?

15. At the command prompt, type `date > file` and press **Enter**.

16. At the command prompt, type `cat file` and press **Enter**. What are the contents of the file and why?

17. At the command prompt, type `date >> file` and press **Enter**.

18. At the command prompt, type `cat file` and press **Enter**. What are the contents of the file and why? Can you tell when each `date` command was run?

19. At the command prompt, type `tr o O /etc/hosts` and press **Enter**. What error message do you receive and why?

20. At the command prompt, type `tr o O </etc/hosts` and press **Enter**. What happened and why?

21. At the command prompt, type `tr o O <<EOF` and press **Enter**. At the secondary prompt, type `oranges` and press **Enter**. Next, type `Toronto` and press **Enter**, type `Donkey Kong` and press **Enter**, and then type `EOF` and press **Enter**. Note the output. What is this type of input redirection called?

22. Type `exit` and press **Enter** to log out of your shell.

Project 7-2

In this hands-on project, you redirect stdout and stdin using pipe metacharacters.

1. Switch to a command-line terminal (tty5) by pressing **Ctrl+Alt+F5** and log in to the terminal using the user name of **root** and the password of **LINUXrocks!**.

2. At the command prompt, type `cat /etc/services` and press **Enter** to view the /etc/services file. Next, type `cat /etc/services | less` at the command prompt and press **Enter** to perform the same task page-by-page. Explain what the | metacharacter does in the previous command. How is this different from the `less /etc/services` command?

3. At the command prompt, type `cat /etc/services | grep NFS` and press **Enter**. How many lines are displayed? Why did you not need to specify a filename with the `grep` command?

4. At the command prompt, type `cat /etc/services | grep NFS | tr F f` and press **Enter**. Explain the output on the terminal screen.

5. At the command prompt, type `cat /etc/services | grep NFS | tr F f | sort -r` and press **Enter**. Explain the output on the terminal screen.

6. At the command prompt, type `cat /etc/services | grep NFS | tr F f | sort -r | tee file` and press **Enter**. Explain the output on the terminal screen. Next, type `cat file` at the command prompt and press **Enter**. What are the contents? Why? What does the `tee` command do in the pipe above?

7. At the command prompt, type `cat /etc/services | grep NFS | tr F f | sort -r | tee file | wc -l` and press **Enter**. Explain the output on the terminal screen. Next, type `cat file` at the command prompt and press **Enter**. What are the contents and why?

8. At the command prompt, type `cat /etc/services | grep NFS | tr F f | sort -r | sed /udp/d | sed /tcp/s/mount/MOUNT/g` and press **Enter**. Explain the output on the terminal screen. Can this output be obtained with the `grep` and `tr` commands instead of `sed`?

9. At the command prompt, type `cat /etc/hosts`. Next, type `cat /etc/hosts | awk '/localhost/ {print $1, $3}'` and press **Enter**. Explain the output on the terminal screen.

10. Type `exit` and press **Enter** to log out of your shell.

Project 7-3

In this hands-on project, you create and use an alias, as well as view and change existing shell variables. In addition to this, you export user-defined variables and load variables automatically upon shell startup.

1. Switch to a command-line terminal (tty5) by pressing **Ctrl+Alt+F5** and log in to the terminal using the user name of **root** and the password of **LINUXrocks!.**

2. At the command prompt, type `set | less` and press **Enter** to view the BASH shell environment variables currently loaded into memory. Scroll through this list using the cursor keys on the keyboard. When finished, press **q** to quit the less utility.

3. At the command prompt, type `env | less` and press **Enter** to view the exported BASH shell environment variables currently loaded into memory. Scroll through this list using the cursor keys on the keyboard. Is this list larger or smaller than the list generated in Step 2? Why? When finished, press **q** to quit the less utility.

4. At the command prompt, type `PS1="Hello There:"` and press **Enter**. What happened and why? Next, type `echo $PS1` at the command prompt and press **Enter** to verify the new value of the PS1 variable.

5. At the command prompt, type `exit` and press **Enter** to log out of the shell. Next, log in to the terminal again using the user name of **root** and the password of **LINUXrocks!.**

What prompt did you receive and why? How could you ensure that the "Hello There: " prompt occurs at every login?

6. At the command prompt, type `vi .bash_profile` and press **Enter**. At the bottom of the file, add the following lines. When finished, save and quit the vi editor.

```
echo -e "Would you like a hello prompt? (y/n) -->\c"
read ANSWER
if [ $ANSWER = "y" -o $ANSWER = "Y" ]
then
PS1="Hello There: "
fi
```

Explain what the preceding lines will perform after each login.

7. At the command prompt, type `exit` and press **Enter** to log out of the shell. Next, log in to the terminal using the user name of **root** and the password of **LINUXrocks!**. When prompted for a hello prompt, type **y** and press **Enter**. What prompt did you receive and why?

8. At the command prompt, type `exit` and press **Enter** to log out of the shell. Next, log in to the terminal using the user name of **root** and the password of **LINUXrocks!**. When prompted for a hello prompt, type **n** and press **Enter** to receive the default prompt.

9. At the command prompt, type `MYVAR="My sample variable"` and press **Enter** to create a variable called MYVAR. Verify its creation by typing `echo $MYVAR` at the command prompt, and press **Enter**.

10. At the command prompt, type `set | grep MYVAR` and press **Enter**. Is the MYVAR variable listed? Why?

11. At the command prompt, type `env | grep MYVAR` and press **Enter**. Is the MYVAR variable listed? Why?

12. At the command prompt, type `export MYVAR` and press **Enter**. Next, type `env | grep MYVAR` at the command prompt and press **Enter**. Is the MYVAR variable listed now? Why?

13. At the command prompt, type `exit` and press **Enter** to log out of the shell. Next, log in to the terminal using the user name of **root** and the password of **LINUXrocks!**.

14. At the command prompt, type `echo $MYVAR` and press **Enter** to view the contents of the MYVAR variable. What is listed and why?

15. At the command prompt, type `vi .bash_profile` and press **Enter**. At the bottom of the file, add the following line. When finished, save and quit the vi editor.

```
export MYVAR="My sample variable"
```

16. At the command prompt, type `exit` and press **Enter** to log out of the shell. Next, log in to the terminal using the user name of **root** and the password of **LINUXrocks!**.

17. At the command prompt, type `echo $MYVAR` and press **Enter** to list the contents of the MYVAR variable. What is listed and why?

18. At the command prompt, type `alias` and press **Enter**. Note the aliases that are present in your shell.

19. At the command prompt, type `alias asample="cd /etc ; cat hosts ; cd ~ ; ls -F"` and press **Enter**. What does this command do?

20. At the command prompt, type `asample` and press **Enter**. What happened and why? What environment file could you add this alias to such that it is executed each time a new BASH shell is created?

21. Type `exit` and press **Enter** to log out of your shell.

Project 7-4

In this hands-on project, you create a basic shell script and execute it on the system.

1. Switch to a command-line terminal (tty5) by pressing **Ctrl+Alt+F5** and log in to the terminal using the user name of **root** and the password of **LINUXrocks!**.

2. At the command prompt, type `vi myscript` and press **Enter** to open a new file for editing called myscript in your home directory.

3. Enter the following text into the myscript file. When finished, save and quit the vi editor.

```
#!/bin/bash
echo -e "This is a sample shell script. \t It displays mounted
filesystems: \a"
df -hT
```

4. At the command prompt, type `ls -l myscript` and press **Enter**. What permissions does the myscript file have? Next, type `bash myscript` at the command prompt and press **Enter**. Did the shell script execute? What do the \t and \a escape sequences do?

5. Next, type `./myscript` at the command prompt and press **Enter**. What error message did you receive and why?

6. At the command prompt, type `chmod u+x myscript` and press **Enter**. Next, type `./myscript` at the command prompt and press **Enter**. Did the script execute? Why?

7. Type `exit` and press **Enter** to log out of your shell.

Project 7-5

In this hands-on project, you create a shell script that uses decision and loop constructs to analyze user input.

1. Switch to a command-line terminal (tty5) by pressing **Ctrl+Alt+F5** and log in to the terminal using the user name of **root** and the password of **LINUXrocks!**.

2. At the command prompt, type `vi diskconfig.sh` and press **Enter** to open a new file for editing called diskconfig.sh in your home directory. Why is it good form to use a .sh extension for shell scripts?

3. Enter the following text into the diskconfig.sh file. As you are typing the contents, ensure that you understand the purpose of each line (reviewing the chapter contents and appropriate man pages as necessary). When finished, save and quit the vi editor.

```
#!/bin/bash
#This script creates a report of our disk configuration

FILENAME=`hostname`
echo "Disk report saved to $FILENAME.report"

echo -e "\n LVM Configuration: \n\n" >>$FILENAME.report
lvscan >>$FILENAME.report

echo -e "\n\n Partition Configuration: \n\n" >>$FILENAME.report
fdisk -l | head -17 >>$FILENAME.report

echo -e "\n\n Mounted Filesystems: \n\n" >>$FILENAME.report
df -hT | grep -v tmp >>$FILENAME.report
```

4. At the command prompt, type **chmod u+x diskconfig.sh** and press **Enter**. Next, type **./diskconfig.sh** at the command prompt and press **Enter**. Note the filename that your report was saved to.

5. At the command prompt, type **less** *filename* where filename is the *filename* you noted in the previous step, and press **Enter**. View the contents. Would this shell script work well to record storage configuration from different systems? Why?

6. At the command prompt, type **vi dirbackup.sh** and press **Enter** to open a new file for editing called dirbackup.sh in your home directory.

7. Enter the following text into the dirbackup.sh file. As you are typing the contents, ensure that you understand the purpose of each line (reviewing the chapter contents and appropriate man pages as necessary; the `tar` backup command will be discussed in Chapter 11 and does not require detailed interpretation here). When finished, save and quit the vi editor.

```
#!/bin/bash
#This script backs up a directory of your choice

if [ $# -ne 1 ]
then
echo "Usage is $0 <directory to back up>"
exit 255
fi

echo "Performing backup....."
sleep 3
tar -zcvf ~/backupfile.tar.gz $1

echo "Backup completed successfully to ~/backupfile.tar.gz"
```

8. At the command prompt, type **chmod u+x dirbackup.sh** and press **Enter**. Next, type **./dirbackup.sh** at the command prompt and press **Enter**. Note the error that you receive because you did not specify a positional parameter. Type **./dirbackup.sh /etc/samba** at the command prompt and press **Enter** to create a backup of the /etc/samba directory within the backupfile.tar.gz file in your home directory.

9. At the command prompt, type **ls -F** and press **Enter**. Was the backupfile.tar.gz file successfully created?

10. At the command prompt, type **vi dirbackup.sh** and press **Enter**. As you are modifying the contents, ensure that you understand the purpose of each change (reviewing the chapter contents and appropriate man pages as necessary). Edit the text inside the dirbackup.sh shell script such that it reads:

```
#!/bin/bash
#This script backs up a directory of your choice

echo -e "What directory do you want to back up?-->\c"
read ANS

echo "Performing backup....."
sleep 3
tar -zcvf ~/backupfile.tar.gz $ANS

echo "Backup completed successfully to ~/backupfile.tar.gz"
```

11. At the command prompt, type **./dirbackup.sh** and press **Enter**. Type **/etc/httpd** and press **Enter** when prompted to back up the /etc/httpd directory to backupfile.tar.gz in your home directory. Note that the backup file does not represent the directory or time the backup was performed.

12. At the command prompt, type **vi dirbackup.sh** and press **Enter**. As you are modifying the contents, ensure that you understand the purpose of each change (reviewing the chapter contents and appropriate man pages as necessary). Edit the text inside the dirbackup.sh shell script such that it reads:

```
#!/bin/bash
#This script backs up a directory of your choice

echo -e "What directory do you want to back up?-->\c"
read ANS

echo "Performing backup....."
sleep 3
FILE=`echo $ANS | sed s#/#-#g`
```

```
DATE=`date +%F`
tar -zcvf ~/backup-$FILE-$DATE.tar.gz $ANS

echo "Backup performed to ~/backup-$FILE-$DATE.tar.gz"
```

13. At the command prompt, type `./dirbackup.sh` and press **Enter**. Type `/etc/httpd` and press **Enter** when prompted to back up the /etc/httpd directory. Note that the filename of the backup now reflects the directory that was backed up as well as the date the backup was performed.

14. At the command prompt, type `vi familydatabase.sh` and press **Enter** to open a new file for editing called familydatabase.sh in your home directory.

15. Enter the following text into the familydatabase.sh file. As you are typing the contents, ensure that you understand the purpose of each line (reviewing the chapter contents and appropriate man pages as necessary). When finished, save and quit the vi editor.

```
#!/bin/bash
while true
do
clear
echo -e "What would you like to do?
Add an entry (a)
Search an entry (s)
Quit (q)
Enter your choice (a/s/q)-->\c"
read ANSWER
case $ANSWER in
a|A ) echo -e "Name of the family member --> \c"
          read NAME
          echo -e "Family member's relation to you -->\c"
          read RELATION
          echo -e "Family member's telephone number --> \c"
          read PHONE
          echo "$NAME\t$RELATION\t$PHONE" >> database
          ;;
s|S ) echo "What word would you like to look for? --> \c"
          read WORD
          grep "$WORD" database
          sleep 4
     ;;
q|Q ) exit
          ;;
*)    echo "You must enter either the letter a or s."
```

```
        sleep 4
        ;;
    esac
    done
```

16. At the command prompt, type **chmod u+x familydatabase.sh** and press **Enter**. Next, type **./familydatabase.sh** at the command prompt and press **Enter**. Type **a** and press **Enter** when prompted and supply the appropriate values for a family member of your choice. Does the menu continue to appear when you have finished entering your record? Type **a** and press **Enter** and supply the appropriate values for a different family member. Type **s** and press **Enter** and supply a piece of information you previously entered for a family member to see the results. Type **x** and press **Enter** to view the usage error. Finally, type **q** and press **Enter** to quit your shell script.

17. Type **exit** and press **Enter** to log out of your shell.

Project 7-6

In this hands-on project, you create a local Git repository for the shell scripts that you created in Project 7-5, and explore Git version control.

1. Switch to a command-line terminal (tty5) by pressing **Ctrl+Alt+F5** and log in to the terminal using the user name of **root** and the password of **LINUXrocks!**.

2. At the command prompt, type **mkdir /shellscripts** and press **Enter**. Next, type **mv diskconfig.sh dirbackup.sh familydatabase.sh /shellscripts** and press **Enter** to move your shell scripts from Project 7-5 to the /shellscripts directory.

3. At the command prompt, type **cd /shellscripts** and press **Enter**. Next, type **git init** and press **Enter** to create a Git repo in your current directory. Finally, type **ls -a** and press **Enter** to verify the creation of the .git subdirectory.

4. At the command prompt, type **git status** and press **Enter**. Note that your shell scripts are detected but not managed by Git yet. Next, type **git add *** and press **Enter** to add your shell scripts to the index. Finally, type **git status** and press **Enter** to verify that your shell scripts are ready for commit.

5. At the command prompt, type **git commit -m "First commit"** and press **Enter**. What error did you receive and why? Next, type **git config --global user.email "root@domain.com"** and press **Enter** to set your email address. Next, type **git config --global user.name "root user"** and press **Enter** to set your user name. Finally, type **git commit -m "First commit"** and press **Enter** to create your first commit.

6. At the command prompt, type **vi diskconfig.sh** and press **Enter**. Add the following lines to the bottom of the diskconfig.sh file. When finished, save and quit the vi editor.

```
echo -e "\n\n RAID Configuration: \n\n" >>$FILENAME.report
mdadm --detail /dev/md0 >>$FILENAME.report
```

7. At the command prompt, type `git status` and press **Enter**. Did Git detect the modification to diskconfig.sh? Next, type `git add *` and press **Enter** to add your shell scripts to the index. Finally, type `git commit -m "Added RAID to diskconfig.sh"` and press **Enter** to create a second commit that represents your change.

8. At the command prompt, type `git log` and press **Enter**. Note the commit identifier next to your original commit (before the RAID section was added). Next, type `git reset --hard commitID` and press **Enter**, where *commitID* is the commit identifier for your original commit. Finally, type `cat diskconfig.sh` and press **Enter**. Was your RAID addition to the diskconfig.sh shell script removed?

9. At the command prompt, type `cd` and press **Enter** to return to your home directory. Next, type `git clone /shellscripts` and press **Enter** to clone your local / shellscripts repo to your home directory. Next, type `cd shellscripts` and press **Enter** to switch to your cloned repo. Finally, type `ls -a` and press **Enter** to verify that your cloned repo contains the same contents as the original repo.

10. At the command prompt, type `git branch` and press **Enter**. What is the default branch called? Next, type `git checkout -b AddRAID` and press **Enter** to create a branch called AddRAID to your cloned repo. Finally, type `git branch` and press **Enter** to verify that your AddRAID branch was added. How can you tell that your AddRAID branch is the active branch in the output?

11. At the command prompt, type `vi diskconfig.sh` and press **Enter**. Add the following lines to the bottom of the diskconfig.sh file. When finished, save and quit the vi editor.

```
echo -e "\n\n RAID Configuration: \n\n" >>$FILENAME.report
mdadm --detail /dev/md0 >>$FILENAME.report
```

12. At the command prompt, type `git add *` and press **Enter** to add your shell scripts to the index within your AddRAID branch. Finally, type `git commit -m "Added RAID to diskconfig.sh"` and press **Enter** to create a commit within your AddRAID branch that represents your change.

13. At the command prompt, type `cat diskconfig.sh` and press **Enter** and note that your RAID modification is shown. Next, type `git checkout master` and press **Enter** to switch back to the master branch of your cloned repo. Finally, type `cat diskconfig.sh` and press **Enter**. Is your RAID modification visible in the master branch?

14. At the command prompt, type `git push origin AddRAID` and press **Enter** to push your AddRAID branch to the original repo. Next, type `cd /shellscripts` and press **Enter** to switch your current directory to the original repo. Finally type `git branch` and press **Enter** to verify that the branch was pushed successfully to the original repo from the cloned repo. Also note that your current branch in the original repo is still set to master.

15. At the command prompt, type `git merge AddRAID` and press **Enter** to merge the changes from the AddRAID branch to your master branch. Next, type `cat diskconfig.sh` and press **Enter**. Is your modification visible in the master branch?

16. At the command prompt, type `cd ~/shellscripts` and press **Enter** to switch your cloned repo in your home directory. Next, type `git pull origin master` and press **Enter** to pull a new copy of the master branch from your original repo. Was the pull successful?

17. Type `exit` and press **Enter** to log out of your shell.

Discovery Exercises

1. Name the command that can be used to do each of the following:
   a. Create an alias called mm that displays only those filesystems that are mounted and contain an ext4 filesystem.
   b. Create and export a variable called NEWHOME that is equivalent to the value contained in the HOME variable.
   c. Find all files that start with the word "host" starting from the /etc directory and save the Standard Output to a file called file1 and the Standard Error to the same file.
   d. Display only the lines from the output of the `set` command that have the word "bash" in them. This output on the terminal screen should be sorted alphabetically.
   e. Display only the user name (first field) in the colon-delimited /etc/passwd file and save the output to a file called users in the current directory.

2. What would happen if the user executed the following commands?

   ```
   cp /etc/hosts ~
   cd
   tr a A <hosts | sort -r |
      pr -d >hosts
   ```

   Explain the output.

3. Recall that only Standard Output can be sent across a pipe to another command.

   Using the information presented in this chapter, how could you send Standard Error across the pipe in the following command?

   ```
   ls /etc/hosts /etc/h | tr h H
   ```

4. Name the test statement that can be used to test the following scenarios:
   a. The user has read permission to the /etc/hosts file.
   b. The user has read and execute permission to the /etc directory.
   c. The contents of the variable $TEST are equal to the string "success."
   d. The contents of the variable $TEST are numerically equal to the contents of the variable $RESULT.
   e. The contents of the variable $TEST are equal to the string "success" and the file /etc/hosts exists.
   f. The contents of the variable $TEST are equal to the string "success," or the number 5, or the contents of the variable $RESULT.

5. Examine the sample /root/.bash_profile file shown next. Using the information presented in this chapter, describe what each line of this file does.

   ```
   # .bash_profile

   # Get the aliases and functions
   if [ -f ~/.bashrc ]; then
   ```

```
    . ~/.bashrc
fi

# User specific environment
    and startup programs

PATH=$PATH:$HOME/bin
BASH_ENV=$HOME/.bashrc
USERNAME="root"

export USERNAME BASH_ENV PATH
```

6. Examine the following shell script and describe its function line-by-line:

```
#!/bin/bash
echo -e "This program copies
    a file to the /stuff
    directory.\n"
echo -e "Which file would you
    like to copy? --> \c"
read FILENAME
mkdir /stuff || echo "The
    /stuff directory could not
    be created."
cp -f $FILENAME /stuff && echo
    "$FILENAME was successfully
    copied to /stuff"
```

7. Examine the following shell script and describe its function line-by-line:

```
#!/bin/bash
#This script backs up the
    Oracle DB

rm -f /SAN/backup-oracle*

if tar -zcvf /SAN/backup-
    oracle-`date +%F`.tar.gz
    /oracledb/*
  then
```

```
    echo "Oracle backup completed
        on `date`" >>/var/log/
        oraclelog

else
    echo "Oracle backup failed on
        `date`" >>/var/log/oraclelog
    mail -s ALERT jason.eckert@
        trios.com </var/log/
        oraclelog
fi
```

8. GitHub.com is one of the most commonly used public Git repositories. Navigate to GitHub.com using a Web browser and create a free account by navigating the appropriate options provided. Following this, create a public repository called shellscripts. Next, on your Fedora Linux virtual machine, run the following commands as root (where *name* is your GitHub account name) to push the contents of the /shellscripts repo from Project 7-6 to GitHub and set GitHub as the original repo. Supply your GitHub username and password when prompted.

```
cd /shellscripts
git remote add origin
    https://github.com/name/
    shellscripts.git
git push -u origin master
```

Finally, log into another terminal as user1 on your Fedora Linux virtual machine and clone your public shellscripts repository from GitHub using the following command (where *name* is your GitHub account name). Verify the results when finished.

```
git clone https://github.
    com/name/shellscripts.git
```

## CHAPTER 8

SYSTEM INITIALIZATION, X WINDOWS, AND LOCALIZATION

After completing this chapter, you will be able to:

Summarize the major steps necessary to boot a Linux system

Detail the configuration of the GRUB boot loader

Explain the UNIX SysV and Systemd system initialization processes

Start, stop, and restart daemons

Configure the system to start and stop daemons upon entering certain runlevels and targets

Identify and explain the purpose of the major Linux GUI components: X Windows, window manager, and desktop environment

Configure X Windows settings and accessibility options

Configure time, time zone, and locale information on a Linux system

In this chapter, you investigate the boot process in greater detail. **You explore how** to configure boot loaders and the process used to start daemons after the kernel has loaded. Additionally, you examine the procedures used to start and stop daemons and set them to start automatically at boot time. Next, you examine the various components the Linux GUI comprises and how to configure these components using common Linux utilities. Finally, you examine the Linux tools and processes used to configure localization options, including locale, date, and time zone information.

The Boot Process

When a computer first initializes, the system BIOS performs a **Power On Self Test (POST)**. Following the POST, the BIOS checks its configuration for boot devices and operating systems to execute. Typically, computers first check for an operating system on removable media devices, such as DVDs and USB flash memory drives, because they can contain installation media for an operating system. If it fails to find an operating system on any of these options, the BIOS usually checks the MBR/GPT on the first hard disk inside the computer.

> **Note** @
>
> Recall that you can alter the order in which boot devices are checked in the computer BIOS.
>
> A computer BIOS can also be configured to boot an operating system from an NFS, HTTP, or FTP server across the network, provided that the computer network interface supports the Preboot Execution Environment (PXE) standard. This process is called **netbooting,** and is primarily used to boot Linux live install media on a computer from across a network in order to perform a new local Linux installation.

The MBR/GPT normally contains the first part of a **boot loader** that can then locate and execute the kernel of the operating system. Alternatively, the MBR/GPT might contain a pointer to a partition on the system that contains a boot loader on the first sector; this partition is referred to as the **active partition**. There can be only one active partition per hard disk.

> **Note** @
>
> In addition to storing the list of all partitions on the hard disk, the MBR/GPT stores the location of the active partition.

If the system has a UEFI BIOS, then boot loader is not loaded from the MBR/GPT or first sector of the active partition; it is instead loaded from the UEFI System Partition by the UEFI BIOS. There can only be one UEFI System Partition per hard disk. If **secure boot** is enabled in the UEFI BIOS, the digital signature of the boot loader within the UEFI System Partition is first checked to ensure that it has not been modified by malware.

Regardless of whether the boot loader is loaded from the MBR/GPT, the first sector of the active partition, or the UEFI System Partition, the remainder of the boot process is the same. The boot loader then executes the Linux kernel from the partition that contains it.

> **Note**
>
> The Linux kernel is stored in the /boot directory and is named vmlinux-<kernel version> if it is not compressed, or vmlinuz-<kernel version> if it is compressed.

After the Linux kernel is loaded into memory, the boot loader is no longer active; instead, the Linux kernel continues to initialize the system by loading daemons into memory. A **daemon** is a system process that performs useful tasks, such as printing, scheduling, and operating system maintenance. The first daemon process on the system is called the **initialize (init) daemon**; it is responsible for loading all other daemons on the system required to bring the system to a usable state in which users can log in and interact with services. The whole process is depicted in Figure 8-1.

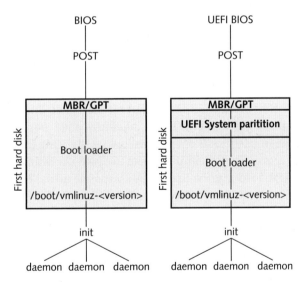

Figure 8-1   The boot process

Boot Loaders

As discussed in the previous section, the primary function of boot loaders during the boot process is to load the Linux kernel into memory. However, boot loaders can perform other functions as well, including passing information to the kernel during system startup and booting other operating systems that are present on the hard disk. Using one boot loader to boot one of several operating systems is known as **multi booting**; the boot loader simply loads a different operating system kernel based on user input.

Unless virtualization software is used, only one operating system can be active at any one time.

The two most common boot loaders used on Linux systems are GRUB and GRUB2.

GRUB Legacy

The original **GRand Unified Bootloader (GRUB)** boot loader was created in 1999 as a replacement boot loader for the original Linux boot loader for hard disks that have an MBR. It supports the booting of several different operating systems, including Linux, macOS, BSD UNIX, Solaris UNIX, and Windows.

Note

The original GRUB boot loader is called **GRUB Legacy** today as it is not used on modern Linux systems. However, because specialized Linux systems typically have a very long lifetime within production environments, it is not uncommon to see a Linux system that still uses GRUB legacy today.

The first major part of the GRUB Legacy boot loader (called Stage 1) typically resides on the MBR. The remaining parts of the boot loader are called Stage 1.5 and Stage 2. Stage 1.5 resides in the unused 30KB of space following the MBR, and Stage 2 resides in the /boot/grub directory. Stage 1 simply points to Stage 1.5, which loads filesystem support and proceeds to load Stage 2. Stage 2 performs the actual boot loader functions and displays a graphical boot loader screen similar to that shown in Figure 8-2.

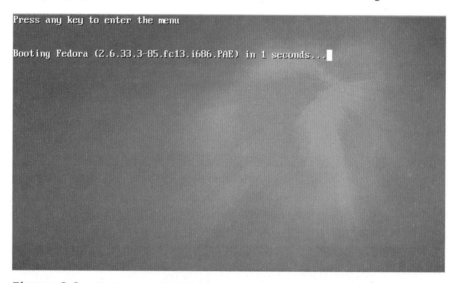

Press any key to enter the menu

Booting Fedora (2.6.33.3-85.fc13.i686.PAE) in 1 seconds...

Figure 8-2 The legacy GRUB boot screen for a Fedora system

> **Note** 📎
>
> Recall that the /boot directory is normally mounted to its own filesystem on most Linux systems; as a result, Stage 2 typically resides on the /boot filesystem alongside the Linux kernel.

You configure GRUB Legacy by editing a configuration file (/boot/grub/grub.conf) that is read directly by the Stage 2 boot loader. An example /boot/grub/grub.conf file for a Fedora system is shown next:

```
[root@server1 ~]# cat /boot/grub/grub.conf
# grub.conf generated by anaconda
#
# Note that you do not have to rerun grub after making changes
# NOTICE:  You do not have a /boot partition.  This means that
#          all kernel and initrd paths are relative to /, eg.
#          root (hd0,0)
#          kernel /boot/vmlinuz-version ro root=/dev/sda1
#          initrd /boot/initrd-[generic-]version.img
boot=/dev/sda
default=0
timeout=5
splashimage=(hd0,0)/boot/grub/splash.xpm.gz
hiddenmenu

title Fedora (2.6.33.3-85.fc13.i686.PAE)
  root (hd0,0)
  kernel /boot/vmlinuz-2.6.33.3-85.fc13.i686.PAE ro root=/dev/sda1 rhgb
quiet
  initrd /boot/initramfs-2.6.33.3-85.fc13.i686.PAE.img
[root@server1 ~]#_
```

> **Note** 📎
>
> Alternatively, you can view and edit the /etc/grub.conf file, which is simply a symbolic link to /boot/grub/grub.conf.
>
> As with shell scripts, lines can be commented out of /boot/grub/grub.conf by preceding those lines with a # symbol.
>
> Some other Linux distributions, such as Ubuntu Linux, use a /boot/grub/menu.lst file in place of /boot/grub/grub.conf to hold GRUB Legacy configuration.

To understand the entries in the /boot/grub/grub.conf file, you must first understand how GRUB refers to partitions on hard disks. Hard disks and partitions on those hard disks are identified by numbers in the following format: (hd<drive#>,<partition#>). Thus, the (hd0,0) notation in the preceding /boot/grub/grub.conf file refers to the first hard disk on the system (regardless of whether it is SCSI, SATA, or PATA) and the first partition on that hard disk, respectively. Similarly, the second partition on the first hard disk is referred to as (hd0,1), and the fourth partition on the third hard disk is referred to as (hd2,3).

In addition, GRUB calls the partition that contains Stage 2 the **GRUB root partition**. Normally, the GRUB root partition is the filesystem that contains the /boot directory and should not be confused with the Linux root filesystem. If your system has a separate partition mounted to /boot, GRUB refers to the file /boot/grub/grub.conf as /grub/grub.conf. If your system does not have a separate filesystem for the /boot directory, this file is simply referred to as /boot/grub/grub.conf in GRUB.

Thus, the example /boot/grub/grub.conf file shown earlier displays a graphical boot screen (splashimage=(hd0,0)/boot/grub/splash.xpm.gz) and boots the default operating system kernel on the first hard drive (default=0) in 5 seconds (timeout=5) without showing any additional menus (hiddenmenu). The default operating system kernel is located on the GRUB root filesystem (root (hd0,0)) and is called /boot/vmlinuz-2.6.33.3-85.fc13.i686.PAE.

The kernel then mounts the root filesystem on /dev/sda1 (root=/dev/sda1) initially as read-only (ro) to avoid problems with the fsck command and uses a special **initramfs** disk filesystem image to load modules into RAM that are needed by the Linux kernel at boot time (initrd /boot/initramfs-2.6.33.3-85.fc13.i686.PAE.img).

Note 📎

Most Linux distributions use a UUID (e.g., root=UUID=42c0fce6-bb79-4218-af1a-0b89316bb7d1) in place of root=/dev/sda1 to identify the partition that holds the root filesystem at boot time.

All other keywords on the kernel line within /boot/grub/grub.conf are used to pass information to the kernel from Stage 2. For example, the keyword rhgb (Red Hat Graphical Boot) tells the Linux kernel to use a graphical boot screen as it is loading daemons, and the keyword quiet tells the Linux kernel to avoid printing errors to the screen during system startup. You can add your own keywords to the kernel line in /boot/grub/grub.conf to control how your Linux kernel is loaded. For example, appending the text nosmp to the kernel line disables Symmetric Multi-Processing

(SMP) support within the Linux kernel. Alternatively, appending the text `mem=16384M` to the `kernel` line forces your Linux kernel to see 16384MB of physical RAM in case your Linux kernel does not detect all of the RAM in your computer properly.

Normally, GRUB Legacy allows users to manipulate the boot loader during system startup; to prevent this, you can optionally password protect GRUB modifications during boot time.

Recall from the /boot/grub/grub.conf file shown earlier that you have 5 seconds after the BIOS POST to interact with the boot screen shown in Figure 8-2. If you press any key within these 5 seconds, you will be presented with a graphical boot menu screen similar to Figure 8-3 that you can use to manipulate the boot process. If you have several Linux kernels installed on your system (from updating your system software), you can select the kernel that you would like to boot, highlight your kernel and press a to append keywords to the kernel line, or press e to edit the entire boot configuration for the kernel listed in /boot/grub/grub.conf at boot time. You can also press c to obtain a grub> prompt where you can enter a variety of commands to view system hardware configuration, find and display files, alter the configuration of GRUB, or boot an operating system kernel. Typing `help` at this grub> prompt will display a list of available commands and their usage.

Figure 8-3   The legacy GRUB boot menu for a Fedora system

If the GRUB Legacy boot loader becomes damaged, you can reinstall it using the `grub-install` **command** that is available on the system or on a live Linux system used for system rescue. To install GRUB Legacy Stage 1 on the MBR of the first SATA hard disk, you can type the following command:

```
[root@server1 ~]# grub-install /dev/sda
Installation finished. No error reported.
This is the contents of the device map /boot/grub/device.map.
Check if this is correct or not. If any of the lines is incorrect,
fix it and re-run the script 'grub-install'.

# this device map was generated by anaconda
(hd0)       /dev/sda
[root@server1 ~]#_
```

Note

Alternatively, you can use the `grub-install /dev/sda1` command to install GRUB Legacy Stage 1 at the beginning of the first primary partition of the same hard disk.

GRUB2

GRand Unified Bootloader version 2 (GRUB2) is the boot loader commonly used on modern Linux systems; it supports storage devices that use either a MBR or GPT, as well as newer storage technologies such as NVMe.

Note

GRUB2 has additional support for systems that do not use the Intel x86_64 architecture, as well as specialized hardware systems. For example, the Sony PlayStation 4 uses the GRUB2 boot loader.

For a system that uses a standard BIOS, GRUB2 has a similar structure to GRUB Legacy. GRUB2 Stage 1 typically resides on the MBR or GPT. On MBR hard disks, Stage 1.5 resides in the unused 30KB of space following the MBR, and on GPT hard disks, Stage 1.5 resides in a BIOS Boot partition that is created for this purpose by the Linux installation program. Stage 2 resides in the /boot/grub directory (or /boot/grub2 directory on some Linux distributions) and loads a terminal-friendly boot loader screen similar to that shown in Figure 8-4. As with GRUB Legacy, you can select the kernel that you would like to boot at the boot loader screen, as well as highlight your kernel and press e to edit the entire boot configuration for the kernel or press c to obtain a prompt where you can enter GRUB configuration commands.

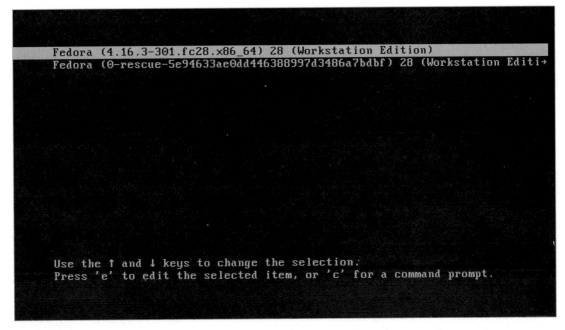

```
Fedora (4.16.3-301.fc28.x86_64) 28 (Workstation Edition)
Fedora (0-rescue-5e94633ae0dd446388997d3486a7bdbf) 28 (Workstation Editi→




Use the ↑ and ↓ keys to change the selection.
Press 'e' to edit the selected item, or 'c' for a command prompt.
```

Figure 8-4   The GRUB2 boot screen on a Fedora 28 system

For a system that uses a UEFI BIOS, all GRUB2 stages are stored entirely on the UEFI System Partition within a UEFI application called grubx64.efi on Intel x64-based systems. If it isn't already present, the UEFI System Partition is created during Linux installation, formatted using the FAT filesystem and mounted to /boot/efi during the Linux boot process. Because the UEFI System Partition can contain boot loaders for multiple different operating systems, grubx64.efi is stored underneath a subdirectory. For example, on Fedora systems, you can find grubx64.efi under /boot/efi/EFI/fedora/ after the Linux system has booted. If the UEFI BIOS has secure boot enabled, you will also find UEFI applications within this subdirectory that store the digital signature information used to ensure that GRUB2 has not been modified by malware; for a Fedora system, these are called shim.efi and shim-fedora.efi.

Note

There is still a /boot/grub (or /boot/grub2) directory on systems that use GRUB2 alongside a UEFI BIOS, but it only contains files that are referenced by GRUB2 after it is fully loaded, such as the background image used for the GRUB boot screen.

After grubx64.efi is executed by the UEFI BIOS, GRUB2 displays the same boot loader screen shown in Figure 8-4, where you can interact with GRUB or boot the Linux kernel.

The main configuration file for GRUB2 is called grub.cfg (or grub2.cfg depending on your Linux distribution); it is stored within the /boot/grub/ (or /boot/grub2/) directory on computers that have a standard BIOS, and within the UEFI System Partition on computers with a UEFI BIOS (e.g., /boot/efi/EFI/fedora/ on Fedora Linux).

Note

Some Linux distributions place a symbolic link to the grub.cfg (or grub2.cfg) file within the / etc directory; on Fedora systems, /etc/grub2.cfg is a symbolic link to /boot/grub2/grub2.cfg, and /etc/grub2-efi.cfg is a symbolic link to /boot/efi/EFI/fedora/grub.cfg.

The syntax of the grub.cfg (or grub2.cfg) file in GRUB2 is different compared to GRUB Legacy, as shown in the following excerpt:

```
set timeout=5

menuentry 'Fedora (4.16.3-301.fc28.x86_64) 28 (Workstation
Edition)' --class fedora --class gnu-linux --class gnu --class os
--unrestricted $menuentry_id_option 'gnulinux-4.16.3-301.fc28.
x86_64 -advanced-9ff25add-035b-4d26-9129-a9da6d0a6fa3' {
        load_video
        set gfxpayload=keep
        insmod gzio
        insmod part_gpt
        insmod ext2
        set root='hd0,gpt2'

        linuxefi /vmlinuz-4.16.3-301.fc28.x86_64 root=UUID=9ff25add-
        035b-4d26-9129-a9da6d0a6fa3 ro resume=UUID=4837de7b-d96e-4edc-
        8d3d-56df0a17ca62 rhgb quiet LANG=en_US.UTF-8

        initrdefi /initramfs-4.16.3-301.fc28.x86_64.img
}
```

Each menu entry at the graphical boot screen is identified by a menuentry paragraph that first loads required hardware support using insmod commands before accessing the GRUB root partition (mounted to /boot). The notation for identifying hard disks in GRUB2 is different from GRUB Legacy; partition numbers start at 1 and are prefixed by msdos for MBR partitions and gpt for GPT partitions. Thus, the set root='hd0,gpt2' notation in the preceding excerpt indicates that the GRUB root partition is the second GPT partition on the first hard disk. Next, the Linux kernel is loaded from the specified file on the GRUB root partition (linuxefi / vmlinuz-4.16.3-301.fc28.x86_64 if the system has a UEFI BIOS, or linux16 / vmlinuz-4.16.3-301.fc28.x86_64 if the system has a standard BIOS). The options following the Linux kernel are used to specify the UUID of the root filesystem that is initially loaded read-only (ro), as well as the use of a graphical boot screen (rhgb) that suppresses errors from being shown during the boot process (quiet). The LANG=en_US.UTF-8 kernel option sets the default locale information that is discussed later in this chapter. As with GRUB Legacy, an initramfs image is used to load modules into RAM that are needed by the Linux kernel at boot time (initrdefi / initramfs-4.16.3-301.fc28.x86_64.img if the system has a UEFI BIOS, or initrd16 /initramfs-4.16.3-301.fc28.x86_64.img if the system has a standard BIOS). By default, GRUB2 stores the last menu entry chosen by the user at the graphical boot screen in the /boot/grub/grubenv (or /boot/grub2/grubenv) file and sets it as the default for the subsequent boot process if you do not select a menu entry within 5 seconds (set timeout=5).

The grub.cfg (or grub2.cfg) file was not meant to be edited manually; instead, it is automatically built via entries within the /etc/default/grub file, and the output of any shell scripts stored within the /etc/grub.d directory. When you install a device driver that needs to be loaded by the boot loader (e.g., disk controller devices), the device driver package will often add a file to the /etc/grub.d directory that provides the necessary configuration. For any other settings, you should add or modify the existing lines within the /etc/default/grub file. A sample /etc/default/grub file on a Fedora 28 system is shown here:

```
[root@server1 ~]# cat /etc/default/grub
GRUB_TIMEOUT=5
GRUB_DISTRIBUTOR="$(sed 's, release .*$,,g' /etc/system-release)"
GRUB_DEFAULT=saved
GRUB_DISABLE_SUBMENU=true
GRUB_TERMINAL_OUTPUT="console"
GRUB_CMDLINE_LINUX="resume=UUID=4837de7b-d96e-4edc-8d3d-56df0a17ca62
rhgb quiet"
GRUB_DISABLE_RECOVERY="true"
[root@server1 ~]#_
```

From the preceding output, you could change the GRUB_TIMEOUT line to modify the number of seconds that the GRUB2 boot loader screen appears before the default operating system is loaded, or add parameters that are passed to the Linux kernel by modifying the GRUB_CMDLINE_LINUX line. Also note that the /etc/default/grub file does not list any operating system information. This is because GRUB2 uses the /etc/grub.d/30_os-prober script to automatically detect available operating system kernels on the system and configure them for use with GRUB2. If you would like to manually set the default operating system kernel listed at the GRUB2 boot loader screen, you can set the GRUB_DEFAULT line to the appropriate line number, starting from 0. For example, to set the second OS line shown in Figure 8-4 (Fedora (0-rescue-5e94633ae0dd446388997d3486a7bdbf)) as the default OS to boot, set GRUB_DEFAULT=1 in the /etc/default/grub file.

After modifying the /etc/default/grub file, or adding scripts to the /etc/grub.d directory, you can run the grub2-mkconfig command to rebuild the /boot/grub/grub.cfg or /boot/grub2/grub.cfg file. For example, to rebuild the /boot/grub2/grub.cfg file, you can use the following:

```
[root@server1 ~]# grub2-mkconfig -o /boot/grub2/grub.cfg
Generating grub.cfg ...
Found linux image: /boot/vmlinuz-3.11.10-301.fc20.x86_64
Found initrd image: /boot/initramfs-3.11.10-301.fc20.x86_64.img
Found linux image: /boot/vmlinuz-0-rescue-034ec8ccdf4642f7a2493195
e11d7df6
Found initrd image: /boot/initramfs-0-rescue-034ec8ccdf4642f7a2493
195e11d7df6.img
done
[root@server1 ~]#_
```

On a system with a UEFI BIOS, you instead specify the location of the grub.cfg (or grub2.cfg) file within the UEFI System Partition alongside the grub2.mkconfig command (e.g. grub2-mkconfig -o /boot/efi/EFI/fedora/grub.cfg).

As with GRUB Legacy, if the GRUB2 boot loader becomes damaged, you can reinstall it. Use the grub2-install command that is available on the system or on a live Linux system used for system rescue. To reinstall GRUB2 Stage 1 on the MBR/GPT of the first SATA hard disk, you can type the following command:

```
[root@server1 ~]# grub2-install /dev/sda
Installation finished. No error reported.
[root@server1 ~]#_
```

Note @

Alternatively, you can use the grub2-install /dev/sda1 command to install GRUB Stage 1 at the beginning of the first primary partition of the same hard disk.

When you update your Linux operating system software, you may receive an updated version of your distribution kernel. In this case, the software update copies the new kernel to the /boot directory, creates a new initramfs to match the new kernel and modifies the GRUB2 configuration to ensure that the new kernel is listed at the top of the graphical boot menu and set as the default for subsequent boot processes.

Invalid entries in the GRUB2 configuration file or a damaged initramfs can prevent the kernel from loading successfully; this is called a **kernel panic,** and will result in a system halt immediately after GRUB attempts to load the Linux kernel. In this case, you will need to edit the GRUB2 configuration file from system rescue or generate a new initramfs using either the `dracut` **command** or `mkinitrd` **command**.

On some Linux distributions that use GRUB2, such as Ubuntu Server 14.04, GRUB2-related pathnames and commands omit the 2 for simplicity. For example, the Ubuntu Server 14.04 GRUB2 configuration file is /boot/grub/grub.cfg, and the `grub-install` and `grub-mkconfig` commands replace the `grub2-install` and `grub2-mkconfig` commands.

Linux Initialization

Recall that after a boot loader loads the Linux operating system kernel into memory, the kernel resumes control and executes the init daemon, which then performs a **system initialization process** to execute other daemons and bring the system into a usable state.

Traditional Linux systems have used a system initialization process from the **UNIX SysV** standard. However, recent Linux distributions have adopted the **Systemd** system initialization process. Systemd is completely compatible with the UNIX SysV standard yet implements new features for managing all system devices, including Linux kernel modules, daemons, filesystems and network sockets. Ubuntu Server 14.04 uses the UNIX SysV system initialization process, whereas Ubuntu 18.04 and Fedora 28 implement the new Systemd system initialization process.

Note

Because Systemd is a recent technology, not all Linux daemons have been rewritten to use it. As a result, many modern Linux distributions that have adopted Systemd still use the UNIX SysV system initialization process to initialize some daemons.

Working with the UNIX SysV System Initialization Process

Most modern Linux systems use two UNIX SysV system initialization processsess: the traditional UNIX SysV system initialization process and the **upstart** system initialization process. In both systems, the init daemon runs a series of scripts to start other daemons on the system to provide system services and ultimately allow users to log in and use the system. Furthermore, the init daemon is responsible for starting and stopping daemons after system initialization, including stopping daemons before the system is halted or rebooted.

Runlevels

Because the init daemon often has to manage several daemons at once, the init daemon categorizes the system into runlevels. A **runlevel** defines the number and type of daemons that are loaded into memory and executed by the kernel on a particular system. At any time, a Linux system might be in any of the seven standard runlevels defined in Table 8-1.

Table 8-1   Linux runlevels

Runlevel	Common name	Description
0	Halt	A system that has no daemons active in memory and is ready to be powered off
1 s S single	Single User Mode	A system that has only enough daemons to allow one user (the root user) to log in and perform system maintenance tasks
2	Multiuser Mode	A system that has most daemons running and allows multiple users the ability to log in and use system services; most common network services other than specialized network services are available in this runlevel as well
3	Extended Multiuser Mode	A system that has the same abilities as Multiuser Mode, yet with all extra networking services started (e.g., SNMP, NFS)
4	Not used	Not normally used, but can be customized to suit your needs
5	Graphical Mode	A system that has the same abilities as Extended Multiuser Mode, yet with a graphical login program; on systems that use the GNOME desktop, this program is called the **GNOME Display Manager (gdm)** and is typically started on tty1 or tty7 to allow for graphical logins
6	Reboot	A special runlevel used to reboot the system

Note 📎

Because the init daemon is responsible for starting and stopping daemons and, hence, changing runlevels, runlevels are often called **initstates**.

To see the current runlevel of the system and the previous runlevel (if runlevels have been changed since system startup), you can use the `runlevel` command, as shown in the following output:

```
[root@server1 ~]# runlevel
N 5
[root@server1 ~]#_
```

The preceding runlevel command indicates that the system is in runlevel 5 and that the most recent runlevel prior to entering this runlevel is nonexistent (N).

To change the runlevel on a running system, you simply need to specify the `init` command followed by the new runlevel; to change from runlevel 5 to runlevel 1 to perform system maintenance tasks, you can use the following commands:

```
[root@server1 ~]# runlevel
N 5
[root@server1 ~]# init 1

*A list of daemons that are being stopped by the init
daemon while the system enters single user mode.*


Telling INIT to go to single user mode.
[root@server1 /]#_
[root@server1 /]# runlevel
5 1
[root@server1 /]#_
```

Note

The **telinit command** can be used in place of the `init` command when changing runlevels. Thus, the command `telinit 1` can instead be used to switch to Single User Mode.

You can also pass options from the boot loader to the Linux kernel to force the system to boot to a particular runlevel. If you append the keyword `single` to the kernel line within the GRUB Legacy or GRUB2 configuration screen, you will boot to Single User Mode.

The /etc/inittab File

Unless you specify otherwise, the init daemon enters the default runlevel indicated in the /etc/inittab file. In the past, the /etc/inittab file contained the entire configuration for the init daemon. However, on systems that use the UNIX SysV system initialization process exclusively today, the /etc/inittab often contains a single uncommented line that configures the default runlevel, as shown here:

```
[root@server1 ~]# cat /etc/inittab
id:5:initdefault:
[root@server1 ~]#_
```

The line `id:5:initdefault:` in the /etc/inittab file tells the init daemon that runlevel 5 is the default runlevel to boot to when initializing the Linux system at system startup.

> **Note** 🖉
>
> Runlevel 5 is the default runlevel in most Linux distributions that have a GUI environment installed.
>
> Ubuntu Server 14.04 does not contain an /etc/inittab file by default but will use it to set the default runlevel if present. Instead, the default runlevel on Ubuntu Server 14.04 is normally set in the /etc/init/rc-sysinit.conf file.

Runtime Configuration Scripts

During the boot process, the init daemon must execute several scripts that prepare the system, start daemons, and eventually bring the system to a usable state. These scripts are called **runtime configuration (rc) scripts**.

On Linux systems that use the traditional UNIX SysV system initialization process, the init daemon identifies the default runlevel in the /etc/inittab file and then proceeds to execute the files within the /etc/rc[runlevel].d directory that start with S or K. If the default runlevel is 5, then the init daemon would execute all files that start with S or K in the /etc/rc5.d directory in alphabetical order. The S or the K indicates whether to Start or Kill (stop) the daemon upon entering this runlevel, respectively. Some sample contents of the /etc/rc.d/rc5.d directory are shown in the following output:

```
[root@server1 ~]# ls /etc/rc5.d
README            S20screen-cleanup   S91apache2
S15bind9          S20zfs-mount        S92tomcat7
S19postgresql     S20zfs-share        S99grub-common
S20postfix        S70dns-clean        S99ondemand
S20rsync          S70pppd-dns         S99rc.local
[root@server1 ~]#_
```

From the preceding output, you can see that the init daemon will start the postfix daemon (S20postfix) upon entering this runlevel. To ensure that the files in the preceding directory are executed in a specific order, a sequence number is added following the S or K at the beginning of the filename. Thus, the file S19postgresql is always executed before the file S20postfix.

Recall that runlevel 1 (Single User Mode) contains only enough daemons for a single user to log in and perform system tasks. If a user tells the init daemon to change to this runlevel using the `init 1` command, the init daemon will execute every file that starts with S or K in the /etc/rc1.d directory. Because few daemons are started in Single User Mode, most files in this directory start with a K, as shown in the following output:

```
[root@server1 ~]# ls /etc/rc1.d
K08tomcat7    K20screen-cleanup   K80ebtables    S70dns-clean
K09apache2    K20zfs-mount        K85bind9       S70pppd-dns
K20postfix    K20zfs-share        README         S90single
K20rsync      K21postgresql       S30killprocs
[root@server1 ~]#_
```

Each file in an /etc/rc[runlevel].d directory is merely a symbolic link to an executable rc script in the /etc/init.d directory that can be used to start or stop a certain daemon, depending on whether the symbolic link filename started with an S (start) or K (kill/stop).

Figure 8-5 illustrates the traditional UNIX SysV system initialization process for a system that boots to runlevel 5.

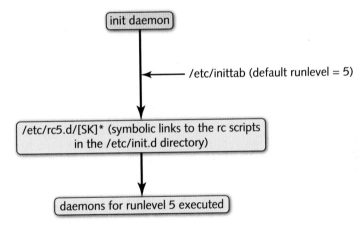

Figure 8-5 A traditional UNIX SysV system initialization process

On Linux systems that use the upstart init system, the /etc/rc[runlevel].d directories are not used. Instead, the init daemon identifies the default runlevel in the /etc/inittab file and then directly executes the rc scripts within the /etc/init.d directory to start or stop the appropriate daemons based on the information specified in the configuration files within the /etc/init directory. Each daemon has a separate configuration file within the /etc/init directory that uses standard wildcard notation to identify the runlevels that it should be started or stopped in. For example, the /etc/init/cron.conf file shown next indicates that the cron daemon should be started in runlevels 2, 3, 4, and 5 ([2345]) and not be stopped in runlevels 2, 3, 4, and 5 ([!2345]):

```
[root@server1 ~]# cat /etc/init/cron.conf
# cron - regular background program processing daemon
#
# cron is a standard UNIX program that runs user-specified programs at
# periodic scheduled times

description     "regular background program processing daemon"

start on runlevel [2345]
stop on runlevel [!2345]

expect fork
respawn

exec cron
[root@server1 ~]#_
```

Figure 8-6 illustrates the upstart system initialization process for a system that boots to runlevel 5.

Figure 8-6 An upstart system initialization process

>
> **Note**
>
> Some daemons are not compatible with the upstart init system. As a result, Linux distributions that use the upstart init system often host several traditional UNIX SysV daemons that are started via entries in the /etc/rc[runlevel].d directories.

Starting and Stopping Daemons Manually

Recall from the preceding section that the init daemon starts daemons at system initialization as well as starts and stops daemons afterwards when the runlevel is changed by executing the rc scripts within the /etc/init.d directory. To manipulate daemons after system startup, you can execute them directly from the /etc/init.d directory with the appropriate argument (start, stop, or restart). For example, to restart the cron daemon, you could run the following command:

```
[root@server1 ~]# /etc/init.d/cron restart
cron stop/waiting
cron start/running, process 3371
[root@server1 ~]#_
```

You can also use the service command to start, stop, or restart any daemons listed within the /etc/init.d directory. For example, you can restart the cron daemon using the following command:

```
[root@server1 ~]# service cron restart
cron stop/waiting
cron start/running, process 3352
[root@server1 ~]#_
```

If you modify a daemon configuration file, you often have to restart a daemon to ensure that the configuration file is reloaded by the daemon. However, some daemons allow you to simply reload configuration files without restarting the daemon; for example, to force the cron daemon to reload its configuration files, you could run the /etc/init.d/cron reload or service cron reload command. You can also see the status of a daemon at any time by using the status argument to the service command or daemon script within the /etc/init.d directory; for example, to see the status of the cron daemon, you could run the /etc/init.d/cron status or service cron status command.

The upstart init system also provides the stop command to stop a daemon, the start command to start a daemon, the restart command to restart a daemon, the reload command to reload the configuration files for a daemon, and the `status` command to view the status of a daemon. Thus, you could also restart the cron daemon using the following command:

```
[root@server1 ~]# restart cron
cron start/running, process 3389
[root@server1 ~]#_
```

Configuring Daemons to Start in a Runlevel

If your Linux distribution uses the upstart init system, then configuring a daemon to start or stop in a particular runlevel is as easy as modifying the associated daemon configuration file in the /etc/init directory, as shown earlier.

However, for systems that use traditional UNIX SysV system initialization, you must create or modify the symbolic links within the /etc/rc[runlevel].d directories. To make this process easier, there are commands that you can use to do this for you. The `chkconfig` command is available on many Linux systems, and can be used to both list and modify the runlevels that a daemon is started in. For example, the following command indicates that the postfix daemon is not started in any runlevel:

```
[root@server1 ~]# chkconfig --list postfix
postfix         0:off 1:off 2:off 3:off 4:off 5:off 6:off
[root@server1 ~]#_
```

To configure the postfix daemon to start in runlevels 3 and 5 and to verify the results, you could run the following commands:

```
[root@server1 ~]# chkconfig --level 35 postfix on
[root@server1 ~]# chkconfig --list postfix
postfix         0:off 1:off 2:off 3:on  4:off 5:on  6:off
[root@server1 ~]#_
```

You can also customize `chkconfig` to manage only the daemons you specify. For example, to remove the ability for `chkconfig` to manage the postfix daemon, you could run the `chkconfig --del postfix` command. Alternatively, the `chkconfig --add postfix` command would allow `chkconfig` to manage the postfix daemon.

Unfortunately, the `chkconfig` command is not available in Ubuntu Server 14.04 by default. Instead, you can use the `update-rc.d command` on Ubuntu Server 14.04 to configure the files within the /etc/rc[runlevel].d directories. First, you should remove any existing symbolic links within the /etc/rc[runlevel].d directories for the postfix daemon using the following command:

```
[root@server1 ~]# update-rc.d -f postfix remove
Removing any system startup links for /etc/init.d/postfix ...
    /etc/rc0.d/K20postfix
    /etc/rc1.d/K20postfix
    /etc/rc2.d/S20postfix
```

```
/etc/rc3.d/S20postfix
/etc/rc4.d/S20postfix
/etc/rc5.d/S20postfix
/etc/rc6.d/K20postfix
[root@server1 ~]#_
```

Next, you can use the `update-rc.d` command to configure the appropriate symbolic links within the /etc/rc[runlevel].d directories for the postfix daemon. Because most daemons are started in runlevels 2 through 5, you can specify the `defaults` keyword to create symbolic links that start the postfix daemon in runlevels 2 through 5, as shown in the following output:

```
[root@server1 ~]# update-rc.d postfix defaults
Adding system startup for /etc/init.d/postfix ...
   /etc/rc0.d/K20postfix -> ../init.d/postfix
   /etc/rc1.d/K20postfix -> ../init.d/postfix
   /etc/rc6.d/K20postfix -> ../init.d/postfix
   /etc/rc2.d/S20postfix -> ../init.d/postfix
   /etc/rc3.d/S20postfix -> ../init.d/postfix
   /etc/rc4.d/S20postfix -> ../init.d/postfix
   /etc/rc5.d/S20postfix -> ../init.d/postfix
[root@server1 ~]#_
```

Alternatively, you can specify to start the postfix daemon only in runlevels 2 and 5 using the following command, which creates the rc scripts using a sequence number of 20:

```
[root@server1 ~]# update-rc.d postfix start 20 2 5 . stop 20 0 1 3 4 6.
update-rc.d: warning:  start runlevel arguments (5) do not match
postfix Default-Start values (2 3 4 5)
update-rc.d: warning:  stop runlevel arguments (1 2 3 4 6) do not
match postfix Default-Stop values (0 1 6)
 Adding system startup for /etc/init.d/postfix ...
   /etc/rc1.d/K00postfix -> ../init.d/postfix
   /etc/rc3.d/K00postfix -> ../init.d/postfix
   /etc/rc4.d/K00postfix -> ../init.d/postfix
   /etc/rc6.d/K00postfix -> ../init.d/postfix
   /etc/rc2.d/S20postfix -> ../init.d/postfix
   /etc/rc5.d/S20postfix -> ../init.d/postfix
[root@server1 ~]#_
```

Working with the Systemd System Initialization Process

Like the UNIX SysV init daemon, the Systemd init daemon is used to start daemons during system initialization as well as start and stop daemons after system initialization. However, Systemd can also be used to start, stop, and configure many other operating system components. To Systemd, each operating system component is called a unit. Daemons are called **service units** because they provide a system service, and runlevels are called **target units** (or **targets**). By default, each target maps to a UNIX SysV runlevel:

- Poweroff.target is the same as Runlevel 0.
- Rescue.target is the same as Runlevel 1 (Single User Mode).
- Multi-user.target is the same as Runlevel 2, 3, and 4.
- Graphical.target is the same as Runlevel 5.
- Reboot.target is the same as Runlevel 6.

Note 📎

The graphical.target first loads all daemons from the multi-user.target.

For ease, many Linux distributions create shortcuts to targets named for the UNIX SysV runlevel; for example, runlevel5.target is often a shortcut to graphical.target, and runlevel1.target is often a shortcut to rescue.target.

The default target on a system that has a GUI environment installed is the graphical.target. To configure your system to instead boot to the multi-user.target, you can update the /etc/systemd/system/default.target symbolic link to point to the correct runlevel using the following command:

```
[root@server1 ~]# ln -s /lib/systemd/system/multi-user.target /
etc/systemd/system/default.target
[root@server1 ~]#_
```

Most of the rc scripts that are used by Systemd to start and stop daemons are stored in the /lib/systemd/system directory and called [daemon].service. For example, the script for the cron daemon on Fedora 28 is /lib/systemd/system/crond.service. To ensure that the cron daemon is started when entering the multi-user.target, you can create a symbolic link to /lib/systemd/system/crond.service called /etc/systemd/system/multi-user.target.wants/crond.service (i.e., the multi-user target wants the crond daemon).

Figure 8-7 illustrates the Systemd system initialization process for a system that boots to multi-user.target.

Figure 8-7   A Systemd system initialization process

To start and stop daemons, as well as configure them to automatically start during system initialization, you can use the `systemctl` **command**. To start, stop, or restart a Systemd daemon, you can specify the appropriate action (start, stop, or restart) and name of the service unit as arguments. For example, to restart the cron daemon on Fedora Linux, you could use the following command:

```
[root@server1 ~]# systemctl restart crond.service
[root@server1 ~]#_
```

To reload the configuration files for the cron daemon on Fedora Linux, you could run the `systemctl reload crond.service` command, and to force Systemd to reload all units, you could run the `systemctl daemon-reload` command. You can also use the `systemctl` command to see detailed information about a particular Systemd daemon. For example, `systemctl status crond.service` would show detailed information about the cron daemon on Fedora Linux.

Without arguments, the `systemctl` command displays a list of all units that are currently executing in memory and their status. You can narrow this list to only services by piping the results to the `grep service` command. Moreover, to see all possible services regardless of whether they are loaded into memory or not, you can add the `-a` (or `--all`) option to the `systemctl` command. The following command displays all Systemd services and their state (dead indicates that it is currently not running):

```
[root@server1 ~]# systemctl -a | grep service | less
abrt-ccpp.service       loaded active exited    Install ABRT coredump
abrt-oops.service       loaded active running   ABRT kernel log watcher
abrt-vmcore.service     loaded active exited    Harvest vmcores for ABRT
abrtd.service           loaded active running   ABRT Automated Bug Repo
acpid.service           loaded active running   ACPI Event Daemon
alsa-store.service      loaded inactive dead    Store Sound Card State
arp-ethers.service      loaded inactive dead    Load static arp entries
atd.service             loaded active running   Job spooling tools
auditd.service          loaded active running   Security Auditing
avahi-daemon.service    loaded active running   Avahi mDNS/DNS-SD Stack
crond.service           loaded active running   Command Scheduler
cups.service            loaded active running   CUPS Printing Service
dbus-org.bluez.service  error  inactive dead    dbus-org.bluez.service
dbus.service            loaded active running   D-Bus System Message Bus
:
```

You can also use the `systemd-analyze` command to view information about Systemd units; for example, to see a list of Systemd units sorted by the time they took to load, you could run the `systemd-analyze blame | less` command.

To configure a Systemd daemon to start in the default target (e.g., multi-user. target), you can use the `enable` argument to the `systemctl` command. For example, to ensure that the cron daemon is started at system initialization, you can run the `systemctl enable crond.service` command, which creates the appropriate symbolic link to /lib/systemd/system/crond.service within the /etc/systemd/system/ multi-user.target.wants/directory. Alternatively, the `systemctl disable crond. service` would prevent the cron daemon from starting when your system is booted by removing the symbolic link to /lib/systemd/system/crond.service within the/etc/ systemd/system/multi-user.target.wants/directory. However, another daemon started in the default target that depends on the cron daemon could potentially start the cron daemon. To fully ensure that the cron daemon cannot be started, you could run the `systemctl mask crond.service` command, which redirects the symbolic link for the cron daemon in /etc/systemd/system/multi-user.target.wants/ to /dev/null.

The `systemctl` command can also be used to change between targets. You can switch to multi-user.target (which is analogous to runlevel 3) by running either the `systemctl isolate multi-user.target` or `systemctl isolate runlevel3.target` command. Alternatively, you can switch to graphical.target (which is analogous to runlevel 5) by running the `systemctl isolate graphical.target` or `systemctl isolate runlevel5.target` command.

You can also create service-specific environment variables that Systemd will load into memory when it starts a particular service. To create a variable called MYVAR with the value SampleValue for use with the cron daemon on Fedora Linux, you could use the command `systemctl edit crond.service` and add the line `Environment=` `"MYVAR=SampleValue"` into the nano editor and save your changes when finished. This line will be stored in a file under the /etc/systemd/system/crond.service.d/ directory that is executed each time Systemd starts the cron daemon.

> **Note** 📎
>
> Systemd provides units to manage many components of the Linux operating system beyond the service and target units discussed in this chapter. For example, you can mount and umount filesystems using Systemd mount units. To create a Systemd mount unit that mounts the filesystem on /dev/sdb1 to the /data directory, you could use the `systemd-mount /dev/` `sdb1 /data` command; this is equivalent to using the `mount /dev/sdb1 /data` command but the mounting process is provided entirely by Systemd and stored in a unit file called data. mount. If you instead use the `systemd-mount -A /dev/sdb1 /data` command, it will create a `data.automount` unit file on the system and Systemd will not actually mount the device until the mount point is accessed by a user. You can also use the `systemd-umount /` `data` command to unmount a filesystem using Systemd. You will examine additional Systemd units in later chapters.
>
> **Advanced Configuration and Power Interface (ACPI)** is a BIOS component that allows operating systems to interface directly to hardware components or provide power management. For example, if you press the power button or close the lid of your laptop computer, it could send a command to your operating system that tells the init daemon to safely shut down (i.e., enter runlevel 0 or shutdown.target). ACPI is often provided by an ACPI daemon (acpid), but can instead be provided entirely by Systemd.

The X Windows System

This chapter has so far focused on performing tasks using a BASH shell command-line interface obtained after logging in to a character terminal. Although most administrators favor the command-line interface, Linux users typically use GUIs for running user programs. Thus, you need to understand the components that make up the Linux GUI. In particular, you need to know how to start, stop, and configure them.

Linux GUI Components

The Linux GUI was designed to function consistently, no matter what video adapter card and monitor are installed on the computer system. It is composed of many components, each of which works separately from the video hardware.

A Linux installation usually includes all of the GUI components listed in Figure 8-8. Together, these GUI components and related programs use over 4GB of storage space on a typical Linux installation.

X Windows

The core component of a Linux GUI is **X Windows**, which provides the ability to draw graphical images in windows that are displayed on a terminal screen. The programs that tell X Windows how to draw the graphics and display the results are known as **X clients**. X clients need not run on the same computer as X Windows; you can use X Windows on one computer to send graphical images to an X client on an entirely different computer by changing the DISPLAY environment variable discussed in Chapter 7. Because of this, X Windows is sometimes referred to as the server component of X Windows, or simply the **X server**.

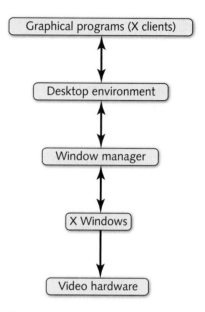

Figure 8-8 Components of the Linux GUI

X Windows was jointly developed by Digital Equipment Corporation (DEC) and the Massachusetts Institute of Technology (MIT) in 1984. At that time, it was code-named Project Athena and was released in 1985 as X Windows in hopes that a new name would be found to replace the X. Shortly thereafter, X Windows was sought by many UNIX vendors; and by 1988, MIT released version 11 release 2 of X Windows (X11R2). Since 1988, X Windows has been maintained by The Open Group, which released version 11 release 6 of X Windows (X11R6) in 1995. Since 2004, X Windows has been maintained as Open Source Software by the **X.org** Foundation.

Wayland is a new version of X Windows designed to replace X.org; it has additional security features and an architecture that makes graphical application development easier. While it is still currently in development, many recent Linux distributions use Wayland as the default X server, but have X.org installed to ensure that Wayland-incompatible applications can still be used.

Note 📎

To find out more about X Windows, visit the X.org Foundation's website at *www.x.org*. To learn more about Wayland, visit *wayland.freedesktop.org*.

When Linux was first released, X Windows was governed by a separate license than the GPL, which restricted the usage of X Windows and its source code. As a result, early Linux distributions used an open source version of X Windows called XFree86.

Window Managers and Desktop Environments

To modify the look and feel of X Windows, you can use a **window manager**. For example, the dimensions and color of windows that are drawn on a graphical screen, as well as the method used to move windows around on a graphical screen, are functions of a window manager.

Note

Window managers that are compatible with Wayland are called **Wayland compositors**.

Many window managers are available for Linux, including those listed in Table 8-2.

Table 8-2   Common Window Managers

Window Manager	Description
Compiz	A highly configurable and expandable window manager based on the Compiz and Beryl window managers that uses 3D acceleration on modern video cards to produce 3D graphical effects, including 3D window behavior and desktop cube workspaces
enlightenment	A highly configurable window manager that allows for multiple desktops with different settings; it is commonly used by the GNOME desktop
fvwm	A window manager based on twm that uses less computer memory and gives the desktop a 3-D look; its full name is "Feeble Virtual Window Manager"
kwin	The window manager used for the KDE desktop
lxde	A window manager specifically designed for use on underpowered systems such as netbooks, mobile devices, and legacy computers; its full name is "Lightweight X Desktop Environment"
metacity	The default window manager used by the GNOME version 1 and 2 desktop environments
mutter	The default window manager used by the GNOME version 3 desktop environment
sawfish	A window manager commonly used for the GNOME desktop. It allows the user to configure most of its settings via tools or scripts
twm	One of the oldest and most basic window managers; its full name is "Tab Window Manager"
wmaker	A window manager that imitates the NeXTSTEP operating system interface that macOS is based on; its full name is "Window Maker"

You can use a window manager alone, or in conjunction with a desktop environment.

A **desktop environment** is a standard set of GUI tools designed to be packaged together, including Web browsers, file managers, and drawing programs. Desktop environments also provide sets of development tools, known as toolkits, that speed up the process of creating new software. As discussed earlier in this book, the two most common desktop environments used on Linux are the **K Desktop Environment (KDE)** and the **GNU Object Model Environment (GNOME)**.

KDE is the traditional desktop environment used on Linux systems. First released by Matthias Ettrich in 1996, KDE uses the **K Window Manager (kwin)** and the **Qt toolkit** for the C++ programming language.

> **Note** 🔗
>
> To learn more about KDE, visit *www.kde.org*.

The Qt toolkit included in KDE was created by a company called Trolltech in Norway in the 1990s. However, it took a while to build a following because, at the time, most open source developers preferred to develop in the C programming language instead of C++. Also, the fact that Qt was not released as Open Source Software until 1998 was a drawback, because most developers preferred source code that was freely modifiable.

As a result of the general dissatisfaction with the Qt toolkit, the GNOME Desktop Environment was created in 1997, and has since become the default desktop environment on most Linux distributions. GNOME 3 is the latest version of GNOME; it uses the **mutter window manager** and the **GTK+ toolkit** for the C programming language. The GTK+ toolkit was originally developed for the GNU Image Manipulation Program (GIMP); like the GIMP, it is open source. The graphical interface components of GNOME 3 are called the **GNOME Shell**. Alternatives to the GNOME Shell have been developed that provide different features, including the mobile-focused **Unity** shell. There are also many desktop environments that are based on GNOME, including the **Cinnamon** desktop environment used by the Linux Mint distribution, and the **MATE** desktop environment used by the Arch Linux and Ubuntu MATE distributions.

Note

To learn more about GNOME, visit *www.gnome.org*.

KDE, GNOME, and GNOME-based desktop environments use system resources, such as memory and CPU time, to provide their graphical interface. As a result, Linux administrators typically do not install a desktop environment on a Linux server, or choose to install a lightweight desktop environment that uses very few system resources. **XFCE** is a common lightweight desktop environment used today.

Note

To learn more about XFCE, visit *xfce.org*.

Note

Desktop environments are often used to run many different programs. As a result, they must provide a mechanism that allows programs to easily communicate with one another for functions such as copy-and-paste. On Linux systems, the **Desktop Bus (D-Bus)** software component is used to provide this functionality.

Starting and Stopping X Windows

As explained earlier in this chapter, when the init daemon boots to runlevel 5 or graphical.target, a program called the gdm is started that displays a graphical login screen. If you click a user account within the gdm and choose the settings icon, you will be able to choose from a list of installed desktop environments or window managers, as shown in Figure 8-9.

Figure 8-9 Selecting a session within the GNOME Display Manager on Fedora 28

Note

The GNOME Display Manager is a variant of the **X Display Manager (xdm)**, which displays a basic graphical login for users. In addition, some Linux distributions use the **KDE Display Manager (kdm)** to display a KDE style graphical login for users. Ubuntu systems use the **LightDM** display manager.

The default desktop environment started by the GNOME Display Manager on Fedora 28 is GNOME using Wayland. However, after you select a particular user, select Plasma using the Session menu, the GNOME Display Manager will continue to use the KDE Plasma as the default desktop environment for the user account unless you choose otherwise.

The GNOME Display Manager is the easiest way to log in and access the desktop environments that are available on your system. If, however, you use runlevel 1 (or rescue.target) or runlevel 2 through 4 (multi-user.target), the GNOME Display Manager is not started by default. In this case, you can type the `startx` command at a character terminal to start X Windows and the default window manager or desktop environment (e.g., GNOME in Fedora 28).

Configuring X Windows

X Windows is the component of the GUI that interfaces with the video hardware in the computer. For X Windows to perform its function, it needs information regarding the mouse, monitor, and video adapter card. This information is normally detected from the associated kernel modules that are loaded at boot time, but can also be specified within configuration files. The keyboard type (e.g., English, US layout) is normally specified manually during the installation process, as shown earlier in Figure 2-9, but can be changed afterwards using the `system-config-keyboard` command within Fedora, or by modifying the appropriate localization options as discussed later in this chapter.

If you use X.org, X Windows stores its configuration in the file /etc/X11/xorg.conf as well as within files stored in the /etcX11/xorg.conf.d/ directory. Although there is no /etc/X11/xorg.conf file in Fedora 28 by default, it will be used if present. Instead, the keyboard type and any user-configured settings are stored in files under the /etc/X11/xorg.conf.d/ directory, and common settings such as the display resolution can be modified using the Displays utility within the GNOME desktop environment. To do this in GNOME, navigate to Activities, Show Applications, Settings, navigate to Devices, Displays, and then select your display to view available settings, as shown in Figure 8-10.

Displays		
	VBX	
Keyboard		
	Orientation	Landscape
Mouse & Touchpad		
Printers		
	Resolution	800 × 600 (4:3)
Removable Media		
	Refresh Rate	59.96 Hz
Thunderbolt		
Wacom Tablet		
	Night Light	Off
Color		

Figure 8-10   Selecting a display resolution

Note

Wayland does not have an xorg.conf equivalent; instead, all manual configuration for Wayland must be performed by the Wayland compositor.

If you choose incompatible X Windows settings, any errors generated will be written to the ~/.xsession-errors file.

Accessibility

Many desktop environments can be configured to suit the needs of users, thus increasing the accessibility of the desktop environment. The tools used to increase accessibility are collectively called **assistive technologies**. You can configure assistive technologies within Fedora 28 using the **Universal Access utility**, as shown in Figure 8-11. To start this utility within the GNOME desktop environment, open the Activities menu and navigate to Show Applications, Settings, Universal Access.

📶 Wi-Fi	Always Show Universal Access Menu OFF
✳ Bluetooth	
🖥 Background	**Seeing**
🔔 Notifications	High Contrast OFF
🔍 Search	Large Text OFF
📷 Region & Language	Cursor Size Default
✷ Universal Access	Zoom Off
⤵ Online Accounts	Screen Reader Off
✋ Privacy	Sound Keys Off
⮜ Sharing	

Figure 8-11   The Universal Access utility

If you turn on the Always Show Universal Access Menu option shown in Figure 8-11, you can enable and disable each assistive technology using the Universal

Access icon in the upper-right corner of the GNOME desktop. Following is a list of the assistive technologies that you can configure within the Universal Access utility or desktop icon:

- High Contrast, which modifies the color scheme to suit those with low vision
- Large Text, which increases the font size of text to suit those with low visionCursor Size, which enlarges the mouse pointer size for easy visibility
- Zoom, which allows you to enable magnification for parts of the screen that your mouse follows, as well as modify the color and crosshair effects during magnification
- Screen Reader, which narrates the text on the active window on the screen
- Sound Keys, which beeps when the Num Lock or Caps Lock keys are pressed
- Visual Alerts, which displays a visual alert in place of beep sounds
- Screen Keyboard, which displays an on-screen keyboard that can be used with a mouse
- Repeat Keys, which simulates multiple key presses when a single key is continually pressed
- Cursor Blinking, which adds a blinking cursor to the current text field
- Typing Assist, which provides three keyboard assistive features:
  - Sticky keys, which simulate simultaneous key presses when two keys are pressed in sequence
  - Slow keys, which add a delay following each key press
  - Bounce keys, which ignore fast duplicate key presses
- Mouse keys, which allow the user to control the mouse using the cursor keys on the keyboard
- Click Assist, which can be used to simulate a right-click by holding down a left-click for a period of time, or trigger a left-click by hovering the mouse pointer over an area of the desktop

You can provide many other assistive technologies if your computer has the appropriate software and hardware. For example, if your system has a braille interface device, you can install braille display software that will allow it to work with the desktop environment. Similarly, you can configure voice recognition software if your system has an audio microphone, or gesture recognition software if your system has a Web camera or trackpad.

Localization

Localization refers to the collective settings on a system that are specific to a specific region within the world. For example, a Linux system within Toronto, Canada, will have different settings compared to a Linux system in Paris, France, including time, time zone, language, character set, and keyboard type. Localization settings are normally chosen during the installation process of the Linux distribution (as shown earlier in Figure 2-8 and 2-9), but can be changed afterwards.

Time Localization

The Linux kernel does not store time information in a format that represents the year, month, day, hour, minute and second as in the output of the date command in Chapter 2. Instead, the Linux kernel stores time as the number of seconds since January 1, 1970 UTC (the birth of UNIX); this is called **epoch time** and can be shown by supplying arguments to the date command, as shown in the following output:

```
[root@server1 ~]# date +%s
1535823499
[root@server1 ~]#_
```

By default, the system obtains the current time from the BIOS on your system. You can view or modify the time within the BIOS using the hwclock **command**. Without arguments, hwclock simply prints the time from the BIOS, but you can specify options to modify the BIOS time as well. For example, the hwclock --set --date='2021-08-20 08:16:00' would set the BIOS time to 8:16 AM on August 20, 2021.

Alternatively, you can set the Linux time using the date command. For example, the command date -s "20 AUG 2021 08:16:00" would set the Linux time to 8:16 AM on August 20, 2021. You could then use the hwclock -w command to set the BIOS time to match the current Linux time to ensure that the correct time is loaded from the BIOS at boot time.

Note

You can also obtain time from a server across a network, such as the Internet, using the **Network Time Protocol (NTP)**. The configuration of NTP will be discussed in Chapter 13.

Time information is dependent on the regional time zone. For example, 8:16 AM in Toronto, Canada, is 2:16 PM in Paris, France. Time zone information is stored in the binary /etc/localtime file, which contains the rules for calculating the time based on your time zone relative to epoch time. This file is normally a copy of, or symbolic link to, the correct file under the /usr/share/zoneinfo/ directory, which stores all zone information files, as shown below:

```
[root@server1 ~]# ll /etc/localtime
lrwxrwxrwx. 1 root root 37 Jul  8 20:13 /etc/localtime -> ../usr/
share/zoneinfo/America/Toronto
[root@server1 ~]#_
```

To change the system time zone, you can copy the appropriate time zone information file from the /usr/share/zoneinfo/ directory to /etc/localtime, or modify the /etc/localtime symbolic link to point to the correct zone information file under the /usr/share/zoneinfo/ directory.

In addition to /etc/localtime, some distributions also have an /etc/timezone text file that contains a reference to the correct time zone file path underneath /usr/share/zoneinfo/ for use by certain applications, as shown in the following output:

```
[root@server1 ~]# cat /etc/timezone
America/Toronto
[root@server1 ~]#_
```

You can also override the default system time zone within your current shell by modifying the contents of the TZ variable. For example, running the export TZ='America/Toronto' command would ensure that any commands that you run in your shell display time information using the Toronto, Canada, time zone. To ensure that the commands within a particular shell script use a particular time zone, set the TZ variable at the beginning of the shell script under the hashpling line. If you are unsure which time zone file you should use with the TZ variable (e.g., America/Toronto), you can run the tzselect command, which will prompt you to answer a series of questions to determine the correct time zone file name.

The timedatectl command can also be used to view and set both the time and time zone information on your system. Without arguments, timedatectl displays system time information. However, you could run the timedatectl set-time "2021-08-20 08:16:00" command to set the system time to 8:16 AM on August 20, 2021, or the timedatectl set-timezone 'America/Toronto' command to set the time zone to Toronto, Canada. You can also use the timedatectl set-ntp true command to ensure that time and time zone information is obtained using NTP.

Format Localization

In addition to time localization, different regions may have different formats used to represent data. This primarily includes the language, but also includes conventions used by the region. For example, while North America often expresses money in the format $4.50 (four dollars and fifty cents), Europe would express the same format as 4,50$. Similarly, Asia typically represents dates in the form YYYYMMDD (Year, Month, Day), whereas the United States typically represents dates in the form MMDDYYYY (Month, Day, Year).

Different languages may also have different character sets that must be represented by software as well as mapped to keyboard keys for input. The **American Standard Code for Information Interchange (ASCII)** character set used on early computers of the 1960s was specific to English characters and thus had no international localization options. It was extended to include some other languages with the introduction of the **ISO-8859** standard, but still lacked many of the extended characters used by these languages. A new standard called **Unicode** extends ASCII to allow for the representation of characters in nearly all languages used worldwide, and the **UTF-8** character set allows software to use one to four 8-bit bytes to represent the characters defined by Unicode.

> **Note**
>
> You can convert data between different character sets using the `iconv` **command**.

Moreover, the same language may have slightly different character sets, keyboard layouts, and formats for different regions; for example, a Canadian French keyboard will differ from a European French keyboard, and Canadian French date and money formats differ from European French date and money formats. As a result, the format localization on most systems includes a language, region, and character set, and is referred to as a **locale**. For example, the en_US.UTF-8 locale represents US regional English, with a UTF-8 character set. If the character set is omitted from the locale, the ASCII character set is assumed; for example, en_US represents US regional English, with an ASCII character set.

Many modern Linux distributions pass the correct locale to the Linux kernel as it is loaded by the GRUB2 boot loader using the LANG option on the kernel line of the GRUB2 configuration file shown in Chapter 7. This instructs Linux to set the LANG variable following boot time to the correct locale. You can also view the contents of /proc/cmdline to see if your Linux kernel was loaded with the LANG option:

```
[root@server1 ~]# cat /proc/cmdline
BOOT_IMAGE=/vmlinuz-4.16.3-301.fc28.x86_64 root=UUID=9ff25add-
035b-4d26-9129-a9da6d0a6fa3 ro resume=UUID=4837de7b-d96e-4edc-
8d3d-56df0a17ca62 rhgb quiet LANG=en_US.UTF-8
[root@server1 ~]#_
```

If the LANG variable was not created by the Linux kernel during boot, it is loaded from a file; on Ubuntu systems, the LANG variable is loaded from /etc/default/locale, and on Fedora systems it is loaded from /etc/locale.conf as shown below:

```
[root@server1 ~]# cat /etc/locale.conf
LANG="en_US.UTF-8"
[root@server1 ~]#_
```

You can display the values for locale variables using the `locale` **command** as shown below:

```
[root@server1 ~]# locale
LANG=en_US.UTF-8
LC_CTYPE="en_US.UTF-8"
LC_NUMERIC="en_US.UTF-8"
LC_TIME="en_US.UTF-8"
LC_COLLATE="en_US.UTF-8"
LC_MONETARY="en_US.UTF-8"
LC_MESSAGES="en_US.UTF-8"
LC_PAPER="en_US.UTF-8"
```

```
LC_NAME="en_US.UTF-8"
LC_ADDRESS="en_US.UTF-8"
LC_TELEPHONE="en_US.UTF-8"
LC_MEASUREMENT="en_US.UTF-8"
LC_IDENTIFICATION="en_US.UTF-8"
LC_ALL=
[root@server1 ~]#_
```

Note from the previous output that the value of the LANG variable is set to en_US.UTF-8. Also note that other format-specific locale variables exist and are set to use the value of LANG by default. This allows users to override the default locale for a particular format type, such as units of measurement. For example, to ensure that operating system components and applications use the Canadian metric system for measurement, you could add the line export LC_MEASUREMENT="en_CA.UTF-8" to a BASH environment file; this will use Canadian regional English with a UTF-8 character set for measurement, and US regional English for all other formats. Alternatively, to ensure that the same locale is used for all format types, you can set the value of the LC_ALL variable, which overrides LANG and all other LC variables. To see a list of all locales that you can use, run the locale -a command.

> **Note** 🖉
>
> The C locale is a standard locale that all UNIX and Linux systems can use. Many Linux administrators add export LANG=C at the beginning of shell scripts (underneath the hashpling line) to ensure that the stdout of any commands within the shell script is not dependent on the locale of the system that executes it. Most shell scripts within a Linux distribution use the C locale to ensure that any stdout can be compared to standardized online documentation for troubleshooting and learning purposes.

You can also use the localectl **command** to view and change locale settings on your system. Without arguments, localectl displays the current locale. To see a list of available locales, you can run the localectl list-locales command, and to set the default locale to en_CA.UTF-8, you can run the localectl set-locale LANG=en_CA.UTF-8 command.

Normally, the keyboard type on a system matches the language and region within the locale (e.g., en_US for US English keyboard, or en_CA for Canadian English keyboard). However, there may be times when you must choose a layout that varies from the regional standard. For example, to ensure that your Linux system can use a US English Apple Macintosh keyboard, you could the localectl set-keymap mac-us command. To see a list of available keyboard types, you can use the localectl list-keymaps command.

Chapter Summary

- The GRUB boot loader is normally loaded by a standard BIOS from the MBR/GPT of a hard disk, or by a UEFI BIOS from the UEFI System Partition. GRUB Legacy supports systems with a standard BIOS and MBR disks, whereas GRUB2 supports both standard and UEFI BIOS systems and MBR/GPT disks.

- After the boot loader loads the Linux kernel, a system initialization process proceeds to load daemons that bring the system to a usable state.

- There are two common system initialization processes: UNIX SysV and Systemd. Modern implementations of UNIX SysV use the upstart system initialization process.

- UNIX SysV uses seven runlevels to categorize a Linux system based on the number and type of daemons loaded in memory. Systemd uses five standard targets that correspond to the seven UNIX SysV runlevels.

- The init daemon is responsible for loading and unloading daemons when switching between runlevels and targets, as well as at system startup and shutdown.

- Daemons are typically executed during system initialization via rc scripts. The /etc/init.d directory contains most UNIX SysV rc scripts, and the /lib/systemd/system and /etc/systemd/system directories contain most Systemd rc scripts.

- You can use a variety of different commands to start, stop, and restart daemons following system inialization. The `service` command is commonly used to start, stop, and restart UNIX SysV daemons, and the `systemctl` command is commonly used to start, stop, and restart Systemd daemons.

- You can use the `chkconfig` or `update-rc.d` commands to configure UNIX SysV daemon startup at boot time, as well as the `systemctl` command to configure Systemd daemon startup at boot time.

- The Linux GUI has several interchangeable components, including the X server, X clients, window manager, and optional desktop environment. You can use assistive technologies to make desktop environments more accessible to users.

- X Windows is the core component of the Linux GUI that draws graphics to the terminal screen. It comes in one of two open source implementations today: X.org and Wayland. The hardware information required by X Windows is automatically detected but can be modified using several utilities.

- You can start the Linux GUI from runlevel 3 by typing `startx` at a command prompt, or from runlevel 5 by using the GNOME Display Manager.

- Linux has many region-specific settings, including time, date, and locale. Locale settings provide region-specific formats, language, and character support; they can be set for an entire system, or for a specific shell or shell script.

Key Terms

active partition
Advanced Configuration
  and Power Interface (ACPI)
American Standard Code for
  Information Interchange
  (ASCII)
assistive technologies
boot loader
chkconfig command
Cinnamon
daemon
Desktop Bus (D-Bus)
desktop environment
dracut command
epoch time
GNOME Display Manager
  (gdm)
GNOME Shell
GNU Object Model
  Environment (GNOME)
GRand Unified Bootloader
  (GRUB)
GRand Unified Bootloader
  version 2 (GRUB2)
GRUB Legacy
GRUB root partition
grub-install command
grub2-install command
grub2-mkconfig command
GTK+ toolkit
hwclock command
iconv command
init command

initialize (init) daemon
initramfs
initstate
ISO-8859
K Desktop Environment
  (KDE)
K Window Manager (kwin)
KDE Display Manager (kdm)
kernel panic
LightDM
locale
locale command
localectl command
localization
MATE
mkinitrd command
multi boot
mutter window manager
netbooting
Network Time Protocol
  (NTP)
Power On Self Test (POST)
Qt toolkit
reload command
restart command
runlevel
runlevel command
runtime configuration (rc)
  scripts
secure boot
service command
service unit
start command

startx command
status command
stop command
system initialization
  process
system-config-keyboard
  command
systemctl command
Systemd
systemd-analyze
  command
target
target unit
telinit command
timedatectl command
tzselect command
Unicode
Unity
Universal Access utility
UNIX SysV
update-rc.d command
upstart
UTF-8
Wayland
Wayland compositor
window manager
X client
X Display Manager (xdm)
X.org
X server
X Windows
XFCE

Review Questions

1. Which command can be used to modify the default locale on the system?
   a. `tzselect`
   b. `cmdline`
   c. `localectl`
   d. `export LANG=C`

2. Which of the following statements is true?
   a. GRUB Legacy can be loaded from a MBR or GPT.
   b. After modifying /etc/default/grub, you must run the `grub2-mkconfig` command before the changes are made to GRUB2.
   c. GRUB2 can only be loaded from a UEFI System Partition.
   d. GRUB needs to be reinstalled after it has been modified.

3. Which directory stores most UNIX SysV rc scripts?
   a. /etc/rc5.d
   b. /etc/rc.d
   c. /etc/init.d
   d. /usr/local/systemd

4. Which runlevel halts the system?
   a. 1
   b. 6
   c. 0
   d. 5

5. Which file does the UNIX SysV init daemon reference on startup to determine the default runlevel?
   a. /etc/initstate
   b. /inittab
   c. /etc/init
   d. /etc/inittab

6. Which command can be used to start X Windows, the window manager, and the default desktop environment?
   a. `startgui`
   b. `startgdm`
   c. `startx`
   d. `gstart`

7. Which of the following statements is true?
   a. Unicode provides the least localization support for different languages.
   b. ASCII is the most common character set used today.
   c. UTF-8 is commonly used to provide Unicode character set support.
   d. ASCII is an extension of the ISO-8859 standard.

8. Which of the following indicates the second MBR partition on the third hard disk drive to GRUB2?
   a. hd2,msdos2
   b. hd4,mbr3
   c. hd3,mbr2
   d. hd2,msdos1

9. Which two implementations of X Windows are commonly used in Linux? (Choose two answers.)
   a. X.org
   b. XFCE
   c. winX
   d. Wayland

10. What is the name of the directory that contains symbolic links to UNIX SysV rc scripts for runlevel 2?
    a. /etc/rc2.d
    b. /etc/init.d/rc2.d
    c. /etc/runlevel/2
    d. /etc/inittab/rc2/d

11. In what directory is Stage 2 of the GRUB2 boot loader stored?
    a. /boot
    b. /root
    c. /bin
    d. /

12. The first daemon loaded on a Linux system is _____.
    a. initstate
    b. inittab
    c. init
    d. linux

13. Which command causes the system to enter Single User Mode?
    a. `init 0`
    b. `init 1`
    c. `init 6`
    d. `initstate 5`

14. Which assistive technology will make a desktop environment more accessible to a person with low vision?
    a. High Contrast
    b. Visual Alerts
    c. Repeat Keys
    d. Click Assist

15. You have recently modified the system time using the date command. What command can you run to ensure that the same time is updated within the system BIOS?
    a. `timedatectl --update`
    b. `tzselect`
    c. `hwclock -w`
    d. `date --set`

16. You want to configure the runlevels that a particular upstart daemon is started in. What should you do?
    a. Run the appropriate `update-rc.d` command.

    b. Modify the contents of the /etc/rc[runlevel].d directories.
    c. Modify the daemon configuration file within the /etc/init directory.
    d. Run the appropriate `systemctl` command.

17. Which of the following Systemd commands can be used to stop a daemon called lala?
    a. `service stop lala`
    b. `systemctl stop lala.service`
    c. `chkconfig stop lala`
    d. `stop lala`

18. Which of the following commands can be used to start a UNIX SysV daemon called lala in runlevels 1, 2, and 3?
    a. `chkconfig --level 123 lala on`
    b. `update-rc.d lala defaults`
    c. `systemctl enable lala 123`
    d. `service enable lala 123`

19. What Systemd target corresponds to runlevel 5?
    a. multi-user.target
    b. graphical.target
    c. system.target
    d. runlevel5.target

20. What kernel option can be specified within a boot loader to force the system to boot to Single User Mode?
    a. `init`
    b. `rescue`
    c. `single`
    d. `telinit`

Hands-On Projects

These projects should be completed in the order given. The hands-on projects presented in this chapter should take a total of three hours to complete. The requirements for this lab include:

- A computer with Fedora Linux installed according to Hands-On Project 2-1 and Ubuntu Server Linux installed according to Hands-On Project 6-7.

Project 8-1

In this hands-on project, you use and configure the GRUB2 boot loader on Fedora 28.

1. Boot your Fedora Linux virtual machine. After your Linux system has been loaded, switch to a command-line terminal (tty5) by pressing **Ctrl+Alt+F5** and log in to the terminal using the user name of **root** and the password of **LINUXrocks!**.

2. At the command prompt, type `less /boot/grub2/grub.cfg` and press **Enter**. Which line sets the default timeout for user interaction at the boot screen? Examine the menuentry paragraphs. Do many of the options match those in the original GRUB bootloader?

3. At the command prompt, type `vi /etc/default/grub` and press **Enter** to edit the GRUB2 configuration file. Change the value of `GRUB_TIMEOUT` to `30`. Save your changes and quit the vi editor.

4. At the command prompt, type `grub2-mkconfig -o /boot/grub2/grub.cfg` and press **Enter** to rebuild the GRUB2 configuration file with your change.

5. Reboot your system by typing `reboot` and pressing **Enter**. At the GRUB2 boot screen, view the available options. How long do you have to interact with the GRUB2 boot loader after POST before the default operating system is booted? Next, press **c** to obtain a command prompt.

6. At the grub> prompt, type `help` and press **Enter** to see a list of available commands, pressing the **spacebar** to cycle through the entire list. Next, type `lspci` and press **Enter** to see a list of detected PCI devices. Following this, type `list_env` and press **Enter** to view the variables present. By default, there should be a single variable called saved_entry that lists the default OS that is booted by GRUB2 (the previously chosen OS stored within /boot/grub/grubenv). Type `reboot` and press **Enter** to reboot your system.

7. At the GRUB2 boot screen, press **e** to edit your configuration. Where did you see these contents recently?

8. Locate the first line that starts with the word "linux" and navigate to the end of this line (the last two keywords on this line should be rhgb and quiet). Add the word `single` after the word quiet and press **F10** to boot your modified configuration. What does this option tell the boot loader to do?

9. Supply your root password of **LINUXrocks!** when prompted.

10. At the command prompt, type `runlevel` and press **Enter**. What is your current runlevel? What is the most recent runlevel?

11. At the command prompt, type `cat /proc/cmdline` and press **Enter**. Note the command that was used to start your current Linux kernel.

12. Reboot your system by typing `reboot` and pressing **Enter**. Allow your system to boot normally.

Project 8-2

In this hands-on project, you explore and configure the SysV and Systemd system initialization processes on Fedora 28.

1. Switch to a command-line terminal (tty5) by pressing **Ctrl+Alt+F5** and log in to the terminal using the user name of **root** and the password of **LINUXrocks!**.

2. At the command prompt, type `runlevel` and press **Enter**. What is your current runlevel? What is the most recent runlevel?

3. At the command prompt, type `cat /etc/inittab` and press **Enter**. View the commented sections. Why is /etc/inittab not used in Fedora 28?

4. At the command prompt, type `ls /lib/systemd/system` and press **Enter**. What do the contents represent?

5. At the command prompt, type `ls /etc/rc.d` and press **Enter**. Do you see init.d and rc[runlevel].d subdirectories? Why?

6. At the command prompt, type `ls /etc/rc.d/init.d` and press **Enter**. Which UNIX SysV daemons are available on Fedora 28?

7. At the command prompt, type `chkconfig --list livesys` and press **Enter**. In which runlevels is the livesys daemon started by default?

8. At the command prompt, type `chkconfig --level 2345 livesys on` and press **Enter** to configure the livesys daemon to start in runlevels 2 through 5. Next, type `ls /etc/rc.d/rc[2-5].d` and press **Enter**. Does the symbolic link to the livesys rc script start with S? Why?

9. At the command prompt, type `init 3` and press **Enter** to switch to runlevel 3 (multi-user.target). Note that you are on tty1 and the gdm is not loaded. Log in to the terminal using the user name of **root** and the password of **LINUXrocks!**.

10. Next, type `runlevel` and press **Enter**. What is your current and most recent runlevel?

11. At the command prompt, type `init 1` and press **Enter** to switch to single user mode (rescue.target). Supply the root password of **LINUXrocks!** when prompted.

12. Next, type `runlevel` and press **Enter**. What is your current and most recent runlevel?

13. At the command prompt, type `systemctl isolate graphical.target` and press **Enter** to switch to runlevel 5 (graphical.target). Note that the gdm is loaded. Press **Ctrl+Alt+F5** and log in to the terminal using the user name of **root** and the password of **LINUXrocks!**.

14. At the command prompt, type `systemctl status crond.service` and press **Enter**. Is the Systemd cron daemon running? Press `q` to return to your command prompt.

15. At the command prompt, type `systemctl restart crond.service` and press **Enter** to restart the cron daemon.

16. At the command prompt, type `systemctl disable crond.service` and press **Enter** to prevent the system from starting the cron daemon in your current runlevel/target. Note that the existing symbolic link in the crond.service rc script is removed. Why was this link from the /etc/systemd/system/multi-user.target.wants directory instead of the /etc/systemd/system/graphical.target.wants directory?

17. At the command prompt, type `systemctl enable crond.service` and press **Enter** to start the cron daemon in your current runlevel/target. Was the symbolic link re-created?

18. At the command prompt, type `service livesys restart` and press **Enter**. Note that Systemd restarted the UNIX SysV netconsole daemon using the `systemctl` command because Systemd is backwards compatible with UNIX SysV.

19. At the command prompt, type `exit` and press **Enter** to log out of your shell.

Project 8-3

In this hands-on project, you configure a basic rc script that is used to execute a shell script (/bootscript.sh) during the Systemd system initialization process on Fedora 28.

1. Switch to a command-line terminal (tty5) by pressing **Ctrl+Alt+F5** and log in to the terminal using the user name of **root** and the password of **LINUXrocks!**.

2. At the command prompt, type `vi /bootscript.sh` and press **Enter**. Add the following lines. When finished, save and quit the vi editor.

```
#!/bin/bash
echo "Boot script started successfully"
```

3. At the command prompt, type `chmod u+x /bootscript.sh` and press **Enter** to ensure that the newly created script can be executed by the system.

4. At the command prompt, type `vi /etc/systemd/system/bootscript.service` and press **Enter**. Add the following lines. When finished, save and quit the vi editor.

```
[Unit]
Description=Sample boot script

[Service]
ExecStart=/bootscript.sh

[Install]
WantedBy=multi-user.target
```

5. At the command prompt, type `systemctl start bootscript.service` and press **Enter**. Next, type `journalctl | tail` at the command prompt and press **Enter**. Did your boot script execute successfully? How can you tell?

6. At the command prompt, type `systemctl enable bootscript.service` and press **Enter**. Why was a symbolic link created in the /etc/systemd/system/multi-user.target.wants/ directory?

7. At the command prompt, type **reboot** and press **Enter**. After the system has rebooted, press **Ctrl+Alt+F5** and log in to the terminal using the user name of **root** and the password of **LINUXrocks!**.

8. At the command prompt, type `journalctl | grep -i "Boot script"` and press **Enter**. Note the timestamps shown. Did your boot script execute successfully during the previous boot?

9. At the command prompt, type **poweroff** and press **Enter** to power off your Fedora Linux virtual machine.

Project 8-4

In this hands-on project, you explore and configure the upstart and SysV system initialization processes on Ubuntu Server 14.04.

1. Boot your Ubuntu Server Linux virtual machine. After your Linux system has been loaded, log into tty1 using the user name of **root** and the password of **LINUXrocks!**.

2. At the command prompt, type **runlevel** and press **Enter**. What is your current runlevel? What is the most recent runlevel?

3. At the command prompt, type `ls /etc/init.d` and press **Enter**. What do the contents represent?

4. At the command prompt, type `ls /etc/init` and press **Enter**. What do the contents represent?

5. At the command prompt, type `cat /etc/init/ssh.conf` and press **Enter**. In which runlevels is the ssh daemon started?

6. At the command prompt, type `restart ssh` and press **Enter**. Why did the restart command successfully `restart` the ssh daemon?

7. At the command prompt, type `ls /etc/rc2.d` and press **Enter**. Are there any traditional UNIX SysV daemons started in your current runlevel? Why? Is the postgresql daemon started before or after the apache2 daemon? Why?

8. At the command prompt, type `restart postgresql` and press **Enter**. Why did you receive an error message?

9. At the command prompt, type `/etc/init.d/postgresql restart` and press **Enter**. Did the postgresql daemon restart?

10. At the command prompt, type `update-rc.d -f postgresql remove` and press **Enter** to remove the symbolic links that start the postgresql daemon. Which runlevels was the postgresql daemon originally started in?

11. At the command prompt, type `update-rc.d postgresql defaults` and press **Enter** to configure the symbolic links to start the postgresql daemon in runlevels 2 through 5.

12. At the command prompt, type `telinit 6` and press **Enter** to reboot your system. Could you have used the `init` command in place of the telinit command?

13. Once your system has rebooted, log into tty1 using the user name of **root** and the password of **LINUXrocks!**.

14. At the command prompt, type **poweroff** and press **Enter** to power off your Ubuntu Server Linux virtual machine.

Project 8-5

In this hands-on project, you start X Windows without the gdm as well as examine X Windows configuration utilities, accessibility options, and localization.

1. Boot your Fedora Linux virtual machine. After your Linux system has been loaded, switch to a command-line terminal (tty5) by pressing **Ctrl+Alt+F5** and log in to the terminal using the user name of **root** and the password of **LINUXrocks!**.

2. At the command prompt, type `init 3` and press **Enter** to switch to runlevel 3 (multi-user.target). Note that the gdm is no longer loaded in tty1. Log into tty1 using the user name of **root** and the password of **LINUXrocks!**.

3. At the command prompt, type `startx` and press **Enter**. What desktop environment was loaded by default and why? Because the root user has not logged into GNOME previously, you will be prompted to choose GNOME preferences.

   a. At the Welcome screen, ensure that **English (United States)** is selected and click **Next**.

   b. At the Input Sources screen, ensure that the English (US) keyboard layout is selected and click Next.

   c. At the Privacy screen, turn off both options and click Next.

   d. At the Online Accounts screen, click Skip to bypass personal account configuration.

   e. On the Ready to Go screen, click **Start using Fedora**.

   f. Close the Getting Started window.

4. Click the power icon in the upper-right corner of the GNOME desktop, click **root**, **Log Out**, and then click **Log Out** again to log out of the GNOME desktop. Were you returned to your original BASH shell on tty1?

5. At the command prompt, type `init 5` and press **Enter** to switch to runlevel 5 (graphical.target). Note that the gdm is now loaded in tty1. Log into the GNOME desktop using your user name and the password of **LINUXrocks!**.

6. Click the **Activities** menu and navigate to **Show Applications**, **Settings**. Navigate to **Devices**, **Displays** and note that you can configure the resolution for your current display, which is limited by the virtualized graphics adapter provided by your hypervisor. Next, click the **Back** button in the upper-left corner of the Settings application and select **Universal Access**. Explore the different assistive technologies available and close the Settings window when finished.

7. Click the **Activities** menu and navigate to **Show Applications**, **Utilities**, **Terminal** to open a command-line terminal. At the command prompt, type `su - root` and press **Enter** to switch to the root user. Supply the root user password of **LINUXrocks!** when prompted.

8. At the command prompt, type `system-config-keyboard` and press **Enter**. Note that your default keyboard matches the localization options you specified during installation, but that you can optionally choose a different keyboard for use with X Windows. Use the **Tab** key to select the **Cancel** button and press **Enter** to quit the Keyboard Selection utility.

9. At the command prompt, type `cat /etc/X11/xorg.conf.d/00-keyboard.conf` and press **Enter**. Note the keyboard localization used by X Windows.
10. At the command prompt, type `locale` and press **Enter**. Which locale is used by default for all format types? Next, type `locale -a | less` and press **Enter**. View the available locales on your system and press `q` to return to your command prompt when finished.
11. At the command prompt, type `cat /etc/locale.conf` and press **Enter**. Next, type `localectl` and press **Enter**. Does the default locale listed by both commands match the output of the previous step?
12. At the command prompt, type `timedatectl` and press **Enter**. Next, type `ll/etc/localtime` and press **Enter**. Does the output of each command indicate the correct time zone information for your system?
13. At the command prompt, type `poweroff` and press **Enter** to power off your Fedora Linux virtual machine.

Discovery Exercises

1. Describe what would happen if you changed the default runlevel/target on your system to runlevel 6 or reboot.target.
2. On your Ubuntu Server 18 virtual machine, explore the available system initialization processes available. Does Ubuntu Server 18 contain Systemd, upstart, or SysV processes? Use the appropriate commands to view, start, and stop daemons, as well as configure them to start within a particular runlevel/target.
3. On your Ubuntu Server 14 virtual machine, perform the same steps that you performed in Project 8-1. In order to accomplish this, you'll need to remember that Ubuntu Server uses slightly different names for GRUB2 configuration files and commands.
4. On your Ubuntu Server 14 virtual machine, use the appropriate commands to explore the localization options available. When finished, explore the same options on your Ubuntu Server 18 virtual machine.
5. Use the Internet to learn more about three Linux window managers or desktop environments that were not discussed in this chapter. For each, describe its common usage and benefits over other window managers and desktop environments. In addition, list how each was developed.

## CHAPTER 9

MANAGING LINUX PROCESSES

After completing this chapter, you will be able to:

Categorize the different types of processes on a Linux system

View processes using standard Linux utilities

Explain the difference between common kill signals

Describe how binary programs and shell scripts are executed

Create and manipulate background processes

Use standard Linux utilities to modify the priority of a process

Schedule commands to execute in the future using the at daemon

Schedule commands to execute repetitively using the cron daemon

A typical Linux system can run thousands of processes simultaneously, including those that you have explored in previous chapters. In this chapter, you focus on viewing and managing processes. In the first part of the chapter, you examine the different types of processes on a Linux system and how to view them and terminate them. You then discover how processes are executed on a system, run in the background, and prioritized. Finally, you examine the various methods used to schedule commands to execute in the future.

Linux Processes

Throughout this book, the terms "program" and "process" are used interchangeably. The same is true in the workplace. However, a fine distinction exists between these two terms. Technically, a **program** is an executable file on the hard disk that can be run when you execute it. A **process**, on the other hand, is a program that is running in memory and on the CPU. In other words, a process is a program in action.

If you start a process while logged in to a terminal, that process runs in that terminal and is labeled a **user process**. Examples of user processes include ls, grep, and find, not to mention most of the other commands that you have executed throughout this book. Recall that a system process that is not associated with a terminal is called a **daemon process**; these processes are typically started on system startup, but you can also start them manually. Most daemon processes provide system services, such as printing, scheduling, and system maintenance, as well as network server services, such as Web servers, database servers, file servers, and print servers.

Every process has a unique **process ID (PID)** that allows the kernel to identify it uniquely. In addition, each process can start an unlimited number of other processes called **child processes**. Conversely, each process must have been started by an existing process called a **parent process**. As a result, each process has a **parent process ID (PPID)**, which identifies the process that started it. An example of the relationship between parent and child processes is depicted in Figure 9-1.

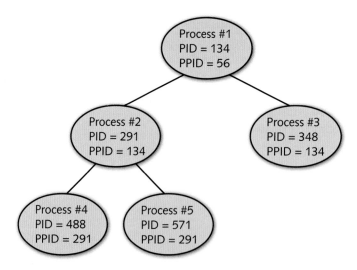

Figure 9-1 Parent and child processes

The first process started by the Linux kernel is the initialize (or init) daemon, which has a PID of 1 and a PPID of 0, the latter of which refers to the kernel itself. The init daemon then starts most other daemons during the system initialization process, including those that allow for user logins. After you log in to the system, the login program starts a BASH shell. The BASH shell then interprets user commands and starts all user processes. Thus, each process on the Linux system can be traced back to the init daemon by examining the series of PPIDs, as shown in Figure 9-2.

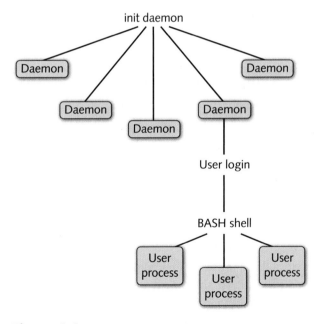

Figure 9-2   Process genealogy

On Linux systems that use the UNIX SysV system initialization process, the init daemon will be listed as `init` within command output. On Linux systems that use the Systemd system initialization process, the init daemon will either be listed as `init` or `systemd` within command output.

Viewing Processes

Although several Linux utilities can view processes, the most versatile and common is the `ps` **command**. Without arguments, the `ps` command simply displays a list of processes that are running in the current shell. The following example shows the output of this command while the user is logged in to tty2:

```
[root@server1 ~]# ps
  PID TTY             TIME CMD
 2159 tty2        00:00:00 bash
 2233 tty2        00:00:00 ps
[root@server1 ~]#_
```

The preceding output shows that two processes were running in the terminal tty2 when the `ps` command executed. The command that started each process (CMD) is listed next to the time it has taken on the CPU (TIME), its PID, and terminal (TTY). In this case, the process took less than one second to run, and so the time elapsed reads nothing. To find out more about these processes, you could instead use the −f, or full, option to the `ps` command, as shown next:

```
[root@server1 ~]# ps -f
UID           PID  PPID  C STIME TTY             TIME CMD
root         2159  2156  0 16:18 tty2        00:00:00 -bash
root         2233  2159  3 16:28 tty2        00:00:00 ps -f
[root@server1 ~]#_
```

This listing provides more information about each process. It displays the user who started the process (UID), the PPID, the time it was started (STIME), as well as the CPU utilization (C), which starts at zero and is incremented with each processor cycle that the process runs on the CPU.

The most valuable information provided by the `ps −f` command is each process's PPID and lineage. The bash process (PID = 2159) displays a shell prompt and interprets user input; it started the `ps` process (PID = 2233) because the `ps` process had a PPID of 2159.

Because daemon processes are not associated with a terminal, they are not displayed by the `ps −f` command. To display an entire list of processes across all terminals and including daemons, you can add the -e option to any ps command, as shown in the following output:

```
[root@server1 ~]# ps -ef
UID        PID  PPID  C STIME TTY       TIME CMD
root         1     0  0 21:22 ?     00:00:00 /usr/lib/systemd/systemd
root         2     0  0 21:22 ?     00:00:00 [kthreadd]
root         3     2  0 21:22 ?     00:00:00 [ksoftirqd/0]
root         5     2  0 21:22 ?     00:00:00 [kworker/0:0H]
root         6     2  0 21:22 ?     00:00:00 [kworker/u128:0]
root         7     2  0 21:22 ?     00:00:00 [migration/0]
root         8     2  0 21:22 ?     00:00:00 [rcu_bh]
root         9     2  0 21:22 ?     00:00:00 [rcu_sched]
root        10     2  0 21:22 ?     00:00:00 [watchdog/0]
root        11     2  0 21:22 ?     00:00:00 [khelper]
root        12     2  0 21:22 ?     00:00:00 [kdevtmpfs]
root        13     2  0 21:22 ?     00:00:00 [netns]
root        14     2  0 21:22 ?     00:00:00 [writeback]
root       394     1  0 21:22 ?     00:00:00 /sbin/auditd -n
root       407   394  0 21:22 ?     00:00:00 /sbin/audispd
root       409   407  0 21:22 ?     00:00:00 /usr/sbin/sedispatch
root       411     1  0 21:22 ?     00:00:00 /usr/sbin/alsactl -s -n
root       418     1  0 21:22 ?     00:00:00 /sbin/rngd -f
root       420     1  0 21:22 ?     00:00:00 /usr/sbin/ModemManager
avahi      422     1  0 21:22 ?     00:00:00 avahi-daemon: running
dbus       424     1  0 21:22 ?     00:00:00 /bin/dbus-daemon --system
chrony     430     1  0 21:22 ?     00:00:00 /usr/sbin/chronyd -u
root       431     1  0 21:22 ?     00:00:00 /usr/sbin/crond -n
root       432     1  0 21:22 ?     00:00:00 /usr/sbin/atd -f
root       435     1  0 21:22 ?     00:00:00 /usr/sbin/abrtd -d -s
root       437     1  0 21:22 ?     00:00:00 /usr/bin/abrt-watch-log
root       441     1  0 21:22 ?     00:00:00 /usr/sbin/gdm
root       446     1  0 21:22 ?     00:00:00 /usr/sbin/mcelog
root       481   441  0 21:22 ?     00:00:00 /usr/libexec/gdm-simple
polkitd    482     1  0 21:22 ?     00:00:00 /usr/lib/polkit-1/polkitd
root       488   481  0 21:22 tty1  00:00:00 /usr/bin/Xorg :0
root       551   481  0 21:22 ?     00:00:00 gdm-session-worker
root       552     1  0 21:22 ?     00:00:00 /usr/sbin/NetworkManager
gdm        842   823  0 21:23 ?     00:00:00 (sd-pam)
gdm        852   551  0 21:23 ?     00:00:00 /usr/bin/gnome-session
gdm        856     1  0 21:23 ?     00:00:00 /usr/bin/dbus-launch
gdm       1018     1  0 21:23 ?     00:00:00 /bin/dbus-daemon --fork
root      1020   552  0 21:23 ?     00:00:00 /sbin/dhclient -d -sf
```

```
gdm        1025     1   0 21:23 ?         00:00:00 /usr/libexec/at-spi-bus
gdm        1045  1025   0 21:23 ?         00:00:00 /bin/dbus-daemon
root       1072     1   0 21:23 ?         00:00:00 /usr/libexec/upowerd
gdm        1077   852   0 21:23 ?         00:00:03 gnome-shell --mode=gdm
colord     1080     1   0 21:23 ?         00:00:00 /usr/libexec/colord
gdm        1087     1   0 21:23 ?         00:00:00 /usr/bin/pulseaudio
gdm        1114  1111   0 21:23 ?         00:00:00 /usr/libexec/ibus-dconf
gdm        1122  1111   0 21:23 ?         00:00:00 /usr/libexec/ibus-engine
gdm        1148     1   0 21:23 ?         00:00:00 /usr/libexec/goa-daemon
root       1164     1   0 21:23 ?         00:00:00 login -- root
root       1174  1171   0 21:23 ?         00:00:00 (sd-pam)
root       1175  1164   0 21:23 tty2      00:00:00 -bash
root       1208     2   0 21:28 ?         00:00:00 [kworker/0:0]
root       1213     1   0 21:31 ?         00:00:00 /usr/sbin/sshd -D
root       1216  1213   0 21:32 ?         00:00:00 sshd: root@pts/0
root       1220  1216   0 21:32 pts/0     00:00:00 -bash
root       1253     2   0 21:33 ?         00:00:00 [kworker/0:2]
root       1260     1   0 21:33 ?         00:00:00 /usr/libexec/packagekitd
root       1742  1220   0 21:33 pts/0     00:00:00 ps -ef
[root@server1 ~]#_
```

As shown in the preceding output, the kernel thread daemon (kthreadd) has a
PID of 2 and starts most subprocesses within the actual Linux kernel because those
subprocesses have a PPID of 2, whereas the init daemon (/usr/lib/systemd/systemd,
PID = 1) starts most other daemons because those daemons have a PPID of 1. In
addition, there is a ? in the TTY column for daemons and kernel subprocesses because
they do not run on a terminal.

Because the output of the ps -ef command can be several hundred lines long on
a Linux server, you usually pipe its output to the less command to send the output
to the terminal screen page-by-page, or to the grep command, which can be used to
display lines containing only certain information. For example, to display only the
BASH shells on the system, you could use the following command:

```
[root@server1 ~]# ps -ef | grep bash
user1      2094  2008   0 14:29 pts/1     00:00:00 -bash
root       2159  2156   0 14:30 tty2      00:00:00 -bash
root       2294  2159   0 14:44 tty2      00:00:00 grep --color=auto bash
[root@server1 ~]#_
```

Notice that the grep bash command is also displayed alongside the BASH
shells in the preceding output because it was running in memory at the time the ps
command was executed. This might not always be the case because the Linux kernel
schedules commands to run based on a variety of factors.

The −e and −f options are the most common options used with the ps command; however, many other options are available. The −l option to the ps command lists even more information about each process than the −f option. An example of using this option to view the processes in the terminal tty2 is shown in the following output:

```
[root@server1 ~]# ps -l
F S   UID   PID  PPID  C PRI  NI ADDR SZ WCHAN  TTY          TIME CMD
4 S     0  2159  2156  0  80   0 -  1238 wait    tty2     00:00:00 bash
4 R     0  2295  2159  2  80   0 -   744 -       tty2     00:00:00 ps
[root@server1 ~]#_
```

The process flag (F) indicates particular features of the process; the flag of 4 in the preceding output indicates that the root user ran the process. The **process state** (S) column is the most valuable to systems administrators because it indicates what the process is currently doing. If a process is not being run on the processor at the current time, you see an S (interruptible sleep) in the process state column; processes are in this state most of the time and are awoken (interrupted) by other processes when they are needed, as seen with bash in the preceding output. You will see an R in this column if the process is currently running on the processor, a D (uninterruptible sleep) if it is waiting for disk access, or a T if it has stopped or is being traced by another process. In addition to these, you might also see a Z in this column, indicating a **zombie process**. When a process finishes executing, the parent process must check to see if it executed successfully and then release the child process's PID so that it can be used again. While a process is waiting for its parent process to release the PID, the process is said to be in a zombie state, because it has finished but still retains a PID. On a busy Linux server, zombie processes can accumulate and prevent new processes from being created; if this occurs, you can kill the parent process of the zombies, as discussed in the next section.

> **Note** 📎
>
> Zombie processes are also known as defunct processes.
> To view a list of zombie processes on your entire system, you could use the ps −el | grep Z command.

Process priority (PRI) is the priority used by the kernel for the process; it is measured between 0 (high priority) and 127 (low priority). The **nice value** (NI) can be used to affect the process priority indirectly; it is measured between −20 (a greater chance of a high priority) and 19 (a greater chance of a lower priority). The ADDR in the preceding output indicates the memory address of the process, whereas the WCHAN indicates what the process is waiting for while sleeping. In addition, the size of the process in memory (SZ) is listed and measured in kilobytes; often, it is roughly equivalent to the size of the executable file on the filesystem.

Some options to the ps command are not prefixed by a dash character; these are referred to as Berkeley style options. The two most common of these are the a option, which lists all processes across terminals, and the x option, which lists processes that do not run on a terminal, as shown in the following output for the first 10 processes on the system:

```
[root@server1 ~]# ps ax | head -11
  PID TTY         STAT    TIME COMMAND
    1 ?           S       0:01 /usr/lib/systemd/systemd
    2 ?           S       0:00 [kthreadd]
    3 ?           S       0:00 [migration/0]
    4 ?           S<      0:00 [ksoftirqd/0]
    5 ?           S       0:00 [watchdog/0]
    6 ?           S       0:00 [migration/1]
    7 ?           S       0:00 [ksoftirqd/1]
    8 ?           S       0:00 [watchdog/1]
    9 ?           S       0:00 [events/0]
   10 ?           S       0:00 [events/1]
[root@server1 ~]#_
```

The columns just listed are equivalent to those discussed earlier; however, the process state column is identified with STAT and might contain additional characters to indicate the full nature of the process state. For example, a W indicates that the process has no contents in memory, a < symbol indicates a high-priority process, and an N indicates a low-priority process.

> **Note**
>
> For a full list of symbols that may be displayed in the STAT or S columns shown in prior output, consult the manual page for the ps command.

Several dozen options to the ps command can be used to display processes and their attributes; the options listed in this section are the most common and are summarized in Table 9-1.

Table 9-1   Common options to the `ps` command

Option	Description
-e	Displays all processes running on terminals as well as processes that do not run on a terminal (daemons)
-f	Displays a full list of information about each process, including the UID, PID, PPID, CPU utilization, start time, terminal, processor time, and command name
-l	Displays a long list of information about each process, including the flag, state, UID, PID, PPID, CPU utilization, priority, nice value, address, size, WCHAN, terminal, and command name
-Z	Displays security-related information about each process (discussed further in Chapter 14)
a	Displays all processes running on terminals
x	Displays all processes that do not run on terminals

The `ps` command is not the only command that can view process information. The kernel exports all process information subdirectories under the /proc directory. Each subdirectory is named for the PID of the process that it contains information for, as shown in the following output:

```
[root@server1 ~]# ls /proc
1      1174   1746   28    407   473   852           irq            slabinfo
10     1175   175    292   409   48    856           kallsyms       softirqs
1018   12     1754   3     411   481   9             kcore          stat
1020   1213   176    307   412   482   acpi          keys           swaps
1025   1216   1760   328   414   488   buddyinfo     key-users      sys
1045   1220   177    350   415   49    bus           kmsg           sysrq
1052   13     178    351   418   5     cgroups       kpagecount     sysvipc
1065   14     179    353   420   551   cmdline       kpageflags     timer_list
1072   15     18     354   421   552   consoles      loadavg        timer_stats
1077   16     180    357   422   58    cpuinfo       locks          tty
1080   164    181    358   424   59    crypto        mdstat         uptime
1087   165    1810   359   430   6     devices       meminfo        version
1097   167    188    370   431   60    diskstats     misc           vmallocinfo
11     168    189    371   432   62    dma           modules        vmstat
1111   169    19     372   435   64    driver        mounts         zoneinfo
1114   17     191    383   437   7     execdomains   mtrr
1117   170    2      384   440   72    fb            net
1122   171    20     385   441   748   filesystems   pagetypeinfo
1144   172    204    386   446   8     fs            partitions
1148   173    205    387   45    814   interrupts    sched_debug
```

```
1164  174   206   388  46   823   iomem        scsi
1171  1745  276   394  47   842   ioports      self
[root@server1 ~]#_
```

Thus, any program that can read from the /proc directory can display process information. For example, the `pstree` **command** displays the lineage of a process by tracing its PPIDs until the init daemon. The first 26 lines of this command are shown in the following output:

```
[root@server1 ~]# pstree | head -26
systemd──┬──ModemManager────2*[{ModemManager}]
         ├──NetworkManager──┬──dhclient
         │                  └──3*[[NetworkManager}]
         ├──2*[abrt-watch-log]
         ├──abrtd
         ├──accounts-daemon────2*[{accounts-daemon}]
         ├──alsactl
         ├──at-spi-bus-laun──┬──dbus-daemon────{dbus-daemon}
         │                   └──3*[{at-spi-bus-laun}]
         ├──at-spi2-registr────{at-spi2-registr}
         ├──atd
         ├──auditd──┬──audispd──┬──sedispatch
         │          │           └──{audispd}
         │          └──{auditd}
         ├──avahi-daemon────avahi-daemon
         ├──bluetoothd
         ├──chronyd
         ├──colord────2*[{colord}]
         ├──crond
         ├──2*[dbus-daemon────{dbus-daemon}]
         ├──dbus-launch
         ├──dconf-service────2*[{dconf-service}]
         ├──firewalld────{firewalld}
         ├──gdm──┬──gdm-simple-slav──┬──Xorg
         │       │                   ├──gdm-session──┬──gnome-session
         │       │                   └──gnome-settings    ├──gnome-shell
[root@server1 ~]#_
```

The most common program used to display processes, aside from ps, is the `top` **command**. The `top` command displays an interactive screen listing processes organized by processor time. Processes that use the most processor time are listed at the top of the screen. An example of the screen that appears when you type the `top` command is shown next:

```
top - 21:55:15 up 32 min,  3 users,  load average: 1.00, 0.99, 0.89
Tasks: 134 total,  1 running, 133 sleeping,  0 stopped,  0 zombie
%Cpu(s): 0.4 us, 0.4 sy, 0.0 ni, 95.9 id, 2.0 wa, 1.1 hi, 0.1 si, 0.0 st
KiB Mem:  2044524 total,  1066848 used,   977676 free,    19880 buffers
KiB Swap: 2097148 total,        0 used,  2097148 free,   255032 cached

  PID USER     PR  NI   VIRT    RES    SHR S %CPU %MEM    TIME+ COMMAND
 1077 gdm      20   0 1518192 150684  36660 R 19.4  7.4  0:33.93 gnome-shell
```

```
2130 root       20    0  123636    1644    1180 R  0.7  0.1   0:00.05 top
   1 root       20    0   51544    7348    2476 S  0.0  0.4   0:00.98 systemd
   2 root       20    0       0       0       0 S  0.0  0.0   0:00.00 kthreadd
   3 root       20    0       0       0       0 S  0.0  0.0   0:00.01 ksoftirqd/0
   5 root        0  -20       0       0       0 S  0.0  0.0   0:00.00 kworker/0:0H
   6 root       20    0       0       0       0 S  0.0  0.0   0:00.02 kworker/u12+
   7 root       rt    0       0       0       0 S  0.0  0.0   0:00.00 migration/0
   8 root       20    0       0       0       0 S  0.0  0.0   0:00.00 rcu_bh
   9 root       20    0       0       0       0 S  0.0  0.0   0:00.34 rcu_sched
  10 root       rt    0       0       0       0 S  0.0  0.0   0:00.00 watchdog/0
  11 root        0  -20       0       0       0 S  0.0  0.0   0:00.00 khelper
  12 root       20    0       0       0       0 S  0.0  0.0   0:00.00 kdevtmpfs
  13 root        0  -20       0       0       0 S  0.0  0.0   0:00.00 netns
  14 root        0  -20       0       0       0 S  0.0  0.0   0:00.00 writeback
  15 root        0  -20       0       0       0 S  0.0  0.0   0:00.00 kintegrityd
  16 root        0  -20       0       0       0 S  0.0  0.0   0:00.00 ioset
```

Note that the top command displays many of the same columns that the ps command does, yet it contains a summary paragraph at the top of the screen and a cursor between the summary paragraph and the process list. From the preceding output, you can see that the gnome-shell uses the most processor time, followed by the top command itself (top) and the init daemon (systemd).

You might come across a process that has encountered an error during execution and continuously uses up system resources. These processes are referred to as **rogue processes** and appear at the top of the listing produced by the top command. The top command can also be used to change the priority of processes or kill them. Thus, you can stop rogue processes from the top command immediately after they are identified. Process priority and killing processes are discussed later in this chapter.

To get a full listing of the different commands that you can use while in the top utility, press h to get a help screen. An example of this help screen is shown next:

```
Help for Interactive Commands - procps-ng version 3.3.12
Window 1:Def: Cumulative mode Off.  System: Delay 3.0 secs; Secure mode Off.

  Z,B,E,e    Global: 'Z' colors; 'B' bold; 'E'/'e' summary/task memory scale
  l,t,m      Toggle Summary: 'l' load avg; 't' task/cpu stats; 'm' memory info
  0,1,2,3,I  Toggle: '0' zeros; '1/2/3' cpus or numa node views; 'I' Irix mode
  f,F,X      Fields: 'f'/'F' add/remove/order/sort; 'X' increase fixed-width

  L,&,<,> .  Locate: 'L'/'&' find/again; Move sort column: '<'/'>' left/right
  R,H,V,J .  Toggle: 'R' Sort; 'H' Threads; 'V' Forest view; 'J' Num justify
  c,i,S,j .  Toggle: 'c' Cmd name/line; 'i' Idle; 'S' Time; 'j' Str justify
  x,y     .  Toggle highlights: 'x' sort field; 'y' running tasks
```

```
z,b      . Toggle: 'z' color/mono; 'b' bold/reverse (only if 'x' or 'y')
u,U,o,O . Filter by: 'u'/'U' effective/any user; 'o'/'O' other criteria
n,#,^O  . Set: 'n'/'#' max tasks displayed; Show: Ctrl+'O' other filter(s)
C,...   . Toggle scroll coordinates msg for: up,down,left,right,home,end

k,r       Manipulate tasks: 'k' kill; 'r' renice
d or s    Set update interval
W,Y       Write configuration file 'W'; Inspect other output 'Y'
q         Quit
          ( commands shown with '.' require a visible task display window )
Press 'h' or '?' for help with Windows,
Type 'q' or <Esc> to continue
```

Killing Processes

As indicated earlier, a large number of rogue and zombie processes use up system resources. When system performance suffers due to these processes, you should send them a **kill signal**, which terminates a process. The most common command used to send kill signals is the `kill` **command**. All told, the `kill` command can send 64 different kill signals to a process. Each of these kill signals operates in a different manner. To view the kill signal names and associated numbers, you can use the `-1` option to the `kill` command, as shown in the following output:

```
[root@server1 ~]# kill -l
 1) SIGHUP        2) SIGINT         3) SIGQUIT       4) SIGILL
 5) SIGTRAP       6) SIGABRT        7) SIGBUS        8) SIGFPE
 9) SIGKILL      10) SIGUSR1       11) SIGSEGV      12) SIGUSR2
13) SIGPIPE      14) SIGALRM       15) SIGTERM      17) SIGCHLD
18) SIGCONT      19) SIGSTOP       20) SIGTSTP      21) SIGTTIN
22) SIGTTOU      23) SIGURG        24) SIGXCPU      25) SIGXFSZ
26) SIGVTALRM    27) SIGPROF       28) SIGWINCH     29) SIGIO
30) SIGPWR       31) SIGSYS        33) SIGRTMIN     34) SIGRTMIN+1
35) SIGRTMIN+2   36) SIGRTMIN+3    37) SIGRTMIN+4   38) SIGRTMIN+5
39) SIGRTMIN+6   40) SIGRTMIN+7    41) SIGRTMIN+8   42) SIGRTMIN+9
43) SIGRTMIN+10  44) SIGRTMIN+11   45) SIGRTMIN+12  46) SIGRTMIN+13
47) SIGRTMIN+14  48) SIGRTMIN+15   49) SIGRTMAX-15  50) SIGRTMAX-14
51) SIGRTMAX-13  52) SIGRTMAX-12   53) SIGRTMAX-11  54) SIGRTMAX-10
55) SIGRTMAX-9   56) SIGRTMAX-8    57) SIGRTMAX-7   58) SIGRTMAX-6
59) SIGRTMAX-5   60) SIGRTMAX-4    61) SIGRTMAX-3   62) SIGRTMAX-2
63) SIGRTMAX-1   64) SIGRTMAX
[root@server1 ~]#_
```

Most of the kill signals listed in the preceding output are not useful for systems administrators. The five most common kill signals used for administration are listed in Table 9-2.

Table 9-2   Common administrative kill signals

Name	Number	Description
SIGHUP	1	Also known as the hang-up signal, it stops a process, then restarts it with the same PID. If you edit the configuration file used by a running daemon, that daemon might be sent a SIGHUP to restart the process; when the daemon starts again, it reads the new configuration file.
SIGINT	2	This signal sends an interrupt signal to a process. Although this signal is one of the weakest kill signals, it works most of the time. When you use the Ctrl+c key combination to kill a currently running process, a SIGINT is actually being sent to the process.
SIGQUIT	3	Also known as a core dump, the quit signal terminates a process by taking the process information in memory and saving it to a file called core on the hard disk in the current working directory. You can use the Ctrl+\ key combination to send a SIGQUIT to a process that is currently running.
SIGTERM	15	The software termination signal is the most common kill signal used by programs to kill other processes. It is the default kill signal used by the `kill` command.
SIGKILL	9	Also known as the absolute kill signal, it forces the Linux kernel to stop executing the process by sending the process's resources to a special device file called /dev/null.

To send a kill signal to a process, you specify the kill signal to send as an option to the `kill` command, followed by the appropriate PID of the process. For example, to send a SIGQUIT to a process called `sample`, you could use the following commands to locate and terminate the process:

```
[root@server1 ~]# ps -ef | grep sample
root       1199      1  0 Jun30 tty3       00:00:00 /sbin/sample
[root@server1 ~]# kill -3 1199
[root@server1 ~]#_
[root@server1 ~]# ps -ef | grep sample
[root@server1 ~]#_
```

Note

The `kill -SIGQUIT 1199` command does the same thing as the `kill -3 1199` command shown in the preceding output.

If you do not specify the kill signal when using the `kill` command, the `kill` command uses the default kill signal, the SIGTERM signal.

When sending a kill signal to several processes, it is often easier to locate the process PIDs using the `pgrep` **command**. The `pgrep` command returns a list of PIDs for processes that match a regular expression, or other criteria. For example, to send a SIGQUIT to all processes started by the user bob whose process name starts with the letters `psql`, you could use the following commands to locate and terminate the process:

```
[root@server1 ~]# pgrep -u bob "^psql"
1344
1501
1522
[root@server1 ~]# kill -3 1344 1501 1522
[root@server1 ~]#_
[root@server1 ~]# pgrep -u bob "^psql"
[root@server1 ~]#_
```

Some processes have the ability to ignore, or **trap**, certain kill signals that are sent to them. The only kill signal that cannot be trapped by any process is the SIGKILL. Thus, if a SIGINT, SIGQUIT, and SIGTERM do not terminate a stubborn process, you can use a SIGKILL to terminate it. However, you should only use SIGKILL as a last resort because it prevents a process from closing open files and other resources properly.

> **Note** @
>
> You can use the `lsof` **(list open files) command** to view the files that a process has open before sending a SIGKILL. For example, to see the files that are used by the process with PID 1399, you can use the `lsof -p 1399` command.

If you send a kill signal to a process that has children, the parent process terminates all of its child processes before terminating itself. Thus, to kill several related processes, you can simply send a kill signal to their parent process. In addition, to kill a zombie process, it is often necessary to send a kill signal to its parent process.

> **Note** @
>
> To prevent a child process from being terminated when the parent process is terminated, you can start the child process with the `nohup` **command**. For example, executing the `nohup cathena` command within your BASH shell would execute the cathena child process without any association to the parent BASH shell process that started it.

Another command that can be used to send kill signals to processes is the `killall` **command**. The `killall` command works similarly to the `kill` command in that it takes the kill signal as an option; however, it uses the process name to kill instead of the PID. This allows multiple processes of the same name to be killed in one command. An example of using the `killall` command to send a SIGQUIT to multiple `sample` processes is shown in the following output:

```
[root@server1 ~]# ps -ef | grep sample
root       1729      1   0 Jun30 tty3     00:00:00 /sbin/sample
root      20198      1   0 Jun30 tty4     00:00:00 /sbin/sample
[root@server1 ~]# killall -3 sample
[root@server1 ~]#_
[root@server1 ~]# ps -ef | grep sample
[root@server1 ~]#_
```

> **Note** 🖉
>
> Alternatively, you could use the command `killall -SIGQUIT sample` to do the same as the `killall -3 sample` command used in the preceding output.
>
> As with the `kill` command, if you do not specify the kill signal when using the `killall` command, it sends a SIGTERM signal by default.

You can also use the `pkill` **command** to kill processes by process name. However, the `pkill` command allows you to identify process names using regular expressions as well as specify other criteria. For example, the `pkill -u bob -3 "^psql"` command will send a SIGQUIT signal to processes started by the bob user that begin with the letters `psql`.

In addition to the `kill`, `killall`, and `pkill` commands, the `top` command can be used to kill processes. While in the top utility, press the k key and supply the appropriate PID and kill signal when prompted.

Process Execution

You can execute three main types of Linux commands:

- Binary programs
- Shell scripts
- Shell functions

Most commands, such as `ls`, `find`, and `grep`, are binary programs that exist on the filesystem until executed. They were written in a certain programming language and compiled into a binary format that only the computer can understand. Other commands, such as `cd` and `exit`, are built into the BASH shell running in memory, and they are called shell functions. Shell scripts can also contain a list of binary programs, shell functions, and special constructs for the shell to execute in order.

When executing compiled programs or shell scripts, the BASH shell that interprets the command you typed creates a new BASH shell. This creation of a new subshell is known as **forking** and is carried out by the fork function in the BASH shell. The new subshell then executes the binary program or shell script using its exec function. After the binary program or shell script has completed, the new BASH shell uses its exit function to kill itself and return control to the original BASH shell. The original BASH shell uses its wait function to wait for the new BASH shell to carry out the aforementioned tasks before returning a prompt to the user. Figure 9-3 depicts this process when a user types the `ls` command at the command line.

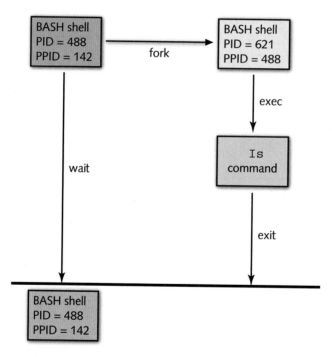

Figure 9-3   Process forking

Running Processes in the Background

As discussed in the previous section, the BASH shell creates, or forks, a subshell to execute most commands on the Linux system. Unfortunately, the original BASH shell must wait for the command in the subshell to finish before displaying a shell prompt to accept new commands. Commands run in this fashion are known as **foreground processes**.

Alternatively, you can omit the wait function shown in Figure 9-3 by appending an ampersand (&) character to the command. Commands run in this fashion are known as **background processes**. When a command is run in the background, the shell immediately returns the shell prompt for the user to enter another command. To run the `sample` command in the background, you can enter the following command:

```
[root@server1 ~]# sample &
[1] 2583
[root@server1 ~]#_
```

> **Note** 🖉
>
> Space characters between the command and the ampersand (&) are optional. In other words, the command `sample&` is equivalent to the command `sample &` used in the preceding output.

The shell returns the PID (2583 in the preceding example) and the background job ID (1 in the preceding example) so that you can manipulate the background job after it has been run. After the process has been started, you can use the ps command to view the PID or the `jobs` **command** to view the background job ID, as shown in the following output:

```
[root@server1 ~]# jobs
[1]+  Running                    sample &
[root@server1 ~]# ps | grep sample
2583 tty2     00:00:00 sample
[root@server1 ~]#_
```

To terminate the background process, you can send a kill signal to the PID (as shown earlier in this chapter), or you can send a kill signal to the background job ID. Background job IDs must be prefixed with a % character. To send a SIGINT signal to the sample background process created earlier, you could use the following `kill` command:

```
[root@server1 ~]# jobs
[1]+  Running                    sample &
[root@server1 ~]# kill -2 %1
[1]+  Interrupt                  sample
[root@server1 ~]# jobs
[root@server1 ~]#_
```

Note

You can also use the `killall -2 sample` command or the `top` utility to terminate the sample background process used in the preceding example.

After a background process has been started, you can move it to the foreground by using the **foreground (fg) command** followed by the background job ID. Similarly, you can pause a foreground process by using the Ctrl+z key combination. You can then send the process to the background with the **background (bg) command**. The Ctrl+z key combination assigns the foreground process a background job ID that is then used as an argument to the `bg` command. To start a sample process in the background and move it to the foreground, then pause it and move it to the background again, you can use the following commands:

```
[root@server1 ~]# sample &
[1]  7519
[root@server1 ~]# fg %1
sample

Ctrl+z

[1]+  Stopped                     sample
[root@server1 ~]# bg %1
[1]+ sample &
[root@server1 ~]# jobs
[1]+  Running                     sample &
[root@server1 ~]#_
```

When there are multiple background processes executing in the shell, the `jobs` command indicates the most recent one with a + symbol, and the second most recent one with a – symbol. If you place the % notation in a command without specifying the background job ID, the command operates on the most recent background process. An example of this is shown in the following output, in which four sample processes are started and sent SIGQUIT kill signals using the % notation:

```
[root@server1 ~]# sample &
[1]  7605
[root@server1 ~]# sample2 &
[2]  7613
[root@server1 ~]# sample3 &
[3]  7621
[root@server1 ~]# sample4 &
[4]  7629
```

```
[root@server1 ~]# jobs
[1]    Running                    sample &
[2]    Running                    sample2 &
[3]-   Running                    sample3 &
[4]+   Running                    sample4 &
[root@server1 ~]# kill -3 %
[root@server1 ~]# jobs
[1]    Running                    sample &
[2]-   Running                    sample2 &
[3]+   Running                    sample3 &
[root@server1 ~]# kill -3 %
[root@server1 ~]# jobs
[1]-   Running                    sample &
[2]+   Running                    sample2 &
[root@server1 ~]# kill -3 %
[root@server1 ~]# jobs
[1]+   Running                    sample &
[root@server1 ~]# kill -3 %
[root@server1 ~]# jobs
[root@server1 ~]#_
```

Process Priorities

Recall that Linux is a multitasking operating system. That is, it can perform several tasks at the same time. Because most computers contain only a single CPU, Linux executes small amounts of each process on the processor in series. This makes it seem to the user as if processes are executing simultaneously. The amount of time a process has to use the CPU is called a **time slice**; the more time slices a process has, the more time it has to execute on the CPU and the faster it executes. Time slices are typically measured in milliseconds. Thus, several hundred processes can be executing on the processor in a single second.

The ps -l command lists the Linux kernel priority (PRI) of a process. This value is directly related to the amount of time slices a process has on the CPU. A PRI of 0 is the most likely to get time slices on the CPU, and a PRI of 127 is the least likely to receive time slices on the CPU. An example of this command is shown next:

```
[root@server1 ~]# ps -l
F S   UID   PID  PPID  C PRI  NI ADDR SZ WCHAN  TTY        TIME CMD
4 S     0  3194  3192  0  75   0 -   1238 wait4  pts/1   00:00:00 bash
4 S     0  3896  3194  0  76   0 -    953 -      pts/1   00:00:00 sleep
4 S     0  3939  3194 13  75   0 -   7015 -      pts/1   00:00:01 gedit
4 R     0  3940  3194  0  77   0 -    632 -      pts/1   00:00:00 ps
[root@server1 ~]#_
```

The bash, sleep, gedit, and ps processes all have different PRI values because the kernel automatically assigns time slices based on several factors. You cannot change the PRI directly, but you can influence it indirectly by assigning a certain nice value to a process. A negative nice value increases the likelihood that the process will receive more time slices, whereas a positive nice value does the opposite. The range of nice values is depicted in Figure 9-4.

−20	0	+19
Most likely to receive time slices; the PRI will be closer to zero	The default nice value for new processes	Least likely to receive time slices; the PRI will be closer to 127

Figure 9-4 The nice value scale

All users can be "nice" to other users of the same computer by lowering the priority of their own processes by increasing their nice value. However, only the root user has the ability to increase the priority of a process by lowering its nice value.

Processes are started with a nice value of 0 by default, as shown in the NI column of the previous ps −1 output. To start a process with a nice value of +19 (low priority), you can use the nice **command** and specify the nice value using the −n option and the command to start. If the -n option is omitted, a nice value of +10 is assumed. To start the ps −1 command with a nice value of +19, you can issue the following command:

```
[root@server1 ~]# nice -n 19 ps -1
F S    UID    PID  PPID  C PRI  NI ADDR SZ WCHAN   TTY        TIME CMD
4 S      0   3194  3192  0  75   0 -    1238 wait4  pts/1   00:00:00 bash
4 S      0   3896  3194  0  76   0 -     953 -      pts/1   00:00:00 sleep
4 S      0   3939  3194  0  76   0 -    7015 -      pts/1   00:00:02 gedit
4 R      0   3946  3194  0  99  19 -     703 -      pts/1   00:00:00 ps
[root@server1 ~]#
```

Notice from the preceding output that NI is 19 for the ps command, as compared to 0 for the bash, sleep, and bash commands. Furthermore, the PRI of 99 for the ps command results in fewer time slices than the PRI of 76 for the sleep and gedit commands and the PRI of 75 for the bash shell.

Conversely, to increase the priority of the ps −1 command, you can use the following command:

```
[root@server1 ~]# nice -n -20 ps -1
F S    UID    PID  PPID  C PRI  NI ADDR SZ WCHAN   TTY        TIME CMD
4 S      0   3194  3192  0  75   0 -    1238 wait4  pts/1   00:00:00 bash
```

```
4 S    0  3896  3194  0  76    0 -     953 -      pts/1   00:00:00 sleep
4 S    0  3939  3194  0  76    0 -    7015 -      pts/1   00:00:02 gedit
4 R    0  3947  3194  0  60  -20 -     687 -      pts/1   00:00:00 ps
[root@server1 ~]#_
```

Note from the preceding output that the nice value of -20 for the ps command resulted in a PRI of 60, which is more likely to receive time slices than the PRI of 76 for the sleep and gedit commands and the PRI of 75 for the bash shell.

Note

On some Linux systems, background processes are given a nice value of 4 by default to lower the chance they will receive time slices.

After a process has been started, you can change its priority by using the renice command and specifying the change to the nice value, as well as the PID of the processes to change. Suppose, for example, three sample processes are currently executing on a terminal:

```
[root@server1 ~]# ps -l
F S   UID   PID  PPID  C PRI  NI ADDR   SZ WCHAN  TTY         TIME CMD
4 S    0  1229  1228  0  71   0 -    617 wait4  pts/0  00:00:00 bash
4 S    0  1990  1229  0  69   0 -    483 nanosl pts/0  00:00:00 sample
4 S    0  2180  1229  0  70   0 -    483 nanosl pts/0  00:00:00 sample
4 S    0  2181  1229  0  71   0 -    483 nanosl pts/0  00:00:00 sample
4 R    0  2196  1229  0  75   0 -    768 -      pts/0  00:00:00 ps
[root@server1 ~]#_
```

To lower priority of the first two sample processes by changing the nice value from 0 to +15 and view the new values, you can execute the following commands:

```
[root@server1 ~]# renice +15 1990 2180
1990 (process ID) old priority 0, new priority 15
2180 (process ID) old priority 0, new priority 15
[root@server1 ~]# ps -l
F S   UID   PID  PPID  C PRI  NI ADDR   SZ WCHAN  TTY      TIME CMD
4 S    0  1229  1228  0  71   0 -    617 wait4  pts/0  00:00:00 bash
4 S    0  1990  1229  0  93  15 -    483 nanosl pts/0  00:00:00 sample
4 S    0  2180  1229  0  96  15 -    483 nanosl pts/0  00:00:00 sample
4 S    0  2181  1229  0  71   0 -    483 nanosl pts/0  00:00:00 sample
4 R    0  2196  1229  0  75   0 -    768 -      pts/0  00:00:00 ps
[root@server1 ~]#_
```

>
>
> You can also use the `top` utility to change the nice value of a running process. Press the `r` key, then supply the PID and the nice value when prompted.
>
>   As with the `nice` command, only the root user can change the nice value to a negative value using the `renice` command.

The root user can use the `renice` command to change the priority of all processes that are owned by a certain user or group. To change the nice value to +15 for all processes owned by the users mary and bob, you could execute the command `renice +15 -u mary bob` at the command prompt. Similarly, to change the nice value to +15 for all processes started by members of the group sys, you could execute the command `renice +15 -g sys` at the command prompt.

Scheduling Commands

Although most processes are begun by users executing commands while logged in to a terminal, at times you might want to schedule a command to execute at some point in the future. For example, scheduling system maintenance commands to run during nonworking hours is good practice, as it does not disrupt normal business activities.

You can use two different daemons to schedule commands: the **at daemon (atd)** and the **cron daemon (crond)**. The at daemon can be used to schedule a command to execute once in the future, whereas the cron daemon is used to schedule a command to execute repeatedly in the future.

Scheduling Commands with atd

To schedule a command or set of commands for execution at a later time by the at daemon, you can specify the time as an argument to the **at command**; some common time formats used with the at command are listed in Table 9-3.

Table 9-3   Common `at` commands

Command	Description
`at 10:15pm`	Schedules commands to run at 10:15 PM on the current date
`at 10:15pm July 15`	Schedules commands to run at 10:15 PM on July 15
`at midnight`	Schedules commands to run at midnight on the current date
`at noon July 15`	Schedules commands to run at noon on July 15
`at teatime`	Schedules commands to run at 4:00 PM on the current date

Table 9-3   Common `at` commands *(continued)*

Command	Description
`at tomorrow`	Schedules commands to run the next day
`at now + 5 minutes`	Schedules commands to run in five minutes
`at now + 10 hours`	Schedules commands to run in 10 hours
`at now + 4 days`	Schedules commands to run in four days
`at now + 2 weeks`	Schedules commands to run in two weeks
`at now` `at batch`	Schedules commands to run immediately

`at 9:00am 01/03/2019`
`at 9:00am 01032019`
`at 9:00am 03.01.2019`
	Schedules commands to run at 9:00 AM on January 3, 2019

After being invoked, the `at` command displays an `at>` prompt allowing you to type commands to be executed, one per line. After the commands have been entered, use the Crtl+d key combination to schedule the commands using atd.

Note 📎

The at daemon uses the current shell's environment when executing scheduled commands. The shell environment and scheduled commands are stored in the /var/spool/at directory on Fedora systems and the /var/spool/cron/atjobs directory on Ubuntu systems.

If the standard output of any command scheduled using atd has not been redirected to a file, it is normally mailed to the user. You can check your local mail by typing `mail` at a command prompt. Because most modern Linux distributions do not install a mail daemon by default, it is important to ensure that the output of any commands scheduled using atd are redirected to a file.

To schedule the commands `date` and `who` to run at 10:15 PM on July 15, you can use the following commands:

```
[root@server1 ~]# at 10:15pm July 15
at> date > /root/atfile
at> who >> /root/atfile
at> Ctrl+d
job 1 at Wed Aug 25 22:15:00 2019
[root@server1 ~]#_
```

As shown in the preceding output, the at command returns an at job ID. You can use this ID to query or remove the scheduled command. To display a list of at job IDs, you can specify the –l option to the at command:

```
[root@server1 ~]# at -l
1         Wed Aug 25 22:15:00 2019 a root
[root@server1 ~]#_
```

Note

Alternatively, you can use the atq **command** to see scheduled at jobs. The atq command is simply a shortcut to the at –l command.

When running the at –l command, a regular user only sees his own scheduled at jobs; however, the root user sees all scheduled at jobs.

To see the contents of the at job listed in the previous output alongside the shell environment at the time the at job was scheduled, you can use the –c option to the at command and specify the appropriate at job ID:

```
[root@server1 ~]# at -c 1
#!/bin/sh
# atrun uid=0 gid=0
# mail root 0
umask 22
XDG_VTNR=2; export XDG_VTNR
XDG_SESSION_ID=1; export XDG_SESSION_ID
HOSTNAME=server1; export HOSTNAME
SHELL=/bin/bash; export SHELL
HISTSIZE=1000; export HISTSIZE
QT_GRAPHICSSYSTEM_CHECKED=1; export QT_GRAPHICSSYSTEM_CHECKED
USER=root; export USER
MAIL=/var/spool/mail/root; export MAIL
PATH=/usr/local/sbin:/usr/local/bin:/sbin:/bin:/usr/sbin:/usr/
bin:/root/bin; export PATH
PWD=/root; export PWD
LANG=en_US.UTF-8; export LANG
KDEDIRS=/usr; export KDEDIRS
HISTCONTROL=ignoredups; export HISTCONTROL
SHLVL=1; export SHLVL
XDG_SEAT=seat0; export XDG_SEAT
HOME=/root; export HOME
LOGNAME=root; export LOGNAME
LESSOPEN=\|\|/usr/bin/lesspipe.sh\ %s; export LESSOPEN
```

```
XDG_RUNTIME_DIR=/run/user/0; export XDG_RUNTIME_DIR
cd /root || {
        echo 'Execution directory inaccessible' >&2
        exit 1
}
${SHELL:-/bin/sh}   <<   'marcinDELIMITER2b2a920e'
date >/root/atfile
who >>/root/atfile
marcinDELIMITER2b2a920e
[root@server1 ~]#_
```

To remove the at job used in the preceding example, specify the –d option to the at command, followed by the appropriate at job ID, as shown in the following output:

```
[root@server1 ~]# at -d 1
[root@server1 ~]# at -l
[root@server1 ~]#_
```

> **Note** 📎
>
> Alternatively, you can use the `atrm 1` command to remove the first at job. The `atrm` **command** is simply a shortcut to the at –d command.

If there are many commands to be scheduled using the at daemon, you can place these commands in a shell script and then schedule the shell script to execute at a later time using the –f option to the at command. An example of scheduling a shell script called myscript using the at command is shown next:

```
[root@server1 ~]# cat myscript
#this is a sample shell script
date > /root/atfile
who >> /root/atfile
[root@server1 ~]# at 10:15pm July 16 -f myscript
job 2 at Wed Aug 25 22:10:00 2019
[root@server1 ~]#_
```

If the /etc/at.allow and /etc/at.deny files do not exist, only the root user is allowed to schedule tasks using the at daemon. To give this ability to other users, create an /etc/at.allow file and add the names of users allowed to use the at daemon, one per line. Conversely, you can use the /etc/at.deny file to deny certain users access to the at daemon; any user not listed in this file is then allowed to use the at daemon. If both files exist, the system checks the /etc/at.allow file and does not process the entries in the /etc/at.deny file.

Note 🖉

On Fedora systems, only an /etc/at.deny file exists by default. Because this file is initially left blank, all users are allowed to use the at daemon. On Ubuntu systems, only an /etc/at.deny file exists by default, and lists daemon user accounts. As a result, the root user and other regular user accounts are allowed to use the at daemon.

Scheduling Commands with cron

The at daemon is useful for scheduling tasks that occur on a certain date in the future but is ill suited for scheduling repetitive tasks, because each task requires its own at job ID. The cron daemon is better suited for repetitive tasks because it uses configuration files called **cron tables** to specify when a command should be executed.

A cron table includes six fields separated by space or tab characters. The first five fields specify the times to run the command, and the sixth field is the absolute pathname to the command to be executed. As with the at command, you can place commands in a shell script and schedule the shell script to run repetitively; in this case, the sixth field is the absolute pathname to the shell script. Each of the fields in a cron table is depicted in Figure 9-5.

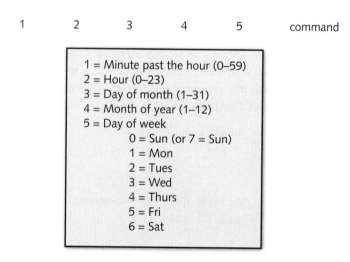

Figure 9-5   User cron table format

Thus, to execute the /root/myscript shell script at 5:20 PM and 5:40 PM Monday to Friday regardless of the day of the month or month of the year, you could use the cron table depicted in Figure 9-6.

1	2	3	4	5	command
20,40	17	*	*	1–5	/root/myscript

Figure 9-6   Sample user cron table entry

The first field in Figure 9-6 specifies the minute past the hour. Because the command must be run at 20 minutes and 40 minutes past the hour, this field has two values, separated by a comma. The second field specifies the time in 24-hour format, with 5 PM being the 17th hour. The third and fourth fields specify the day of month and month of year, respectively, to run the command. Because the command might run during any month regardless of the day of month, both fields use the * wildcard shell metacharacter to match all values. The final field indicates the day of the week to run the command; as with the first field, the command must be run on multiple days, but a range of days was specified (day 1 to day 5).

Two types of cron tables are used by the cron daemon: user cron tables and system cron tables. User cron tables represent tasks that individual users schedule and exist in the /var/spool/cron directory on Fedora systems and the /var/spool/cron/crontabs directory on Ubuntu systems. System cron tables contain system tasks and exist in the /etc/crontab file as well as the /etc/cron.d directory.

User Cron Tables

On a newly installed Fedora system, all users have the ability to schedule tasks using the cron daemon because the /etc/cron.deny file has no contents. However, if you create an /etc/cron.allow file and add a list of users to it, only those users will be able to schedule tasks using the cron daemon. All other users are denied. Conversely, you can modify the /etc/cron.deny file to list those users who are denied the ability to schedule tasks. Thus, any users not listed in this file are allowed to schedule tasks only. If both files exist, only the /etc/cron.allow file is processed. If neither file exists, all users are allowed to schedule tasks, which is the case on a newly installed Ubuntu system.

To create or edit a user cron table, you can use the –e option to the `crontab` command, which opens the vi editor. You can then enter the appropriate cron table entries. Suppose, for example, that the root user executed the `crontab -e` command on a Fedora system. To schedule /bin/command1 to run at 4:30 AM every Friday and /bin/command2 to run at 2:00 PM on the first day of every month, you can add the following lines while in the vi editor:

```
30 4 * * 5 /bin/command1
0 14 1 * * /bin/command2
~
~
~
```

```
~
~
~
~
~
~
~
~
~
~
~
~
"/tmp/crontab.4101"   2L 41C
```

When the user saves the changes and quits the vi editor, the information is stored in the file /var/spool/cron/*username*, where *username* is the name of the user who executed the `crontab` -e command. In the preceding example, the file would be named /var/spool/cron/root.

To list your user cron table, you can use the -l option to the `crontab` command. The following output lists the cron table created earlier:

```
[root@server1 ~]# crontab -l
30 4 * * 5 /bin/command1
0 14 1 * * /bin/command2
[root@server1 ~]#_
```

Furthermore, to remove a cron table and all scheduled jobs, you can use the -r option to the `crontab` command, as illustrated next:

```
[root@server1 ~]# crontab -r
[root@server1 ~]# crontab -l
no crontab for root
[root@server1 ~]#_
```

The root user can edit, list, or remove any other user's cron table by using the -u option to the `crontab` command followed by the user name. For example, to edit the cron table for the user mary, the root user could use the command `crontab` -e -u mary at the command prompt. Similarly, to list and remove mary's cron table, the root user could execute the commands `crontab` -l -u mary and `crontab` -r -u mary, respectively.

System Cron Tables

Linux systems are typically scheduled to run many commands during nonbusiness hours. These commands might perform system maintenance, back up data, or run CPU-intensive programs. Most of these commands are scheduled by the cron daemon from entries in the system cron table /etc/crontab, which can only be edited by the root user. The default /etc/crontab file on a Fedora system is shown in the following output:

```
[root@server1 ~]# cat /etc/crontab
SHELL=/bin/bash
PATH=/sbin:/bin:/usr/sbin:/usr/bin
MAILTO=root
# For details see man 4 crontabs
# Example of job definition:
# .---------------- minute (0 - 59)
# |  .------------- hour (0 - 23)
# |  |  .---------- day of month (1 - 31)
# |  |  |  .------- month (1 - 12) OR jan,feb,mar,apr ...
# |  |  |  |  .---- day of week (0 - 6) (Sunday=0 or 7) OR
# |  |  |  |  |        sun,mon,tue,wed,thu,fri,sat
# |  |  |  |  |
# *  *  *  *  * user-name command to be executed
[root@server1 ~]#_
```

The initial section of the cron table specifies the environment used while executing commands. The remainder of the file contains comments that identify the format of a cron table entry. If you add your own cron table entries to the bottom of this file, they will be executed as the root user. Alternatively, you may prefix the command within a system cron table entry with the user account that it should be executed as. For example, the /bin/cleanup command shown in the following output will be executed as the apache user every Friday at 11:30 PM:

```
[root@server1 ~]# cat /etc/crontab
SHELL=/bin/bash
PATH=/sbin:/bin:/usr/sbin:/usr/bin
MAILTO=root
# For details see man 4 crontabs
# Example of job definition:
# .---------------- minute (0 - 59)
# |  .------------- hour (0 - 23)
# |  |  .---------- day of month (1 - 31)
# |  |  |  .------- month (1 - 12) OR jan,feb,mar,apr ...
# |  |  |  |  .---- day of week (0 - 6) (Sunday=0 or 7) OR
# |  |  |  |  |        sun,mon,tue,wed,thu,fri,sat
# |  |  |  |  |
# *  *  *  *  * user-name command to be executed
  30 23  *  *  5    apache  /bin/cleanup
[root@server1 ~]#_
```

You can also place a cron table with the same information in the /etc/cron.d directory. Any cron tables found in this directory can have the same format as /etc/crontab and are run by the system. In the following example, the cron daemon is configured to run the `sa1` command every 10 minutes as the root user, and the `sa2` command at 11:53 PM as the root user each day:

```
[root@server1 ~]# cat /etc/cron.d/sysstat
# Run system activity accounting tool every 10 minutes
*/10 * * * * root /usr/lib/sa/sa1 -S DISK 1 1
# Generate a daily summary of process accounting at 23:53
53 23 * * * root /usr/lib/sa/sa2 -A
[root@server1 ~]#_
```

> **Note** 🖉
>
> The `watch` **command** can be used instead of the cron daemon for scheduling very frequent tasks. For example, to run the `sa1` command shown in the previous output every 1 minute (60 seconds), you could run the `watch -n 60 /usr/lib/sa/sa1 -S DISK 1 1` command.

Many administrative tasks are performed on an hourly, daily, weekly, or monthly basis. If you have a task of this type, you don't need to create a system cron table. Instead, you can place a shell script that runs the appropriate commands in one of the following directories:

- Scripts that should be executed hourly in the /etc/cron.hourly/ directory
- Scripts that should be executed daily in the /etc/cron.daily/ directory
- Scripts that should be executed weekly in the /etc/cron.weekly/ directory
- Scripts that should be executed monthly in the /etc/cron.monthly/ directory

On Fedora systems, the cron daemon runs the /etc/cron.d/0hourly script, which executes the contents of the /etc/cron.hourly directory 1 minute past the hour, every hour on the hour. The /etc/cron.hourly/0anacron file starts the anacron daemon, which then executes the contents of the /etc/cron.daily/, /etc/cron.weekly/, and /etc/cron.monthy/ directories at the times specified in /etc/anacrontab.

On Ubuntu systems, cron table entries within the /etc/crontab file are used to execute the contents of the /etc/cron.hourly, as well as the contents of the /etc/cron.daily/, /etc/cron.weekly/, and /etc/cron.monthy/ directories using the anacron daemon.

> **Note** 📎
>
> If the computer is powered off during the time of a scheduled task, the cron daemon will simply not execute the task. This is why cron tables within the /etc/cron.daily/, /etc/cron.weekly/, and /etc/cron.monthy/ directories are often executed by the anacron daemon, which will resume task execution at the next available time if the computer is powered off during the time of a scheduled task.

Chapter Summary

- Processes are programs that are executing on the system.
- User processes are run in the same terminal the user executed them on, whereas daemon processes are system processes that do not run on a terminal.
- Every process has a parent process associated with it and, optionally, several child processes.
- Process information is stored in the /proc filesystem. You can use the `ps`, `pstree`, `psgrep`, and `top` commands to view this information.
- Zombie and rogue processes that exist for long periods of time use up system resources and should be killed to improve system performance.
- You can send kill signals to a process using the `kill`, `killall`, `pkill`, and `top` commands.

- The BASH shell creates, or forks, a subshell to execute most commands.
- Processes can be run in the background by appending an & to the command name. The BASH shell assigns each background process a background job ID such that it can be manipulated afterward.
- The priority of a process can be affected indirectly by altering its nice value; nice values range from –20 (high priority) to +19 (low priority). Only the root user can increase the priority of a process.
- You can use the at and cron daemons to schedule commands to run at a later time. The at daemon schedules tasks to occur once at a later time, whereas the cron daemon uses cron tables to schedule tasks to occur repetitively in the future.

Key Terms

`at` **command**
at daemon (atd)
`atq` **command**
`atrm` **command**

`background` **(bg) command**
background process
child process
cron daemon (crond)

cron table
`crontab` **command**
daemon process
`foreground` **(fg) command**

foreground process	nohup command	ps command
forking	parent process	pstree command
jobs command	parent process ID (PPID)	renice command
kill command	pgrep command	rogue process
kill signal	pkill command	time slice
killall command	process	top command
lsof (list open files) command	process ID (PID)	trap
nice command	process priority	user process
nice value	process state	watch command
	program	zombie process

Review Questions

1. Which command entered without arguments is used to display a list of processes running in the current shell?
   a. pgrep
   b. list
   c. pid
   d. ps

2. Which of the following statements is true? (Choose all that apply.)
   a. If /etc/at.allow exists, only users listed in it can use the at command.
   b. If /etc/cron.allow exists, only users listed in it can use the cron command.
   c. If /etc/cron.deny exists and /etc/cron. allow does not exist, any user not listed in /etc/cron.deny can use the cron command.
   d. If /etc/cron.allow and /etc/cron.deny exist, only users listed in the former can use the cron command, and any users listed in the latter are denied access to the cron command.
   e. If a user is listed in both /etc/cron. allow and /etc/cron.deny, then /etc/ cron.deny takes precedence and the user cannot access the crontab command.

3. Where are individual user tasks scheduled to run with the cron daemon stored on a Fedora system?
   a. /etc/crontab
   b. /etc/cron/*username*
   c. /var/spool/cron
   d. /var/spool/cron/*username*

4. Which process has a PID of 1 and a PPID of 0?
   a. the kernel itself
   b. ps
   c. init/systemd
   d. top

5. A process spawning or initiating another process is referred to as _____.
   a. a child process
   b. forking
   c. branching
   d. parenting

6. As daemon processes are not associated with terminals, you must use an option such as -e alongside the ps command to view them. True or False?

7. Which of the following commands will most likely increase the chance of a process receiving more time slices?
   a. renice 0
   b. renice 15
   c. renice -12
   d. renice 19

8. How can you bypass the wait function and send a user process to the background?
   a. This cannot happen once a process is executing; it can be done only when the command is started by placing an ampersand (&) after it.
   b. This cannot happen; only daemon processes can run in the background.
   c. You can use the ps command.
   d. You can use the Ctrl+z key combination and the bg command.

9. The at command is used to _____.
   a. schedule processes to run periodically in the background
   b. schedule processes to run periodically on a recurring basis in the future
   c. schedule processes to run at a single instance in the future
   d. schedule processes to run in the foreground

10. What command is used to view and modify user jobs scheduled to run with cron?
    a. crontab
    b. cron
    c. ps
    d. sched

11. Every process has a process ID and a _____.
    a. fork process
    b. daemon
    c. child process
    d. parent process

12. The pkill command terminates _____.
    a. all instances of a process with the same PPID
    b. all instances of a process with the same PID
    c. all instances of a process with the same priority

d. all instances of a process with the same name matched by a regular expression

13. Nice values are used to affect process priorities using a range between _____.
    a. 0 and 20
    b. 0 and -19
    c. -19 and 20
    d. -20 and 19

14. What is the name given to a process not associated with a terminal?
    a. child process
    b. parent process
    c. user process
    d. daemon process

15. To kill a process running in the background, you must place a % character before its process ID. True or False?

16. What kill level signal cannot be trapped?
    a. 1
    b. 9
    c. 3
    d. 15

17. A runaway process that is faulty and consuming mass amounts of system resources _____.
    a. is a zombie process
    b. is an orphaned process
    c. has a PPID of Z
    d. is a rogue process

18. When you run the ps command, how are daemon processes recognized?
    a. The terminal is listed as ttyo.
    b. There is a question mark in the TTY column.
    c. There is an asterisk in the STIME column.
    d. There is a "d" for daemon in the terminal identification column.

19. Which command is used to gain real-time information about processes running on the system, with the most processor-intensive processes appearing at the beginning of the list?

a. ps

b. ps -elf

c. top

d. pstree

20. Which command can be used to see processes running in the background?

a. bg

b. jobs

c. ps -%

d. fg

Hands-On Projects

These projects should be completed in the order given. The hands-on projects presented in this chapter should take a total of three hours to complete. The requirements for this lab include:

- A computer with Fedora Linux installed according to Hands-On Project 2-1

Project 9-1

In this hands-on project, you view characteristics of processes using the ps command.

1. Boot your Fedora Linux virtual machine. After your Linux system has been loaded, switch to a command-line terminal (tty5) by pressing **Ctrl+Alt+F5** and log in to the terminal using the user name of **root** and the password of **LINUXrocks!**.

2. At the command prompt, type **ps -ef | less** and press **Enter** to view the first processes started on the entire Linux system.

3. Fill in the following information from the data displayed on the terminal screen after typing the command:

   a. Which process has a Process ID of 1? (PID=1) _____

   b. What character do most processes have in the terminal column (tty)? _____

   c. What does this character in the terminal column indicate? _____

   d. Which user started most of these processes? _____

   e. Most processes that are displayed on the screen are started by a certain parent process indicated in the Parent Process ID column (PPID). Which process is the parent to most processes? _____

   Type **q** at the MORE prompt to quit.

4. At the command prompt, type **ps -el | less** and press **Enter** to view the process states for the first processes started on the entire Linux system.

5. Fill in the following information from the data displayed on the terminal screen after typing the command:

   a. What character exists in the State (S) column for most processes, and what does this character indicate? _____

b. What range of numbers is it possible to have in the Nice (NI) column? _____

c. Which processes have the number 4 in the Flag (F) column, and what does this number indicate? _____

Type **q** at the MORE prompt to quit.

6. At the command prompt, type **ps –el | grep Z** and press **Enter** to display zombie processes on your Linux system. Are there any zombie processes indicated in the State (S) column?

7. Type **exit** and press **Enter** to log out of your shell.

Project 9-2

In this hands-on project, you use kill signals to terminate processes on your system.

1. On your Fedora Linux virtual machine, switch to a command-line terminal (tty5) by pressing **Ctrl+Alt+F5** and log in to the terminal using the user name of **root** and the password of **LINUXrocks!**.

2. At the command prompt, type **ps –ef | grep bash** and press **Enter** to view the BASH shells that are running in memory on your computer. Record the PID of the BASH shell running in your terminal (tty5): _____.

3. At the command prompt, type **pgrep -t tty5 bash** and press **Enter** to view the PID of BASH shells that are running in memory within your terminal (tty5).

   Does the PID shown match the one from Step 2?

4. At the command prompt, type **kill –l** and press **Enter** to list the available kill signals that you can send to a process.

5. At the command prompt, type **kill -2 PID** (where PID is the PID that you recorded in Question 2) and press **Enter**. Did your shell terminate?

6. At the command prompt, type **kill -3 PID** (where PID is the PID that you recorded in Question 2) and press **Enter**. Did your shell terminate?

7. At the command prompt, type **kill -15 PID** (where PID is the PID that you recorded in Question 2) and press **Enter**. Did your shell terminate?

8. At the command prompt, **type kill -9 PID** (where PID is the PID that you recorded in Question 2) and press **Enter**. Did your shell terminate? Why did this command work when the others did not?

Project 9-3

In this hands-on project, you run processes in the background, kill them using the `kill`, `killall`, and `pgrep` commands, and change their priorities using the `nice` and `renice` commands.

1. On your Fedora Linux virtual machine, switch to a command-line terminal (tty5) by pressing **Ctrl+Alt+F5** and log in to the terminal using the user name of **root** and the password of **LINUXrocks!**.

2. At the command prompt, type `sleep 6000` and press **Enter** to start the `sleep` command, which waits 6000 seconds in the foreground. Do you get your prompt back after you enter this command? Why? Send the process a SIGINT signal by typing the **Ctrl+c** key combination.

3. At the command prompt, type `sleep 6000&` and press **Enter** to start the `sleep` command, which waits 6000 seconds in the background. Observe the background Job ID and PID that is returned.

4. Bring the background sleep process to the foreground by typing `fg %1` at the command prompt, then press **Enter**. Send the process a SIGINT signal by typing the **Ctrl+c** key combination.

5. Place another `sleep` command in memory by typing the `sleep 6000&` command and pressing **Enter**. Repeat this command three more times to place a total of four `sleep` commands in memory.

6. At the command prompt, type `jobs` and press **Enter** to view the jobs running in the background. What does the + symbol indicate?

7. At the command prompt, type `kill %` and press **Enter** to terminate the most recent process. Next, type `jobs` and press **Enter** to view the results.

8. At the command prompt, type `kill %1` and press **Enter** to terminate background job #1. Next, type `jobs` and press **Enter** to view the results.

9. At the command prompt, type `killall sleep` and press **Enter** to terminate the remaining sleep processes in memory. Verify that there are no more sleep processes in memory by typing the `jobs` command, then press **Enter**.

10. Place a `sleep` command in memory by typing `sleep 6000&` at a command prompt and pressing **Enter**.

11. Place a `sleep` command in memory with a lower priority by typing `nice -n 19 sleep 6000&` at a command prompt and pressing **Enter**.

12. Verify that these two processes have different nice values by typing the command `ps -el | grep sleep` at the command prompt and pressing **Enter**. Record the PID of the process with a nice value of 0:_____.

13. At the command prompt, type `renice +10 PID` (where PID is the PID you recorded in the previous question) to change the priority of the process. Type the command `ps -el | grep sleep` and press **Enter** to verify the new priority.

14. At the command prompt, type `pkill -t tty5 sleep` to kill all sleep processes running within your terminal (tty5).

15. Type `exit` and press **Enter** to log out of your shell.

Project 9-4

In this hands-on project, you view and manage processes using the top command-line utility.

1. On your Fedora Linux virtual machine, switch to a command-line terminal (tty5) by pressing **Ctrl+Alt+F5** and log in to the terminal using the user name of **root** and the password of **LINUXrocks!**.

2. At the command prompt, type **top** and press **Enter**.
3. From the output on the terminal screen, record the following information:
   a. Number of processes: _____
   b. Number of sleeping processes: _____
   c. Amount of total memory (K): _____
   d. Amount of total swap memory (K): _____
4. While in the top utility, press the **h** key and observe the output. When finished, press any key to return to the previous top output.
5. By observing the output under the COMMAND column on your terminal screen, identify the PID of the top command in the output and record it here: _____
6. Type **r** in the top utility to change the priority of a running process. When asked which process to change (renice), type the **PID** from the previous question. When asked which value to use, type **10** to lower the priority of the top process to 10. Does this new priority take effect immediately?
7. Type **k** in the top utility to send a kill signal to a process. When asked which process, type the **PID** used in the previous question. When asked which signal to send, type **2** to send a SIGINT signal. Did the top utility terminate?
8. At the command prompt, type **top** and press **Enter**.
9. By observing the output under the COMMAND column on your terminal screen, identify the PID of the top command in the output and record it here:_____
10. Type **k** in the top utility to send a kill signal to a process. When asked which process, type the **PID** from the previous question. When asked which signal to send, type **15** to send a SIGTERM signal. Did the SIGTERM signal allow top to exit cleanly?
11. At the command prompt, type **clear** and press **Enter** to clear the screen.
12. Type **exit** and press **Enter** to log out of your shell.

Project 9-5

In this hands-on project, you schedule processes using the at and cron daemons.

1. On your Fedora Linux virtual machine, switch to a command-line terminal (tty5) by pressing **Ctrl+Alt+F5** and log in to the terminal using the user name of **root** and the password of **LINUXrocks!**.
2. Schedule processes to run 1 minute in the future by typing the command **at now + 1 minute** at a command prompt, then press **Enter**.
3. When the at> prompt appears, type **date > /root/datefile** and press **Enter**.
4. When the second at> prompt appears, type **who >> /root/datefile** and press **Enter**.
5. When the third at> prompt appears, press the **Ctrl+d** key combination to finish the scheduling and observe the output. When will your job run? Where will the output of the date and who commands be sent?
6. In approximately one minute, type **cat datefile** and press **Enter**. View the output from your scheduled at job.

7. At the command prompt, type `crontab -l` and press **Enter** to list your cron table. Do you have one?

8. At the command prompt, type `crontab -e` and press **Enter** to edit a new cron table for the root user. When the vi editor appears, add the line:`30 20 *  * 5 /bin/false`

9. When you finish typing, save and quit the vi editor and observe the output on the terminal screen.

10. At the command prompt, type `crontab -l` and press **Enter** to list your cron table. When will the `/bin/false` command run?

11. At the command prompt, type `cat /var/spool/cron/root` and press **Enter** to list your cron table from the cron directory. Is it the same as the output from the previous command?

12. At the command prompt, type `crontab -r` and press **Enter** to remove your cron table.

13. At the command prompt, type `ls /etc/cron.daily` and press **Enter**. Are there any scripts that will be run daily on your system?

14. At the command prompt, type `ls /etc/cron.d` and press **Enter**. Are there any custom system cron tables on your system?

15. At the command prompt, type `cat /etc/cron.d/raid-check` and press **Enter**. When is the raid-check command run by the cron daemon?

16. Type `exit` and press **Enter** to log out of your shell.

Project 9-6

In this hands-on project, you view information that is exported by the Linux kernel to the /proc directory.

1. On your Fedora Linux virtual machine, switch to a command-line terminal (tty5) by pressing **Ctrl+Alt+F5** and log in to the terminal using the user name of **root** and the password of **LINUXrocks!**.

2. At the command prompt, type `cd /proc` and press **Enter** to change your current directory to /proc. Then type `ls` to list the directory contents and examine the output on the terminal screen. Why are the subdirectories named using numbers?

3. At the command prompt, type `cat meminfo | less` and press **Enter** to list information about total and available memory. How does the value for total memory (MemTotal) compare to the information from Step 3 in Project 9-4?

4. At the command prompt, type `cat swaps` and press **Enter** to list information about total and available swap memory. How does the value for total swap memory (Size) compare to the information from Step 3 in Project 9-4?

5. At the command prompt, type `cd 1` and press **Enter** to enter the subdirectory that contains information about the init daemon (PID = 1).

6. At the command prompt, type `ls` and press **Enter** to list the files in the /proc/1 directory. Next, type `cat status | less` and press **Enter**. What is the state of the init (systemd) daemon? Does it list the correct PID and PPID?

7. Type `exit` and press **Enter** to log out of your shell.

Discovery Exercises

1. Type the command **sleep 5** at a command prompt and press Enter. When did you receive your shell prompt? Explain the events that occurred by referencing Figure 9-3. Next, type **exec sleep 5** at a command prompt and press Enter. What happened? Can you explain the results using Figure 9-3? Redraw Figure 9-3 to indicate what happens when a command is directly executed.

2. Using the man or info pages, research four more options to the ps command. What processes does each option display? What information is given about each process?

3. Log in to the GNOME desktop on your Fedora system as user1 and open a command-line terminal. At a shell prompt, type **xeyes** to execute the xeyes program. Does the terminal window stay open? Click the terminal window to bring it to the foreground. Do you see your shell prompt? Why? Close your terminal window. What happened to the xeyes program and why?

   Next, open another command-line terminal and type **xeyes&** at the command prompt to execute the xeyes program in the background. Click the terminal window to bring it to the foreground. Do you see your shell prompt? Why? Close your terminal window. What happened to the xeyes program and why?

   Finally, open another command-line terminal and type **nohup xeyes&** at the command prompt to execute the xeyes program in the background from the nohup command. Click the terminal window to bring it to the foreground and press **Enter**. Close your terminal. Visit the nohup manual page to explain why the xeyes program is still available.

4. You are the systems administrator for a large trust company. Most of the Linux servers in the company host databases that are accessed frequently by company employees. One particular Linux server has been reported as being very slow today. Upon further investigation using the top utility, you have found a rogue process that is wasting a great deal of system resources. Unfortunately, the rogue process is a database maintenance program and should be killed with caution. Which kill signal would you send this process and why? If the rogue process traps this signal, which other kill signals would you try? Which command could you use as a last resort to kill the rogue process? What command can list the files that could be impacted if you terminate the rogue process?

5. Write the lines that you could use in your user cron table to schedule the **/bin/myscript** command to run:
   a. every Wednesday afternoon at 2:15 PM
   b. every hour on the hour every day of the week
   c. every 15 minutes on the first of every month
   d. only on February 25th at 6:00 PM
   e. on the first Monday of every month at 12:10 PM

6. Time-permitting, perform Project 9-1 through 9-6 on your Ubuntu Server virtual machine. Note any differences between the Fedora and Ubuntu distributions.

## CHAPTER 10

COMMON ADMINISTRATIVE TASKS

After completing this chapter, you will be able to:

Set up, manage, and print to printers on a Linux system

Understand the purpose of log files and how they are administered

Create, modify, manage, and delete user and group accounts

In previous chapters, you learned how to administer filesystems, X Windows, system startup, and processes. In this chapter, you examine other essential areas of Linux administration. First, you learn about the print process and how to administer and set up printers, followed by a discussion on viewing and managing log files. Finally, you examine system databases that store user and group information, and the utilities that can be used to create, modify, and delete user and group accounts on a Linux system.

Printer Administration

Many users commonly need to print files on a Linux system, and printing log files and system configuration information is good procedure in case of a system failure. Thus, a firm understanding of how to set up, manage, and print to printers is vital for those who set up and administer Linux servers.

The Common UNIX Printing System

Today, the most common printing system used on Linux computers is the **Common Unix Printing System (CUPS)**, which was developed by Apple, Inc. Fundamental to using CUPS on a Linux system is an understanding of how information is sent to a printer. A set of information sent to a printer at the same time is called a **print job**. Print jobs can consist of a file, several files, or the output of a command. To send a print job to a printer, you must first use the `lp` **command** and specify what to print.

Next, the **CUPS daemon (cupsd)** assigns the print job a unique **print job ID** and places a copy of the print job into a temporary directory on the filesystem called the **print queue**, provided the printer is accepting requests. If the printer is rejecting requests, the CUPS daemon displays an error message stating that the printer is not accepting print jobs.

Note

Accepting print jobs into a print queue is called **spooling** or **queuing**.

The print queue for a printer is typically /var/spool/cups. Regardless of how many printers you have on your Linux system, all print jobs are sent to the same directory.

When a print job is in the print queue, it is ready to be printed. If the printer is enabled and ready to accept the print job, the CUPS daemon sends the print job from the print queue to the printer and removes the copy of the print job in the print queue. Conversely, if the printer is disabled, the print job remains in the print queue.

Note

Sending print jobs from a print queue to a printer is commonly called printing.

An example of this process for a printer called printer1 is illustrated in Figure 10-1.

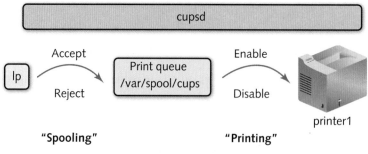

Figure 10-1   The print process

To see a list of all printers on the system and their status, you can use the −t (total) option to the `lpstat` **command**, as shown in the following output:

```
[root@server1 ~]# lpstat -t
scheduler is running
system default destination: printer1
device for printer1: parallel: /dev/lp0
printer1 accepting requests since Thu 26 Aug 2019 08:34:30 AM EDT
printer printer1 is idle. enabled since Thu 26 Aug 2019 08:42:23 AM EDT
[root@server1 ~]# _
```

This output indicates the system has only one printer, called *printer1*, that it prints to a printer connected to the first parallel port on the computer (`parallel:/dev/lp0`), and that no print jobs are in its print queue. In addition, the CUPS daemon (`scheduler`) is running and accepting jobs into the print queue for this printer. The CUPS daemon sends print jobs from the print queue to the printer because the printer is enabled.

You can manipulate the status of a printer using the `cupsaccept`, `cupsreject`, `cupsenable`, or `cupsdisable` **command** followed by the printer name. To enable spooling and disable printing for the printer *printer1*, you can use the following commands:

```
[root@server1 ~]# cupsaccept printer1
[root@server1 ~]# cupsdisable printer1
[root@server1 ~]# lpstat -t
scheduler is running
system default destination: printer1
device for printer1: parallel: /dev/lp0
printer1 accepting requests since Thu 26 Aug 2019 08:51:21 AM EDT
printer printer1 disabled since Thu 26 Aug 2019 08:51:21 AM EDT -
        Paused
[root@server1 ~]# _
```

Any print jobs now sent to the printer *printer1* are sent to the print queue but remain in the print queue until the printer is started again.

You can also use the −r option to the `cupsdisable` and `cupsreject` commands to specify a reason for the action, as shown in the following output:

```
[root@server1 ~]# cupsdisable -r "Changing toner cartridge"
printer1
[root@server1 ~]# lpstat -t
scheduler is running
```

```
system default destination: printer1
device for printer1: parallel:/dev/lp0
printer1 accepting requests since Thu 26 Aug 2015 08:51:21 AM EDT
printer printer1 disabled since Thu 26 Aug 2015 08:51:21 AM EDT -
        Changing toner cartridge
[root@server1 ~]# _
```

Managing Print Jobs

Recall that you create a print job by using the lp command. To print a copy of the /etc/inittab file to the printer *printer1* shown in earlier examples, you can use the following command, which returns a print job ID that you can use to manipulate the print job afterward:

```
[root@server1 ~]# lp -d printer1 /etc/inittab
request id is printer1-1 (1 file(s))
[root@server1 ~]# _
```

The lp command uses the -d option to specify the destination printer name. If you omit this option, the lp command assumes the default printer on the system. Because *printer1* is the only printer on the system making it the default printer, the command lp /etc/inittab is equivalent to the one used in the preceding output.

Note 📎

You can set the default printer for all users on your system by using the lpoptions -d printername command, where printername is the name of the default printer. This information is stored in the /etc/cups/lpoptions file.

You can specify your own default printer by adding the line default printername to the .lpoptions file in your home directory, where printername is the name of the default printer. Alternatively, you can use the PRINTER or LPDEST variables to set the default printer. For example, to specify *printer2* as the default printer, you can add either the line export PRINTER=printer2 or the line export LPDEST=printer2 to an environment file in your home directory, such as .bash_profile.

Table 10-1 lists some common options to the lp command.

Table 10-1   Common options to the **lp** command

Option	Description
-d printer name	Specifies the name of the destination printer
-i print job ID	Specifies a certain print job ID to modify
-n number	Prints a certain *number* of copies
-m	Mails you confirmation of print job completion
-o option	Specifies certain printing options; common printing options include the following: cpi=*number*—Sets the characters per inch to *number* landscape—Prints in landscape orientation number-up=*number*—Prints *number* pages on a single page, where *number* is 1, 2, or 4 sides=*string*—Sets double-sided printing, where *string* is either "two-sided-short-edge" or "two-sided-long-edge"
-q priority	Specifies a print job priority from 1 (low priority) to 100 (high priority); by default, all print jobs have a priority of 50

You can also specify several files to print using a single lp command by including the files as arguments. In this case, the system creates only one print job to print all of the files. To print the files /etc/hosts and /etc/issue to the printer *printer1*, you can execute the following command:

```
[root@server1 ~]# lp -d printer1 /etc/hosts /etc/issue
request id is printer1-2 (2 file(s))
[root@server1 ~]# _
```

The lp command accepts information from Standard Input, so you can place the lp command at the end of a pipe to print information. To print a list of logged-in users, you can use the following pipe:

```
[root@server1 ~]# who | lp -d printer1
request id is printer1-3 (1 file(s))
[root@server1 ~]# _
```

To see a list of print jobs in the queue for *printer1*, you can use the `lpstat` command. Without arguments, this command displays all jobs in the print queue that you have printed:

```
[root@server1 ~]# lpstat
printer1-1          root        2048    Thu 26 Aug 2019 08:54:18 AM EDT
printer1-2          root        3072    Thu 26 Aug 2019 08:54:33 AM EDT
printer1-3          root        1024    Thu 26 Aug 2019 08:54:49 AM EDT
[root@server1 ~]# _
```

Table 10-2 lists other options that you can use with the `lpstat` command.

Table 10-2 Common options to the `lpstat` command

Option	Description
-a	Displays a list of printers that are accepting print jobs
-d	Displays the default destination printer
-o printername	Displays the print jobs in the print queue for `printername` only
-p	Displays a list of printers that are enabled
-r	Shows whether the CUPS daemon (scheduler) is running
-s	Shows printer and printer status information
-t	Shows all information about printers and their print jobs

To remove a print job from the print queue, you can use the `cancel` command followed by the IDs of the print jobs to remove. To remove the print job IDs printer1-1 and printer1-2 created earlier, you can use the following command:

```
[root@server1 ~]# cancel printer1-1 printer1-2
[root@server1 ~]# lpstat
printer1-3          root        3072    Thu 26 Aug 2015 08:54:49 AM EDT
[root@server1 ~]# _
```

You can also remove all jobs started by a certain user by specifying the –u option to the `cancel` command followed by the user name. To remove all jobs in a print queue, you can use the –a option to the `cancel` command, as shown in the following example, which removes all jobs destined for printer1:

```
[root@server1 ~]# cancel -a printer1
[root@server1 ~]# lpstat
[root@server1 ~]# _
```

Not all users might be allowed access to a certain printer. As a result, you can restrict access to certain printers by using the `lpadmin` command. For example, to deny all users other than root and user1 from printing to the *printer1* printer created earlier, you can use the following command:

```
[root@server1 ~]# lpadmin -u allow:root,user1 -u deny:all -d
printer1
[root@server1 ~]# _
```

The LPD Printing System

Although CUPS is the preferred printing system for Linux computers today, many legacy Linux systems use the traditional **Line Printer Daemon (LPD)** printing system. In this printing system, you use the `lpr` **command** to print documents to the print queue much like the `lp` command. You can use the `lpc` **command** to view the status of printers, the `lpq` **command** to view print jobs in the print queue, much like the `lpstat` command, and the `lprm` **command** to remove print jobs, much like the `cancel` command.

For those who are accustomed to using the LPD printing system, CUPS contains versions of the `lpr`, `lpc`, `lpq`, and `lprm` commands. The following output displays the status of all printers on the system, prints two copies of /etc/inittab to *printer1*, views the print job in the queue, and removes the print job:

```
[root@server1 ~]# lpc status
printer1:
      printing is enabled
      queuing is enabled
      no entries
      daemon present
[root@server1 ~]# lpr -#2 -P printer1 /etc/inittab
[root@server1 ~]# lpq
printer1 is ready and printing
Rank     Owner    Job     File(s)              Total Size
1st      root     1       inittab              2048 bytes
[root@server1 ~]# lprm 1
[root@server1 ~]# lpq
printer1 is ready
no entries
[root@server1 ~]# _
```

Configuring Printers

Recall that the core component of printing is the CUPS daemon, which accepts print jobs into a queue and sends them to the printer. The file that contains settings for the CUPS daemon is /etc/cups/cupsd.conf, and the file that contains the configuration information for each printer installed on the system is /etc/cups/printers.conf. By default, the CUPS daemon detects locally connected and network-shared printers and automatically adds an entry for them in the /etc/cups/printers.conf file using a name based on the printer model number (e.g., HP Laserjet 6M). For any printers that the CUPS daemon does not detect and configure, you must provide the necessary information.

Because the format of the /etc/cups/printers.conf file is rigid, it is safer to use a program to create or modify its entries. You can provide a series of options to the lpadmin command discussed earlier to configure a printer on the system, or you can use one of several graphical utilities within a desktop environment that can do the same. On Fedora Linux, you can use the **Printers tool** within the GNOME desktop (shown in Figure 10-2) to create new printers, print a test page, view print jobs, control spooling, and specify basic printing options. You can access the Printers tool within the GNOME desktop environment on Fedora 28 by navigating to the Activities menu, Show Applications, Settings, Devices, Printers.

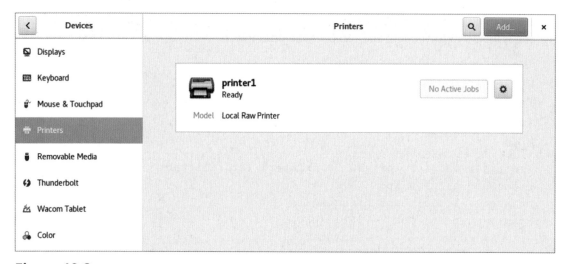

Figure 10-2   The Printers tool

To manually add a printer using the Printers tool, you can click the Unlock button in the upper-right corner and supply your account password, and then click the Add button that appears in its place, as shown in Figure 10-2. The Printers tool prompts you to select your device from a list of detected printers, or specify the name or IP address of a printer on the network.

> **Note**
>
> The Printers tool provides for a quick and easy method of configuring and managing printers on a system. It does not allow you to specify detailed printer configuration when adding a printer.

The most comprehensive way to create and manage CUPS printers is by using the **CUPS Web administration tool**, which allows Linux administrators to create and manage all printer settings. You can access the CUPS Web administration tool using a Web browser on TCP port 631 by navigating to *http://servername:631*, as shown in Figure 10-3.

CUPS.org   Home   Administration   Classes   Help   Jobs   Printers

CUPS 2.2.6

CUPS is the standards-based, open source printing system developed by Apple Inc. for macOS® and other UNIX®-like operating systems.

CUPS for Users	**CUPS for Administrators**	**CUPS for Developers**
Overview of CUPS	Adding Printers and Classes	Introduction to CUPS Programming
Command-Line Printing and Options	Managing Operation Policies	CUPS API
User Forum	Using Network Printers	Filter and Backend Programming
	cupsd.conf Reference	HTTP and IPP APIs
		Developer Forum

Figure 10-3   The CUPS Web administration tool

To create a new printer using this tool, select the Administration tab, click Add Printer, and log in using the root user name and password. You are then prompted to choose the type of printer, as shown in Figure 10-4. You can choose to print to a printer connected to a local serial, parallel, or USB port, to a printer connected to the network using Hewlett-Packard JetDirect technology, or to a printer that is shared on a remote computer across a network with the **Internet Printing Protocol (IPP)**, the Line Printer Daemon (LPD), or the Windows (SAMBA) printing service.

CUPS.org Home Administration Classes Help Jobs Printers

Add Printer

Add Printer

Local Printers: ○ HP Printer (HPLIP)
○ HP Fax (HPLIP)

Discovered Network Printers:

Other Network Printers: ○ Internet Printing Protocol (http)
○ Internet Printing Protocol (https)
○ Backend Error Handler
○ LPD/LPR Host or Printer
○ Internet Printing Protocol (ipps)
○ AppSocket/HP JetDirect
○ Internet Printing Protocol (ipp)
○ Windows Printer via SAMBA

[Continue]

Figure 10-4   Selecting the printer type for a new printer

Note

The local HP Printer selections shown in Figure 10-4 can be used to configure other brands of locally connected printers as well.

After selecting a printer type, you specify information related to the printer type (e.g., the network address for a network printer), as well as a printer name, description, manufacturer and model, default printer options, and whether to share the printer using IPP to other systems on the network.

After creating a printer, you can use the other options available on the Administration tab of the CUPS Web administration tool to configure and manage the CUPS printing service, as shown in Figure 10-5.

The Find New Printers button shown in Figure 10-5 performs a detailed local and network search for new printer devices. The Manage Printers button (which switches to the Printers tab) allows you to configure individual printer settings.

CUPS also allows you to configure collections of printers to use as a single unit. These collections are called **printer classes**. When you print to a printer class, the print job is sent to the first available printer in the printer class. Printer classes are often

Figure 10-5 CUPS administration options

used in larger organizations, where multiple printers are stored in a print room. To create a printer class, select the Add Class button shown in Figure 10-5, supply a name and description for the new class, and then choose the printers to include in the class. Next, you can click the Manage Classes button (which switches to the Classes tab) to configure settings for your new printer class.

Clicking Manage Jobs shown in Figure 10-5 (which switches to the Jobs tab) allows you to view, modify, and delete print jobs in the queue. Regular users can also access the CUPS Web administration tool and select the Jobs tab to manage their own jobs after logging in with their user name and password.

The Server section shown in Figure 10-5 allows you to edit the CUPS configuration file, access log files, and perform advanced functions. Select the Allow remote administration option to access the CUPS Web administration tool from other computers on the network. By selecting the Share printers connected to this system and Allow printing from the Internet options, IPP printer sharing will be enabled for all printers that allow IPP printer sharing in their settings. To configure a shared printer on a remote system using IPP, you can specify the URL *http://servername:631/ printers/printername* when adding the printer.

Note 🖉

To allow for IPP printer sharing, any firewalls must allow TCP ports 80, 443, and 631. Firewall configuration is discussed in Chapter 14.

Log File Administration

To identify and troubleshoot problems on a Linux system, you must view the events that occur over time. Because administrators cannot observe all events that take place on a Linux system, most daemons record information and error messages to files stored on the filesystem. These files are referred to as **log files** and are typically stored in the /var/log directory.

Many programs store their log files in subdirectories of the /var/log directory. For example, the /var/log/samba directory contains the log files created by the samba file-sharing daemons. Table 10-3 lists some common log files that you may find in the /var/log directory, depending on your Linux distribution.

Table 10-3 Common Linux log files found in /var/log

Log file	Description
auth.log	Contains a history of all authentication requests on the system by users and daemons
btmp	Contains a history of failed login sessions; must be viewed using the `lastb` command
boot.log	Contains basic information regarding daemon startup obtained during system initialization
cron	Contains information and error messages generated by the cron and at daemons
dmesg	Contains detected hardware information obtained during system startup
kern.log	Contains information and error messages generated by the kernel
mail.log	Contains information and error messages generated by the sendmail or postfix daemon
secure	Contains information and error messages regarding network access generated by daemons such as sshd and xinetd
wtmp	Contains a history of all login sessions; must be viewed using the `last` or `who` commands
rpmpkgs yum.log dnf.rpm.log	Contains messages for actions taken and packages installed by the Red Hat Package Manager
dpkg.log	Contains messages for actions taken and packages installed by the Debian Package Manager
xferlog	Contains information and error messages generated by the FTP daemon

Table 10-3   Common Linux log files found in **/var/log** (*continued*)

Log file	Description
Xorg.0.log	Contains information and error messages generated by X Windows
lastlog	Contains a list of users and their last login time; must be viewed using the `lastlog` command
messages syslog	Contains detailed information regarding daemon startup obtained at system initialization as well as important system messages produced after system initialization

Daemons that provide a service to other computers on the network typically manage their own log files within the /var/log directory. The logging for other daemons and operating system components is performed by a logging daemon. The two most common logging daemons used on Linux systems today are the **System Log Daemon (rsyslogd)** and the **Systemd Journal Daemon (journald)**.

Note 📎

Many third-party software suites can monitor different systems on the network; these software suites provide a small program that is installed on each Linux server (called an *agent*) that collects the events logged by rsyslogd or journald, and sends them to a central monitoring server on the network.

Working with the System Log Daemon

The System Log Daemon (rsyslogd) is the traditional and most common logging daemon used on Linux systems. When this daemon is loaded upon system startup, it creates a socket (/dev/log) for other system processes to write to. It then reads any information written to this socket and saves the information in the appropriate log file according to entries in the /etc/rsyslog.conf file and any files within the /etc/rsyslog.d directory. A sample /etc/rsyslog.conf file is shown in the following output:

```
[root@server1 ~]# cat /etc/rsyslog.conf
#### MODULES ####
$ModLoad imuxsock.so   # provides support for local system logging
(e.g. via logger command)
$ModLoad imklog.so   # provides kernel logging support (previously
done by rklogd)
#$ModLoad immark.so   # provides --MARK-- message capability
```

```
# Provides UDP syslog reception
#$ModLoad imudp
#$UDPServerRun 514

# Provides TCP syslog reception
#$ModLoad imtcp
#$InputTCPServerRun 514


#### RULES ####
# Log all kernel messages to the console.
# Logging much else clutters up the screen.
#kern.*                                  /dev/console

# Log anything (except mail) of level info or higher.
# Don't log private authentication messages!
*.info;mail.none;news.none;authpriv.none;cron.none  /var/log/messages

# The authpriv file has restricted access.
authpriv.*                              /var/log/secure

# Log all the mail messages in one place.
mail.*                                  -/var/log/maillog

# Log cron stuff
cron.*                                  /var/log/cron

# Everybody gets emergency messages
*.emerg                                     *

# Save news errors of level crit and higher in a special file.
uucp,news.crit                          /var/log/spooler

# Save boot messages also to boot.log
local7.*                                /var/log/boot.log

# INN
news.=crit                              /var/log/news/news.crit
news.=err                               /var/log/news/news.err
news.notice                             /var/log/news/news.notice
news.=debug                             /var/log/news/news.debug
[root@server1 ~]# _
```

> **Note** 🖉
>
> On legacy Linux systems, the System Log Daemon is represented by syslogd and configured using the /etc/syslog.conf file.

Lines in the /etc/rsyslog.conf file or in files within the /etc/rsyslog.d directory that start with a # character are comments. All other entries have the following format:

```
facility.priority     /var/log/logfile
```

The **facility** is the area of the system to listen to, whereas the **priority** refers to the importance of the information. For example, a facility of kern and priority of warning indicates that the System Log Daemon should listen for kernel messages of priority warning and more serious. When found, the System Log Daemon places these messages in the /var/log/logfile file. This entry would read as follows:

```
kern.warning     /var/log/logfile
```

To only log warning messages from the kernel to /var/log/logfile, you can use the following entry instead:

```
kern.=warning     /var/log/logfile
```

Alternatively, you can log all error messages from the kernel to /var/log/logfile by using the * wildcard, as shown in the following entry:

```
kern.*     /var/log/logfile
```

In addition, you can specify multiple facilities and priorities. To log all error messages except warnings from the kernel to /var/log/logfile, you can use the following entry:

```
kern.*;kern.!=warn     /var/log/logfile
```

To log all error messages from the kernel and news daemons, you can use the following entry:

```
kern,news.*     /var/log/logfile
```

To log all warnings from all facilities except for the kernel, you can use the "none" keyword, as shown in following entry:

```
*.=warn;kern.none     /var/log/logfile
```

You can also prefix the pathname to the log file in any entry to ensure that the system synchronizes changes to the disk immediately after a new event occurs, as shown in the following entry:

```
*.=warn;kern.none     -/var/log/logfile
```

Table 10-4 describes the different facilities available and their descriptions.

Table 10-4 Facilities used by the System Log Daemon

Facility	Description
auth or security	Specifies messages from the login system, such as the login program, the getty program, and the su command
authpriv	Specifies messages from the login system when authenticating users across the network or to system databases
cron	Specifies messages from the cron and at daemons
daemon	Specifies messages from system daemons such as the FTP daemon
kern	Specifies messages from the Linux kernel
lpr	Specifies messages from the printing system (lpd)
mail	Specifies messages from the email system (sendmail)
mark	Specifies time stamps used by syslogd; used internally only
news	Specifies messages from the Inter Network News daemon and other USENET daemons
syslog	Specifies messages from the syslog daemon
user	Specifies messages from user processes
uucp	Specifies messages from the uucp (UNIX to UNIX copy) daemon
local0-7	Specifies local messages; these are not used by default but can be defined for custom use

Table 10-5 displays the different priorities available listed in ascending order.

Table 10-5 Priorities used by the System Log Daemon

Priority	Description
debug	Indicates all information from a certain facility
info	Indicates normal information messages as a result of system operations
notice	Indicates information that should be noted for future reference, yet does not indicate a problem
warning or warn	Indicates messages that might be the result of an error but are not critical to system operations

Table 10-5   **Priorities used by the System Log Daemon** *(continued)*

Priority	Description
error or err	Indicates all other error messages not described by other priorities
crit	Indicates system critical errors such as hard disk failure
alert	Indicates an error that should be rectified immediately, such as a corrupt system database
emerg or panic	Indicates very serious system conditions that would normally be broadcast to all users

The /etc/rsyslog.conf file may also send logging information to another computer using the format `facility.priority @hostname:portnumber`; however the remote computer must have the modules that listen on either the TCP or UDP protocol uncommented in the /etc/rsyslog.conf file. For example, by uncommenting the same lines shown next in the /etc/rsyslog.conf file, you allow your system to accept incoming requests from another System Log Daemon on TCP and UDP port 514 (the default System Log Daemon port):

```
# Provides UDP syslog reception
$ModLoad imudp
$UDPServerRun 514

# Provides TCP syslog reception
$ModLoad imtcp
$InputTCPServerRun 514
```

Working with the Systemd Journal Daemon

The Systemd Journal Daemon (journald) replaces the System Log Daemon on Linux distributions that use Systemd. As with the System Log Daemon, journald creates a socket (/dev/log) for other system processes to write to and reads any information that is written to this socket. However, the events logged are not controlled by specific rules. Instead, journald logs all information to a database under the /var/log/journal directory structure, and events are tagged with labels that identify the same facility and priority information that you examined earlier with the rsyslogd daemon.

Note

You can configure daemon settings for journald by editing its configuration file /etc/systemd/journald.conf. For example, to configure journald to forward all events to the System Log Daemon, you could uncomment and configure the ForwardToSyslog=yes line within /etc/systemd/journald.conf and restart journald.

To view events within the journald database, you can use the same `journalctl` command introduced in Chapter 6 to view boot-related messages. If you type `journalctl` at a command prompt and press the Tab key, you will see a multipage list of areas and criteria that can be queried, as shown in the following sample excerpt:

```
_AUDIT_ID=                   PROBLEM_UUID=
_AUDIT_LOGINUID=             PULSE_BACKTRACE=
_AUDIT_SESSION=              QT_CATEGORY=
_AUDIT_TYPE=                 REALMD_OPERATION=
AVAILABLE=                   SEAT_ID=
AVAILABLE_PRETTY=            _SELINUX_CONTEXT=
BOLT_LOG_CONTEXT=            SESSION_ID=
BOLT_TOPIC=                  _SOURCE_MONOTONIC_TIMESTAMP=
BOLT_VERSION=                _SOURCE_REALTIME_TIMESTAMP=
_BOOT_ID=                    _STREAM_ID=
_CAP_EFFECTIVE=              SYSLOG_FACILITY=
_CMDLINE=                    SYSLOG_IDENTIFIER=
CODE_FILE=                   SYSLOG_PID=
CODE_FUNC=                   _SYSTEMD_CGROUP=
CODE_LINE=                   _SYSTEMD_INVOCATION_ID=
_COMM=                       _SYSTEMD_OWNER_UID=
--More--
```

Say, for example, that you want to search for information in the logs from a particular command on the system. You can type `journalctl _COMM=` and press the Tab key to see a multipage list of the available commands that perform logging via journald on the system, as shown in the following sample excerpt:

```
akonadi_maildir   gdm-x-session     korgac            sshd
akonadi_mailfil   gnome-clocks      kscreen_backend   start-pulseaudi
akonadi_migrati   gnome-contacts-   ksmserver         su
akonadi_newmail   gnome-control-c   ksmserver-logou   sudo
akonadiserver     gnome-documents   kwin_x11          (systemd)
alsactl           gnome-initial-s   logger            systemd
```

anacron	gnome-keyring-d	login	systemd-coredum
atd	gnome-session-b	lvm	systemd-fsck
at-spi2-registr	gnome-session-f	mcelog	systemd-hiberna
at-spi-bus-laun	gnome-shell	ModemManager	systemd-hostnam
audispd	gnome-shell-cal	mount	systemd-journal
auditd	gnome-software	mtp-probe	systemd-logind
augenrules	gnome-terminal-	netconsole	systemd-tty-ask
avahi-daemon	gnome-welcome-t	NetworkManager	systemd-udevd
backlighthelper	goa-daemon	nm-dispatcher	systemd-vconsol
baloo_file	goa-identity-se	obexd	tracker-extract
bash	groupadd	org_kde_powerde	tracker-miner-a
boltd	gsd-color	packagekitd	tracker-miner-f
bootscript.sh	gsd-media-keys	passwd	tracker-store
canberra-gtk-pl	gsd-print-notif	PK-Backend	udisksd
chronyd	gsd-rfkill	plasmashell	umount
colord	gsd-sharing	plymouthd	unbound-anchor
crond	gsd-smartcard	polkitd	unix_chkpwd

```
--More--
```

To see the logs from the cron daemon (crond), you can run the command `journalctl _COMM=crond | less` because the output will likely have many lines. However, when troubleshooting an issue regarding the cron daemon, it is more useful to narrow the time period. The following command displays crond log entries from 1:00 pm (13:00) until 2:00 pm (14:00) from the current day:

```
[root@server1 ~]# journalctl _COMM=crond --since "13:00" --until
"14:00"
-- Logs begin at Tue 2019-09-16 21:56:29 EDT, end at Tue 2019-10-
14 20:43:32 EDT
Oct 14 13:50:58 server1 crond[457]: (CRON) INFO (RANDOM_DELAY will
be scaled with factor 30% if used.)
Oct 14 13:50:59 server1 crond[457]: (CRON) INFO (running with
inotify support)
[root@server1 ~]# _
```

The time format used within the `journalctl` command follows the standard YYYY-MM-DD HH-MM-SS. Thus, to obtain crond events since 5:30 pm (17:30) on August 22, 2019, you could instead run the `journalctl _COMM=crond --since "2019-08-22 17:30:00"` command.

You can also query events related to a specific process or daemon if you specify the path name to the executable file or PID. For example, because the Systemd init daemon has a path of /usr/lib/systemd/systemd and a PID of 1, you could run the `journalctl /usr/lib/systemd/systemd` command or the `journalctl _PID=1` command to view events related to the Systemd init daemon.

> **Note** 📎
>
> You can use the `systemd-cat` **command** or `logger` **command** to add custom log file entries to the journald database; for example, you could use the `echo "Backup of $DIR completed successfully at `date`" | systemd-cat` command or the `logger "Backup of $DIR completed successfully at `date`"` command within a shell script to log a message to the journald database indicating that a backup of a directory within the $DIR variable was completed at a particular time. The `logger` command can also be used to add custom log file entries on a system that uses the System Log Daemon; simply specify the `-p facility.priority` option alongside the `logger` command to control how the events are logged.

Managing Log Files and the journald Database

Although log files and the journald database contain important system information, they might take up unnecessary space on the filesystem over time because journald is configured to use persistent storage by default. However, you can uncomment and configure the line Storage=volatile within /etc/systemd/journald.conf to ensure that events are only stored in memory and not on the filesystem. Alternatively, you could limit the amount of space on the filesystem that journald will use to store events by uncommenting and configuring the SystemMaxUse line in /etc/systemd/journald. conf. For example, SystemMaxUse=75M would limit the database to 75MB, and the oldest events would be deleted as new events are logged. To prevent key older events from being overwritten, you can create a shell script that executes the appropriate `journalctl` commands and either prints the results or saves them to a text file. You can then configure the cron daemon to execute this shell script periodically, as discussed in Chapter 9.

For log files within the /var/log directory, you can periodically clear their contents to reclaim space on the filesystem.

> **Note** 📎
>
> Do not remove log files, because the permissions and ownership will be removed as well.
>
> Before clearing important log files, it is good form to save them to a different location or print their contents for future reference.

To clear a log file, recall that you can use a > redirection symbol. The following commands display the size of the /var/log/boot.log file before and after it has been printed and cleared:

```
[root@server1 ~]# ls -l /var/log/boot.log
-rw-------   1 root      root       21705 Aug 27 10:52 /var/log/
boot.log
[root@server1 ~]# lp -d printer1 /var/log/boot.log
[root@server1 ~]# >/var/log/boot.log
[root@server1 ~]# ls -l /var/log/boot.log
-rw-------   1 root      root           0 Aug 27 10:52 /var/log/
boot.log
[root@server1 ~]# _
```

Alternatively, you can schedule the `logrotate` command to back up and clear log files from entries stored in the /etc/logrotate.conf file and files stored in the /etc/logrotate.d directory. The `logrotate` command typically renames (or rotates) log files on a cyclic basis; the log file will be renamed to contain a numeric or date extension, and a new log file will be created to accept system information. You can specify the type of extension as well as the number of log files that are kept. If configured to keep only two copies of old log files, then after two log rotations, the oldest log file will automatically be removed.

An example of the /etc/logrotate.conf file is shown in the following output:

```
[root@server1 ~]# cat /etc/logrotate.conf
# see "man logrotate" for details
# rotate log files weekly
weekly

# keep 4 weeks worth of backlogs
rotate 4

# create new (empty) log files after rotating old ones
create

# use date as a suffix of the rotated file
dateext

# uncomment this if you want your log files compressed
#compress

# RPM packages drop log rotation information into this directory
include /etc/logrotate.d
```

```
# no packages own wtmp and btmp -- we'll rotate them here
/var/log/wtmp {
    monthly
    create 0664 root utmp
    minsize 1M
    rotate 1
}

/var/log/btmp {
    missingok
    monthly
    create 0600 root utmp
    rotate 1
}

[root@server1 ~]# _
```

In the preceding output, any # characters indicate a comment and are ignored. The other lines indicate that log files contained in this file and all other files in the /etc/logrotate.d directory (include /etc/logrotate.d) are rotated on a weekly basis unless otherwise specified (weekly) using a date extension (dateext), and up to 4 weeks of log files will be kept (rotate 4).

The bottom of the /etc/logrotate.conf file has two entries that override these values. For the file /var/log/wtmp, this rotation occurs monthly instead of weekly, only if the size of the log file is greater than 1MB. Only one old log file is kept, and the new log file created has the permissions 0664(rw-rw-r--), the owner root, and the group utmp. For the file /var/log/btmp, this rotation occurs monthly instead of weekly, and no errors are reported if the log file is missing. Only one old log file is kept, and the new log file created has the permissions 0600 (rw------), the owner root, and the group utmp.

Most rotation information within /etc/logrotate.conf is overridden from files stored in the /etc/logrotate.d directory. Take the file /etc/logrotate.d/psacct as an example:

```
[root@server1 ~]# cat /etc/logrotate.d/psacct
# Logrotate file for psacct RPM

/var/account/pacct {
    compress
    delaycompress
    notifempty
    daily
    rotate 31
    create 0600 root root
    postrotate
        if /usr/bin/systemctl --quiet is-active psacct.service ; then
```

```
            /usr/sbin/accton /var/account/pacct
      fi
   endscript
}
[root@server1 ~]# _
```

This file indicates that the /var/account/pacct file should be rotated daily if it is not empty, and that new log files will be owned by the `root` user/group and have the permissions `0600` (rw-------). Up to 31 old log files will be kept and compressed, but only on the next rotation (`delaycompress`). In addition, the `/usr/sbin/ accton /var/account/pacct` command is run after each rotation if the `/usr/bin/ systemctl --quiet is-active psacct.service` command returns true.

On most Linux systems, the `logrotate` command is automatically scheduled to run daily via the file /etc/cron.daily/logrotate; however, you might choose to run it manually by typing `logrotate /etc/logrotate.conf` at a command prompt.

Over time, the `logrotate` command generates several copies of each log file, as shown in the following listing of the /var/log directory:

```
[root@server1 ~]# ls /var/log
anaconda                  dnf.rpm.log-20190826    messages-20190918
audit                     dnf.rpm.log-20190911    pluto
blivet-gui                dnf.rpm.log-20190918    ppp
boot.log                  firewalld               README
btmp                      gdm                     sa
btmp-20190911             glusterfs               samba
chrony                    hawkey.log              secure
cron                      hawkey.log-20190819     secure-20190819
cron-20190819             hawkey.log-20190826     secure-20190826
cron-20190826             hawkey.log-20190911     secure-20190911
cron-20190911             hawkey.log-20190918     secure-20190918
cron-20190918             httpd                   speech-dispatcher
cups                      journal                 spooler
dnf.librepo.log           lastlog                 spooler-20190819
dnf.librepo.log-20190819  libvirt                 spooler-20190826
dnf.librepo.log-20190826  maillog                 spooler-20190911
dnf.librepo.log-20190911  maillog-20190819        spooler-20190918
dnf.librepo.log-20190918  maillog-20190826        sssd
dnf.log                   maillog-20190911        tallylog
dnf.log-20190819          maillog-20190918        vbox
dnf.log-20190826          mariadb                 vmware-vmusr.log
dnf.log-20190911          messages                wtmp
dnf.log-20190918          messages-20190819       Xorg.0.log
dnf.rpm.log               messages-20190826       Xorg.1.log
dnf.rpm.log-20190819      messages-20190911
[root@server1 ~]# _
```

Given the preceding output, the most recent events for the cron daemon are recorded in the cron file, followed by the cron-20190819 file, followed by the cron-20190826 file, the cron-20190911 file, and the cron-20190918 file.

Administering Users and Groups

You must log in to a Linux system with a valid user name and password before a BASH shell is granted. This process is called **authentication** because the user name and password are authenticated against a system database that contains all **user account** information. Authenticated users are then granted access to files, directories, and other resources on the system based on their user account.

The system database that contains user account information typically consists of two files: /etc/passwd and /etc/shadow. Every user typically has a line that describes the user account in /etc/passwd and a line that contains the encrypted password and expiration information in /etc/shadow.

Legacy Linux systems stored the encrypted password in the /etc/passwd file and did not use an /etc/shadow file at all. This is considered poor security today because processes often require access to the user information in /etc/passwd. Storing the encrypted password in a separate file that cannot be accessed by processes prevents a process from obtaining all user account information. By default, Linux configures passwords using an /etc/shadow file. However, you can use the `pwunconv` command to revert to using an /etc/passwd file only, or the `pwconv` command to configure the system again using an /etc/shadow file for password storage.

Each line of the /etc/passwd file has the following colon-delimited format:

```
name:password:UID:GID:GECOS:homedirectory:shell
```

The name in the preceding output refers to the name of the user. If an /etc/shadow is not used, the password field contains the encrypted password for the user; otherwise, it just contains an x character as a placeholder for the password stored in /etc/shadow.

The **User Identifier (UID)** specifies the unique User ID that is assigned to each user. Typically, UIDs that are less than 1000 refer to user accounts that are used by daemons when logging in to the system. The root user always has a UID of zero.

The **Group Identifier (GID)** is the primary Group ID for the user. Each user can be a member of several groups, but only one of those groups can be the primary group. The **primary group** of a user is the group that is made the group owner of any file or directory that the user creates. Similarly, when a user creates a file or directory, that user becomes the owner of that file or directory.

GECOS represents an optional text description of the user; this information was originally used in the **General Electric Comprehensive Operating System (GECOS)**. The last two fields represent the absolute pathname to the user's home directory and the shell, respectively.

An example of an **/etc/passwd** file is shown next:

```
[root@server1 ~]# cat /etc/passwd
root:x:0:0:root:/root:/bin/bash
bin:x:1:1:bin:/bin:/sbin/nologin
daemon:x:2:2:daemon:/sbin:/sbin/nologin
adm:x:3:4:adm:/var/adm:/sbin/nologin
lp:x:4:7:lp:/var/spool/lpd:/sbin/nologin
sync:x:5:0:sync:/sbin:/bin/sync
shutdown:x:6:0:shutdown:/sbin:/sbin/shutdown
halt:x:7:0:halt:/sbin:/sbin/halt
mail:x:8:12:mail:/var/spool/mail:/sbin/nologin
operator:x:11:0:operator:/root:/sbin/nologin
games:x:12:100:games:/usr/games:/sbin/nologin
ftp:x:14:50:FTP User:/var/ftp:/sbin/nologin
nobody:x:65534:65534:Kernel Overflow User:/:/sbin/nologin
apache:x:48:48:Apache:/usr/share/httpd:/sbin/nologin
dbus:x:81:81:System message bus:/:/sbin/nologin
pulse:x:171:171:PulseAudio System Daemon:/var/run/pulse:/sbin/nologin
chrony:x:994:988::/var/lib/chrony:/sbin/nologin
dnsmasq:x:987:987:Dnsmasq DHCP and DNS server:/var/lib/dnsmasq:/
sbin/nologin
rpc:x:32:32:Rpcbind Daemon:/var/lib/rpcbind:/sbin/nologin
usbmuxd:x:113:113:usbmuxd user:/:/sbin/nologin
openvpn:x:986:986:OpenVPN:/etc/openvpn:/sbin/nologin
radvd:x:75:75:radvd user:/:/sbin/nologin
saslauth:x:985:76:Saslauthd user:/run/saslauthd:/sbin/nologin
abrt:x:173:173::/etc/abrt:/sbin/nologin
pipewire:x:982:980:PipeWire System
Daemon:/var/run/pipewire:/sbin/nologin
gdm:x:42:42::/var/lib/gdm:/sbin/nologin
rpcuser:x:29:29:RPC Service User:/var/lib/nfs:/sbin/nologin
user1:x:1000:1000:Jason Eckert:/home/user1:/bin/bash
[root@server1 ~]# _
```

The root user is usually listed at the top of the /etc/passwd file, as just shown, followed by user accounts used by daemons when logging in to the system, followed by regular user accounts. The final line of the preceding output indicates that the user user1 has a UID of 1000, a primary GID of 1000, a GECOS of "Jason Eckert" the home directory /home/user1, and uses the BASH shell.

Like /etc/passwd, the /etc/shadow file is colon-delimited yet has the following format:

```
name:password:lastchange:min:max:warn:disable1:disable2:
```

Although the first two fields in the /etc/shadow file are the same as those in /etc/passwd, the contents of the password field are different. The password field in the /etc/shadow file contains the encrypted password, whereas the password field in /etc/passwd contains an x character, because it is not used.

The lastchange field represents the date of the most recent password change; it is measured in the number of days since January 1, 1970. For example, the number 10957 represents January 1, 2000, because January 1, 2000 is 10957 days after January 1, 1970.

> **Note** 🖉
>
> Traditionally, a calendar date was represented by a number indicating the number of days since January 1, 1970. Many calendar dates found in configuration files follow the same convention.

To prevent unauthorized access to a Linux system, it is good form to change passwords for user accounts regularly. To ensure that passwords are changed, you can set them to expire at certain intervals. The next three fields of the /etc/shadow file indicate information about password expiration: min represents the number of days a user must wait before he changes his password after receiving a new one, max represents the number of days a user can use the same password without changing it, and warn represents the number of days a user is warned to change his password before it expires.

By default on most Linux systems, min is equal to zero days, max is equal to 99999 days, and warn is equal to seven days. This means you can change your password immediately after receiving a new one, your password expires in 99999 days, and you are warned seven days before your password needs to be changed.

When a password has expired, the user is still allowed to log in to the system for a certain period of time, after which point the user is disabled from logging in. The number of days a user account is disabled after a password expires is represented by the disable1 field in /etc/shadow. In addition, you can choose to disable a user from logging in at a certain date, such as the end of an employment contract. The disable2 field in /etc/shadow represents the number of days since January 1, 1970 that a user account will be disabled.

An example /etc/shadow file is shown next:

```
[root@server1 ~]# cat /etc/shadow
root:$6$PpnHJ3rl/6OouP9G$cKhZbi96b9UxfkHOt4ahHvrW9V73vg9BLqiEHKFOfcIAvktJ.
fP2V9RoFkxgz6tcW9LlEspV2FN1j4g5vy90M1:17745:0:99999:7:::
bin:*:17589:0:99999:7:::
daemon:*:17589:0:99999:7:::
adm:*:17589:0:99999:7:::
```

```
lp:*:17589:0:99999:7:::
sync:*:17589:0:99999:7:::
shutdown:*:17589:0:99999:7:::
halt:*:17589:0:99999:7:::
mail:*:17589:0:99999:7:::
operator:*:17589:0:99999:7:::
games:*:17589:0:99999:7:::
ftp:*:17589:0:99999:7:::
nobody:*:17589:0:99999:7:::
apache:!!:17646::::::
dbus:!!:17646::::::
pulse:!!:17646::::::
chrony:!!:17646::::::
dnsmasq:!!:17646::::::
rpc:!!:17646:0:99999:7:::
usbmuxd:!!:17646::::::
openvpn:!!:17646::::::
radvd:!!:17646::::::
saslauth:!!:17646::::::
abrt:!!:17646::::::
pipewire:!!:17646::::::
gdm:!!:17646::::::
rpcuser:!!:17646::::::
user1:$6$YQ.IzyVU9.QVZgxK$hQbMxA0TNdWNF5Aeefa9.2WBKnbm2pofKZSeARUW
XuzZTj.UyYcwRVqVBVikYz8/HauSBLgy2ar2Yw7X8UplM.:17721:0:99999:7:::
[root@server1 ~]# _
```

Note from the preceding output that most user accounts used by daemons do not receive an encrypted password.

Although every user must have a primary group listed in the /etc/passwd file, each user can be a member of multiple groups. All groups and their members are listed in the /etc/group file. The /etc/group file has the following colon-delimited fields:

```
name:password:GID:members
```

The first field is the name of the group, followed by a group password.

Note

The password field usually contains an x, because group passwords are rarely used. If group passwords are used on your system, you need to specify a password to change your primary group membership using the newgrp command discussed later in this chapter. These passwords are set using the gpasswd command and can be stored in the /etc/gshadow file for added security. Refer to the gpasswd manual or info page for more information.

The GID represents the unique Group ID for the group, and the members field indicates the list of group members. An example /etc/group file is shown next:

```
[root@server1 ~]# cat /etc/group
root:x:0:
bin:x:1:root,bin,daemon
daemon:x:2:
sys:x:3:
adm:x:4:
tty:x:5:
disk:x:6:
lp:x:7:
mem:x:8:
kmem:x:9:
wheel:x:10:user1
cdrom:x:11:
mail:x:12:
man:x:15:
dialout:x:18:
floppy:x:19:
games:x:20:
tape:x:33:
video:x:39:
ftp:x:50:
lock:x:54:
audio:x:63:
users:x:100:
nobody:x:65534:
utmp:x:22:
apache:x:48:
ssh_keys:x:999:
input:x:998:
kvm:x:36:qemu
render:x:997:
dbus:x:81:
dip:x:40:
pulse:x:171:
avahi:x:70:
chrony:x:988:
saslauth:x:76:
abrt:x:173:
pipewire:x:980:
```

```
gdm:x:42:
rpcuser:x:29:
sshd:x:74:
slocate:x:21:
user1:x:1000:
[root@server1 ~]# _
```

From the preceding output, the "bin" group has a GID of 1 and three users as members: root, bin, and daemon. Similarly, the wheel group has a GID of 10 and user1 as a member.

> **Note** 📎
>
> The wheel group is a special group that provides its members with the ability to run the su and sudo commands; as a result, the first user that you create during a Linux installation is added to the wheel group to allow them to set the root password using the sudo command. Some Linux distributions, including Ubuntu, use the sudo group in place of the wheel group.
>
> You can also use the getent **command** to view the entries within system databases such as /etc/passwd, /etc/shadow, /etc/group, and /etc/gshadow; for example, getent shadow will display the entries within the shadow database (/etc/shadow).

Creating User Accounts

You can create user accounts on the Linux system by using the useradd **command**, specifying the user name as an argument, as shown next:

```
[root@server1 ~]# useradd bobg
[root@server1 ~]# _
```

In this case, all other information, such as the UID, shell, and home directory location, is taken from two files that contain user account creation default values.

The first file, /etc/login.defs, contains parameters that set the default location for email, password expiration information, minimum password length, and the range of UIDs and GIDs available for use. In addition, it determines whether home directories will be automatically made during user creation, as well as the password hash algorithm used to store passwords within /etc/shadow.

A sample /etc/login.defs file is depicted in the following example:

```
[root@server1 ~]# cat /etc/login.defs
# *REQUIRED*
# Directory where mailboxes reside, _or_ name of file, relative to the
# home directory.  If you _do_ define both, MAIL_DIR takes precedence.
```

```
# QMAIL_DIR is for Qmail
#
#QMAIL_DIR   Maildir
MAIL_DIR   /var/spool/mail
#MAIL_FILE   .mail

# Password aging controls:
#
# PASS_MAX_DAYS    Maximum number of days a password may be used.
# PASS_MIN_DAYS    Minimum number of days allowed between password
changes.
# PASS_MIN_LEN     Minimum acceptable password length.
# PASS_WARN_AGE    Number of days warning before a password expires.
#
PASS_MAX_DAYS       99999
PASS_MIN_DAYS       0
PASS_MIN_LEN        5
PASS_WARN_AGE       7


#
# Min/max values for automatic uid selection in useradd
#
UID_MIN                 1000
UID_MAX                 60000
# System accounts
SYS_UID_MIN             201
SYS_UID_MAX             999


#
# Min/max values for automatic gid selection in groupadd
#
GID_MIN                 100
GID_MAX                 60000
# System accounts
SYS_GID_MIN             201
SYS_GID_MAX             999


#
# If defined, this command is run when removing a user.
# It should remove any at/cron/print jobs etc. owned by
```

```
# the user to be removed (passed as the first argument).
#
#USERDEL_CMD   /usr/sbin/userdel_local


#
# If useradd should create home directories for users by default
# On RH systems, we do. This option is overridden with the -m flag on
# useradd command line.
#
CREATE_HOME   yes


# The permission mask is initialized to this value. If not specified,
# the permission mask will be initialized to 022.
UMASK              077


# This enables userdel to remove user groups if no members exist.
#
USERGROUPS_ENAB yes


# Use SHA512 to encrypt password.
ENCRYPT_METHOD SHA512
[root@server1 ~]# _
```

The second file, /etc/default/useradd, contains information regarding the default primary group, the location of home directories, the default number of days to disable accounts with expired passwords, the date to disable user accounts, the shell used, and the skeleton directory used. The **skeleton directory**, which is /etc/skel on most Linux systems, contains files that are copied to all new users' home directories when the home directory is created. Most of these files are environment files, such as .bash_profile and .bashrc.

A sample /etc/default/useradd file is shown in the following output:

```
[root@server1 ~]# cat /etc/default/useradd
# useradd defaults file
GROUP=100
HOME=/home
INACTIVE=-1
EXPIRE=
SHELL=/bin/bash
SKEL=/etc/skel
CREATE_MAIL_SPOOL=yes
[root@server1 ~]# _
```

To override any of the default parameters for a user in the /etc/login.defs and /etc/default/useradd files, you can specify options to the useradd command when creating user accounts. For example, to create a user named maryj with a UID of 762, you can use the –u option to the useradd command, as shown in the following example:

```
[root@server1 ~]# useradd -u 762 maryj
[root@server1 ~]# _
```

Table 10-6 lists some common options available to the useradd command and their descriptions.

Table 10-6 Common options to the `useradd` command

Option	Description
`-c "description"`	Adds a description for the user to the GECOS field of /etc/passwd
`-d homedirectory`	Specifies the absolute pathname to the user's home directory
`-e expirydate`	Specifies a date to disable the account from logging in
`-f days`	Specifies the number of days until a user account with an expired password is disabled
`-g group`	Specifies the primary group for the user account; on most Linux distributions, a group is created with the same name as the user and made the primary group for that user via the USERGROUPS_ENAB entry in the /etc/login.defs file
`-G group1,group2,etc.`	Specifies all other group memberships for the user account
`-m`	Specifies that a home directory should be created for the user account; on most Linux distributions, home directories are created for all users by default via the CREATE_HOME entry in the /etc/login.defs file
`-k directory`	Specifies the skeleton directory used when copying files to a new home directory
`-s shell`	Specifies the absolute pathname to the shell used for the user account
`-u UID`	Specifies the UID of the user account

After a user account has been added, the password field in the /etc/shadow file contains either two ! characters or a single * character, indicating that no password has been set for the user account. To set the password, type the passwd command, type the name of the new user account at a command prompt, and then supply the appropriate password when prompted. An example of setting the password for the bobg user is shown in the following:

```
[root@server1 ~]# passwd bobg
Changing password for user bobg.
New UNIX password:
Retype new UNIX password:
passwd: all authentication tokens updated successfully.
[root@server1 ~]# _
```

> **Note** 📎
>
> Without arguments, the `passwd` command changes the password for the current user.
>
> All user accounts must have a password set before they are used to log in to the system.
>
> The root user can set the password on any user account using the `passwd` command; however, regular users can change their password only using this command.
>
> Passwords should be difficult to guess and contain a combination of uppercase, lowercase, and special characters to increase system security. An example of a good password is C2Jr1;Pwr.

Modifying User Accounts

To modify the information regarding a user account after creation, you can edit the /etc/passwd or /etc/shadow file. This is not recommended, however, because typographical errors in these files might prevent the system from functioning. Instead, it's better to use the `usermod` command, which you can use to modify most information regarding user accounts. For example, to change the login name of the user bobg to barbg, you can use the -l option to the `usermod` command:

```
[root@server1 ~]# usermod -l barbg bobg
[root@server1 ~]# _
```

Table 10-7 displays a complete list of options used with the `usermod` command to modify user accounts.

Table 10-7 Common options to the `usermod` command

Option	Description
`-c "description"`	Specifies a new description for the user in the GECOS field of /etc/passwd
`-d homedirectory`	Specifies the absolute pathname to a new home directory
`-e expirydate`	Specifies a date to disable the account from logging in
`-f days`	Specifies the number of days until a user account with an expired password is disabled
`-g group`	Specifies a new primary group for the user account
`-G group1,group2,etc.`	Specifies all other group memberships for the user account
`-l name`	Specifies a new login name
`-s shell`	Specifies the absolute pathname to a new shell used for the user account
`-u UID`	Specifies a new UID for the user account

> **Note**
>
> If installed, the `finger` command can be used to view information about users. This information is stored in the GECOS field of /etc/passwd. As a result, instead of using the `-c` option to the `usermod` command, users can change their own GECOS, or finger information, using the `chfn` **command**.

The only user account information that the `usermod` command cannot modify is the password expiration information stored in /etc/shadow (min, max, warn), discussed earlier. To change this information, you can use the `chage` **command** with the appropriate option. For example, to specify that the user bobg must wait two days before changing his password after receiving a new password, as well as to specify that his password expires every 50 days with seven days of warning prior to expiration, you can use the following options to the `chage` command:

```
[root@server1 ~]# chage -m 2 -M 50 -W 7 bobg
[root@server1 ~]# _
```

> **Note**
>
> You can also use the `chage` command to view password expiration information. For example, the `chage -l bobg` command displays the password expiration information for the user bobg.

Sometimes it's necessary to **lock an account**—that is, to temporarily prevent a user from logging in. To lock an account, you can use the command `usermod -L username` at the command prompt. This places a ! character at the beginning of the encrypted password field in the /etc/shadow file. To unlock the account, type `usermod -U username` at the command prompt, which removes the ! character from the password field in the /etc/shadow file.

Alternatively, you can use the `passwd -l username` command to lock a user account, and the `passwd -u username` command to unlock a user account. These commands place and remove two ! characters at the beginning of the encrypted password field in the /etc/shadow file, respectively.

Yet another method commonly used to lock a user account is to change the shell specified in /etc/passwd for a user account from /bin/bash to an invalid shell such as /bin/false or /sbin/nologin. Without a valid shell, a user cannot use the system. To lock a user account this way, you can edit the /etc/passwd file and make the appropriate change, use the -s option to the `usermod` command, or use the `chsh` **command**. The following example uses the `chsh` command to change the shell to /bin/false for the user bobg:

```
[root@server1 ~]# chsh -s /bin/false bobg
Changing shell for bobg.
chsh: Warning: "/bin/false" is not listed in /etc/shells
Shell changed.
[root@server1 ~]# _
```

Deleting User Accounts

To delete a user account, you can use the `userdel` **command** and specify the user name as an argument. This removes entries from the /etc/passwd and /etc/shadow files corresponding to the user account. Furthermore, you can specify the -r option to the `userdel` command to remove the home directory for the user and all of its contents.

When a user account is deleted, any files that were previously owned by the user become owned by a number that represents the UID of the deleted user. Any future user account that is given the same UID then becomes the owner of those files.

Suppose, for example, that the user bobg leaves the company. To delete bobg's user account and display the ownership of his old files, you can use the following commands:

```
[root@server1 ~]# userdel bobg
[root@server1 ~]# ls -la /home/bobg
total 52
drwx------    4 1002      1002          4096 Jul 17 15:37 .
drwxr-xr-x    5 root      root          4096 Jul 17 15:37 ..
-rw-r--r--    1 1002      1002            24 Jul 17 15:37 .bash_logout
-rw-r--r--    1 1002      1002           191 Jul 17 15:37 .bash_profile
```

```
-rw-r--r--      1 1002      1002           124 Jul 17 15:37 .bashrc
-rw-r--r--      1 1002      1002          5542 Jul 17 15:37 .canna
-rw-r--r--      1 1002      1002           820 Jul 17 15:37 .emacs
-rw-r--r--      1 1002      1002           118 Jul 17 15:37 .gtkrc
-rw-r--r--      3 1002      1002          4096 Jul 17 15:37 .kde
drwxr-xr-x      2 1002      1002          4096 Jul 17 15:37 .xemacs
-rw-r--r--      1 1002      1002          3511 Jul 17 15:37 .zshrc
[root@server1 ~]# _
```

From the preceding output, you can see that the UID of the bobg user was 1002. Now suppose the company hires Sue—that is, the user sueb—to replace bobg. You can then assign the UID of 1002 to Sue's user account. Although she will have her own home directory (/home/sueb), she will also own all of bobg's old files within /home/bobg and otherwise. She can then copy the files that she needs to her own home directory and remove any files that she doesn't need as part of her job function.

To create the user sueb with a UID of 1002 and list the ownership of the files in bobg's home directory, you can use the following commands:

```
[root@server1 ~]# useradd -u 1002 sueb
[root@server1 ~]# ls -la /home/bobg
total 52
drwx------      4 sueb       sueb          4096 Jul 17 15:37 .
drwxr-xr-x      5 root       root          4096 Jul 17 18:56 ..
-rw-r--r--      1 sueb       sueb            24 Jul 17 15:37 .bash_logout
-rw-r--r--      1 sueb       sueb           191 Jul 17 15:37 .bash_profile
-rw-r--r--      1 sueb       sueb           124 Jul 17 15:37 .bashrc
-rw-r--r--      1 sueb       sueb          5542 Jul 17 15:37 .canna
-rw-r--r--      1 sueb       sueb           820 Jul 17 15:37 .emacs
-rw-r--r--      1 sueb       sueb           118 Jul 17 15:37 .gtkrc
-rw-r--r--      3 sueb       sueb          4096 Jul 17 15:37 .kde
drwxr-xr-x      2 sueb       sueb          4096 Jul 17 15:37 .xemacs
-rw-r--r--      1 sueb       sueb          3511 Jul 17 15:37 .zshrc
[root@server1 ~]# _
```

Managing Groups

By far, the easiest way to add groups to a system is to edit the /etc/group file using a text editor. Another method is to use the groupadd command. To add a group called group1 to the system and assign it a GID of 492, you can use the following command:

```
[root@server1 ~]# groupadd -g 492 group1
[root@server1 ~]# _
```

Then, you can use the -G option to the usermod command to add members to the group. To add the user maryj to this group and view the addition, you can use the following usermod command:

```
[root@server1 ~]# usermod -G group1 maryj
[root@server1 ~]# tail -1 /etc/group
group1:x:492:maryj
[root@server1 ~]# _
```

You can use the groupmod **command** to modify the group name and GID and the groupdel **command** to remove groups from the system.

To see a list of groups of which you are a member, run the groups **command**; to see the GIDs for each group, run the id **command**. Each command always lists the primary group first. The following output shows sample output of these commands when executed by the root user:

```
[root@server1 ~]# groups
root bin daemon sys adm disk wheel
[root@server1 ~]# id
uid=0(root) gid=0(root) groups=0(root),1(bin),2(daemon),3(sys),4(a
dm),6(disk),10(wheel)
[root@server1 ~]# _
```

In the preceding output the primary group for the root user is the root group. This group is attached as the group owner for all files that are created by the root user, as shown in the following output:

```
[root@server1 ~]# touch samplefile1
[root@server1 ~]# ls -l samplefile1
-rw-r--r--   1 root      root           0 Aug 27 19:22 sample-
file1 [root@server1 ~]# _
```

To change the primary group temporarily to another group that is listed in the output of the groups and id commands, you can use the newgrp command. Any new files created afterward will then have the new group owner. The following output demonstrates how changing the primary group for the root user affects file ownership:

```
[root@server1 ~]# newgrp sys
[root@server1 root]# id
uid=0(root) gid=3(sys)
groups=0(root),1(bin),2(daemon),3(sys),4(adm),6(disk),10(wheel)
[root@server1 ~]# touch samplefile2
[root@server1 ~]# ls -l samplefile2
-rw-r--r--   1 root      sys            0 Aug 27 19:28 samplefile2
[root@server1 ~]# _
```

Although command-line utilities are commonly used to administer users and groups, you can instead use a graphical utility to create, modify, and delete user and group accounts on the system. These utilities run the appropriate command-line utility in the background. To create and manage users and groups in Fedora 28 from within a desktop environment, you can open a terminal application in the desktop environment, switch to the root user, and run the `system-config-users` command to open the User Manager utility shown in Figure 10-6.

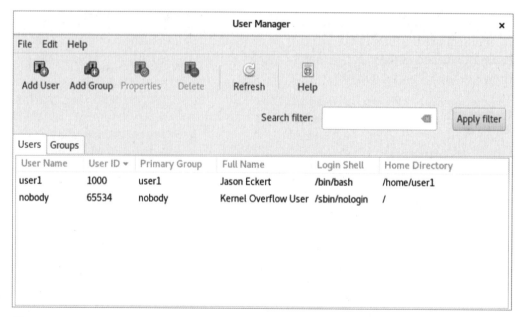

Figure 10-6 Configuring users and groups within a desktop environment

Chapter Summary

- Print jobs are spooled to a print queue before being printed to a printer.
- You can configure spooling or printing for a printer by using the cupsaccept, cupsreject, cupsenable, and cupsdisable commands.
- Print jobs are created using the lp command, can be viewed in the print queue using the lpstat command, and are removed from the print queue using the cancel command.
- You can configure printers using the lpadmin command, the CUPS Web administration tool, or by modifying the /etc/cups/printers.conf file.
- Most log files on a Linux system are stored in the /var/log directory.
- System events are typically logged to files by the System Log Daemon (rsyslogd) or to a database by the Systemd Journal Daemon (journald).

- You can use the jounalctl command to view the contents of the journald database.
- Log files should be cleared or rotated over time to save disk space; the logrotate utility can be used to rotate log files.
- User and group account information is typically stored in the /etc/passwd, /etc/shadow, and /etc/group files.
- You can use the useradd command to create users and the groupadd command to create groups.
- All users must have a valid password before logging in to a Linux system.
- Users can be modified with the usermod, chage, chfn, chsh, and passwd commands, and groups can be modified using the groupmod command.
- The userdel and groupdel commands can be used to remove users and groups from the system, respectively.

Key Terms

agent
authentication
cancel command
chage command
chfn command
chsh command
Common Unix Printing System (CUPS)
CUPS daemon (cupsd)
CUPS Web administration tool
cupsaccept command
cupsdisable command

cupsenable command
cupsreject command
facility
General Electric Comprehensive Operating System (GECOS)
getent command
Group Identifier (GID)
groupadd command
groupdel command
groupmod command
groups command
id command

Internet Printing Protocol (IPP)
journalctl command
Line Printer Daemon (LPD)
lock an account
log file
logger command
logrotate command
lp command
lpadmin command
lpc command
lpq command
lpr command

lprm command

lpstat command

newgrp command

passwd command

primary group

print job

print job ID

print queue

printer class

Printers tool

priority

pwconv command

pwunconv command

queuing

skeleton directory

spooling

System Log Daemon
(rsyslogd)

Systemd Journal Daemon
(journald)

systemd-cat command

user account

User Identifier (UID)

useradd command

userdel command

usermod command

Review Questions

1. The process of sending print jobs from the print queue to the printer is called

   _____.

   a. spooling
   b. queuing
   c. redirecting
   d. printing

2. You can clear a log file simply by redirecting nothing into it. True or False?

3. When a printer is disabled, _____.

   a. the print queue does not accept jobs and sends a message to the user noting that the printer is unavailable
   b. the print queue accepts jobs into the print queue and holds them there until the printer is enabled again
   c. the printer appears as offline when an lp request is sent
   d. the print queue redirects all print jobs sent to it to /dev/null

4. What is the term used to describe a user providing a user name and password to log in to a system?

   a. validation
   b. authorization
   c. login
   d. authentication

5. Which command can you use to lock a user account?

   a. lock username
   b. secure username
   c. usermod -L username
   d. useradd -L username

6. Which command can be used to temporarily alter the primary group associated with a given user?

   a. usermod
   b. chggrp
   c. gpasswd
   d. newgrp

7. Which command can be used to send a print job to the default printer named Printer1? (Choose all that apply.)

   a. lp -d Printer1 file
   b. lp Printer1 file
   c. lp file
   d. lp -m Printer1 file

8. What is the name of the file that contains a listing of all users on the system and their home directories?

   a. /etc/passwd
   b. /etc/users
   c. /etc/shadow
   d. /etc/password

9. UIDs and GIDs are unique to the system and, once used, can never be reused. True or False?

10. What is the name of the utility used to rotate log files?
    a. syslog
    b. jetpack
    c. logrotate
    d. logbackup

11. You can lock a user account by changing the default login shell to an invalid shell in /etc/passwd. True or False?

12. When a printer is rejecting requests, _____.
    a. the print queue does not accept jobs and sends a message to the user noting that the printer is unavailable
    b. the print queue accepts jobs into the print queue and holds them there until the printer is accepting requests again
    c. the printer appears as offline when an `lp` request is sent
    d. the print queue redirects all print jobs sent to it to /dev/null

13. When referring to the /etc/rsyslog.conf file, _____ specifies information from a certain area of the system, whereas _____ is the level of importance of that information.
    a. section, priority
    b. service, precedents
    c. process, degree
    d. facility, priority

14. Most log files on the system are found in which directory?
    a. /etc/logfiles
    b. /etc/log
    c. /var/log
    d. /dev/log

15. Which file contains default information such as UID and GID ranges and minimum password length to be used at user creation?
    a. /etc/skel
    b. /etc/passwd
    c. /etc/login.defs
    d. /etc/default/useradd

16. What command can you use to view journald log entries on a system that uses Systemd?
    a. `less`
    b. `journalctl`
    c. `syslog`
    d. `catlog`

17. Which command would you use to unlock a user account?
    a. `unlock username`
    b. `open username`
    c. `passwd -u username`
    d. `useradd -U username`

18. Along with a listing of user accounts, the /etc/passwd file contains information on account expiry. True or False?

19. You use `lpstat` and determine that a user named User1 has placed two large print jobs in the queue for Printer1 that have yet to start printing. They have print job IDs of Printer1-17 and Printer1-21, respectively. Which command would you use to remove these two jobs from the print queue?
    a. `cancel Printer1-17 Printer1-21`
    b. `cancel -u Printer1-17 Printer1-21`
    c. `cancel -a Printer1-17 Printer1-21`
    d. `cancel 17 21`

20. Which command is used to delete a user account?
    a. `usermod -d username`
    b. `del username`
    c. `userdel username`
    d. `rm username`

Hands-On Projects

These projects should be completed in the order given. The hands-on projects presented in this chapter should take a total of three hours to complete. The requirements for this lab include:

- A computer with Fedora Linux installed according to Hands-On Project 2-1 and Ubuntu Server 14 Linux installed according to Hands-On Project 6-7.

Project 10-1

In this hands-on project, you use commands to create and configure a printer as well as submit and manage print jobs.

1. Boot your Fedora Linux virtual machine. After your Linux system has been loaded, switch to a command-line terminal (tty5) by pressing **Ctrl+Alt+F5** and log in to the terminal using the user name of **root** and the password of **LINUXrocks!**.

2. At the command prompt, type `lpadmin -p printer1 -E -v /dev/null -m raw` and press **Enter** to create a sample printer called printer1 that prints to the /dev/null device using a raw print driver.

3. At the command prompt, type `lpoptions -d printer1` and press **Enter** to ensure that printer1 is the default printer on the system.

4. At the terminal screen prompt, type `cat /etc/cups/printers.conf` and press **Enter**. Do you see an entry for printer1 that prints to /dev/null?

5. At the command prompt, type `lpstat -t` and press **Enter**. Is the CUPS daemon running? Is printer1 enabled and accepting requests? Is printer1 the default printer on the system?

6. At the command prompt, type `cupsdisable -r "To keep print jobs in the queue" printer1` and press **Enter** to disable printer1 with an appropriate reason. Next, type `lpstat -t` at the command prompt and press **Enter**. Is printer1 disabled with a reason?

7. At the command prompt, type `lp -n 2 /etc/inittab` and press **Enter** to print two copies of /etc/inittab to printer1. What is the print job ID? Why did you not need to specify the printer name when running the `lp` command?

8. At the command prompt, type `lp /etc/hosts /etc/nsswitch.conf` and press **Enter** to print the /etc/hosts and /etc/nsswitch.conf files. What is the print job ID?

9. At the command prompt, type `mount | lp` and press **Enter** to print the output of the `mount` command to printer1. What is the print job ID?

10. At the command prompt, type `lpstat` and press **Enter**. Are your print jobs shown in the queue? How long will they remain in the queue and why?

11. At the command prompt, type `ls /var/spool/cups` and press **Enter**. You should notice contents within this directory for your three print jobs. The data for your print jobs should have file names that start with d, and the settings for your print jobs should

have file names that start with c. Type `cat /var/spool/cups/d00001-001` at the command prompt and press **Enter** to view the data for the first print job on the system. What is shown and why?

12. At the command prompt, type `cancel printer1-1` and press **Enter** to remove the first print job from the queue. Next, type `lpstat printer1` at the command prompt and press **Enter**. Has the printer1-1 job been removed?

13. At the command prompt, type `lpc status` and press **Enter** to view the status of CUPS using the traditional BSD `lpc` command. Is the CUPS daemon running? Is the status of printing and spooling correct? Next, type `lpq` at the command prompt and press **Enter**. Do you see the two remaining jobs in the print queue for printer1? Do the job numbers displayed correspond with the job numbers in the `lpstat` output from the previous step?

14. At the command prompt, type `lpr -#2 /etc/inittab` and press **Enter** to print two copies of /etc/inittab to the default printer using the traditional BSD `lpr` command. Next, type `lpq` at the command prompt and press **Enter**. Do you see an additional job in the print queue? What is the job ID?

15. At the command prompt, type `lprm 4` and press **Enter** to remove the most recent print job that you submitted. Next, type `lpq` at the command prompt and press **Enter**. Was print job 4 removed successfully?

16. Type `exit` and press **Enter** to log out of your shell.

Project 10-2

In this hands-on project, you submit a print job from a graphical program as well as explore the Printers tool and the CUPS Web administration tool.

1. On your Fedora Linux virtual machine, switch to tty1 by pressing **Ctrl+Alt+F1** and log in to the GNOME desktop using your user name and the password of **LINUXrocks!**.

2. In the GNOME desktop, click the **Activities** menu, select the **Show Applications** icon, and click **LibreOffice Writer**. Type a line of your choice within the document, select the **File** menu, and choose **Print**. Is printer1 listed as the default printer? Click **OK** to print one copy of your document. Close the LibreOffice Writer window and click **Don't Save** when prompted.

3. In the GNOME desktop, click the **Activities** menu, select the **Show Applications** icon, and click **Settings** to open the Settings window. Navigate to **Devices**, **Printers** to open the graphical Printers tool and note that printer1 is displayed, and that a button indicating the number of jobs within the queue is shown.

4. In the Printers tool, click the **1 Job** button and note that your recently submitted print job is shown. Why aren't the two other print jobs in the printer1 queue shown? Close the printer1 - Active Jobs window when finished.

5. In the Printers tool, click the settings (cog wheel) icon and select **Printing Options**. Next, click **Test Page** to submit a test page print job and close the printer1 window when

finished. Note that the button indicating the number of jobs displays 2 Jobs. Click the **2 Jobs** button, click the **Stop** icon to remove the job from the queue, and then close the printer1 – Active Jobs window. Close the Printers tool when finished.

6. In the GNOME desktop, click the **Activities** menu and select the **Firefox** icon. Enter the address **localhost:631** in the navigation dialog box and press **Enter** to access the CUPS Web administration tool.

7. In the CUPS Web administration tool, highlight the **Administration** tab and select the **Allow remote administration**, **Share printers connected to this system**, and **Allow printing from the Internet** options. Click the **Change Settings** button to activate your changes. Supply the user name **root** and password **LINUXrocks!** when prompted and click **OK**.

> **Note** 📎
>
> Note that if your configuration is not applied, you will not be able to access the CUPS Web administration tool; in this case, you will need to log into a BASH shell as the root user and restart the CUPS daemon using the `systemctl restart cups.service` command.

8. On the Administration tab of the CUPS Web administration tool, click **Add Class**, supply a name of **SampleClass**, select **printer1**, and click **Add Class**.

9. Highlight the **Printers** tab of the CUPS Web administration tool and click **printer1**. Select the **Maintenance** drop-down menu and note the maintenance tasks that you can perform for printer1. Next, select the **Administration** drop-down menu and note the administrative tasks that you can perform for printer1. View the print jobs at the bottom of the page and note the management functions that you can perform for each one.

10. Highlight the **Jobs** tab of the CUPS Web administration tool. Are the jobs shown the same as those shown on the Printers tab for printer1? Can you perform the same management functions for each job?

11. Highlight the **Classes** tab of the CUPS Web administration tool and click **SampleClass**. Select the **Maintenance** drop-down menu and note the maintenance tasks that you can perform for printer1. Next, select the **Administration** drop-down menu and note the administrative tasks that you can perform for printer1. Do these options match those shown on the Printers tab for printer1?

12. Close the Firefox Web browser window and switch to a command-line terminal (tty5) by pressing **Ctrl+Alt+F5** and log in to the terminal using the user name of **root** and the password of **LINUXrocks!**.

13. At the command prompt, type `lpstat -t` and press **Enter**. Is your SampleClass shown in the output? Why is user1 listed as the user for the most recent print job?

14. At the command prompt, type `lp -d SampleClass /etc/hosts` and press **Enter** to print a copy of /etc/hosts to the SampleClass printer class. Why does the print job ID reflect the printer class name and not printer1?

15. At the command prompt, type `lpstat -t` and press **Enter**. Is the print job submitted to your printer class shown?

16. At the command prompt, type `cancel -a printer1 SampleClass` and press **Enter** to remove all print jobs in the queue for printer1 and SampleClass. Next, type `lpstat -t` and press **Enter** to verify that no print jobs exist within the print queue.

17. Type `exit` and press **Enter** to log out of your shell.

Project 10-3

In this hands-on project, you view the configuration of the System Log Daemon and the logrotate utility on Ubuntu Server 14 Linux.

1. Boot your Ubuntu Server 14 Linux virtual machine. After your Linux system has been loaded, log into tty1 using the user name of **root** and the password of **LINUXrocks!**.

2. At the command prompt, type `ls -l /dev/log` and press **Enter**. What is the file type? Which daemon on Ubuntu Server 14 Linux uses this file and what is its purpose?

3. At the command prompt, type `less /etc/rsyslog.conf` and press **Enter** to view the configuration file for the System Log Daemon. Are there any entries that specify facilities, priorities, or log file locations? What does the last line of the file specify? Press **q** when finished to quit the less utility.

4. At the command prompt, type `less /etc/rsyslog.d/50-default.conf` and press **Enter**. Where do kernel messages of any priority get logged to by default? What does the – character next to the filename indicate? Press **q** when finished to quit the less utility.

5. At the command prompt, type `tail /var/log/kern.log` and press **Enter**. Observe the entries.

6. At the command prompt, type `ls /var/log/cups` and press **Enter**. What daemon creates the log files within the /var/log/cups directory?

7. At the command prompt, type `cat /etc/cron.daily/logrotate` and press **Enter** to observe the `logrotate` command that is run each day.

8. At the command prompt, type `less /etc/logrotate.conf` and press **Enter** to view the configuration file for the `logrotate` command. How many copies of old log files are kept by default? When finished, press **q** to quit the less utility.

9. At the command prompt, type `ls /etc/logrotate.d` and press **Enter**. How many files are in this directory? Will entries in these files override the same entries in /etc/logrotate.conf?

10. At the command prompt, type `cat /etc/logrotate.d/cups-daemon` and press **Enter**. How many copies of old log files are kept for the log files in the /var/log/cups directory? Will the log files be rotated if they contain no contents?

11. Type `exit` and press **Enter** to log out of your shell.

Project 10-4

In this hands-on project, you view the configuration and log entries created by the Systemd Journal Daemon as well as the configuration of the logrotate utility on Fedora Linux.

1. On your Fedora Linux virtual machine, switch to a command-line terminal (tty5) by pressing **Ctrl+Alt+F5** and log in to the terminal using the user name of **root** and the password of **LINUXrocks!**.

2. At the command prompt, type `ls -l /dev/log` and press **Enter**. Note that /dev/log is a symbolic link to /run/systemd/journal/dev-log on Fedora Linux. Next, type `ls -l /run/systemd/journal/dev-log` and press **Enter**. What is the file type? Which daemon on Fedora Linux uses this file and what is its purpose?

3. At the command prompt, type `cat /etc/systemd/journald.conf` and press **Enter** to view the configuration file for the Systemd Journal Daemon. What line could you uncomment and configure to set a maximum size for the journald database?

4. At the command prompt, type `journalctl _COMM=` and press the **Tab** key twice. Which keyword could you use to view log entries from the GNOME display manager? Press **Ctrl+c** to return to your command prompt. Next, type `journalctl _COMM=gdm` and press **Enter** to view log entries from the GNOME display manager. Are entries shown for multiple days?

5. At the command prompt, type `journalctl _COMM=gdm --since "5:00"` and press **Enter** to view log entries from the GNOME display manager since 5:00am.

6. At the command prompt, type `which crond` and press **Enter**. What is the path to the cron daemon executable file? Next, type `journalctl /usr/sbin/crond --since "5:00"` and press **Enter**. Note the entries shown.

7. At the command prompt, type `ls /var/log` and press **Enter**. Observe the entries. Are there log files within /var/log created by daemons that do not log entries via journald?

8. At the command prompt, type `ls /var/log/cups` and press **Enter**. Are the contents similar to those from Step 6 in Project 10-3?

9. At the command prompt, type `cat /etc/cron.daily/logrotate` and press **Enter** to observe the `logrotate` command that is run each day.

10. At the command prompt, type `less /etc/logrotate.conf` and press **Enter** to view the configuration file for the `logrotate` command. How often are log files rotated, and how many copies of old log files are kept by default? When finished, press **q** to quit the less utility.

11. At the command prompt, type `ls /etc/logrotate.d` and press **Enter**. How many files are in this directory? Will entries in these files override the same entries in /etc/logrotate.conf?

12. At the command prompt, type `cat /etc/logrotate.d/cups` and press **Enter**. How many copies of old log files are kept for the log files in the /var/log/cups directory? Will the log files be rotated if they contain no contents?

13. Type `exit` and press **Enter** to log out of your shell.

Project 10-5

In this hands-on project, you observe user account databases on Fedora Linux and create a user account using command-line utilities.

1. On your Fedora Linux virtual machine, switch to a command-line terminal (tty5) by pressing **Ctrl+Alt+F5** and log in to the terminal using the user name of **root** and the password of **LINUXrocks!**.

2. At the command prompt, type `less /etc/passwd` and press **Enter**. Where is the line that describes the root user located in this file? Where is the line that describes the user1 user in this file? How many daemon accounts are present? What is in the password field for all accounts? When finished, press the **q** key to quit the less utility.

3. At the command prompt, type `ls -l /etc/passwd` and press **Enter**. Who is the owner and group owner of this file? Who has permission to read this file?

4. At the command prompt, type `less /etc/shadow` and press **Enter**. What is in the password field for the root user and user1 user accounts? What is in the password field for most daemon accounts? Press the **q** key to quit the less utility.

5. At the command prompt, type `ls -l /etc/shadow` and press **Enter**. Who is the owner and group owner of this file? Who has permission to read this file? Compare the permissions for /etc/shadow to those of /etc/passwd obtained in Step 3 and explain the difference.

6. At the command prompt, type `pwunconv` and press **Enter**. Next, type `less /etc/shadow` at the command prompt and press **Enter**. What error message do you receive? Why?

7. At the command prompt, type `less /etc/passwd` and press **Enter**. What is in the password field for the root and user1 accounts? Why? When finished, press the **q** key to quit the less utility.

8. At the command prompt, type `pwconv` and press **Enter**. What does the `pwconv` command do?

9. Next, type `less /etc/shadow` at the command prompt and press **Enter**. Verify that the file has contents and press **q** when finished. Next, type `less /etc/passwd` at the command prompt and press **Enter**. Verify that the file has contents and press **q** when finished.

10. At the command prompt, type `cat /etc/default/useradd` and press **Enter**. What is the default shell used when creating users? What is the default location of the skel directory used when creating users? Where are user home directories created by default?

11. At the command prompt, type `ls -a /etc/skel` and press **Enter**. What files are stored in this directory? What is the purpose of this directory when creating users?

12. At the command prompt, type `cp /etc/inittab /etc/skel` and press **Enter** to create a copy of the init table in the /etc/skel directory.

13. At the command prompt, type `useradd -m bozo` and press **Enter**. What does the -m option specify? From where is the default shell and home directory information taken?

14. At the command prompt, type `less /etc/login.defs` and press **Enter**. Observe the entries and descriptive comments. Did you need to specify the `-m` option to the `useradd` command in Step 13? Explain. Press the **q** key to quit the less utility.

15. At the command prompt, type `cat /etc/passwd` and press **Enter**. What shell and home directory does bozo have? What is bozo's UID?

16. At the command prompt, type `cat /etc/shadow` and press **Enter**. Does bozo have a password? Can bozo log in to the system?

17. At the command prompt, type `passwd bozo` and press **Enter**. Enter the password of **LINUXrocks!** and press **Enter**. Enter the password of **LINUXrocks!** again to confirm and press **Enter**.

18. At the command prompt, type `ls -a /home/bozo` and press **Enter**. How many files are in this directory? Compare this list to the one obtained in Step 11. Is the `inittab` file present?

19. Type `exit` and press **Enter** to log out of your shell.

Project 10-6

In this hands-on project, you modify user accounts on Fedora Linux using command-line utilities.

1. On your Fedora Linux virtual machine, switch to a command-line terminal (tty5) by pressing **Ctrl+Alt+F5** and log in to the terminal using the user name of **root** and the password of **LINUXrocks!**.

2. At the command prompt, type `grep bozo /etc/passwd` and press **Enter**. Note the line used to describe the user bozo.

3. At the command prompt, type `grep bozo /etc/shadow` and press **Enter**. Note the line used to describe the user bozo.

4. At the command prompt, type `usermod -l bozo2 bozo` and press **Enter** to change the login name for the user bozo to bozo2. Next, type `grep bozo /etc/passwd` at the command prompt and press **Enter**. Was the login name changed from bozo to bozo2? Was the UID changed? Was the home directory changed?

5. At the command prompt, type `usermod -l bozo bozo2` and press **Enter** to change the login name for the user bozo2 back to bozo.

6. At the command prompt, type `usermod -u 666 bozo` and press **Enter** to change the UID of the user bozo to 666. Next, type `grep bozo /etc/passwd` at the command prompt and press **Enter**. Was the UID changed?

7. At the command prompt, type `usermod -f 14 bozo` and press **Enter** to disable bozo's user account 14 days after the password expires. Next, type `grep bozo /etc/shadow` at the command prompt and press **Enter**. Which field was changed?

8. At the command prompt, type `usermod -e "01/01/2028" bozo` and press **Enter** to expire bozo's user account on January 1, 2028. Next, type `grep bozo /etc/shadow` at the command prompt and press **Enter**. Which field was changed? What does the number represent in this field?

9. At the command prompt, type `chage -m 2 bozo` and press **Enter** to require that the user bozo wait at least two days before making password changes. Next, type `grep bozo /etc/shadow` at the command prompt and press **Enter**. Which field was changed?

10. At the command prompt, type `chage -M 40 bozo` and press **Enter** to require that the user bozo change passwords every 40 days. Next, type `grep bozo /etc/shadow` at the command prompt and press **Enter**. Which field was changed?

11. At the command prompt, type `chage -W 5 bozo` and press **Enter** to warn the user bozo five days before a password change is required. Next, type `grep bozo /etc/shadow` at the command prompt and press **Enter**. Which field was changed?

12. Type `exit` and press **Enter** to log out of your shell.

Project 10-7

In this hands-on project, you lock and unlock user accounts on Fedora Linux using command-line utilities.

1. On your Fedora Linux virtual machine, switch to a command-line terminal (tty5) by pressing **Ctrl+Alt+F5** and log in to the terminal using the user name of **root** and the password of **LINUXrocks!**.

2. At the command prompt, type `grep bozo /etc/shadow` and press **Enter**. Note the encrypted password for bozo's user account.

3. At the command prompt, type `passwd -l bozo` and press **Enter** to lock bozo's user account.

4. At the command prompt, type `grep bozo /etc/shadow` and press **Enter**. What has been changed regarding the original encrypted password noted in Step 2?

5. Switch to a different command-line terminal (tty6) by pressing **Ctrl+Alt+F6** and attempt to log in to the terminal using the user name of **bozo** and the password of **LINUXrocks!**. Were you successful?

6. Switch back to tty5 by pressing **Ctrl+Alt+F5**.

7. At the command prompt, type `passwd -u bozo` and press **Enter** to unlock bozo's user account.

8. At the command prompt, type `grep bozo /etc/shadow` and press **Enter**. Compare the encrypted password for bozo's user account to the one noted in Step 2.

9. Switch to tty6 by pressing **Ctrl+Alt+F6** and attempt to log in to the terminal using the user name of **bozo** and the password of **LINUXrocks!**. Were you successful?

10. Type `exit` and press **Enter** to log out of your shell.

11. Switch back to tty5 by pressing **Ctrl+Alt+F5**.

12. At the command prompt, type `chsh -s /bin/false bozo` and press **Enter** to change bozo's shell to /bin/false. What message did you receive? Was the shell changed? Type `grep bozo /etc/passwd` at a command prompt to verify that the shell was changed to /bin/false for bozo's user account.

13. Switch to tty6 by pressing **Ctrl+Alt+F6** and attempt to log in to the terminal using the user name of **bozo** and the password of **LINUXrocks!**. Were you successful?

14. Switch back to tty5 by pressing **Ctrl+Alt+F5**.
15. At the command prompt, type `chsh -s /bin/bash bozo` and press **Enter** to change bozo's shell to /bin/bash.
16. Switch to tty6 by pressing **Ctrl+Alt+F6** and attempt to log in to the terminal using the user name of **bozo** and the password of **LINUXrocks!**. Were you successful?
17. Type `exit` and press **Enter** to log out of your shell.
18. Switch back to tty5 by pressing **Ctrl+Alt+F5**.
19. Type `exit` and press **Enter** to log out of your shell.

Project 10-8

In this hands-on project, you remove a user account on Fedora Linux and create a new user account in its place using command-line utilities.

1. On your Fedora Linux virtual machine, switch to a command-line terminal (tty5) by pressing **Ctrl+Alt+F5** and log in to the terminal using the user name of **root** and the password of **LINUXrocks!**.
2. At the command prompt, type `ls -la /home/bozo` and press **Enter**. Who owns most files in this directory? Why?
3. At the command prompt, type `userdel bozo` and press **Enter**. Was the home directory removed for bozo as well?
4. At the command prompt, type `ls -la /home/bozo` and press **Enter**. Who owns most files in this directory? Why?
5. At the command prompt, type `useradd -m -u 666 bozoette` and press **Enter**. What do the `-m` and the `-u` options do in this command?
6. At the command prompt, type `passwd bozoette` and press **Enter**. Enter the password of **LINUXrocks!** and press **Enter**. Enter the password of **LINUXrocks!** again to confirm and press **Enter**.
7. At the command prompt, type `grep bozoette /etc/passwd` and press **Enter**. What is bozoette's home directory? What is bozoette's UID?
8. At the command prompt, type `ls -la /home/bozo` and press **Enter**. Who owns most files in this directory? Why? Can bozoette manage these files?
9. Type `exit` and press **Enter** to log out of your shell.

Project 10-9

In this hands-on project, you create, use, and delete groups on Fedora Linux using command-line utilities.

1. On your Fedora Linux virtual machine, switch to a command-line terminal (tty5) by pressing **Ctrl+Alt+F5**, and log in to the terminal using the user name of **root** and the password of **LINUXrocks!**.
2. At the command prompt, type `vi /etc/group` and press **Enter** to open the /etc/group file in the vi editor. Add a line to the bottom of this file that reads:
   `groupies:x:1234:root,bozoette`

This adds a group to the system with a GID of 1234, the members root, and bozoette. When finished, save and quit the vi editor.

3. Switch to a different command-line terminal (tty6) by pressing **Ctrl+Alt+F6** and log in to the terminal using the user name of **bozoette** and the password of **LINUXrocks!**.

4. At the command prompt, type `groups` and press **Enter**. Of which groups is bozoette a member?

5. At the command prompt, type `id` and press **Enter**. Which group is the primary group for the user bozoette?

6. At the command prompt, type `touch file1` and press **Enter** to create a new file called file1 in the current directory.

7. At the command prompt, type `ls -l` and press **Enter**. Who is the owner and group owner of the file file1? Why?

8. At the command prompt, type `newgrp groupies` and press **Enter** to temporarily change bozoette's primary group to groupies.

9. At the command prompt, type `touch file2` and press **Enter** to create a new file called file2 in the current directory.

10. At the command prompt, type `ls -l` and press **Enter**. Who is the owner and group owner of the file file2? Why?

11. Type `exit` and press **Enter** to log out of the new shell created when you used the `newgrp` command. Next, type `exit` and press **Enter** to log out of your shell.

12. Switch back to tty5 by pressing **Ctrl+Alt+F5**.

13. At the command prompt, type `groupdel groupies` and press **Enter** to remove the group groupies from the system. Which file is edited by the `groupdel` command?

14. Type `exit` and press **Enter** to log out of your shell.

Discovery Exercises

1. Which entry could you add to /etc/rsyslog.conf to:
   a. Log all critical messages from the kernel to /var/log/alert
   b. Log all messages from the user processes to /var/log/userlog
   c. Log all debug messages and those with a more serious status from the printing daemon to /var/log/printer
   d. Log all messages except notices from the mail daemon to /var/log/mailman
   e. Log all alerts and critical error messages to /var/log/serious
   f. Log all warnings and errors from the kernel and the printing daemon to /var/log/shared

2. Use the man or info pages to find a description of the –D option to the `useradd` command. What does this option do? What file does it edit? Use this option with the `useradd` command to set the date that all new user accounts will be disabled to March 5, 2055. What command did you use?

3. In Project 10-2, you enabled the remote administration and IPP print sharing options within the CUPS remote administration tool on your Fedora Linux virtual machine. However, in order to access CUPS remotely or print to your shared IPP printers, you must allow the ports for the HTTP (TCP port 80), HTTPS (TCP port 443), and IPP (TCP port 631) protocols in the firewall that is enabled by default in Fedora 20. Run the following commands to enable those ports:

```
firewall-cmd --add-service
http
firewall-cmd --add-service
https
firewall-cmd --add-service
ipp
```

Next, use the `ifconfig` command to determine the IP address of your Fedora Linux virtual machine. Following this, access the CUPS administration website using the Web browser on your Windows host computer (URL: http://IP address:631). Finally, add a new printer within Control Panel on your Windows host computer that prints to the URL http://IP address:631/printers/printer1. Print to this new printer from a Windows program of your choice and verify that the job was submitted to the printer1 print queue using the `lpstat -t` command on your Fedora Linux virtual machine.

4. The CUPS commands introduced in this chapter work identically on both Fedora 28 and Ubuntu Server 14.04 systems. Because remote administration of the CUPS Web administration tool is disabled by default and Ubuntu Server 14.04 does not contain a GUI environment that allows you to access a Web browser and the CUPS Web administration tool, you must manually enable remote administration within the /etc/cups/cupsd.conf file.

On your Ubuntu Server Linux virtual machine, edit the /etc/cups/cupsd. conf file and change the line that reads `Listen localhost:631` to `Port 631` as well as add three `Allow from all` lines within the access sections, as shown here:

```
 # Restrict access to the
server...
<Location />
  Order allow,deny
  Allow from all
</Location>

# Restrict access to the
admin pages...
<Location /admin>
  Order allow,deny
  Allow from all
</Location>

# Restrict access to
configuration files...
<Location /admin/conf>
  AuthType Default
  Require user @SYSTEM
  Order allow,deny
  Allow from all
</Location>
```

Next, save your changes, run the `service cups restart` command to restart the CUPS daemon, and run the `ifconfig` command to determine the IP address of your Ubuntu Server Linux virtual machine. Finally, access the CUPS administration website using the Web browser on your Windows host computer (URL: http://IP address:631).

5. When adding several user accounts, you might want to use the `newusers` utility, which can process a text file full of entries to add user accounts. Use the man or info page to find out how to use this utility, and use it to add three users. When finished, view the /etc/passwd, /etc/shadow, and /etc/group files to verify that the users were added successfully.

6. Write commands to accomplish the following (use the manual or info pages if necessary):

   a. Create a user with a login name of bsmith, a UID of 733, a GECOS field entry of "accounting manager," and a password of Gxj234

   b. Delete the user jdoe, but leave the home directory intact

   c. Change the properties of the existing user wjones such that the user has a new comment field of "shipping" and an account expiry of March 23, 2032

   d. Lock the account of wjenkins

   e. Change the password of bsmith to We34Rt

   f. Change the properties of the existing user tbanks such that the user is a member of the managers group and has a login name of artbanks

   g. Create a user with the same UID and primary group as root and a login name of wjones

   h. Change the primary group of the user wsmith to root

   i. Add the users tbanks and jdoe to the group acctg

## CHAPTER 11

COMPRESSION, SYSTEM BACKUP, AND SOFTWARE INSTALLATION

After completing this chapter, you will be able to:

Outline the features of common compression utilities

Compress and decompress files using common compression utilities

Perform system backups using the `tar`, `cpio`, `dump`, and `dd` commands

View and extract archives using the `tar`, `cpio`, `restore`, and `dd` commands

Use burning software to back up files to CD and DVD

Describe common types of Linux software

Compile and install software packages from source code

Install, manage, and remove software packages using the Red Hat Package Manager (RPM) and Debian Package Manager (DPM)

Identify and support shared libraries used by software

In the preceding chapter, you examined common administrative tasks that are performed on a regular basis. In this chapter, you learn common data- and software-related tasks that are performed frequently. You begin this chapter by learning about utilities commonly used to compress files on filesystems, followed by a discussion of system backup and archiving utilities. Finally, you learn about the different forms of software available for Linux systems, how to compile source code into functional programs, as well as the features and usage of the Red Hat Package Manager (RPM) and Debian Package Manager (DPM).

Compression

At times, you might want to reduce the size of a file or set of files due to limited disk space. You might also want to compress files that are sent across the Internet to decrease transfer time. In either case, you can choose from several utilities that reduce a file's size by stripping out certain patterns of data via a process known as **compression**. The standard set of instructions used to compress a file is known as a **compression algorithm**. To decompress a file, you run the compression algorithm in reverse.

Because compression utilities use compression algorithms in different ways, they achieve different rates of compression, or **compression ratios**, for similar files types. To calculate the compression ratio for a utility, you subtract the compressed percentage from 100. For example, if a compression utility compresses a file to 52 percent of its original size, it has a compression ratio of 48 percent.

Many compression utilities are available to Linux users; this section examines the five most common:

- compress
- GNU zip
- xz
- zip
- bzip2

Using `compress`

The `compress` **command** is one of the oldest compression utilities common to most UNIX and Linux systems. Its compression algorithm, which is called Adaptive Lempel-Ziv coding (LZW), has an average compression ratio of 40–50 percent.

To compress a file using `compress`, you specify the files to compress as arguments. Each file is renamed with a `.Z` filename extension to indicate that it is compressed. In addition, you can use the `-v` (verbose) option to the `compress` command to display the compression ratio during compression. The following output displays the filenames and size of the samplefile and samplefile2 files before and after compression:

```
[root@server1 ~]# ls -l
total 28
drwx------    3 root     root          4096 Jul 21 08:15 Desktop
-rw-r--r--    1 root     root         27298 Jul 21 08:15 samplefile
```

```
-rw-rw-r--    1 root      root           540 Jul 21 08:18 samplefile2
[root@server1 ~]# compress -v samplefile samplefile2
samplefile:  -- replaced with samplefile.Z Compression: 59.65%
samplefile2:  -- replaced with samplefile2.Z Compression: 37.22%
[root@server1 root]# ls -l
total 20
drwx------    3 root      root          4096 Jul 21 08:15 Desktop
-rw-rw-r--    1 root      root           339 Jul 21 08:18 samplefile2.Z
-rw-r--r--    1 root      root         11013 Jul 21 08:15 samplefile.Z
[root@server1 ~]# _
```

> **Note** 🖉
>
> The compress command is not installed on most Linux distributions by default. To install it from a software repository on the Internet, you can run the dnf install ncompress command as the root user on Fedora 28, or the apt-get install ncompress command as the root user on Ubuntu Server.
>
> The compress command preserves the original ownership, modification, and access time for each file that it compresses.
>
> By default, compress does not compress symbolic links, hard links, or very small files unless you use the -f option.
>
> You can compress all of the files in a certain directory by using the -r option and specifying the directory name as an argument to the compress command.

After compression, the zcat command can be used to display the contents of a compressed file, as shown in the following output:

```
[root@server1 ~]# zcat samplefile2.Z
Hi there, I hope this day finds you well.

Unfortunately we were not able to make it to your dining
room this year while vacationing in Algonquin Park - I
especially wished to see the model of the Highland Inn
and the train station in the dining room.

I have been reading on the history of Algonquin Park but
no where could I find a description of where the Highland
Inn was originally located on Cache lake.
```

If it is no trouble, could you kindly let me know such that
I need not wait until next year when I visit your lodge?

Regards,
Mackenzie Elizabeth

[root@server1 ~]# _

Note 📎

You can also use the `zmore` **command** and `zless` **command** to view the contents of
a compressed file page by page, or the `zgrep` **command** to search the contents of a
compressed file.

To decompress files that have been compressed with the `compress` command, use
the `uncompress` **command** followed by the names of the files to be decompressed.
This restores the original filename. The following output decompresses and displays
the filenames for the samplefile.Z and samplefile2.Z files created earlier:

```
[root@server1 ~]# uncompress -v samplefile.Z samplefile2.Z
samplefile.Z:           59.7% -- replaced with samplefile
samplefile2.Z:          37.2% -- replaced with samplefile2
[root@server1 ~]# ls -l
total 28
drwx------    3 root      root        4096 Jul 21 08:15 Desktop
-rw-r--r--    1 root      root       27298 Jul 21 08:15 samplefile
-rw-rw-r--    1 root      root         540 Jul 21 08:18 samplefile2
[root@server1 ~]# _
```

Note 📎

The `uncompress` command prompts you for confirmation if any existing files will be
overwritten during decompression. To prevent this confirmation, you can use the `-f` option
to the `uncompress` command.

You can omit the `.Z` extension when using the `uncompress` command. The command
`uncompress -v samplefile samplefile2` would achieve the same results as the command shown in the preceding output.

Furthermore, the compress utility is a filter command that can take information from Standard Input and send it to Standard Output. For example, to send the output of the who command to the compress utility and save the compressed information to a file called file.Z, you can execute the following command:

```
[root@server1 ~]# who | compress -v >file.Z
Compression: 17.0%
[root@server1 ~]# _
```

Following this, you can display the contents of file.Z using the zcat command, or decompress it using the uncompress command, as shown in the following output:

```
[root@server1 ~]# zcat file.Z
root       pts/1     Jul 20 19:22 (3.0.0.2)
root       tty5      Jul 15 19:03
root       pts/1     Jul 17 19:58
[root@server1 root]# uncompress -v file.Z
file.Z:         17.0% -- replaced with file
[root@server1 ~]# _
```

Table 11-1 provides a summary of options commonly used with the compress utility.

Table 11-1   Common options used with the compress utility

Option	Description
-c	When used with the uncompress command, it displays the contents of the compressed file to Standard Output (same function as the zcat command).
-f	When used with the compress command, it can be used to compress linked files. When used with the uncompress command, it overwrites any existing files without prompting the user.
-r	Specifies to compress or decompress all files recursively within a specified directory.
-v	Displays verbose output (compression ratio and filenames) during compression and decompression.

Using GNU zip

GNU zip uses a Lempel-Ziv compression algorithm (LZ77) that varies slightly from the one used by the compress command. Typically, this algorithm yields better compression than the one used by compress. The average compression ratio for GNU zip is 60–70 percent. To compress files using GNU zip, you can use the gzip command.

Like compress, linked files are not compressed by the gzip command unless the -f option is given, and the -r option can be used to compress all files in a certain directory. In addition, the ownership, modification, and access times of compressed files are preserved by default, and the -v option to the gzip command can be used to display the compression ratio and filename. However, gzip uses the .gz filename extension by default.

To compress the samplefile and samplefile2 files shown earlier and view the compression ratio, you can use the following command:

```
[root@server1 ~]# gzip -v samplefile samplefile2
samplefile:        82.2% -- replaced with samplefile.gz
samplefile2:       65.0% -- replaced with samplefile2.gz
[root@server1 ~]# _
```

Because GNU zip uses the same fundamental compression algorithm as compress, you can use the zcat, zmore, zless, and zgrep commands to send the contents of a gzip-compressed file to Standard Output. Similarly, the gzip command can accept information via Standard Input. Thus, to compress the output of the date command to a file called file.gz and view its contents afterward, you can use the following commands:

```
[root@server1 ~]# date | gzip -v >file.gz
-6.9%
[root@server1 ~]# zcat file.gz
Sun Jul 25 19:24:56 EDT 2019
[root@server1 ~]# _
```

To decompress the file.gz file in the preceding output, you can use the -d option to the gzip command, or the gunzip **command**, as shown in the following output:

```
[root@server1 ~]# gunzip -v file.gz
file.gz:        -6.9% -- replaced with file
[root@server1 ~]# _
```

Like the uncompress command, the gunzip command prompts you to overwrite existing files unless the -f option is specified. Furthermore, you can omit the .gz extension when decompressing files, as shown in the following example:

```
[root@server1 ~]# ls -l
total 20
drwx------    3 root     root         4096 Jul 21 08:15 Desktop
-rw-rw-r--    1 root     root          219 Jul 21 08:18 samplefile2.gz
-rw-r--r--    1 root     root         4898 Jul 21 08:15 samplefile.gz
```

```
[root@server1 ~]# gunzip -v samplefile samplefile2
samplefile.gz:      82.2% -- replaced with samplefile
samplefile2.gz:     65.0% -- replaced with samplefile2
[root@server1 ~]# ls -1
total 28
drwx------   3 root      root          4096 Jul 21 08:15 Desktop
-rw-r--r--   1 root      root         27298 Jul 21 08:15 samplefile
-rw-rw-r--   1 root      root           540 Jul 21 08:18 samplefile2
[root@server1 ~]# _
```

One of the largest advantages that gzip has over compress is its ability to control the level of compression via a numeric option. The -1 option is also known as fast compression and results in a lower compression ratio. Alternatively, the -9 option is known as best compression and results in the highest compression ratio at the expense of time. If no level of compression is specified, the gzip command assumes the -6 option.

The following command compresses the samplefile file shown earlier using fast compression and displays the compression ratio:

```
[root@server1 ~]# gzip -v -1 samplefile
samplefile:      78.8% -- replaced with samplefile.gz
[root@server1 ~]# _
```

Notice from the preceding output that samplefile was compressed with a compression ratio of 78.8 percent, which is lower than the compression ratio of 82.2 percent obtained earlier when samplefile was compressed with the default level of 6.

Note

You need not specify the level of compression when decompressing files, as it is built into the compressed file itself.

Many more options are available to gzip than to compress, and many of these options have a POSIX option equivalent. Table 11-2 shows a list of these options.

Table 11-2 Common GNU zip options

Option	Description
-#	When used with the gzip command, it specifies how thorough the compression will be, where # can be the number 1–9. The option -1 represents fast compression, which takes less time to compress but results in a lower compression ratio. The option -9 represents thorough compression, which takes more time but results in a higher compression ratio.
--best	When used with the gzip command, it results in a higher compression ratio; same as the -9 option.
-c --stdout --to-stdout	Displays the contents of the compressed file to Standard Output (same function as the zcat command) when used with the gunzip command.
-d --decompress --uncompress	Decompresses the files specified (same as the gunzip command) when used with the gzip command.
-f --force	Compresses linked files and files with special permissions set when used with the gzip command. When used with the gunzip command, it overwrites any existing files without prompting the user.
--fast	When used with the gzip command, it results in a lower compression ratio; same as the -1 option.
-h --help	Displays the syntax and available options for the gzip and gunzip commands.
-l --list	Lists the compression ratio for files that have been compressed with gzip.
-n --no-name	Does not allow gzip and gunzip to preserve the original modification and access time for files.
-q --quiet	Suppresses all warning messages.
-r --recursive	Specifies to compress or decompress all files recursively within a specified directory.
-S .suffix --suffix .suffix	Specifies a file suffix other than .gz when compressing or decompressing files.
-t --test	Performs a test decompression such that a user can view any error messages before decompression, when used with the gunzip command; it does not decompress files.
-v --verbose	Displays verbose output (compression ratio and filenames) during compression and decompression.

Using xz

Like compress and gzip, the **xz command** can be used to compress files and Standard Input using a Lempel-Ziv compression algorithm (LZMA); however, it uses a different implementation that typically yields a higher compression ratio compared to compress and gzip for most files (60-80 percent, on average). Additionally, xz uses the .xz extension for compressed files by default, and implements the same gzip options shown in Table 11-2 with the exception of -n and -r. To decompress xz-compressed files, you can use the -d option to the xz command, or the unxz command.

The following example compresses the samplefile and samplefile2 files shown earlier with the highest possible compression ratio using xz, as well as decompresses the same files using unxz.

```
[root@server1 ~]# ls -l
total 20
drwx------    3 root     root        4096 Jul 21 08:15 Desktop
-rw-r--r--    1 root     root       27298 Jul 21 08:15 samplefile
-rw-rw-r--    1 root     root         540 Jul 21 08:18 samplefile2
[root@server1 ~]# xz -v -9 samplefile samplefile2
samplefile (1/2)
  100 %          4,632 B / 26.7 KiB = 0.170

samplefile2 (2/2)
  100 %            264 B / 540 B = 0.489
[root@server1 ~]# ls -l
total 28
drwx------    3 root     root        4096 Jul 21 08:15 Desktop
-rw-r--r--    1 root     root        4632 Jul 21 08:15 samplefile.xz
-rw-rw-r--    1 root     root         264 Jul 21 08:18 samplefile2.xz
[root@server1 ~]# unxz -v samplefile.xz samplefile2.xz
samplefile.xz (1/2)
  100 %          4,632 B / 26.7 KiB = 0.170

samplefile2.xz (2/2)
  100 %            264 B / 540 B = 0.489
[root@server1 ~]# ls -l
total 20
drwx------    3 root     root        4096 Jul 21 08:15 Desktop
-rw-r--r--    1 root     root       27298 Jul 21 08:15 samplefile
-rw-rw-r--    1 root     root         540 Jul 21 08:18 samplefile2
[root@server1 ~]# _
```

Note 📎

Unlike uncompress and gunzip, you must include the filename extension when decompressing files using the unxz command.

You can use the **xzcat, xzmore, xzless,** or **xzgrep command** to send the contents of an xz-compressed file to Standard Output.

Using zip

The **zip command** is a Linux implementation of the cross-platform PKZIP utility, which was originally designed to compress multiple files into a single compressed file. Because it compresses files and Standard Input using the same implementation of the Lempel-Ziv compression algorithm that gzip uses, it often yields a similar compression ratio on average. The zip command compresses linked files, as well as preserves file ownership, modification, and access time during compression. While there is no default file extension used for zip-compressed archives, .zip is often used by convention.

Note 📎

The zip command is not installed on Ubuntu Server by default. To install it from a software repository on the Internet, you can run the apt-get install zip command as the root user.

The following example compresses the samplefile and samplefile2 files shown earlier into a single samplefile.zip file and displays the compression ratio (-v) during the process:

```
[root@server1 ~]# ls -l
total 20
drwx------    3 root     root          4096 Jul 21 08:15 Desktop
-rw-r--r--    1 root     root         27298 Jul 21 08:15 samplefile
-rw-rw-r--    1 root     root           540 Jul 21 08:18 samplefile2
[root@server1 ~]# zip -v samplefile.zip samplefile samplefile2
  adding: samplefile   (in=27298) (out=4869) (deflated 82%)
  adding: samplefile2  (in=540) (out=189) (deflated 65%)
total bytes=27838, compressed=5058 -> 82% savings
```

```
[root@server1 ~]# ls -l
total 22
drwx------    3 root      root          4096 Jul 21 08:15 Desktop
-rw-r--r--    1 root      root         27298 Jul 21 08:15 samplefile
-rw-rw-r--    1 root      root           540 Jul 21 08:18 samplefile2
-rw-r--r--    1 root      root          5378 Jul 22 07:28 samplefile.zip
[root@server1 ~]# _
```

> **Note**
>
> You can use the `zcat`, `zmore`, `zless`, or `zgrep` commands to send the contents of a zip-compressed file to Standard Output.

To view the contents of, or extract a zip-compressed file, you can use the `unzip` command. The following example views the contents of the samplefile.zip archive, and then extracts those contents to the current folder:

```
[root@server1 ~]# unzip -v samplefile.zip
Archive:  samplefile.zip
 Length   Method    Size  Cmpr    Date      Time   CRC-32    Name
--------  ------   ------- ----  ---------- -----  --------  ----
   27298  Defl:N     4869  82%  2019-06-21 08:15  a57ea058  samplefile
     540  Defl:N      189  65%  2019-06-21 08:18  b6509945  samplefile2
--------           ------- ---                             -------
   27838              5058  82%                             2 files
[root@server1 ~]# unzip samplefile.zip
Archive:  samplefile.zip
  inflating: samplefile
  inflating: samplefile2
[root@server1 ~]# ls -l
total 22
drwx------    3 root      root          4096 Jul 21 08:15 Desktop
-rw-r--r--    1 root      root         27298 Jul 21 08:15 samplefile
-rw-rw-r--    1 root      root           540 Jul 21 08:18 samplefile2
-rw-r--r--    1 root      root          5378 Jul 22 07:28 samplefile.zip
[root@server1 ~]# _
```

Table 11-3 provides a summary of options commonly used with the zip utility.

Table 11-3 Common options used with the zip utility

Option	Description
-#	When used with the zip command, it specifies how thorough the compression will be, where # can be the number 1–9. The option -1 represents fast compression, which takes less time to compress but results in a lower compression ratio. The option -9 represents thorough compression, which takes more time but results in a higher compression ratio.
-c	Displays the contents of the compressed file to Standard Output (same function as the zcat command) when used with the unzip command.
-d directory	When used with the unzip command, it extracts the contents of the zip-compressed file to the specified directory.
-e	When used with the zip command, it encrypts the contents of the zip-compressed file using a password that the user is prompted to enter following the command. The user will be prompted for this password when using the unzip command.
-h --help	Displays the syntax and available options for the zip and unzip commands.
-m --move	When used with the zip command, it moves the specified files into the zip-compressed file.
-q --quiet	Suppresses all warning messages.
-r --recurse-path	When used with the zip command, it compresses all files recursively within a specified directory.
-v --verbose	When used with the zip command, it displays the compression ratio and filenames. When used with the unzip command, it displays the contents and compression ratios of the files within the zip-compressed file.

Using bzip2

The bzip2 command differs from the compress, gzip, zip, and xz commands previously discussed in that it uses the Burrows-Wheeler Block Sorting Huffman Coding algorithm when compressing files, which is better suited to compressing already compressed files as well as files with binary data contents. It provides a compression ratio of 60–80 percent on average.

As with compress and gzip, symbolic links are only compressed if the -f option is used, and the -v option can be used to display compression ratios. Also, file ownership, modification, and access time are preserved during compression.

The filename extension given to files compressed with bzip2 is .bz2. To compress the samplefile and samplefile2 files and view their compression ratios and filenames, you can use the following commands:

```
[root@server1 ~]# bzip2 -v samplefile samplefile2
samplefile: 5.044:1, 1.586 bits/byte, 80.17% saved, 27298 in, 5412 out.
samplefile2: 2.101:1, 3.807 bits/byte, 52.41% saved, 540 in, 257 out.
[root@server1 ~]# ls -l
total 16
drwx------    3 root       root          4096 Jul 21 08:15 Desktop
-rw-rw-r--    1 root       root           257 Jul 21 08:18 samplefile2.bz2
-rw-r--r--    1 root       root          5412 Jul 21 08:15 samplefile.bz2
[root@server1 ~]# _
```

Because the compression algorithm is different from the one used by compress, gzip, zip, and xz, you must use the bzcat command to display the contents of bzip2-compressed files to Standard Output, as shown in the following example:

```
[root@server1 ~]# bzcat samplefile2.bz2
Hi there, I hope this day finds you well.

Unfortunately we were not able to make it to your dining
room this year while vacationing in Algonquin Park - I
especially wished to see the model of the Highland Inn
and the train station in the dining room.

I have been reading on the history of Algonquin Park but
no where could I find a description of where the Highland
Inn was originally located on Cache lake.

If it is no trouble, could you kindly let me know such that
I need not wait until next year when I visit your lodge?

Regards,
Mackenzie Elizabeth

[root@server1 ~]# _
```

> **Note**
>
> You can also use the bzmore and bzless commands to view the contents of a bzip2-compressed file page by page, or the bzgrep command to search the contents of a bzip2-compressed file.

To decompress files, you can use the `bunzip2` **command** followed by the filename(s) to decompress; the following command decompresses the samplefile.bz2 and samplefile2.bz2 files created earlier and displays the results:

```
[root@server1 ~]# bunzip2 -v samplefile.bz2 samplefile2.bz2
  samplefile.bz2:   done
  samplefile2.bz2: done
[root@server1 ~]# _
```

If any files are about to be overwritten, the `bunzip2` command prompts the user for confirmation. To skip this confirmation, you can include the `-f` option. Table 11-4 lists other common options used with the bzip2 utility.

Table 11-4 Common options used with the bzip2 utility

Option	Description
`-#`	When used with the `bzip2` command, it specifies the block size used during compression; `-1` indicates a block size of 100KB, whereas `-9` indicates a block size of 900KB.
`-c` `--stdout`	Displays the contents of the compressed file to Standard Output when used with the `bunzip2` command.
`-d` `--decompress`	Decompresses the files specified (same as the `bunzip2` command) when used with the `bzip2` command.
`-f` `--force`	Compresses symbolic links when used with the `bzip2` command. When used with the `bunzip2` command, it overwrites any existing files without prompting the user.
`-k` `--keep`	Keeps the original file during compression; a new file is created with the extension `.bz2`.
`-q` `--quiet`	Suppresses all warning messages.
`-s` `--small`	Minimizes memory usage during compression.
`-t` `--test`	Performs a test decompression when used with the `bunzip2` command, such that a user can view any error messages before decompression; it does not decompress files.
`-v` `--verbose`	Displays verbose output (compression ratio) during compression and decompression.

System Backup

It's a good idea to create backup copies of files and directories regularly and store them at an alternate location. You can then distribute these backup copies to other computers or use them to restore files lost as a result of a system failure or user error. This entire process is known as **system backup**, and the backup copies of files and directories are called **archives**.

You can create an archive on many types of media, such as tapes, CDs, and DVDs. Alternatively, you can create an archive within a single file stored in an existing filesystem on a USB flash drive, hard disk, or SSD. Traditionally, tapes were used to back up data, and while some organizations still use tapes to store archives, most archives are stored within files on a filesystem today. Larger backups are typically performed to files stored on hard disks, while smaller backups are typically performed to files stored on USB flash drives. Some organizations perform smaller backups to DVDs, which require special disc burning software described later in this chapter.

Table 11-5 shows a list of some common device files used for tape devices.

Table 11-5	Common tape device files
Device file	**Description**
/dev/st0	First SCSI tape device (rewinding)
/dev/st1	Second SCSI tape device (rewinding)
/dev/st2	Third SCSI tape device (rewinding)
/dev/nst0	First SCSI tape device (nonrewinding)
/dev/ht0	First ATAPI IDE tape device (rewinding)
/dev/nht0	First ATAPI IDE tape device (nonrewinding)

After creating an archive within a file on a filesystem, it is good practice to copy that file to another server across the Internet; this is called an **offsite backup** and ensures that data can be recovered following a catastrophic event, such as a building fire. You can use the `sftp` **(secure FTP) command**, `scp` **(secure copy) command** or `rsync` **(remote sync) command** to copy an archive file to a remote server across the Internet; you examine these commands in later chapters.

A typical Linux system can include hundreds of thousands of files, but you don't have to include all of them in an archive. For example, you don't have to include temporary files in the /tmp and /var/tmp directories.

As a rule of thumb, you should back up files used by system services. For example, you should back up website content files if the Linux computer is used as a Web server, and database files if the Linux computer hosts a database server. In addition, you should back up user files from home directories and any important system configuration files such as /etc/passwd. Operating system components and programs such as grep and vi need not be backed up because they can be reinstalled in the event of a system failure.

After files have been selected for system backup, you can use a backup utility to copy the files to the appropriate media or archive file on a filesystem. Several backup utilities are available to Linux administrators. The most common are the following:

- tape archive (tar)
- copy in/out (cpio)
- dump/restore
- dd
- disc burning software

Note 🖉

In addition to the utilities mentioned here, many third-party commercial backup software suites can be used to back up data on multiple computers across the network; common examples include Arcserve Backup, Veritas NetBackup, NetApp, and Acronis Backup.

While software RAID, ZFS, and BTRFS can be configured to perform fault tolerance for data, you should still regularly back up the data stored on these volumes to ensure that data can be recovered if an entire software RAID, ZFS, or BTRFS volume fails.

Some storage technologies provide features that can provide duplicate copies of data for backup purposes. For example, ZFS supports snapshot clones, which can be used to create backup copies of ZFS filesystems, and the LVM supports automatic mirroring of logical volumes, which can be used to store backup copies of logical volumes on different physical volumes.

Using tape archive (tar)

The **tape archive (tar)** utility is one of the oldest, most widely used backup utilities and is executed via the **tar command**. It can create an archive in a file on a filesystem or directly on a device.

Like the compression utilities discussed earlier, the tar command accepts options to determine the location of the archive and the action to perform on the archive. Any arguments specified to the tar command list the file(s) to place in the archive. Table 11-6 lists common options used with the tar command.

Table 11-6   Common options used with the `tar` command

Option	Description

`-A`
`--catenate`
`--concatenate`
	Appends whole archives to another archive

`-c` `--create`	Creates a new archive
`--exclude PATTERN`	Excludes files that have a matching *PATTERN* in their filename when creating an archive
`-f FILENAME` `--file FILENAME`	Specifies the location of the archive (*FILENAME*); it can be a file on a filesystem or a device file
`-h` `--dereference`	Prevents tar from backing up symbolic links; instead, tar backs up the target files of symbolic links
`-j` `--bzip`	Compresses/decompresses the archive using the `bzip2` utility
`-J` `--xz`	Compresses/decompresses the archive using the `xz` utility
`-P` `--absolute-paths`	Stores filenames in an archive using absolute pathnames
`-r` `--append`	Appends files to an existing archive
`--remove-files`	Removes files after adding them to an archive
`-t` `--list`	Lists the filename contents (table of contents) of an existing archive
`-u` `--update`	Appends files to an existing archive only if they are newer than the same filename inside the archive
`-v` `--verbose`	Displays verbose output (file and directory information) when manipulating archives

`-w`
`--interactive`
`--confirmation`
	Prompts the user for confirmation of each action

`-W` `--verify`	Verifies the contents of each archive after creation

(continues)

Table 11-6   Common options used with the `tar` command *(continued)*

Option	Description
-x --extract --get	Extracts the contents of an archive
-z --gzip --ungzip	Compresses/decompresses the archive using the `gzip` utility
-Z --compress --uncompress	Compresses/decompresses the archive using the `compress` utility

To create an archive called /backup.tar that contains the contents of the current directory and view the results, you can use the following commands:

```
[root@server1 ~]# tar -cvf /backup.tar   *
Desktop/
Desktop/Home.desktop
Desktop/trash.desktop
samplefile
samplefile2
[root@server1 ~]# ls -l /backup.tar
-rw-r--r--    1 root      root          40960 Jul 27 10:49 /backup.tar
[root@server1 ~]# _
```

Note from the preceding command that the `-f` option is followed by the pathname of the archive and that the `*` metacharacter indicates that all files in the current directory will be added to this archive. Also note that files are backed up recursively by default and stored using relative pathnames; to force the use of absolute pathnames when creating archives, use the `-P` option to the `tar` command.

Note

The filename used for an archive need not have an extension. However, it is good practice to name archive files with an extension to identify their contents, as with /backup.tar in the preceding example.

The tar utility cannot back up device files or files with filenames longer than 255 characters.

After creating an archive, you can view its detailed contents by specifying the −t (table of contents) option to the tar command and the archive to view. For example, to view the detailed contents of the /backup.tar archive created earlier, you can issue the following command:

```
[root@server1 ~]# tar -tvf /backup.tar
drwx------ root/root        0 2019-07-21 08:15 Desktop/
-rw-r--r-- root/root     3595 2019-06-21 20:32 Desktop/Home.desktop
-rw-r--r-- root/root     3595 2019-06-21 20:32 Desktop/trash.desktop
-rw-r--r-- root/root    20239 2019-07-21 08:15 samplefile
-rw-rw-r-- root/root      574 2019-07-21 08:18 samplefile2
[root@server1 ~]# _
```

You can use the −x option with the tar command to extract a specified archive. To extract the contents of the /backup.tar file to a new directory called /tartest and view the results, you can issue the following commands:

```
[root@server1 ~]# mkdir /tartest
[root@server1 ~]# cd /tartest
[root@server1 tartest]# tar -xvf /backup.tar
Desktop/
Desktop/Home.desktop
Desktop/trash.desktop
samplefile
samplefile2
[root@server1 tartest]# ls -F
Desktop/   samplefile   samplefile2
[root@server1 tartest]# _
```

After an archive has been created in a file on a filesystem, that file can be sent to other computers across a network or the Internet. This is the most common form of backup today and a common method used to distribute software across the Internet. Unfortunately, the tar utility does not compress files inside the archive. Thus, the time needed to transfer the archive across a network is high. To reduce transfer times, you can compress the archive using a compression utility before transmission. Because this is a common task, the tar command accepts options that allow you to compress an archive immediately after creation using the compress, gzip, xz, or bzip2 command.

To create a gzip-compressed archive called /backup.tar.gz that contains the contents of the current directory and view the results, you can use the following commands:

```
[root@server1 ~]# tar -zcvf /backup.tar.gz   *
Desktop/
Desktop/Home.desktop
Desktop/trash.desktop
```

```
samplefile
samplefile2
[root@server1 ~]# ls -l /backup.tar*
-rw-r--r--   1 root     root        40960 Jul 27 10:49 /backup.tar
-rw-r--r--   1 root     root        12207 Jul 27 11:18 /backup.tar.gz
[root@server1 ~]# _
```

Note in the preceding output that the −z option indicated compression using the gzip utility, and that we chose to end the filename with the .tar.gz extension. In addition, the size of the /backup.tar.gz file is much less than the /backup.tar file created earlier.

> **Note**
>
> Filenames that end with the .tar.gz or .tgz extension are commonly called **tarballs** because they represent compressed tar archives.

To view the contents of a gzip-compressed archive, you must use the −z option in addition to the −t option followed by the archive to view. The detailed contents of the /backup.tar.gz file can be viewed using the following command:

```
[root@server1 ~]# tar -ztvf /backup.tar.gz
drwx------ root/root        0 2015-07-21 08:15 Desktop/
-rw-r--r-- root/root     3595 2015-06-21 20:32 Desktop/Home.desktop
-rw-r--r-- root/root     3595 2015-06-21 20:32 Desktop/trash.desktop
-rw-r--r-- root/root    20239 2015-07-21 08:15 samplefile
-rw-rw-r-- root/root      574 2015-07-21 08:18 samplefile2
[root@server1 ~]# _
```

Similarly, when extracting a gzip-compressed archive, you must supply the −z option to the tar command. To extract the contents of the /backup.tar.gz file to a new directory called /tartest2 and view the results, you can issue the following commands:

```
[root@server1 ~]# mkdir /tartest2
[root@server1 ~]# cd /tartest2
[root@server1 tartest2]# tar -zxvf /backup.tar.gz
Desktop/
Desktop/Home.desktop
Desktop/trash.desktop
samplefile
samplefile2
[root@server1 tartest2]# ls -F
Desktop/  samplefile  samplefile2
[root@server1 tartest2]# _
```

Backing up files to a compressed archive on a filesystem is useful when you plan to transfer the archived data across a network. However, you can use tar to back up data directly to a device such as a tape. To back up files to a device, you can use the -f option to the tar command to specify the pathname to the appropriate device file. Files are then transferred directly to the device, overwriting any other data or filesystems that might be present.

For example, to create an archive on the first rewinding SCSI tape device containing the contents of the current directory, you can use the following command:

```
[root@server1 ~]# tar -cvf /dev/st0   *
Desktop/
Desktop/Home.desktop
Desktop/trash.desktop
samplefile
samplefile2
[root@server1 ~]#
```

You can then view the contents of the archive on the tape device used in the preceding example using the command tar -tvf /dev/st0 or extract the contents of the archive on the tape device using the command tar -xvf /dev/st0 in a similar fashion to the examples shown earlier.

Because tape devices can hold large amounts of information, you might want to add to a tar archive that already exists on the tape device. To do this, replace the -c option with the -r option when using the tar utility. For example, to append a file called samplefile3 to the archive created in the previous output and view the results, you can use the following commands:

```
[root@server1 ~]# tar -rvf /dev/st0 samplefile3
samplefile3
[root@server1 ~]# tar -tvf /dev/st0
drwx------ root/root        0 2019-07-21 08:15 Desktop/
-rw-r--r-- root/root     3595 2019-06-21 20:32 Desktop/Home.desktop
-rw-r--r-- root/root     3595 2019-06-21 20:32 Desktop/trash.desktop
-rw-r--r-- root/root    20239 2019-07-21 08:15 samplefile
-rw-rw-r-- root/root      574 2019-07-21 08:18 samplefile2
-rw-r--r-- root/root      147 2019-07-27 16:15 samplefile3
[root@server1 ~]# _
```

Using copy in/out (cpio)

Another common backup utility is **copy in/out (cpio)**, which can be executed via the cpio **command**. Although cpio uses options similar to tar, it has some added features, including long filenames and the ability to back up device files.

Because its primary use is to back up files in case of system failure, cpio uses absolute pathnames by default when archiving. In addition, cpio normally takes a list of files to archive from Standard Input and sends the files "out" to the archive specified by the -o option. Conversely, when extracting an archive, you must include the -I option to indicate the archive from which to read "in" files.

Table 11-7 provides a list of commonly used options to the cpio command and their descriptions.

Table 11-7 Common options used with the cpio utility

Option	Description
-A --append	Appends files to an existing archive
-B	Changes the default block size from 512 bytes to 5KB, thus speeding up the transfer of information
-c	Uses a storage format (SVR4) that is widely recognized by different versions of cpio for UNIX and Linux
-d --make-directories	Creates directories as needed during extraction
-i --extract	Reads files from an archive
-I FILENAME	Represents the input archive; it is the file or device file of the archive used when viewing or extracting files
-L --dereference	Prevents cpio from backing up symbolic links; instead, cpio backs up the target files of symbolic links
--no-absolute-filenames	Stores filenames in an archive using relative pathnames
-o --create	Creates a new archive
-O FILENAME	Represents the output archive; it is the file or device file of the target archive when backing up files
-t --list	Lists the filename contents (table of contents) of an existing archive
-u --unconditional	Overwrites existing files during extraction without prompting for user confirmation
-v --verbose	Displays verbose output (file and directory information) when manipulating archives

To create an archive using cpio, you must first generate a list of filenames. You can do this using the find command. To list all filenames under the /root/sample directory, you can use the following command:

```
[root@server1 ~]# find /root/sample
/root/sample
/root/sample/samplefile
/root/sample/samplefile2
[root@server1 ~]# _
```

Next, you can send this list via Standard Input to the cpio command. For example, to verbosely back up all files in /root/sample to the first SCSI tape device using a block size of 5KB and a common format, you can use the following command:

```
[root@server1 ~]# find /root/sample | cpio -vocB -O /dev/st0
/root/sample
/root/sample/samplefile
/root/sample/samplefile2
5 blocks
[root@server1 ~]# _
```

To view the verbose table of contents of this archive, you can use the following command:

```
[root@server1 ~]# cpio -vitB -I /dev/st0
drwxr-xr-x   2 root   root       0  Jul 27 13:40 /root/sample
-rw-r--r--   1 root   root   20239  Jul 21 08:15 /root/sample/samplefile
-rw-rw-r--   1 root   root     574  Jul 21 08:18 /root/sample/samplefile2
5 blocks
[root@server1 ~]# _
```

Following this, you can extract the archive on /dev/sto, creating directories and overwriting files as needed by using the following command:

```
[root@server1 ~]# cpio -vicduB -I /dev/st0
/root/sample
/root/sample/samplefile
/root/sample/samplefile2
5 blocks
[root@server1 ~]# _
```

Like tar, the cpio command can be used to create an archive on a file on the filesystem; to do this, specify the filename after the –O option. To create an archive called /root/sample.cpio that contains the files from the directory /root/sample, using a block size of 5KB as well as a common header, and to view the results, you can issue the following commands:

```
[root@server1 ~]# find /root/sample | cpio -vocB -O
/root/sample.cpio
/root/sample
/root/sample/samplefile
/root/sample/samplefile2
5 blocks
[root@server1 ~]# ls -l sample.cpio
-rw-rw-rw-    1 root   root     25600 Jul 27 13:45 sample.cpio
[root@server1 ~]# _
```

As with the tar utility, cpio archive filenames need not have an extension to identify their contents. However, it is good practice to use extensions, as shown with /root/sample.cpio in the preceding example.

Using dump/restore

Like tar and cpio, the **dump command** can be used to back up files and directories to a device or to a file on the filesystem, and the **restore command** can be used to restore those files and directories. However, dump and restore can only work with files on ext2, ext3, and ext4 filesystems.

> **Note** 📎
>
> The dump and restore commands are not installed on Fedora 28 or Ubuntu Server by default. To install them from a software repository on the Internet, you can run the dnf install dump command as the root user on Fedora 28, or the apt-get install dump command as the root user on Ubuntu Server.

Although dump can be used to back up only certain files and directories, it was designed to back up entire filesystems to an archive and keep track of these filesystems in a file called /etc/dumpdates. Because archiving all data on a filesystem (known as a **full backup**) might take a long time, you can choose to perform a full backup only on weekends and incremental backups each evening during the week. An **incremental backup** backs up only the data that has been changed since the last backup. In the case of a system failure, you can restore the information from the full backup and then restore the information from all subsequent incremental backups in sequential order. You can perform up to nine different incremental backups using dump; number 0 represents a full backup, whereas numbers 1 through 9 represent incremental backups.

Suppose, for example, that you perform a full backup of the /dev/sda3 filesystem on Sunday, perform incremental backups from Monday to Wednesday, and on Thursday the /dev/sda3 filesystem becomes corrupted, as depicted in Figure 11-1.

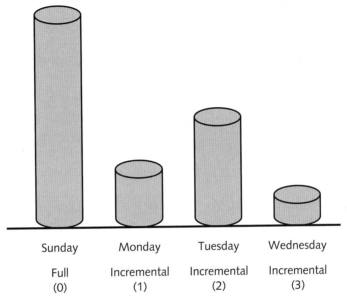

Sunday	Monday	Tuesday	Wednesday
Full	Incremental	Incremental	Incremental
(0)	(1)	(2)	(3)

Figure 11-1   A sample backup strategy

After the filesystem has been re-created, you should restore the full backup (0) followed by the first incremental backup (1), the second incremental backup (2), and the third incremental backup (3) to ensure that data has been properly recovered.

Note 📎

Differential backups are an alternative to incremental backups; they back up only the data that has been changed since the last full backup. This allows you to recover data by restoring a full backup followed by the most recent differential backup only. While dump/restore cannot perform differential backups, many third-party software suites can.

The `dump` and `restore` commands have many options available; Table 11-8 provides a list of these options.

Table 11-8	Common options used with `dump/restore`

Option	Description
`-#`	Specifies the type of backup when used with the `dump` command; if # is 0, a full backup is performed. If # is 1 through 9, the appropriate incremental backup is performed.
`-b SIZE`	When used with the `dump` command, it specifies a certain block size to use in kilobytes; the default block size is 10KB.
`-f FILENAME`	Specifies the pathname to the archive; the `FILENAME` can be a file on a filesystem or a device file.
`-u`	Specifies to update the /etc/dumpdates file after a successful backup.
`-n`	When used with the `dump` command, it notifies the user if any errors occur and when the backup has completed.
`-r`	Extracts an entire archive when used with the `restore` command.
`-x FILENAME`	Extracts a certain file or files represented by `FILENAME` when used with the `restore` command.
`-i`	Restores files interactively, prompting the user for confirmation for all actions, when used with the `restore` command.
`-t`	Lists the filename contents (table of contents) of an existing archive when used with the `restore` command.
`-v`	Displays verbose output (file and directory information) when manipulating archives.

Take, for example, the output from the following df command:

```
[root@server1 ~]# df
Filesystem              1K-blocks      Used Available Use% Mounted on
/dev/sda1               30237648    6885728  21815920   24% /
tmpfs                     480640        272    480368    1% /dev/shm
/dev/sda3               15481840     169484  14525924    2% /data
[root@server1 ~]# _
```

To perform a full backup of the /data partition (/dev/sda3) to the first rewinding SCSI tape device and update the /etc/dumpdates file when completed, you can issue the following command:

```
[root@server1 ~]# dump -0uf /dev/st0 /dev/sda3
  DUMP: Date of this level 0 dump: Sat Aug 28 10:39:12 2019
  DUMP: Dumping /dev/sda3 (/data) to /dev/st0
  DUMP: Label: none
  DUMP: Writing 10 Kilobyte records
  DUMP: mapping (Pass I) [regular files]
  DUMP: mapping (Pass II) [directories]
```

```
  DUMP: estimated 300 blocks.
  DUMP: Volume 1 started with block 1 at: Sat Aug 28 10:39:12 2019
  DUMP: dumping (Pass III) [directories]
  DUMP: dumping (Pass IV) [regular files]
  DUMP: Closing /dev/sda3
  DUMP: Volume 1 completed at: Sat Aug 28 10:39:12 2019
  DUMP: Volume 1 290 blocks (0.28MB)
  DUMP: 290 blocks (0.28MB) on 1 volume(s)
  DUMP: finished in less than a second
  DUMP: Date of this level 0 dump: Sat Aug 28 10:39:12 2019
  DUMP: Date this dump completed:  Sat Aug 28 10:39:12 2019
  DUMP: Average transfer rate: 0 kB/s
  DUMP: DUMP IS DONE
[root@server1 ~]# _
```

> **Note** 🖉
>
> Alternatively, you can specify the filesystem mount point when using the `dump` command.
> The command `dump -0uf /dev/st0 /data` is equivalent to the one used in the preceding
> example.
> To create a dump archive within a file, you can specify a filename instead of a device file.
> For example, the `dump -0uf /data-archive.dump /data` would create the same archive
> used in the preceding example within the /data-archive.dump file.

The contents of the /etc/dumpdates file now indicate that a full backup has taken place:

```
[root@server1 ~]# cat /etc/dumpdates
/dev/sda3 0 Sat Aug 28 10:39:12 2019 -0400
[root@server1 ~]# _
```

To perform the first incremental backup and view the contents of the /etc/
dumpdates file, you can place a new tape into the SCSI tape drive and issue the
following commands:

```
[root@server1 ~]# dump -1uf /dev/st0 /dev/sda3
  DUMP: Date of this level 1 dump: Sat Aug 28 10:41:09 2019
  DUMP: Date of last level 0 dump: Sat Aug 28 10:39:12 2019
  DUMP: Dumping /dev/sda3 (/data) to /dev/st0
  DUMP: Label: none
  DUMP: Writing 10 Kilobyte records
  DUMP: mapping (Pass I) [regular files]
  DUMP: mapping (Pass II) [directories]
```

```
DUMP: estimated 255 blocks.
DUMP: Volume 1 started with block 1 at: Sat Aug 28 10:41:10 2019
DUMP: dumping (Pass III) [directories]
DUMP: dumping (Pass IV) [regular files]
DUMP: Closing /dev/sda3
DUMP: Volume 1 completed at: Sat Aug 28 10:41:10 2019
DUMP: Volume 1 250 blocks (0.24MB)
DUMP: 250 blocks (0.24MB) on 1 volume(s)
DUMP: finished in less than a second
DUMP: Date of this level 1 dump: Sat Aug 28 10:41:09 2019
DUMP: Date this dump completed:  Sat Aug 28 10:41:10 2019
DUMP: Average transfer rate: 0 kB/s
DUMP: DUMP IS DONE
[root@server1 ~]# cat /etc/dumpdates
/dev/sda3 0 Sat Aug 28 10:39:12 2019 -0400
/dev/sda3 1 Sat Aug 28 10:41:09 2019 -0400
[root@server1 ~]# _
```

To view the contents of an archive, you can specify the -t option to the restore command followed by the archive information. To view the contents of the full backup performed earlier, you can place the appropriate tape into the tape drive and execute the following command:

```
[root@server1 ~]# restore -tf /dev/st0
Dump    date: Sat Aug 28 10:39:12 2019
Dumped from: the epoch
Level 0 dump of /data on server1.class.com:/dev/sda3
Label: none
        2  .
       11  ./lost+found
       12  ./inittab
       13  ./hosts
       14  ./issue
       17  ./aquota.user
       15  ./aquota.group
[root@server1 ~]# _
```

To extract the full backup shown in the preceding output, you can specify the -r option to the restore command followed by the archive information. In addition, you can specify the -v option to list the filenames restored, as shown in the following example:

```
[root@server1 ~]# restore -vrf /dev/st0
Verify tape and initialize maps
```

```
Input is from a local file/pipe
Input block size is 32
Dump    date: Sat Aug 28 10:39:12 2019
Dumped from: the epoch
Level 0 dump of /data on server1.class.com:/dev/sda3
Label: none
Begin level 0 restore
Initialize symbol table.
Extract directories from tape
Calculate extraction list.
Make node ./lost+found
Extract new leaves.
Check pointing the restore
extract file ./inittab
extract file ./hosts
extract file ./issue
extract file ./aquota.group
extract file ./aquota.user
Add links
Set directory mode, owner, and times.
Check the symbol table.
Check pointing the restore
[root@server1 ~]# _
```

Using dd

Unlike the `tar`, `cpio`, and `dump` commands, which back up data in a file-based format, the **dd command** backs up data block by block to an archive device or file, without keeping track of the files that the blocks comprise. This type of backup is called an **image backup** and is often used to create archives of entire filesystems or disk structures (e.g., MBR).

At minimum, the `dd` command requires an input file (`if`) and an output file (`of`) option to be specified. For example, to create an image backup of the filesystem on /dev/sda2 within the archive file /sda2.img, you could use the following command:

```
[root@server1 ~]# dd if=/dev/sda2 of=/sda2.img
2097152+0 records in
2097152+0 records out
1073741824 bytes (1.1 GB, 1.0 GiB) copied, 9.29465 s, 116 MB/s
[root@server1 ~]# _
```

Note

By default, the dd command copies information 512 bytes at a time, but you can modify this behavior using the bs (block size) option. For example, `dd if=/dev/sda2 of=/sda2.img bs=1M` would transfer information 1MB at a time, which would result in a faster transfer rate compared to the default.

To restore the filesystem on /dev/sda2 from the /sda2.img archive file, you could unmount the existing filesystem from /dev/sda2 and run the dd command with the input and output files reversed:

```
[root@server1 ~]# umount /dev/sda2
[root@server1 ~]# dd if=/sda2.img of=/dev/sda2
2097152+0 records in
2097152+0 records out
1073741824 bytes (1.1 GB, 1.0 GiB) copied, 44.7753 s, 24.0 MB/s
[root@server1 ~]# _
```

Following this, you can remount the filesystem normally and access the data within.

Note

The dd command can also be used to back up specific storage locations, such as the MBR, which uses the first 512 bytes of a disk device. For example, to back up the MBR on /dev/sda to the /MBRarchive.img file, you could use the `dd if=/dev/sda of=/MBRarchive.img bs=512 count=1` command.

Using Disc Burning Software

The backup utilities you've examined thus far are primarily used to create archive files on filesystems or tape devices. To create an archive on CD or DVD media, you must use a program that allows you to select the data to copy, organize that data, build a CD or DVD filesystem, and write the entire filesystem (including the data) to the CD or DVD. Recall from Chapter 2 that the programs that can be used to do this are called disc burning software. Figure 11-2 shows the **Brasero** disc burning software. You can install Brasero on a Fedora 28 system using the `dnf install brasero` command as the root user, and launch it from the GNOME desktop by navigating to Activities, Show Applications, Brasero. You can then click the Data project button shown in Figure 11-2, select the data that you wish to back up, and click Burn to write it to your CD or DVD drive.

Figure 11-2   The Brasero disc burning software

Software Installation

Primary responsibilities of most Linux administrators typically include installing and maintaining software packages. Software for Linux can consist of binary files that have been precompiled to run on certain hardware architectures such as 64-bit Intel (x86_64), or as source code, which must be compiled on the local architecture before use. The largest advantage to obtaining and compiling source code is that the source code is not created for a particular hardware architecture. After being compiled, the program executes natively on the architecture from which it was compiled.

Note 📎

The most common method for obtaining software for Linux is via the Internet. Appendix C lists some common websites that host Linux Open Source Software for download.

When downloading software files from the Internet, you may notice that the Internet site lists a **checksum** value for the file, which was calculated from the exact file contents. To ensure that the file was received in its entirety after you download it, you should verify that the checksum value is still the same. You can use one of several *sum **commands**, depending on the algorithm used to create the checksum. For example, you can use the md5sum programfile command to check an MD5 checksum, the sha1sum programfile command to check an SHA-1 checksum, the sha256sum programfile command to check an SHA-256 checksum, or the sha512sum programfile command to check an SHA-512 checksum.

Precompiled binary programs can also be distributed in tarball format, but they are typically distributed in a format for use with a package manager. Recall from Chapter 1 that a **package manager** provides a standard format for distributing programs as well as a central database to store information about software packages installed on the system; this allows software packages to be queried and easily uninstalled. Many Linux distributions today, including Fedora, use the **Red Hat Package Manager (RPM)**. However, Debian and Debian-based Linux distributions, such as Ubuntu Linux, use the **Debian Package Manager (DPM)**.

> **Note**
>
> RPM and DPM are used by nearly all mainstream Linux distributions. However, they are not the only package managers available on Linux systems. For example, Arch Linux uses the Pacman package manager, and Gentoo Linux uses the Portage package manager.

Compiling Source Code into Programs

Program source code is typically obtained by cloning an online git repository as described in Chapter 7, or by downloading a tarball that contains the source code and extracting its contents. If your system has a GUI installed, you can download a source code tarball from the Internet using a Web browser. Alternatively, if your system does not have a GUI installed, you can use the `wget` **(Web get) command** or `curl` **(client for URLs) command** to download a source code tarball. For example, to download a sample source code tarball called sample.tar.gz from https://sample.com to your current directory, you could use the `wget https://sample.com/sample.tar.gz` or `curl https://sample.com/sample.tar.gz --output sample.tar.gz` command.

After you clone a git repository of source code, or download and extract the contents of a source code tarball, there will be a subdirectory under the current directory containing the source code. This directory typically contains a text file that starts with README or INSTALL with information about the program and instructions for installation.

While inside the source code directory, the first step to installation is to run the `configure` program. This performs a preliminary check for system requirements and creates a list of what to compile inside a file called Makefile in the current directory.

Next, you can type the `make` command, which looks for the Makefile file and uses the information in it to compile the source code into binary programs using the appropriate compiler program for the local hardware architecture. For example, software written in the C programming language is compiled using the **GNU C Compiler (gcc)**. After compilation, the binary files the program comprises remain in the source code directory. To install the compiled program on your system, you must type `make install` to copy the newly compiled executable files to a directory listed in your PATH variable, as well as copy supporting files, such as man pages, to the correct location on the filesystem.

Note 📎

Most Linux programs compiled from source code are installed to a subdirectory of the /usr/local directory after compilation.

After the program has been compiled and copied to the correct location on the filesystem, you can remove the source code directory and its contents from the system.

Suppose, for example, that you download the source code tarball for conky (a desktop system monitor app) version 1.9.0 from the Internet at *sourceforge.net*:

```
[root@server1 ~]# ls -F
Desktop/    conky-1.9.0.tar.bz2
[root@server1 ~]# _
```

The first step to installing this program is to extract the contents of the tarball, which will create a directory containing the source code and supporting files. Next, you can move to this directory and view the file contents, as shown in the following output:

```
[root@server1 ~]# tar -jxf conky-1.9.0.tar.bz2
[root@server1 ~]# ls -F
Desktop/    conky-1.9.0/    conky-1.9.0.tar.bz2
[root@server1 ~]# cd conky-1.9.0
[root@server1 conky-1.9.0]# ls -F
aclocal.m4       config.rpath*    data/          ltmain.sh      NEWS
AUTHORS          config.sub*      depcomp*       lua/           README
autogen.sh*      configure*       doc/           m4/            src/
ChangeLog        configure.ac     extras/        Makefile.am    text2c.sh
compile*         configure.ac.in  INSTALL        Makefile.in    TODO
config.guess*    COPYING          install-sh*    missing*
[root@server1 conky-1.9.0]# _
```

In the preceding output, you can see that a README, INSTALL, and configure file exist and that the configure file is executable. To execute the configure shell script without using the PATH variable, you can enter the following command:

```
[root@server1 conky-1.9.0]# ./configure
checking for a BSD-compatible install... /usr/bin/install -c
checking whether build environment is sane... yes
checking for a thread-safe mkdir -p... /usr/bin/mkdir -p
checking for gawk... gawk
checking whether make sets $(MAKE)... yes
checking for gcc... gcc
checking whether the C compiler works... yes
checking for C compiler default output file name... a.out
checking for suffix of executables...
checking whether we are cross compiling... no
checking for suffix of object files... o
checking whether we are using the GNU C compiler... yes
checking whether gcc accepts -g... yes
checking for gcc option to accept ISO C89... none needed
checking for style of include used by make... GNU
checking dependency style of gcc... gcc3
checking build system type... x86_64-unknown-linux-gnu

<Additional contents omitted here>

[root@server1 conky-1.9.0]# _
```

If the configure shell script produces errors instead of running successfully, you will likely need to install the specified **shared library** necessary to support the program, often using a package manager as described later in this chapter. Shared libraries are files that contain executable code that can be used by multiple, different programs; rather than implementing that code within a program, most program developers reuse the code from a shared library to save time. If the required shared library is for an optional program features, you can instead choose to disable the optional program feature by specifying an option to the configure script. To see a list of available options for your configure script, you can run the ./configure --help command.

After the configure script has run successfully, a Makefile exists in the current directory, as shown in the following output:

```
[root@server1 conky-1.9.0]# head -2 Makefile
# Makefile.in generated by automake 1.11.5 from Makefile.am.
# Makefile.  Generated from Makefile.in by configure.
[root@server1 conky-1.9.0]# _
```

This Makefile contains most of the information and commands necessary to compile the program. Some program source code that you download might contain commented lines that you need to uncomment to enable certain features of the program or to allow the program to compile on your computer architecture. Instructions for these commented areas are documented in the Makefile itself; thus, it is good form to read the Makefile after you run the configure script. You can also edit the Makefile if you want to change the location to which the program is installed. For example, the line `prefix=/usr/local` within the Makefile installs the program to subdirectories under /usr/local.

Next, you must compile the program according to the settings stored in the Makefile by typing the `make` command while in the source code directory. This typically uses the **gcc command** to compile the source code files, as shown in the following output:

```
[root@server1 conky-1.9.0]# make
Making all in src
make[1]: Entering directory '/home/user1/Downloads/conky-1.9.0/src'
make  all-am
make[2]: Entering directory '/home/user1/Downloads/conky-1.9.0/src'
gcc -DHAVE_CONFIG_H -I. -
DSYSTEM_CONFIG_FILE=\"/usr/local/etc/conky/conky.conf\" -
DPACKAGE_LIBDIR=\"/usr/local/lib/conky\"   -I/usr/include/freetype2 -
I/usr/include/libpng16 -I/usr/include/uuid  -I/usr/include/glib-2.0 -
I/usr/lib64/glib-2.0/include  -Wall -W  -MT conky-conf_cookie.o -MD -MP
-MF .deps/conky-conf_cookie.Tpo -c -o conky-conf_cookie.o `test -f
'conf_cookie.c' || echo './'`conf_cookie.c
mv -f .deps/conky-conf_cookie.Tpo .deps/conky-conf_cookie.Po
gcc -DHAVE_CONFIG_H -I. -
DSYSTEM_CONFIG_FILE=\"/usr/local/etc/conky/conky.conf\" -
DPACKAGE_LIBDIR=\"/usr/local/lib/conky\"   -I/usr/include/freetype2 -
I/usr/include/libpng16 -I/usr/include/uuid  -I/usr/include/glib-2.0 -
I/usr/lib64/glib-2.0/include  -Wall -W  -MT conky-mpd.o -MD -MP -MF
.deps/conky-mpd.Tpo -c -o conky-mpd.o `test -f 'mpd.c' || echo
'./'`mpd.c
mv -f .deps/conky-mpd.Tpo .deps/conky-mpd.Po
gcc -DHAVE_CONFIG_H -I. -
DSYSTEM_CONFIG_FILE=\"/usr/local/etc/conky/conky.conf\" -
DPACKAGE_LIBDIR=\"/usr/local/lib/conky\"   -I/usr/include/freetype2 -
I/usr/include/libpng16 -I/usr/include/uuid  -I/usr/include/glib-2.0 -
I/usr/lib64/glib-2.0/include  -Wall -W  -MT conky-libmpdclient.o -MD -
MP -MF .deps/conky-libmpdclient.Tpo -c -o conky-libmpdclient.o `test -f
'libmpdclient.c' || echo './'`libmpdclient.c
mv -f .deps/conky-libmpdclient.Tpo .deps/conky-libmpdclient.Po
```

```
gcc -DHAVE_CONFIG_H -I. -
DSYSTEM_CONFIG_FILE=\"/usr/local/etc/conky/conky.conf\" -
DPACKAGE_LIBDIR=\"/usr/local/lib/conky\"   -I/usr/include/freetype2 -
I/usr/include/libpng16 -I/usr/include/uuid  -I/usr/include/glib-2.0 -
I/usr/lib64/glib-2.0/include  -Wall -W  -MT conky-moc.o -MD -MP -MF
.deps/conky-moc.Tpo -c -o conky-moc.o `test -f 'moc.c' || echo
'./'`moc.c
mv -f .deps/conky-moc.Tpo .deps/conky-moc.Po

<Additional gcc commands omitted here>

[root@server1 conky-1.9.0]# _
```

After you compile the source code files, you can copy the program files to the correct location on the filesystem by typing the following command:

```
[root@server1 conky-1.9.0]# make install
Making install in src
make[1]: Entering directory '/root/conky-1.9.0/src'
make  install-am
make[2]: Entering directory '/root/conky-1.9.0/src'
make[3]: Entering directory '/root/conky-1.9.0/src'
 /usr/bin/mkdir -p '/usr/local/bin'
  /bin/sh ../libtool    --mode=install /usr/bin/install -c conky
'/usr/local/bin'
libtool: install: /usr/bin/install -c conky /usr/local/bin/conky
make[3]: Nothing to be done for 'install-data-am'.
make[3]: Leaving directory '/root/conky-1.9.0/src'
make[2]: Leaving directory '/root/conky-1.9.0/src'
make[1]: Leaving directory '/root/conky-1.9.0/src'
Making install in doc
make[1]: Entering directory '/root/conky-1.9.0/doc'
make[2]: Entering directory '/root/conky-1.9.0/doc'
make[2]: Nothing to be done for 'install-exec-am'.
 /usr/bin/mkdir -p '/usr/local/share/man/man1'
 /usr/bin/install -c -m 644 conky.1 '/usr/local/share/man/man1'
make[2]: Leaving directory '/root/conky-1.9.0/doc'
make[1]: Leaving directory '/root/conky-1.9.0/doc'

<Additional contents omitted here>

[root@server1 conky-1.9.0]# _
```

After the program files are copied to the appropriate directories, you can remove the source code directory and tarball and locate the main binary file for the program, as shown in the following example:

```
[root@server1 conky-1.9.0]# cd ..
[root@server1 ~]# rm -Rf conky-1.9.0
[root@server1 ~]# rm -f conky-1.9.0.tar.bz2
[root@server1 ~]# which conky
/usr/local/bin/conky
[root@server1 ~]# _
```

Finally, you can view the conky manual page, and then switch to a desktop environment running on X.org and run the command conky& within a graphical terminal to execute the conky program, as shown in Figure 11-3.

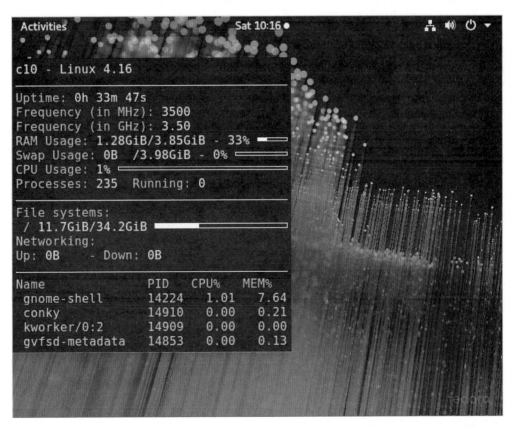

Figure 11-3   The conky program

Working with the Red Hat Package Manager (RPM)

RPM is the most widely used format for Linux software distributed via the Internet on distributions derived from Red Hat Linux. RPM packages have filenames that indicate the hardware architecture for which the software was compiled and end with the .rpm extension. The following output indicates that the bluefish RPM package (a Web page editor) version 2.2.10-8 was compiled for Fedora 28 (fc28) on the Intel x86_64 platform:

```
[root@server1 ~]# ls -F
Desktop/        bluefish-2.2.10-8.fc28.x86_64.rpm
[root@server1 ~]# _
```

To install an RPM package, you can use the -i option to the rpm command. In addition, you can use the -v and -h options to print the verbose information and hash marks, respectively, during installation.

Some RPM packages require that other RPM packages or shared libraries be installed on your system first. This type of relationship is known as a **package dependency**. If you attempt to install an RPM package that has package dependencies, you receive an error message that indicates the packages and shared libraries that need to be installed first. After installing these prerequisites, you can successfully install your desired RPM package. Say, for example, that you download the RPM package for the bluefish Web page editor and run the following command to install it:

```
[root@server1 ~]# rpm -ivh bluefish-2.2.10-8.fc28.x86_64.rpm
error: Failed dependencies:
bluefish-shared-data = 2.2.10-8.fc28 is needed by
    bluefish-2.2.10-8.fc28.x86_64
libgucharmap_2_90.so.7()(64bit) is needed by
    bluefish-2.2.10-8.fc28.x86_64
[root@server1 ~]# _
```

The error shown in the preceding output indicates that there are two package dependencies for the bluefish RPM package called bluefish-shared-data and libgucharmap. Consequently, you must download the bluefish-shared-data package and libgucharmap shared library (part of the gucharmap-libs package) for your architecture. Following this, you can run the following command to install all three packages:

```
[root@server1 ~]# rpm -ivh bluefish.x86_64 2.2.10-8.fc28
bluefish-shared-data.noarch 2.2.10-8.fc28 gucharmap-libs.x86_64
10.0.4-1.fc28
Preparing...                          #################### [100%]
Updating / installing...
 1:bluefish.x86_64 2.2.10-8.fc28       #################### [100%]
 2:shared-data.noarch 2.2.10-8.fc28    #################### [100%]
 3:gucharmap-libs.x86_64 10.0.4-1.fc28 #################### [100%]
[root@server1 ~]# _
```

After you install an RPM package, the RPM database (stored within files in the /var/ lib/rpm directory) is updated to contain information about the package and the files contained within. To query the full package name after installation, you can use the -q (query) option to the rpm command followed by the common name of the package:

```
[root@server1 ~]# rpm -q bluefish
bluefish-2.2.10-8.fc28.x86_64
[root@server1 ~]# _
```

In addition, you can add the -i (info) option to the preceding command to display the detailed package information for the bluefish package:

```
[root@server1 ~]# rpm -qi bluefish
Name         : bluefish
Version      : 2.2.10
Release      : 8.fc28
Architecture: x86_64
Install Date: Sat 29 Sep 2019 11:29:11 AM EDT
Group        : Unspecified
Size         : 1635419
License      : GPLv3+
Signature    : RSA/SHA256, Tue 13 Feb 2019 04:34:43 AM EST, Key ID
e08e7e629db62fb1
Source RPM   : bluefish-2.2.10-8.fc28.src.rpm
Build Date   : Tue 13 Feb 2019 04:29:42 AM EST
Build Host   : buildvm-10.phx2.fedoraproject.org
Relocations  : (not relocatable)
Packager     : Fedora Project
Vendor       : Fedora Project
URL          : http://bluefish.openoffice.n/
Summary      : Web development application for experienced users
Description  :
Bluefish is a powerful editor for experienced web designers
and programmers. Bluefish supports many programming and markup
languages, but it focuses on editing dynamic and interactive
websites.
[root@server1 ~]# _
```

Because the Red Hat Package Manager keeps track of all installed files, you can find the executable file for the bluefish program by using the -q and -l (list) options followed by the RPM package name to list all files contained within the package. The following command lists the first 10 files in the bluefish package:

```
[root@server1 ~]# rpm -ql bluefish
/usr/bin/bluefish
/usr/lib64/bluefish
```

```
/usr/lib64/bluefish/about.so
/usr/lib64/bluefish/charmap.so
/usr/lib64/bluefish/entities.so
/usr/lib64/bluefish/htmlbar.so
/usr/lib64/bluefish/infbrowser.so
/usr/lib64/bluefish/snippets.so
/usr/lib64/bluefish/zencoding.so
/usr/share/licenses/bluefish
/usr/share/licenses/bluefish/COPYING
[root@server1 ~]# _
```

From the preceding output, you can see that the pathname to the executable file is /usr/bin/bluefish, which resides in a directory in the PATH variable. Upon execution in a desktop environment, you see the screen depicted in Figure 11-4.

Figure 11-4 The bluefish program

Conversely, you can find out to which RPM package a certain file belongs by using the –q and –f (file) options with the rpm command, followed by the filename:

```
[root@server1 ~]# rpm -qf /usr/bin/bluefish
bluefish-2.2.10-8.fc28.x86_64
[root@server1 ~]# _
```

To remove an RPM package from the system, you can use the –e option to the rpm command; all files that belong to the package will be removed as well. To remove the bluefish and bluefish-shared-data RPM packages and verify the deletion, you can use the following commands:

```
[root@server1 ~]# rpm -e bluefish bluefish-shared-data
[root@server1 ~]# rpm -q bluefish bluefish-shared-data
package bluefish is not installed
package bluefish-shared-data is not installed
[root@server1 ~]# _
```

Table 11-9 displays a list of common options used with the rpm command.

Table 11-9   Common options used with the rpm command

Option	Description
-a --all	Displays all package names installed on the system (when used with the -q option)
-c --configfiles	Displays the locations of the configuration files for a package installed on the system (when used with the -q option)
--dump	Displays detailed information regarding configuration files for a package installed on the system (when used following the -q and -c options)
-e --erase	Removes a specified package from the system
-F --freshen	Upgrades a specified package only if an older version exists on the system
-f --file	Displays the package to which the specified file belongs (when used with the -q option)
-h --hash	Prints hash marks on the screen to indicate installation progress (when used with the -i option)
-i --install	Installs a specified package (provided the -q option is not used)
-i --info	Displays full information about the specified package (when used with the -q option)
-K	When used before a filename argument, validates the checksum listed within the RPM file
-l --list	Lists the filenames the specified package comprises (when used with the -q option)
--nodeps	Forces the RPM to avoid checking for dependencies before installing packages (when used following the -i option)

(continues)

Table 11-9   Common options used with the `rpm` command *(continued)*

Option	Description
`-q` `--query`	Queries information about packages on the system
`--test`	Performs a test installation only (when used with the `-i` option)
`-U` `--upgrade`	Upgrades a specified package; the package is installed even if no older version exists on the system
`-V` `--verify`	Verifies the location of all files that belong to the specified package
`-v`	Prints verbose information when installing or manipulating packages

Note 📎

RPM packages can also be converted to cpio archives using the `rpm2cpio` **command**. This allows you to easily inspect or extract file contents from an RPM package without installing the package on the system.

There are thousands of different RPM packages available for free download on Internet servers called **software repositories**. Moreover, each RPM on a software repository may have several package dependencies. Luckily, you can use the `yum` **(Yellowdog Updater Modified) command** to search Internet software repositories for RPM packages that map to your architecture, and automatically install or upgrade those packages on your system. Prior to installing the desired RPM package, the `yum` command also downloads and installs any package dependencies. The /etc/yum.conf and /etc/yum.repos.d/* files are used to specify the locations of Internet software repositories.

While many current Linux distributions still use the `yum` command, Fedora 28 and some other Linux distributions use the `dnf` **(Dandified YUM) command** alongside the repository information stored in the /etc/yum.conf and /etc/yum.repos.d/* files.

Note 📎

The `dnf` command is simply a faster version of the `yum` command that provides the same core options and functionality.

The SUSE and openSUSE Linux distributions use the `zypper` **command** to provide the same functionality as the `yum` command.

To install a particular RPM package and its dependencies following a Fedora 28 installation, you can use the `dnf install packagename` command. Multiple software packages can be installed using a single `dnf` command. For example, the `dnf install package1name package2name package3name` command will install three packages, including any package dependencies.

> **Note** 🖇
>
> You have used the `dnf` command in previous chapters to install several programs on your Fedora 28 virtual machine from software repositories on the Internet.

Because newer versions of RPM packages are frequently added to software repositories, you can also upgrade an installed package to the latest version using the `dnf update packagename` command, or the `dnf upgrade packagename` command (which also removes any obsolete packages during the process). For example, to upgrade your BASH shell to the latest version, you could use the following command and press `y` when prompted to download and install the latest packages:

```
[root@server1 ~]# dnf upgrade bash
Last metadata expiration check: 0:56:17 ago on Sat 29 Sep 2019 11:12:29
Dependencies resolved.
================================================================
 Package        Arch         Version            Repository    Size
================================================================
Upgrading:
 bash           x86_64       4.4.23-1.fc28      updates       1.5 M

Transaction Summary
================================================================
Upgrade  1 Package

Total download size:  1.5 M
Is this ok [y/N]:  y
Downloading Packages:
bash-4.4.23-1.fc28.x86_64.rpm            831 kB/s | 1.5 MB      00:01
----------------------------------------------------------------
Total                                    670 kB/s | 1.5 MB      00:02
```

```
Running transaction check
Transaction check succeeded.
Running transaction test
Transaction test succeeded.
Running transaction
  Preparing         :                                        1/1
  Upgrading         : bash-4.4.23-1.fc28.x86_64              1/2
  Running scriptlet: bash-4.4.23-1.fc28.x86_64              1/2
  Cleanup           : bash-4.4.19-2.fc28.x86_64              2/2
  Running scriptlet: bash-4.4.19-2.fc28.x86_64              2/2
  Verifying         : bash-4.4.23-1.fc28.x86_64              1/2
  Verifying         : bash-4.4.19-2.fc28.x86_64              2/2
Upgraded:
  bash.x86_64 4.4.23-1.fc28

Complete!
[root@server1 ~]# _
```

> **Note** 🖉
>
> Without a package name argument, the dnf update command will attempt to update all installed packages. You can also use the dnf check-update command to check for installed software updates.

Note from the previous output that the dnf command did not find any other package dependencies for BASH that needed updating. You may also find that the dnf command tries several different software repositories that contain the necessary software (called **software mirrors**) before finding one that accepts a connection. This is common, because software repositories limit their concurrent download connections to allow for fast download. When a software repository reaches its concurrent connection limit, it returns a negative response to the dnf command and the dnf command searches for the RPM package on the next software mirror listed in the repository configuration files.

In some cases, you may not know the exact RPM package name to use alongside the dnf command. Luckily, you can use the dnf search keyword command to search a software repository by keyword, or the dnf list available command to list available RPM packages. The dnf grouplist available command will display a list of package group names that are available for installation. A **package group** is a group of related RPM packages that are often installed together to provide a key function. For example, to install the Development Tools package group on Fedora 28 (which contains a core set of development libraries and commands), you can use the `dnf groupinstall "Development Tools"` command.

You can use the `dnf repolist` command to view the software repositories that are configured within the /etc/yum.conf and /etc/yum.repos.d/* files on your system. Many software authors host their RPM packages on private software repositories and include instructions on their website that guide you through the process of adding the private software repository to your repository configuration files (usually by installing a special RPM package). For example, if you want to install the VideoLAN VLC media player on Fedora 28, you can access the instructions for Fedora 28 from the VideoLAN website (*www.videolan.org*). Because the VideoLAN VLC media player is hosted on the private RPM Fusion software repository, the VideoLAN website instructs you to run the `dnf install https://download1.rpmfusion.org/free/fedora/ rpmfusion-free-release-$(rpm -E %fedora).noarch.rpm` command to install the appropriate files to the /etc/yum.repos.d directory that list the locations of the RPM fusion repositories. Next, you can run the `dnf install vlc` command to install the VLC media player.

Note

The `dnf` command caches repository information and packages. You can run the `dnf clean all` command to clear these caches, which is often used to fix `dnf`-related problems.

The `dnf` command can also be used to view and manage installed RPM packages. The `dnf list installed` command will list installed RPM packages, the `dnf grouplist installed` command will list installed package groups, the `dnf info packagename` command will display detailed information for an installed RPM package, and the `dnf groupinfo packagegroupname` command will display the contents of a package group. You can also use the `dnf remove packagename` command to remove an installed RPM package, or the `dnf groupremove packagegroupname` command to remove all of the RPM packages within a particular package group.

Each Linux distribution includes a graphical software app that provides desktop users with an easy method for managing the software on the system as well as installing or updating packages from available software repositories on the Internet. Similarly, any packages downloaded within a desktop environment are opened by this graphical software app by default, which automatically downloads and installs any dependencies before installing the package.

On Fedora 28, the graphical **Software utility** shown in Figure 11-5 is used to view, manage, and install software within a desktop environment. To start the Software utility within the GNOME desktop environment, navigate to Activities, Software.

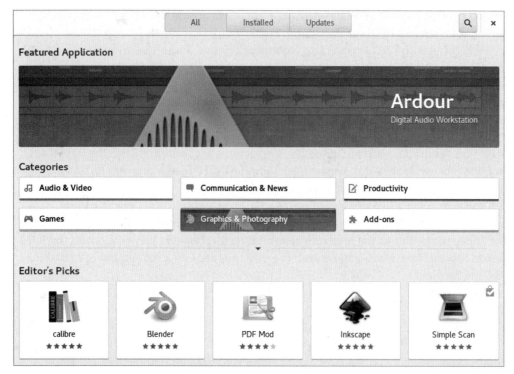

Figure 11-5 The Software utility

Working with the Debian Package Manager (DPM)

The Debian Package Manager (DPM) is used by default on Linux distributions based on the Debian Linux distribution, such as Ubuntu Linux. Like RPM packages, DPM packages contain software that has been precompiled for a specific platform, and they may have package dependencies. However, DPM packages use the .deb extension and are installed and maintained by the **dpkg command**. For example, to install the bluefish Web page editor on an Ubuntu Linux system from the downloaded DPM file bluefish_2.2.6-1_amd64.deb, you can use the dpkg -i bluefish_2.2.6-1_amd64.deb command. Table 11-10 displays a list of common options used with the dpkg command.

> **Note** 📎
>
> The amd64 architecture is identical to the x86_64 architecture; you will often find amd64 used in place of x86_64 within DPM package names.
>
> Some DPM packages prompt you to supply configuration options during installation. You can use **dpkg-reconfigure command** after package installation to modify these configuration options.

Table 11-10 Common options used with the `dpkg` command

Option	Description
`-i` `--install`	Installs a specified package
`--ignore-depends`	Ignores any dependency checking for a specified package
`-l` `--list`	Displays information for a specified package by name or wildcard pattern (or all packages if no argument is given); it may also be used with the `dpkg-query` command
`-L` `--listfiles`	Displays the files that comprise a specified package; it may also be used with the `dpkg-query` command
`-p` `--print-avail`	Displays detailed package information for a specified package; it may also be used with the `dpkg-query` command
`-P` `--purge`	Removes a specified package from the system, including any configuration files used by the package
`-r` `--remove`	Removes a specified package from the system, excluding any configuration files used by the package
`-S` `--search`	Displays the package to which the specified file belongs; it may also be used with the `dpkg-query` command
`-s` `--status`	Displays the status for a specified package; it may also be used with the `dpkg-query` command
`--test`	Performs a test installation only (when used with the `-i` option)
`-V` `--verify`	Verifies the location of all files that belong to the specified package

After you install a DPM package, the DPM database (stored within files in the /var/lib/dpkg directory) is updated to contain information about the package and the files contained within. As with the RPM, you can query package information for installed packages. For example, to list information about the BASH shell package, you can use the following command:

```
[root@server1 ~]# dpkg -l bash
Desired=Unknown/Install/Remove/Purge/Hold
| Status=Not/Inst/Conf-files/Unpacked/halF-conf/Half-inst/trig-
aWait/Trig-pend
```

```
|/ Err?=(none)/Reinst-required (Status,Err: uppercase=bad)
||/ Name            Version       Architecture Description
+++-=============-============-============-=====================
ii  bash           4.4.18-2ubun amd64        GNU Bourne Again SHell
[root@server1 ~]# _
```

Note

You can instead use the `dpkg-query` **command** when searching for DPM package
information. The `dpkg-query` command takes the same search arguments as the `dpkg`
command.

Alternatively, you could use the following command to list detailed information
about the BASH shell package:

```
[root@server1 ~]# dpkg -p bash
Package: bash
Essential: yes
Priority: required
Section: shells
Installed-Size: 1588
Origin: Ubuntu
Maintainer: Ubuntu Developers <ubuntu-devel-discuss@lists.ubuntu.com>
Bugs: https://bugs.launchpad.net/ubuntu/+filebug
Architecture: amd64
Multi-Arch: foreign
Version: 4.4.18-2ubuntu1
Replaces: bash-completion (<< 20060301-0), bash-doc (<= 2.05-1)
Depends: base-files (>= 2.1.12), debianutils (>= 2.15)
Pre-Depends: libc6 (>= 2.15), libtinfo5 (>= 6)
Recommends: bash-completion (>= 20060301-0)
Suggests: bash-doc
Conflicts: bash-completion (<< 20060301-0)
Filename: pool/main/b/bash/bash_4.4.18-2ubuntu1_amd64.deb
Size: 614184
MD5sum: bb172fdca61d926fe61d8e642876f369
Description: GNU Bourne Again SHell
Original-Maintainer: Matthias Klose <doko@debian.org>
SHA1: ff433274a20b8d832387d4a2fecaabd2786d98b1
SHA256:
5895e980d1fc874906d27823ab31eeb65cfe1d059936b9d6d304bfee02c8995c
```

```
Homepage: http://tiswww.case.edu/php/chet/bash/bashtop.html
Task: minimal
Description-md5: 3522aa7b4374048d6450e348a5bb45d9
Supported: 5y
[root@server1 ~]# _
```

Because the Debian Package Manager keeps track of all installed files, you can also list the files that belong to a DPM package, verify DPM package contents, or search for the DPM package name for a specified file using the appropriate options from Table 11-10. For example, the following command lists the first 10 files in the BASH shell DPM package:

```
[root@server1 ~]# dpkg -L bash | head
/.
/bin
/bin/bash
/etc
/etc/bash.bashrc
/etc/skel
/etc/skel/.bash_logout
/etc/skel/.bashrc
/etc/skel/.profile
/usr
[root@server1 ~]# _
```

As with RPM, most DPM packages are hosted on Internet software repositories for free download. To download and install DPM packages, including any package dependencies, you can use the apt **(Advanced Package Tool) command** or apt-get command. You can search available repository information using the apt command or the apt-cache **command**.

> Note
>
> The apt command is a newer alternative to the apt-get and apt-cache commands. It uses the same core options, but provides more detailed and useful output on the terminal screen. As a result, this section focuses primarily on the apt command.
>
> In Chapter 6, you used the apt-get command to install the DPM packages required for ZFS, as well as used the apt command to install the DPM package for the lsscsi command on your Ubuntu Server 18 virtual machine.

The apt command is as easy to use as the dnf command with the RPM. For example, to install the nmap DPM package (a network port scanner) from an Internet software repository, you could run the following command:

```
[root@server1 ~]# apt install nmap
Reading package lists... Done
Building dependency tree
Reading state information... Done
The following additional packages will be installed:
  libblas3 liblinear3 liblua5.3-0
Suggested packages:
  liblinear-tools liblinear-dev ndiff
The following NEW packages will be installed:
  libblas3 liblinear3 liblua5.3-0 nmap
0 upgraded, 4 newly installed, 0 to remove and 40 not upgraded.
Need to get 5,471 kB of archives.
After this operation, 25.0 MB of additional disk space will be used.
Do you want to continue? [Y/n] y
Get:1 http://archive.ubuntu.com/ubuntu bionic/main amd64 libblas3 amd64
3.7.1-4ubuntu1 [140 kB]
Get:2 http://archive.ubuntu.com/ubuntu bionic/main amd64 liblinear3
amd64 2.1.0+dfsg-2 [39.3 kB]
Get:3 http://archive.ubuntu.com/ubuntu bionic/main amd64 liblua5.3-0
amd64 5.3.3-1 [119 kB]
Get:4 http://archive.ubuntu.com/ubuntu bionic/main amd64 nmap amd64
7.60-1ubuntu5 [5,174 kB]
Fetched 5,471 kB in 7s (790 kB/s)
Selecting previously unselected package libblas3:amd64.
(Reading database ... 102756 files and directories currently
installed.)
Preparing to unpack .../libblas3_3.7.1-4ubuntu1_amd64.deb ...
Unpacking libblas3:amd64 (3.7.1-4ubuntu1) ...
Selecting previously unselected package liblinear3:amd64.
Preparing to unpack .../liblinear3_2.1.0+dfsg-2_amd64.deb ...
Unpacking liblinear3:amd64 (2.1.0+dfsg-2) ...
Selecting previously unselected package liblua5.3-0:amd64.
Preparing to unpack .../liblua5.3-0_5.3.3-1_amd64.deb ...
Unpacking liblua5.3-0:amd64 (5.3.3-1) ...
Selecting previously unselected package nmap.
Preparing to unpack .../nmap_7.60-1ubuntu5_amd64.deb ...
Unpacking nmap (7.60-1ubuntu5) ...
```

```
Setting up libblas3:amd64 (3.7.1-4ubuntu1) ...
update-alternatives: using /usr/lib/x86_64-linux-gnu/blas/libblas.
so.3 to provide /usr/lib/x86_64-linux-gnu/libblas.so.3 (libblas.
so.3-x86_64-linux-gnu) in auto mode
Processing triggers for libc-bin (2.27-3ubuntu1) ...
Processing triggers for man-db (2.8.3-2) ...
Setting up liblinear3:amd64 (2.1.0+dfsg-2) ...
Setting up liblua5.3-0:amd64 (5.3.3-1) ...
Setting up nmap (7.60-1ubuntu5) ...
Processing triggers for libc-bin (2.27-3ubuntu1) ...
[root@server1 ~]# _
```

To remove the nmap DPM package, excluding any nmap configuration files, you could use the `apt remove nmap` command. Alternatively, you could use the `apt purge nmap` command to remove the nmap DPM package, including all nmap configuration files. If you remove a package, the package dependencies are not removed; however, you can use the `apt autoremove` command to remove package dependencies that are no longer required by programs on the system.

You can also use the `apt update` command to update the list of available DPM packages from Internet software repositories, as well as the `apt upgrade` command to upgrade the DPM packages on your system to the latest versions based on the updated package list.

> **Note** 📎
>
> All of the `apt` commands discussed thus far have an `apt-get` equivalent. For example, the `apt install nmap` command is equivalent to the `apt-get install nmap` command, and the `apt purge nmap` command is equivalent to the `apt-get purge nmap` command.

DPM repository information is stored in the /etc/apt/sources.list file and files within the /etc/apt/sources.list.d directory. You can add new repositories using the `add-apt-repository` **command** and search available repository and package information using either the `apt` or `apt-cache` command. For example, to search software repositories for DPM packages that contain the word nmap, you could use the `apt search nmap` or `apt-cache search nmap` command. To list all DPM packages available on software repositories, you could use the `apt search .` or `apt-cache search .` command. To view detailed information regarding the nmap package, use the `apt show nmap` or `apt-cache show nmap` command.

Note

You used the `add-apt-repository` command in Chapter 6 to add the ZFS software repository to your Ubuntu Server 18 virtual machine.

You can also use the **Aptitude** utility (shown in Figure 11-6) to install, query, and remove DPM packages. You can start this utility by executing the `aptitude` `command` in a command-line or graphical terminal. In a command-line terminal, you can access the different Aptitude menus by pressing the Ctrl+t key combination. The `aptitude` command also accepts many of the same arguments as `apt` and `apt-get`. For example, `aptitude install nmap` will install the nmap DPM package from an Internet repository, `aptitude remove nmap` will remove the installed nmap DPM package (excluding nmap configuration files), and `aptitude purge nmap` will remove the installed nmap DPM package (including nmap configuration files).

```
Actions  Undo  Package  Resolver  Search  Options  Views  Help
C-T: Menu  ?: Help  q: Quit  u: Update  g: Preview/Download/Install/Remove Pkgs
aptitude 0.8.10 @ ubuntu18
--- Upgradable Packages (40)
--- Installed Packages (507)
--- Not Installed Packages (60748)
--- Virtual Packages (6661)
--- Tasks (22727)




A newer version of these packages is available.

This group contains 40 packages.
```

Figure 11-6   The Aptitude utility

Note

The Aptitude utility is not installed in Ubuntu 18 by default. It can be installed using the `apt` `install aptitude` command.

Understanding Shared Libraries

Recall that when you install an RPM or DPM package, the package manager does a preliminary check to ensure that all shared libraries and prerequisite packages (package dependencies) required for the program to work properly have been installed. If you are using yum, dnf zypper, apt-get, or apt to install the package, then the package dependencies are automatically downloaded and installed; however, if you are using the rpm or dpkg command to install the package, then the installation will fail if the package dependencies are not installed. Similarly, when you compile a program from source code, the configure script checks for shared library dependencies; if those shared libraries are not present, the configure script will fail to create the Makefile necessary to compile the program.

If you uninstall an RPM or DPM package, including packages that contain shared libraries, the removal process normally stops if that package is a dependency for another package. However, this dependency check sometimes fails, the package dependency is removed from the system, and any programs that require the package dependency will fail to execute properly. Furthermore, if you remove an RPM or DPM package containing a shared library that is a dependency for other programs that were compiled from source code on the system, the removal process will be unaware that the package is a dependency. In this case, the package will be removed from the system and the programs that were compiled from source code that require the shared library will fail to execute.

Shared libraries are typically installed under the /lib, /lib64, /usr/lib, or /usr/lib64 directories. To identify which shared libraries are required by a certain program, you can use the **ldd command**. For example, the following output displays the shared libraries required by the /bin/bash program:

```
[root@server1 ~]# ldd /bin/bash
linux-vdso.so.1 (0x00007ffda81db000)
libtinfo.so.5 => /lib/x86_64-linux-gnu/libtinfo.so.5
(0x00007f9c9d000)
libdl.so.2 => /lib/x86_64-linux-gnu/libdl.so.2 (0x00007f9f39a99000)
libc.so.6 => /lib/x86_64-linux-gnu/libc.so.6 (0x00007f9f396a8000)
/lib64/ld-linux-x86-64.so.2 (0x00007f9f3a1e1000)
[root@server1 ~]# _
```

If any shared libraries listed by the ldd command are missing, the ldd command will identify them as "not found" in the output. In this case, you can locate the appropriate RPM or DPM package that contains the library and install it on your system. After downloading and installing any shared libraries, it is good practice to run the **ldconfig command** to ensure that the list of shared library directories (/etc/ld.so.conf) and the list of shared libraries (/etc/ld.so.cache) are updated. Alternatively, you can create a variable in your BASH shell called LD_LIBRARY_PATH that lists the directories that contain the shared libraries.

Sometimes, the files that comprise a shared library can become corrupted. If this is the case, output of the `ldd` command will not report any problems, but the programs that depend on the shared library will produce errors that identify the shared library that is not functioning properly. In this case, you should reinstall the RPM or DPM package that contains the shared library to remedy these errors. For example, to reinstall the samplelibrary RPM package, you could use the `dnf resinstall samplelibrary` command, and to reinstall the samplelibrary DPM package, you could use the `apt install --reinstall samplelibrary` command.

Chapter Summary

- Many compression utilities are available for Linux systems; each of them uses a different compression algorithm and produces a different compression ratio.

- Files can be backed up to an archive using a backup utility. To back up files to CD or DVD, you must use burning software instead of a backup utility.

- The `tar` command is the most common backup utility used today; it is typically used to create compressed archives called tarballs.

- The source code for Linux software can be obtained and compiled afterward using the GNU C Compiler; most source code is available in tarball format via the Internet.

- Package managers install and manage compiled software of the same format. The Red Hat Package Manager (RPM) and Debian Package Manager (DPM) are the most common package managers available for Linux systems today.

- In addition to managing and removing installed RPM packages, you can install and upgrade RPM packages from software repositories on the Internet using the `dnf`, `yum`, or `zypper` commands, depending on your Linux distribution. You can also use the `rpm` command to query installed RPM packages as well as perform RPM package management.

- In addition to managing and removing installed DPM packages, you can install or upgrade DPM packages from software repositories on the Internet using the `apt` and `apt-get` commands. You can also use the `dpkg` command to view installed DPM packages or perform DPM package management.

- Most programs depend on shared libraries for functionality. If a shared library is removed from the system, dependent programs will encounter errors.

Key Terms

`*sum` commands
`add-apt-repository`
  command
`apt` (Advanced Package
  Tool) command
`apt-cache` command
`apt-get` command
Aptitude
`aptitude` command
archive
Brasero
`bunzip2` command
`bzcat` command
`bzgrep` command
`bzip2` command
`bzless` command
`bzmore` command
checksum
`compress` command
compression
compression algorithm
compression ratio
`cpio` (copy in/out) command
`curl` (client for URLs)
  command
`dd` command
Debian Package Manager
  (DPM)

differential backup
`dnf` (Dandified YUM)
  command
`dpkg` command
`dpkg-query` command
`dpkg-reconfigure`
  command
`dump` command
full backup
`gcc` (GNU C Compiler)
  command
`gzip` (GNU zip) command
`gunzip` command
image backup
incremental backup
`ldconfig` command
`ldd` command
offsite backup
package dependency
package group
package manager
Red Hat Package Manager
  (RPM)
`restore` command
`rpm` command
`rpm2cpio` command
`rsync` (remote sync)
  command

`scp` (secure copy) command
`sftp` (secure FTP) command
shared library
software mirror
software repositories
Software utility
system backup
`tar` (tape archive)
  command
tarball
`uncompress` command
`unxz` command
`unzip` command
`wget` (Web get) command
`xz` command
`xzcat` command
`xzgrep` command
`xzless` command
`xzmore` command
`yum` (Yellowdog Updater
  Modified) command
`zcat` command
`zgrep` command
`zip` command
`zless` command
`zmore` command
`zypper` command

Review Questions

1. Most source code is typically available on the Internet in tarball format or as a git repository. True or False?

2. Which dump level indicates a full backup?
   - **a.** 0
   - **b.** 9
   - **c.** 1
   - **d.** f

3. Which filename extension indicates a tarball?
   - **a.** .tar.xz
   - **b.** .cpio
   - **c.** .dump
   - **d.** .tar

4. Files that have been compressed
   using the xz utility typically have the
   _____ extension.
   a. .zip
   b. .gz
   c. .xz
   d. .bz2

5. The bzip2 and gzip utilities use similar
   compression algorithms. True or False?

6. When compiling source code into a
   binary program, which command does
   the compiling using the GNU C Compiler?
   a. `tar`
   b. `./configure`
   c. `make`
   d. `make install`

7. The `-9` option to the gzip command
   results in a higher compression ratio.
   True or False?

8. You have created a full backup and four
   incremental backups. In which order
   must you restore these backups?
   a. 0, 1, 2, 3, 4
   b. 0, 4, 3, 2, 1
   c. 4, 3, 2, 1, 0
   d. 1, 2, 3, 4, 0

9. Which of the following commands
   extracts an archive?
   a. `cpio -vocBL /dev/fd0`
   b. `cpio -vicdu -I /dev/fd0`
   c. `cpio -vicdu -O /dev/fd0`
   d. `cpio -vti -I /dev/fd0`

10. The Debian Package Manager (DPM) is
    the default package manager used by
    Fedora 28. True or False?

11. Which of the following commands can
    be used to list the files contained within
    an installed RPM package?
    a. `rpm -qa packagename`
    b. `rpm -qi packagename`
    c. `rpm -ql packagename`
    d. `rpm -q packagename`

12. Which of the following commands can
    be used to remove the test DPM package,
    including any test configuration files?
    a. `dpkg remove test`
    b. `apt remove test`
    c. `dpkg purge test`
    d. `apt purge test`

13. To install a new program from RPM
    software repositories on the Internet,
    you can use the `dnf update`
    `programname` command. True or False?

14. Which command can be used to create
    an image backup of a partition?
    a. `tar`
    b. `dd`
    c. `dump`
    d. `cpio`

15. Which of the following commands
    should be run following the installation
    of a shared library to update the /etc/
    ld.so.conf and /etc/ld.so.cache files?
    a. `ldd`
    b. `updatedb`
    c. `ldconfig`
    d. `dpkg-reconfigure`

16. Which option to the `dpkg` command can
    be used to list the files that comprise a
    package?
    a. `-l`
    b. `-L`
    c. `-s`
    d. `-i`

17. Which option to the `rpm` command can
    be used to remove a package from the
    system?
    a. `-r`
    b. `-e`
    c. `-u`
    d. `-U`

18. Which of the following commands creates an archive?
    a. tar -cvf /dev/st0
    b. tar -xvf /dev/st0
    c. tar -tvf /dev/st0
    d. tar -zcvf /dev/st0 *

19. When compiling source code into a binary program, which command performs a system check and creates the Makefile?
    a. tar
    b. ./configure
    c. make
    d. make install

20. Which of the following commands can be used to search for packages that contain the word "oobla" on RPM software repositories?
    a. yum search oobla
    b. rpm -qS oobla
    c. yum list oobla
    d. rpm -ql oobla

Hands-On Projects

These projects should be completed in the order given. The hands-on projects presented in this chapter should take a total of three hours to complete. The requirements for this lab include the following:

- A computer with Fedora Linux installed according to Hands-On Project 2-1 and Ubuntu Server 18 Linux installed according to Hands-On Project 6-1.

Project 11-1

In this hands-on project, you use common compression utilities to compress and uncompress information on Fedora 28.

1. Boot your Fedora Linux virtual machine. After your Linux system has been loaded, switch to a command-line terminal (tty5) by pressing **Ctrl+Alt+F5** and log in to the terminal using the user name of **root** and the password of **LINUXrocks!**.

2. At the command prompt, type **dnf install ncompress** and press **Enter**. Press **y** when prompted to complete the installation of the ncompress RPM package (and any package dependencies).

3. At the command prompt, type **cp /etc/services ~** and press **Enter** to make a copy of the /etc/services file in your home directory. Next, type **ls -l services** at the command prompt and press **Enter**. How large is the services file?

4. At the command prompt, type **compress -v services** and press **Enter** to compress the services file. What was the compression ratio? Next, type **ls -l services*** at the command prompt and press **Enter**. What extension does the services file have and how large is it?

5. At the command prompt, type `uncompress -v services.Z` and press **Enter** to decompress the services file.

6. At the command prompt, type `mkdir compressed; cp /etc/hosts /etc/inittab compress` and press **Enter** to create a subdirectory called compressed and copy the hosts and inittab file to it.

7. At the command prompt, type `compress -vr compressed` and press **Enter** to compress the contents of the Desktop subdirectory. Next, type `ls -l compressed` at the command prompt and press **Enter** to view the contents of the Desktop directory. Which files were compressed? If there were symbolic links in this directory, how could you force the compress utility to compress these files as well?

8. At the command prompt, type `uncompress -vr Desktop` and press **Enter** to decompress the contents of the Desktop subdirectory.

9. At the command prompt, type `ps -ef | compress -v >psfile.Z` and press **Enter** to compress the output of the `ps -ef` command to a file called psfile.Z. What was the compression ratio?

10. At the command prompt, type `zless psfile.Z` and press **Enter** to view the compressed contents of the psfile.Z file. When finished, press **q** to quit the more utility.

11. At the command prompt, type `zip -v compressed.zip compressed/*` and press **Enter** to compress the contents of the Desktop subdirectory into a single compressed. zip file. What compression ratio did you obtain overall?

12. At the command prompt, type `unzip -v compressed.zip` and press **Enter** to view the contents of compressed.zip. Next, type `unzip compressed.zip` and press **Enter** to extract the contents of compressed.zip. Press **A** when prompted to overwrite all existing files during decompression.

13. At the command prompt, type `gzip -v services` and press **Enter** to compress the services file. What was the compression ratio? How does this ratio compare to the one obtained in Step 4? Why? Next, type `ls -l services*` at the command prompt and press **Enter**. What extension does the services file have and how large is it?

14. At the command prompt, type `gunzip -v services.gz` and press **Enter** to decompress the services file.

15. At the command prompt, type `gzip -v -9 services` and press **Enter** to compress the services file. What was the compression ratio? Why?

16. At the command prompt, type `gunzip -v services.gz` and press **Enter** to decompress the services file.

17. At the command prompt, type `gzip -v -1 services` and press **Enter** to compress the services file. What was the compression ratio? Why?

18. At the command prompt, type `gunzip -v services.gz` and press **Enter** to decompress the services file.

19. At the command prompt, type `xz -v -9 services` and press **Enter** to compress the services file. What was the compression ratio? Why was it larger than that shown in Step 13?

20. At the command prompt, type `unxz -v services.xz` and press **Enter** to decompress the services file.

21. At the command prompt, type `bzip2 -v services` and press **Enter** to compress the services file. What was the compression ratio? How does this compare to the ratios from Step 4, Step 13, and Step 19? Next, type `ls -l services*` at the command prompt and press **Enter**. What extension does the services file have and how large is it?

22. At the command prompt, type `bunzip2 -v services.bz2` and press **Enter** to decompress the services file.

23. Type `exit` and press **Enter** to log out of your shell.

Project 11-2

In this hands-on project, you create, view, and extract archives using the `tar` utility.

1. On your Fedora Linux virtual machine, switch to a command-line terminal (tty5) by pressing **Ctrl+Alt+F5** and log in to the terminal using the user name of **root** and the password of **LINUXrocks!**.

2. At the command prompt, type `tar -cvf test1.tar /etc/samba` and press **Enter** to create an archive called test1.tar in the current directory that contains the /etc/samba directory and its contents. Next, type `ls -l test1.tar` at the command prompt and press **Enter**. How large is the test1.tar file?

3. At the command prompt, type `tar -tvf test1.tar` and press **Enter**. What is displayed?

4. At the command prompt, type `mkdir /new1` and press **Enter**. Next, type `cd /new1` at the command prompt and press **Enter** to change the current directory to the /new1 directory.

5. At the command prompt, type `tar -xvf /root/test1.tar` and press **Enter** to extract the contents of the test1.tar archive. Next, type `ls -RF` at the command prompt and press **Enter** to view the contents of the /new1 directory. Was the extraction successful?

6. At the command prompt, type `cd` and press **Enter** to return to your home directory.

7. At the command prompt, type `tar -zcvf test2.tar.gz /etc/samba` and press **Enter** to create a `gzip`-compressed archive called test2.tar.gz in the current directory that contains the /etc/samba directory and its contents. Next, type `ls -l test2.tar.gz` at the command prompt and press **Enter**. How large is the test2.tar.gz file? How does this compare to the size obtained for test1.tar in Step 2? Why?

8. At the command prompt, type `tar -ztvf test2.tar.gz` and press **Enter**. What is displayed?

9. At the command prompt, type `mkdir /new2` and press **Enter**. Next, type `cd /new2` at the command prompt and press **Enter** to change the current directory to the /new2 directory.

10. At the command prompt, type `tar -zxvf /root/test2.tar.gz` and press **Enter** to uncompress and extract the contents of the test2.tar.gz archive. Next, type `ls -RF` at the command prompt and press **Enter** to view the contents of the /new2 directory. Was the extraction successful?

11. At the command prompt, type `cd` and press **Enter** to return to your home directory.

12. At the command prompt, type `rm -Rf /new[12]` and press **Enter** to remove the directories created in this hands-on project.

13. At the command prompt, type `rm -f test*` and press **Enter** to remove the tar archives created in this hands-on project.

14. Type `exit` and press **Enter** to log out of your shell.

Project 11-3

In this hands-on project, you create, view, and extract archives using the `cpio`, `dump`, and `dd` utilities.

1. On your Fedora Linux virtual machine, switch to a command-line terminal (tty5) by pressing **Ctrl+Alt+F5** and log in to the terminal using the user name of **root** and the password of **LINUXrocks!**.

2. At the command prompt, type `find /etc/samba | cpio -ovcBL -O test.cpio` and press **Enter** to create an archive in the file test.cpio that contains the /etc/samba directory and its contents. What does each option indicate in the aforementioned command?

3. At the command prompt, type `cpio -ivtB -I test.cpio` and press **Enter**. What is displayed? What does each option indicate in the aforementioned command?

4. At the command prompt, type `cpio -ivcdumB -I test.cpio` and press **Enter** to extract the contents of the archive in the test.cpio file. To what location were the files extracted? Were any files overwritten? What does each option indicate in the aforementioned command?

5. At the command prompt, type `dnf install dump` and press **Enter**. Press `y` when prompted to complete the installation of the dump RPM package (and any package dependencies).

6. At the command prompt, type `dump -0uf test.dump /dev/sda1` and press **Enter** to create an archive of the /boot filesystem in the archive file test.dump. What type of backup was performed? Will the /etc/dumpdates file be updated?

7. At the command prompt, type `cat /etc/dumpdates` and press **Enter**. Does the file indicate your full backup and time?

8. At the command prompt, type `mkdir /new` and press **Enter**. Next, type `cd /new` at the command prompt and press **Enter** to change the current directory to the /new directory.

9. At the command prompt, type `restore -rf /root/test.dump` and press **Enter**.

10. Type `ls -F` at the command prompt and press **Enter** to view the contents of the /new directory. What is displayed? Were absolute or relative pathnames used during the restore operation?

11. At the command prompt, type **cd** and press **Enter** to return to your home directory.

12. At the command prompt, type **dd if=/dev/sda1 of=test.img** and press **Enter** to create an image backup of your /boot filesystem.

13. At the command prompt, type **ls -l test.img test.dump** and press **Enter**. Why is the boot.img file much larger than the test.dump file, even though both were used to back up the /boot filesystem?

14. At the command prompt, type **rm –Rf /new** and press **Enter** to remove the directory created in this hands-on project.

15. At the command prompt, type **rm –f /root/test*** and press **Enter** to remove the archives created in this hands-on project.

16. Type **exit** and press **Enter** to log out of your shell.

Project 11-4

In this hands-on project, you compile and install the conky program from source code.

1. On your Fedora Linux virtual machine, switch to tty1 by pressing **Ctrl+Alt+F1** and log in to the GNOME desktop using the user name of **user1** and the password of **LINUXrocks!**.

2. Open the Firefox Web browser and download the source code tarball for conky 1.9.0 (conky-1.9.0.tar.bz2) from *sourceforge.net*. Save the source code tarball to the default location (/home/user1/Downloads).

3. Next, switch to a command-line terminal (tty5) by pressing **Ctrl+Alt+F5** and log in to the terminal using the user name of **root** and the password of **LINUXrocks!**.

4. At the command prompt, type **dnf groupinstall "Development Tools"** and press **Enter** to install the compiler tools from a software repository.

5. At the command prompt, type **dnf install ncurses-devel lua-devel glib2-devel libX11-devel libXext-devel libXft-devel** and press **Enter** to install the development libraries needed for conky from a software repository.

6. At the command prompt, type **cp ~user1/Downloads/conky-1.9.0.tar.bz2 ~** and press **Enter** to copy the conky source code tarball to your home directory.

7. At the command prompt, type **tar –jxvf conky-1.9.0.tar.bz2** and press **Enter** to uncompress and extract the contents of the tarball. Next, type **ls -F** at the command prompt and press **Enter**. What directory was created?

8. At the command prompt, type **cd conky-1.9.0** and press **Enter**. Next, type **ls -F** at the command prompt and press **Enter**. Is there an executable configure program? Are there README and INSTALL files present?

9. At the command prompt, type **./configure --help | less** and press **Enter** to see the available options to the configure script. Next, type **./configure --disable-xdamage** and press **Enter** to run the configure script without xdamage support. What does the configure script do? Near the bottom of the output, can you see whether the Makefile was created successfully?

10. At the command prompt, type **make** and press **Enter**. What does the make program do? Which program compiles the different parts of the program?

11. At the command prompt, type **make install** and press **Enter**. What does the `make install` command do?

12. At the command prompt, type **cd** and press **Enter** to return to your home directory. Next, type **rm –Rf conky-1.9.0** to remove the source code directory for conky.

13. At the command prompt, type **which conky** and press **Enter**. Which directory contains the conky executable program? Is a central database updated with this information?

14. At the command prompt, type **man conky** and press **Enter**. View the available options for the `conky` command and press **q** to quit when finished.

15. Type **exit** and press **Enter** to log out of your shell.

16. Switch to your GNOME desktop by pressing **Ctrl+Alt+F2** and open a graphical terminal. At the graphical terminal command prompt, type **conky&** and press **Enter** to run the conky program. Why is it good form to execute graphical programs in the background within a graphical terminal?

17. Log out of your GNOME desktop.

Project 11-5

In this hands-on project, you query, remove, and install the ncompress RPM package.

1. On your Fedora Linux virtual machine, switch to a command-line terminal (tty5) by pressing **Ctrl+Alt+F5** and log in to the terminal using the user name of **root** and the password of **LINUXrocks!**.

2. At the command prompt, type **rpm –qa | less** and press **Enter** to view the RPM packages installed on your computer. Are there many of them? Briefly scroll through the list and press **q** when finished to exit the less utility.

3. At the command prompt, type **rpm –q ncompress** and press **Enter**. Is the ncompress RPM package installed on your computer? When did you install it?

4. At the command prompt, type **rpm –qi ncompress** and press **Enter** to view the information about the ncompress RPM package. What license does this package use?

5. At the command prompt, type **rpm –ql ncompress** and press **Enter** to view the locations of all files that belong to the ncompress package. What directory holds the compress and uncompress executables?

6. At the command prompt, type **ldd /usr/bin/compress** and press **Enter** to view the shared libraries needed by /usr/bin/compress. Were any libraries marked as not found?

7. At the command prompt, type **rpm –e ncompress** and press **Enter**. What does this option to the `rpm` command do?

8. At the command prompt, type **rpm –q ncompress** and press **Enter**. Is the ncompress RPM package installed?

9. At the command prompt, type **dnf search ncompress** and press **Enter**. Is the ncompress RPM package listed? Press **q** to quit the less utility.

10. At the command prompt, type `dnf list available | grep ncompress` and press **Enter**. Is the ncompress RPM package available for installation from a software repository?

11. At the command prompt, type `dnf install ncompress` and press **Enter**. Press `y` when prompted to complete the installation. Next, type `rpm -q ncompress` and press **Enter** to verify that the installation completed successfully.

12. Type **exit** and press **Enter** to log out of your shell.

Project 11-6

In this hands-on project, you install, query, and remove the ncompress DPM package.

1. Boot your Ubuntu Server 18 virtual machine, and log into tty1 using the user name of **root** and the password of **LINUXrocks!**.

2. At the command prompt, type `dpkg -l | less` and press **Enter** to view the DPM packages installed on your computer. Are there many of them? Briefly scroll through the list and press `q` when finished to exit the less utility.

3. At the command prompt, type `dpkg -l ncompress` and press **Enter**. Is the ncompress DPM package installed on your computer?

4. At the command prompt, type `apt-cache search compress | grep ncompress` and press **Enter**. Is ncompress listed? What other command can be used instead of apt-cache to search for programs within online repositories?

5. At the command prompt, type `apt install ncompress` and press **Enter** to install the ncompress DPM package from a software repository. What other command could you have used to perform the same action?

6. At the command prompt, type `dpkg -L ncompress` and press **Enter** to list the files that comprise the ncompress package. Next, type `dpkg -l ncompress` at the command prompt and press **Enter** to view the detailed information about the ncompress package.

7. At the command prompt, type `apt purge ncompress` and press **Enter**. Press `y` when prompted. What does the purge option do? What other command could you have used to perform the same action?

8. At the command prompt, type `apt install aptitude` and press **Enter** to install the Aptitude utility.

9. At the command prompt, type `aptitude install ncompress` and press **Enter**. What does this command do?

10. Type **exit** and press **Enter** to log out of your shell.

Discovery Exercises

1. Write the command that can be used to perform the following:
   a. Compress the symbolic link /root/sfile using the compress utility and display the compression ratio.
   b. Compress the contents of the directory /root/dir1 using the gzip utility and display the compression ratio.
   c. View the contents of the file /root/letter.zip.
   d. Compress the file /root/letter using xz fast compression.
   e. Find the compression ratio of the file /root/letter.gz.
   f. Perform a test compression of the file /root/sample using the bzip2 utility.
   g. Compress the file /root/sample using the bzip2 utility while minimizing memory usage during the compression.

2. Write the command that can be used to perform the following:
   a. Back up the contents of the /var directory (which contains symbolically linked files) to the second nonrewinding SCSI tape device on the system using the tar utility.
   b. Append the file /etc/inittab to the archive created in Exercise 2a.
   c. Create a tarball called /stuff.tar.gz that contains all files in the /root/stuff directory.
   d. Use the cpio utility to back up all files in the /var directory (which contains symbolically linked files) to the first

rewinding IDE tape device that has a block size of 5KB.
   e. Perform a full filesystem backup of the /var filesystem using the dump utility and record the event in the /etc/dumpdates file.
   f. Create an image of the /dev/sdb4 filesystem to the /sdb4.img file.
   g. View the contents of the archives created in Exercises 2a, 2c, 2d, and 2e.
   h. Extract the contents of the archives created in Exercises 2a and 2c to the /root directory.
   i. Extract the contents of the archives created in Exercises 2d and 2e to their original locations.
   j. Restore the image of the /dev/sdb4 filesystem created in Exercise 2f.

3. On your Fedora 28 virtual machine, log into a terminal as the root user and run the `git clone https://github.com/bartobri/no-more-secrets.git` command to obtain the source code for the **sneakers** and **nms** (no-more-secrets) programs depicted in the movie Sneakers (1992). Next, change to the cloned repository directory to view the contents. Is there a configure script? Why? Is there a README file? View the contents of the README.md file to learn how the developer intended for these programs to be compiled and used. Follow the instructions in the README.md file to compile your programs. When finished, execute the programs within your terminal to test them.

4. On your Fedora 28 virtual machine, log into a GNOME on X.org desktop and use your Firefox Web browser to download the xbill-2.1-9.fc28.x86_64.rpm package (a graphical game) from *www.rpmfind. net*. Use the Files application to open and install your RPM package using the Software utility, which will download any dependencies necessary for the xbill package. Finally, use the appropriate rpm and dnf commands to explore the installed program and execute the xbill program within a graphical terminal.

5. While the package managers discussed in this chapter are the most common way to install software on Linux systems today, the packages that they work with are distribution-specific, because different Linux distributions often organize their package and shared library locations differently. For example, conky-1.10.8-2.fc28.x86_64. rpm is an RPM package that has been modified to work on 64-bit (x86_64) Fedora 28 (fc28) Linux distributions only.

Several new package managers have been recently developed that provide universal packages that work on any Linux distribution that have the package manager installed. The most common of these include **Flatpak** (which is installed by default on Fedora 28) and **Snappy** (which is installed by default on Ubuntu Server 18). Both Flatpak and Snappy download self-contained images of software that are either stored in a subdirectory of /var or /snap for programs that should be visible system-wide, or within a subdirectory under the user's home directory for user-specific programs. A limited number of packages exist in Flatpak and Snappy format on Internet repositories, but you can search for, install, and manage them using the flatpak (Flatpak) or snap (Snappy) commands.

a. On your Ubuntu Server 18 virtual machine, log into a terminal as the root user and run the snap install powershell –classic command to install the Microsoft PowerShell Snappy package from an Internet software repository. Next, run the snap list powershell, snap info powershell, and which powershell commands to view information about the package and the directory it was installed to. Finally, run the powershell command to execute the PowerShell program.

b. On your Fedora Linux virtual machine, log into a terminal as the root user and run the flatpak --system remote-add --if-not-exists flathub https:// flathub.org/repo/flathub. flatpakrepo command to add the flathub Flatpak repository to your Flatpak package manager. Next, run the flatpak search vlc command to search the online Flatpak repositories for the VLC media player Flatpak package, and then run flatpak install flathub org. videolan.VLC to install it from the remote flathub repository. After it is installed, run the `flatpak list vlc` and `ls /var/lib/flatpak/app` commands to view information about the package and the directory it was installed to. Finally, log into the GNOME desktop and run the VLC program (Activities, Show Applications, VLC media player).

6. Download the installation ISO image for openSUSE Leap 15 Linux (64-bit) from *opensuse.org* and install it within a new virtual machine called openSUSE Linux that has the same settings as your Fedora Linux virtual machine. Next, explore the man page for the `zypper` command. Are the options similar to `yum` and `dnf`? Next, search for and install a software package of your choice using the `zypper` command. Finally, use the appropriate `zypper` commands to view package information and remove your package.

## CHAPTER 12

NETWORK CONFIGURATION

After completing this chapter, you will be able to:

Describe the purpose and types of networks, protocols, and media access methods

Explain the basic configuration of IP

Configure a network interface to use IP

Configure a PPP interface

Describe the purpose of host names and how they are resolved to IP addresses

Configure IP routing

Identify common network services

Use command-line and graphical utilities to perform remote administration

Throughout this book, you have examined the installation and administration of local Linux services. This chapter focuses on configuring Linux to participate on a network. First, you become acquainted with some common network terminology, then you learn about IP and the procedure for configuring a network interface. Next, you learn about the Domain Name Space and the processes by which host names are resolved to IP addresses. Finally, you learn how to configure IP routing as well as how to set up and use various utilities to perform remote administration of a Linux system.

Networks

Most functions that computers perform today involve the sharing of information between computers. Information is usually transmitted from computer to computer via media such as fiber optic, telephone, coaxial, or unshielded twisted pair (UTP) cable, but it can also be transmitted via wireless media such as radio, micro, or infrared waves. These media typically interact directly with a peripheral card on the computer, such as a network interface or modem device.

A **network** consists of two or more computers that are linked via media in order to exchange information. Networks that connect computers within close proximity are called **local area networks (LANs)**, whereas networks that connect computers separated by large distances are called **wide area networks (WANs)**.

Many companies use LANs to allow employees to connect to databases and other shared resources such as shared files and printers. Home users can also use LANs to connect several home computers together. As an alternative, home users can use a WAN to connect home computers to an **Internet service provider (ISP)** to gain access to resources such as websites on the worldwide public network called the Internet.

> **Note** 📎
>
> The Internet (the name is short for "internetwork") is merely several interconnected public networks. Both home and company networks can be part of the Internet. Special computers called **routers** transfer information from one network to another.

Network media serve as the conduit for information as it travels across a network. But sending information through this conduit is not enough. In order for the devices on the network to make sense of this information, it must be organized according to a set of rules, or protocols. A network **protocol** breaks information down into **packets** that can be recognized by workstations, routers, and other devices on a network.

While you can configure many network protocols in Linux, nearly all Linux computers use the following three protocols by default:

- **Transmission Control Protocol/Internet Protocol (TCP/IP)**, which provides reliable communication of packets across the Internet.
- **User Datagram Protocol/Internet Protocol (UDP/IP)**, which provides fast, yet unreliable communication of packets across the Internet.
- **Internet Control Message Protocol (ICMP)**, which is used to send network-related information and error messages across the Internet.

> **Note** 📎
>
> While both TCP/IP and UDP/IP can send information packets across the Internet, TCP/IP is the most common network protocol used today, and the one that we'll focus on within this chapter.
>
> When transmitting information across a WAN, you might use a WAN protocol in addition to a specific LAN protocol to format packets for safer transmission. The most common WAN protocol is **Point-to-Point Protocol (PPP)**.

Another important part of the puzzle, the **media access method**, is a set of rules that govern how the various devices on the network share the network media. The media access method is usually contained within the hardware on the network interface or modem. Although many media access methods are available, the one most commonly used to send packets onto network media is called **Ethernet**. It ensures that any packets are retransmitted onto the network if a network error occurs. Another media access method, **Token Ring**, controls which computer has the ability to transmit information by passing a special packet of information, called a token, around the network. Only the computer that currently has the token can transmit information.

> **Note** 📎
>
> **Wireless-Fidelity (Wi-Fi)** LANs also use Ethernet to place packets onto the network medium (in this case, the air).

The IP Protocol

TCP/IP is actually a set, or suite, of protocols with two core components: TCP and IP. Together, these two protocols ensure that information packets travel across a network as quickly as possible, without getting lost or mislabeled.

When you transfer information across a network such as the Internet, that information is often divided into many thousands of small IP packets. Each of these packets may take a different physical route when reaching its destination as routers can transfer information to multiple interconnected networks. TCP ensures that packets can be assembled in the correct order at their destination regardless of the order in which they arrive. Additionally, TCP ensures that any lost packets are retransmitted.

Note

UDP is an alternative to TCP that does not provide packet ordering or retransmission.

IP is responsible for labeling each packet with the destination address. As a result, each computer that participates on an IP network must have a valid **Internet Protocol (IP) address** that identifies itself to the IP protocol. Nearly all computers on the Internet use a version of the IP protocol called **IP version 4 (IPv4)**. However, a smaller number of computers use a next-generation IP protocol called **IP version 6 (IPv6)**. We will examine the structure and configuration of IPv4 and IPv6 in this chapter.

The IPv4 Protocol

To participate on an IPv4 network, your computer must have a valid IP address as well as a **subnet mask**. Optionally, you can configure a **default gateway** to participate on larger networks such as the Internet.

IPv4 Addresses

An IP address is a unique number assigned to the computer that identifies itself on the network, similar to a unique postal address that identifies your location in the world. If any two computers on the same network have the same IP address, it is impossible for information to be correctly delivered to them. Directed communication from one computer to another single computer using IP is referred to as a **unicast**.

The most common format for IPv4 addresses is four numbers called **octets** that are separated by periods. Each octet represents an 8-bit binary number (0–255). An example of an IP address in this notation is 192.168.5.69.

You can convert between decimal and binary by recognizing that an 8-bit binary number represents the decimal binary powers of two in the following order:

128 64 32 16 8 4 2 1

Thus, the number 255 is 11111111 (128+64+32+16+8+4+2+1) in binary, and the number 69 is 01000101 (64+4+1) in binary. When the computer looks at an IP address, the numbers are converted to binary. To learn more about binary/decimal number conversion, visit *www.wikihow.com/Convert-from-Decimal-to-Binary*.

All IPv4 addresses are composed of two parts: the network ID and the host ID. The **network ID** represents the network on which the computer is located, whereas the **host ID** represents a single computer on that network. No two computers on the same network can have the same host ID; however, two computers on different networks can have the same host ID.

The network ID and the host ID are similar to postal mailing addresses, which are made up of a street name and a house number. The street name is similar to a network ID. No two streets in the same city can have the same name, just as no two networks can have the same network ID. The host ID is like the house number. Two houses can have the same house number as long as they are on different streets, just as two computers can have the same host ID as long as they are on different networks.

Only computers with the same network ID can communicate with each other without the use of a router. This allows administrators to logically separate computers on a network; computers in the Accounting Department could use one network ID, whereas computers in the Sales Department could use a different network number. If the two departments are connected by a router, computers in the Accounting Department can communicate with computers in the Sales Department and vice versa.

> **Note** 🖉
>
> If your IP network is not connected to the Internet, the choice of IP address is entirely up to you. However, if your network is connected to the Internet, you might need to use preselected IP addresses for the computers on your network. IP addresses that can be used on the public Internet are assigned by your Internet service provider.
>
> The IP address 127.0.0.1 is called the loopback IP address. It always refers to the local computer. In other words, on your computer, 127.0.0.1 refers to your computer. On your coworker's computer, 127.0.0.1 refers to your coworker's computer.

Subnet Masks

Each computer with an IPv4 address must also be configured with a subnet mask to define which part of its IP address is the network ID and which part is the host ID. Subnet masks are composed of four octets, just like an IP address. The simplest subnet masks use only the values 0 and 255. An octet in a subnet mask containing 255 is part of the network ID. An octet in a subnet mask containing 0 is part of the host ID. Your computer uses the binary process called **ANDing** to find the network ID. ANDing is a mathematical operation that compares two binary digits and gives a result of 1 or 0. If both binary digits being compared have a value of 1, the result is 1. If one digit is 0 and the other is 1, or if both digits are 0, the result is 0.

When an IP address is ANDed with a subnet mask, the result is the network ID. Figure 12-1 shows an example of how the network ID and host ID of an IP address can be calculated using the subnet mask.

Thus, the IP address shown in Figure 12-1 identifies the first computer (host portion 0.1) on the 144.58 network (network portion 144.58).

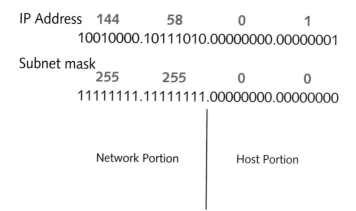

Figure 12-1 A sample IP address and subnet mask

Note

IP addresses and their subnet masks are often written using the **classless interdomain routing (CIDR) notation**. For example, the notation 144.58.0.1/16 refers to the IP address 144.58.0.1 with a 16-bit subnet mask (255.255.0.0).

The IP addresses 0.0.0.0 and 255.255.255.255 cannot be assigned to a host computer because they refer to all networks and all computers on all networks, respectively. Similarly, using the number 255 (all 1s in binary format) in an IP address can specify many hosts. For example, the IP address 192.168.131.255 refers to all hosts on the 192.168.131 network; this IP address is also called the **broadcast** address for the 192.168.131 network.

Note

A computer uses its IP address and subnet mask to determine what network it is on. If two computers are on the same network, they can deliver packets directly to each other. If two computers are on different networks, they must use a router to communicate.

Default Gateway

Typically, all computers on a LAN are configured with the same network ID and different host IDs. A LAN can connect to another LAN by means of a router, which has IP addresses for both LANs and can forward packets to and from each network. Each computer on a LAN can contain the IP address of a router in its IP configuration; any packets that are not destined for the local LAN are then sent to the router, which can forward the packet to the appropriate network or to another router. The IP address of the network interface on the router to which you send packets is called the default gateway.

A router is often a dedicated hardware device from a vendor such as Cisco, D-Link, or HP. Other times, a router is actually a computer with multiple network cards. The one consistent feature of routers, regardless of the manufacturer, is that they can distinguish between different networks and move (or route) packets between them. A router has an IP address on every network to which it is attached. When a computer sends a packet to the default gateway for further delivery, the address of the router must be on the same network as the computer, as computers can send packets directly to devices only on their own network.

IPv4 Classes and Subnetting

IPv4 addresses are divided into classes to make them easier to manage. The class of an IP address defines the default subnet mask of the device using that address. All of the IP address classes can be identified by the first octet of the address, as shown in Table 12-1.

Table 12-1   IP address classes

Class	Subnet mask	First octet	Maximum number of networks	Maximum number of hosts	Example IP address
A	255.0.0.0	1–127	127	16,777,214	3.4.1.99
B	255.255.0.0	128–191	16,384	65,534	144.129.188.1
C	255.255.255.0	192–223	2,097,152	254	192.168.1.1
D	N/A	224–239	N/A	N/A	224.0.2.1
E	N/A	240–254	N/A	N/A	N/A

Class A addresses use 8 bits for the network ID and 24 bits for the host ID. You can see this is true by looking at the subnet mask, 255.0.0.0. The value of the first octet will always be somewhere in the range 1 to 127. This means there are only 127 potential Class A networks available for the entire Internet. Class A networks are only assigned to very large companies and Internet providers.

Class B addresses, which are identified by the subnet mask 255.255.0.0, use 16 bits for the network ID and 16 bits for the host ID. The value of the first octet ranges from 128 to 191. There are 16,384 Class B networks, with 65,534 hosts on each network. Class B networks are assigned to many larger organizations, such as governments, universities, and companies with several thousand users.

Class C addresses, which are identified by the subnet mask 255.255.255.0, use 24 bits for the network ID and 8 bits for the host ID. The value of the first octet ranges from 192 to 223. There are 2,097,152 Class C networks, with 254 hosts on each network. Although there are very many Class C networks, they have a relatively small number of hosts; thus, they are suited only to smaller organizations.

Class D addresses are not divided into networks, and they cannot be assigned to computers as IP addresses; instead, Class D addresses are used for multicasting. **Multicast** addresses are used by groups of computers. A packet addressed to a multicast address is delivered to each computer in the multicast group. This is better than a broadcast message because routers can be configured to allow multicast traffic to move from one network to another. In addition, all computers on the network process broadcasts, while only computers that are part of that multicast group process multicasts. Streaming media and network conferencing software often use multicasting to communicate to several computers at once.

Like Class D addresses, Class E addresses are not typically assigned to a computer. Class E addresses are considered experimental and are reserved for future use.

Notice from Table 12-1 that Class A and B networks can have many thousands or millions of hosts on a single network. Because this is not practically manageable, Class A and B networks are typically subnetted. **Subnetting** is the process in which a single large network is subdivided into several smaller networks to control traffic flow and improve manageability. After a network has been subnetted, a router is required to move packets from one subnet to another.

Note

You can subnet any Class A, B, or C network.

To subnet a network, you take some bits from the host ID and give them to the network ID. Suppose, for example, that you want to divide the 3.0.0.0/8 network into 17 subnets. The binary representation of this network is:

```
3.0.0.0   = 00000011.00000000.00000000.00000000
255.0.0.0 = 11111111.00000000.00000000.00000000
```

You then borrow some bits from the host portion of the subnet mask. Because the number of combinations of binary numbers can be represented in binary powers of two, and because valid subnet masks do not contain all 0s or 1s, you can use the equation 2^n to represent the minimum number of subnets required, where n is the number of binary bits that are borrowed from the host portion of the subnet mask. For our example, this is represented as:

$$2^n \geq 15$$

Thus, $n = 4$ (because $2^3 = 8$ is less than 15, but $2^4 = 16$ is greater than 15). Following this, our subnet mask borrows four bits from the default Class A subnet mask:

```
255.240.0.0 = 11111111.11110000.00000000.00000000
```

Similarly, because there are 20 zeros in the preceding subnet mask, you can use the $2^n - 2$ equation to identify the number of hosts per subnet (the -2 accounts for the broadcast and network address for the subnet):

```
2²⁰ - 2 = number of hosts per subnet
        = 1,048,574 hosts per subnet
```

You can then work out the IP address ranges for each of the network ranges. Because four bits in the second octet were not borrowed during subnetting, the ranges of IP addresses that can be given to each subnet must be in ranges of $2^4 = 16$. Thus, the first five ranges that can be given to different subnets on the 3.0.0.0/8 network that use the subnet mask 255.240.0.0 are as follows:

```
3.0.0.1-3.15.255.254
3.16.0.1-3.31.255.254
3.32.0.1-3.47.255.254
3.48.0.1-3.63.255.254
3.64.0.1-3.79.255.254
```

From the preceding ranges, a computer with the IP address 3.34.0.6/12 cannot communicate with the computer 3.31.0.99/12 because they are on different subnets. To communicate, there must be a router between them.

> **Note**
>
> When subnetting a Class C network, ensure that you discard the first and last IP address in each range to account for the broadcast and network address for the subnet.

The IPv6 Protocol

As the Internet grew in the 1990s, ISPs realized that the number of IP addresses available using IPv4 was inadequate to accommodate future growth. As a result, the IPv6 protocol was designed in 1998 to accommodate far more IP addresses. IPv6 uses 128 bits to identify computers, whereas IPv4 only uses 32 bits (4 octets). This allows IPv6 to address up to 340,282,366,920,938,463,463,374,607,431,768,211,456 (or 340 trillion trillion trillion) unique computers.

IPv6 IP addresses are written using 8 colon-delimited 16-bit hexadecimal numbers—for example, 2001:0db8:3c4d:0015:0000:0000:adb6:ef12. If an IPv6

IP address contains 0000 segments, they are often omitted in most notation, thus 2001:0db8:3c4d:0015:::adb6:ef12 is equivalent to 2001:0db8:3c4d:0015:0000:0000:adb6:ef12. The IPv6 loopback address is 0000:0000:0000:0000:0000:0000:0000:0001, but it is often referred to as ::1 for simplicity.

> **Note**
>
> Unlike our traditional decimal numbering scheme, hexadecimal uses an expanded numbering system that includes the letters A through F in addition to the numbers 0–9. Thus, the number 10 is called A in hexadecimal, the number 11 is called B in hexadecimal, the number 12 is called C in hexadecimal, the number 13 is called D in hexadecimal, the number 14 is called E in hexadecimal, and the number 15 is called F in hexadecimal.

Although IPv6 addresses can be expressed several ways, the first half (64 bits) of an IPv6 address identifies your network (the network ID); the first 48 bits are typically assigned by your ISP and identify your organization uniquely on the public Internet, and the following 16 bits can be used to identify unique subnets within your organization. The last 64 bits of an IPv6 address is used to uniquely identify a computer in your LAN (the host ID), and is often generated from the unique hardware address on each computer's network interface.

> **Note**
>
> The hardware address on a network interface is a 48-bit hexadecimal number called the **Media Access Control (MAC) address** that is unique for each network interface manufactured. Ethernet translates IPv4 and IPv6-addressed packets into MAC-addressed frames before sending it to the nearest host or router.

Although most operating systems today support IPv6, few networks and computers on the Internet have adopted it. In 2018, Google reported that less than 20 percent of all computers in any country have adopted IPv6. Most computers that have adopted IPv6 are small Internet-connected devices that are collectively referred to as the **Internet of Things (IoT)**. Some example IoT devices include the NEST smart thermostat and the Google Home personal assistant; both of which run the Linux operating system. IoT devices often use an IPv6 address that can be accessed by an online app, and the IPv6 traffic they send is often encapsulated in IPv4 traffic using a protocol such as **Teredo** to allow it to work within IPv4-only networks.

This slow adoption of IPv6 is primarily the result of two technologies that allow IPv4 to address many more computers than was previously possible: **proxy servers** and **Network Address Translation (NAT)** routers.

Proxy servers and NAT routers are computers or hardware devices that have an IP address and access to a network such as the Internet. Other computers on the network can use a proxy server or NAT router to obtain network or Internet resources on their behalf. Moreover, there are three reserved ranges of IPv4 addresses that are not distributed to computers on the Internet and are intended only for use behind a proxy server or NAT router:

- The entire 10.0.0.0 Class A network (10.0.0.0/8)
- The 172.16 through 172.31 Class B networks (172.16–31.0.0/16)
- The 192.168 Class C networks (192.168.0–255.0/24)

Thus, a computer behind a proxy server in Iceland and a computer behind a NAT router in Seattle could use the same IPv4 address—say, 10.0.5.4—without problems because each of these computers only requests Internet resources using its own proxy server or NAT router. A company may use a Cisco NAT router, for example, to allow other networks and computers in the company to gain access to the Internet. Similarly, a high-speed home Internet modem typically functions as a NAT router to allow multiple computers in your home to access the Internet.

Most computers in the world today obtain Internet access via a proxy server or NAT router. Because these computers share IPv4 addresses on a reserved network range, rather than using a unique IP address, the number of available IPv4 addresses has remained high and slowed the adoption of IPv6.

Configuring a Network Interface

Linux computers in a business environment typically connect to the company network via a wired or wireless network interface. At home, people typically connect to the Internet by means of a network interface, using technologies such as Fiber optic, cellular wireless, Wi-Fi, Digital Subscriber Line (DSL), and Broadband Cable Networks (BCNs).

Recall from Chapter 6 that network interface drivers are provided by modules that are inserted into the Linux kernel at boot time and given an alias that can be used to refer to the network interface afterwards. To view the driver modules and associated aliases for network interfaces in your system, you can use the `lshw –class network` command. On legacy Linux systems, such as Ubuntu 14, the first wired Ethernet network interface is called eth0, the second wired Ethernet network interface is called eth1, and so on. Similarly, the first wireless Ethernet network interface on a legacy Linux system is called wlan0, the second wireless Ethernet network interface in your system is called wlan1, and so on. Most modern Linux systems that use Systemd provide a more descriptive name for network interfaces that reflect the location of the hardware in the system. For example, enpos3 refers to the wired Ethernet network interface on PCI bus 00 slot 03, and wlp8so refers to the wireless Ethernet network interface on PCI bus 08 slot 00.

Note 📎

The network interface aliases displayed by the `lshw -class network` command on a modern Linux system should match the PCI bus information associated with the network interface hardware displayed by the `lspci` command.

You can also use the `ethtool` **command** to display detailed information for network hardware. For example, `ethtool -i enp0s3` will display driver information for the enp0s3 network interface.

After a driver module for a network interface has been loaded into the Linux kernel and given an alias, you can configure it to use IP. The `ifconfig` **(interface configuration) command** can be used to assign an IP configuration to a network interface as well as view the configuration of all network interfaces in the computer. To assign eth0 the IP address of 3.4.5.6 with a subnet mask of 255.0.0.0 and broadcast address of 3.255.255.255, you can use the following command at the command prompt:

```
ifconfig eth0 3.4.5.6 netmask 255.0.0.0 broadcast 3.255.255.255
```

Alternatively, you can receive IP configuration from a Dynamic Host Configuration Protocol (DHCP) or Boot Protocol (BOOTP) server on the network. To obtain and configure IP information from a server on the network, you can use the `dhclient` **command**; for example, `dhclient eth0` would attempt to obtain IP configuration from the network connected to eth0.

The process of obtaining an IP address for your network interface varies, depending on whether your computer is on an IPv4 or IPv6 network. If you attempt to obtain IPv4 configuration for your network interface from a DHCP or BOOTP server and no DHCP or BOOTP server exists on your network, your system will assign an IPv4 address of 169.254.*x.x* where *.x.x* is a randomly generated host ID. This automatic assignment feature is called **Automatic Private IP Addressing (APIPA)**. If your network has IPv6-configured routers, an IPv6 address is automatically assigned to each network interface. This is because network interfaces use **Internet Control Message Protocol version 6 (ICMPv6)** router discovery messages to probe their network for IPv6 configuration information. Alternatively, you can obtain your IPv6 configuration from a DHCP server on the network. If there are no IPv6-configured routers or DHCP servers on your network from which you can obtain an IPv6 configuration for your network interface, your system will assign an IPv6 APIPA address that begins with FE80 and ends with the last half of your network interface's MAC address.

Note

A single network interface can have both an IPv4 and an IPv6 address. Each address can be used to access the Internet using the IPv4 and IPv6 protocols, respectively.

To view the configuration of all interfaces, you can use the `ifconfig` command without any arguments, as shown in the following output:

```
[root@server1 ~]# ifconfig
eth0: flags=4163<UP,BROADCAST,RUNNING,MULTICAST>  mtu 1500
        inet 3.4.5.6  netmask 255.0.0.0  broadcast 3.255.255.255
        inet6 fe80::280:c6ff:fef9:1b8c prefixlen 64  scopeid 0x20<link>
        ether 00:80:C6:F9:1B:8C  txqueuelen 1000  (Ethernet)
        RX packets 1550  bytes 611332 (597.0 KiB)
        RX errors 0  dropped 0  overruns 0  frame 0
        TX packets 722  bytes 62170 (60.7 KiB)
        TX errors 0  dropped 0 overruns 0  carrier 0  collisions 0

lo: flags=73<UP,LOOPBACK,RUNNING>  mtu 65536
        inet 127.0.0.1  netmask 255.0.0.0
        inet6 ::1  prefixlen 128  scopeid 0x10<host>
        loop  txqueuelen 0  (Local Loopback)
        RX packets 4  bytes 340 (340.0 B)
        RX errors 0  dropped 0  overruns 0  frame 0
        TX packets 4  bytes 340 (340.0 B)
        TX errors 0  dropped 0 overruns 0  carrier 0  collisions 0
[root@server1 ~]# _
```

The output of the `ifconfig` command shows that the etho network interface has an IPv4 address of `3.4.5.6` and an IPv6 address of `fe80::280:c6ff:fef9:1b8c` that you can tell was automatically configured by the system because the end of the IPv6 is identical to the last half of the MAC address (`ether 00:80:C6:F9:1B:8C`). It also shows receive (RX) and transmit (TX) statistics and the special loopback adapter (`lo`) with the IPv4 address 127.0.0.1 and IPv6 address ::1; these IP addresses represent the local computer and are required on all computers that use IP.

Note

You can also use the `-i` option to the **netstat command** to show interface statistics.

Note

The `iwconfig` command is similar to the `ifconfig` command, but only displays the configuration of wireless network interfaces in your system. You can also use the `iwconfig` command to set additional parameters for wireless network interfaces, such as frequency and channel.

If you restart the computer, the IP information configured for eth0 will be lost. To allow the system to activate and configure the IP information for an interface at each boot time, you can place entries in a configuration file that is read at boot time by your Linux distribution when activating the network. For Fedora 28 systems, you can add entries to the /etc/sysconfig/network-scripts/ifcfg-*interface* file, where *interface* is the name of the network interface. An example of the configuration file for enp0s3 is shown in the following output:

```
[root@server1 ~]# cat /etc/sysconfig/network-scripts/ifcfg-enp0s3
TYPE=Ethernet
PROXY_METHOD=none
BROWSER_ONLY=no
BOOTPROTO=none
DEFROUTE=yes
IPV4_FAILURE_FATAL=no
IPV6INIT=yes
IPV6_AUTOCONF=yes
IPV6_DEFROUTE=yes
IPV6_FAILURE_FATAL=no
IPV6_ADDR_GEN_MODE=stable-privacy
NAME=enp0s3
UUID=73473ce3-931b-3481-9a31-455bc94de56d
ONBOOT=yes
AUTOCONNECT_PRIORITY=-999
DEVICE=enp0s3
IPADDR=3.4.5.6
PREFIX=8
GATEWAY=3.0.0.254
DNS1=8.8.8.8
DNS2=8.8.4.4
[root@server1 ~]# _
```

The entries in the preceding output indicate that the IP configuration for the Ethernet adapter (enp0s3) will be activated at boot time (ONBOOT=yes) and IPv6 will be automatically configured using ICMPv6 if an IPv6-configured router is available

(IPV6_AUTOCONF=yes). The network interface does not obtain information from a DHCP server (BOOTPROTO=none). IPv4 is instead configured using the IP address 3.4.5.6, an 8-bit subnet mask of 255.0.0.0 (PREFIX=8), and a default gateway of 3.0.0.254. To resolve Internet names, the first DNS server queried will be 8.8.8.8, followed by 8.8.4.4 if the first DNS server is unavailable (DNS1=8.8.8.8, DNS2=8.8.4.4). Also, you can change the BOOTPROTO=none line to BOOTPROTO=dhcp to obtain all IP configuration information from a DHCP server on the network.

After editing the /etc/sysconfig/network-scripts/ifcfg-eth0 file, you do not need to reboot your system to have the new IP configuration take effect. Instead, you can run the command ifdown eth0 to unconfigure the eth0 network interface, followed by ifup eth0 to configure the eth0 network interface using the settings in the /etc/sysconfig/network-scripts/ifcfg-eth0 file. Alternatively, you can use the ifconfig eth0 down and ifconfig eth0 up commands to deactivate and activate the eth0 network interface.

> **Note** 📎
>
> You can optionally use the /etc/sysconfig/network file in Fedora 28 to store network configuration settings that should be shared by all network interfaces on the system.

Ubuntu Linux systems don't store network configuration within files under the /etc/sysconfig/network-scripts directory. On legacy systems, such as Ubuntu Server 14, all network interfaces are configured from information stored within the /etc/network/interfaces file. A sample /etc/network/interfaces file that has an IP address (3.4.5.6) manually assigned to eth0 is shown in the following output:

```
[root@server1 ~]# cat /etc/network/interfaces
# This file describes the network interfaces available on your system
# and how to activate them.  For more information, see interfaces(5).

# The loopback network interface
auto lo
iface lo inet loopback

# The primary network interface
auto eth0
iface eth0 inet static
address 3.4.5.6
netmask 255.0.0.0
gateway 3.0.0.254
dns-nameservers 8.8.8.8 8.8.4.4
[root@server1 ~]# _
```

To instead use DHCP configuration for eth0, you can change the line `iface eth0 inet static` to `iface eth0 inet dhcp` and remove the `address`, `netmask`, and `gateway` lines in the preceding example and then reload your configuration by using the `ifdown eth0` command followed by the `ifup eth0` command, as you would in Fedora Linux, to deactivate and activate the network interface.

On modern Ubuntu systems, such as Ubuntu Server 18, **NetPlan** is used to configure network interfaces; it allows for easy integration with the cloud-init system that Ubuntu uses to create new virtual machines within a cloud environment. NetPlan uses *.yaml files stored within the /etc/netplan directory to configure network interfaces. A sample /etc/netplan/50-cloud-init.yaml file that has an IP address (3.4.5.6) manually assigned to enpos3 is shown in the following output:

```
[root@server1 ~]# cat /etc/netplan/50-cloud-init.yaml
cat /etc/netplan/50-cloud-init.yaml
# This file is generated from information provided by the
datasource.
#Changes to it will not persist across an instance. To disable
#cloud-init's network configuration capabilities, write a file
#/etc/cloud/cloud.cfg.d/99-disable-network-config.cfg with the
#following:
network: {config: disabled}
network:
    ethernets:
        enp0s3:
            dhcp4: no
            addresses: [3.4.5.6/8]
            gateway4: 3.0.0.254
            nameservers:
              addresses: [8.8.8.8,8.8.4.4]
    version: 2
[root@server1 ~]# _
```

To instead use DHCP configuration for enpos3, you can change the line `dhcp4: no` to read `dhcp4: yes` or `dhcp4: true` and reload your configuration by using the `netplan apply` command.

Note 📎

YAML (YAML Ain't Markup Language) is a file format that uses the `attribute: value` syntax defined by JSON (JavaScript Object Notation), but with additional support for comments. Due to its simplicity, YAML is increasingly being used to provide configuration information for modern Linux systems and cloud-related services.

To make the configuration of a network interface easier, you may access your configuration from within a GUI environment. Most Linux distributions contain a graphical network configuration tool that can be run if a GUI environment is installed. On Fedora 28, you can configure IP on your network interfaces using the **Network utility**. To do this, you can navigate to Activities, Show Applications, Settings, Network, and click the cog wheel icon next to your wired or wireless network interface shown in Figure 12-2.

Figure 12-2   The Network utility

Portable computers with a GUI environment often have both a wired and wireless network interface, and connect to a wide variety of networks at different times. To simplify the switching and management of these networks, a daemon called **NetworkManager** is often used on Linux distributions that have a GUI environment, including the Fedora 28 Workstation distribution. If your system is running NetworkManager, you can additionally use the `nmcli` **command** to view or modify connection information. Without arguments, `nmcli` displays information about each network interface, and indicates the active connection as shown in the following output:

```
[root@server1 ~]# nmcli
wlp8s0: connected to CLASSWIFI
        "Qualcomm Atheros AR93xx Wireless Network Adapter (Killer
            Wireless-N 1103 Half-size Mini PCIe Card [AR9380])"
        wifi (ath9k), B8:76:3F:16:F9:F4, hw, mtu 1500
        ip4 default
        inet4 192.168.1.101/24
        route4 0.0.0.0/0
        route4 192.168.1.0/24
        inet6 fe80::3157:d86d:5da1:2292/64
        route6 ff00::/8
        route6 fe80::/64
        route6 fe80::/64
```

```
enp7s0: unavailable
        "Qualcomm Atheros AR8151 v2.0 Gigabit Ethernet"
        ethernet (atl1c), B8:CA:3A:D5:61:A9, hw, mtu 1500

lo: unmanaged
        "lo"
        loopback (unknown), 00:00:00:00:00:00, sw, mtu 65536

DNS configuration:
        servers: 192.168.1.1
        interface: wlp8s0

Use "nmcli device show" to get complete information about known
devices and "nmcli connection show" to get an overview on active
connection profiles.

Consult nmcli(1) and nmcli-examples(5) manual pages for complete
usage details.
[root@server1 ~]# _
```

In the previous output, the wireless Ethernet network interface wlp8so is connected to a wireless network called CLASSWIFI. On a Fedora system, NetworkManager will store the network configuration for this connection in a separate file called /etc/sysconfig/network-scripts/ifcfg-CLASSWIFI. It can then be reused if the system connects to the network in the future. This is especially useful if you manually configure IP addresses for a wireless network, such as a home or work network; each time you connect to the wireless network, the IP address information you configured previously will automatically be applied from the associated configuration file. To see a list of all wired and wireless networks that NetworkManager has connected to in the past, you can run the nmcli conn show command as shown in the following output:

```
[root@server1 ~]# nmcli conn show
NAME          UUID                                    TYPE      DEVICE
CLASSWIFI     562a0a70-7944-4621-ac4d-35572f08b1ed    wifi      wlp8s0
Starbucks     59683e0b-5e1d-405c-b88f-8289899b60bd    wifi      --
McDonalds     0dc84378-4e04-4b43-a7fc-2ce25cff9401    wifi      --
HomeWifi      1966c022-8cc5-422c-9fcf-1fdfd8cdef4e    wifi      --
enp7s0        f1b34bb3-b621-36d0-bdd0-c23e646c9a51    ethernet  --
[root@server1 ~]# _
```

Systemd also contains a daemon called **Systemd-networkd** that provides the same functionality as NetworkManager. You can use the `networkctl command` to view and modify connection information for Systemd-network; without arguments, it displays information about each network interface, including the active connection. The following output indicates that enpos3 is actively connected and managed by Systemd-networkd:

```
[root@server1 ~]# networkctl
IDX LINK              TYPE           OPERATIONAL        SETUP
  1 lo                loopback       carrier            unmanaged
  2 enp0s3            ether          routable           configured
  3 wlp8s0            ether          no-carrier         unmanaged

3 links listed.
[root@server1 ~]# _
```

Note

Both NetworkManager and Systemd-networkd are optional network helper daemons, and only one can be active at any time.

After a network interface has been configured to use IP, you should test the configuration by using the `ping` **(Packet Internet Groper) command**. The `ping` command sends an ICMP packet to another IP address and awaits a response. By default, the `ping` command sends packets continuously every second until the Ctrl+c key combination is pressed; to send only five ping requests to the loopback interface, you can use the `-c` option to the `ping` command, as shown in the following example:

```
[root@server1 ~]# ping -c 5 127.0.0.1
PING 127.0.0.1 (127.0.0.1) 56(84) bytes of data.
64 bytes from 127.0.0.1: icmp_seq=0 ttl=64 time=0.154 ms
64 bytes from 127.0.0.1: icmp_seq=1 ttl=64 time=0.109 ms
64 bytes from 127.0.0.1: icmp_seq=2 ttl=64 time=0.110 ms
64 bytes from 127.0.0.1: icmp_seq=3 ttl=64 time=0.119 ms
64 bytes from 127.0.0.1: icmp_seq=4 ttl=64 time=0.111 ms

--- 127.0.0.1 ping statistics ---
5 packets transmitted, 5 received, 0% packet loss, time 3999ms
rtt min/avg/max/mdev = 0.109/0.120/0.154/0.020 ms
[root@server1 ~]# _
```

Note

If the `ping` command fails to receive any responses from the loopback interface, there is a problem with IP itself.

Next, you need to test whether the Linux computer can ping other computers on the same network; the following command can be used to send five ping requests to the computer that has the IP address 3.0.0.2 configured:

```
[root@server1 ~]# ping -c 5 3.0.0.2
PING 3.0.0.2 (3.0.0.2) 56(84) bytes of data.
64 bytes from 3.0.0.2: icmp_seq=0 ttl=128 time=0.448 ms
64 bytes from 3.0.0.2: icmp_seq=1 ttl=128 time=0.401 ms
64 bytes from 3.0.0.2: icmp_seq=2 ttl=128 time=0.403 ms
64 bytes from 3.0.0.2: icmp_seq=3 ttl=128 time=0.419 ms
64 bytes from 3.0.0.2: icmp_seq=4 ttl=128 time=0.439 ms

--- 3.0.0.2 ping statistics ---
5 packets transmitted, 5 received, 0% packet loss, time 4001ms
rtt min/avg/max/mdev = 0.401/0.422/0.448/0.018 ms
[root@server1 ~]# _
```

Note

If the `ping` command fails to receive any responses from other computers on the network, there is a problem with the network media.

You can use the `ping6` **command** to send an ICMP6 message to an IPv6 address.

Configuring a PPP Interface

Instead of configuring IP to run on a network interface to gain network access, you can run IP over serial lines (such as telephone lines) using the PPP WAN protocol. Three common technologies use PPP to connect computers to the Internet or other networks:

- Modems
- ISDN
- DSL

Modem (modulator-demodulator) devices use PPP to send IP information across normal telephone lines; they were the most common method for home users to gain Internet access in the 1990s. Modem connections are considered slow today compared to most other technologies; most modems can only transmit data at 56KB/s. Because modems transmit information on a serial port, the system typically makes a symbolic link called /dev/modem that points to the correct serial port device, such as /dev/ttyS0 for COM1.

Integrated Services Digital Network (ISDN) is a set of standards designed for transmitting voice, video, and data over normal copper telephone lines. It allows data to be transferred at 128KB/s. ISDN uses an ISDN modem device to connect to a different type of media than regular phone lines. Although ISDN is popular in Europe, it does not have a large presence in North America.

One of the most popular connection technologies in North America is DSL. DSL has many variants, such as Asynchronous DSL (ADSL), which is the most common DSL used in homes across North America, and High-bit-rate DSL (HDSL), which is common in business environments; for simplification, all variants of DSL are referred to as xDSL. You use an Ethernet network interface to connect to a DSL modem using IP and PPP; as a result, DSL connections are said to use **PPP over Ethernet (PPPoE)**. The DSL modem then transmits information across normal telephone lines at speeds that can exceed 100MB/s.

Because modem, ISDN, and DSL connections require additional configuration information that is specific to the ISP, they are not normally configured during the Linux installation and must be configured manually.

Configuring a PPP connection requires support for PPP compiled into the kernel or available as a module, the PPP daemon (pppd), and a series of supporting utilities such as the chat program, which is used to communicate with a modem. PPP configuration in the past was tedious at best; you needed to create a chat script that contained the necessary information to establish a PPP connection (user name, password, and so on), a connection script that contained device parameters used by the PPP daemon, as well as use a program such as minicom to initiate network communication. Because the IP configuration is typically assigned by the ISP to which you connect, it rarely needs to be configured during the process.

Because modems and ISDN modems are relatively rare today, modern Linux distributions typically don't ship with a graphical configuration tool by default. However, you can download and install the **Modem Manager utility** to configure modems and ISDN modems. On a Fedora 28 system, you can run the `dnf install modem-manager-gui` command as the root user to install this package, and then navigate to Activities, Show Applications, Modem Manager GUI to start the Modem Manager shown in Figure 12-3. The Modem Manager automatically detects any modem or ISDN hardware in your computer and allows you to configure the associated ISP configuration, including the ISP account username and password.

Figure 12-3   The Modem Manager utility

DSL connections are very common today. As a result, nearly all modem Linux distributions contain a utility that can configure your network interface to work with a DSL modem. On Fedora 28, you can either execute the `pppoe-setup` **command** at a command-line terminal or the `nm-connection-editor` **command** within a terminal in a GUI environment. The `nm-connection-editor` command starts the graphical **Network Connections tool** shown in Figure 12-4, which is a component of NetworkManager. If you click the + button shown in Figure 12-4 and choose your device type (DSL/PPPoE), the Network Connections tool will attempt to detect your DSL modem and prompt you to supply the ISP account username and password.

Figure 12-4   The Network Connections utility

 Note

In addition to DSL, the Network Connections tool can also be used to configure many other network technologies, including:

- Overlay networks, including **Virtual Private Network (VPN)** connections that provide an encrypted virtual IP network on top of the existing unencrypted IP network.
- Specialized technologies, such as Infiniband, that allow network interfaces to communicate directly to each other using **Remote Direct Memory Access (RDMA)**.
- **Bonding** (also called **aggregation**), in which two separate network interfaces connected to the same network can be combined to provide fault tolerance (in an active/passive configuration) or load balancing of network traffic to achieve higher transmission rates.
- **Bridging**, in which two network interfaces connected to separate networks provide for seamless connectivity between the networks.

To configure a DSL connection on a system without a GUI environment that contains NetworkManager, you can execute the `nmtui` **command** to start a text version of the Network Connections tool, or run the `nmcli` command with the appropriate options. If NetworkManager is not installed (the default on Ubuntu Server), you can instead execute the `pppoeconf` **command**, which will open a basic graphical screen within your terminal and scan for DSL devices, as shown in Figure 12-5. If a DSL device is found, you will be prompted to supply the ISP account username and password to complete the configuration.

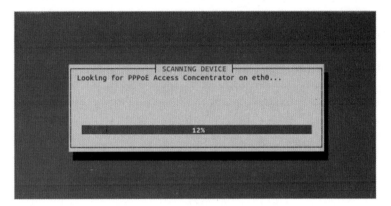

Figure 12-5   The pppoeconf utility

After a PPP modem, ISDN, or DSL connection has been configured, it will normally be activated automatically at boot time like other network interfaces on the system. On a Fedora 28 system, you will notice a new file for the connection within the /etc/sysconfig/network-scripts directory. On an Ubuntu Server 14 system, there will an additional paragraph added to the /etc/network/interfaces file, and on an Ubuntu Server 18 system, there will be an additional YAML configuration file within the /etc/netplan directory. Other configuration used by the PPP daemon is stored within the /etc/ppp and /etc/isdn directories. It is good form to double-check the passwords used to connect to the ISP because incorrect passwords represent the most common problem with PPP connections. These passwords are stored in two files: /etc/ppp/pap-secrets (Password Authentication Protocol secrets) and /etc/ppp/chap-secrets (Challenge Handshake Authentication Protocol secrets). If the ISP accepts passwords sent across the network in text form, the /etc/ppp/pap-secrets file is consulted for the correct password; however, if the ISP requires a more secure method for validating the identity of a user, the passwords in the /etc/ppp/chap-secrets file are used. When you configure a PPP connection, this information is automatically added to both files, as shown in the following output:

```
[root@server1 ~]# cat /etc/ppp/pap-secrets
# Secrets for authentication using PAP
# client        server   secret                  IP addresses
####### system-config-network will overwrite this part!!! (begin) ####
"user1"         "isp"    "secret"
####### system-config-network will overwrite this part!!! (end) ######
```

```
[root@server1 ~]# cat /etc/ppp/chap-secrets
# Secrets for authentication using CHAP
# client         server   secret                IP addresses
####### system-config-network will overwrite this part!!! (begin) ####
"user1"          "isp"    "secret"
####### system-config-network will overwrite this part!!! (end) ######
[root@server1 ~]# _
```

After a PPP device has been configured, the `ifconfig` command indicates the PPP interface using the appropriate name; pppo is typically used for the first modem or xDSL device, and ipppo is typically used for the first ISDN device. The following output shows the IP configuration (obtained from the ISP) when the first xDSL interface (pppo) is activated:

```
[root@server1 ~]# ifconfig
eth0      Link encap:EthernetHWaddr 00:80:C6:F9:1B:8C
          inet addr:3.4.5.6  Bcast:3.255.255.255  Mask:255.0.0.0
          inet6addr: fe80::280:c6ff:fef9:1b8c/64 Scope:Link
          UP BROADCAST RUNNING MULTICAST  MTU:1500  Metric:1
          RX packets:47 errors:0 dropped:0 overruns:0 frame:0
          TX packets:13 errors:5 dropped:0 overruns:0 carrier:5
          collisions:0 txqueuelen:1000
          RX bytes:5560 (5.4 Kb)  TX bytes:770 (770.0 b)
          Interrupt:10 Base address:0x8000

lo        Link encap:LocalLoopback
          inet6addr: ::1/128 Scope:Host
          UP LOOPBACK RUNNING  MTU:16436  Metric:1
          RX packets:3142 errors:0 dropped:0 overruns:0 frame:0
          TX packets:3142 errors:0 dropped:0 overruns:0 carrier:0
          collisions:0 txqueuelen:0
          RX bytes:3443414 (3.2 Mb)  TX bytes:3443414 (3.2 Mb)

ppp0      Link encap:Point-to-Point Protocol
          inet addr:65.95.13.217  P-t-P:65.95.13.1 Mask:255.255.255.255
          UP POINTOPOINT RUNNING NOARP MULTICAST  MTU:1492  Metric:1
          RX packets:15 errors:0 dropped:0 overruns:0 frame:0
          TX packets:31 errors:0 dropped:0 overruns:0 carrier:0
          collisions:0 txqueuelen:3
          RX bytes:1448 (1.4 Kb)  TX bytes:3088 (3.0 Kb)
[root@server1 ~]# _
```

Name Resolution

Computers that communicate on an IP network identify themselves using unique IP addresses; however, this identification scheme is impractical for human use because it is difficult to remember IP addresses. As a result, every computer on a network is identified by a name that makes sense to humans, such as "Accounting1" or "ReceptionKiosk." Because each computer on a network is called a host, the name assigned to an individual computer is its **host name**.

For computers that require a presence on the Internet, simple host names are rarely used. Instead, they are given a host name called a **fully qualified domain name (FQDN)** according to a hierarchical naming scheme called **Domain Name Space (DNS)**. At the top of the Domain Name Space is the root domain, which is really just a theoretical starting point for the branching, tree-like structure. Below the root domain are the top-level domain names, which identify the type of organization in which a network is located. For example, the com domain is primarily used for business, or commercial, networks. Several second-level domains exist under each top-level domain name to identify the name of the organization, and simple host names are listed under the second-level domains. Figure 12-6 shows a portion of the Domain Name Space.

Note

For simplicity, FQDNs are often referred to as host names.

Thus, the host computer shown in Figure 12-6 has an FQDN of *www.linux.org*.

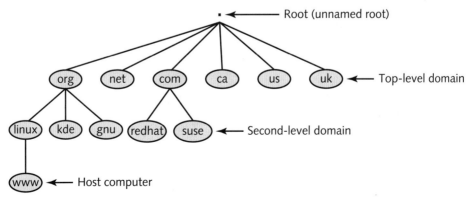

Figure 12-6   The domain name space

Note

The host name www (World Wide Web) is often used by servers that host Web pages.

Second-level domains must be purchased and registered with an ISP in order to be recognized by other computers on the Internet. You can use the `whois` **command** to obtain registration information about any domain within the Domain Name Space. For example, to obtain information about the organization responsible for maintaining the linux.org domain, you can use the following command:

```
[root@server1 ~]# whois linux.org | head -25
[Querying whois.pir.org]
[whois.pir.org]
Domain Name: LINUX.ORG
Registry Domain ID: D2338975-LROR
Registrar WHOIS Server: whois.networksolutions.com
Registrar URL: http://www.networksolutions.com
Updated Date: 2018-03-12T17:00:11Z
Creation Date: 1994-05-10T04:00:00Z
Registry Expiry Date: 2027-05-11T04:00:00Z
Registrar Registration Expiration Date:
Registrar: Network Solutions, LLC
Registrar IANA ID: 2
Registrar Abuse Contact Email: abuse@web.com
Registrar Abuse Contact Phone: +1.8003337680
Reseller:
Domain Status: clientTransferProhibited
https://icann.org/epp#clientTransferProhibited
Registrant Organization: Linux Online, Inc
Registrant State/Province: NY
Registrant Country: US
Name Server: MARK.NS.CLOUDFLARE.COM
Name Server: LIA.NS.CLOUDFLARE.COM
DNSSEC: unsigned
URL of the ICANN Whois Inaccuracy Complaint Form
https://www.icann.org/wicf/)
>>> Last update of WHOIS database: 2018-10-14T01:41:56Z <<<
[root@server1 ~]# _
```

You can view or set the host name for a Linux computer using the `hostname` **command**, as shown in the following output:

```
[root@server1 ~]# hostname
server1.class.com
```

```
[root@server1 ~]# hostname computer1.sampledomain.com
[root@server1 ~]# hostname
computer1.sampledomain.com
[root@server1 ~]# _
```

To configure the host name shown in the preceding output at every boot time, modify the HOSTNAME line in the /etc/hostname file, or run the `hostnamectl` **command**. For example, the commands in the following output set the host name to computer1.sampledomain.com and verify the configuration within /etc/hostname:

```
[root@server1 ~]# hostnamectl set-hostname computer1.sampledomain.com
[root@server1 ~]# cat /etc/hostname
computer1.sampledomain.com
[root@server1 ~]# _
```

> **Note**
>
> Many network server daemons record the system host name in their configuration files during installation. As a result, some Linux server distributions prompt you for the host name during the Linux installation to ensure that you don't need to modify network server daemon configuration files afterwards.

Although host names are easier to use when specifying computers on the network, IP cannot use them to identify computers. Thus, you must map host names to their associated IP addresses so that applications that contact other computers across the network can find the appropriate IP address for a host name.

The simplest method for mapping host names to IP addresses is by placing entries into the /etc/hosts file, as shown in the following example:

```
[root@server1 ~]# cat /etc/hosts
127.0.0.1   server1 server1.class.com localhost localhost.localdomain
::1         server1 server1.class.com localhost6 localhost6.localdomain6
3.0.0.2  ftp.sampledomain.com fileserver
10.3.0.1    alpha
[root@server1 ~]# _
```

> **Note**
>
> You can also use the *getent hosts* command to view the contents of the /etc/hosts file.

The entries in the preceding output identify the local computer, 127.0.0.1, by the host names server1, server1.class.com, localhost, and localhost.localdomain. Similarly, you can use the host name ftp.sampledomain.com or fileserver to refer to the computer with the IP address of 3.0.0.2. Also, the computer with the IP address of 10.3.0.1 can be referred to using the name alpha.

Because it would be cumbersome to list names for all hosts on the Internet in the /etc/hosts file, ISPs can list FQDNs in DNS servers on the Internet. Applications can then ask DNS servers for the IP address associated with a certain FQDN. To configure your system to resolve names to IP addresses by contacting a DNS server, you can specify the IP address of the DNS server in the /etc/resolv.conf file. This file can contain up to three DNS servers; if the first DNS server is unavailable, the system attempts to contact the second DNS server, followed by the third DNS server listed in the file. An example /etc/resolv.conf file is shown in the following output:

```
[root@server1 ~]# cat /etc/resolv.conf
nameserver 209.121.197.2
nameserver 192.139.188.144
nameserver 6.0.4.211
[root@server1 ~]# _
```

Each network interface can have a different set of DNS servers that it uses for name resolution. To do this, you can specify the DNS servers within the IP configuration file for the network interface as shown earlier in this chapter. In this case, the DNS servers listed within the IP configuration file for the network interface are written to the /etc/resolv.conf file when the interface is activated.

> **Note** 📎
>
> On Ubuntu Server 14.04, the /etc/resolv.conf file is built dynamically at each boot. To manually add a DNS server, add the appropriate lines to /etc/resolvconf/resolv.conf.d/base and they will be incorporated into /etc/resolv.conf on each subsequent boot.
>
> On Linux distributions that use Systemd, the Systemd-resolved service handles name resolution requests. This service queries the DNS servers listed in the /etc/resolv.conf file on most Linux distributions, but may instead be configured to use the /run/systemd/resolve/stub-resolv.conf file; in this case /etc/resolv.conf is merely a symlink to /run/systemd/resolve/stub-resolv.conf.
>
> To test the DNS configuration by resolving a host name or FQDN to an IP address, you can supply the host name or FQDN as an argument to the nslookup, dig, or host **command** at a command prompt.

When you specify a host name while using a certain application, that application must then resolve that host name to the appropriate IP address by searching either the local /etc/hosts file or a DNS server. The method that applications use to resolve host names is determined by the "hosts:" line in the /etc/nsswitch.conf file; an example of this file is shown in the following output:

```
[root@server1 ~]# grep hosts /etc/nsswitch.conf
hosts:          files dns
[root@server1 ~]# _
```

The preceding output indicates that applications first try to resolve host names using the /etc/hosts file (files). If unsuccessful, applications contact the DNS servers listed in the /etc/resolv.conf file (dns).

On older Linux computers, the /etc/host.conf file was used instead of /etc/nsswitch.conf; the /etc/host.conf file still exists today to support older programs and should contain the same name resolution order as /etc/nsswitch.conf if older programs are installed. An example /etc/host.conf file that tells applications to search the /etc/hosts file (hosts) followed by DNS servers (bind) is shown in the following output:

```
[root@server1 ~]# cat /etc/host.conf
multi on
order hosts,bind
[root@server1 ~]# _
```

Routing

Every computer on a network maintains a list of IP networks so that packets are sent to the appropriate location; this list is called a **route table** and is stored in system memory. To see the route table, you can use the `route` **command**, as shown in the following output:

```
[root@server1 ~]# route
Kernel IP routing table
Destination     Gateway          Genmask         Flags Metric Ref    Use Iface
10.0.0.0        *                255.255.0.0     U     2      0        0 wlan0
192.168.0.0     *                255.255.0.0     U     0      0        0 eth0
127.0.0.0       *                255.0.0.0       U     0      0        0 lo
default         192.168.0.1      0.0.0.0         UG    0      0        0 eth0
[root@server1 ~]# _
```

> **Note** 📎
>
> The `netstat -r` command is equivalent to the `route` command.
>
> The /etc/networks file contains aliases for IP networks. The "default" line in the previous output refers to the 0.0.0.0 network because the /etc/networks file provides an alias for the 0.0.0.0 network called "default." To view the route table without aliases, supply the –n option to the `route` or netstat -r command.

The route table shown in the preceding output indicates that all packets destined for the 10.0.0.0 network will be sent to the device wlan0. Similarly, all packets destined for the 192.168.0.0 network will be sent to the device eth0 and packets destined for the 127.0.0.0 network will be sent to the loopback adapter (`lo`). Packets that must be sent to any other network will be sent to the default gateway; the final line in the preceding output indicates that the default gateway is a computer with the IP address 192.168.0.1, via the eth0 device.

> **Note** 📎
>
> The default gateway is normally specified within the IP configuration file for the network interface as shown earlier in this chapter, and loaded when the network interface is activated.

If your computer has more than one network interface configured, the route table will have more entries that define the available IP networks; computers that have more than one network interface are called **multihomed hosts**. Multihomed hosts can be configured to forward packets from one interface to another to aid a packet in reaching its destination; this process is commonly called **routing** or **IP forwarding**. To enable routing on your Linux computer, place the number 1 in the file /proc/sys/net/ipv4/ip_forward for IPv4 or /proc/sys/net/ipv6/conf/all/forwarding for IPv6, as shown in the following output:

```
[root@server1 ~]# cat /proc/sys/net/ipv4/ip_forward
0
[root@server1 ~]# cat /proc/sys/net/ipv6/conf/all/forwarding
0
[root@server1 ~]# echo 1 > /proc/sys/net/ipv4/ip_forward
[root@server1 ~]# echo 1 > /proc/sys/net/ipv6/conf/all/forwarding
[root@server1 ~]# cat /proc/sys/net/ipv4/ip_forward
1
[root@server1 ~]# cat /proc/sys/net/ipv6/conf/all/forwarding
1
[root@server1 ~]# _
```

Note

The `sysctl` **command** can also be used to modify the contents of files under the /proc/sys directory. For example, `sysctl net.ipv4.ip_forward = 1` would be equivalent to the `echo 1 > /proc/sys/net/ipv4/ip_forward` command.

To enable IPv4 routing at every boot, ensure that the line `net.ipv4.ip_forward = 1` exists in the /etc/sysctl.conf file. To enable IPv6 routing at every boot, ensure that the line `net.ipv6.conf.default.forwarding = 1` exists in the /etc/sysctl.conf file.

If your computer has more than one network interface and routing is enabled, your computer will route packets only to networks for which it has a network interface. On larger networks, however, you might have several routers, in which case packets might have to travel through several routers to reach their destination. Because routers only know the networks to which they are directly connected, you might need to add entries to the route table on a router so that it knows where to send packets that are destined for a remote network. Suppose, for example, your organization has three IP networks (1.0.0.0/8, 2.0.0.0/8, and 3.0.0.0/8) divided by two routers, as shown in Figure 12-7.

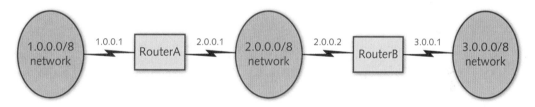

Figure 12-7   A sample routed network

RouterA has an entry in its route table that says it is connected to: 1) the 1.0.0.0/8 network via the network interface that has the IP address 1.0.0.1; and 2) the 2.0.0.0/8 network via the network interface that has the IP address 2.0.0.1. These two routes are automatically established when IP is configured. If RouterA receives a packet that is destined for the 3.0.0.0/8 network, it does not know where to forward it because it does not have a route for the 3.0.0.0/8 network in its routing table. To add the appropriate route to the 3.0.0.0/8 network on RouterA, you can run the following command on RouterA:

```
[root@server1 ~]# route add -net 3.0.0.0 netmask 255.0.0.0 gw 2.0.0.2
[root@server1 ~]# _
```

Now, RouterA sends any packets destined for the 3.0.0.0/8 network to the computer 2.0.0.2 (RouterB). RouterB then forwards the packets to the 3.0.0.0/8 network because it has a route in its route table that says it is connected to the 3.0.0.0/8 network via the network interface that has the IP address 3.0.0.1.

Similarly, for RouterB to forward packets it receives destined for the 1.0.0.0/8 network, it must have a route that sends those packets to RouterA via the interface 2.0.0.1:

```
[root@server1 ~]# route add -net 1.0.0.0 netmask 255.0.0.0 gw 2.0.0.1
[root@server1 ~]# _
```

> ## Note
>
> You can use the `route del <route>` command to remove entries from the route table.
>
> The `ip` **command** can also be used to view and manipulate the route table. For example, the command `ip route add 1.0.0.0/8 via 2.0.0.1` can be used to add the route shown in the previous output to the route table, and the command `ip route show` can display the route table.
>
> The contents of the route table are lost when the computer is powered off; to load the additional route shown in the previous output to the route table at every boot time, add the line `1.0.0.0/8 via 2.0.0.1 dev interface` to the /etc/sysconfig/network-scripts/route-interface file on a Fedora 28 system, or add the line `up route add -net 1.0.0.0 netmask 255.0.0.0 gw 2.0.0.1` to the network interface section of the /etc/network/interfaces file on an Ubuntu Server 14 system. For Ubuntu 18, you can add the following lines within the network interface section of the YAML file under the /etc/netplan directory:
>
> ```
>   routes:
>   - to: 1.0.0.0/8
>   via: 2.0.0.1
> ```
>
> You can also use a routing protocol on routers within your network to automate the addition of routes to the routing table. Two common routing protocols are Routing Information Protocol (RIP) and Open Shortest Path First (OSPF). If you install the quagga package, you can configure the RIP and OSPF routing protocols using the `zebra` **command**.

Because the list of all routes on large networks such as the Internet is too large to be stored in a route table on a router, most routers are configured with a default gateway. Any packets that are addressed to a destination that is not listed in the route table are sent to the default gateway, which is a router that can forward the packet to the appropriate network or to the router's own default gateway and so on until the packets reach their destination.

If computers on your network are unable to connect to other computers on a remote network, the problem is likely routing-related. A common utility used to troubleshoot routing is the `traceroute` **command**; it displays all routers between the current computer and a remote computer. To trace the path from the local computer to the computer with the IP address 3.4.5.6, you can use the following command:

```
[root@server1 ~]# traceroute 3.4.5.6
traceroute to 3.4.5.6 (3.4.5.6), 30 hops max, 38 byte packets
1   linksys (192.168.0.1)   2.048 ms   0.560 ms   0.489 ms
2   apban.pso.com (7.43.111.2)   2.560 ms   0.660 ms   0.429 ms
3   tfs.ihtfcid.net (3.0.0.1)   3.521 ms   0.513 ms   0.499 ms
4   srl.lala.com (3.4.5.6)   5.028 ms   0.710 ms   0.554 ms
[root@server1 ~]# _
```

> **Note**
>
> Two common alternatives to the `traceroute` command include the `tracepath` **command** and the `mtr` **command**.
>
> To trace an IPv6 route, you can use the `mtr`, `traceroute6`, or `tracepath6` **command**.

Network Services

Recall from Chapter 1 that Linux provides a wide variety of services that are available to users across a network. Before you are able to configure the appropriate network services to meet your organization's needs, you must first identify the types and features of network services.

Network services are processes that run on your computer and provide some type of valuable service for client computers on the network. They are often represented by a series of daemon processes that listen for certain requests on the network. Daemons identify the packets to which they should respond using a **port** number that uniquely identifies each network service. Different daemons listen for different port numbers. A port number is like an apartment number for the delivery of mail. The network ID of the IP address ensures that the packet is delivered to the correct street (network); the host ID ensures that the packet is delivered to the correct building (host); and the transport layer protocol and port number ensure that the packet is delivered to the proper apartment in the building (service).

Ports and their associated protocols are defined in the /etc/services file. To see to which port the telnet daemon listens, you can use the following command:

```
[root@server1 ~]# grep telnet /etc/services
telnet          23/tcp
telnet          23/udp
rtelnet         107/tcp             # Remote Telnet
rtelnet         107/udp
telnets         992/tcp
telnets         992/udp
skytelnet       1618/tcp            # skytelnet
skytelnet       1618/udp            # skytelnet
hp-3000-telnet  2564/tcp            # HP 3000 NS/VT block mode telnet
hp-3000-telnet  2564/udp            # HP 3000 NS/VT block mode telnet
tl1-telnet      3083/tcp            # TL1-TELNET
tl1-telnet      3083/udp            # TL1-TELNET
telnetcpcd      3696/tcp            # Telnet Com Port Control
telnetcpcd      3696/udp            # Telnet Com Port Control
scpi-telnet     5024/tcp            # SCPI-TELNET
scpi-telnet     5024/udp            # SCPI-TELNET
ktelnet         6623/tcp            # Kerberos V5 Telnet
ktelnet         6623/udp            # Kerberos V5 Telnet
[root@server1 ~]# _
```

The preceding output indicates that the telnet daemon listens on port 23 using both TCP/IP and UDP/IP.

Ports range in number from 0 to 65534. The ports 0–1023 are called **well-known ports** because they represent commonly used services. Table 12-2 provides a list of common well-known ports.

Table 12-2 Common well-known ports

Service	Port
FTP	TCP 20, 21
Secure Shell (SSH)	TCP 22
Telnet	TCP 23
SMTP	TCP 25
HTTP / HTTPS	TCP 80 / TCP 443
rlogin	TCP 513
DNS	TCP 53, UDP 53
Trivial FTP (TFTP)	UDP 69

Table 12-2   Common well-known ports *(continued)*

Service	Port
NNTP / NNTPS	TCP 119 / TCP 563
POP3 / POP3S	TCP 110 / TCP 995
IMAP4 / IMAP4S	TCP 143 / TCP 993
NTP	TCP 123, UDP 123
SNMP	TCP 161, TCP 162, UDP 161, UDP 162
NetBIOS	TCP 139, UDP 139
SMB/CIFS	TCP 445, UDP 445
Syslog	TCP 514, UDP 514
LDAP / LDAPS	TCP 389, UDP 389 / TCP 636, UDP 636

Note

Many protocols have a secure version that uses encrypted communication. For example, secure HTTP is called HTTPS and uses a different port number as a result.

You can use the `netstat` or `ss` **(socket statistics) command** to display active TCP/IP and UDP/IP connections on your system; the `netstat -t` or `ss -t` command will display active TCP/IP connections, whereas the `netstat -u` or `ss -u` command will display active UDP/IP connections.

Network utilities can connect to daemons that provide network services directly; these daemons are called **stand-alone daemons**. Alternatively, network utilities can connect to network services via the **Extended Internet Super Daemon (xinetd)**, which starts the appropriate daemon to provide the network service as needed. This structure is shown in Figure 12-8.

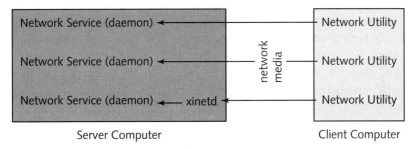

Figure 12-8   Interacting with network services

> **Note**
>
> The xinetd daemon is an extended version of the original Internet Super Daemon (inetd) that was available on legacy UNIX and Linux systems.

Because xinetd only starts daemons on demand to conserve memory and other system resources, it is often used on smaller Linux systems, such as IoT devices. On larger Linux systems, xinetd is optionally used to start and manage connections for smaller network daemons such as telnet and rlogin. Ubuntu Server 14, Ubuntu Server 18, and Fedora 28 systems do not contain the xinetd daemon by default, but you can install it from a software repository.

The xinetd daemon is configured via entries within the /etc/xinetd.conf file. Normally, this file incorporates all of the files in the /etc/xinetd.d directory as well. Most daemons that are managed by xinetd are configured by files in the /etc/xinetd.d directory named after the daemons. For example, if you install the telnet daemon, you can configure it to be started by xinetd via the /etc/xinetd.d/telnet file, as shown in the following output:

```
[root@server1 ~]# cat /etc/xinetd.d/telnet
service telnet
{
    flags           = REUSE
    socket_type     = stream
    wait            = no
    user            = root
    server          = /usr/sbin/in.telnetd
    log_on_failure  += USERID
    disable         = no
}
[root@server1 ~]# _
```

Large network daemons are rarely started by xinetd. Instead, they are stand-alone daemons that are started at boot time from rc scripts as part of the UNIX SysV or Systemd system initialization process.

Many stand-alone and xinetd-managed daemons also have one or more configuration files that control how they operate. Most of these configuration files contain many commented lines that indicate the usage of certain configuration parameters. As a result, these configuration files can be very large; the main configuration file used by the Apache Web Server is often several hundred lines long. In addition to this, most stand-alone network daemons do not use the system log daemon (rsyslogd) or Systemd journal daemon (journald) to log information related to their operation. Instead, they log this information themselves to subdirectories of the same name under the /var/log directory. For example, log files for the Samba daemon are located in the /var/log/samba directory.

Table 12-3 lists the names and features of network services that are commonly found on Linux computers that participate in a network environment. You'll learn how to configure many of these network services in this chapter as well as within Chapter 13.

Table 12-3	Common network services		
Network service	Type	Port	Description
Apache Web Server (httpd)	Stand-alone	TCP 80 TCP 443	Serves Web pages using HTTP/HTTPS to other computers on the network that have a Web browser Configuration file: /etc/httpd/conf/httpd.conf or /etc/apache2/apache2.conf
BIND / DNS Server (named)	Stand-alone	TCP 53 UDP 53	Resolves fully qualified domain names to IP addresses for a certain namespace on the Internet Configuration file: /etc/named.conf
DHCP Server (dhcpd)	Stand-alone	UDP 67 UDP 68	Provides IP configuration for computers on a network Configuration file: /etc/dhcp/dhcpd.conf
Washington University FTP Server (in.ftpd)	xinetd	TCP 20 TCP 21 UDP 69	Transfers files to and accepts files from other computers on the network with an FTP utility Configuration file: /etc/ftpaccess Hosts denied FTP access: /etc/ftphosts Users denied FTP access: /etc/ftpusers FTP data compression: /etc/ftpconversions
Very Secure FTP Server (vsftpd)	Stand-alone	TCP 20 TCP 21 UDP 69	Transfers files to and accepts files from other computers on the network with an FTP utility Configuration file: /etc/vsftpd/vsftpd.conf or /etc/vsftpd.conf Users denied FTP access: /etc/vsftpd/ftpusers or /etc/ftpusers
Internetwork News Server (innd)	Stand-alone	TCP 119 TCP 563	Accepts and manages newsgroup postings and transfers them to other news servers Configuration file: /etc/news/inn.conf
NFS Server (rpc.nfsd)	Stand-alone	TCP 2049	Shares files to other computers on the network that have an NFS client utility Configuration file: /etc/exports
POP3 Server (ipop3d)	Stand-alone	TCP 110 TCP 995	Allows users with an email reader to obtain email from the server using the Post Office Protocol version 3

(continues)

Table 12-3 Common network services *(continued)*

Network service	Type	Port	Description
IMAP4 Server (imapd)	Stand-alone	TCP 143 TCP 993	Allows users with an email reader to obtain email from the server using the Intenet Message Access Protocol
Sendmail Email Server (sendmail)	Stand-alone	TCP 25	Accepts and sends email to users or other email servers on the Internet using the Simple Mail Transfer Protocol (SMTP) Configuration file: /etc/sendmail.cf
Postfix Email Server (postfix)	Stand-alone	TCP 25	Accepts and sends email to users or other email servers on the Internet using the Simple Mail Transfer Protocol (SMTP) Configuration file: /etc/postfix/main.cf
rlogin Daemon (in.rlogind)	xinetd	TCP 513	Allows users who use the `rlogin` and `rcp` utilities the ability to copy files and obtain shells on other computers on the network
rsh Daemon (in.rshd)	xinetd	TCP 514	Allows users who use the `rsh` utility the ability to run commands on other computers on the network
Samba Server (smbd & nmbd)	Stand-alone	TCP 137 TCP 138 TCP 139 TCP 445	Allows Windows users to view shared files and printers on a Linux server Configuration file: /etc/samba/smb.conf
Secure Shell Daemon (sshd)	Stand-alone	TCP 22	Provides a secure alternative to the `telnet`, `rlogin`, and `rsh` utilities by using encrypted communication Configuration file: /etc/ssh/sshd_config
Squid Proxy Server (squid)	Stand-alone	TCP 3128	Allows computers on a network to share one connection to the Internet. It is also known as a proxy server Configuration file: /etc/squid/squid.conf
telnet Daemon (in.telnetd)	xinetd	TCP 23	Allows users who have a telnet utility the ability to log in to the system from across the network and obtain a shell
X.org (X11)	stand-alone	TCP 6000	Allows users who use X.org to obtain graphics from another X.org computer across the network using the XDMCP protocol. You can specify the hosts that can connect to X.org using the `xhost` command. Alternatively, you can use the `xauth` command to generate credentials (stored in ~/.Xauthority) that are used to connect to a remote X.org server.

To ensure that a service is responding to client requests, you can use the `ncat` **(net cat) command** to interact with it. For example, to interact with the sshd service running on port 22 on the local computer (127.0.0.1), you could run the `ncat 127.0.0.1 22` command and view the output. If the service doesn't display any output, you can often restart the daemon (sshd) to fix the problem.

> **Note**
>
> Many Linux distributions create a symlink to the `ncat` command called `nc`.

Remote Administration

As we discussed in Chapter 6, Linux servers are typically installed on a rackmount server system that is located on a rack in a server room and administered remotely. There are several ways to perform command-line and graphical administration of remote Linux servers, including telnet, remote commands, Secure Shell (SSH), and Virtual Network Computing (VNC).

Telnet

The easiest way to perform administration on a remote Linux computer is via a command-line interface. The `telnet` **command** has traditionally been used to obtain a command-line shell on remote UNIX and Linux servers across the network that run a telnet server daemon. Nearly all Macintosh, Linux, and UNIX systems come with a `telnet` command. For Windows systems, you can download the free **Putty** program at *www.chiark.greenend.org.uk/~sgtatham/putty/* to start a telnet session to another computer.

The telnet server daemon is not installed by default on most modern Linux distributions, but it can easily be installed from a software repository. On systems that use the Systemd system initialization process, such as Fedora 28, the telnet server daemon is managed directly by Systemd as a socket unit (telnet.socket). On systems that use the Sys Vinit system initialization process, such as Ubuntu Server 14, the telnet server daemon is managed by xinetd.

> **Note**
>
> By default, you are prevented from logging in and obtaining a shell as the root user to certain network services such as telnet due to entries in the /etc/securetty file. Removing or renaming this file allows the root user to log in and receive a shell across the network using the `telnet` command.

After the telnet daemon has been configured, you can connect to it from a remote computer. To do this, specify the host name or IP address of the target computer to the `telnet` command and log in with the appropriate user name and password. A shell obtained during a telnet session runs on a pseudo terminal (a terminal that does not obtain input directly from the computer keyboard) rather than a local terminal, and it works much the same way a normal shell does; you can execute commands and use the `exit` command to kill the BASH shell and end the session. A sample telnet session is shown in the following output using a computer with a host name of server1:

```
[root@server1 ~]# telnet server1
Trying 192.168.1.105...
Connected to server1.
Escape character is '^]'.


Kernel 4.16.3-301.fc28.x86_64 on an x86_64 (0)
server1 login: root
Password: LINUXrocks!
Last login: Fri Oct 24 16:55:33 from 192.168.1.100
[root@server1 ~]# who
(unknown) :0              2019-10-24 16:15 (:0)
root      tty2           2019-10-24 16:16
root      pts/0          2019-10-24 16:55 (server1)
[root@server1 ~]# exit
logout
Connection closed by foreign host.
[root@server1 ~]# _
```

Secure Shell (SSH)

Although the `telnet` command can be quickly used to perform remote administration, it doesn't encrypt the information that passes between computers. **Secure Shell (SSH)** was designed as a secure replacement for telnet (and other legacy commands, such as `rsh`, `rlogin`, and `rcp`) that encrypts information that passes across the network. As a result, the SSH daemon (sshd) is installed by default on most Linux distributions.

Note

On Fedora 28, sshd is installed by default but not set to start automatically at boot time.

To connect to a remote Linux computer running sshd, you can use the `ssh` **command** followed by the host name or IP address of the target computer. For example, you can connect to a computer with the host name of appserver using the `ssh appserver` command. Your local user name will be passed to the server automatically during the SSH request, and you will be prompted to supply the password for the same user on the target computer. If you need to log in using a different user name on the remote appserver computer, you can instead use the `ssh -1 username appserver` command or the `ssh username@appserver` command. A sample `ssh` session is shown in the following output:

```
[root@server1 ~]# ssh root@appserver
root@appserver's password:
Last login: Thu Sep  2 14:29:06 2019 from 10.0.1.3
[root@server1 ~]# who
root     :0              Aug 10 14:13
root     pts/8           Aug 10 14:14 (:0.0)
root     pts/9           Aug 10 14:14 (10.0.1.3)
[root@server1 root]# exit
logout
Connection to appserver closed.
[root@server1 ~]# _
```

> **Note**
>
> You can also use the Putty program on a Windows computer to connect to sshd running on a Linux, UNIX, or macOS computer.

SSH can also be used to transfer files between computers. For example, to transfer the /root/sample file on a remote computer called appserver to the /var directory on the local computer, you could run the following command:

```
[root@server1 ~]# ssh root@appserver cat /root/sample > /var/sample
root@appserver's password:
[root@server1 ~]# _
```

Similarly, to transfer the /root/sample file on the local computer to the /var directory on a remote computer called appserver, you could run the following command:

```
[root@server1 ~]# ssh root@appserver cat </root/sample ">" /var/sample
root@appserver's password:
[root@server1 ~]# _
```

Alternatively, you can use the `scp` command to copy files using SSH. For example, to transfer the /root/sample file on a remote computer called appserver to the /var directory on the local computer, you could run the following `scp` command:

```
[root@server1 ~]# scp root@appserver:/root/sample /var
root@appserver's password:
[root@server1 ~]# _
```

Similarly, to copy the /root/sample file to the /var directory on appserver, you could use the following `scp` command:

```
[root@server1 ~]# scp /root/sample root@appserver:/var
root@appserver's password:
[root@server1 ~]# _
```

Many Linux utilities have built-in support for SSH, including `rsync`, which can also be used to copy files to other computers. For example, to copy the /root/sample file using `rsync` with SSH encryption to the /var directory on appserver, you could run the following `rsync` command:

```
[root@server1 ~]# rsync -e ssh /root/sample root@appserver:/var
root@appserver's password:
[root@server1 ~]# _
```

Although SSH is used to perform command-line administration of remote systems, the –X option to the `ssh` command can be used to tunnel X Windows information through the SSH connection if you are using the `ssh` command within a GUI environment. For example, if you start a command-line terminal within a GNOME desktop and run the command `ssh –X root@appserver`, you will receive a command prompt where you can type commands as you would in any command-line SSH session. However, if you type a graphical command (e.g., `gnome-control-center`), you will execute the graphical utility on appserver across the SSH tunnel. All graphics, keystrokes, and mouse movement will be passed between X Windows on appserver and X Windows on the local system.

Understanding SSH Host and User Keys

SSH uses symmetric encryption to encrypt the data that is sent over the network, but requires asymmetric encryption to securely communicate the symmetric encryption key between the two computers at the beginning of the SSH connection. This asymmetric encryption requires that each computer running sshd have a public key and private key for the various asymmetric encryption algorithms supported by SSH (DSA, RSA, ECDSA, and ED25519); these keys are called the **SSH host keys** and are stored in the /etc/ssh directory as shown in the following output:

```
[root@server1 ~]# ls /etc/ssh | grep key
ssh_host_dsa_key
ssh_host_dsa_key.pub
```

```
ssh_host_ecdsa_key
ssh_host_ecdsa_key.pub
ssh_host_ed25519_key
ssh_host_ed25519_key.pub
ssh_host_rsa_key
ssh_host_rsa_key.pub
[root@server1 ~]# _
```

In the previous output, the ssh_host_ecdsa_key file contains the ECDSA private key for the host, whereas the ssh_host_ecdsa_key.pub file contains the ECDSA public key for the host. At the beginning of the SSH connection, the two computers negotiate the strongest asymmetric encryption algorithm that is supported by both computers.

When you connect to a new computer for the first time using SSH, you will be prompted to accept the encryption fingerprint for the target computer, which is stored in ~/.ssh/known_hosts for subsequent connections. If the target computer's encryption keys are regenerated, you will need to remove the old key from the ~/.ssh/known_hosts file before you connect again.

Note

You can regenerate the host keys used by sshd using the `ssh-keygen` command.

To make authenticating to remote SSH hosts easier, you can generate a public key and private key for your user account for use with SSH using the `ssh-keygen` command; these keys are called SSH user keys and are stored in the ~/.ssh directory. For example, the ~/.ssh/id_rsa file contains the RSA private key for your user, and the ~/.ssh/id_rsa.pub file contains the RSA public key for your user. SSH user keys can be used in place of a password when connecting to trusted computers. To do this, you use the `ssh-copy-id` **command** to copy your public key to the user account on each computer that you would like to connect to without supplying a password. The target computer will store your public key in the ~/.ssh/authorized_keys file for each user account you specified with the `ssh-copy-id` command. The following example generates SSH user keys for the root user on server1, copies them to the root user account on server2, and then connects to server2 as the root user without specifying a password:

```
[root@server1 ~]# ssh-keygen
Generating public/private rsa key pair.
Enter file in which to save the key (/root/.ssh/id_rsa):
Enter passphrase (empty for no passphrase):
Enter same passphrase again:
```

```
Your identification has been saved in /root/.ssh/id_rsa.
Your public key has been saved in /root/.ssh/id_rsa.pub.
The key fingerprint is:
SHA256:1Zu0U5EsQWcM1dFWNHvYK07YB5D8uQhgp/XuRACP5PQ root@dhcppc10
The key's randomart image is:
+---[RSA 2048]----+
|        +..=B*o.=+|
|       +O++.*=..o=|
|      .o=E*.o.ooo|
|      . + Boo. o|
|       S O..+.o |
|         =o.o   |
|        o  .    |
|      |    .     |
|      |          |
+----[SHA256]-----+
[root@server1 ~]# ls .ssh
id_rsa   id_rsa.pub   known_hosts
[root@server1 ~]# ssh-copy-id -i root@server2
/usr/bin/ssh-copy-id: INFO: Source of key(s) to be installed: "/
root/.ssh/id_rsa.pub"
/usr/bin/ssh-copy-id: INFO: attempting to log in with the new
key(s), to filter out any that are already installed
/usr/bin/ssh-copy-id: INFO: 1 key(s) remain to be installed -- if
you are prompted now it is to install the new keys
root@server2's password: **********

Number of key(s) added: 1

Now try logging into the machine, with:   "ssh 'root@server2'"
and check to make sure that only the key(s) you wanted were added.

[root@server1 ~]# ssh root@server2
Last login: Sun Oct 14 20:17:41 2019 from server1
[root@server2 ~]# ls .ssh
authorized_keys
[root@server2 ~]# _
```

Note from the ssh-keygen command in the previous output that no passphrase was supplied to protect the private key. If you supply a passphrase, then you will need to supply that passphrase each time you use the private key, including each time you connect to another computer using your SSH user keys. To prevent this, you can use the **ssh-agent command** to start the SSH agent process on your computer and run the **ssh-add command** to add your private key to this process (supplying your passphrase when prompted). The SSH agent process will then automatically supply your passphrase when your SSH user keys are used to connect to other computers.

Configuring SSH

You can configure the functionality of sshd by editing the /etc/ssh/sshd_config file. Most of this file is commented and should only be edited to change the default settings that sshd uses when servicing SSH clients. The most commonly changed options in this file are those that deal with authentication and encryption. For example, to allow the root user to log into SSH, you can modify the value of the `PermitRootLogin` line to `yes` within /etc/ssh/sshd_config and restart sshd.

> **Note** 📎
>
> On Ubuntu Server, root access via SSH is denied by default. This is considered good security practice because malicious software on the Internet often attempts to log in as the root user. In this case, you can access SSH as a regular user and then use the `su` command to switch to the root user to perform administrative tasks.

Recall that the data communicated across the network with SSH is encrypted using a symmetric encryption algorithm that is negotiated at the beginning of the SSH connection, after the SSH host keys have been exchanged. Each symmetric encryption algorithm differs in its method of encryption and the cryptography key lengths used to encrypt data; the longer the key length, the more difficult it is for malicious users to decode the data. The main types of symmetric encryption supported by sshd are as follows:

- Triple Data Encryption Standard (3DES), which encrypts blocks of data in three stages using a 168-bit key length
- Advanced Encryption Standard (AES), an improvement on 3DES encryption and is available in 128-, 192-, and 256-bit key lengths
- Blowfish, an encryption algorithm that is much faster than 3DES and can use keys up to 448 bits in length
- Carlisle Adams Stafford Tavares (CAST), a general-purpose encryption similar to 3DES that is commonly available using a 128-bit key length
- ARCfour, a fast encryption algorithm that operates on streams of data instead of blocks of data and uses variable-length keys up to 2048 bits in length

In addition, all of the aforementioned types of encryption except ARCfour typically use Cipher Block Chaining (CBC), which can be used to encrypt larger amounts of data.

Client computers can use a /etc/ssh/ssh_config or ~/ssh/ssh_config file to set SSH options for use with the `ssh` command, including the symmetric encryption types that can be used, because the SSH client is responsible for randomly generating the symmetric encryption key at the beginning of the SSH connection. However, the encryption types on the client computer must match those supported by the SSH server for a connection to be successful.

Virtual Network Computing (VNC)

Like the -X option of ssh, **Virtual Network Computing (VNC)** is another graphical option for administrating a Linux system remotely. After installing a VNC server daemon on a computer, other computers that run a VNC client can connect to the VNC server daemon across a network to obtain a full desktop environment. VNC uses a special platform-independent protocol called Remote FrameBuffer (RFB) to transfer graphics, mouse movements, and keystrokes across the network.

> **Note** 📎
>
> VNC server software and client software exist for Linux, UNIX, Mac, and Windows systems. This allows you to use a single technology to obtain the desktop of all of the Linux, UNIX, macOS, and Windows systems on your network.
>
> Because X Windows is not installed on Ubuntu Server by default, we'll focus on the configuration of VNC on Fedora 28 in this section. However, the steps are similar on other Linux distributions.

On Fedora 28, you can install a VNC server by running the dnf install tigervnc-server command. Next, you can set a VNC connection password for a user using the **vncpasswd command**. The VNC password is stored in the ~/.vnc/passwd file; for user1, the VNC password will be stored in the /home/user1/.vnc/passwd file. Finally, you can run the **vncserver command** as the user you specified the VNC password for; this will start a VNC server process with the next available display number, starting from 1.

> **Note** 📎
>
> By default, the VNC server process listens on port 5900 + display number. For display number 1, the VNC server will listen on port 5901, for display number 2, the VNC server will listen on port 5902, and so on.

Other computers can then connect to the VNC server using a **VNC viewer** program, such as RealVNC. When using a VNC viewer program to connect to a remote VNC server, you can specify the server name or IP address, port, and display number using the syntax *server:port:display*. For example, to connect to the VNC server that uses display number 1 on the computer server1.class.com, you could use the syntax server1.class.com:5901:1. You will then obtain a desktop session on the remote computer, as shown in Figure 12-9.

Figure 12-9   A remote VNC session

Many VNC viewers allow you to specify the server name or IP address and either the port or display number. For example, you could specify `server1.class.com:5901` or `server1.class.com:1` within a VNC viewer to connect to the server shown in Figure 12-9.

You can use the remote or local port forwarding feature of SSH to encrypt the traffic sent by other services, such as VNC. For example, if you run the command `ssh -R 5901:server1.class.com:5901 bob@client1.class.com`, bob on the client1.class.com computer can start a VNC viewer and connect to *client1.class.com:5901* in order to access the VNC server running on port 5901 on *server1.class.com* via SSH. Alternatively, you can run the `ssh -L 5901:localhost:5901 bob@server1.class.com` command on your computer to start an SSH session that forwards any local traffic on port 5901 to *server1.class.com* on port 5901 as bob. Following this, you can start a VNC viewer and connect to *localhost:5901* in order to access the VNC server running on port 5901 on *server1.class.com* via SSH.

To configure a VNC server process to run persistently, you must create a VNC Systemd service unit that specifies the user and display number. To create a VNC Systemd service unit that listens on the third X Windows display, you can use the following command to copy it from the /lib/systemd/system/vncserver@.service template:

```
[root@server1 ~]# cp /lib/systemd/system/vncserver@.service /lib/
systemd/system/vncserver@:3.service
[root@server1 ~]# _
```

> **Note** 🔗
>
> On systems that do not use the Systemd system initialization system, the /etc/sysconfig/vncservers configuration file is used in place of /lib/systemd/system/vncserver@:3.service.

Next, you must edit the VNC server configuration file and, at minimum, modify the line(s) that indicate(s) the user that can connect (replace <user> with a valid username).

Following this, you must ensure that the user specified within the VNC Systemd service unit file has a VNC connection password set. Finally, you can start the VNC service unit for the display number, and configure it to start automatically at system initialization. For display number 3, you can use the following commands:

```
[root@server1 ~]# systemctl enable vncserver@:3.service
[root@server1 ~]# systemctl start vncserver@:3.service
[root@server1 ~]# _
```

> **Note** 🔗
>
> There are many alternatives to VNC that provide for remote access to Linux desktops, including Xrdp, which uses the Microsoft Remote Desktop Protocol, and NoMachine, which uses the proprietary NX protocol.

Chapter Summary

- A network is a collection of connected computers that share information.

- A protocol is a set of rules that define the format of information that is transmitted across a network. TCP/IP is the standard protocol used by the Internet and most networks.

- Each computer on an IP network must have a valid IPv4 or IPv6 address.

- The IPv4 configuration of a network interface can be specified manually, obtained automatically from a DHCP or BOOTP server, or autoconfigured by the system.

- The IPv6 configuration of a network interface can be obtained from a router using ICMPv6, from a DHCP server, or autoconfigured by the system.

- On a Fedora 28 system, the /etc/sysconfig/ network-scripts directory contains the configuration for network interfaces. On an Ubuntu 18 system, the /etc/netplan directory contains the configuration for network interfaces, and on an Ubuntu Server 14 system, network interface

configuration is stored within the /etc/ network/interfaces file.

- Host names are computer names that, unlike IP addresses, are easy for humans to remember. Host names that are generated by the hierarchical Domain Name Space are called FQDNs.

- Host names must be resolved to an IP address before network communication can take place.

- Routers are devices that forward IP packets from one network to another. Each computer and router has a route table that it uses to determine how IP packets are forwarded.

- Network services are started by a stand-alone daemon, or by xinetd on demand. In either case, they listen for requests on a certain port.

- There are many ways to remotely administer a Linux system. You can perform command-line administration remotely via the `telnet` and `ssh` commands. For graphical remote administration, you can use the `ssh -X` command or VNC.

Key Terms

aggregation
ANDing
Automatic Private IP
  Addressing (APIPA)
bonding
bridging
broadcast
classless interdomain
  routing (CIDR) notation

default gateway
`dhclient` **command**
`dig` **command**
Domain Name Space
  (DNS)
Ethernet
`ethtool` **command**
Extended Internet Super
  Daemon (xinetd)

fully qualified domain
  name (FQDN)
`host` **command**
host ID
host name
`hostname` **command**
`hostnamectl` **command**
`ifconfig` **(interface**
  configuration) command

Internet Control Message Protocol (ICMP)

Internet Control Message Protocol version 6 (ICMPv6)

Internet of Things (IoT)

Internet Protocol (IP) address

Internet service provider (ISP)

`ip` command

IP forwarding

IP version 4 (IPv4)

IP version 6 (IPv6)

`iwconfig` command

local area network (LAN)

Media Access Control (MAC) address

media access method

Modem Manager utility

`mtr` command

multicast

multihomed hosts

`ncat` (net cat) command

NetPlan

`netstat` command

network

Network Address Translation (NAT)

Network Connections tool

network ID

network service

Network utility

`networkctl` command

NetworkManager

`nm-connection-editor` command

`nmcli` command

`nmtui` command

`nslookup` command

octet

packet

`ping` (Packet Internet Groper) command

`ping6` command

Point-to-Point Protocol (PPP)

port

PPP over Ethernet (PPPoE)

`pppoe-setup` command

`pppoeconf` command

protocol

proxy server

Putty

Remote Direct Memory Access (RDMA)

`route` command

route table

router

routing

Secure Shell (SSH)

`ss` (socket statistics) command

`ssh` command

SSH host keys

`ssh-add` command

`ssh-agent` command

`ssh-copy-id` command

`ssh-keygen` command

stand-alone daemon

subnet mask

subnetting

`sysctl` command

Systemd-networkd

`telnet` command

Teredo

Token Ring

`tracepath` command

`tracepath6` command

`traceroute` command

`traceroute6` command

Transmission Control Protocol/Internet Protocol (TCP/IP)

unicast

User Datagram Protocol/ Internet Protocol (UDP/IP)

Virtual Network Computing (VNC)

Virtual Private Network (VPN)

VNC viewer

`vncpasswd` command

`vncserver` command

well-known ports

`whois` command

wide area network (WAN)

Wireless-Fidelity (Wi-Fi)

YAML (YAML Ain't Markup Language)

`zebra` command

Review Questions

1. The NetworkManager or Systemd-networkd components must be installed on a Linux system in order to configure an IP address on a network interface. True or False?

2. Which Windows program is often used to connect to a Linux server via SSH?
   a. SSHD
   b. Putty
   c. Rdesktop
   d. mstsc

3. Stand-alone daemons are started on demand using xinetd. True or False?

4. Which file stores the IP addresses of the DNS servers used to resolve host names if no DNS servers are specified within the network configuration file for the network interface?
   a. /etc/hosts
   b. /etc/host.conf
   c. /etc/resolve
   d. /etc/resolv.conf

5. To test DNS configuration by resolving a host name to an IP address, which command or commands can you use? (Choose all that apply.)
   a. nslookup *hostname*
   b. dig *hostname*
   c. host *hostname*
   d. resolve *hostname*

6. Which two commands can be used to modify the route table on a Linux computer? (Choose two answers.)
   a. route
   b. ipconfig
   c. ip
   d. traceroute

7. Which file holds the methods to be used and the order in which they will be applied for host name resolution?
   a. /etc/nsswitch.conf
   b. /etc/resolve.conf
   c. /etc/hosts
   d. /etc/dns.conf

8. What are two means available to resolve a host name to the appropriate IP address? (Choose two answers.)
   a. DHCP
   b. DNS
   c. /etc/hosts
   d. /etc/resolve.conf

9. SSH encrypts all traffic that passes across the network, whereas telnet does not. True or False?

10. You want to generate SSH keys for your user account and copy them to a remote computer to simplify future SSH authentication. What two commands can you use to perform these actions? (Choose two answers.)
    a. ssh-keygen
    b. ssh-add
    c. ssh-copy-id
    d. ssh-agent

11. Which of the following can be used to provide graphical remote administration? (Choose all that apply.)
    a. telnet
    b. ssh -X
    c. ssh
    d. VNC

12. The daemons associated with network services listen for network traffic associated with a particular _____.
    a. station
    b. port
    c. IP address
    d. allocation number

13. The IP address of 127.0.0.1 is also referred to as the _____.
    a. local address
    b. lookup address
    c. local host
    d. loopback address

14. The line that configures the host name for the computer at boot time can be found in /etc/hostname. True or False?

15. Which commands can be used to display TCP/IP connections on your Linux system? (Choose all that apply.)
    a. netstat -t
    b. mtr
    c. traceroute show
    d. ss -t

16. Which of the following port numbers is associated with SSH?
    a. 22
    b. 137
    c. 49
    d. 23

17. Which file would you modify to permanently change the IP address of a network interface on a Fedora 28 system?
    a. /etc/sysconfig/network-scripts/ifcfg-enp8so
    b. /etc/sysconfig/network
    c. /etc/netplan/50-cloud-init.yaml
    d. /etc/network/interfaces

18. Before a computer can use a router, with what configuration information must it be provided?
    a. routing table
    b. subnet mask
    c. default gateway
    d. default router

19. Which of the following are stand-alone daemons? (Choose all that apply.)
    a. Apache (httpd)
    b. Washington University FTP (in.ftpd)
    c. telnet (in.telnetd)
    d. DNS (named)

20. Which of the following utilities can be used to check IP configuration and test network connectivity? (Choose all that apply.)
    a. `ifconfig`
    b. `iwconfig`
    c. `ping`
    d. `nmcli`

Hands-On Projects

These projects should be completed in the order given. The hands-on projects presented in this chapter should take a total of three hours to complete. The requirements for this lab include:

- A computer with Fedora Linux installed according to Hands-On Project 2-1, and Ubuntu Server 14 Linux installed according to Hands-On Project 6-7.

Project 12-1

In this hands-on project, you explore the IP configuration of the network interface on your Fedora Linux, Ubuntu Server 14 Linux, and Ubuntu Server 18 Linux virtual machines.

1. Boot your Fedora Linux virtual machine. After your Linux system has been loaded, switch to a command-line terminal (tty5) by pressing **Ctrl+Alt+F5** and log in to the terminal using the user name of **root** and the password of **LINUXrocks!**.

2. At the command prompt, type `nmcli connection show` and press **Enter**. Note the name of your wired network interface.

3. At the command prompt, type `ifconfig` and press **Enter**. Does your network interface have an IP configuration? From where was this configuration obtained?

4. At the command prompt, type `cat /etc/sysconfig/network-scripts/ifcfg-interface` and press **Enter**, where *interface* is the name of your network interface. What is the BOOTPROTO line equal to?

5. Switch to tty1 by pressing **Ctrl+Alt+F1** and log into the GNOME desktop using your user account and the password of **LINUXrocks!**.

6. Navigate to the **Activities** menu, **Show Applications**, **Settings** and click **Network**. Note the IPv4 and IPv6 configuration for your Wired network interface.

7. Next, click the cog wheel icon next to your wired network adapter, highlight the **IPv4** tab and select **Manual**. Supply an appropriate IP address, netmask, default gateway, and DNS server information for your classroom network and click **Apply**. Log out of the GNOME desktop when finished.

8. Switch back to tty5 by pressing **Ctrl+Alt+F5**. At the command prompt, type `ifdown interface` and press **Enter**, where *interface* is the name of your network interface. Next, type `ifconfig` and press **Enter**. Does your network interface have an IP configuration?

9. At the command prompt, type `ifup interface` and press **Enter**, where *interface* is the name of your network interface. Next, type `ifconfig` and press **Enter**. What IP configuration does your network interface have?

10. At the command prompt, type `nmcli` and press **Enter**. Does NetworkManager indicate that your network interface is actively connected?

11. At the command prompt, type `cat /etc/sysconfig/network-scripts/ifcfg-interface` and press **Enter**, where *interface* is the name of your wired network interface. Is your manual IP configuration listed?

12. At the command prompt, type `ping interfaceIP` and press **Enter**, where *interfaceIP* is the IPv4 address of your network interface. Do you receive ping responses from your network interface? Press **Ctrl+c** when finished to quit the `ping` command.

13. At the command prompt, type `netstat -i` and press **Enter**. View the statistics for your network interfaces. If necessary, consult the netstat manual page to determine the meaning of each column displayed.

14. Type `exit` and press **Enter** to log out of your shell.

15. Boot your Ubuntu Server 14 Linux virtual machine. After your Linux system has been loaded, log into tty1 using the user name of **root** and the password of **LINUXrocks!**.

16. At the command prompt, type `ifconfig` and press **Enter**. What IPv4 and IPv6 configuration do you see for eth0?

17. At the command prompt, type `cat /etc/network/interfaces` and press **Enter**. Is IP information obtained automatically for eth0? What lines could you modify and add to this file to manually set the IP configuration?

18. At the command prompt, type `ifdown eth0 ; ifup eth0` and press **Enter**. When would you normally run this command?

19. Type `exit` and press **Enter** to log out of your shell.

20. Boot your Ubuntu Server 18 Linux virtual machine. After your Linux system has been loaded, log into tty1 using the user name of **root** and the password of **LINUXrocks!**.

21. At the command prompt, type `lshw -C network` and press **Enter**. Note the logical name of your wired network interface.

22. At the command prompt, type `ifconfig` and press **Enter**. What IPv4 and IPv6 configuration do you see for your network interface, and from where was it obtained?

23. At the command prompt, type `networkctl` and press **Enter**. Is your network interface currently managed by Systemd-networkd?

24. At the command prompt, type `cat /etc/netplan/50-cloud-init.yaml` and press **Enter**. Is IP information obtained automatically for your network interface? What lines could you modify and add to this file to manually set the IP configuration?

25. At the command prompt, type `netplan apply` and press **Enter**. When would you normally run this command?

26. Type `exit` and press **Enter** to log out of your shell.

Project 12-2

In this hands-on project, you examine the host name configuration on your Fedora Linux virtual machine, as well as resolve host names.

1. On your Fedora Linux virtual machine, switch to a command-line terminal (tty5) by pressing **Ctrl+Alt+F5** and log in to the terminal using the user name of **root** and the password of **LINUXrocks!**.

2. At the command prompt, type `hostname` and press **Enter**. What is your host name? Next, type `cat /etc/hostname` at the command prompt and press **Enter**. What host name is listed here? Why?

3. At the command prompt, type `cat /etc/resolv.conf` and press **Enter**. What Linux component added the DNS server information to this file?

4. At the command prompt, type `less /etc/nsswitch.conf` and press **Enter**. Will files such as /etc/hosts be used for name resolution before DNS? Press **q** to quit the less utility.

5. Edit the **/etc/hosts** file with a text editor such as vi. Add a line to the bottom of the file that reads:

   ```
   1.2.3.4 fakehost.fakedomain.com sample
   ```
   When finished, save your changes and quit the editor.

6. At the command prompt, type `host localhost` and press **Enter**. Was the name resolved correctly? Next, type `host fakehost.fakedomain.com` and press **Enter**. Was the name resolved correctly?

7. At the command prompt, type `host www.kernel.org` and press **Enter**. Note the IPv4 and IPv6 address returned for www.kernel.org. Is there another name for www.kernel.org?

8. At the command prompt, type `nslookup www.kernel.org` and press **Enter**. How do you know that this information came from your ISP's DNS server?

9. At the command prompt, type the command `dig www.kernel.org` and press **Enter**. What additional information does dig provide compared to the nslookup and host utilities?

10. Type `exit` and press **Enter** to log out of your shell.

Project 12-3

In this hands-on project, you view and configure the route table on your Fedora Linux virtual machine as well as view and test your routing configuration.

1. On your Fedora Linux virtual machine, switch to a command-line terminal (tty5) by pressing **Ctrl+Alt+F5** and log in to the terminal using the user name of **root** and the password of **LINUXrocks!**.

2. At the command prompt, type `route -n` and press **Enter**. What entries are listed? What does each entry represent? What IPv4 address is listed as your default gateway? What other commands can be used to list the route table?

3. At the command prompt, type `ip route add 1.0.0.0/8 via` *gwIP* and press **Enter**, where *gwIP* is the IPv4 address of your default gateway.

4. At the command prompt, type `route -n` and press **Enter**. Is the route added in Step 3 visible? Will this route interfere with traffic that is sent to the 1.0.0.0 network? Explain.

5. At the command prompt, type `traceroute www.kernel.org` and press **Enter**. How many routers are used to pass your packet to the ftp.kernel.org computer?

6. At the command prompt, type `tracepath www.kernel.org` and press **Enter**. Is the same path taken? If not, explain why.

7. At the command prompt, type `mtr www.kernel.org` and press **Enter**. What information does mtr provide in addition to traceroute and tracepath? Press **q** to quit the mtr utility.

8. At the command prompt, type the command `cat /proc/sys/net/ipv4/ip_forward` and press **Enter**. Is your system configured as an IPv4 router? Next, type the command `cat /proc/sys/net/ipv6/conf/all/forwarding` and press **Enter**. Is your system configured as an IPv6 router? What file could you modify to set IP forwarding at boot time?

9. Type `exit` and press **Enter** to log out of your shell.

Project 12-4

In this hands-on project, you install and configure the Extended Internet Super Daemon and telnet server daemon on your Ubuntu Server 14 Linux virtual machine. Next, you test remote administration of your Ubuntu Server 14 Linux virtual machine using the `telnet` command on your Ubuntu host as well as the Putty program on your Windows host. Finally, you install the telnet server daemon on your Fedora Linux virtual machine and perform remote administration using a telnet session.

1. On your Ubuntu Server Linux virtual machine, log into tty1 using the user name of **root** and the password of **LINUXrocks!**.

2. At the command prompt, type `apt-get install xinetd telnetd` and press **Enter**.

3. Edit the **/etc/xinetd.d/telnet** file (it will be a new file) with a text editor such as vi and add the following contents:

```
service telnet
{
disable = no
flags = REUSE
socket_type = stream
wait = no
user = root
server = /usr/sbin/in.telnetd
log_on_failure += USERID
}
```

When finished, save your changes and quit the editor.

4. At the command prompt, type `service xinetd restart` and press **Enter** to restart the Extended Internet Super Daemon.

5. At the command prompt, type `telnet localhost` and press **Enter**. Supply the user name of **user1** and password of **LINUXrocks!** when prompted.

6. Next, type `who` at the command prompt and press **Enter**. Are you using a pseudoterminal through a local connection?

7. Type `exit` and press **Enter** to log out of your remote shell.

8. At the command prompt, type `telnet localhost` and press **Enter**. Supply the user name of **root** when prompted. What error did you receive after entering the user name of root? Press **Ctrl+c** to return to your command prompt.

9. At the command prompt, type `mv /etc/securetty /etc/securetty.backup` and press **Enter**.

10. At the command prompt, type `telnet localhost` and press **Enter**. Supply the user name of **root** and password of **LINUXrocks!** when prompted.

11. Type `exit` and press **Enter** to log out of your remote shell. Finally, type `exit` and press **Enter** to log out of your local shell.

12. On your Windows host, use a Web browser to download the putty.exe program from **www.chiark.greenend.org.uk/~sgtatham/putty/download.html** and save the executable file on your Windows desktop.

13. Double-click the putty.exe file on your Windows desktop. What is the default connection type? Select **Telnet** as the connection type, enter the IP address of your Ubuntu Server 14 Linux virtual machine in the Host Name (or IP address) box, and click **Open**. Log into your Ubuntu Server Linux virtual machine using the user name of **root** and password of **LINUXrocks!**. Next, type `who` at the command prompt and press **Enter**. What is listed in brackets next to your pseudoterminal session and why?

14. Type `exit` and press **Enter** to log out of your remote shell (this closes the Putty program).

15. On your Fedora Linux virtual machine, switch to a command-line terminal (tty5) by pressing **Ctrl+Alt+F5** and log in to the terminal using the user name of **root** and the password of **LINUXrocks!**.

16. At the command prompt, type `telnet IP`, where `IP` is the IP address of your Ubuntu Server 14 Linux virtual machine, and press **Enter**. Supply the user name of **root** and password of **LINUXrocks!** when prompted.

17. At the command prompt, type `who` and press **Enter**. What is listed in brackets next to your pseudoterminal session and why? Type `exit` and press **Enter** to log out of your remote shell.

18. At the command prompt, type `dnf install telnet-server` and press **Enter** to install the telnet daemon on your Fedora Linux virtual machine. Press **y** when prompted to complete the installation.

19. At the command prompt, type `systemctl start telnet.socket` and press **Enter** to start the telnet daemon. Next, type `systemctl enable telnet.socket` and press **Enter** to start the telnet daemon at boot time.

20. At the command prompt, type `telnet localhost` and press **Enter**. Supply the user name of **root** and password of **LINUXrocks!** when prompted. Note that your root login was successful because the Fedora 28 does not contain an /etc/securetty file by default. Type `exit` and press **Enter** to log out of your remote shell.

21. At the command prompt, type `firewall-cmd --add-service telnet` and press **Enter** to add an exception to the firewall on your Fedora Linux virtual machine for telnet. Next, type `firewall-cmd --add-service telnet --permanent` and press **Enter** to provide the same exception at boot time. We discuss firewalls in Chapter 14.

22. Next, type `exit` and press **Enter** to log out of your shell.

23. On your Windows host, double-click the putty.exe file on your desktop. Select **Telnet** as the connection type, enter the IP address of your Fedora Linux virtual machine in the Host Name (or IP address) box, and click **Open**. Log into your Fedora Linux virtual machine using the user name of **root** and password of **LINUXrocks!**.

24. Next, type `who` at the command prompt and press **Enter**. What is listed in brackets next to your pseudoterminal session and why? Type `exit` and press **Enter** to log out of your remote shell (this closes the Putty program).

Project 12-5

In this hands-on project, you configure SSH on your Ubuntu Server 14 Linux and Fedora Linux virtual machines. Additionally, you perform remote administration of your Ubuntu Server 14 Linux and Fedora Linux virtual machines using SSH.

1. On your Fedora Linux virtual machine, switch to a command-line terminal (tty5) by pressing **Ctrl+Alt+F5** and log in to the terminal using the user name of **root** and the password of **LINUXrocks!**.

2. At the command prompt, type `ps -ef | grep sshd` and press **Enter**. Is the SSH daemon started by default?

3. At the command prompt, type `systemctl enable sshd.service ; systemctl start sshd.service` and press **Enter** to start the SSH daemon and ensure that it is started at boot time.

4. At the command prompt, type `nc localhost 22` and press **Enter** to interact with the SSH daemon listening on port 22. What is displayed on the screen, and what does this indicate? Press **Ctrl+c** to return to your command prompt.

5. At the command prompt, type `ssh root@localhost` and press **Enter**. When prompted to accept the negotiated SSH host keys of the target system, type `yes` and press **Enter**. Next supply the root user's password of **LINUXrocks!** and press **Enter**.

6. At the command prompt, type `who` and press **Enter**. Are you on a pseudoterminal? Next, type `ss -t` and press **Enter** to view your TCP connections. Is your SSH connection listed?

7. At the command prompt, type `exit` and press **Enter** to log out of your remote shell. Next, type `ss -t` and press **Enter**. Is your SSH connection listed?

8. At the command prompt, type `cat .ssh/known_hosts` and press **Enter**. Note the cached SSH host keys from the target computer (localhost).

9. Switch to a graphical terminal by pressing **Ctrl+Alt+F1** and log in to the GNOME desktop on X.Org using your user account and the password of **LINUXrocks!**. Next, open a command-line terminal (Activities, Show Applications, Utilities, Terminal).

10. At the command prompt, type `ssh -X root@localhost` and press **Enter**. When prompted to accept the negotiated SSH host keys of the target system, type `yes` and press **Enter**. Supply the root user's password of **LINUXrocks!** and press **Enter** when prompted.

11. At the command prompt, type `system-config-abrt` and press **Enter**. Note that this command starts the remote Problem Reporting Configuration utility (used to configure the abrtd daemon) in a graphical window through your SSH session. Close the Problem Reporting Configuration utility, type `exit`, and press **Enter** to close your remote shell. Log out of the GNOME desktop when finished.

12. Switch back to tty5 by pressing **Ctrl+Alt+F5** and type `ssh user1@IP`, where *IP* is the IP address of your Ubuntu Server 14 Linux virtual machine. When prompted to accept the negotiated SSH host keys of the target system, type `yes` and press **Enter**. Supply the root user password of **LINUXrocks!** when prompted. Why is the SSH daemon started by default in Ubuntu Server?

13. At the command prompt, type `su - root` and press **Enter**. Supply the root user password of **LINUXrocks!** when prompted to obtain a root shell.

14. At the command prompt, type `vi /etc/ssh/sshd_config` and press **Enter**. Modify the **PermitRootLogin without-password** line such that it reads **PermitRootLogin yes**, save your changes, and quit the vi editor.

15. At the command prompt, type `service ssh reload` and press **Enter** to force the SSH daemon to reload its configuration file.

16. Type `exit` and press **Enter** to log out of your remote shell.

17. At the command prompt, type `ssh root@IP`, where `IP` is the IP address of your Ubuntu Server Linux virtual machine, and supply the root user password of **LINUXrocks!** when prompted. Next, type `exit` and press **Enter** to log out of your remote shell.

18. At the command prompt, type `ssh-keygen` and press **Enter** to generate SSH user keys for the root user account on your Fedora Linux virtual machine. Press **Enter** to accept the default location of your SSH user private key (/root/.ssh/id_rsa). Press **Enter**, and then press **Enter** again to prevent the use of a passphrase.

19. At the command prompt, type `ssh-copy-id -i root@IP`, where `IP` is the IP address of your Ubuntu Server 14 Linux virtual machine, and supply the root user password of **LINUXrocks!** when prompted. What does this command do?

20. At the command prompt, type `ssh root@IP`, where `IP` is the IP address of your Ubuntu Server Linux virtual machine. Were you prompted for a password? Why? Next, type `cat .ssh/authorized_keys` and press **Enter** to view the root user's SSH user keys from your Fedora Linux virtual machine. Finally, type `exit` and press **Enter** to log out of your remote shell.

21. At the command prompt, type `ssh root@IP cat /etc/issue > /root/downloaded_issue` and press **Enter**, where `IP` is the IP address of your Ubuntu Server 14 virtual machine. Next, type `cat downloaded_issue` and press **Enter**. Was the /etc/issue file transferred successfully to your system via SSH?

22. At the command prompt, type `less /etc/ssh/ssh_config` and press **Enter**. Examine the SSH client options available and press **q** when finished.

23. Type `exit` and press **Enter** to log out of your shell.

24. On your Windows host, double-click the putty.exe file on your desktop. Note that the default connection type is SSH, enter the IP address of your Fedora Linux virtual machine in the Host Name (or IP address) box, and click **Open**. Log into your Fedora Linux virtual machine using the user name of **root** and password of **LINUXrocks!**. When finished, type `exit` and press **Enter** to log out of your remote shell.

25. On your Windows host, double-click the putty.exe file on your desktop. Note that the default connection type is SSH, enter the IP address of your Ubuntu Server Linux virtual machine in the Host Name (or IP address) box, and click **Open**. Log into your Ubuntu Server Linux virtual machine using the user name of **root** and password of **LINUXrocks!**. When finished, type `exit` and press **Enter** to log out of your remote shell.

Project 12-6

In this hands-on project, you configure a VNC server on your Fedora Linux virtual machine and connect to it remotely from your Windows host.

1. On your Fedora Linux virtual machine, switch to a command-line terminal (tty5) by pressing **Ctrl+Alt+F5** and log in to the terminal using the user name of **root** and the password of **LINUXrocks!**.

2. At the command prompt, type `dnf install tigervnc-server` and press **Enter**. Press **y** when prompted to complete the installation of the tiger VNC server.

3. At the command prompt, type `firewall-cmd --add-service vnc-server` and press **Enter** to add a firewall exception for the VNC server. Next, type `firewall-cmd --add-service vnc-server --permanent` and press **Enter** to ensure that this firewall exception is also created at boot time.

4. Switch to a graphical terminal by pressing **Ctrl+Alt+F1** and log in to the GNOME desktop on X.Org using your user account and the password of **LINUXrocks!**. Next, open a command-line terminal (Activities, Show Applications, Utilities, Terminal).

5. At the command prompt, type `vncpasswd` and press **Enter** to set a VNC password. Supply a password of **LINUXrocks!** when prompted (twice). When prompted to set a view-only password, type **n** and press Enter.

6. At the command prompt, type `vncserver` and press **Enter** to start a VNC server process as your user account (user1). Note the display number that was chosen from the output.

7. On your Windows host, open a Web browser and download the RealVNC Viewer for Windows EXE program from **https://www.realvnc.com/download/viewer/**. Install the program when finished and open the program following installation.

8. In the VNC Viewer program, enter `IP:590n` in the VNC Server dialog box, where `IP` is the IP address of your Fedora Linux virtual machine and `n` is the display number that you noted in Step 6 and press **Enter**. When warned that you are about to connect using an unencrypted session, click **Continue**, supply the VNC password of **LINUXrocks!** and click **OK**. Explore your user1 desktop and close the VNC Viewer window when finished.

Discovery Exercises

1. Assuming that your company uses the Class A network 100.0.0.0/8, with what subnet mask would you need to configure all computers on the network to divide this network 11 times to match the company's 11 departments? How many hosts can you have per network? What are the first five ranges of addresses that you can assign to different departments?

2. In Project 12-1, you manually configured the IPv4 settings for the network interface on your Fedora Linux virtual machine, as well as viewed the IPv4 configuration for the network interfaces on your Ubuntu Server 14 Linux and Ubuntu Server 18 Linux virtual machines. On your Ubuntu Server 14 Linux virtual machine, perform a manual IPv4 configuration of the network interface using values appropriate for your classroom network, and test your configuration when finished. Next, perform a manual IPv4 configuration for the network interface on your Ubuntu Server 18 Linux virtual machine using values appropriate for your classroom network, and test your configuration when finished.

3. In Project 12-5, you used the following method to transfer a file from a remote system to your local computer:
```
ssh remotecomputer cat
remotefile > localfile
```

Using your knowledge of redirection, briefly describe how this command achieves this transfer. Can this command be used to transfer a binary file? Explain. What `scp` command would be an alternative to this command?

4. In Project 12-5, you used the Putty SSH client to perform remote administration of two Linux systems from your Windows 10 host computer. Windows 10 also includes the Windows Subsystem for Linux (WSL) feature that allows you to install a full Linux system that runs concurrently with your Windows 10 kernel for development use (not virtualized). IT administrators often take advantage of this feature to perform remote administration of Linux systems from their Windows 10 desktop.

On your Windows 10 host, navigate to **Start**, **Settings**, **Update & Security**. Highlight **For developers** in the left pane, select **Developer mode** and click **Yes** when prompted. Next, navigate to **Start**, **Settings**, **Apps**, and click **Programs and Features**. In the Programs and Features window, select **Turn Windows features on or off**, select the **Windows Subsystem for Linux** and click **OK**. Click **Restart now** when prompted. After your system has rebooted, log in and navigate to **Start**, **Microsoft Store**. Search for **Linux** and note the Apps that represent different Linux distributions that are available. Select the **Ubuntu** app and click **Get** to install it; this will download and install the Ubuntu Linux distribution for Windows 10 within the WSL. After the download has completed, click **Launch** and specify a Linux username and password of your choice when prompted.

Take a few moments to explore the system. Next, connect to your Linux virtual machines using SSH from your WSL. Finally, generate SSH user keys within your WSL and add them to your Linux virtual machines to allow for easy authentication from Windows 10. Note that you can enter the WSL at any time by typing **bash** at any PowerShell or command prompt within Windows 10.

5. In Project 12-6, you started the VNC server on your Fedora Linux virtual machine manually as user1. Take the appropriate steps (outlined in this chapter) to configure and enable a Systemd unit file for the VNC service that is activated at boot time and allows user1 to connect to display number 3.

6. There are many alternatives to VNC for graphical remote administration of Linux systems. One of the most common alternatives is Xrdp. Use the Internet to research how to install and enable Xrdp on your Fedora Linux virtual machine. Next, connect to your Xrdp server from your Windows 10 computer by navigating to Start, Remote Desktop Connection and specifying the IP address of your Fedora Linux virtual machine.

## CHAPTER 13

CONFIGURING NETWORK SERVICES AND CLOUD TECHNOLOGIES

After completing this chapter, you will be able to:

Configure infrastructure network services, including DHCP, DNS, and NTP

Configure Web services using the Apache Web server

Configure file-sharing services, including Samba, NFS, and FTP

Configure email services using Postfix

Configure database services using PostgreSQL

Describe how virtualization and containers are created and used within cloud environments

Configure containers using Docker

Identify the components that comprise a CD workflow

In the previous chapter, you examined the concepts and procedures that allow Linux to participate on a network. You also learned about the network services that are commonly used on Linux systems, including those that are used for remote administration. In this chapter, you examine the configuration of network services that provide infrastructure, Web, file sharing, email, and database services to users across a network. Additionally, you explore how network services and apps are hosted within cloud environments, as well as learn the components and processes that allow developers to continually deploy their apps to the cloud.

Infrastructure Services

Some networking services provide network configuration and support for other computers on a network in the form of TCP/IP configuration, name resolution, and time management. These services, which are collectively called **infrastructure services**, include DHCP, DNS, and NTP.

DHCP

Recall from the previous chapter that your network interface can be configured manually, or automatically using Dynamic Host Configuration Protocol (DHCP). If your network interface is configured using DHCP, it sends a DHCP broadcast on the network requesting IP configuration information. If a DHCP server on the network has a range of IP addresses available, it leases an IP address to the client computer for a certain period of time; after this lease has expired, the client computer must send another DHCP request. Because DHCP servers keep track of the IP addresses they lease to client computers, they can ensure that no two computers receive the same IP address. If two computers are accidentally configured manually with the same IP address, neither would be able to communicate using the IP protocol.

DHCP servers can also send client computers other IP configuration information, such as the default gateway and the DNS server they should use.

The DHCP Lease Process

The process by which a DHCP client requests IP configuration from a DHCP server involves several stages. First, the client sends a request (DHCPDISCOVER packet) to all hosts on the network. In reply, a DHCP server sends an offer (DHCPOFFER packet) that contains a potential IP configuration. The DHCP client then selects (accepts) the offer by sending a DHCPREQUEST packet to the associated DHCP server. Next, the DHCP server sends to the client an acknowledgment indicating the amount of time the client can use the IP configuration (DHCPACK packet). Finally, the client configures itself with the IP configuration. This process is illustrated in Figure 13-1.

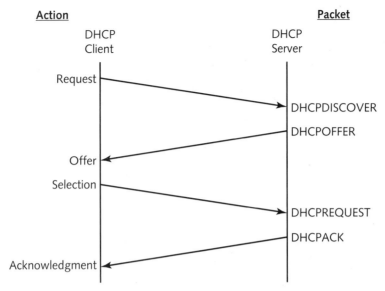

Figure 13-1   The DHCP lease process

> **Note** 📎
>
> If your network has multiple DHCP servers, DHCP clients will accept the first offer that they receive and decline all other offers by sending a DHCPDECLINE packet to the other DHCP servers.

Halfway through the time period specified by its lease (i.e., at 50 percent of its lease), the DHCP client will send another DHCPREQUEST packet to its DHCP server to renew its IP configuration. If its DHCP server is unreachable, it will try to renew its IP configuration again at 87.5 percent of its lease by sending a DHCPDISCOVER packet to all hosts on the network to allow any DHCP server on the network to respond with an offer. After the lease is up, the DHCP client discards its IP configuration obtained from the DHCP server and automatically configures the network interface using APIPA (the IPv4 169.254.0.0 network, or IPv6 FE80 network).

To configure your Linux system as a DHCP server, you must first install the DHCP daemon, which is available from online software repositories. The two most common DHCP daemons available for Linux are the **DHCP daemon (dhcpd)** and **BusyBox DHCP daemon (udhcpd)**.

Configuring a Linux DHCP Server Using dhcpd

Most Linux systems, including Fedora 28 and Ubuntu Server 18, use the dhcpd daemon to provide for DHCP functionality on the network. To configure a system using dhcpd, you must add lines to the appropriate configuration files to list the appropriate IP address range for your network, as well as lease information and other IP configuration options. The dhcpd configuration files for IPv4 and IPv6 are as follows:

- /etc/dhcp/dhcpd.conf stores IPv4 configuration
- /etc/dhcp/dhcpd6.conf stores IPv6 configuration

Note 📎

You don't need to configure the /etc/dhcp/dhcpd.conf file unless you want to configure IPv4 clients. Similarly, you don't need to configure the /etc/dhcp/dhcpd6.conf file unless you want to configure IPv6 clients.

You can refer to the manual page for the dhcpd.conf file to obtain a complete list of parameters that can be configured within the /etc/dhcp/dhcpd.conf and /etc/dhcp/dhcpd6 .conf files.

An example /etc/dhcp/dhcpd.conf file that leases IPv4 addresses on the 192.168.1.0/24 network is shown in the following output:

```
[root@server1 ~]# cat /etc/dhcp/dhcpd.conf
default-lease-time 36000;
option routers 192.168.1.254;
option domain-name-servers 192.168.1.200;
subnet 192.168.1.0 netmask 255.255.255.0 {
range 192.168.1.1 192.168.1.100;
}
[root@server1 ~]# _
```

Note from the preceding output that the DHCP server leases clients an IP address between 192.168.1.1 and 192.168.1.100 for 36,000 seconds. In addition, the DHCP server configures the client with a default gateway of 192.168.1.254 and a DNS server of 192.168.1.200.

After the /etc/dhcp/dhcpd.conf file has been configured with the appropriate information, you can start dhcpd as well as configure it to start at boot time.

To view current DHCP leases, you can examine the /var/lib/dhcpd/dhcpd.leases file for IPv4 leases and the /var/lib/dhcpd/dhcpd6.leases file for IPv6 leases.

Configuring a Linux DHCP Server Using udhcpd

Some Linux systems, including Ubuntu Server 14.04, use the udhcpd daemon to provide for IPv4 DHCP functionality on the network. To configure an Ubuntu Server14.04 system using udhcpd, you must first change the DHCPD_ENABLED="no" line within the /etc/default/udhcpd file to read DHCPD_ENABLED="yes" and save your changes. Next, you must specify the appropriate IP address range for your network as well as lease information and other IP configuration options within the /etc/udhcpd. conf. The following udhcpd.conf file leases clients an IP address between 192.168.1.1 and 192.168.1.100 on eth0 for 36,000 seconds as well as configures the client with a default gateway of 192.168.1.254 and a DNS server of 192.168.1.200:

```
[root@server1 ~]# cat /etc/udhcpd.conf
start           192.168.1.1
end             192.168.1.100
interface       eth0
option  subnet  255.255.255.0
option  router  192.168.1.254
option  dns     192.168.1.200
option  lease   36000
lease_file      /var/lib/misc/udhcpd.leases
[root@server1 ~]# _
```

Also note from the preceding output that the location of the file that stores IPv4 lease information (/var/lib/misc/udhcpd.leases) is also set within the /etc/udhcpd.conf file. If you do not specify the location of a lease file within /etc/udhcpd.conf, you can still view DHCP lease information by executing the **dumpleases command**.

Finally, you can start udhcpd and configure it to start at boot time.

DNS

Recall that DNS is a hierarchical namespace used to identify computers on large TCP/IP networks such as the Internet. Each part of this namespace is called a **zone**, and DNS servers contain all host name information for a zone. DNS servers typically resolve FQDNs to IP addresses (called a **forward lookup**), but they can also resolve IP addresses to FQDNs (called a **reverse lookup**).

The DNS Lookup Process

When you contact a Web server on the Internet using a Web browser, the Web browser performs a forward lookup of the FQDN such that it can contact the IP address of the Web server. This forward lookup can be performed by a DNS server or a series of DNS servers. The whole process used to resolve the FQDN *www.linux.org* is illustrated in Figure 13-2.

Figure 13-2 The DNS lookup process

In the first step from Figure 13-2, the Linux computer sends a forward lookup request for *www.linux.org* to the DNS server that is configured in network interface properties or /etc/resolv.conf; this is typically the DNS server at your ISP. If the ISP DNS server has recently resolved the FQDN and placed the result in its local DNS cache, you receive the response immediately (a DNS lookup query that generates a reply from a DNS cache is called an **iterative query**). If it has not, the ISP DNS server normally contacts the DNS server for the .org top-level zone (Step 2) and repeats the forward lookup request for *www.linux.org* (called a **recursive query**). The .org DNS server will not contain the IP address for the *www.linux.org* computer in its zone, but will reply with the IP address of the DNS server for the linux.org zone (Step 3).

> **Note** 📎
>
> All DNS servers contain a **DNS cache file** that contains the IP addresses of DNS servers that hold top-level DNS zones.

Your ISP DNS server then contacts the DNS server for the linux.org zone (Step 4) and repeats the forward lookup request for *www.linux.org* (another recursive query). The DNS server for the linux.org domain contains a record that lists the IP address for the *www.linux.org* computer and returns this IP address to the ISP DNS server (Step 5). The ISP DNS server then caches and returns the result to the client Web browser (Step 6), which then uses the IP address to connect to the Web server (Step 7).

> **Note** 📎
>
> Each zone typically has more than one DNS server to ensure that names can be resolved if one server is unavailable. The first DNS server in a zone is called the **master** or **primary DNS server**, and all additional DNS servers are called **slave** or **secondary DNS servers**. New zone information is added to the master DNS server; slave DNS servers periodically copy the new records from the master DNS server in a process known as a **zone transfer**.

Configuring a Linux DNS Server

To configure your Linux computer as a DNS server, you must install and configure the DNS name daemon (named) for a specific zone and add resource records that list FQDNs for computers in that zone as well as their associated IP addresses. Table 13-1 lists the files that can be used to configure this zone information.

Table 13-1   Common zone configuration files

File	Description
/etc/named.conf	Contains the list of DNS zones and their type (master/slave) that the name daemon will manage.
/var/named/*zone_name*.db or /var/named/*zone_name*.zone	Contains **resource records** used to perform forward lookups for a particular *zone_name*. Lines in this file have a type that determines the kind of resource record: • A (add host) records map FQDNs to IPv4 addresses. • AAAA (add host) records map FQDNs to IPv6 addresses. • CNAME (canonical name) records provide additional aliases for A records. • NS (name server) records provide the names of DNS servers for the zone. • MX (mail exchange) records provide the IP address for the email server for a zone. • SOA (start of authority) determines the parameters used for zone transfers as well as how long information can be cached by the computer performing the forward or reverse lookup (called the **Time-To-Live (TTL)**).
/var/named/*reverse_network_ID*.in-addr.arpa or /var/named/*network_ID*.db or /var/named/*network_ID*.zone	Contains resource records of type PTR (pointer), which list names used for reverse lookups for a particular network. The network is incorporated into the filename itself; for example, the filename that contains PTR records for the 192.168.1.0 IPv4 network would be called 1.168.192.in-addr.arpa or 192.168.1.db or 192.168.1.zone.
/var/named/named.local & /var/named/named.ip6.local or /var/named/named.localhost or /var/named/named.loopback	Contains PTR records used to identify the loopback adapter (127.0.0.1 for IPv4, ::1 for IPv6).
/var/named/named.ca or /var/named/named.root	Contains the IP addresses of top-level DNS servers; it is commonly called the DNS cache file.

Note

The name and location of zone configuration files can differ between Linux distributions. For example, on Ubuntu Server Linux, the zone configuration files listed in Table 13-1 are stored within the /etc/bind directory by default. A set of default zone files is also created within this directory that follow the naming convention db.zonetype.

The files listed in Table 13-1 have a standard format called **Berkeley Internet Name Domain (BIND)** and are difficult to create manually. As a result, it is best to copy and modify sample zone configuration files, or use a graphical utility to create these files. You can install a graphical **BIND configuration utility** within Fedora 28 using the `dnf install system-config-bind` command (this will install named if not already installed). Next, you can run the `system-config-bind-gui` command at a BASH terminal prompt within a desktop environment and configure the appropriate zones, as shown in Figure 13-3.

Figure 13-3   The BIND configuration utility

After you configure the appropriate zones within the graphical BIND utility shown in Figure 13-3, you must click the Save button to save your configuration to the /etc/named.conf file and the appropriate files within the /var/named directory.

After the files that contain the zone information have been created, you can start the DNS name daemon to provide DNS services on the network, as well as configure the DNS name daemon to start at boot time.

> **Note** 📎
>
> The name of the DNS name daemon differs in each Linux distribution. For example, to restart named on Fedora 28, you can use the `systemctl restart named.service` command. However, to restart named on Ubuntu Server, you use the `systemctl restart bind9 .service` command on Ubuntu Server 18, or the `service bind9 restart` command on Ubuntu Server 14.
>
> If you modify any zone files (for example, to add resource records), you must restart the DNS name daemon for those changes to take effect.

Recall from Chapter 12 that you can use the `dig` command to test name resolution. The `dig` command can also query the records that exist on a specific DNS server using the format `dig @server record type`, where `server` is the name or IP address of the DNS server, `record` is the name of the resource record or domain, and `type` is the type of record (A, CNAME, PTR, MX, NS, SOA, ANY, etc.). This is especially useful if you want to see whether a zone from a primary (master) DNS server to a secondary (slave) DNS server was successful. You can query the secondary DNS server to find out whether the new records have been added.

NTP

Most system components and network services require the correct date and time in order to function properly, as well as log events at the correct time. Recall from Chapter 8 that the BIOS on each computer contains a system clock that stores the date and time used to generate the time localization needed by the Linux system during the boot process. After the boot process has completed, many Linux systems obtain their time information from other servers on the network using the Network Time Protocol (NTP). This ensures that the time used by system components and network services remains correct if the system clock is modified or contains inaccurate time information.

NTP is one of the oldest Internet protocols still commonly used on the Internet. It is designed to simplify the setting of time and date information on computers across the Internet using TCP or UDP port 123. The two NTP daemons that are commonly used on Linux systems are the **NTP daemon (ntpd)** and **Chrony NTP daemon (chronyd)**.

Note

NTP is an optional time service. Some Linux distributions, such as Ubuntu Server 18, do not install an NTP daemon during the installation process. In this case, all time information is obtained from the system clock at boot time.

Understanding NTP Strata

NTP uses a hierarchical series of time sources called **strata**. Stratum 0 is at the top of this hierarchy and consists of atomic devices or GPS clocks. Stratum 1 devices obtain their time directly from Stratum 0 devices; stratum 2 devices obtain their time from Stratum 1 servers, and so on. This organization is shown in Figure 13-4.

Figure 13-4   A sample strata structure

The stratum is not an indication of quality or reliability because NTP servers typically obtain time information from multiple time sources (NTP servers) and use an algorithm to determine the most reliable time information. As a result, it is common to find a Stratum 3 device that is more accurate than a Stratum 2 device.

Note

NTP supports up to 256 strata.
Most Internet time servers, such as *time.apple.com*, are Stratum 1 devices.

Working with ntpd

Legacy Linux systems use ntpd to provide for NTP functionality. It can act as both an NTP client to obtain time from an Internet time server or an NTP server that other computers can query for time information. Although Linux distributions typically install ntpd during the Linux installation process, it can be installed from a software repository if it is not available.

To configure a Linux system as an NTP client using ntpd, you can modify the /etc/ntp.conf file and add lines for different NTP servers the client can query. These servers could be any strata or combinations of different strata.

For example, the following lines in /etc/ntp.conf query three time servers: ntp.research.gov, ntp.redhat.com, and o.fedora.pool.ntp.org.

```
server ntp.research.gov
server ntp.redhat.com
server 0.fedora.pool.ntp.org
```

> **Note** 📎
>
> Each of the FQDNs listed in the preceding output may point to multiple servers as NTP servers typically have several A (host) records in DNS that list the name FQDN for different IP addresses. This allows NTP requests to be spread across all servers to reduce server load.

If your time differs significantly from the time on these time servers, you must first stop ntpd and then run the **ntpdate command** to manually synchronize the time. You might need to run the ntpdate command several times until the time difference (or **offset**) is far less than 1 second. After manually synchronizing the time in this way, you can start the ntpd daemon again. This process is shown in the following output:

```
[root@server1 ~]# service ntpd stop
Shutting down ntpd:                                        [  OK  ]
[root@server1 ~]# ntpdate -u 0.fedora.pool.ntp.org
4 Sep 15:03:43 ntpdate[2908]: adjust time server 206.248.190.142
offset 0.977783 sec
[root@server1 ~]# ntpdate -u 0.fedora.pool.ntp.org
4 Sep 15:03:53 ntpdate[2909]: adjust time server 206.248.190.142
offset 0.001751 sec
[root@server1 ~]# ntpdate -u 0.fedora.pool.ntp.org
4 Sep 15:04:01 ntpdate[2910]: adjust time server 206.248.190.142
offset 0.001291 sec
[root@server1 ~]# service ntpd start
Starting ntpd:                                            [  OK  ]
[root@server1 ~]# _
```

After restarting the ntpd daemon, you can use the `ntpq` **command** to see what actual time servers you are synchronizing with. Because time varies greatly by location, NTP uses a **jitter** buffer to store the difference between the same time measurements from different NTP servers. The jitter information is used by NTP when determining the most reliable time when several NTP servers are queried for time information. The ntpq -p command shows the offset and jitter in milliseconds, as shown here:

```
[root@server1 ~]# ntpq -p
remote        refid           st t when poll reach  delay   offset jitter
==============================================================================
ox.eicat.ca 139.78.135.14   2  u    6   64    3   28.662  11.138  0.046
adelaide.ph 142.3.100.15    3  u    2   64    3   62.211  30.870  0.574
one.trx.com 209.51.161.238 2  u    3   64    3   43.329  22.867  0.190
[root@server1 ~]# _
```

By default, the NTP daemon is not configured as an NTP server because the /etc/ntp.conf file has only a single NTP `restrict` line:

```
restrict 127.0.0.1
```

This line allows your local client to query the NTP daemon for time information with no restrictions. If you want to allow other computers to query your NTP daemon (ntpd) for time information, edit the /etc/ntp.conf file again and add a line that identifies the specific computers or networks that are allowed to query your NTP daemon. For example, the following line within /etc/ntp.conf allows all computers on the 192.168.1.0 network to query your NTP daemon for time information but prevents other computers from modifying your NTP server configuration (`nomodify notrap`).

```
restrict 192.168.1.0 mask 255.255.255.0 nomodify notrap
```

Note

If you modify the /etc/ntp.conf file, you must restart ntpd for those changes to take effect.

Working with chronyd

Most modern Linux distributions, such as Fedora 28, use chronyd in place of ntpd, because it offers a faster response time and is backwards-compatible with ntpd. It uses the /etc/chrony.conf configuration file. You can add the location of NTP servers to query for time information, as well as add lines that allow other NTP servers to query you on a particular subnet. The line `pool 0.fedora.pool.ntp.org iburst` would configure chronyd to obtain time information from the pool of servers identified by the host name o.fedora.pool.ntp.org using fast clock synchronization (`iburst`). Rather than using a `restrict` line to allow other NTP clients to query your time as seen earlier in /etc/ntp.conf, you can add the line `allow` *subnet* to /etc/chrony.conf. For example, the line `allow 192.168.1/24` would allow NTP clients to connect from the 192.168.1.0 network (with a 24-bit subnet mask of 255.255.255.0).

For management, chronyd uses the **chronyc command** to provide the functionality that the `ntpdate` and `ntpq` commands do with ntpd. For example, to view the servers that you are currently polling for time, run the `chronyc sources` command, as shown here:

```
[root@server1 ~]# chronyc sources
210 Number of sources = 4
MS Name/IP address      Stratum Poll LastRx Last sample
===============================================================================
^+ 209.167.68.100          2     6     22    +11ms [  +11ms] +/-    87ms
^+ 66.102.79.92            2     6     32   +3556us [+3669us] +/-    62ms
^+ ox.eicat.ca             2     6     42   -4311us [-4198us] +/-    75ms
^* 216.234.161.11          2     6     50    -41us [  +72us] +/-    81ms
[root@server1 ~]# _
```

When run without arguments, the `chronyc` command provides an interactive chronyc> prompt that you can use to type additional commands. Typing `help` at the chronyc> prompt will display a list of common commands, including `polltarget` (which can be used to poll a specified NTP server) and `settime` (which can be used to manually set the date and time to a specified value).

Nearly all desktop environments installed today obtain time from an Internet time server using NTP and allow for NTP client configuration using a graphical application. For example, to obtain time from an Internet time server using chronyd on a Fedora 20 system, you can navigate to the Activities menu, Show Applications, Settings, Details, Date & Time within the GNOME desktop to open the **Date & Time utility** shown in Figure 13-5.

Figure 13-5 The Date & Time utility

Source: Used with permissions from Microsoft

Web Services

Apache is the world's most common Web server. It started as the HTTP Daemon (httpd) developed by Rob McCool for the NCSA (National Center for Supercomputing Applications) at the University of Illinois. In the early 1990s, Rob McCool became too busy to continue the project single-handedly, so he released the source code for httpd under the GPL. Open Source Software developers then made patches to this code, with each patch improving one component of the system. These patches gave rise to the name Apache server (a patchy server). After these early days, the Apache Group of Open Source Developers took over development of Apache. To learn more about this group, go to *www.apache.org*.

Recall that Web servers hand out HTML files and other Web content using the HyperText Transfer Protocol (HTTP) from a specific directory in the directory tree. This directory is called the **document root** directory and contains the default website that is used on the server. On most systems, the default document root directory is /var/www/html, and the default document that is handed out from this directory is index.html. The main configuration file for Apache differs based on your Linux distribution. On Fedora, the main Apache configuration file is /etc/httpd/conf/httpd.conf, and for Ubuntu Server, the main Apache configuration file is /etc/apache2/apache2.conf. Each line in the httpd.conf file is called a **directive**. Table 13-2 lists some common directives.

> **Note** 📎
>
> The main Apache configuration file often references several other configuration files that contain directives used by Apache.
>
> The name of the Apache service differs in each Linux distribution. For example, to install Apache on Fedora 28, you can install the httpd package and use the command `systemctl start httpd.service` to start Apache. However, to install Apache on Ubuntu Server, you install the apache2 package, and use the `service apache2 start` command (Ubuntu 14) or `systemctl start apache2.service` command (Ubuntu 18) to start Apache.

Table 13-2   Common Apache configuration file directives

Directive	What it specifies
`Listen 80`	Apache daemon will listen for HTTP requests on port 80.
`ServerName server1.class.com`	Name of the local server is server1.class.com.
`DocumentRoot "/var/www/html"`	Document root directory is /var/www/html on the local computer.

(continues)

Table 13-2 Common Apache configuration file directives *(continued)*

Directive	What it specifies
`DirectoryIndex index.html`	Index.html file in the document root directory will be sent to clients who request an HTML document.
`ServerRoot /etc/httpd`	All paths listed within the /etc/httpd/conf/httpd.conf file are relative to the /etc/httpd directory.
`ErrorLog logs/error_log`	All Apache daemon messages will be written to the /etc/httpd/logs/error_log file.
`CustomLog logs/access_log combined`	All Web requests will be written to the /etc/httpd/logs/access_log file using a combined log format.
`MaxClients 150`	Maximum number of simultaneous requests cannot exceed 150.
`User apache`	Apache daemon will run as the "apache" local user account.
`Group apache`	Apache daemon will run as the "apache" local group account.
`Include configurationfile`	Include directives that are listed in the specified configuration file.
`IncludeOptional configurationfile`	Include directives that are listed in the specified configuration file, if it exists.

`<Directory /var/www/html>`
`Order allow,deny`
`Allow from all`
`Deny from 192.168.1.51`
`</Directory>`
	All hosts are allowed to access HTML files and other Web content from the /var/www/html directory except for the computer with the IP address 192.168.1.51.

The default settings in the httpd.conf file are sufficient for most simple Web servers; thus, you only need to copy the appropriate HTML files to the /var/www/html directory, including the index.html file, start Apache to host Web content on your network, and ensure that Apache is started automatically at boot time. Client computers can then enter the location *http://servername_or_IPaddress* in their Web browser to obtain the default Web page. Each time a client request is received by the Apache Web server (called a **Web page hit**), a separate httpd daemon is started to service the request.

Note 📎

You can also use the `curl` command at a BASH prompt to obtain a Web page. For example, the `curl http://127.0.0.1/` command can be used to test your local Apache Web server to ensure that your Apache Web server is sending the correct Web page to clients.

On a busy Web server, there may be several hundred httpd daemons running on the system responding to client requests. The first httpd daemon is started as the root user and is used to start all other httpd daemons. These non-root httpd daemons are started as a regular user account to prevent privileged access to the system. For example, the `User apache` directive shown in Table 13-2 will ensure that non-root httpd daemons are started as the apache user. In this case, any Web content must have Linux permissions that allow it to be readable by the apache user. When you restart Apache, the root httpd daemon is restarted, which in turn restarts all other httpd daemons. If you change the HTML content inside the document root directory, you do not need to restart Apache. However, if you change the contents of an Apache configuration file, you need to restart Apache to activate those changes.

> **Note** 📎
>
> The `apachectl` **command** is useful when managing Apache. The `apachectl graceful` command can be used to restart Apache without dropping any client connections, whereas the `apachectl configtest` command checks the syntax of lines within Apache configuration files and notes any errors.
>
> The `ab` **(Apache benchmark) command** can be used to monitor the performance of the Apache Web server by sending null requests to it. To send 1000 requests to the local Apache Web server (100 at a time), you could use the `ab -n1000 -c100 http://127.0.0.1/` command.
>
> Another popular Web server used on Linux systems is Nginx. You can learn more about Nginx at *www.nginx.com*.

File-Sharing Services

Many file-sharing services are available on Linux systems. Each is tailored for a specific purpose and has a different configuration method. The most common include Samba, NFS, and FTP.

Samba

Microsoft Windows is the most commonly used client computer operating system, so you need to know how to configure your Linux system to communicate with Windows computers. Windows computers format TCP/IP data using the **Server Message Blocks (SMB)** protocol. To share information with Windows client computers, you can use the Samba daemon (smbd), which emulates the SMB protocol. In addition, Windows computers advertise their computer names using the **NetBIOS** protocol. To create and advertise a NetBIOS name that Windows computers can use to connect to your Linux server, you can use the NetBIOS name daemon (nmbd).

Note

NetBIOS names can be up to 15 characters long and are normally resolved on the network using a WINS (Windows Internet Name Service) server or NetBIOS broadcasts. All NetBIOS names that are successfully resolved are placed in a NetBIOS name cache to speed future access to the same servers. The `nmblookup` **command** can be used to test NetBIOS name resolution in Linux.

Because of the widespread popularity of SMB, nearly all operating systems, including UNIX, Linux, macOS, and Microsoft Windows, can connect to directories that are shared using the SMB protocol.

SMB is sometimes referred to as the Common Internet File System (CIFS).

Configuring a Samba Server

When a Windows client computer accesses a shared directory using SMB, the Windows user name and password are transmitted alongside the request in case the shared directory allows access to certain users only. As a result, you should first create local Linux user accounts for each Windows user and create a Samba password for them using the `smbpasswd` **command** that matches the password that they use on their Windows computer, as shown in the following output:

```
[root@server1 ~]# useradd mary
[root@server1 ~]# passwd mary
Changing password for user mary.
New UNIX password:
Retype new UNIX password:
passwd: all authentication tokens updated successfully.
[root@server1 ~]# smbpasswd -a mary
New SMB password:
Retype new SMB password:
Added user mary.
[root@server1 ~]# _
```

Following this, you can edit the main configuration file for Samba, /etc/samba/smb.conf. Like the Apache configuration file, the smb.conf contains directives that can be used to set your NetBIOS name, server settings, shared directories, and shared printers. On most Linux systems, the default settings within the smb.conf file shares all CUPS printers and home directories (for recognized Windows users). However, you need to add a line under the `[global]` section of this file to set your NetBIOS name. For example, to set your NetBIOS name to server1, you could add the directive `netbios name = server1` to the smb.conf file. As with Apache, if you change the smb.conf file, you must restart the Samba and NetBIOS name daemons.

Note

You can use the `testparm` **command** to ensure that the /etc/samba/smb.conf file has no syntax errors. As a result, it is good practice to run this command after you edit the /etc/samba/smb.conf file.

Connecting to a Samba Server

After configuring Samba, you should test its functionality to ensure that it is functioning normally. To do this, you could log into a Windows client, open File Explorer, and browse to the name of your Samba server under the Network section, or enter *Samba_server* within File Explorer or the Search dialog box, where *Samba_server* is the NetBIOS name or IP address of your Samba server. If successful, the Windows operating system will open a new window that displays your home directory, shared printers, and other shared directories that you have permission to access, as shown in Figure 13-6.

Figure 13-6   Accessing a Samba server from a Windows client

Source: Used with permissions from Microsoft

Alternatively, you could connect to your Samba server using the `smbclient` **command** on your Linux computer. To do this, log into a BASH terminal using the login information for an established Windows user account. Then run the `smbclient` `-L` *Samba_server* command, where *Samba_server* is the NetBIOS name or IP address of your Samba server. This connects your computer to the Samba server using your current user account credentials and lists the shared directories and available printers, as shown in the following sample output:

```
[root@server1 ~]# smbclient -L server1
Enter root's password:
Domain=[WORKGROUP] OS=[Unix] Server=[Samba 4.7.6-Ubuntu]

    Sharename       Type        Comment
    ---------       ----        -------
    IPC$            IPC         IPC Service(server1 server (Samba,Ubuntu))
    print$          Disk        Printer Drivers
    printer1        Printer     printer1
Domain=[WORKGROUP] OS=[Unix] Server=[Samba 4.7.6-Ubuntu]
    stuff           Disk        Good Stuff


    Server                      Comment
    ---------                   -------
    ALIENWARE
    SERVER1                     server1 server (Samba, Ubuntu)


    Workgroup                   Master
    ---------                   -------
    WORKGROUP                   SERVER1
[root@server1 ~]# _
```

Note

You can use the smbclient command to connect to both Samba and Windows servers.

Additionally, you can use the smbclient command to display an FTP-like interface for transferring files to and from shared directories on Samba or Windows servers. The following output demonstrates how to connect to the stuff shared directory on server1 using an FTP-like interface:

```
[root@server1 root]# smbclient //server1/stuff
Enter root's password:
Domain=[MYGROUP] OS=[Unix] Server=[ Samba 4.7.6-Ubuntu]
smb: \> dir
    .                       D        0  Mon Sep  6 22:28:12 2019
    ..                      D        0  Mon Sep  6 22:28:12 2019
    Final Exam.doc          A    26624  Mon Sep  6 23:17:30 2019
    homework questions.doc  A    46080  Mon Sep  6 23:33:03 2019
    Part 0.DOC              A    13312  Mon Sep  6 23:27:51 2019
    Part 1.DOC              A    35328  Mon Sep  6 23:24:44 2019
```

```
    Part 2.doc                      A      70656   Mon Sep   6 23:25:28 2019
    Part 3.DOC                      A      38912   Mon Sep   6 23:26:07 2019
    Part 4.doc                      A      75776   Mon Sep   6 23:26:57 2019
    Part 5.DOC                      A      26624   Mon Sep   6 23:27:23 2019
    Part 6.doc                      A      59904   Mon Sep   6 23:05:32 2019
    TOC.doc                         A      58880   Mon Sep   6 23:09:16 2019
39032 blocks of size 262144. 14180 blocks available

smb: \> help
?                  allinfo         altname          archive         backup
blocksize          cancel          case_sensitive   cd              chmod
chown              close           del              dir             du
echo               exit            get              getfacl         geteas
hardlink           help            history          iosize          lcd
link               lock            lowercase        ls              l
mask               md              mget             mkdir           more
mput               newer           notify           open            posix
posix_encrypt      posix_open      posix_mkdir      posix_rmdir     posix_unlink
print              prompt          put              pwd             q
queue              quit            readlink         rd              recurse
reget              rename          reput            rm              rmdir
showacls           setea           setmode          stat            symlink
tar                tarmode         timeout          translate       unlock
volume             vuid            wdel             logon           listconnect
showconnect        tcon            tdis             tid             logoff
..                 !
smb: \> get TOC.doc
getting file \TOC.doc of size 58880 as TOC.doc (16.0 KiloBytes/sec)
(average 16.0 KiloBytes/sec)
smb: \> exit
[root@server1 root]# _
```

NFS

Network File System (NFS) allows UNIX, Linux, macOS, and Windows computers to share files transparently. In NFS, one computer shares (or **exports**) a directory in the directory tree by placing the name of that directory in the /etc/exports file. The other computer can then access that directory across the network by using the mount command to mount the remote directory on the local computer.

Configuring a Linux NFS Server

To configure an NFS server in Linux, perform the following steps:

1. Install the NFS server package from a software repository.
2. Create a directory that contains the information to share with client computers. Although you can use an existing directory, try to avoid doing so because you

might accidentally give client computers the ability to view or modify existing system files.

3. Edit the /etc/exports file and add a line that lists the directory to share and the appropriate options. For example, the following lines in the /etc/exports file share the /source directory to the computer server1, allowing users to read and write data and ensuring that the root user is treated as an anonymous user on the NFS server, as well as share the /admin directory to all users, allowing users to read and write data:

```
/source   server1(rw,root_squash)
/admin    *(rw)
```

4. Save your changes to the /etc/exports file and return to the command prompt.
5. Run the command exportfs -a to update the list of exported filesystems in memory from the /etc/exports file.
6. Restart the NFS daemon.

Note 📎

The name of the NFS server package differs based on Linux distribution. On Fedora, you can install the nfs-utils package, and on Ubuntu Server you can install the nfs-kernel-server package.

The name of the NFS daemon is nfsd. To restart this daemon on Fedora 28, you can use the systemctl restart nfs.service command. Alternatively, you can use the service nfs-kernel-server restart command on Ubuntu Server 14, or the systemctl restart nfs-kernel-server.service command on Ubuntu Server 18 to restart nfsd.

Connecting to a Linux NFS Server

You can see a list of available NFS shared directories on a remote server using the showmount **command**. For example, to see a list of the shared directories on the server nfs.sampledomain.com, you could use the following command:

```
[root@server1 ~]# showmount -e nfs.sampledomain.com
Export list for 192.168.1.104:
/var *
[root@server1 ~]# _
```

From the preceding output, the /var directory on the nfs.sampledomain.com server is shared to all hosts (*).

To access files using NFS, you mount a directory from a remote NFS server on the network to a directory on your local computer. That is, you specify the nfs filesystem type, server name or IP address, remote directory, and local directory as arguments to the mount command. For example, to mount the /var directory on the remote computer named nfs.sampledomain.com (IP address 192.168.0.1) to the /mnt directory on the local computer using NFS and view the results, you can use the following commands:

```
[root@server1 ~]# mount -t nfs nfs.sampledomain.com:/var /mnt
[root@server1 ~]# mount | grep nfs
192.168.0.1:/var on /mnt type nfs (rw,vers=4,clientaddr=
192.168.0.5)
[root@server1 ~]# ls /mnt
arpwatch   ftpkerberos   lock   mailman    nis        run     tux
cachegdm   lib           log    mars_nwe   opt        spool   www
dbiptraf   local         mail   named      preserve   tmpyp
[root@server1 ~]# _
```

After running these commands, you can use the /mnt directory as any other local directory, with all file operations performed in the /var directory on the remote computer. You can then dismount the NFS filesystem using the umount command.

FTP

The protocol most commonly used to transfer files on public networks is the **File Transfer Protocol (FTP)**. FTP hosts files differently than NFS. In anonymous access, a special directory is available to any user who wants to connect to the FTP server. Alternatively, users can log in, via an FTP client program, to a home directory on the FTP server.

Configuring a Linux FTP Server

The traditional FTP server program is the Washington University FTP daemon (wu-ftpd). However, most Linux systems today use the **Very Secure FTP daemon (vsftpd)**, which provides additional security features, including support for SSH using **Secure FTP (SFTP)**. This stand-alone daemon is much easier to configure than wu-ftpd. The following steps show how to configure vsftpd to host files that can be downloaded from a client computer by user1 after user1 logs in with a valid password:

1. Create a directory under user1's home directory and ensure that user1 owns this directory. This directory will be used to host the files.
2. Edit the /etc/vsftpd.conf file and modify the appropriate commented options to control what actions the vsftpd daemon will allow from FTP clients. This includes:
   a. Whether to allow anonymous connections
   b. Whether to allow local user connections
   c. Whether to allow users to upload files
   d. Whether to prevent users from accessing files outside their home directory (called a "chroot jail")
3. Start the vsftpd daemon and ensure that it is started at boot time.

When you connect to the vsftpd daemon using an FTP client utility, you are prompted to log in. If you log in as the user "anonymous," you will be placed in the / var/ftp or /srv/ftp directory, depending on your Linux distribution. Alternatively, if you log in as a valid user account on the system, you will be placed in that user's home directory.

> **Note** 📎
>
> The root user is not allowed to connect to vsftpd by default. To log in as the root user to vsftpd, you must remove the line `root` from the /etc/ftpusers and /etc/user_list files, if they exist.
>
> On Fedora Linux, the configuration files for vsftpd are stored within the /etc/vsftpd directory. For example, the configuration file for vsftpd on Fedora 28 would be /etc/vsftpd/ vsftpd.conf.

Connecting to a Linux FTP Server

Most Web browsers have a built-in FTP utility that allows you to access files and directories on a remote computer. To connect to an FTP server using a Web browser, specify the location *ftp://servername_or_IPaddress* in your Web browser for anonymous access or the location *ftp://user:password@servername_or_IPaddress* to log in with a particular user account and password. A sample FTP session within a Web browser is shown in Figure 13-7.

Figure 13-7 Using a Web browser FTP client

Clicking a file displayed in Figure 13-7 displays a dialog box that allows you to save the file to the appropriate location on a local filesystem.

Most operating systems also come with a command-line FTP utility that can connect to an FTP server. To use such a utility, you specify the host name or IP address of an FTP server as an argument to the `ftp` **command** for standard FTP, or the `sftp` **command** for Secure FTP (SFTP). This opens a connection that allows the transfer of files to and from that computer. You can then log in as a valid user on that computer, in which case you are automatically placed in your home directory. Alternatively, you can log in as the user "anonymous" and be placed in the /var/ftp or /srv/ftp directory, depending on your Linux distribution. After you are logged in, you receive an interactive prompt that accepts FTP commands. A list of common FTP commands is shown in Table 13-3.

> **Note**
>
> Most FTP servers require you enter a password when logging in as the anonymous user via a command-line FTP utility; this value you specify for this password is irrelevant.
>
> The `ftp` command will prompt you for a username and password when connecting to an FTP server, whereas the `sftp` command assumes the current user name and prompts only for a password. To connect as a different user using SFTP, you can use the `sftp username@ servername_or_IPaddress` command.
>
> If the SFTP server does not allow SSH logins as the root user, you will not be able to connect using SFTP as the root user, because SFTP negotiates SSH encryption prior to starting the FTP session.

Table 13-3 Common FTP commands

Command	Description
`help`	Displays a list of commands
`pwd`	Displays the current directory on the remote computer
`dir` `ls`	Displays a directory listing from the remote computer
`cd directory`	Changes the current directory to `directory` on the remote computer
`lcd directory`	Changes the current directory to `directory` on the local computer
`get filename`	Downloads the `filename` to the current directory on the local computer
`ascii`	Specifies text file downloads for standard FTP connections (default)

(continues)

Table 13-3 Common FTP commands *(continued)*

Command	Description
binary	Specifies binary file downloads for standard FTP connections
mget *filename*	Downloads the file named *filename* to the current directory on the local computer; it also allows the use of wildcard metacharacters to specify the *filename*
put *filename*	Uploads the *filename* from the current directory on the local computer to the current directory on the remote computer
mput *filename*	Uploads the *filename* from the current directory on the local computer to the current directory on the remote computer; it also allows the use of wildcard metacharacters to specify the *filename*
!	Runs a shell on the local computer
close	Closes the standard FTP connection to the remote computer
open *hostname or IP*	Opens a standard FTP connection to the *hostname or IP* address specified
bye quit	Quits the FTP utility

The exact output displayed during an FTP session varies slightly depending on the version of the FTP software used on the FTP server. The following output is an example of using the ftp command to connect to an FTP server named ftp.sampledomain.com as the root user:

```
[root@server1 ~]# ftp ftp.sampledomain.com
Connected to ftp.sampledomain.com.
220 (vsFTPd 2.2.2)
Name (ftp.sampledomain.com:root): root
331 Please specify the password.
Password:
230 Login successful.
Remote system type is UNIX.
Using binary mode to transfer files.
ftp>
```

The current directory on the remote computer is the home directory for the root user in the preceding output. To verify this and see a list of files to download, you can use the following commands at the ftp> prompt:

```
ftp> pwd
257 "/root"
ftp> ls
```

```
227 Entering Passive Mode (192,168,0,1,56,88).
150 Here comes the directory listing.
total 2064
-rw-r--r--    1 root      root           1756 Aug 14  08:48  file1
-rw-r--r--    1 root      root            160 Aug 14  08:48  file2
-rw-r--r--    1 root      root        1039996 Aug 14  08:39  file3
drwxr-xr-x    2 root      root           4096 Aug 14  08:50  stuff
226 Directory send OK.
ftp>
```

The preceding output shows three files and one subdirectory. To download file3 to the current directory on the local computer, you can use the following command:

```
ftp> get file3
local: file3 remote: file3
227 Entering Passive Mode (192,168,0,1,137,37)
150 Opening BINARY mode data connection for file3 (1039996 bytes).
226 Transfer complete.
ftp>
```

Similarly, to change the current directory on the remote computer to /root/ stuff and upload a copy of file4 from the current directory on the local computer to it, as well as view the results and then exit the ftp utility, you can use the following commands at the ftp> prompt:

```
ftp> cd stuff
250 Directory successfully changed.
ftp> pwd
257 "/root/stuff"
ftp> mput file4
mput file4? y
227 Entering Passive Mode (192,168,0,1,70,109)
150 Opening BINARY mode data connection for file4.
226 Transfer complete.
929 bytes sent in 0.00019 seconds (4.8e+03 Kbytes/s)
ftp> ls
227 Entering Passive Mode (192,168,0,1,235,35)
150 Opening ASCII mode data connection for directory listing.
total 8
-rw-r--r--    1 root      root            929 Aug 14 09:26 file4
226 Transfer complete.
ftp> bye
221 Goodbye.
[root@server1 ~]# _
```

Note

In addition to using a Web browser or command-line FTP/SFTP client included with your computer's operating system, you can choose from many third-party graphical FTP/SFTP client programs, such as FileZilla.

Email Services

Email servers typically accept email and route it over the Internet using Simple Mail Transfer Protocol (SMTP) or Enhanced Simple Mail Transfer Protocol (ESMTP) on TCP port 25. Additionally, client computers can retrieve email from email servers using a variety of protocols such as Post Office Protocol (POP) or Internet Message Access Protocol (IMAP). Client computers can also send email to email servers using SMTP/ESMTP for later relay on the Internet.

Note

Most email servers provide the functions of the Mail Transfer Agent (MTA) and Mail Delivery Agent (MDA) described earlier in Chapter 1.

To relay email to other servers on the Internet, an email server must look up the name of the target email server in the domain's MX (Mail Exchanger) records, which are stored on a public DNS server. For example, if your local email server needs to send email to jason.eckert@trios.com, the email server locates the name of the target email server by looking up the MX record for the trios.com domain. It then resolves the target email server name to the appropriate IP address using the A (host) record for the server on the public DNS server.

Daemons and other system components on Linux systems traditionally relied on email to send important information to the root user. Because Systemd can be used to log detailed daemon information intended for the root user, many modern Linux distributions that use Systemd do not install an email daemon by default, but an email daemon can easily be added afterwards from a software repository. The most common email daemon used on modern Linux systems is **Postfix**.

The Postfix daemon is configured by default to accept email on TCP port 25 and route it to the appropriate user on the Linux system. To test this, you can use the `telnet` command with port 25 as an argument. This displays a Welcome banner that identifies the email server, as shown in the following output. Additionally, you can use the EHLO command to test ESMTP support and the HELO command to test SMTP support, as shown in the following output:

```
[root@server1 ~]# telnet localhost 25
Connected to localhost.
Escape character is '^]'.
220 server1.class.com ESMTP Postfix
EHLO sample.com
250-server1.class.com
250-PIPELINING
250-SIZE 10240000
250-VRFY
250-ETRN
250-ENHANCEDSTATUSCODES
250-8BITMIME
250 DSN
HELO sample.com
250 server1.class.com
quit
221 2.0.0 Bye
Connection closed by foreign host.
[root@server1 ~]# _
```

To check your email on your local Linux system, you can use the mail **command**, as shown here:

```
[root@server1 ~]# mail
Mail version 8.1.2 01/15/2019.  Type ? for help.
"/var/spool/mail/root": 13 messages 6 new 10 unread
U  1 Cron Daemon          Sat Jul 11 07:01  26/981   "Cron"
U  2 logwatch@localhost.1  Mon Jul 20 11:43  42/1528  "Logwatch"
U  3 logwatch@localhost.1  Tue Jul 21 12:32 151/4669
N  4 jason.eckert@trios.c  Wed Sep 29 15:53  11/430
& 4
Message 4:
From jason.eckert@trios.com Wed Sep 29 15:53:25 2019
Return-Path: <jason.eckert@trios.com>
Date: Wed, 29 Sep 2019 15:52:36 -0400
From: jason.eckert@trios.com
Status: R

Hey dude

& q
[root@server1 ~]# _
```

Note 📎

The `mail` command is an example of a Mail User Agent (MUA), as described in Chapter 1.

Email for each user is stored within a file named for the user in the /var/spool/mail directory. For example, the email for the bob user will be stored within the /var/spool/mail/bob file.

To forward email, users can create a ~/.forward file that lists a target email address. Any email sent to the user will automatically be forwarded to the target email address.

The `mailq` **command** can be used to troubleshoot email delivery. By default, `mailq` displays any email messages awaiting delivery alongside the reason that they were not delivered.

The /etc/aliases file contains other email names that are used to identify the different users on the system. From the entries in the /etc/aliases file shown next, you can use the names postmaster, bin, daemon, or adm to refer to the root user:

```
[root@server1 ~]# head -17 /etc/aliases
# See man 5 aliases for format
postmaster:  root
bin:         root
daemon:      root
adm:         root
[root@server1 ~]# _
```

If you modify the /etc/aliases file, you need to run the `newaliases` **command** in order to rebuild the aliases database (/etc/aliases.db) based on the entries in the /etc/aliases file. Only the aliases database is used by the Postfix daemon.

While Postfix is normally configured to accept and route local email only, you can also configure it to relay email to other servers on the Internet as well as accept connections from email clients on your network using POP and IMAP. To do this, you must edit its configuration file: /etc/postfix/main.cf. A common set of lines that you should modify or add at minimum is listed in Table 13-4.

Table 13-4   Sample lines in /etc/postfix/main.cf to modify or add when configuring Postfix

Line	Change
`mydomain = sample.com`	Sets the email domain name; changes to desired name
`myorigin = $mydomain`	Sets local access to the domain name
`inet_interfaces = all`	Configures Postfix to listen for email on all interfaces
`mydestination = $myhostname, localhost.$mydomain, localhost, $mydomain`	Configures destination domain for email
`mynetworks_style = class`	Trusts email from computers on the local network

Database Services

Databases are large files that store important information in the form of **tables**. A table organizes information into a list. Within the list, the set of information about a particular item is called a **record**. For example, in a list of customer mailing addresses, a single record would contain a customer's first name, last name, street address, city, state, and Zip code. The various categories of information within a record are called **fields**. For example, in our customer mailing address example, one field contains the city information, one contains the state information, and so on.

Most databases consist of dozens or hundreds of tables that store information used by applications. For example, accounting software typically stores financial data within a database. In large databases, information within certain tables can be related to information within other tables in the same database. These databases are called **relational databases**, and the tables within are usually linked by a common field. Figure 13-8 shows a simple relational database that consists of two tables with a related EmployeeID field.

EmployeeID	FirstName	LastName	Address	ZIP	Home Phone	Mobile Phone
A518	Bob	Smith	14 Wallington St.	49288	555-123-1399	555-144-2039
A827	Jill	Sagan	51 York Ave. N.	49282	555-132-1039	
A988	Frank	Kertz	623 Queen St.	44922	555-209-1039	555-199-2938
A472	Bethany	Weber	82 Shepherd Ave.	49100	555-299-0199	555-203-1000
A381	John	Lauer	55 Rooshill Ave.	49288	555-123-2883	555-203-2811

Common field

EmployeeID	Week	Hours	MgrOK
A518	08/20/20	37	Yes
A827	08/20/20	40	Yes
A988	08/20/20	40	Yes
A472	08/20/20	40	Yes
A381	08/20/20	22	Yes
A518	08/27/20	40	Yes
A827	08/27/20	35	Yes
A988	08/27/20	0	Yes
A472	08/27/20	40	Yes
A381	08/27/20	22	Yes

Field names

Record

Figure 13-8   A simple relational database structure

Structured Query Language (SQL) is a special programming language used to store and access the data in databases. The database server programs that allow users to access and update the data stored within a database are called **SQL servers**. Table 13-5 lists common SQL statements that are used to manipulate data on SQL servers.

Table 13-5   Common SQL statements

Command	Description
CREATE DATABASE database_name	Creates a database
DROP DATABASE database_name	Deletes a database
CREATE TABLE table_name field_definitions	Creates a table within a database
DROP TABLE table_name	Deletes a table within a database
INSERT INTO table_name VALUES record	Inserts a new record within a table
UPDATE table_name SET record_modifications	Modifies records within a table
DELETE FROM table_name record	Deletes a record within a table
SELECT * FROM table_name	Displays all records within a table
SELECT fields FROM table_name WHERE criteria	Displays one or more fields for records within a table that meet specific criteria
SELECT fields FROM table_name GROUP BY field	Displays one or more fields for records within a table and groups the results according to the values within a common field
SELECT fields FROM table_name ORDER BY field [ASC/DESC]	Displays one or more fields for records within a table and sorts the results in ascending or descending order according to the values within a common field
SELECT fields FROM table1 INNER JOIN table2 ON table1.common_field = table2.common_field	Displays one or more fields for records within two related tables (table1 and table2) that have a common field; only records that have matching information within the common field in both tables are displayed
SELECT fields FROM table1 LEFT OUTER JOIN table2_name ON table1_name.common_field = table2_name.common_field	Displays one or more fields for all records within table1 and any records within table2 that have matching information within a common field
SELECT fields FROM table1 RIGHT OUTER JOIN table2_name ON table1_name.common_field = table2_name.common_field	Displays one or more fields for all records within table2 and any records within table1 that have matching information within a common field
CREATE USER user_name WITH PASSWORD password	Creates a user that can access the SQL server
GRANT permissions ON table1 TO user_name	Assigns permissions to a user that give the user the ability to work with the table, where permissions can include INSERT, UPDATE, SELECT, or DELETE

SQL servers usually offer advanced backup, repair, replication, and recovery utilities for the data within the database. In addition, SQL servers can store multiple databases, and they allow programs to access these databases from across the network. Thus, a single SQL server can store the data needed by all programs that exist on servers and client computers within the network. Although several SQL servers are available for Linux, PostgreSQL is one of the most widely used.

Configuring PostgreSQL

PostgreSQL is a powerful SQL server that provides a large number of features. Although some Linux server distributions allow you to install PostgreSQL during the Linux installation process, you can easily install it from a software repository afterwards. During installation, the PostgreSQL installation creates a postgres user within the /etc/passwd and /etc/shadow files that has a home directory of /var/lib/postgresql and a shell of /bin/bash.

Next, you can prepare PostgreSQL for use by following these steps:

1. Assign the postgres user a password using the `passwd postgres` command.
2. Optionally modify the PostgreSQL configuration file, postgresql.conf. The location of this file differs depending on your Linux distribution, but it is often stored under the /var/lib/postgresql directory or the /etc/postgresql directory.
3. Start the PostgreSQL daemon and configure it to start at boot time.

Configuring PostgreSQL Databases

To configure PostgreSQL databases, you must first log in as the postgres user. Next, you can execute one of several PostgreSQL command-line utilities to create and manage databases. These commands are summarized in Table 13-6.

Table 13-6 PostgreSQL command-line utilities

Command	Description
clusterdb	Associates a PostgreSQL database to another database on a different server
createdb	Creates a PostgreSQL database
createlang	Allows a new programming language to be used with PostgreSQL
createuser	Creates a PostgreSQL user
dropdb	Deletes a PostgreSQL database
droplang	Removes support for a programming language within PostgreSQL
dropuser	Deletes a PostgreSQL user
pg_dump	Backs up PostgreSQL database settings
pg_dumpall	Backs up PostgreSQL database cluster settings

(continues)

Table 13-6	PostgreSQL command-line utilities *(continued)*
Command	**Description**
pg_restore	Restores PostgreSQL database settings
psql	The PostgreSQL utility
reindexdb	Reindexes a PostgreSQL database
vacuumdb	Analyzes and regenerates internal PostgreSQL database statistics

For example, to create a database called sampledb after logging in as the postgres user, you could use the following command:

```
[postgres@server1 ~]$ createdb sampledb
[postgres@server1 ~]$ _
```

Next, you can run the psql command to connect to the employee database using the interactive **PostgreSQL utility**, where you can obtain information about the SQL statements and psql commands that can perform most database administration.

```
[postgres@server1 ~]$ psql sampledb
psql (9.3.4)
Type "help" for help.

sampledb=# help
You are using psql, the command-line interface to PostgreSQL.
Type:  \copyright for distribution terms
       \h for help with SQL commands
       \? for help with psql commands
       \g or terminate with semicolon to execute query
       \q to quit
sampledb=# _
```

You can create tables and add records within the PostgreSQL utility using the appropriate SQL statements. The following output shows how to create a table called "employee" with three fields (Name, Dept, Title) that each allow 20 characters of information, add three employee records, and display the results.

```
sampledb=# CREATE TABLE employee (Name char(20), Dept char(20),
Title char(20));
CREATE TABLE
sampledb=# INSERT INTO employee VALUES ('Jeff Smith','Research','Analyst');
INSERT 0 1
sampledb=# INSERT INTO employee VALUES ('Mary Wong','Accounting','Manager');
INSERT 0 1
```

```
sampledb=# INSERT INTO employee VALUES ('Pat Clarke','Marketing',
'Coordinator');
INSERT 0 1
sampledb=# SELECT * from employee;
         name        |        dept         |        title
---------------------+---------------------+---------------------
 Jeff Smith          | Research            | Analyst
 Mary Wong           | Accounting          | Manager
 Pat Clarke          | Marketing           | Coordinator
(3 rows)

sampledb=# _
```

> **Note** 📎
>
> Each SQL statement that is entered within the PostgreSQL utility must end with a ; metacharacter.

In addition to SQL statements, the PostgreSQL utility has many built-in commands. These commands, which are prefixed with a \ character, can be used to obtain database information or perform functions within the PostgreSQL utility. The most common of these built-in commands are listed in Table 13-7.

Table 13-7   Common built-in PostgreSQL utility commands

Command	Description
\l	Lists available databases
\c database_name	Connects to a different database
\d	Lists the tables within the current database
\d table_name	Lists the fields within a table
\q	Exits the PostgreSQL utility

Working with Cloud Technologies

During the 1990s, most resources on the Internet consisted of simple Web pages stored on Web servers that could be accessed remotely across the Internet using a Web browser. Together, these Web servers were collectively referred to as the World Wide Web. Today, complex Web apps (and the data they access) are the most common Internet-accessible resource, and the servers that host them are collectively referred to as the cloud instead of the World Wide Web.

Recall from Chapter 1 that organizations that provide access to the Web apps running in their data center are called cloud providers, and may provide public access to their data center, or may keep the access to their data center private to their own organization. Also recall that you can host Web apps on a cloud server in three ways: Software as a Service (SaaS), Platform as a Service (PaaS), and Infrastructure as a Service (IaaS).

With IaaS, the cloud provider offers a cloud platform that provides Internet access, IP addressing, and FQDN name resolution to virtual machines that you create on their hypervisor. You must manage each virtual machine as you would any other operating system, including installing and managing all of the software, and the Web apps that users will access from across the Internet. This structure is shown in Figure 13-9.

Figure 13-9 A Sample IaaS structure

PaaS allows you to run Web app containers within the cloud. Unlike virtual machines, containers do not have a complete operating system. Instead, a container is a subset of an operating system comprised of one or more apps, and the supporting operating system files needed by those apps. As a result, containers must be run on an existing operating system, as shown in Figure 13-10.

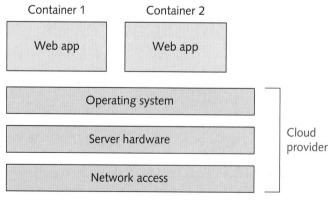

Figure 13-10 A Sample PaaS structure

When you run a container, the container apps are executed in a way that is isolated from apps running within other containers and the underlying operating system; this type of execution is often called **sandboxing**. To allow each container app to be uniquely identified on the network, each container functions as a virtual operating system with a unique name and IP address.

While separate virtual machines could instead be used to run apps on the same computer in an isolated fashion, containers are much smaller and use far less underlying system resources as a result. This makes containers well-suited for cloud providers, where resource efficiency and scalability are important for controlling data center costs.

Say, for example, that you create an IoT device that can be controlled remotely from a Web app running on a cloud provider, and that you plan on selling thousands of these devices to customers. In this case, you don't need to create a large, complex Web app that is designed to connect to thousands of devices simultaneously, and hosted within a large virtual machine on a cloud provider. Instead, you can create a small, simple Web app that can connect to a single device, and run that Web app within a container that can be run thousands of times on a cloud provider. When a customer connects to their device, a new container is run on the cloud provider to start a unique copy of the Web app for that customer's device. Similarly, when a customer disconnects from their device, the cloud provider stops running the customer's container to free up system resources.

Note

IaaS can also use containers. In this case, the containers are run on the operating system within a virtual machine hosted on a cloud provider.

Unlike IaaS and PaaS, SaaS uses no virtual machines or containers. Instead, the SaaS cloud provider maintains all aspects of the network, hardware and operating system; it merely executes the Web app that you provide. This structure is shown in Figure 13-11.

Figure 13-11   A Sample SaaS structure

Note

Most cloud providers, such as Amazon Web Services and Microsoft Azure, allow you to choose between SaaS, PaaS, and IaaS.

Because Linux doesn't require expensive operating system licensing in addition to cloud provider costs, it's the operating system that is most commonly used by SaaS, PaaS, and IaaS.

The words "as a service" are commonly used for marketing purposes. For example, Mobile as a Service (MaaS) can be used to describe cloud apps that manage smartphone devices, whereas Database as a Service (DBaaS) can be used to describe database apps available in the cloud. These terms are collectively referred to as **Anything as a Service (XaaS)**, and represent specific uses of either SaaS, PaaS, or IaaS.

In addition to the storage needed for a virtual machine or container, many Web apps need to store large amounts of data on a cloud provider. One option is to store this data on a filesystem within a virtual hard disk file that is provided by the cloud provider; this type of storage is called **block storage**, and the cloud provider charges you based on the total amount of storage that you select for your virtual hard disk file. Because block storage is fast, it is often used for storing database files, but is normally associated with a single virtual machine or container only. Another storage option that most cloud providers offer is called **object storage**. Object storage allows Web apps to directly store objects, such as pictures, files, and video using an HTTP request that is sent to the cloud provider's object storage service. While object storage is slower than block storage, it is often less expensive as you are charged only for the space that is used by the objects you've stored. In addition, object storage can easily be shared by several virtual machines or containers. Web apps that need to store and share thousands of pictures, files, and video typically use object storage.

Note

Block storage is often referred to as a **persistent volume**, and object storage is often called **Binary Large Object (BLOB) storage**.

If you work as a Linux administrator within a cloud environment, you will need a solid understanding of how containers work, the process used to create virtual machines and containers within the cloud, and the process used to push new versions of Web apps to cloud providers for testing.

Working with Containers

Operating systems need to contain specialized software that allows containers to run. The most common container software used today is **Docker**, which consists of a Docker daemon and a series of operating system frameworks that support it. Nearly all Docker configuration is performed using the `docker` **command**, which is often referred to as the **Docker client** program.

Note

Docker is available for most operating systems, including Linux, UNIX, macOS, and Windows. On most Linux systems, you can install the docker package from an RPM, DPM, or Snappy repository to obtain Docker.

Docker provides an online repository of preconfigured container images that you can download and run on your system. This repository is called **Docker Hub**, and can be used to host public container images available to anyone, or private container images that are only available to your user account on Docker Hub.

Note

You can create a free Docker Hub user account at *hub.docker.com*.

To search Docker Hub for public container images, you can use the `docker search` command. For example, to search for a container image for Alpine Linux, you could use the following command:

```
[root@server1 ~]# docker search alpine | less
NAME                        DESCRIPTION
alpine                      A minimal Docker image based on Alpine Linux...
mhart/alpine-node           Minimal Node.js built on Alpine Linux
anapsix/alpine-java         Oracle Java 8 (and 7) with GLIBC 2.28 over A...
gliderlabs/alpine           Image based on Alpine Linux will help you wi...
frolvlad/alpine-glibc       Alpine Docker image with glibc (~12MB)
alpine/git                  A simple git container running in alpine li...
kiasaki/alpine-postgres     PostgreSQL docker image based on Alpine Linux
zzrot/alpine-caddy          Caddy Server Docker Container running on Alp...
easypi/alpine-arm           AlpineLinux for RaspberryPi
davidcaste/alpine-tomcat    Apache Tomcat 7/8 using Oracle Java 7/8 with...
byrnedo/alpine-curl         Alpine linux with curl installed and set :
[root@server1 ~]# _
```

The first result listed (alpine) is an official public Docker container image because it has a single name under the root of Docker Hub. Alternatively, the second result listed (mhart/alpine-node) is a container image called alpine-node hosted publicly by the user mhart. To download the latest version of the official Alpine Linux container image from Docker Hub, you can run the following command:

```
[root@server1 ~]# docker pull alpine
Using default tag: latest
latest: Pulling from library/alpine
4fe2ade4980c: Pull complete
Digest:
sha256:621c2f39f8133acb8e64023a94dbdf0d5ca81896102b9e57c0dc184cadaf5528
Status: Downloaded newer image for alpine:latest
[root@server1 ~]# _
```

Container images on Docker Hub can have different versions, much like files within a git repository. The docker pull alpine command is essentially the same as docker pull alpine:latest (latest version of the alpine container). However, you can instead pull older versions of a container; for example, docker pull alpine:3.6 would pull an older version (3.6) of the official Alpine Linux container. Downloaded container images are normally stored under the /var/lib/docker directory, or /var/snap/docker/common/var-lib-docker directory if you installed Docker using Snappy.

To view downloaded container images, you can use the docker images command. The following command indicates that the latest version of the Alpine Linux container image has been downloaded and is 4.41MB in size:

```
[root@server1 ~]# docker images
REPOSITORY    TAG         IMAGE ID         CREATED        SIZE
alpine        latest      196d12cf6ab1     6 weeks ago    4.41MB
[root@server1 ~]# _
```

After you have a container image downloaded on your system, you can run copies of it as many times as you wish. To run a copy of the Alpine Linux container image on your Linux operating system and have it execute the echo Hi command, you could run the following docker command:

```
[root@server1 ~]# docker run alpine echo Hi
Hi
[root@server1 ~]# _
```

After the echo Hi command has completed executing, Docker stops running the container, releasing any resources it used back to the operating system. You can view currently running containers using the docker ps command, as well as see any previously run containers using the docker ps -a command. The following output demonstrates that the Alpine Linux container we ran in the previous output is no longer running, executed the `echo Hi` command 5 seconds ago, and exited successfully (exit status = 0) 4 seconds ago:

```
[root@server1 ~]# docker ps
CONTAINER ID   IMAGE   COMMAND   CREATED   STATUS        PORTS NAMES
[root@server1 ~]# _
[root@server1 ~]# docker ps -a
CONTAINER ID   IMAGE   COMMAND   CREATED   STATUS        PORTS NAMES
18280cdaf3bb   alpine  "echo Hi" 5s ago   Exited(0)4s ago   nice_cray
[root@server1 ~]# _
```

Note from the previous output that a random name was generated for the container during execution (`nice_cray`) because a name was not specified with the docker run command. This name is not mandatory, because all containers automatically receive a unique container ID when they are run that can be used to identify them afterwards.

Recall that containers can be identified uniquely on the network, as well as provide a sandboxed Linux environment to the Web apps that they contain. To demonstrate this, the following commands run another copy of the Alpine Linux container image that interactively (`-it`) executes a shell (`sh`) to allow us to explore the filesystem, processes, host name, and IP configuration until we close the shell using the `exit` command:

```
[root@server1 ~]# docker run -it alpine sh
/ # ls
bin     etc    lib     mnt     root    sbin    sys     usr
dev     home   media   proc    run     srv     tmp     var
/ # ls /etc
TZ                init.d          mtab            resolv.conf
alpine-release    inittab         network         securetty
apk               issue           opt             services
conf.d            localtime       os-release      shadow
crontabs          logrotate.d     passwd          shells
fstab             modprobe.d      periodic        ssl
group             modules         profile         sysctl.conf
hostname          modules-load.d  profile.d       sysctl.d
hosts             motd            protocols       udhcpd.conf
/ # ps -ef
PID    USER     TIME   COMMAND
    1 root      0:00 sh
    8 root      0:00 ps -ef
/ # hostname
260d4f5b3308
```

```
/ # ifconfig
eth0      Link encap:Ethernet  HWaddr 02:42:AC:11:00:02
          inet addr:172.17.0.2  Bcast:172.17.255.255   Mask:255.255.0.0
          UP BROADCAST RUNNING MULTICAST  MTU:1500  Metric:1
          RX packets:10 errors:0 dropped:0 overruns:0 frame:0
          TX packets:0 errors:0 dropped:0 overruns:0 carrier:0
          collisions:0 txqueuelen:0
          RX bytes:836 (836.0 B)  TX bytes:0 (0.0 B)

lo        Link encap:Local Loopback
          inet addr:127.0.0.1  Mask:255.0.0.0
          UP LOOPBACK RUNNING  MTU:65536  Metric:1
          RX packets:0 errors:0 dropped:0 overruns:0 frame:0
          TX packets:0 errors:0 dropped:0 overruns:0 carrier:0
          collisions:0 txqueuelen:1000
          RX bytes:0 (0.0 B)  TX bytes:0 (0.0 B)
/ # exit
[root@server1 ~]# _
[root@server1 ~]# docker ps
CONTAINER ID   IMAGE  COMMAND    CREATED    STATUS              PORTS NAMES
[root@server1 ~]# docker ps -a
CONTAINER ID   IMAGE  COMMAND    CREATED    STATUS              PORTS NAMES
260d4f5b3308   alpine "sh"       20s ago    Exited(0)1s ago     misty_tom
18280cdaf3bb   alpine "echo Hi"  3m ago     Exited(0)3m ago     nice_cray
[root@server1 ~]# _
```

The docker ps -a command shown in the previous output lists both Alpine Linux containers that we have run previously, and the container ID is used as the host name for the container by default. Because the list of previously run containers may grow large over time, you can run the docker container prune command to automatically remove any stopped containers that you don't plan to rerun in the future.

Although each container maintains a unique IP address and host name, any Web apps that run within a container can be made available to the underlying operating system running the container on a unique port number. This simplifies the process of connecting to a Web app running on a cloud provider, because you only need to know the host name of the underlying operating system running the container, and the port number it is using for your particular copy of the Web app.

Say, for example, that you downloaded a private container image from Docker Hub called ex/webapp that is a copy of the Alpine Linux container with the Apache Web server and Javascript framework installed, as well as a Javascript Web app (app.js) that is designed to manage a customer's IoT device across the Internet on port 80. You could then configure a user-accessible website to automatically run a copy of this container image for each customer that wishes to manage their IoT device, and map port 80 for the associated Web app to a unique port on the underlying operating system for each customer. In the following output, three copies of the ex/webapp container are run; each one is named for the customer (cust1, cust2, and cust3), and port 80 is mapped to a unique port number on the underlying operating system for each customer (36001, 36002, and 36003):

```
[root@server1 ~]# docker run -d -p 36001:80 --name cust1
ex/webapp
436be848fefd0da097eb711375a8dbded01d05c979ca944f14dd8ac9ab3fc585
[root@server1 ~]# docker run -d -p 36002:80 --name cust2 ex/webapp
cfcb44e2d4ce2d1fefd6ba63e051d0a4691b22cae3eb96a01ef9e532fe5fb96e
[root@server1 ~]# docker run -d -p 36003:80 --name cust3 ex/webapp
55a8677432743667a43d78ac477b654cee0a823a2c1084d85c0e8d20a827c851
[root@server1 ~]# _
[root@server1 ~]# docker ps
CONTAINER ID   IMAGE       COMMAND     CREATED   STATUS   PORTS          NAMES
55a867743274   ex/webapp   "app.js"    37s ago   Up 36s   36003->80/tcp  cust3
cfcb44e2d4ce   ex/webapp   "app.js"    44s ago   Up 43s   36002->80/tcp  cust2
436be848fefd   ex/webapp   "app.js"    51s ago   Up 50s   36001->80/tcp  cust1
[root@server1 ~]# _
```

The -d option of the docker run command shown in the previous output detaches the container from your terminal and keeps the container running until you stop it using the docker stop command. For example, the docker stop cust2 command would stop executing the cust2 container and release the resources it used to the underlying operating system; this could be triggered automatically when the cust2 logs off of the website used to manage their IoT device. Similarly, when cust2 logs into the website at a later time to manage their IoT device, the website could trigger the docker start cust2 command to run the container again.

You can also access a shell within a running container using the docker exec command. For example, docker exec -it cfcb44e2d4ce sh would connect to the cust2 container (using the container ID) and run a shell interactively for you to make configuration changes.

> ### Note ✐
>
> You can use the --help option with any docker command to obtain available options and usage information. For example, docker --help will display general options and usage for the docker command, and docker run --help will display options and usage for the docker run command.

Creating Containers and Virtual Machines within the Cloud

Because cloud providers can run thousands of containers and virtual machines within their data center, it is important to automate the process of creating new containers or virtual machines. This is often called **build automation** and involves copying a container or virtual machine template and then customizing it to suit your needs.

Container templates are often container images hosted on Docker Hub; the PaaS cloud provider pulls the container images that you specify from Docker Hub and runs them on the operating system. Most IaaS cloud providers supply several preconfigured virtual machine templates for you to choose from, but you can modify them or replace them with ones that you have created. Each virtual machine template is comprised of a virtual hard disk file (containing a preinstalled operating system) alongside one or more files that define the virtual machine settings, such as memory and virtual hardware required. Most virtual machine settings for cloud hosts are stored in **Open Virtualization Format (OVF)** files that use a `.ovf` extension.

> **Note**
>
> You can combine virtual hard disk and virtual machine settings files into a single file called a **virtual appliance** that can be easily imported within an IaaS cloud provider. A common virtual appliance format is **Open Virtualization Archive (OVA)**, which combines a virtual hard disk file and `.ovf` file into a single tar archive file that uses a `.ova` extension.
>
> Rather than copying a virtual machine template, you instead can choose to manually install an operating system to a virtual hard disk file from installation source files on an IaaS cloud provider.

To customize a copy of a container image or virtual machine template that is running on a cloud provider, you can use automated **configuration management (CM)** software. CM software allows you to add apps, modify existing configuration settings, or perform administrative tasks required for a specific container or virtual machine, or a series of related containers or virtual machines. The containers and virtual machines managed by CM software are collectively called the **inventory**, and each individual container or virtual machine is called an **inventory member**. Many CM software packages are available that you can install on a server to manage your inventory; each one provides different methods for configuring inventory members. Most CM software packages require that software agents are installed on each inventory member. However, some CM software packages are **agentless**; they connect to inventory members using SSH to perform all configuration management. Moreover, some CM software requires that you define the individual procedures that must be executed on inventory members within a script file (called **imperative configuration**), whereas other CM software only requires that you specify the attributes (e.g., apps and settings) that the inventory members must have within a configuration file (called **declarative configuration**).

Following is an example YAML file that provides a declarative configuration for three inventory members (server1, server2, and server3) that can be used by CM software to install Apache (httpd) using yum, add a home page (index.html), start Apache, create a new file (/tmp/httplog) using touch, and add a new user named fred that receives a BASH shell upon login:

```
---
- name: Sample Declarative Configuration
  hosts: server1,server2,server3
  become: true
  tasks:
  - name: Install Apache
    yum:
      name: httpd
      state: present


  - name: Add Home Page
    template:
      src: https://sample.com/source/index.html
      dest: /var/www/html/index.html
  - name: Start Apache
    service:
      name: httpd
      state: started
  - name: Create file
    file:
      path: /tmp/httplog
      state: touch
  - name: Create user
    user:
      name: fred
      shell: /bin/bash
```

Note

Some common CM software examples include Puppet, Chef, and Ansible. Puppet provides agent-based declarative configuration, Chef provides agent-based imperative configuration, and Ansible provides agentless declarative configuration.

The terms **infrastructure automation** and **Infrastructure as Code (IaC)** are often used to describe the practice of using build automation and CM to provide a functional cloud infrastructure.

Many CM software packages can also be configured to copy and run the appropriate container or virtual machine template on a cloud provider before customizing the container or virtual machine; this functionality is often referred to as **orchestration** as it involves the coordination of multiple automated tasks.

Some alternatives to CM are supported by many cloud providers for virtual machines. One alternative used on modern Linux distributions is **cloud-init**, which reads YAML configuration files to add apps, modify existing configuration settings, or perform administrative tasks at boot time. Many cloud providers, such as Amazon Web Services, allow you to customize a virtual machine template for a Linux distribution that uses cloud-init by providing a custom cloud-init configuration file; when the virtual machine is started, the cloud-init configuration file is automatically applied.

Another alternative to CM is **Kickstart**, which is a component of the Anaconda installation program used by many Linux distributions. Kickstart is only run during the installation of the operating system, and reads the entries within a Kickstart configuration file to set system configuration. Many cloud providers allow you to supply a Kickstart configuration file when creating a new virtual machine of a distribution that uses Anaconda. In this case, the virtual machine is not copied from a template; instead, it is installed from an installation ISO image using the system configuration specified within the Kickstart configuration file.

Note

Ubuntu Server 18 uses cloud-init, and stores cloud-init configuration files under the /etc/cloud directory.

Fedora Linux uses the Anaconda installation program. Following an installation of Fedora Linux, a sample Kickstart configuration file is written to /root/anaconda-ks.cfg that contains the configuration settings chosen during the installation program.

Understanding Continuous Deployment

Recall that most cloud providers are used to host Web apps for an organization within a container or virtual machine; these Web apps are created by developers within the organization and revised on a continual basis to fix bugs and incorporate new features. While developers create new versions of the Web app on their workstation, they need to test these new versions on the cloud provider to ensure that they work as expected before replacing the existing cloud-hosted Web app with the new version. As part of the development process, new versions of the Web app may need to be tested on a cloud provider several times per day. Each new version will require that a new container or virtual machine be created with the correct settings for the Web app using build automation and CM software. Additional software may also be required to move the Web app from the developer workstation to the new container or virtual machine on the cloud provider, as well as ensure that the Web app is ready for execution. This entire process is called a **continuous deployment (CD)** workflow, and the Linux administrators that manage this workflow are called **devops** because they are system operators (ops) that support Web app development (dev).

Because you can use many different technologies and tools to build software, you can choose from hundreds of available software packages when creating CD workflows. Figure 13-12 illustrates a sample workflow that allows developers to push new versions of a Java Web app to virtual machines within the cloud.

Figure 13-12   A sample CD workflow

The first step shown in Figure 13-12 involves developers pushing a new version of their Java source code to a Git server. Next, Jenkins software running on a cloud provider obtains the new version of the Java source code (step 2) and compiles it into binary form using Maven software (step 3). This compiled Java Web app is then sent to Ansible software (step 4), which creates a new virtual machine for testing using build automation and CM, as well as executes the Java Web app on it.

At this point, the new version of the Web app is now running on a server in the cloud and can be tested. If this new version doesn't work as expected, the virtual machine is removed and the whole process is repeated for another new version of the Web app. However, if this new version of the Web app works as expected, the underlying virtual machine used to test the Web app will replace the publicly accessible virtual machine running the old version of the Web app, and customers on the Internet will immediately have access to the new version.

Not all CD workflows are as complex as the one shown in Figure 13-12. For smaller Web apps, CD functionality may be provided by the Git server. One example of this is GitLab.com, which provides a CD feature called GitLab runners to provide build automation and CM for Web apps that are created by developers. To use GitLab runners, you must first create a .gitlab-ci.yml file that lists a container image from Docker Hub, CM settings for the container, and the Web app commands that must be executed. Next, you can configure the GitLab runner to execute the Web app on the appropriate cloud provider. This simplified CD workflow is shown in Figure 13-13.

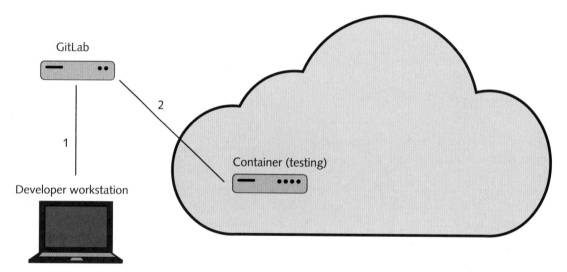

Figure 13-13 A GitLab workflow

Chapter Summary

- DHCP, DNS, and NTP are called infrastructure services as they provide network-related services to other computers on the network.

- DHCP servers lease other computers an IPv4 or IPv6 configuration. The two most common DHCP servers are dhcpd and udhcpd.

- DNS servers provide name resolution services for other computers on the network. Each DNS server can contain several zones that store resource records for names that can be resolved.

- Linux computers can use the system time stored within the computer BIOS or obtain their time from an NTP server across the network. NTP servers obtain their time from other NTP servers in a hierarchical organization that consists of several strata. The two most common NTP servers are ntpd and chronyd.

- The Apache server shares Web pages from its document root directory to computers on the network using the HTTP protocol.

- Samba can be used to share files to Linux, UNIX, macOS, and Windows computers using the SMB protocol.

- NFS can be used to share files amongst Linux, UNIX, macOS, and Windows systems that have NFS server or client software installed. NFS clients access files on NFS servers by mounting shared directories.

- FTP can be used to share files to any computer that has an FTP client utility and is the most common method for file sharing on the Internet. The most common FTP daemon on modern Linux systems is vsftpd.

- Email servers deliver email messages from one user to another on your system. They also accept new email messages from users and relay it to other email servers on the Internet for delivery. The most common email server used on Linux systems is Postfix.

- Many large applications store their data within databases on a database server. These applications use SQL statements to add, manipulate, and retrieve information within a database across the network. PostgreSQL is a common database server that provides advanced configuration and utilities.

- Servers on the Internet that host Web apps and the associated data are collectively called the cloud, and the data centers that host these servers are called cloud providers. Cloud providers typically provide block or object storage to store Web app data.

- SaaS cloud providers run Web apps directly, PaaS cloud providers run Web apps within a container, and IaaS cloud providers run Web apps within a virtual machine. Docker is the most common container software used within cloud environments.

- Build automation and CM software are typically used to create containers and virtual machines within cloud environments.

- Developers regularly push new versions of their Web app to a cloud provider for testing using a process called CD. Linux administrators that configure CD software are called devops.

Key Terms

ab **(Apache benchmark)**
  command
agentless
Anything as a Service
  (XaaS)
apachectl **command**

Berkeley Internet Name
  Domain (BIND)
Binary Large Object (BLOB)
  storage
BIND configuration utility
block storage

build automation
BusyBox DHCP daemon
  (udhcpd)
Chrony NTP daemon
  (chronyd)
chronyc **command**

cloud-init
configuration management
 (CM)
continuous deployment (CD)
database
Date & Time utility
declarative configuration
devop
DHCP daemon (dhcpd)
directive
DNS cache file
Docker
Docker client
`docker` command
Docker Hub
document root
`dumpleases` command
exports
field
File Transfer Protocol (FTP)
forward lookup
`ftp` command
imperative configuration
Infrastructure as Code
 (IaC)
infrastructure automation
infrastructure services
inventory

inventory member
iterative query
jitter
Kickstart
`mail` command
`mailq` command
master DNS server
NetBIOS
Network File System
 (NFS)
`newaliases` command
`nmblookup` command
NTP daemon (ntpd)
`ntpdate` command
`ntpq` command
object storage
offset
Open Virtualization
 Archive (OVA)
Open Virtualization
 Format (OVF)
orchestration
persistent volume
Postfix
PostgreSQL
PostgreSQL utility
primary DNS server
`psql` command

record
recursive query
relational database
resource records
reverse lookup
sandboxing
secondary DNS server
Secure FTP (SFTP)
Server Message Blocks
 (SMB)
`sftp` command
`showmount` command
slave DNS server
`smbclient` command
`smbpasswd` command
SQL server
strata
Structured Query Language
 (SQL)
table
`testparm` command
Time-To-Live (TTL)
Very Secure FTP daemon
 (vsftpd)
virtual appliance
Web page hit
zone
zone transfer

Review Questions

1. PaaS cloud providers host sandboxed Web apps using containers for scalability. True or False?

2. Which file stores the Apache configuration in Fedora 28?
   a. /etc/apache2/httpd.conf
   b. /etc/apache2.conf
   c. /etc/httpd.conf
   d. /etc/httpd/conf/httpd.conf

3. Which DNS resource record is an alias to other records?
   a. A
   b. AAAA
   c. CNAME
   d. NS

4. You can purchase object storage from a cloud provider to provide persistent filesystem-based storage. True or False?

5. Which command can be used to connect to check the /etc/samba/smb.conf file for syntax errors?
   a. `apachectl`
   b. `sambactl`
   c. `testparm`
   d. `psql`

6. You have modified the /etc/aliases file to include a new email alias. However, when you send email to the alias, it cannot be delivered. What should you do?
   a. Add the line to the /etc/aliases.db file instead.
   b. Run the `newaliases` command.
   c. Restart the Postfix daemon.
   d. Log out of the system and then log back into the system and resend the email.

7. Which command within the command-line FTP utility can be used to change the current directory on the local computer?
   a. `cd`
   b. `dir`
   c. `lcd`
   d. `get`

8. Which command can be used to list containers that are currently running on the operating system only?
   a. `docker ps`
   b. `docker ps -a`
   c. `docker run`
   d. `docker exec`

9. Which of the following must you perform to share a directory using NFS? (Choose all that apply.)
   a. Edit the /etc/exports file.
   b. Mount the directory to the /etc/exports directory using the `mount` command.
   c. Run the `exportfs -a` command.
   d. Start or restart the NFS daemons.

10. DHCP clients send a DHCPREQUEST packet when they require a new IP configuration. True or False?

11. Which command can be used to connect to a remote Windows share called data on the server called fileserver?
   a. `smbclient -L fileserver:data`
   b. `smbclient -L //fileserver/data`
   c. `smbclient //fileserver/data`
   d. `smbclient \\fileserver\data`

12. The lines within the Apache configuration file that modify the functionality of the Apache are called directives. True or False?

13. Which of the following can be used to create a database within PostgreSQL? (Choose all that apply.)
   a. the CREATE DATABASE statement within the PostgreSQL utility.
   b. the ADD DATABASE statement within the PostgreSQL utility.
   c. the `adddb` command.
   d. the `createdb` command.

14. Stratum 1 NTP servers do not obtain time information from other NTP servers. True or False?

15. What must you do to transform your computer into a DNS server? (Choose all that apply.)
   a. Create zone files.
   b. Create resource records for DNS lookups.
   c. Create NIS maps.
   d. Run the name daemon (named).

16. What directory are you placed in when you log in as the anonymous user to an Ubuntu Server 18 FTP server?
   a. /srv/ftp
   b. /var/www/ftp
   c. /home/anonymous
   d. /var/ftp/pub

17. Chronyd is an NTP daemon that offers a faster response time compared to the ntpd daemon. True or False?

18. Which term is used to describe the process of pushing new versions of a Web app to a cloud provider for testing?
    a. IaC
    b. Build automation
    c. CD
    d. Infrastructure automation

19. Which command can you use to synchronize ntpd with an NTP time source?
    a. `ntp`
    b. `ntpquery`
    c. `ntpq`
    d. `hwclock`

20. Mary is a system administrator in your organization. She has recently made changes to the DHCP configuration file, but the DHCP daemon does not seem to recognize the new changes. What should she do?
    a. Log in as the root user and reedit the configuration file.
    b. Run the `dhcpconf` command to edit the configuration file.
    c. Restart the DHCP daemon.
    d. Restart the xinetd daemon.

Hands-On Projects

These projects should be completed in the order given. The hands-on projects presented in this chapter should take a total of three hours to complete. The requirements for this lab include:

- A computer with Fedora Linux installed according to Hands-On Project 2-1, Ubuntu Server 18 Linux installed according to Hands-On Project 6-1, and Ubuntu Server 14 Linux installed according to Hands-On Project 6-7.

Project 13-1

In this hands-on project, you configure the DHCP daemon on your Fedora Linux virtual machine and test your configuration by obtaining an IPv4 address from your Ubuntu Server 14 Linux virtual machine.

1. Boot your Fedora Linux virtual machine. After your Linux system has been loaded, switch to a command-line terminal (tty5) by pressing **Ctrl+Alt+F5** and log in to the terminal using the user name of **root** and the password of **LINUXrocks!**.

2. At the command prompt, type **dnf install dhcp** and press **Enter** to install the DHCP server daemon. Type **y** and press **Enter** when prompted to continue the installation.

3. Edit the **/etc/dhcp/dhcpd.conf** file with a text editor by adding the following lines:

```
default-lease-time 72000;
option routers IP_address_of_your_class_default_gateway;
option domain-name-servers IP_address_of_your_class_DNS_server;
subnet class_network netmask subnet_mask {
    range class_network.50 class_network.100;
}
```

For example, if your class uses the 192.168.1 network (subnet mask 255.255.255.0) and a default gateway and DNS server of 192.168.1.254, you would add the following lines:

```
default-lease-time 72000;
option routers 192.168.1.254;
option domain-name-servers 192.168.1.254;
subnet 192.168.1.0 netmask 255.255.255.0 {
    range 192.168.1.50 192.168.1.100;
}
```

When finished, save your changes and quit the editor.

4. At the command prompt, type `systemctl start dhcpd.service` and press **Enter** to start the DHCP daemon.

5. At the command prompt, type `ps -ef | grep dhcpd` and press **Enter** to ensure that the DHCP daemon has loaded successfully. If the DHCP daemon is not listed, check for errors in your /etc/dhcp/dhcpd.conf file and repeat the previous step.

6. At the command prompt, type `firewall-cmd --add-service dhcp` and press **Enter** to allow DHCP traffic through the firewall on your Fedora Linux virtual machine. Firewalls will be discussed in Chapter 14.

7. Next, boot your Ubuntu Server 14 Linux virtual machine and log into tty1 using the user name of **root** and the password of **LINUXrocks!**.

8. At the command prompt, type `dhclient eth0` and press **Enter** to request a DHCP address.

9. Return to your Fedora Linux virtual machine. At the command prompt, type `cat /var/lib/dhcpd/dhcpd.leases` and press **Enter**. Note the line that details the lease information.

10. At the command prompt, type `systemctl stop dhcpd.service` and press **Enter** to stop the DHCP daemon. Next, type `exit` and press **Enter** to log out of your shell.

11. Return to your Ubuntu Server 14 virtual machine. At the command prompt, type `poweroff` and press **Enter** to shut down the system. What IP configuration will be configured on your Ubuntu Server 14 Linux virtual machine when it is powered on again and why?

Project 13-2

In this hands-on project, you configure and test the DNS daemon on your Fedora Linux virtual machine.

1. On your Fedora Linux virtual machine, switch to a command-line terminal (tty5) by pressing **Ctrl+Alt+F5** and log in to the terminal using the user name of **root** and the password of **LINUXrocks!**.

2. At the command prompt, type `dnf install bind` and press **Enter** to install BIND (the named daemon). Type `y` and press **Enter** when prompted to continue the installation.

3. Create and edit the **/var/named/example.com.dns** file with a text editor by adding the following lines:

```
$ORIGIN example.com.
$TTL 86400
@ SOA     dns1.example.com. hostmaster.example.com. (
      1           ; serial
      21600       ; refresh after 6 hours
      3600        ; retry after 1 hour
      604800      ; expire after 1 week
      86400 )     ; minimum TTL of 1 day
;
;
NS dns1.example.com.
dns1   A   192.168.1.1
;
;
@ MX   10 mail.example.com.
mail   A   192.168.1.2
;
;
server1    A      192.168.1.3
server2    A      192.168.1.4
ftp CNAME server1.example.com.
www CNAME server2.example.com.
;
;
```

When finished, save your changes and quit the editor.

4. At the command prompt, type `chgrp named /var/named/example.com.dns` and press **Enter** to change the group ownership of the example.com.dns zone file. Next, type `chmod 640 /var/named/example.com.dns` and press **Enter** to allow named to read the contents of the example.com.dns zone file.

5. Edit the **/etc/named.conf** file with a text editor. Under the line that reads:

```
        allow-query { localhost; };
```

add the following line:

```
        forwarders { IP_address_of_your_class_DNS_server; };
```

6. At the bottom of the file, add the following lines that identify your example.com.dns zone file:

```
zone "example.com" IN {
  type master;
  file "example.com.dns";
    allow-update { none; };
};
```

When finished, save your changes and quit the editor.

7. At the command prompt, type `systemctl start named.service` and press **Enter** to start the DNS name daemon.

8. Edit the /etc/resolv.conf file with a text editor and remove any existing nameserver lines. Add the line `nameserver 127.0.0.1` to ensure that your Linux computer uses the local DNS server daemon for name resolution. Save your changes and quit the editor when finished.

9. At the command prompt, type `host server1.example.com` and press **Enter**. Was the name resolved successfully?

10. At the command prompt, type `host ftp.example.com` and press **Enter**. Was the name resolved successfully?

11. At the command prompt, type `nslookup server2.example.com` and press **Enter**. Was the name resolved successfully?

12. At the command prompt, type `nslookup www.example.com` and press **Enter**. Was the name resolved successfully?

13. At the command prompt, type `dig @localhost example.com ANY` and press **Enter**. Are your resources records returned successfully?

14. At the command prompt, type `host www.linux.org` and press **Enter**. Explain why the name was resolved successfully.

15. At the command prompt, type `less /var/named/named.ca` and press **Enter**. View the entries. What do these entries represent?

16. Type `exit` and press **Enter** to log out of your shell.

Project 13-3

In this hands-on project, you install and explore the NTP daemon on your Ubuntu Server 14 Linux virtual machine as well as explore the Chrony NTP daemon on your Fedora Linux virtual machine.

1. Boot your Ubuntu Server 14 Linux virtual machine and log into tty1 using the user name of **root** and the password of **LINUXrocks!**.

2. At the command prompt, type `apt-get install ntpd` and press **Enter**. Press **y** when prompted to install the NTP daemon. Next, type `ps -ef | grep ntpd` and press **Enter** to verify that the NTP daemon is running.

3. At the command prompt, type the `less /etc/ntp.conf` command. What lines indicate that your system is configured as an NTP client? Is your system configured as an NTP server? If not, what line could you modify to allow computers on your network to query your NTP server?

4. At the command prompt, type `service ntp stop` and press **Enter** to stop the NTP daemon.

5. At the command prompt, type `ntpdate -u 0.ubuntu.pool.ntp.org` and press **Enter** to synchronize your clock with the first time server listed in /etc/ntp.conf. Repeat this command several times until the offset is very low.

6. At the command prompt, type `service ntp start` and press **Enter** to start the NTP daemon.

7. At the command prompt, type `ntpq -p` and press **Enter** to view information about the time servers that you are synchronizing with (peers).

8. Type `exit` and press **Enter** to log out of your shell.

9. On your Fedora Linux virtual machine, switch to a graphical terminal by pressing **Ctrl+Alt+F1** and log in to the GNOME desktop with the user name **user1** and the password of **LINUXrocks!**.

10. Navigate to **Activities**, **Show Applications**, **Settings**, **Details**, **Date & Time**. Is time information obtained automatically from the Internet using NTP by default? Close the Settings window when finished.

11. Navigate to **Activities**, **Show Applications**, **Utilities**, **Terminal** to open a graphical terminal application.

12. At the command prompt, type `su - root` and press **Enter**. Supply the password of `LINUXrocks!` and press **Enter** when prompted to switch to the root user.

13. At the command prompt, type `less /etc/chrony.conf` and press **Enter**. What lines indicate that your system is configured as an NTP client? Is your system configured as an NTP server? If not, what line could you modify to allow computers on your network to query your NTP server?

14. At the command prompt, type `chronyc sources -v` and press **Enter** to view information about the time servers that you are synchronizing with (peers).

15. Close the terminal application and log out of the GNOME desktop when finished.

Project 13-4

In this hands-on project, you configure the Apache Web server on your Fedora Linux virtual machine and test daemon permissions to files on the system.

1. On your Fedora Linux virtual machine, switch to a command-line terminal (tty5) by pressing **Ctrl+Alt+F5** and log in to the terminal using the user name of **root** and the password of **LINUXrocks!**.

2. At the command prompt, type `dnf install httpd` and press **Enter**. Press **y** when prompted to complete the installation of the Apache Web server.

3. At the command prompt, type `grep DocumentRoot /etc/httpd/conf/httpd.conf` and press **Enter**. What is the document root directory?

4. At the command prompt, type `grep DirectoryIndex /etc/httpd/conf/httpd.conf` and press **Enter**. What file(s) will automatically be handed out by the Apache daemon from the document root directory?

5. At the command prompt, type `grep "User " /etc/httpd/conf/httpd.conf` and press **Enter**. What user does the Apache daemon run as locally?

6. At the command prompt, type `grep "Group " /etc/httpd/conf/httpd.conf` and press **Enter**. What group does the Apache daemon run as locally?

7. At the command prompt, type `apachectl configtest` and press **Enter**. Are there any syntax errors within your /etc/httpd/conf/httpd.conf file?

8. Edit the `/var/www/html/index.html` file with a text editor such as vi. Are there any entries? Add the following lines:

```
<html>
<body>
<h1>My sample website</h1>
</body>
</html>
```

When finished, save your changes and quit the editor.

9. At the command prompt, type `systemctl start httpd.service` and press **Enter** to start the Apache Web server.

10. At the command prompt, type `curl http://127.0.0.1/` and press **Enter**. Was your Web page successfully returned by Apache?

11. At the command prompt, type `ab -n 1000 http://127.0.0.1/` and press **Enter**. How long did Apache take to respond to 1000 requests?

12. At the command prompt, type `less /etc/httpd/logs/access_log` and press **Enter**. How many Web page hits are shown? Explain.

13. At the command prompt, type `firewall-cmd --add-service http` and press **Enter** to allow inbound HTTP connections in your firewall.

14. On your Windows host, open a Web browser and navigate to the location **http://IPaddress** (where *IPaddress* is the IP address of your Fedora Linux virtual machine). Is your Web page displayed?

15. Return to tty5 on your Fedora Linux virtual machine. At the command prompt, type `ls -l /var/www/html/index.html` and press **Enter**. Who owns the file? What is the group owner? What category do the Apache daemons use when they run as the user apache and group apache?

16. At the command prompt, type `chmod 640 /var/www/html/index.html` and press **Enter**.

17. In the Web browser on your Windows host, refresh the Web page for **http://IPaddress** (where *IPaddress* is the IP address of your Fedora Linux virtual machine). What error do you receive and why?

18. Return to tty5 on your Fedora Linux virtual machine. At the command prompt, type `chmod 644 /var/www/html/index.html` and press **Enter**.

19. In the Web browser on your Windows host, refresh the Web page for **http://*IPaddress*** (where *IPaddress* is the IP address of your Fedora Linux virtual machine). Does your page display properly now? Close the Web browser on your Windows host.

20. Return to tty5 on your Fedora Linux virtual machine, type `poweroff`, and press **Enter** to shut down your virtual machine.

Project 13-5

In this hands-on project, you configure and test Samba file sharing on your Ubuntu Server 18 Linux virtual machine.

1. Boot your Ubuntu Server 18 Linux virtual machine, log into tty1 using the user name of **root** and the password of **LINUXrocks!**.

2. At the command prompt, type `apt install samba` and press **Enter** to install the Samba file-sharing daemons.

3. Edit the **/etc/samba/smb.conf** file with the vi text editor. Spend a few minutes examining the comments within this file to understand the available Samba configuration options. Under the Share Definitions section, notice that the only two shares configured by default are the [printers] share (which shares all printers to Windows hosts) and the hidden [print$] share (which shares print drivers to Windows hosts).

4. Add the following line underneath the [global] line in this file, where *hostname* is the host name configured on your Ubuntu Server Linux virtual machine:

```
netbios name = hostname
```

5. Uncomment/modify the following section that shares out all home directories to users who authenticate successfully:

```
[homes]
comment = Home Directories
browseable = yes
read only = no
```

6. Next, add the following share definition to the bottom of the file to share out the /etc directory to all users as read-only:

```
[etc]
comment = The etc directory
path = /etc
browseable = yes
guest ok = yes
read only = yes
```

7. When finished, save your changes and quit the editor.

8. At the command prompt, type `testparm` and press **Enter**. Were any syntax errors reported within /etc/samba/smb.conf? Press **Enter** to view your Samba configuration.

9. At the command prompt, type `systemctl restart smbd` and press **Enter** to restart the Samba daemons.

10. At the command prompt, type `smbpasswd -a root` and press **Enter**. When prompted, supply the password **LINUXrocks!**. Repeat the same password when prompted a second time.

11. At the command prompt, type `smbclient -L 127.0.0.1` and press **Enter**. Supply your Samba password of **LINUXrocks!** when prompted. Do you see your shared home directory? Do you see any printer shares?

12. At the command prompt, type `smbclient //127.0.0.1/root` and press **Enter**. Supply your Samba password of **LINUXrocks!** when prompted.

13. At the smb:\> prompt, type `dir` and press **Enter**. Are you in your home directory?

14. At the smb:\> prompt, type `exit` and press **Enter**.

15. At the command prompt type `poweroff` and press **Enter** to shut down your virtual machine.

16. On your Windows host, add a local user account called **root** with a password of **LINUXrocks!** that has administrative ability on your PC. Next, log in to your Windows host as the root user and start your Ubuntu Server 18 Linux virtual machine.

17. After your Ubuntu Server 18 Linux virtual machine has started, open the Run dialog box on your Windows host, type **\\IPaddress**, and press **Enter**. What shared directories and printers do you see and why? Are you able to copy files from your Windows host to your home directory share? Are you able to copy files from your Windows host to your /etc directory share? Explain.

18. Close the File Explorer window when finished.

Project 13-6

In this hands-on project, you export the /etc directory using NFS on your Ubuntu Server 18 Linux virtual machine and access it from your Fedora Linux virtual machine.

1. On your Ubuntu Server 18 Linux virtual machine, log into tty1 using the user name of **root** and the password of **LINUXrocks!**.

2. At the command prompt, type `apt install nfs-kernel-server` and press **Enter** to install NFS.

3. Edit the /etc/exports file with the vi text editor and add a line that reads:

   ```
   /etc    *(rw)
   ```

   When finished, save your changes and quit the editor.

4. At the command prompt, type `exportfs -a` and press **Enter**. Next, type `systemctl restart nfs-kernel-server` and press **Enter** to restart NFS.

5. Type `exit` and press **Enter** to log out of your shell.

6. Boot your Fedora Linux virtual machine. After your Linux system has been loaded, switch to a command-line terminal (tty5) by pressing **Ctrl+Alt+F5** and log in to the terminal using the user name of **root** and the password of **LINUXrocks!**.

7. At the command prompt, type `dnf install nfs-utils` and press **Enter**. Press `y` when prompted to complete the installation of NFS.

8. At the command prompt, type `mount -t nfs IPaddress:/etc /mnt` (where *IPaddress* is the IP address of your Ubuntu Server Linux virtual machine) and press **Enter**.

9. At the command prompt, type `df -hT` and press **Enter**. What is mounted to the /mnt directory?

10. At the command prompt, type `ls -F /mnt` and press **Enter**. What directory are you observing? Type `cat /mnt/issue` at the command prompt and press **Enter**. Can you tell that the issue file is on your Ubuntu Server Linux virtual machine?

11. At the command prompt, type `umount /mnt` and press **Enter** to unmount the NFS filesystem.

12. Type `exit` and press **Enter** to log out of your shell.

Project 13-7

In this hands-on project, you install and configure the Very Secure FTP daemon on your Ubuntu Server 18 Linux virtual machine, as well as transfer files using FTP and SFTP.

1. On your Ubuntu Server Linux virtual machine, log into tty1 using the user name of **root** and the password of **LINUXrocks!**.

2. At the command prompt, type `apt install vsftpd` and press **Enter** to install vsftpd.

3. At the command prompt, type `cp /etc/hosts ~user1/file1 ; cp /etc/hosts ~user1/file2 ; cp /etc/hosts /srv/ftp/file3` and press **Enter** to create two copies of the file /etc/hosts within user1's home directory called file1 and file2 as well as a copy of the file /etc/hosts within the /srv/ftp directory called file3.

4. Edit the /etc/vsftpd.conf file using the vi editor. Take a few moments to read the options in this file and the comments that describe each option. Next, uncomment the `write_enable=YES` line, modify the anonymous_enable line to read `anonymous_enable=YES`, save your changes, and quit the vi editor.

5. At the command prompt, type `systemctl restart vsftpd` and press **Enter** to restart vsftpd.

6. At the command prompt, type `ftp localhost` and press **Enter**. Log in as **user1** using the password **LINUXrocks!** when prompted.

7. At the ftp> prompt, type `dir` and press **Enter** to list the contents of the /home/user1 directory.

8. At the ftp> prompt, type `lcd /etc` and press **Enter** to change the current working directory on the FTP client to /etc.

9. At the ftp> prompt, type `put issue` and press **Enter** to upload the issue file to the remote FTP server.

10. At the ftp> prompt, type `dir` and press **Enter** to list the contents of the /home/user1 directory. Was the issue file uploaded successfully?

11. At the ftp> prompt, type `lcd /` and press **Enter** to change the current working directory on the FTP client to /.

12. At the ftp> prompt, type `get issue` and press **Enter** to download the issue file to the / directory on the local computer.

13. At the ftp> prompt, type `mget file*` and press **Enter** to download file1 and file2 to the / directory on the local computer.

14. At the ftp> prompt, type `help` and press **Enter** to list the commands available within the FTP client program.

15. At the ftp> prompt, type `bye` and press **Enter** to exit the FTP client program.

16. At the command prompt, type `ls /` and press **Enter**. Were the issue file, file1, and file2 downloaded to the / directory successfully?

17. At the command prompt, type `ftp localhost` and press **Enter**. Log in as **anonymous** using the password **nothing** when prompted (the actual password is not relevant for the anonymous user; you could use any password).

18. At the ftp> prompt, type `dir` and press **Enter** to list the contents of the /var/ftp directory.

19. At the ftp> prompt, type `lcd /` and press **Enter** to change the current working directory on the FTP client to /.

20. At the ftp> prompt, type `get file3` and press **Enter** to download the hosts file to the / directory on the local computer.

21. At the ftp> prompt, type `bye` and press **Enter** to exit the FTP client program.

22. At the command prompt, type `ls /` and press **Enter**. Was file3 downloaded to the / directory successfully?

23. At the command prompt, type `ftp localhost` and press **Enter**. Log in as the **root** user and the password **LINUXrocks!** when prompted. Were you able to log in? At the ftp> prompt, type `bye` and press **Enter** to exit the FTP client program.

24. Edit the /etc/ftpusers file using the vi editor and remove the following line:

    ```
    root
    ```

    When finished, save your changes and quit the editor.

25. At the command prompt, type `ftp localhost` and press **Enter**. Log in as the **root** user with the password **LINUXrocks!** when prompted.

26. At the ftp> prompt, type `dir` and press **Enter** to list the contents of the /root directory.

27. At the ftp> prompt, type `bye` and press **Enter** to exit the FTP client program.

28. At the command prompt, type `sftp user1@localhost` and press **Enter**. Type `yes` when prompted to accept the SSH user keys and then supply the password **LINUXrocks!** when prompted.

29. At the sftp> prompt, type `dir` and press **Enter** to list the contents of the /home/user1 directory.

30. At the sftp> prompt, type `lcd /etc` and press **Enter** to change the current working directory on the SFTP client to /etc.

31. At the sftp> prompt, type `put fstab` and press **Enter** to upload the fstab file to the remote SFTP server.

32. At the sftp> prompt, type `dir` and press **Enter** to list the contents of the /home/user1 directory. Was the fstab file uploaded successfully?

33. At the sftp> prompt, type **help** and press **Enter** to list the commands available within the SFTP client program.

34. At the sftp> prompt, type **bye** and press **Enter** to exit the SFTP client program.

35. At the command prompt, type **ls ~user1** and press **Enter**. Is the fstab file present?

36. Type **exit** and press **Enter** to log out of your shell.

37. On your Windows host, open a Web browser and enter the location **ftp://IPaddress**, where *IPaddress* is the IP address of your Ubuntu Server 18 Linux virtual machine. What directory are you placed in and why? Next, enter the location **ftp://user1:LINUXrocks!@IPaddress**, where *IPaddress* is the IP address of your Ubuntu Server 18 Linux virtual machine. What directory are you placed in and why? Close your Web browser when finished.

38. On your Windows host, download and install the free FileZilla FTP client program from *https://filezilla-project.org/*. Next, open the FileZilla program and enter **sftp://IPaddress** in the Host dialog box (where *IPaddress* is the IP address of your Ubuntu Server 18 Linux virtual machine). Next, enter **user1** in the Username dialog box and **LINUXrocks!** in the Password dialog box and click **Quickconnect**. Explore copying files between your Windows host and Ubuntu Server Linux virtual machine, and close FileZilla when finished.

Project 13-8

In this hands-on project, you explore the Postfix email daemon on your Ubuntu Server 18 Linux virtual machine.

1. On your Ubuntu Server 18 Linux virtual machine, log in to tty1 using the user name of **root** and the password of **LINUXrocks!**.

2. At the command prompt, type **apt install postfix** and press **Enter**. When prompted for the general type of mail configuration, ensure that **Internet Site** is selected and select **OK**. At the Postfix Configuration screen, select **OK** to accept the default system mail name.

3. Edit the /etc/aliases file with a text editor and add the following line:

```
webmaster: user1
```

When finished, save your changes and quit the editor.

4. At the command prompt, type **newaliases** and press **Enter** to update the aliases database using the information within the /etc/aliases file.

5. At the command prompt, type **apt install mailutils** and press **Enter**. Press **y** when prompted to continue the installation of the mail utilities package.

6. At the command prompt, type **mail webmaster** and press **Enter** to compose a new email message to user1. Press **Enter** at the Cc: prompt. At the Subject: prompt, type **Test email** and press **Enter**. Next, type **This is a test email that will be delivered using the Postfix daemon** and press **Enter**. Next, press **Ctrl+d** to complete and send the email message.

7. At the command prompt, type **su - user1** to switch to a new shell as user1.

8. At the command prompt, type `mail` to check your mailbox for email messages. Type `1` and press **Enter** to read the first message. Type `q` and press **Enter** when finished to exit the mail program.

9. At the command prompt, type `exit` and press **Enter** to return to your root shell.

10. At the command prompt, type `telnet localhost 25` and press **Enter**. Can you tell that you are interacting with the Postfix daemon?

11. Type `EHLO localhost` and press **Enter**. Does your Postfix daemon support 8-bit MIME? How do you know? Type `quit` and press **Enter** to quit the telnet session.

12. Type `exit` and press **Enter** to log out of your shell.

Project 13-9

In this hands-on project, you create, query, and manage a database using PostgreSQL on your Ubuntu Server 18 Linux virtual machine.

1. On your Ubuntu Server 18 Linux virtual machine, log into tty1 using the user name of **root** and the password of **LINUXrocks!**.

2. At the command prompt, type `apt install postgresql` and press **Enter** to install PostgreSQL.

3. At the command prompt, type `passwd postgres` and press **Enter**. Type a password of **LINUXrocks!** and press **Enter** at both prompts to set a password of LINUXrocks! for the postgres user account.

4. At the command prompt, type `su - postgres` and press **Enter** to start a new shell as the postgres user.

5. At the command prompt, type `createdb sales` and press **Enter**.

6. At the command prompt, type `psql sales` and press **Enter** to start the PostgreSQL utility.

7. At the sales=# prompt, type `\l` and press **Enter** to view the databases on your PostgreSQL server. The postgres database stores all information used internally by the PostgreSQL server, and the template databases are used when creating new databases. Note that your sales database is listed and uses the UTF-8 character set for information.

8. At the sales=# prompt, type `CREATE TABLE customer (Name char(20),Address char(40),Balance char(10));` and press **Enter** to create a customer table that has three fields (Name, Address, Balance).

9. At the sales=# prompt, type `\d` and press **Enter** to view the tables within your database. Is the customer database listed?

10. At the sales=# prompt, type `\d customer` and press **Enter** to view the fields within the customer table. How many characters are allowed in each of the three fields?

11. At the sales=# prompt, type `INSERT INTO customer VALUES (Lily Bopeep','123 Rutherford Lane','526.80');` and press **Enter** to add a record to your table.

12. At the sales=# prompt, type `INSERT INTO customer VALUES ('Harvey Lipshitz','51 King Street','122.19');` and press **Enter** to add a record to your table.

13. At the sales=# prompt, type **INSERT INTO customer VALUES ('John Escobar','14-6919 Franklin Drive','709.66');** and press **Enter** to add a record to your table.

14. At the sales=# prompt, type **SELECT * from customer;** and press **Enter** to view all records within your table.

15. At the sales=# prompt, type **SELECT * from customer ORDER BY Balance DESC;** and press **Enter** to view all records within your table in descending order by balance.

16. At the sales=# prompt, type **SELECT * from customer WHERE Name = 'Harvey Lipshitz';** and press **Enter** to view the record for Harvey Lipshitz.

17. At the sales=# prompt, type **CREATE USER bob WITH PASSWORD 'supersecret';** and press **Enter** to create a user account within PostgreSQL that can access the customer database.

18. At the sales=# prompt, type **GRANT ALL PRIVILEGES ON customer TO bob** and press **Enter** to grant SELECT, UPDATE, DELETE, and INSERT permission on the customer table to the bob user.

19. At the sales=# prompt, type **\q** and press **Enter** to quit the PostgreSQL utility.

20. Type **exit** and press **Enter** to log out of your shell.

Project 13-10

In this hands-on project, you install Docker on your Ubuntu Server 18 Linux virtual machine and run multiple copies of the Apache container image from Docker Hub.

1. On your Ubuntu Server 18 Linux virtual machine, log into tty1 using the user name of **root** and the password of **LINUXrocks!**.

2. At the command prompt, type **snap install docker** and press **Enter** to install Docker using Snappy.

3. At the command prompt, type **docker search apache | less** and press **Enter**. Note that the Apache HTTP Server Project official Docker image is called httpd and press **q** to return to your command prompt.

4. At the command prompt, type **docker pull httpd** and press **Enter** to download the latest version of the official httpd container image from Docker Hub.

5. At the command prompt, type **docker images** and press **Enter**. Is your httpd container image listed?

6. At the command prompt, type **docker run -d -p 50001:80 --name site1 httpd** and press **Enter** to run a detached copy of your httpd container image called site1 and map port 80 for the Apache Web server to port 50001 within the underlying Ubuntu Server 18 operating system.

7. At the command prompt, type **docker run -d -p 50002:80 --name site2 httpd** and press **Enter** to run a detached copy of your httpd container image called site2 and map port 80 for the Apache Web server to port 50002 within the underlying Ubuntu Server 18 operating system.

8. At the command prompt, type **docker ps** and press **Enter**. Note that both containers are running. Is port 80 mapped to the correct port in the underlying operating system

for each container? What IP address in the output identifies the underlying operating system?

9. At the command prompt, type **docker exec -it** *containerID* **sh** and press **Enter**, where *containerID* is the container ID of the site1 container. This will start a shell within your site1 container.

10. At the site1 container shell prompt, type **ls** and press **Enter**. Note the contents of the / filesystem. Next, type **apachectl start** and press **Enter**. Was the Apache daemon already running?

11. At the site1 container shell prompt, type **cd htdocs** and press **Enter** to enter the Apache document root directory in the site1 container. Next, type **echo "<html><body><h1>Site 1 works!</h1></body></html>" > index.html** and press **Enter** to write a simple Web page to the index.html file within the Apache document root directory. Finally, type **exit** and press **Enter** to log out of your shell within the site1 container.

12. At the command prompt, type **docker exec -it** *containerID* **sh** and press **Enter**, where *containerID* is the container ID of the site2 container. This will start a shell within your site2 container.

13. At the site2 container shell prompt, type **cd htdocs** and press **Enter** to enter the Apache document root directory in the site2 container. Next, type **echo "<html><body><h1>Site 2 works!</h1></body></html>" > index.html** and press **Enter** to write a simple Web page to the index.html file within the Apache document root directory. Finally, type **exit** and press **Enter** to log out of your shell within the site2 container.

14. On your Windows host, open a Web browser and connect to the URL **http://*IP*:50001**, where *IP* is the IP address of your Ubuntu Server 18 Linux virtual machine. Is the Web page from your site1 container shown? Next, connect to the URL **http://*IP*:50002**, where *IP* is the IP address of your Ubuntu Server 18 Linux virtual machine. Is the Web page from your site2 container shown? Leave your Web browser open.

15. Return to tty1 on your Ubuntu Server 18 Linux virtual machine. Type **docker stop site2** and press **Enter** to stop running the site2 container. Next, type **docker ps** and press **Enter** to verify that the site2 container is no longer running.

16. On your Windows host, refresh the Web page from your site2 container (**http://*IP*:50002**, where *IP* is the IP address of your Ubuntu Server 18 Linux virtual machine). Is the Web page from your site2 container available? Leave your Web browser open.

17. Return to tty1 on your Ubuntu Server 18 Linux virtual machine. Type **docker start site2** and press **Enter** to re-run the site2 container. Next, type **docker ps** and press **Enter** to verify that the site2 container is running.

18. On your Windows host, refresh the Web page from your site2 container (**http://*IP*:50002**, where *IP* is the IP address of your Ubuntu Server 18 Linux virtual machine). Is the Web page from your site2 container available? Close your Web browser when finished.

19. Return to tty1 on your Ubuntu Server 18 Linux virtual machine. Type `docker stop site1 site2` and press **Enter** to stop the site1 and site2 containers. Next, type `docker ps` and press **Enter** to verify that no containers are running.

20. At the command prompt, type `docker ps -a` and press **Enter** and note the status of your two containers. Type `docker container prune` and press **Enter** to remove any stopped containers. Finally type `docker ps -a` and press **Enter** to verify that the site1 and site2 containers have been removed from the list.

21. Type `exit` and press **Enter** to log out of your shell.

Project 13-11

In this hands-on project, you run two Web apps within a GitLab runner to demonstrate build automation, CM, and CD.

1. On your Windows host, open a Web browser and create a free account at GitLab.com. Next, log into GitLab.com, select the **Projects** menu and choose **Your projects**. Click **New project**, supply the name **SampleCDworkflow** in the Project name dialog box and click **Create project**.

2. On your Ubuntu Server 18 Linux virtual machine, log into tty1 using the user name of **root** and the password of **LINUXrocks!**.

3. At the command prompt, type `wget https://gitlab.com/gitlab-examples/ nodejs/-/archive/master/nodejs-master.tar.gz` and press **Enter** to download a tarball that contains two JavaScript Node.js Web apps and a GitLab runner configuration file. Next, type `tar -zxvf nodejs-master.tar.gz ; cd nodejs-master` and press **Enter** to extract the contents of the tarball and change to the directory that was created.

4. At the command prompt, type `cat .gitlab-ci.yml` and press **Enter** to view the GitLab runner configuration used for build automation and CM. Note the following:

    a. The **image: node:4.2.2** line advises the GitLab runner to obtain and run the **node:4.2.2** container image from Docker Hub.

    b. The **test_async:** section represents the first Web app that will be executed within the container using the commands listed within the **script:** subsection.

    c. The **test_db:** section represents the second Web app that will be executed within the container using the commands listed within the **script:** subsection. The **services:** subsection requires a second container image (**postgres:9.5.0**) be downloaded from Docker Hub and run to provide a PostgreSQL database server.

5. At the command prompt, type `git config --global user.email "root@domain .com"` and press **Enter** to set your email address. Next, type `git config --global user.name "root user"` and press **Enter** to set your user name.

6. At the command prompt, type `git init` and press **Enter** to turn your current directory into a Git repository. Next, type `git remote add origin https://gitlab.com/ username/samplecdworkflow.git` and press **Enter**, where *username* is your GitLab user name. This will set the origin of the Git repository to your new project on GitLab.com.

7. At the command prompt, type `git add .` and press **Enter** to stage the files within your current repository. Next, type `git commit -m "Initial commit"` and press **Enter** to create your first commit. Finally, type `git push -u origin master` and press **Enter** to push your committed repository to GitLab. Supply your GitLab username and password when prompted to complete the process.

8. Type `exit` and press **Enter** to log out of your shell.

9. On your Windows host, open a Web browser and go into your account at GitLab. com. Next, select the **Projects** menu, choose **Your projects** and click your **SampleCDworkflow** project. In the left pane, click **CI / CD** and choose **Pipelines**. Click **Run Pipeline** and then **Create pipeline** to execute your .gitlab-ci.yml file on the free Digital Ocean cloud provider. Digital Ocean provides its services for free to GitLab runners when it has resources available; as a result, you may have to wait a few minutes for your containers to be created and the test_async and test_db Web apps to be executed. Click **test_async** and **test_db** in turn to see them execute within the Digital Ocean cloud provider, and view the output of each Web app.

10. Close your Web browser when finished.

Discovery Exercises

1. In Project 13-1, you configured the DHCP daemon (dhcpd) on your Fedora Linux virtual machine. On your Ubuntu Server 14 Linux virtual machine, install and configure udhcpd to provide the same functionality described in Project 13-1, and test your settings by configuring your Fedora Linux virtual machine as a DHCP client that obtains IPv4 configuration from udhcpd. Finally, restore your original configuration.

2. In Project 13-2, you installed and configured the DNS daemon (named) on your Fedora Linux virtual machine. Install the graphical BIND configuration utility on your Fedora Linux virtual machine and experiment with adding a new zone file that hosts forward lookup records. When finished, examine the files that were created and modified, and test your configuration.

3. In Project 13-3, you examined the NTP configuration on your Ubuntu Server 14 and Fedora Linux virtual machines. Install and configure the Chrony NTP daemon on your Ubuntu Server 18 virtual machine to share time information to other computers on your classroom network. Next, edit the NTP configuration files on your Ubuntu Server 14 and Fedora Linux virtual machines to obtain time information from your Ubuntu Server 18 virtual machine and test the results using the appropriate commands. Next, restore your original configuration.

4. In Project 13-4, you installed and configured the Apache Web server on your Fedora Linux virtual machine. Install the Apache Web server on your Ubuntu Server 18 Linux virtual machine and perform the same configuration tasks.

Note any pathname and configuration file differences.

5. The file-sharing servers discussed in this chapter (vsftpd, NFS, and Samba) were installed and configured on your Ubuntu Server 18 Linux virtual machine during Projects 13-5, 13-6, and 13-7. Install the same file-sharing servers on your Fedora Linux virtual machine and perform the same configuration tasks. Note any pathname and configuration file differences.

6. Ansible is one of the most common CM software tools used today for agentless configuration of virtual machines and containers; it stores the configuration that needs to be applied to each inventory member using YAML files called Ansible Playbooks. Use the Internet to research the installation, configuration, and usage of Ansible. Next, install Ansible on your Fedora Linux virtual machine and create an Ansible Playbook that can be used to create a new user called AnsibleTest on your Ubuntu Server 18 Linux virtual machine. Test your configuration when finished.

## CHAPTER 14

SECURITY, TROUBLESHOOTING, AND PERFORMANCE

After completing this chapter, you will be able to:

Describe the different facets of Linux security

Increase the security of a Linux computer

Describe and outline good troubleshooting practices

Effectively troubleshoot common hardware, application, filesystem, and network problems

Monitor system performance

Identify and fix common performance problems

Throughout this textbook, you have examined the various components that comprise a Linux system. In this chapter, you learn how to secure, troubleshoot, and monitor the performance of these components. First, you learn security concepts, good security practices, as well as the utilities that you can use to prevent both local and network-related security breaches. Next, you explore troubleshooting procedures, common system problems, and performance monitoring utilities.

Security

In the past decade, hundreds of new services have been made available to Linux systems, and the number of Linux users has risen to tens of millions. In addition, Linux systems hosted by organizations and cloud providers are typically made available across networks such as the Internet. As a result, Linux is more prone today to security loopholes and attacks both locally and from across networks. To protect your Linux computer from unauthorized access and network attacks, you should take steps to improve local and network security.

Securing the Local Computer

A key component in providing security within an organization involves securing local access to each computer on the network. This involves limiting physical and operating system access, providing secure root user access, using encryption to protect data, and using secure system administration practices.

Limiting Physical Access

One of the most important security-related practices is to limit access to the physical Linux computer itself. If a malicious user has access to the Linux computer, that user could boot the computer using a USB flash drive, CD, or DVD that contains a small operating system and use it to access files within the filesystems on the hard disk of the Linux computer without having to log in to the operating system installed on the hard disk. To prevent this, you should lock important computers, such as Linux servers, in a specific room to which only Linux administrators or trusted users have key access. This room is commonly called a **server closet**. Unfortunately, some Linux computers, such as Linux workstations, must be located in public areas. For these computers, you should remove the CD and DVD drives from the computer. In addition, you should configure the computer BIOS to prevent booting from the USB ports, as well as ensure that a system BIOS password is set to prevent other users from changing the boot order.

> **Note** 📎
>
> Both GRUB and GRUB2 allow you to specify a password within their configuration file that must be supplied at boot time before the Linux kernel is loaded. However, this will not prevent someone with physical access to the computer from booting the system from a USB flash drive, CD, or DVD to gain access to the underlying filesystems.
>
> To prevent users from spreading viruses and malware stored on personal USB flash drivers inadvertently, some organizations disable all access to USB ports on workstations. Other organizations discourage the use of USB flash drives for the same reason.

Some organizations use publicly accessible Linux computers running secure kiosk software to provide information to visitors. Normally, the Linux computer running the kiosk software is locked within a cabinet or display enclosure to prevent users from accessing the USB ports. However, malicious users will often attempt to reboot the computer using the Ctrl+Alt+Del key combination and interact with the operating system before the kiosk software is loaded. As a result, it is good security to prevent publicly accessible Linux systems from rebooting when the Ctrl+Alt+Del key combination is used. To do this on a system that uses SysV init, you can comment the line that contains the `ctrlaltdel` action within the /etc/inittab file and restart the init daemon. For systems that use upstart init, you can comment the line that contains the `shutdown` command within the /etc/init/control-alt-delete.conf file and restart the init daemon. For systems that use Systemd, you can run the `systemctl mask ctrl-alt-del.target` command to prevent the Ctrl+Alt+Del key combination from rebooting the system.

Limiting Access to the Operating System

In addition to limiting physical access to the physical Linux computer, it is important to provide mechanisms that limit unauthorized access to the Linux operating system. Enforcing complex passwords when users change their password, and locking user accounts after multiple invalid password attempts are the most common ways used to limit unauthorized access to systems. To enable password enforcement or user account lockout, you can configure the appropriate **Pluggable Authentication Module (PAM)** on your Linux system by editing the appropriate file within the /etc/pam.d directory. On Fedora systems, you can modify the /etc/pam.d/password-auth or /etc/pam.d /system-auth file, and on Ubuntu systems, you can modify the /etc/pam.d/common -password or /etc/pam.d/common-auth file. For example, to ensure that users create passwords that are a minimum of 10 characters (`minlen=10`), and contain at least one number (`dcredit=1`), one uppercase character (`ucredit=1`), one lowercase character (`lcredit=1`), and four characters that are different from their previous password (`difok=4`), you could add the following line to the appropriate file within the /etc /pam.d directory:

```
password requisite pam_cracklib.so minlen=10 dcredit=1 ucredit=1
lcredit=1 difok=4
```

Note that the PAM used to enforce password complexity is called pam_cracklib.so. To lock user accounts after multiple invalid logins, you can use either pam_tally2.so or pam_faillock.so. For example, to use pam_tally2.so to lock users after they attempt to log in unsuccessfully three times (`deny=3`) within 300 seconds (`unlock_time=300`), you could add the following line to the appropriate file within the /etc/pam.d directory:

```
auth required pam_tally2.so deny=3 unlock_time=300
```

To enforce the same account lockout settings using pam_faillock.so, you could instead add the following line to the appropriate file within the /etc/pam.d directory:

```
auth required pam_faillock.so preauth deny=3 unlock_time=300
```

If a user supplies an incorrect password three times within 300 seconds, they will be unable to log into the system until their user account is unlocked. You can use the **pam_tally2** command to list users who have been locked out by pam_tally2.so, and the `faillock` **command** to list users who have been locked out by pam_faillock.so. To unlock a user named bob that was locked with pam_tally2.so, you can use the `pam_tally2 --reset --user bob` command, and to unlock a user named mary that was locked out using pam_faillock.so, you can use the `faillock --reset --user mary` command.

Authentication services, such as Microsoft Active Directory, can also be used to limit unauthorized access to the operating system. Most authentication services use a secure protocol, such as Kerberos, to authenticate users, as well as store user information and authentication requirements within a **Lightweight Directory Access Protocol (LDAP)** database. For example, the information within an LDAP database could be used to ensure that only users that are part of the Accounting group are allowed to log into computers within the Accounting Department.

You can configure your Linux system to log in to an authentication service using Kerberos by installing the Kerberos package for your Linux distribution. Next, you must supply the name of your authentication service and servers within the /etc/krb5.conf file. Following this, you can use the `kinit` **command** to log into your authentication service; for example, `kinit jason.eckert@trios.com` would log into the trios.com authentication service as the user jason.eckert using Kerberos and enforce the restrictions for the user jason.eckert within the associated LDAP database.

> ### Note 📎
>
> You can use the `klist` **command** to view your Kerberos authentication information.
> Most Linux distributions integrate `kinit` functionality into the display manager login screen to ensure that authentication services are used to authenticate users exclusively. Additionally, you can add the `password sufficient pam_ldap.so` line to the appropriate files within the /etc/pam.d directory to ensure that all areas of the system attempt to log into the LDAP database provided by an authentication service using Kerberos before attempting local authentication.

Some organizations use other software- and hardware-based authentication methods in addition to a user name and password to further limit access to the operating system; this practice is called **multi-factor authentication**. For example, a Linux system with a **biometric** thumbprint reader and the associated software installed will prompt you to scan your thumbprint to further prove your identity after supplying your user name and password. Alternatively, a Linux system with RSA SecurID software installed will prompt you to type in the **One Time Password (OTP)** stored on your RSA SecureID token device after supplying your user name and password. This OTP is changed frequently using an algorithm that is the same within the RSA SecurID token device and RSA SecurID software installed on the Linux system for your user account; by providing the correct OTP, you prove that you have the correct RSA SecurID token device.

Another important security consideration is to limit access to graphical desktops and shells. If you walk away from your workstation for a few minutes and leave yourself logged in to the system, another person can use your operating system while you are away. To avoid this, you should exit your command-line shell, or lock your desktop environment screen before leaving the computer. To lock your screen within the GNOME desktop, you can access the drop-down menu in the upper-right corner of the desktop and choose the lock icon. To use your desktop again, you need to enter your password.

Providing Secure Root User Access

If you have root access to a Linux system, it is important to minimize the time that you are logged in as the root user to reduce the chance that another user can access your terminal if you accidentally leave your system without locking your desktop or exiting your shell. It is best practice to create a regular user account that you can use to check emails and perform other day-to-day tasks. Recall from Chapter 2 that you can then use the su command to obtain root access only when you need to perform an administrative task. When you are finished, you can use the exit command to return to your previous shell, where you are logged in as a regular user account.

> **Note**
>
> The root user can use the su command to switch to any other user account without specifying the user account password.

Still, some regular users, such as software developers, need to run certain commands as the root user in certain situations. Instead of giving them the root password, it is best to give them the ability to run certain commands as the root user via the **sudo command**. The sudo command checks the /etc/sudoers file to see if you have rights to run a certain command as a different user. The following /etc/sudoers file gives the software developers, mary and bob, the ability to run the kill and killall commands as the root user on the computers server1 and server2:

```
[root@server1 ~]# cat /etc/sudoers
User_Alias SD = mary, bob
Cmnd_Alias KILL = /usr/bin/kill, /usr/bin/killall
Host_Alias SERVERS = server1, server2

SD      SERVERS = (root) KILL
[root@server1 ~]#_
```

Now, if mary needs to kill the cron daemon on server1 (which was started as the root user) to test a program that she wrote, she needs to use the sudo command, as shown in the following output, and supply her own password:

```
[mary@server1 ~]$ ps -ef |grep crond
root        2281      1  0 21:20 ?        00:00:00 /usr/sbin/crond -n
[mary@server1 ~]$ kill -9 2281
-bash: kill: (2281) - Operation not permitted
[mary@server1 ~]$ sudo kill -9 2281
[sudo] password for mary: *********
[mary@server1 ~]$_
```

Recall that the first regular user created on most modern Linux distributions is automatically assigned to the wheel group. Members of the wheel group are granted permission to perform all system administration tasks using the %wheel ALL = (ALL) ALL line within the /etc/sudoers file, including setting the root user password following installation. As a Linux administrator, you can choose to log into a regular user account that is a member of the wheel group to perform all administrative tasks; in this case, each system administration command you run must be prefixed with the sudo command. Additionally, you can use the sudoedit command while logged into a regular user account that is a member of the wheel group to edit text files, such as configuration files, as the root user. The sudoedit command opens text files using the default text editor on the system, which can be modified using the EDITOR environment variable.

> **Note** 🖉
>
> On Ubuntu systems, the sudo group is used in place of the wheel group.
>
> The root user does not have write permission to the /etc/sudoers file by default, but has the ability to supersede all file permissions. As a result, when editing the /etc/sudoers file as the root user within the vi editor, you must use :w! when saving your changes to ensure that the vi editor allows you to supersede the underlying file permissions. Alternatively, you can use the visudo command to edit the /etc/sudoers file as the root user; this command edits a copy of /etc/sudoers using the default text editor on the system, and then replaces /etc/sudoers with this copy when you exit the text editor.

Using Encryption to Protect Data

Encryption can be used to prevent someone with physical access to your files from reading them. This is especially important on computers that can be easily stolen, such as laptop computers and computers that are in publicly accessible areas. For these systems, it's often best to use **Linux Unified Key Setup (LUKS)** to encrypt entire filesystems using AES symmetric encryption. It is best to configure LUKS on each filesystem during Linux installation; for example, you can select the Encrypt check box within Figure 2-11 to encrypt the contents of the root (/) filesystem using LUKS, and supply a passphrase of your choice when prompted. The passphrase serves as the symmetric encryption key used to decrypt the contents of the filesystem, and must be specified each time the filesystem is mounted.

To set up LUKS after installation, you can run the `cryptsetup` command. For example, to configure LUKS encryption on the empty /dev/sdb1 partition, you could run the following command and supply a passphrase when prompted:

```
[root@server1 ~]# cryptsetup luksFormat /dev/sdb1
WARNING!
========
This will overwrite data on /dev/sdb1 irrevocably.

Are you sure? (Type uppercase yes): YES
Enter passphrase for /dev/sdb1: ********
Verify passphrase: ********
[root@server1 ~]#_
```

Next, you can make the encrypted /dev/sdb1 partition available to the Linux device mapper as a volume and create a filesystem on the mapped volume. To make /dev/sdb1 available as a volume called securedata and create an ext4 filesystem on the mapped volume (/dev/mapper/securedata), you could run the following commands:

```
[root@server1 ~]# cryptsetup luksOpen /dev/sdb1 securedata
Enter passphrase for /dev/sdb1: ********
[root@server1 ~]# mkfs -t ext4 /dev/mapper/securedata
mke2fs 1.43.8 (1-Jan-2018)
Creating filesystem with 2096379 4k blocks and 524288 inodes
Filesystem UUID: dc3e7bb4-bda4-4aaa-b499-8a96875e57b1
Superblock backups stored on blocks:
    32768, 98304, 163840, 229376, 294912, 819200, 884736, 1605632

Allocating group tables: done
Writing inode tables: done
Creating journal (16384 blocks): done
Writing superblocks and filesystem accounting information: done

[root@server1 ~]#_
```

After the filesystem has been created, you can create a mount point directory and mount the mapped volume to it as you would any other filesystem. The following commands create a /securedata mount point directory, mount the securedata volume to it, and examine the contents:

```
[root@server1 ~]# mkdir /securedata
[root@server1 ~]# mount /dev/mapper/securedata /securedata
[root@server1 ~]# ls /securedata
lost+found
[root@server1 ~]#_
```

To ensure that the encrypted volume in the previous example is mounted at boot time, you must add the line securedata /dev/sdb1 to the /etc/crypttab file, as well as add the line /dev/mapper/securedata /securedata ext4 defaults 0 0 to the /etc/fstab file. Each time you boot your computer, you will be prompted to supply the passphrase needed to unlock the encrypted securedata volume, as shown in Figure 14-1.

Figure 14-1   Providing a LUKS passphrase at boot time

You can instead choose to encrypt only specific files that contain sensitive information using **GNU Privacy Guard (GPG)**. Because GPG uses asymmetric encryption, you must create a GPG public/private key pair using the gpg **command** as shown in the following output:

```
[root@server1 ~]# gpg --gen-key
gpg (GnuPG) 1.4.22; Copyright (C) 2015 Free Software Foundation, Inc.
This is free software: you are free to change and redistribute it.
There is NO WARRANTY, to the extent permitted by law.
```

```
Please select what kind of key you want:
    (1) RSA and RSA (default)
    (2) DSA and Elgamal
    (3) DSA (sign only)
    (4) RSA (sign only)
Your selection? 1
RSA keys may be between 1024 and 4096 bits long.
What keysize do you want? (2048) 2048
Requested keysize is 2048 bits
Please specify how long the key should be valid.
                    0 = key does not expire
        <n>  = key expires in n days
        <n>w = key expires in n weeks
        <n>m = key expires in n months
        <n>y = key expires in n years
Key is valid for? (0) 0
Key does not expire at all
Is this correct? (y/N) y

You need a user ID to identify your key; the software constructs the
user ID from the Real Name, Comment and Email Address in this form:
    "Heinrich Heine (Der Dichter) <heinrichh@duesseldorf.de>"

Real name: Jason Eckert
Email address: jason.eckert@trios.com
Comment: These are my GPG keys
You selected this USER-ID:
    "Jason Eckert (These are my GPG keys) <jason.eckert@trios.com>"

Change (N)ame, (C)omment, (E)mail or (O)kay/(Q)uit? O
You need a Passphrase to protect your secret key: ***********
gpg: key 8FD8C0FA marked as ultimately trusted
public and secret key created and signed.

gpg: checking the trustdb
gpg: 3 marginal(s) needed, 1 complete(s) needed, PGP trust model
gpg: depth: 0  valid:   1  signed:   0  trust: 0-, 0q, 0n, 0m, 0f, 1u
pub   2048R/8FD8C0FA 2019-11-17
Key fingerprint = C478 827E E846 1E42 2497  C498 DE93 BAC2 8FD8 C0FA
uid   Jason Eckert (These are my GPG keys) <jason.eckert@trios.com>
sub   2048R/8C8F080D 2019-11-17
[root@server1 ~]#_
```

The private key generated by the `gpg --gen-key` command is protected by a passphrase that you supply; this passphrase must be supplied each time the private key is used to digitally sign or decrypt files. Moreover, the GPG public/private key pair is stored in the ~/.gnupg directory alongside any other GPG configuration options.

After creating a GPG public/private key pair, you can use the `gpg` command to encrypt, decrypt, and digitally sign files on the filesystem. The following output demonstrates how to encrypt and digitally sign the topsecretdata text file, creating a topsecretdata.gpg file that can be decrypted by jason.eckert@trios.com:

```
[root@server1 ~]# file topsecretdata
topsecretdata: UTF-8 Unicode text
[root@server1 ~]# gpg --encrypt --sign -r jason.eckert@trios.com
topsecretdata


You need a passphrase to unlock the secret key for
user: "Jason Eckert (These are my GPG keys) <jason.eckert@trios.com>"
2048-bit RSA key, ID 8FD8C0FA, created 2019-11-17 ***********

[root@server1 ~]# file topsecretdata.gpg
topsecretdata.gpg: PGP RSA encrypted session key - keyid: D3E5FE7C
D088F8C RSA (Encrypt or Sign) 2048b
[root@server1 ~]#_
```

To verify the digital signature and decrypt a file that was digitally signed and encrypted with GPG, you can supply the file name as an argument to the `gpg` command. For example, the following commands verify the digital signature and decrypt the topsecretdata.gpg file created earlier, as well as validate the results:

```
[root@server1 ~]# gpg topsecretdata.gpg
You need a passphrase to unlock the secret key for
user: "Jason Eckert (These are my GPG keys) <jason.eckert@trios.com>"
2048-bit RSA key, ID 8C8F080D, created 2019-11-17 (main key ID
8FD8C0FA) ***********

gpg: encrypted with 2048-bit RSA key, ID 8C8F080D, created 2019-11-17
      "Jason Eckert (These are my GPG keys) <jason.eckert@trios.com>"
gpg: Signature made Sat 17 Nov 2019 07:06:55 PM EST using RSA key
ID 8FD8C0FA
gpg: Good signature from "Jason Eckert (These are my GPG keys)
<jason.eckert@trios.com>"
[root@server1 ~]# file topsecretdata
topsecretdata: UTF-8 Unicode text
[root@server1 ~]#_
```

> **Note** 📎
>
> To prevent having to enter your GPG passphrase each time you digitally sign or decrypt a file, you can start the **GPG agent** daemon, which prompts you for your passphrase once and supplies it automatically within GPG commands during the remainder of your login session. To learn how to start the GPG agent daemon for your user account, view the `gpg-agent` manual page.

Practicing Secure Linux Administration

Other considerations for securing the local computer involve using secure Linux administration practices. For example, ensuring that users do not have unnecessary file and directory permissions will minimize the chance that they could gain access to sensitive documents on the local system. Similarly, restricting the users who are allowed to schedule commands using the /etc/cron.allow, /etc/cron.deny, /etc/at.allow, and /etc/at.deny files would prevent a malicious user from scheduling tasks that could detract from system performance.

Moreover, if the available space on the root (/) filesystem is exhausted, the Linux system will crash. To prevent this, you could create separate filesystems for the /home, /tmp, /usr, and /var directories. In this case, if a user downloads a large number of files to their home directory, only the /home filesystem is affected. Similarly, if a program writes a large amount of data under the /tmp, /usr, or /var directories, only the filesystems mounted to those directories are affected, and the Linux system remains available.

To remind users of secure computer etiquette techniques, or the acceptable computer use policy used by your organization, you can add a **login banner**. Login banners are messages that are displayed on the screen after a user logs into the system. To create a login banner, you can place the appropriate text within the /etc/motd (message of the day) file.

Protecting Against Network Attacks

Recall from Chapter 12 that network services listen for network traffic on a certain port number and interact with that traffic. As long as network services exist on a computer, there is always the possibility that hackers with network access can manipulate the network service by interacting with it in unusual ways. Network attacks may exploit a weakness with a particular service, compromise an authentication mechanism to gain access to the system, or even replace data used by the network service in memory with malicious data (called a **buffer overrun**). There are many ways to minimize the chance of a network attack, including reducing the number of network services, using encryption, limiting system and client access, using secure file permissions, changing default ports, updating software, running vulnerability scanners, as well as using firewalls, SELinux, and AppArmor.

Reducing the Number of Network Services

The first step in securing your computer against network attacks is to minimize the number of network services running. If you run only the minimum number of network services necessary for your organization, you minimize the avenues that a hacker can use to gain access to systems. To see what network services are running on your network, you can run the `nmap` **(network mapper) command.** The following output demonstrates how `nmap` can be used to determine the number of services running on the server1 computer:

```
[root@server1 ~]# nmap -sT server1.class.com
Starting Nmap 7.60 ( http://nmap.org ) at 2019-11-01 15:14 EDT
Nmap scan report for server1.class.com (192.168.1.105)
Host is up (0.0019s latency).
rDNS record for 192.168.1.105: server1.class.com
Not shown: 995 closed ports
PORT      STATE SERVICE
22/tcp    open  ssh
23/tcp    open  telnet
111/tcp   open  rpcbind
631/tcp   open  ipp
5903/tcp  open  vnc-3

Nmap done: 1 IP address (1 host up) scanned in 0.13 seconds
[root@server1 ~]#_
```

Note

The `nmap` command is not normally installed on a Linux distribution by default, but can be added from a software repository.

From the preceding output, you can determine which services are running on your computer by viewing the service name or by searching the descriptions for the port numbers in the /etc/services file or on the Internet. For services that are not needed, ensure that they are not started automatically when entering your default runlevel. It is also important to ensure that services that do not provide encryption are minimized on your systems, as these services are more prone to network attacks. For example, the telnet service shown in the preceding output is unnecessary because the ssh service provides the same functionality, but with encryption. As a result, it is good form to stop the telnet service on this system, and ensure that it isn't started when entering the default runlevel. For services that must be used because they are essential to your organization, you can take certain steps to ensure that they are as secure as possible, as described in the following sections.

> **Note**
>
> Some common network services that should be stopped or removed on a system if they are not used include printing (IPP, LPD, Samba), file sharing (FTP, NFS, Samba), email (Sendmail, Postfix), and legacy services that do not use encryption (telnet, rsh, finger).

Using Encryption

When possible, you should use network services that support encryption using SSH tunneling or SSL/TLS and configure those services to reject unencrypted connections. For example, the vsftpd daemon discussed in Chapter 13 supports both SFTP (FTP + SSH) as well as FTPS (FTP + SSL/TLS) encrypted connections. However, SFTP and unencrypted FTP are allowed by default. To prevent unencrypted FTP connections, you could force any connections that do not use SFTP to use FTPS by adding the following two lines to the vsftpd.conf file, and restarting the vsftpd daemon afterwards:

```
ssl_enable=YES
force_local_logins_ssl=YES
```

Recall from Chapter 1 that SSL/TLS uses a certificate to protect the integrity of the public key stored on the server. This server certificate contains a checksum of the public key that is digitally signed by a trusted CA. Before using the server's public key to encrypt data, each client decrypts the digital signature within the certificate and compares the checksum within to a checksum of the server's public key to ensure that it has not been modified by a hacker.

> **Note**
>
> When discussing certificates, checksums are often called **hashes** or **message digests**.

By default, most services generate a **self-signed certificate** for SSL/TLS, which includes a public key that is digitally signed by the server computer, and not a trusted CA. Because self-signed certificates can easily be modified by hackers, it is important that you replace this self-signed certificate with one that is obtained from a public CA, or a CA within your organization.

If you must run network services that do not provide encryption, you can use a VPN overlay network that adds encryption to existing network traffic. VPNs can be used to provide encryption for IP packets destined for another computer (called **transport mode**), or provide encryption for all IP packets that travel between two routers (called **tunnel mode**). There are many types of VPN technologies available, including IP Security (IPSec), Layer 2 Tunneling Protocol (L2TP), Point-to-Point Tunneling Protocol (PPTP), OpenVPN, Cisco AnyConnect, SSL/TLS, SSH, and Datagram TLS (DTLS). After you configure VPN software on a server or router, clients can connect to the VPN prior to accessing network services to ensure that their traffic is encrypted across the network. You can connect to a VPN on Fedora Linux by clicking the + symbol next to VPN within the Network utility shown in Figure 12-2, or by clicking the + symbol within the Network Connections utility shown in Figure 12-4.

Limiting System Access for Network Services

Regardless of whether encryption is used with a network service, you should also take steps to limit the access that network services have to the underlying operating system. First, you should ensure that network service daemons are not run as the root user on the system when possible. If a hacker gains access to your system via a network service daemon run as the root user, the hacker has root access as well. Many network daemons, such as Apache, set the user account by which they execute in their configuration files.

Similarly, for daemons such as Apache that run as a non-root user, you should ensure that the shell listed in /etc/passwd for the daemon is set to an invalid shell, such as /sbin/nologin. If a hacker attempted to remotely log into the system using a well-known daemon account, she would not be able to get a BASH shell. Instead, the /sbin/nologin merely prints the warning listed in the /etc/nologin.txt file to the screen and exits. If the /etc/nologin.txt file doesn't exist, the /sbin/nologin program prints a standard warning.

Limiting Client Access

By default, network services allow any client to connect. If you use network services that are started by xinetd, you can use TCP wrappers to specify the computers that are allowed to connect to the network service. A **TCP wrapper** is a program (/usr/sbin/tcpd) that can start a network daemon. To enable TCP wrappers, you must modify the appropriate file in the /etc/xinetd.d directory and start the network daemon as an argument to the TCP wrapper. For the telnet daemon started by xinetd, you modify the /etc/xinetd.d/telnet file, as shown in the following example:

```
[root@server1 ~]# cat /etc/xinetd.d/telnet
# default: on
# description: The telnet server serves telnet sessions; it uses \
```

```
#        unencrypted username/password pairs for authentication.
service telnet
{
    flags               = REUSE
    socket_type         = stream
    wait                = no
    user                = root
    server              = /usr/sbin/tcpd
    server_args         = /usr/sbin/in.telnetd
    log_on_failure      += USERID
    disable             = no
}
[root@server1 ~]#_
```

Now, the telnet daemon (/usr/sbin/in.telnetd) will be started by the TCP wrapper (/usr/sbin/tcpd). Before a TCP wrapper starts a network daemon, it first checks the /etc/hosts.allow and /etc/hosts.deny files. The following /etc/hosts.allow and /etc /hosts.deny files only give the computers client1 and client2 the ability to connect to your telnet server.

```
[root@server1 ~]# cat /etc/hosts.deny
in.telnetd:  ALL
[root@server1 ~]#_
[root@server1 ~]# cat /etc/hosts.allow
in.telnetd:  client1, client2
[root@server1 ~]#_
```

TCP wrapper functionality is not only limited to daemons started by xinetd. Some standalone daemons that provide network services can be configured to check the /etc/hosts.deny and /etc/hosts.allow file before granting access. Additionally, many network services can be configured to forward connection requests to a **Remote Dial In User Service (RADIUS)** or **Terminal Access Controller Access Control System Plus (TACACS+)** server before granting access. In addition to providing centralized authentication, RADIUS and TACACS+ servers allow you to create policies that specify the computers that are allowed to connect to your service.

Using Secure File Permissions

Another important component of network security involves local file permissions. If everyone had read permission on the /etc/shadow file, any user could read the encrypted passwords for all user accounts, including the root user, and possibly decrypt the password using a decryption program. Fortunately, the default permissions on the /etc/shadow file allow read permission for the root user only to minimize this possibility. However, similar permission problems exist with many other important files, including those used by network services.

Take, for example, the Apache Web server discussed in Chapter 13. Apache daemons are run as the user apache and the group apache by default. These daemons read HTML files from the document root directory such that they can give the information to client Web browsers. The following directory listing from a sample document root directory shows that the Apache daemons also have write permission because they own the index.html file:

```
[root@server1 ~]# ls -l /var/www/html
total 64
-rw-r----- 1 apache apache 61156 Sep 5 08:36 index.html
[root@server1 ~]#_
```

Thus, if a hacker was able to manipulate an Apache daemon, the hacker would have write access to the index.html file and would be able to modify it. It is secure practice to ensure that the index.html is owned by the Web developer (who needs to modify the file) and that the Apache daemons are given read access only through membership in the group category. If your Web developer logs into the system as the user account webma, you could perform the following commands to change the permissions on the Web content and verify the results:

```
[root@server1 ~]# chown webma /var/www/html/index.html
[root@server1 ~]# ls -l /var/www/html
total 64
-rw-r----- 1 webma apache 61156 Sep 5 08:36 index.html
[root@server1 ~]#_
```

In addition to examining regular permissions, you should minimize the number of files that have the SUID and SGID special permissions set, as these files can be executed by a hacker that gains access to the system to perform tasks as a privileged user. To find all files on the system that have the SUID permission set, you can use the find / -perm /u=s command, and to find all files that have the SGID permission set, you can use the find / -perm /g=s command.

Changing Default Ports

Recall from Chapter 12 that most network services use well-known ports; these ports are commonly searched by hackers when they are looking for systems to attack. Many daemons that provide network services allow you to specify a non-default port number in their configuration file to thwart hackers. For instance, if you change the port number within your Apache Web server configuration file to TCP port 8019, then a hacker who is scanning for Web services running on the default TCP port 80 for HTTP will not locate the Web service running on your computer unless they examine other ports. However, any users that wish to connect to your Web server must specify TCP port 8019 within their Web browser, because Web browsers connect to TCP port 80 by default. For example, if your Web server uses a FQDN of webserver.example.com, you will need to ensure that clients connect to http://webserver.example.com:8019 within their Web browser.

Updating Network Service Software

Because network attacks are regularly reported in the security and open source communities, new versions of network services usually include security-related fixes. As such, these new versions are more resilient to network attacks. Because of this, it is good form to periodically check for new versions of network services, install them, and check the associated documentation for new security-related parameters that can be set in the configuration file.

Running Vulnerability Scanners

Many organizations maintain databases of known vulnerabilities for operating systems and network services, as well as the associated fixes. Most vulnerabilities are given a unique **Common Vulnerabilities and Exposures (CVE)** number for identification. Other vulnerabilities may not use CVE numbers for identification. For example, the Open Web Application Security Project (OWASP) maintains a database of known Web app vulnerabilities by category, with many of these vulnerabilities identified by a **Common Weakness Enumeration (CWE)** number.

There are many **vulnerability scanner** software packages that you can install and run to scan the systems on your network for the vulnerabilities listed within multiple online vulnerability databases. If vulnerabilities are found, the vulnerability scanner software will identify the steps needed to fix these vulnerabilities, which could include a configuration change, software update, or firewall rule change. By scanning the systems on your network periodically using a vulnerability scanner, and taking the recommended actions to fix detected vulnerabilities, you dramatically reduce the chance that a hacker could exploit a software vulnerability on the computers within your network environment.

> **Note** 📎
>
> Open Vulnerability Assessment System (OpenVAS) is a popular vulnerability scanner available for Linux systems. It can be used to scan Windows, Linux, and UNIX systems for known vulnerabilities.

Vulnerability scanners are often incorporated into **Security Information and Event Management (SIEM)** software suites. SIEM can be used to continually monitor the systems on your network for vulnerabilities or attacks, and alert you when one is discovered.

> **Note** 📎
>
> Alienvault Open Source SIEM (OSSIM) is a popular SIEM software suite that can be used to monitor the security of a wide variety of systems on a network.

Configuring a Firewall

Another method that you can use to ensure that network services are as secure as possible is to configure a firewall on your Linux computer using a component of the Linux kernel called **netfilter**. Recall from Chapter 1 that firewalls can be used in your organization to block unwanted network traffic; as a result, firewalls are typically enabled on router interfaces.

Netfilter discards certain network packets according to **chains** of **rules** that are stored in your computer's memory. By default, you can specify firewall rules for three types of chains:

- INPUT chain, for network packets destined for your computer
- FORWARD chain, for network packets that must pass through your computer (if the computer is a router)
- OUTPUT chain, for network packets that originate from your computer

Note

Netfilter can also be used to configure a Linux computer with two or more network interfaces as a NAT router. To do this, you would use the PREROUTING, OUTPUT, and POSTROUTING chains. Consult the `iptables` manual page for more information.

In most cases, no rules exist for the INPUT, FORWARD, or OUTPUT chains after a Linux installation. To create rules that are used for each chain, you must use the `iptables` **command**. Rules can be based on the source IP address, destination IP address, protocol used (TCP, UDP, ICMP), or packet status. For example, to flush all previous rules from memory, specify that forwarded packets are dropped by default, and that packets are only to be forwarded if they originate from the 192.168.1.0 network, you can use the following commands:

```
[root@server1 ~]# iptables -F
[root@server1 ~]# iptables -P FORWARD DROP
[root@server1 ~]# iptables -A FORWARD -s 192.168.1.0/24 -j ACCEPT
[root@server1 ~]#
```

You can then verify the list of rules for each chain in memory by using the following command:

```
[root@server1 ~]# iptables -L
Chain INPUT (policy ACCEPT)
target     prot opt source               destination

Chain FORWARD (policy DROP)
target     prot opt source               destination
ACCEPT     all  --  192.168.1.0/24       anywhere
```

```
Chain OUTPUT (policy ACCEPT)
target       prot opt source                   destination
[root@server1 ~]#_
```

The previous firewall example uses static packet filtering rules. Most technologies today start by using a specific port and then switch to a random port above 32768. A good example of this is SSH. The first SSH packet is addressed to port 22, but the port number is changed in the return packet to a random port above 32768 for subsequent traffic. In a static filter, you would need to allow traffic for all ports above 32768 in order to use SSH.

Instead of doing this, you can use a dynamic (or stateful) packet filter rule by specifying the −m state option to the iptables command. **Stateful packet filters** remember traffic that was originally allowed in an existing session and adjust their rules appropriately. For example, to forward all packets from your internal interface eth1 to your external interface eth0 on your Linux router that are addressed to port 22, you could use the following command:

```
[root@server1 ~]# iptables −A FORWARD −i eth1 −o eth0 −m state
--state NEW -dport 22 -j ACCEPT
[root@server1 ~]#_
```

Next, you can allow all subsequent packets that are part of an allowed existing session, as shown in the following output (remember that only SSH is allowed):

```
[root@server1 ~]# iptables −A FORWARD −i eth1 −o eth0 −m state
--state ESTABLISHED,RELATED -j ACCEPT
[root@server1 ~]#_
```

Table 14-1 provides a list of common options to the iptables command.

Table 14-1   Common iptables Options

Option	Description
-s address	Specifies the source address of packets for a rule
-d address	Specifies the destination address of packets for a rule
-sport port#	Specifies the source port number for a rule
-dport port#	Specifies the destination port number for a rule
-p protocol	Specifies the protocol type for a rule
-i interface	Specifies the input network interface
-o interface	Specifies the output network interface
-j action	Specifies the action that is taken for a rule; common actions include ACCEPT (allow), DROP (disallow), REJECT (disallow and return ICMP error to the source computer), and LOG (allow and log event information)

(continues)

Table 14-1 Common iptables Options (*continued*)

Option	Description
`-m match`	Specifies a match parameter that should be used within the rule; the most common match used is `state`, which creates a stateful packet filtering firewall
`-A chain`	Specifies the chain used
`-L chain`	Lists rules for a certain chain; if no chain is given, all chains are listed
`-P policy`	Specifies the default policy for a certain chain type
`-D number`	Deletes a rule for a chain specified by additional arguments; rules start at number 1
`-R number`	Replaces a rule for a chain specified by additional arguments; rules start at number 1
`-F chain`	Removes all rules for a certain chain; if no chain is specified, it removes all rules for all chains

Note

The order in which firewall rules are defined is the order in which they are applied. Normally, firewall rules are defined to first DROP all traffic destined for the computer (the INPUT chain) and allow only specific traffic by port number.

You can block multiple hosts and networks using a single `iptables` command. To do this, you must first create an **IP set** using the **`ipset` command** that includes the appropriate hosts and networks. Next, you can specify the IP set within your `iptables` command using the `-m set --match-set IPsetname` options, where IPsetname is the name of the IP set you created.

To configure firewall rules for IPv6, you can use the **`ip6tables` command**.

Because chains and rules are stored in memory, they are lost when your computer is shut down. To ensure that they are loaded on each boot on a Fedora 28 system, run the `iptables-save > /etc/sysconfig/iptables` command to save all current chains and rules to the /etc/sysconfig/iptables file. To ensure that they are loaded on each boot on an Ubuntu Server system, you can install the iptables-persistent package and run the `iptables-save > /etc/iptables/rules.v4` command.

There are many software packages that examine the log files on your system for invalid access attempts and automatically update netfilter firewall rules to prevent similar attempts. DenyHosts and Fail2ban are common examples of software packages that provide this functionality.

Ubuntu Linux systems can optionally use the **Uncomplicated Firewall (UFW)** system to provide easy configuration of stateful netfilter firewall rules via the **`ufw` (Uncomplicated Firewall) command**. By default, there are no firewall rules configured on Ubuntu Server distributions; to enable default firewall rules at boot time that deny incoming traffic, but allow outgoing traffic, you can run the following commands:

```
[root@server1 ~]# ufw enable
Firewall is active and enabled on system startup
[root@server1 ~]# ufw default deny incoming
Default incoming policy changed to 'deny'
(be sure to update your rules accordingly)
[root@server1 ~]# ufw default allow outgoing
Default outgoing policy changed to 'allow'
(be sure to update your rules accordingly)
[root@server1 ~]#_
```

By default, only incoming SSH is allowed after enabling UFW. However, you can provide firewall exceptions for other services running on Ubuntu Server. For example, to allow telnet connections, you could use the following command:

```
[root@server1 ~]# ufw allow telnet
Rule updated
Rule updated (v6)
[root@server1 ~]#_
```

Alternatively, you could provide firewall exceptions by protocol and port number, as well as source and destination. For example, to allow TCP port 80 and 443 traffic from any host to any host, you could use the following command:

```
[root@server1 ~]# ufw allow proto tcp from any to any port 80,443
Rule updated
Rule updated (v6)
[root@server1 ~]#_
```

You can also enable UFW logging using the `ufw logging on` command; this will write all firewall access to the system log, and could be used by other programs to locate malicious network traffic.

To view your current Ubuntu Firewall rules, you can use the following command:

```
[root@server1 ~]# ufw status verbose
Status: active
Logging: on (low)
Default: deny (incoming), allow (outgoing), deny (routed)
New profiles: skip

To                         Action        From
--                         ------        ----
22/tcp                     ALLOW IN      Anywhere
23/tcp                     ALLOW IN      Anywhere
```

```
80,443/tcp              ALLOW IN      Anywhere
22/tcp (v6)             ALLOW IN      Anywhere (v6)
23/tcp (v6)             ALLOW IN      Anywhere (v6)
80,443/tcp (v6)         ALLOW IN      Anywhere (v6)
[root@server1 ~]#_
```

Note

To view a list of common `ufw` arguments, you can run the `ufw help` command or view the `ufw` manual page.

Ubuntu Firewall loads default firewall rules from the /etc/default/ufw file at boot time; all other firewall rules are loaded from files under the /etc/ufw directory. The `ufw` command automatically updates these files to ensure that any firewall configuration you perform is also performed at boot time.

Because firewall rules can quickly become complex, many Linux distributions, such as Fedora 28, implement a **firewall daemon (firewalld)** that can configure netfilter firewall rules with more flexibility through the use of network zones and service names. A **network zone** defines the level of trust for network connections and can be mutable (modification to its definition is allowed) or immutable (its definition cannot be changed). Table 14-2 lists common network zones used by firewalld.

Table 14-2   Common Network Zones

Network zone	Type	Description
drop	Immutable	Deny all incoming connections; outgoing ones are accepted
block	Immutable	Deny all incoming connections, with ICMP host-prohibited messages issued to the sender
trusted	Immutable	Allow all network connections
public	Mutable	Public areas, do not trust other computers
external	Mutable	For computers with masquerading enabled, protecting a local network
dmz	Mutable	For computers publicly accessible with restricted access
work	Mutable	For trusted work areas
home	Mutable	For trusted home network connections
internal	Mutable	For internal network, restrict incoming connections

Network zones allow you to maintain different sets of firewall rules for different environments. When you connect to a new network using a laptop computer, NetworkManager will prompt you to choose the network zone that you wish to use with firewalld for your particular environment. If you choose the work network zone, firewalld will allow file sharing traffic by default. Alternatively, if you choose the public network zone, firewalld will prevent file sharing traffic by default.

The default network zone used on your system is defined in the /etc/firewalld/firewalld.conf file, and custom network zone configuration is stored in the /etc/firewalld/zones directory. You can manage network zones and firewall rules that allow or deny traffic by service or port through the use of the `firewall-cmd` **command.** Some common options to the `firewall-cmd` command are listed in Table 14-3.

Table 14-3   **Common firewall-cmd Options**

Option	Description
`--get-zones`	Displays all available network zones
`--get-services`	Displays a list of names used by firewalld to identify network services
`--get-default-zone`	Specifies the source port number for a rule
`--set-default-zone=zone`	Specifies the destination port number for a rule
`--get-active-zones`	Displays the network interfaces that are active for each network zone
`--list-all-zones`	Displays the services that are enabled (allowed) for each network zone
`--list-all`	Displays the services that are enabled (allowed) for the current network zone
`--zone=zone --list-all`	Displays the services that are enabled (allowed) for the specified network zone (*zone*)
`--add-service=service`	Enable (allow) the specified *service* within the current network zone
`--add-service=service` `--permanent`	Ensure that the specified *service* is enabled (allowed) within the current network zone at boot time
`--add-port=port`	Enable (allow) the specified *port* within the current network zone
`--add-port=port` `--permanent`	Ensure that the specified *port* is enabled (allowed) within the current network zone at boot time
`--remove-service=service`	Disable (disallow) the specified *service* within the current network zone
`--remove-service=service --permanent`	Ensure that the specified *service* is disabled (disallowed) within the current network zone at boot time

(continues)

Table 14-3   Common firewall-cmd Options *(continued)*

Option	Description
`--remove-port=port`	Disable (disallow) the specified *port* within the current network zone
`--remove-port=port` `--permanent`	Ensure that the specified *port* is disabled (disallowed) within the current network zone at boot time
`--query-service=service`	Returns yes if the specified *service* is enabled (allowed) within the current network zone, and no if it is not
`--query-port=port`	Returns yes if the specified *port* is enabled (allowed) within the current network zone, and no if it is not

To define a stateful firewall exception for postgresql in your default (current) network zone and also ensure that this exception is loaded at boot time, you could use the following commands:

```
[root@server1 ~]# firewall-cmd --add-service=postgresql
success
[root@server1 ~]# firewall-cmd --permanent --add-service=postgresql
success
[root@server1 ~]#_
```

You can instead define a stateful firewall exception for traffic by port number. For example, to define a firewall exception for SSH (TCP port 22) in your default (current) network zone and also ensure that this exception is loaded at boot time, you could use the following commands:

```
[root@server1 ~]# firewall-cmd --add-port=22/tcp
success
[root@server1 ~]# firewall-cmd --permanent --add-port=22/tcp
success
[root@server1 ~]#_
```

Note 📎

You used the `firewall-cmd` command during the hands-on projects in Chapter 13 to allow traffic destined to your Fedora Linux virtual machine by service name.

Many Linux distributions also provide a graphical firewall configuration utility that can be used to configure netfilter by service name or port. On Fedora 28, the **Firewall Configuration utility** shown in Figure 14-2 automatically creates netfilter rules based on your selections via firewalld. These rules are activated immediately because the Configuration drop-down dialog box shown in Figure 14-2 is set to Runtime by default; to set rules that are loaded at boot time, you must select Permanent from the Configuration drop-down dialog box. You can start the Firewall Configuration utility within the GNOME desktop by opening the Activities menu and navigating to Show Applications, Sundry, Firewall.

Figure 14-2   The Firewall Configuration utility

Configuring SELinux

Security Enhanced Linux (SELinux) is a series of kernel patches and utilities created by the National Security Agency (NSA) that enforce security on your system using policies that prevent applications from being used to access resources and system components in insecure ways. SELinux adds a **label** to each file, directory, and process. Preconfigured SELinux policies contain rules that identify the process labels that should be allowed to access certain file and directory labels. When SELinux is enabled, the Linux kernel enforces the rules within the SELinux security policies to prevent processes from accessing areas of the system that could pose a security concern.

> **Note**
>
> SELinux is enabled by default in Fedora Linux.

Recall from Chapter 3 that a period (.) immediately following the mode of a file or directory within output of the `ls -l` command indicates that the file or directory has an SELinux label. To view the SELinux labels for files and directories, you can add the `-Z` option to the `ls` command. This is shown in the following output for the index. html file within the Apache document root directory on a Fedora system (/var/www /html):

```
[root@server1 html]# pwd
/var/www/html
[root@server1 html]# ls -l
total 4
-rw-r-----. 1 apache root 46 Nov 16 17:32 index.html
[root@server1 html]# ls -Z
unconfined_u:object_r:httpd_sys_content_t:s0 index.html
[root@server1 html]#_
```

The previous output indicates that the index.html file has an SELinux label of `unconfined_u:object_r:httpd_sys_content_t:s0`. SELinux labels consist of the following four colon (:) delimited sections:

```
user:role:type:level
```

The `user` section identifies the Linux user type, and the `role` section identifies the category the user belongs to within SELinux policies; for most user-generated files, these will be `unconfined_u` (unconfined user) and `object_r` (object access role), respectively.

The `type` section is the most important part of an SELinux label; it defines the classification of the file or directory. Only processes that contain the same classification prefix will normally be allowed to access the file or directory within SELinux policy rules. In the previous output, the index.html has a classification of `httpd_sys_content_t` (Apache system content type); thus, only processes that have a classification of `httpd_t` (Apache type) will be permitted to access the index.html file. To view the SELinux labels for processes, you can add the `-Z` option to the `ps` command. The following output indicates that the currently running Apache processes contain a `httpd_t` classification and will be able to access the index.html shown earlier as a result:

```
[root@server1 html]# ps -eZ | grep httpd
system_u:system_r:httpd_t:s0     1625 ?          00:00:00 httpd
system_u:system_r:httpd_t:s0     1626 ?          00:00:00 httpd
system_u:system_r:httpd_t:s0     1628 ?          00:00:00 httpd
system_u:system_r:httpd_t:s0     1629 ?          00:00:00 httpd
system_u:system_r:httpd_t:s0     1630 ?          00:00:00 httpd
[root@server1 html]#_
```

The level section is an optional attribute; it is only used if you extend SELinux functionality to use **Multi-Level Security (MLS)** or **Multi-Category Security (MCS)**. MLS can be used to restrict access to files, based on additional attributes provided by the organization (e.g., Top-Secret, Confidential, Public), whereas MCS can be used to restrict similar process types from accessing one another.

> **Note** 📎
>
> You can use the `seinfo` **command** to view the values available on your system for SELinux label sections. For example, `seinfo -u` displays user values, `seinfo -r` displays role values, and `seinfo -t` displays type values.

To enable SELinux, you can edit the /etc/selinux/config file and set one of the following SELINUX options:

- `SELINUX = enforcing` (policy settings are enforced by SELinux)
- `SELINUX = permissive` (SELinux generates warnings only and logs events)
- `SELINUX = disabled` (SELinux is disabled)

Next, you can select an SELINUX policy by configuring one of the following SELINUXTYPE options within the /etc/selinux/config file:

- `SELINUXTYPE = targeted` (all network daemons are protected)
- `SELINUXTYPE = minimum` (only critical network daemons are protected)
- `SELINUXTYPE = mls` (use MLS attributes instead of type classifications)

Most Linux systems that use SELinux have definitions for the targeted policy that protect the system from malicious applications that can damage system files or compromise security. After modifying the /etc/selinux/config file to enable SELinux, you must reboot to relabel the existing files on the system. Following this, you can use the `sestatus` **command** to view your current SELinux status:

```
[root@server1 ~]# sestatus -v
SELinux status:                 enabled
SELinuxfs mount:                /sys/fs/selinux
SELinux root directory:         /etc/selinux
Loaded policy name:             targeted
Current mode:                   enforcing
Mode from config file:          enforcing
Policy MLS status:              enabled
Policy deny_unknown status:     allowed
Memory protection checking:     actual (secure)
Max kernel policy version:      31
```

```
Process contexts:
Current context:        unconfined_u:unconfined_r:unconfined_t:s0-s0:c0.
                        c1023
Init context:           system_u:system_r:init_t:s0
/usr/sbin/sshd          system_u:system_r:sshd_t:s0-s0:c0.c1023

File contexts:
Controlling terminal:   unconfined_u:object_r:user_devpts_t:s0
/etc/passwd             system_u:object_r:passwd_file_t:s0
/etc/shadow             system_u:object_r:shadow_t:s0
/bin/bash               system_u:object_r:shell_exec_t:s0
/bin/login              system_u:object_r:login_exec_t:s0
/bin/sh                 system_u:object_r:bin_t:s0 -> system_u:object_r:
                        shell_exec_t:s0
/sbin/agetty            system_u:object_r:getty_exec_t:s0
/sbin/init              system_u:object_r:bin_t:s0 -> system_u:object_r:
                        init_exec_t:s0
/usr/sbin/sshd          system_u:object_r:sshd_exec_t:s0 [root@server1 ~]#_
```

Note from the previous output that the system is enforcing the targeted
SELinux policy. Sometimes, SELinux blocks network services from accessing files
and directories that you would like the services to access. To determine whether a
network service problem is the result of SELinux enforcement, you can temporarily
change the SELinux mode from enforcing to permissive. If the problem is no longer
present in permissive mode, then SELinux enforcement is the cause. You can use
the `setenforce` **command** to easily switch between enforcing and permissive
mode, as well as use the `getenforce` **command** to view your current mode. This is
demonstrated in the following output:

```
[root@server1 ~]# getenforce
Enforcing
[root@server1 ~]# setenforce permissive
[root@server1 ~]# getenforce
Permissive
[root@server1 ~]# setenforce enforcing
[root@server1 ~]# getenforce
Enforcing
[root@server1 ~]#_
```

In most cases, SELinux enforcement problems are the result of an incorrect label
applied to files and directories. SELinux automatically labels files and directories on
the first boot after SELinux is enabled, as well as when new files and directories are
created. If you copy a file that has an SELinux label to another directory, SELinux will
set the correct label on the newly created copy in the target directory. However, if you

move a file that has an SELinux label to a new directory, the files will retain its original SELinux label, because a new file was not created in the process. This is illustrated in the following output, in which an index.html is moved from the root user's home directory to the /var/www/html directory:

```
[root@server1 ~]# ls -Z index.html
unconfined_u:object_r:admin_home_t:s0 index.html
[root@server1 ~]# mv index.html /var/www/html
[root@server1 ~]# ls -Z /var/www/html/index.html
unconfined_u:object_r:admin_home_t:s0 /var/www/html/index.html
[root@server1 ~]#_
```

Because the index.html in the previous output retains its original classification following the move operation, it cannot be read by the Apache daemon, as SELinux prevents Apache from reading files that do not have a httpd_ classification. Consequently, clients will receive an HTTP 403 Forbidden error when attempting to access the Web page in their Web browser. To remedy the issue, you can manually change the classification of the /var/www/html/index.html file to the correct classification (httpd_sys_content_t) using the chcon **command** as shown in the following output:

```
[root@server1 ~]# chcon -t httpd_sys_content_t /var/www/html/index.html
[root@server1 ~]# ls -Z /var/www/html/index.html
unconfined_u:object_r:httpd_sys_content_t:s0 /var/www/html/index.html
[root@server1 ~]#_
```

You can also use the **restorecon command** to force SELinux to relabel a file using the correct classification. For example, the restorecon /var/www/html/index. html command could have been used in place of the chcon command in the previous output to set the correct classification on the /var/www/html/index.html file.

> **Note** 📎
>
> To force SELinux to relabel all files on the system during the next boot time, you can create a /.autorelabel file using the touch /.autorelabel command.

Not all SELinux problems that you may encounter are related to incorrect labelling. For example, the default SELinux targeted policy does not allow the Apache daemon to read Web content within user home directories. As a result, if you enable home directory hosting within Apache, SELinux will prevent the feature from working. To remedy the issue, you can change the targeted policy settings by modifying the appropriate files within the /etc/selinux/targeted directory. Alternatively, you can locate the policy setting that allows Apache to read Web content within user home directories using the `getsebool` command, and modify that setting using the `setsebool` command. This is demonstrated in the following output:

```
[root@server1 ~]# getsebool -a | grep httpd | grep home
httpd_enable_homedirs --> off
[root@server1 ~]# setsebool -P httpd_enable_homedirs on
[root@server1 ~]# getsebool -a | grep httpd | grep home
httpd_enable_homedirs --> on
[root@server1 ~]#_
```

On systems that use SELinux, the auditd daemon listens to kernel system calls and logs SELinux-related events to the /var/log/audit/audit.log file. You can view this log file to identify problems related to SELinux enforcement. Additionally, you can use the `audit2why` command to generate easy-to-read descriptions of SELinux-related events within /var/log /audit/audit.log using the `audit2why < /var/log/audit/audit.log` command. These descriptions are often very helpful in determining the cause of an SELinux restriction.

Configuring AppArmor

AppArmor is an alternative to SELinux that provides a similar type of protection for programs that access system resources. It consists of a kernel module and a series of utilities that provide restrictions for individual programs on a Linux system. Restrictions for each program are stored within text files named for the program under the /etc/apparmor.d directory; each text file is called an **AppArmor profile**. For example, the AppArmor profile for the CUPS daemon (/usr/sbin/cupsd) would be stored within the /etc/apparmor.d/usr.sbin.cupsd file.

Note

AppArmor is enabled by default in Ubuntu Linux.

AppArmor profiles can be enforced by AppArmor (called enforce mode) or used to generate warnings and log events only (called complain mode). To view the AppArmor profiles configured for each mode, as well as the active processes on the system that are being managed by AppArmor, you can run the `aa-status` command, as shown here:

```
[root@server1 ~]# aa-status
apparmor module is loaded.
35 profiles are loaded.
34 profiles are in enforce mode.
    /sbin/dhclient
    /usr/bin/lxc-start
    /usr/bin/man
```

```
/usr/lib/NetworkManager/nm-dhcp-client.action
/usr/lib/NetworkManager/nm-dhcp-helper
/usr/lib/connman/scripts/dhclient-script
/usr/lib/cups/backend/cups-pdf
/usr/lib/snapd/snap-confine
/usr/lib/snapd/snap-confine//mount-namespace-capture-helper
/usr/sbin/chronyd
/usr/sbin/cups-browsed
/usr/sbin/cupsd
/usr/sbin/cupsd//third_party
/usr/sbin/tcpdump
docker-default
lxc-container-default
lxc-container-default-cgns
lxc-container-default-with-mounting
lxc-container-default-with-nesting
man_filter
man_groff
snap-update-ns.core
snap-update-ns.docker
snap-update-ns.notepad3
snap-update-ns.powershell
snap.core.hook.configure
snap.docker.compose
snap.docker.docker
snap.docker.dockerd
snap.docker.help
snap.docker.hook.install
snap.docker.hook.post-refresh
snap.docker.machine
snap.notepad3.notepad3
1 profiles are in complain mode.
snap.powershell.powershell
5 processes have profiles defined.
5 processes are in enforce mode.
/usr/sbin/chronyd (1520)
/usr/sbin/cups-browsed (10622)
/usr/sbin/cupsd (10621)
snap.docker.dockerd (1447)
snap.docker.dockerd (2028)
0 processes are in complain mode.
0 processes are unconfined but have a profile defined.
[root@server1 ~]#_
```

Note from the previous output that 34 AppArmor profiles are loaded and set to enforce mode, while 1 AppArmor profile is loaded and set to complain mode. However, only 5 processes that match these AppArmor profiles are currently started, and all of them are set to enforce mode. Moreover, there are 0 processes running that do not have a matching AppArmor profile; these processes are referred to as unconfined processes within the previous output, and can also be shown using the `aa-unconfined` **command**.

To switch an AppArmor profile to enforce mode, you can use the `aa-enforce` **command**. Alternatively, you can use the `aa-complain` **command** to switch an AppArmor profile to complain mode, or the `aa-disable` **command** to disable an AppArmor profile. For example, to switch the CUPS daemon AppArmor profile (/etc /apparmor.d/usr.sbin.cupsd) to complain mode, you could run the following command:

```
[root@server1 ~]# aa-complain /etc/apparmor.d/usr.sbin.cupsd
Setting /etc/apparmor.d/usr.sbin.cupsd to complain mode.
[root@server1 ~]#_
```

> **Note** 🔗
>
> Although AppArmor is installed by default on Ubuntu Server, you must install the apparmor-utils package from a software repository in order to use the `aa-unconfined`, `aa-enforce`, `aa-complain`, and `aa-disable` commands.

As with SELinux, AppArmor may inadvertently block network services from accessing desired resources. To determine if an enforced AppArmor profile is the cause of the problem, you can temporarily set the AppArmor profile for the network service to complain mode. If this remedies the problem, then you can adjust the appropriate settings within the AppArmor profile for the network service in the /etc/apparmor.d directory and set the AppArmor profile to enforce mode afterwards. For problems that affect multiple AppArmor profiles, you can often modify the settings within a text file under the /etc/apparmor.d/tunables directory. For example, if you change the location of user home directories from /home to /users on a Linux system, many AppArmor profiles will prevent network services from accessing home directory content. In this case, you can modify the line `@{HOMEDIRS}=/home/` to read `@{HOMEDIRS}=/users /` within the /etc/apparmor.d/tunables/home file.

> **Note** 🔗
>
> To view the available settings that you can configure within an AppArmor profile, you can view the `apparmor.d` manual page.

Troubleshooting Methodology

After you have successfully installed Linux, you must configure services on the system, secure local and network access, document settings, as well as maintain the system's integrity over time. This includes monitoring, proactive maintenance, and reactive maintenance, as illustrated in Figure 14-3.

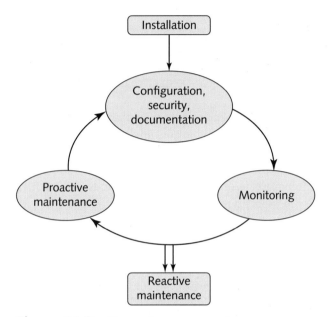

Figure 14-3   The maintenance cycle

Monitoring, the activity on which Linux administrators spend the most time, involves examining log files and running performance utilities periodically to identify problems and their causes. **Proactive maintenance** involves taking the required steps to minimize the chance of future problems as well as their impact. Performing regular system backups and identifying potential problem areas are examples of proactive maintenance. All proactive maintenance tasks should be documented for future reference. This information, along with any data backups, is vital to the reconstruction of your system, should it suffer catastrophic failure.

Reactive maintenance is used to correct problems when they arise during monitoring. When a problem is solved, it needs to be documented and the system adjusted proactively to reduce the likelihood that the same problem will occur in the future. Furthermore, documenting the solution to problems creates a template for action, allowing subsequent or similar problems to be remedied faster.

> **Note** 📎
>
> Any system **documentation** should either be printed and kept in a log book, or stored within a file on a separate computer because this information might be lost during a system failure. Many organizations store system documentation within their help desk ticketing software, which is backed up regularly to ensure that the documentation is not lost during a system failure.

Reactive maintenance is further composed of many tasks known as **troubleshooting procedures**, which can be used to efficiently solve a problem in a systematic manner.

When a problem occurs, you need to gather as much information about the problem as possible. This might include examining system log files, viewing the contents of the /proc and /sys filesystems, or running information utilities, such as `ps` or `lsblk`. In addition, you might research the symptoms of the problem on the Internet; many technology-related websites list commands and log files that can be used to check for certain problems.

> **Note** 📎
>
> The `tail -f /path/to/logfile` command opens a specific log file for continuous viewing; this allows you to see entries as they are added, which is useful when gathering information about system problems. If your system uses Systemd, you can use the `--follow` option to the `journalctl` command to do the same. For example, to view chronyd events as they are added, you can use the `journalctl _COMM=chronyd --follow` command.

Following this, you need to try to isolate the problem by examining the information gathered. Determine whether the problem is persistent or intermittent and whether it affects all users or just one.

Given this information, you might then generate a list of possible causes and solutions organized by placing the most probable solution at the top of the list and the least probable solution at the bottom of the list. Using the Internet at this stage is beneficial because solutions for many Linux problems are posted on websites that can be found by performing a Google search for key words related to the problem. In addition, posting the problem on a Linux-related forum website will likely generate many possible solutions.

Next, you need to implement and test each possible solution for results until the problem is resolved. When implementing possible solutions, it is very important that you only apply one change at a time. If you make multiple modifications, it will be unclear as to what worked and why.

After the problem has been solved, document the solution for future reference and proceed to take proactive maintenance measures to reduce the chance of the same problem recurring in the future. These troubleshooting procedures are outlined in Figure 14-4.

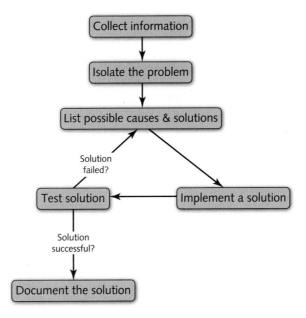

Figure 14-4   Common troubleshooting procedures

The troubleshooting procedures listed in Figure 14-4 serve as a guideline only. You might need to alter your approach for certain problems. Remember, troubleshooting is an art that you will begin to master only with practice. There are, however, two golden rules that should guide you during any troubleshooting process:

- *Prioritize problems*—If you need to solve multiple problems, prioritize the problems according to severity and spend the most time on the most severe problems. Becoming fixated on a small problem and ignoring larger issues results in much lower productivity. If a problem is too difficult to solve in a given period of time, it is good practice to ask for help.
- *Try to solve the root of the problem*—Some solutions might appear successful in the short term yet fail over the long term because of an underlying problem. Effective troubleshooting requires good instincts, which in turn comes from a solid knowledge of the system hardware and configuration. To avoid missing the underlying cause of any problem, try to justify why a certain solution was successful. If it is unclear why a certain solution was successful, it is likely that you have missed an underlying cause to the problem that might need to be remedied in the future to prevent the same problem from recurring.

Resolving Common System Problems

The possible problems that can arise on Linux systems are too numerous to list here. However, as a troubleshooter, you'll most often face a set of the common problems described in this section. Most Linux problems can be divided into four categories: hardware-related, application-related, filesystem-related, and network-related.

Hardware-Related Problems

Hardware devices within a computer fall into one of several categories, and each category has different troubleshooting practices. When troubleshooting peripheral devices, such as monitors, keyboards, printers, and mice, first ensure that they are properly connected to the port on the computer. If a monitor has a loose connection to the display port, the picture will be distorted or unavailable. Similarly, if a USB mouse, printer, or keyboard becomes unresponsive, it may not be seated properly in the USB port of the computer. An incorrect keymap can also cause a keyboard to become unresponsive; in this case you can connect another keyboard and run the `system-config-keyboard` or `localectl` command and select the correct keymap. In rare cases, the peripheral device or port itself may be faulty, or the associated hardware within the computer that controls the peripheral device may have failed.

When troubleshooting hardware devices, such as video cards and network interface cards, first ensure that the card is seated properly in the slot on the computer motherboard, and that the proper device driver module is loaded by the Linux kernel. You can use the commands listed in Table 6-2 to determine whether the Linux has the correct device driver module for your hardware, and proceed to install the correct one if necessary. If the hardware device is physically present but not listed by the commands within Table 6-2, you can use the `dmidecode` **command** to list the BIOS information about the device, which can be searched online to locate a device driver module. In rare cases, the hardware device may not have a Linux device driver, and will not be usable within Linux as a result.

Memory failures can result in a wide range of erratic behavior within Linux, including frozen applications and kernel panics. If you suspect a memory failure, you can run the memtest86 utility from Linux installation media to test and identify a faulty memory stick.

Many problems that affect storage devices, such as hard disks and SSDs, are related to the speed of the underlying storage device itself. If too many processes write to a slow storage device, users will experience problems reading and writing data to the filesystems on that device. In some cases, you can modify how the Linux kernel writes to the hard disk or SSD to fix read and write problems on a busy system. By default, the Linux kernel uses a scheduling method called completely fair queuing (cfq) when writing to storage devices, but this can be changed to either noop (no operation) or deadline to improve performance under certain situations. For example, to modify the scheduling method used for the first SATA hard disk (sda) to use noop instead of cfq, and verify the results, you could run the following commands:

```
[root@server1 ~]# cat /sys/block/sda/queue/scheduler
noop deadline [cfq]
[root@server1 ~]# echo noop > /sys/block/sda/queue/scheduler
[root@server1 ~]# cat /sys/block/sda/queue/scheduler
[noop] deadline cfq
[root@server1 ~]#_
```

If modifying the scheduling method results in better performance, you can ensure that the scheduler is set at boot time by modifying the GRUB bootloader. For example, to ensure that the noop scheduling method is used at boot time, you could append `elevator=noop` to the `GRUB_CMDLINE_LINUX` line within /etc/default/grub and run the appropriate `grub2-mkconfig` command to rebuild the GRUB configuration files.

Other storage-related problems may be related to device access. For example, if a SATA or SCSI cable becomes unseated, the associated hard disk or SSD will not be visible by the system. Similarly, a SCSI controller can sometimes fail to detect a hard disk that is properly connected to it. In this case, you can force the SCSI controller to rescan the SCSI bus for connected devices; for the first SCSI bus, you could run the `echo "- - -" > /sys/class/scsi_host/host0/scan` command.

Removable storage device access problems can usually be solved by writing a udev rule that dictates how the udev daemon processes the device when it is inserted into the system. For example, to give members of the developer group the ability to mount a particular Verbatim USB storage device in order to perform backups, you could add a udev rule to a text file that has a .rules extension within the /etc/udev/rules.d directory (e.g., /etc/udev/rules.d/VerbatimUSB.rules). To do this, you must first insert the Verbatim USB storage device and locate its bus and device ID using the `lsusb` command:

```
[root@server1 ~]# lsusb
Bus 001 Device 004: ID 18a5:024a Verbatim, Ltd
Bus 001 Device 003: ID 05ac:828d Apple, Inc.
Bus 001 Device 002: ID 80ee:0021 VirtualBox USB Tablet
Bus 001 Device 001: ID 1d6b:0001 Linux Foundation 1.1 root hub
[root@server1 ~]#_
```

Next, you can use the bus ID (001) and device ID (004) shown in the previous output within the following `udevadm` **command** to identify its unique attributes:

```
[root@server1 ~]# udevadm info -a -p $(udevadm info -q path -n /
dev/bus/usb/001/004)
```

```
looking at device '/devices/pci0000:00/0000:00:06.0/usb1/1-3':
  KERNEL=="1-3"
  SUBSYSTEM=="usb"
  DRIVER=="usb"
  ATTR{authorized}=="1"
  ATTR{avoid_reset_quirk}=="0"
  ATTR{bConfigurationValue}=="1"
  ATTR{bDeviceClass}=="00"
  ATTR{bDeviceProtocol}=="00"
  ATTR{bDeviceSubClass}=="00"
  ATTR{bMaxPacketSize0}=="64"
  ATTR{bMaxPower}=="200mA"
  ATTR{bNumConfigurations}=="1"
  ATTR{bNumInterfaces}==" 1"
  ATTR{bcdDevice}=="0100"
  ATTR{bmAttributes}=="80"
  ATTR{busnum}=="1"
  ATTR{configuration}==""
  ATTR{devnum}=="4"
  ATTR{devpath}=="3"
  ATTR{idProduct}=="024a"
  ATTR{idVendor}=="18a5"
  ATTR{ltm_capable}=="no"
  ATTR{manufacturer}=="Verbatim"
  ATTR{maxchild}=="0"
  ATTR{product}=="STORE N GO"
  ATTR{quirks}=="0x0"
  ATTR{removable}=="unknown"
  ATTR{serial}=="070B43C65D99D047"
  ATTR{speed}=="12"
  ATTR{urbnum}=="1385"
  ATTR{version}==" 1.10"

<<<additional output omitted>>>

[root@server1 ~]#_
```

From the previous output, you could use the product attribute (ATTR{product}
=="STORE N GO") alongside the device subsystem type (SUBSYSTEM=="usb") to
uniquely identify the USB storage device within a udev rule. Thus, to ensure that
members of the developer group can mount this particular USB storage device, you
could add the line SUBSYSTEMS=="usb", ATTRS{product}=="STORE N GO",

GROUP="developers" to the /etc/udev/rules.d/VerbatimUSB.rules file. Next, you could run the udevadm control -R command to force udev to reload the new rules from the /etc/udev/rules directory.

> **Note** 📎
>
> You can also write udev rules that trigger an event when a device is inserted into the system. To learn more about udev rules, view the udevadm manual page.

Because hard disks and SSDs are used frequently, they are the most common hardware component to fail on Linux systems. If the Linux system uses a fault tolerant storage configuration, such as hardware or software RAID 1 or 5, or a fault tolerant ZFS or BTRFS volume, the data on the failed hard disk or SSD can be regenerated after you replace the failed device as discussed in Chapter 6.

If, however, the Linux system does not use a fault tolerant storage configuration, and the hard disk or SSD that failed contained partitions that were mounted on noncritical directories, such as /home or /var, then you can perform the following steps to recover the data:

1. Power down the computer and replace the failed hard disk or SSD.
2. Boot the Linux system.
3. Create partitions on the replaced hard disk or SSD.
4. Optionally configure LVM logical volumes from the partitions created in Step 3.
5. Use the mkfs (or equivalent) command to create filesystems on the partitions or LVM logical volumes.
6. Restore the original data using a backup utility (e.g., tar, restore, or cpio).
7. Ensure that /etc/fstab has the appropriate entries to mount the filesystems at system startup.

Alternatively, if the hard disk or SSD that contains the **/** filesystem fails, you can perform the following steps:

1. Power down the computer and replace the failed hard disk or SSD.
2. Reinstall Linux on the new hard disk or SSD (remembering to recreate the original partition and volume structure during installation).
3. Restore the original configuration and data files using a backup utility (e.g., tar, restore, or cpio).

Application-Related Problems

Applications can fail during execution for a number of reasons, including missing dependencies, system configuration, process restrictions, or conflicting applications.

Recall from Chapter 11 that most applications depend on shared program libraries and other prerequisite packages. If a shared library or prerequisite package is removed from the system, the application may crash or work with limited functionality. You can use the -V option to the rpm or dpkg command to determine if a package is missing a file or prerequisite package, as well as use the ldd command to identify missing libraries for an application. Additionally, an application can fail following an update if the updated version is incompatible with existing software or shared libraries on the system.

Restrictive file permissions, incorrect file ownership, missing environment variables, SELinux, and AppArmor may prevent a process from accessing files needed for the process to run properly. However, processes can also be restricted by a number of other constraints that can prevent them from executing properly. Recall that all processes require a PID from the system process table. Too many processes running on the system can use all available PIDs in the process table; this is typically the result of a large number of zombie processes. Killing the parent process of the zombie processes then frees several entries in the process table.

In addition, processes can initiate numerous connections to files on the filesystem in addition to Standard Input, Standard Output, and Standard Error. These connections are called **file handles**. The shell restricts the number of file handles that programs can open to 1024 by default on most systems; to increase the maximum number of file handles to 5000, you can run the command ulimit –n 5000. The ulimit **command** can also be used to increase the number of processes that users can start in a shell; this might be required for programs that start a great deal of child processes. For example, to increase the maximum number of user processes to 30000, you can use the command ulimit –u 30000.

To isolate application problems that are not related to missing dependencies or restrictions, you should first check the log file produced by the application. Most application log files are stored in the /var/log directory or subdirectories of the /var/log directory named for the application. Even if an application stores its log files elsewhere, it usually hard links or symbolically links its log files to files within the /var/log directory. For example, to view the errors for the Apache daemon, you can view the appropriate log files created by the Apache daemon under the /var/log/httpd directory on Fedora systems, or the /var/log/apache2 directory on Ubuntu systems.

Applications might also run into difficulties gaining resources during execution and stop functioning. Often, restarting the process using a SIGHUP solves this problem. This condition might also be caused by another process on the system that attempts to use the same resources. To determine if this is the case, attempt to start the application when fewer processes are loaded, such as in single user mode (runlevel 1). If resource conflict seems to be the cause of the problem, check the Internet for a newer version of the application or an application fix. Many Linux distributions start the **Automatic Bug Reporting Tool Daemon (abrtd)** by default to send any application crash data to an online bug reporting site, such as Bugzilla. This information is then distributed to the appropriate open source developers, who can create an updated version of the program that fixes the issue.

Filesystem-Related Problems

Filesystems are accessed frequently by the operating system as they provide the storage for most user and system files. Accordingly, filesystem limits, corruption, and bad blocks are the most common filesystem-related problems that Linux administrators encounter.

Problems that prevent users from creating or saving data to files are often the result of a user quota on a filesystem. You can use the `quota -u username` command to determine whether a user has reached their quota limit, and the `edquota -u username` command to modify the quota limits for that user. Similarly, users will encounter errors creating or saving to files on a filesystem if that filesystem has no data blocks or inodes available. You can use the `df` command to list the available data blocks for each filesystem, and the `df -i` command to list the available inodes within each filesystem's inode table. If there are no free data blocks, or the inode table has no free inodes, you can remove files, or move files to another filesystem to remedy the issue. If the filesystem is stored on a LVM, RAID, ZFS, or BTRFS volume, you can instead add storage and extend the filesystem to remedy the problem.

Filesystem corruption or bad blocks can cause a wide range of problems, including missing files, errors when opening files, very slow write requests, errors printed to the console, and failure to mount. Running the appropriate filesystem repair utility (e.g., `fsck`) can be used to remedy these problems. More specifically, if you suspect corruption or bad blocks for a filesystem mounted to a noncritical directory, such as /home or /var, you should perform the following troubleshooting steps:

1. Unmount the filesystem, if mounted.
2. Run the `fsck` (or equivalent) command on the filesystem device.
3. If the `fsck` (or equivalent) command cannot repair the filesystem, use the `mkfs` (or equivalent) command to re-create the filesystem and restore the original data for the filesystem using a backup utility.

Note

Do not restore data onto a damaged filesystem; ensure that the filesystem has been recreated first.

If the root (/) filesystem becomes corrupted, the system is unstable and must be turned off. Following this, you can perform the following troubleshooting steps:

1. Boot your system from your installation or live media to perform system rescue, as described in Chapter 6.
2. Run the `fsck` (or equivalent) command on the root (/) filesystem device.

3. If the `fsck` (or equivalent) command cannot repair the root (/) filesystem, use the `mkfs` (or equivalent) command to re-create the filesystem and restore the original data for the filesystem using a backup utility.
4. Boot your system normally following the system rescue.

Network-Related Problems

Problems related to the network are common within most environments. The most common network issues that Linux administrators encounter relate to network connectivity, network service access, and network latency.

Network Connectivity Issues

If you are unable to connect to other computers on the network from a Linux system, first determine if the network interface is active and has an IP address (e.g., using the `ifconfig` command). If an IP configuration is not available on a wired network interface, check to ensure that the Ethernet cable is connected to the Ethernet port on the computer, and run the appropriate command to activate the interface. For a wireless network interface, reconnect to your wireless access point within NetworkManager or your desktop environment. Next, check to ensure that you have the correct IP settings configured for your network interface. If your network interface uses DHCP to obtain IP settings, also ensure that the DHCP server is available on the network and has not exhausted its range of IP addresses.

Following this, you should test connectivity to the IP address of your network interface (e.g., using the `ping IP_address` command). If you do not receive a successful response, then the driver module for your network interface has experienced a failure that can be solved by rebooting the system.

> **Note** 🖇
>
> When using the `ping` command, it is best to choose a target computer that does not have a firewall enabled. Firewalls often block ICMP, preventing the `ping` command from receiving a successful response. In this case, you can determine whether the target computer was contacted successfully following a `ping` command by looking for the target computer's IP address in the MAC address cache on your computer. You can use the **arp command** to display the MAC address cache.

Next, you should test connectivity to an IP address on the same LAN as your network interface (e.g., using the `ping IP_address` command). If you are unable to connect to other computers on your LAN, you may need to reboot your switch or wireless access point.

After testing local LAN access, you should test connectivity to an IP address on another LAN, or a public IP address on the Internet (e.g., using the `ping IP_address` command). If you are unable to connect to computers outside of your LAN, you may not have the correct default gateway route configured within your route table, or a router between your computer and the target IP address has failed, contains incorrect configuration, or is experiencing high load. You can supply the target IP address as an argument to the `traceroute`, `tracepath`, or `mtr` command to determine which router is the source of the problem.

If you can access both local and remote LANs from your system by IP address, then the issue is likely due to name resolution. Test connectivity to the FQDN of a computer on the network (e.g., using the `ping FQDN` command). If connectivity to the computer's FQDN fails, then ensure that your system has the correct DNS server configured for name resolution, and that the DNS server is available on the network. If the DNS server is unavailable, you can specify an alternate DNS server within your system configuration to obtain network connectivity.

> **Note** 🖉
>
> If your server runs as a virtual machine, you should also verify the network type used by the virtual machine. Most virtual machines bridge the virtual network adapter within the virtual machine to the physical network adapter in the computer in order to allow the virtual machine to function as a host directly on the LAN. You can use the `brctl` **command** to view or modify the bridge configuration used by the Linux kernel for your network adapter.

Network Service Issues

If clients are unable to contact a particular network service running on your server from across the network, you should start troubleshooting at the server itself. First determine if the network service is running (e.g., using the `ps -ef | grep service_name` command), and start it if necessary. If the network service fails to start, then check system and application log entries to determine the nature of the problem. Incorrect network service configuration file entries, SELinux and AppArmor restrictions, and other network services that are listening to the same port number can prevent a network service from starting successfully.

Next, determine if the network service is listening on the correct port number (e.g., using the `netstat` command). If the network service is configured to listen to a non-standard port number, then client programs will also need to specify the non-standard port number for a connection to be successful.

Following this, attempt to interact with the network service locally to see if it is responding to requests on the correct port number. For example, to interact with the local Apache daemon listening on port 80, you could run the `ncat localhost 80` command and see if the Apache daemon interacts with the `ncat` command. If there is no response, you may need to restart the Apache daemon or verify that it has the correct settings within its configuration files.

If the network service is responding to requests, you should attempt to access the network service from the local computer using an appropriate client program. For example, to obtain the default Web page from the local Apache daemon, you could run the `curl http://localhost/` command. If you are unable to obtain the default Web page, then local file permissions on the Web page file, SELinux or AppArmor restrictions, or incorrect Apache configuration could be the cause.

Finally, you should attempt to access the network service from another computer on the network. If you are able to access a network service locally, but are unable to access the same network service from across a network, then a firewall on the server or network is likely preventing the access. To remedy the issue, you can allow the protocol name or port number in the appropriate firewall configuration.

Network Latency Issues

Sometimes, a network is properly configured, but the time it takes for network services to respond to requests is very high, or users receive occasional timeout errors when attempting to connect to a network service. This problem is called **network latency**, and can occur when a network is saturated with traffic, or has limited bandwidth.

To determine if a particular network service or application is saturating the network, you can examine the traffic that is passing to and from your network interface using the `tcpdump` **command**, or **Wireshark**. Wireshark normally runs as a graphical program within a desktop environment, but can also be run from a command line terminal using the `tshark` **command**. If, for example, you notice a very large number of DHCPDISCOVER or DHCPREQUEST packets on the network, then the DHCP server service is likely unavailable, and the client computers attempting to renew their IP configuration are saturating the network with DHCP requests.

To determine if the network bandwidth is the cause of network latency, you can measure the available bandwidth between two computers on the network using the `iperf` **command**. On the first computer, you run the `iperf -s` command to start a bandwidth measuring server process, and on the second computer, you pass the IP address of the first computer as an argument to the `iperf -c` command to measure the available bandwidth. Say, for example, that a computer on the network with the IP address 192.168.1.103 has executed the `iperf -s` command. You could then run the following command on your computer to test the bandwidth available between your computer and the computer with the IP address 192.168.1.103:

```
[root@server1 ~]# iperf -c 192.168.1.103
------------------------------------------------------------
Client connecting to 192.168.1.103, TCP port 5001
TCP window size: 85.0 KByte (default)
------------------------------------------------------------
```

```
[  3] local 10.0.0.2 port 48216 connected with 192.168.1.103 port 5001
[ ID] Interval        Transfer     Bandwidth
[  3]  0.0-10.0 sec  8.00 MBytes  2.58 Kbits/sec
[root@server1 ~]#_
```

> **Note** 🖉
>
> Most computers communicate with multiple systems simultaneously. To measure the bandwidth from your network interface to each system that your computer is communicating with, you can use the `iftop` **command**.

In some cases, network latency can be caused by firewall devices that are restricting network throughput, or by a malfunctioning network interface, switch, or router that is dropping IP packets instead of processing them. In this case, rebooting the affected device often remedies the problem. If network latency affects a single computer, then there is likely an application on that computer that is sending or receiving a large amount of data on the network interface. Stopping applications in order can help you identify which one is causing the problem.

Performance Monitoring

Some problems that you will encounter on a Linux system are not as noticeable as those discussed in the previous section. Such problems affect the overall performance of the Linux system. Like the problems discussed earlier, performance problems can be caused by hardware, applications, filesystem issues, or network traffic.

Hardware that is improperly configured might still work, but at a slower speed. In addition, when hardware ages, it might start to malfunction by sending large amounts of information to the CPU when not in use. This process, known as **jabbering**, can slow down a CPU and, hence, the rest of the Linux system. To avoid this hardware malfunction, most companies retire computer equipment after two to three years of use.

Applications can also affect the overall performance of a system. Processes that require too many system resources monopolize the CPU, memory, and peripheral devices. Poor performance can also be the result of too many processes running on a computer, processes that make a great deal of read/write requests to the hard disk (such as databases), processes that send or receive large amounts of information on the network, rogue processes, or **memory leaks**. Memory leaks are processes that enter a state that allows them to continually use more memory, until the memory within the system is exhausted. To remedy most application performance issues, you can remove applications from the system to free up system resources. If the applications are needed for business activity, you can instead choose to move them to another Linux system that has more free system resources.

Application performance problems can also sometimes be remedied by altering the hardware. Upgrading or adding another CPU allows the Linux system to execute processes faster and reduce the number of processes running concurrently on the CPU. Alternatively, some peripheral devices can perform a great deal of processing that is normally performed by the CPU; this is known as **bus mastering**. Using bus mastering peripheral components reduces the amount of processing the CPU must perform and, hence, increases system speed. Most modern server systems use bus mastering disk controllers and network interfaces as a result.

Adding RAM to the computer also increases system speed because it gives processes more working space in memory and the system will send much less information to and from the swap partition. Because the operating system, peripheral components, and all processes use RAM constantly, adding RAM to any system often has a profound impact on system performance.

In addition, replacing slower hard disk drives with faster ones or SSDs improves the performance of programs that require frequent access to filesystems. SAS and NVMe devices typically have faster access speeds and are commonly used within modern Linux servers for this reason.

To make it easier to identify performance problems, you should run performance utilities on a healthy Linux system on a regular basis during normal business hours and store the results in a file or log book that can be easily accessed. The average results of these performance utilities are known as **baseline** values because they represent normal system activity. When performance issues arise, you can compare the output of performance utilities to the baseline values. Values that have changed dramatically from the baseline can help you pinpoint the source of the performance problem.

Although many performance utilities are available to Linux administrators, the most common of these belong to the sysstat package, described next.

Monitoring Performance with sysstat Utilities

The **System Statistics (sysstat) package** contains a wide range of utilities that monitor the system using information from the /proc directory and system devices. The sysstat package isn't added during the installation process on most Linux distributions but can be installed from a software repository afterwards.

To monitor CPU performance, you can use the mpstat **(multiple processor statistics) command**. Without arguments, the mpstat command gives average CPU statistics for all processors on the system since the most previous system boot, as shown in the following output:

```
[root@server1 ~]# mpstat
Linux 4.16.3-301.fc28.x86_64 (server1)   11/01/2019 _x86_64_   (2 CPU)

06:38:42 PM CPU  %usr %nice %sys %iowait %irq %soft %steal %guest %gnice %idle
06:38:42 PM all  17.53 1.48 6.21   11.73 0.19  0.00   0.00   0.00   0.00 62.85
[root@server1 ~]#_
```

> **Note** 📎
>
> If your system has multiple CPUs, you can measure the performance of a single CPU by specifying the `-P #` option to the `mpstat` command, where # represents the number of the processor starting from zero. Thus, the command `mpstat -P 0` displays statistics for the first processor on the system.

The `%usr` value shown in the preceding output indicates the percentage of time the processor spent executing user programs and daemons, whereas the `%nice` value indicates the percentage of time the processor spent executing user programs and daemons that had nondefault nice values. These numbers combined should be greater than the value of `%sys`, which indicates the amount of time the system spent maintaining itself such that it can execute user programs and daemons.

> **Note** 📎
>
> A system that has a high `%sys` compared to `%usr` and `%nice` is likely executing too many resource-intensive programs.

The `%iowait` value indicates the percentage of time the CPU was idle when an outstanding disk I/O request existed. The `%irq` and `%soft` values indicate the percentage of time the CPU is using to respond to normal interrupts and interrupts that span multiple CPUs, respectively. If these three values rapidly increase over time, the CPU cannot keep up with the number of requests it receives from software. If you have virtualization software installed, the `%guest` value indicates the percentage of time the CPU is executing another virtual CPU, the `%gnice` value indicates the percentage of time the processor spent executing user programs and daemons in the virtual CPU that had nondefault nice values, and the `%steal` indicates the percentage of time the CPU is waiting to respond to virtual CPU requests.

The `%idle` value indicates the percentage of time the CPU did not spend executing tasks. Although it might be zero for short periods of time, `%idle` should be greater than 25 percent over a long period of time.

> **Note** 📎
>
> A system that has a `%idle` of less than 25 percent over a long period of time might require faster or additional CPUs.

Although the average values given by the mpstat command are very useful in determining the CPU health of a Linux system, you might choose to take current measurements using mpstat. To do this, specify the interval in seconds and number of measurements as arguments to the mpstat command. For example, the following command takes five current measurements, one per second:

```
[root@server1 ~]# mpstat 1 5
Linux 4.16.3-301.fc28.x86_64 (server1)   11/01/2019 _x86_64_   (2 CPU)

07:05:10 AM CPU   %usr %nice   %sys %iowait   %irq %soft %steal %guest %gnice %idle
07:05:11 AM all   8.91  1.98   0.00    0.00   0.99  0.00   0.00   0.00   0.00 88.12
07:05:12 AM all   7.07  2.02   0.00    0.00   0.00  0.00   0.00   0.00   0.00 90.91
07:05:13 AM all   7.92  1.98   0.99    0.00   0.00  0.00   0.00   0.00   0.00 89.11
07:05:14 AM all   7.07  2.02   0.00    0.00   0.00  0.00   0.00   0.00   0.00 90.91
07:05:15 AM all   6.93  2.97   0.99    0.00   0.00  0.00   0.00   0.00   0.00 89.11
Average:    all   7.58  2.20   0.40    0.00   0.20  0.00   0.00   0.00   0.00 89.62
[root@server1 ~]#_
```

The preceding output must be used with caution because it was taken over a short period of time. If, for example, the %idle values are under 25 percent on average, they are not necessarily abnormal because the system might be performing a CPU-intensive task during the short time the statistics were taken.

To view CPU statistics for each process running on the system, you can instead run the pidstat **(PID statistics) command**:

```
[root@server1 ~]# pidstat | head
Linux 4.16.3-301.fc28.x86_64 (server1)   11/01/2019 _x86_64_   (2 CPU)

05:04:34 PM UID   PID  %usr %system %guest %wait  %CPU CPU  Command
05:04:34 PM   0     1  0.00    0.01   0.00  0.01  0.01   0  systemd
05:04:34 PM   0     7  0.00    0.00   0.00  0.00  0.00   0  ksoftirqd/0
05:04:34 PM   0     8  0.00    0.00   0.00  0.01  0.00   0  rcu_sched
05:04:34 PM   0    11  0.00    0.00   0.00  0.00  0.00   0  watchdog/0
05:04:34 PM   0   325  0.00    0.00   0.00  0.01  0.00   0  kworker/0:1H
05:04:34 PM   0   346  0.00    0.00   0.00  0.00  0.00   0  jbd2/sda3-8
05:04:34 PM   0   438  0.00    0.00   0.00  0.00  0.00   0  systemd-journal
[root@server1 ~]#_
```

The pidstat command is often used to determine the CPU performance of a single process. For example, the pidstat | grep crond command would display CPU performance for the cron daemon.

Another command, iostat **(input/output statistics)**, measures the flow of information to and from disk devices. Without any arguments, the iostat command displays CPU statistics similar to mpstat, followed by statistics for each disk device on the system. If your Linux system has one SATA hard disk drive (/dev/sda), the iostat command produces output similar to the following:

```
[root@server1 ~]# iostat
Linux 4.16.3-301.fc28.x86_64 (server1)   11/01/2019 _x86_64_  (2 CPU)

avg-cpu:   %user   %nice %system %iowait  %steal    %idle
           0.10    0.01    0.15    0.39    0.00    99.35

Device:             tps   kB_read/s   kB_wrtn/s    kB_read    kB_wrtn
sda                0.76      20.94        5.51     1619316     426256
dm-0               0.00       0.01        0.00         890          8
dm-1               0.00       0.01        0.00         472          0

[root@server1 ~]#_
```

The output from iostat displays the number of transfers per second (tps) as well as the number of kilobytes read per second (kB_read/s) and written per second (kB_wrtn/s), followed by the total number of kilobytes read (kB_read) and written (kB_wrtn) for the device since the last boot. An increase over time in these values indicates an increase in disk usage by processes. If this increase results in slow performance, the hard disks should be replaced with faster ones, or SSDs. Like mpstat, the iostat command can take current measurements of the system. To do this, specify the interval in seconds, followed by the number of measurements as arguments to the iostat command.

Although mpstat, pidstat, and iostat can be used to get quick information about system performance, they are limited in their abilities. The **sar (system activity reporter) command** can be used to display far more information than other utilities within the sysstat package. As such, it is the most widely used performance monitoring tool on UNIX and Linux systems.

By default, sar commands are scheduled using the cron daemon to run every 10 minutes on Fedora systems. On Ubuntu systems, you must set ENABLED="true" within the /etc/default/sysstat file to schedule sar commands to run every 10 minutes via the cron daemon. All performance information obtained is logged to a file in the /var/log/sa directory (Fedora) or /var/log/sysstat directory (Ubuntu) called sa#, where # represents the day of the month. If today were the 14th day of the month, the output from the sar command that is run every 10 minutes would be logged to the file sa14. Next month, this file will be overwritten on the 14th day. In other words, only one month of records is kept at any one time.

Note @

You can change the sar logging interval by editing the /etc/cron.d/sysstat cron table.

Without arguments, the `sar` command displays the CPU statistics taken every 10 minutes for the current day, as shown in the following output:

```
[root@server1 ~]# sar
Linux 4.16.3-301.fc28.x86_64 (server1)   11/01/2019 _x86_64_   (2 CPU)

03:40:01 AM    CPU    %user    %nice    %system    %iowait    %steal    %idle
03:50:01 AM    all    0.06     0.00     0.13       0.27       0.00      99.54
04:00:01 AM    all    0.06     0.00     0.12       0.23       0.00      99.58
04:10:01 AM    all    0.08     0.00     0.14       0.19       0.00      99.60
04:20:01 AM    all    0.06     0.00     0.13       0.38       0.00      99.43
04:30:01 AM    all    0.06     0.00     0.12       0.20       0.00      99.61
04:40:01 AM    all    0.05     0.00     0.12       0.24       0.00      99.59
04:50:01 AM    all    0.06     0.00     0.12       0.21       0.00      99.61
05:00:01 AM    all    0.07     0.00     0.12       0.22       0.00      99.59
05:10:01 AM    all    0.08     0.00     0.13       0.19       0.00      99.59
05:20:01 AM    all    0.06     0.00     0.12       0.37       0.00      99.45
05:30:01 AM    all    0.07     0.00     0.12       0.20       0.00      99.61
05:40:01 AM    all    0.06     0.00     0.13       0.28       0.00      99.53
05:50:01 AM    all    0.06     0.00     0.12       0.22       0.00      99.60
06:00:01 AM    all    0.07     0.00     0.12       0.22       0.00      99.59
06:10:01 AM    all    0.08     0.00     0.14       0.18       0.00      99.60
06:20:01 AM    all    0.06     0.00     0.12       0.36       0.00      99.46
06:30:01 AM    all    0.07     0.00     0.13       0.20       0.00      99.60
06:40:01 AM    all    0.07     0.00     0.13       0.24       0.00      99.57
06:50:01 AM    all    0.06     0.00     0.13       0.26       0.00      99.56
07:00:01 AM    all    0.10     0.00     0.15       0.27       0.00      99.49
07:10:01 AM    all    0.09     0.00     0.15       0.31       0.00      99.45
07:20:01 AM    all    1.79     0.00     0.99       4.19       0.00      93.04
Average:       all    0.11     0.05     0.15       0.35       0.00      99.34
[root@server1 ~]#_
```

To view the CPU statistics for the 6th of the month, you can specify the pathname to the appropriate file using the `-f` option to the `sar` command:

```
[root@server1 ~]# sar -f /var/log/sa/sa06 | head
Linux 4.16.3-301.fc28.x86_64 (server1)   11/01/2019 _x86_64_   (2 CPU)

12:00:01 AM    CPU    %user    %nice    %system    %iowait    %steal    %idle
12:10:01 AM    all    0.07     0.00     0.14       0.56       0.00      99.22
12:20:01 AM    all    0.07     0.00     0.14       0.51       0.00      99.28
12:30:01 AM    all    0.07     0.00     0.13       0.53       0.00      99.28
12:40:01 AM    all    0.06     0.00     0.13       0.58       0.00      99.22
```

```
12:50:01 AM    all    0.07    0.00    0.13    0.54    0.00    99.26
01:00:01 AM    all    0.07    0.00    0.13    0.58    0.00    99.22
01:10:01 AM    all    0.07    0.00    0.14    0.60    0.00    99.19
[root@server1 ~]#_
```

You must use the -f option to the sar command to view files in the /var/log/sa
(or /var/log/sysstat) directory with the aforementioned filenames because they contain
binary information. A sar text report is also written to the /var/log/sa/sar# file (or /
var/log/sysstat/sar# file) at the end of each day, where # represents the day of the
month. To view a sar report file, you can use any text command, such as less.

As with the iostat and mpstat commands, the sar command can be used to
take current system measurements. To take four CPU statistics every two seconds, you
can use the following command:

```
[root@server1 ~]# sar 2 4
Linux 4.16.3-301.fc28.x86_64 (server1)   11/01/2019 _x86_64_   (2 CPU)

08:24:41 AM    CPU    %user   %nice   %system   %iowait   %steal   %idle
08:24:43 AM    all    0.00    0.00    0.50      0.00      0.00     99.50
08:24:45 AM    all    0.00    0.00    0.25      0.00      0.00     99.75
08:24:47 AM    all    0.25    0.00    0.76      0.00      0.00     98.99
08:24:49 AM    all    0.00    0.00    0.27      0.00      0.00     99.73
Average:       all    0.06    0.00    0.45      0.00      0.00     99.49
[root@server1 ~]#_
```

Although the sar command displays CPU statistics by default, you can display
different statistics by specifying options to the sar command. Table 14-4 lists common
options used with the sar command.

Table 14-4   Common Options to the sar Command

Option	Description
-A	Displays the most information; this option is equivalent to all options
-b	Displays Input/Output statistics
-B	Displays swap statistics
-d	Displays Input/Output statistics for each block device on the system
-f file_name	Displays information from the specified file; these files typically reside in the /var/log/sa directory
-n ALL	Reports all network statistics
-o file_name	Saves the output to a file in binary format

(continues)

Table 14-4	Common Options to the `sar` Command (*continued*)
Option	**Description**
`-P CPU#`	Specifies statistics for a single CPU (the first CPU is 0, the second CPU is 1, and so on)
`-q`	Displays statistics for the processor queue
`-r`	Displays memory and swap statistics
`-u`	Displays CPU statistics; this is the default action when no options are specified
`-v`	Displays kernel-related filesystem statistics
`-W`	Displays swapping statistics

From Table 14-4, you can see that the –b and –d options to the `sar` command display information similar to the output of the `iostat` command. In addition, the –u option displays CPU statistics equivalent to the output of the `mpstat` command.

Another important option to the `sar` command is –q, which shows processor queue statistics. A processor queue is an area of RAM that stores information temporarily for quick retrieval by the CPU. To view processor queue statistics every five seconds, you can execute the following command:

```
[root@server1 ~]# sar -q 1 5
Linux 4.16.3-301.fc28.x86_64 (server1)   11/01/2019 _x86_64_   (2 CPU)

08:34:36 AM   runq-sz   plist-sz   ldavg-1   ldavg-5   ldavg-15   blocked
08:34:37 AM         0        252      0.00      0.00       0.00         0
08:34:38 AM         0        252      0.00      0.00       0.00         0
08:34:39 AM         0        252      0.00      0.00       0.00         0
08:34:40 AM         0        252      0.00      0.00       0.00         0
08:34:41 AM         0        252      0.00      0.00       0.00         0
Average:            0        252      0.00      0.00       0.00         0
[root@server1 ~]#_
```

The `runq-sz` (run queue size) indicates the number of processes that are waiting for execution on the processor run queue. For most Intel architectures, this number is typically 2 or less on average.

Note 🖉

A `runq-sz` much greater than 2 for long periods of time indicates that the CPU is too slow to respond to system requests.

The `plist-sz` (process list size) value indicates the number of processes currently running in memory, and the `ldavg-1` (load average – 1 minute), `ldavg-5` (load average – 5 minutes), and `ldavg-15` (load average – 15 minutes) values represent an average CPU load for the last 1 minute, 5 minutes, and 15 minutes, respectively. These four statistics display an overall picture of processor activity. A rapid increase in these values is typically caused by CPU-intensive software that is running on the system.

> **Note**
>
> When interpreting load average values on a single CPU system, a load average of 1.00 represents 100% load; thus, a load average of 0.80 indicates that the system is 20% underloaded, and a load average of 1.20 indicates that the system is 20% overloaded. For systems that have multiple CPUs, load average values are multiplied by the number of CPUs; thus, a load average of 2.00 on a dual CPU system represents 100% load.

The `blocked` value represents the number of tasks currently blocked from completion because they are waiting for I/O requests to complete. If this value is high, there are likely one or more storage devices that cannot keep up with system requests.

Recall that all Linux systems use a swap partition to store information that cannot fit into physical memory; this information is sent to and from the swap partition in units called pages. The number of pages that are sent to the swap partition (`pswpin/s`) and the pages that are taken from the swap partition (`pswpout/s`) can be viewed using the `-W` option to the `sar` command, as shown in the following output:

```
[root@server1 ~]# sar -W 1 5
Linux 4.16.3-301.fc28.x86_64 (server1)   11/01/2019 _x86_64_   (2 CPU)

08:37:01 AM   pswpin/s pswpout/s
08:37:02 AM      0.00      0.00
08:37:03 AM      0.00      0.00
08:37:04 AM      0.00      0.00
08:37:05 AM      0.00      0.00
08:37:06 AM      0.00      0.00
Average:         0.00      0.00
[root@server1 ~]#_
```

If a large number of pages are being sent to and taken from the swap partition, the system will suffer from slower performance. To remedy this, you can add more physical memory (RAM) to the system.

Other Performance Monitoring Utilities

The sysstat package utilities are not the only performance-monitoring utilities available on Linux systems. Many regular system utilities display performance information in addition to other system information. For example, the w command introduced in Chapter 2 displays the system load average values for the last 1, 5, and 15 minutes in addition to user session information. Similarly, the uptime **command** displays these same system load average values in addition to the time since the previous boot. If you only wish to view system load average values, you can instead use the tload **command**.

The top command discussed in Chapter 9 also displays CPU statistics, memory usage, swap usage, and average CPU load at the top of the screen, as shown here:

```
top - 08:40:07 up 22:43,  3 users,   load average: 0.00, 0.00, 0.00
Tasks: 166 total, 1 running, 165 sleeping, 0 stopped, 0 zombie
Cpu(s): 0.5%us, 0.3%sy, 0.0%ni, 99.2%id, 0.0%wa, 0.0%hi, 0.0%si, 0.0%st
KiB Mem:    961284 total,   814576 used,   146708 free,   126036 buffers
KiB Swap: 4095992 total,      212 used, 4095780 free,   480740 cached

  PID USER      PR  NI   VIRT  RES   SHR S %CPU %MEM    TIME+   COMMAND
 5693 root      20   0   2696 1120   852 R  1.0  0.1  0:00.08  top
    1 root      20   0   2828 1312  1144 S  0.0  0.1  0:01.43  init
    2 root      20   0      0    0     0 S  0.0  0.0  0:00.00  kthreadd
    3 root      RT   0      0    0     0 S  0.0  0.0  0:00.01  migration/0
    4 root      20   0      0    0     0 S  0.0  0.0  0:00.11  ksoftirqd/0
    5 root      RT   0      0    0     0 S  0.0  0.0  0:00.00  watchdog/0
    6 root      RT   0      0    0     0 S  0.0  0.0  0:00.01  migration/1
    7 root      20   0      0    0     0 S  0.0  0.0  0:00.45  ksoftirqd/1
    8 root      RT   0      0    0     0 S  0.0  0.0  0:00.00  watchdog/1
    9 root      20   0      0    0     0 S  0.0  0.0  0:00.66  events/0
   10 root      20   0      0    0     0 S  0.0  0.0  0:00.57  events/1
   11 root      20   0      0    0     0 S  0.0  0.0  0:00.00  cpuset
   12 root      20   0      0    0     0 S  0.0  0.0  0:00.00  khelper
```

The **free command** can be used to display the total amounts of physical and swap memory in Kilobytes and their utilizations, as shown in the following output:

```
[root@server1 ~]# free
           total      used      free   shared  buff/cache   available
Mem:     4038984   1251200   1160484     5664     1627300     2516148
Swap:    4170748         0   4170748
[root@server1 ~]#_
```

The Linux kernel reserves some memory for temporary filessytems (shared) and to hold requests from hardware devices (buff/cache); the total memory in the preceding output is calculated with and without these values to indicate how much memory the system has reserved. The output from the preceding `free` command indicates that there is sufficient memory in the system because little swap is used and a great deal of free physical memory is available.

Like the free utility, the **vmstat command** can be used to indicate whether more physical memory is required by measuring swap performance:

```
[root@server1 ~]# vmstat
procs  ---------memory---------- -swap-  --io-- system -----cpu-----
 r  b   swpd   free    buff   cache  si   so  bi   bo   in cs us sy id wa st
 1  0    212 146496 126144 480752   0    0   5    2   49 51  0  0 99  0  0
[root@server1 ~]#_
```

The previous output indicates more information than the `free` command used earlier, including the following:

- The number of processes waiting to be run (`r`)
- The number of sleeping processes (`b`)
- The amount of swap memory used, in Kilobytes (`swpd`)
- The amount of free physical memory (`free`)
- The amount of memory used by buffers, in Kilobytes (`buff`)
- The amount of memory used as cache (`cache`)
- The amount of memory in Kilobytes per second swapped in to the disk (`si`)
- The amount of memory in Kilobytes per second swapped out to the disk (`so`)
- The number of blocks per second sent to block devices (`bi`)
- The number of blocks per second received from block devices (`bo`)
- The number of interrupts sent to the CPU per second (`in`)
- The number of context changes sent to the CPU per second (`cs`)
- The CPU user time (`us`)
- The CPU system time (`sy`)
- The CPU idle time (`id`)
- The time spent waiting for I/O (`wa`)
- The time stolen from a virtual machine (`st`)

Thus, the output from vmstat shown previously indicates that little swap memory is being used because `swpd` is 212 KB and `si` and `so` are both zero; however, it also indicates that the reason for this is that the system is not running many processes at the current time (`r=1`, `id=99`).

The `iotop` **(input/output top) command** is similar to the `top` command, but instead displays the processes on the system sorted by the most disk I/O usage, as shown here:

```
Total DISK READ :     0.00 B/s | Total DISK WRITE :     0.00 B/s
Actual DISK READ:     0.00 B/s | Actual DISK WRITE:     0.00 B/s
```

```
  TID PRIO USER DISK READ  DISK WRITE  SWAPIN      IO>    COMMAND
 7033 be/4 root  0.00 B/s    0.00 B/s  0.00 %   0.01 % [kworker/0:1]
    1 be/4 root  0.00 B/s    0.00 B/s  0.00 %   0.00 % systemd
    2 be/4 root  0.00 B/s    0.00 B/s  0.00 %   0.00 % [kthreadd]
    4 be/0 root  0.00 B/s    0.00 B/s  0.00 %   0.00 % [kworker/0:0H]
    6 be/0 root  0.00 B/s    0.00 B/s  0.00 %   0.00 % [mm_percpu_wq]
    7 be/4 root  0.00 B/s    0.00 B/s  0.00 %   0.00 % [ksoftirqd/0]
    8 be/4 root  0.00 B/s    0.00 B/s  0.00 %   0.00 % [rcu_sched]
    9 be/4 root  0.00 B/s    0.00 B/s  0.00 %   0.00 % [rcu_bh]
   10 rt/4 root  0.00 B/s    0.00 B/s  0.00 %   0.00 % [migration/0]
   11 rt/4 root  0.00 B/s    0.00 B/s  0.00 %   0.00 % [watchdog/0]
   12 be/4 root  0.00 B/s    0.00 B/s  0.00 %   0.00 % [cpuhp/0]
   13 be/4 root  0.00 B/s    0.00 B/s  0.00 %   0.00 % [kdevtmpfs]
   14 be/0 root  0.00 B/s    0.00 B/s  0.00 %   0.00 % [netns]
   15 be/4 root  0.00 B/s    0.00 B/s  0.00 %   0.00 % [rcu_tasks_kthre]
   16 be/4 root  0.00 B/s    0.00 B/s  0.00 %   0.00 % [kauditd]
   17 be/4 root  0.00 B/s    0.00 B/s  0.00 %   0.00 % [oom_reaper]
   18 be/0 root  0.00 B/s    0.00 B/s  0.00 %   0.00 % [writeback]
   19 be/4 root  0.00 B/s    0.00 B/s  0.00 %   0.00 % [kcompact]
```

The thread ID (TID) column in the previous output identifies the PID of each process. The blocks that are read (DISK READ) and written (DISK WRITE) per second are listed next to each process, as are the percentage of swap (SWAPIN) and total I/O operations (IO>) for each process.

To monitor the performance of a specific storage device, you can use the ioping (input/output ping) command and press Ctrl+c when finished to display overall statistics. For example, the following ioping command is used to monitor the performance of /dev/sda:

```
[root@server1 ~]# ioping /dev/sda
4 KiB <<< /dev/sda (block device 50 GiB): request=1 time=1.03 ms (warmup)
4 KiB <<< /dev/sda (block device 50 GiB): request=2 time=1.32 ms
4 KiB <<< /dev/sda (block device 50 GiB): request=3 time=241.8 us
4 KiB <<< /dev/sda (block device 50 GiB): request=4 time=1.10 ms
4 KiB <<< /dev/sda (block device 50 GiB): request=5 time=1.11 ms
4 KiB <<< /dev/sda (block device 50 GiB): request=6 time=1.07 ms
^c
--- /dev/sda (block device 50 GiB) ioping statistics ---
5 requests completed in 4.84 ms, 20 KiB read, 1.03 k iops, 4.04 MiB/s
generated 6 requests in 5.66 s, 24 KiB, 1 iops, 4.24 KiB/s
min/avg/max/mdev = 241.8 us / 968.0 us / 1.32 ms / 373.8 us
[root@server1 ~]#_
```

The time it takes for /dev/sda to respond to an ioping request depends on the speed of the underlying storage device hardware, but is often measured in milliseconds (ms) or microseconds (us). By monitoring the output of `ioping` as you start applications, you can measure the impact that the applications have on your storage devices. Similarly, by comparing `ioping` output on a system that has application performance issues to a baseline measurement taken earlier, you can determine if the storage devices are the cause of the issue.

Chapter Summary

- Securing a Linux computer involves performing tasks that increase local security as well as minimize the chance of network attacks.

- By restricting access to your computer and Linux operating system, minimizing the use of the root account, encrypting files, and practicing secure administration, you greatly improve local Linux security.

- Stopping unused network services, encrypting network traffic, limiting system and client access, configuring secure file permissions, changing default ports, updating network service software, performing vulnerability scans, implementing firewalls, and enabling SELinux or AppArmor can greatly reduce the chance of network attacks.

- After installing, configuring, and securing a system, Linux administrators monitor the system, perform proactive and reactive maintenance, and document important system information.

- Common troubleshooting procedures involve collecting data to isolate and determine the cause of system problems as well as implementing and testing solutions that can be documented for future use.

- Hardware-related problems on Linux systems can come from a wide range of hardware devices, including peripheral devices, adapter cards, memory, and storage devices.

- Missing dependencies, system restrictions, and resource conflicts are common causes of application-related problems.

- Quota and filesystem limits, filesystem corruption, and bad blocks are common causes of filesystem-related problems.

- Network-related problems can prevent network connectivity and access to network services, as well as cause latency between computers on a network.

- System performance is affected by a variety of factors, including the amount of RAM, CPU, and storage device speed, and process load.

- Using performance monitoring utilities to create a baseline is helpful when diagnosing performance problems in the future. The sysstat package contains many useful performance monitoring commands.

Key Terms

`aa-complain` command
`aa-disable` command
`aa-enforce` command
`aa-status` command
`aa-unconfined` command
AppArmor
AppArmor profile
`arp` command
`audit2why` command
Automatic Bug Reporting
  Tool Daemon (abrtd)
baseline
biometric
`brctl` command
buffer overrun
bus mastering
chains
`chcon` command
Common Vulnerabilities
  and Exposures (CVE)
Common Weakness
  Enumeration (CWE)
`cryptsetup` command
`dmidecode` command
documentation
`faillock` command
file handles
Firewall Configuration
  utility
firewall daemon (firewalld)
`firewall-cmd` command
`free` command
`getenforce` command
`getsebool` command
GNU Privacy Guard (GPG)
GPG Agent
`gpg` command
hash
`iftop` command
`ioping` (input/output ping)
  command

`iostat` (input/output
  statistics) command
`iotop` (input/output top)
  command
IP set
`iperf` command
`ipset` command
`iptables` command
`ip6tables` command
jabbering
`kinit` command
`klist` command
label
Lightweight Directory
  Access Protocol (LDAP)
Linux Unified Key Setup
  (LUKS)
login banner
memory leak
message digest
monitoring
`mpstat` (multiple processor
  statistics) command
Multi-Category Security (MCS)
multi-factor authentication
Multi-Level Security (MLS)
netfilter
network latency
network zone
`nmap` (network mapper)
  command
One Time Password (OTP)
`pam_tally2` command
`pidstat` (PID statistics)
  command
Pluggable Authentication
  Module (PAM)
proactive maintenance
reactive maintenance
Remote Dial In User Service
  (RADIUS)

`restorecon` command
rules
`sar` (system activity
  reporter) command
Security Enhanced Linux
  (SELinux)
Security Information and
  Event Management (SIEM)
`seinfo` command
self-signed certificate
server closet
`sestatus` command
`setenforce` command
`setsebool` command
stateful packet filter
`sudo` command
`sudoedit` command
System Statistics (sysstat)
  package
TCP wrapper
`tcpdump` command
Terminal Access Controller
  Access Control System
  Plus (TACACS+)
`tload` command
transport mode
troubleshooting
  procedures
`tshark` command
tunnel mode
`udevadm` command
`ufw` (Uncomplicated
  Firewall) command
`ulimit` command
Uncomplicated Firewall
  (UFW)
`uptime` command
`visudo` command
`vmstat` command
vulnerability scanner
Wireshark

Review Questions

1. On which part of the maintenance cycle do Linux administrators spend the most time?
   a. monitoring
   b. proactive maintenance
   c. reactive maintenance
   d. documentation

2. Which of the following files is likely to be found in the /var/log/sa directory on a Fedora system over time?
   a. 15
   b. sa39
   c. sa19
   d. 00

3. Network latency issues are often caused by SELinux or AppArmor restrictions. True or False?

4. Which of the following commands can be used to display memory statistics? (Choose all that apply.)
   a. `free`
   b. `sar`
   c. `vmstat`
   d. `iostat`

5. Which option can be added to the `ls` or `ps` command to view the SELinux label?
   a. `-s`
   b. `-S`
   c. `-L`
   d. `-Z`

6. To set udev rules on a Linux system, you must add the appropriate line to a file within the /etc/udev/rules.d directory. True or False?

7. What type of iptables chain targets traffic that is destined for the local computer?
   a. INPUT
   b. ROUTE
   c. FORWARD
   d. OUTPUT

8. Which of the following steps is not a common troubleshooting procedure?
   a. Test the solution.
   b. Isolate the problem.
   c. Delegate responsibility.
   d. Collect information.

9. Which of the following firewalld commands can be used to allow incoming SSH connections the next time the system is booted?
   a. `firewall-cmd --add-service ssh`
   b. `firewall-cmd --add-port 22/tcp`
   c. `firewall-cmd --add-port 22/udp`
   d. `firewall-cmd --add-service ssh --permanent`

10. Which file contains information regarding the users, computers, and commands used by the `sudo` command?
    a. /etc/sudo
    b. /etc/su.cfg
    c. /etc/sudo.cfg
    d. /etc/sudoers

11. Which command can increase the number of filehandles that programs can open in a shell?
    a. `ldd`
    b. `ulimit`
    c. `lba32`
    d. `top`

12. The pam_tally2.so PAM can be used to enforce complex passwords on a Linux system. True or False?

13. Which of the following actions should you first take to secure your Linux computer against network attacks?
    a. Change permissions on key system files.
    b. Ensure that only necessary services are running.
    c. Run a checksum for each file used by network services.
    d. Configure entries in the /etc/sudoers file.

14. What will the command `sar -W 3 50` do?
    a. Take 3 swap statistics every 50 seconds.
    b. Take 50 swap statistics every 3 seconds.
    c. Take 3 CPU statistics every 50 seconds.
    d. Take 50 CPU statistics every 3 seconds.

15. Which of the following commands can be used to scan the available ports on computers within your organization?
    a. `traceroute`
    b. `tracert`
    c. `nmap`
    d. `sudo`

16. Which of the following UFW commands can be used to view configured firewall rules?
    a. `ufw`
    b. `ufw status`
    c. `ufw show`
    d. `ufwdisplay`

17. Which of the following technologies can encrypt files stored on a filesystem within a Linux system? (Choose all that apply.)
    a. SSL/TLS
    b. LUKS
    c. GPG
    d. L2TP

18. When the `fsck` command cannot repair a non-root (/) filesystem, you should immediately restore all data from backup. True or False?

19. When performing a `sar -u` command, you notice that %idle is consistently 10 percent. Is this good or bad?
    a. Good, because the processor should be idle more than 5 percent of the time
    b. Good, because the processor is idle 90 percent of the time
    c. Bad, because the processor is idle 10 percent of the time and perhaps a faster CPU is required
    d. Bad, because the processor is idle 10 percent of the time and perhaps a new hard disk is required

20. What are best practices for securing a Linux server? (Choose all that apply.)
    a. Lock the server in a server closet.
    b. Ensure that you are logged in as the root user to the server at all times.
    c. Ensure that SELinux or AppArmor is used to protect key services.
    d. Use encryption for files and network traffic.

Hands-On Projects

These projects should be completed in the order given. The hands-on projects presented in this chapter should take a total of three hours to complete. The requirements for this lab include:

- A computer with Fedora Linux installed according to Hands-On Project 2-1, and Ubuntu Server 18 Linux installed according to Hands-On Project 6-1.

Project 14-1

In this hands-on project, you install the sysstat package on your Fedora Linux virtual machine and monitor system performance using the command-line utilities included within the package.

1. Boot your Fedora Linux virtual machine. After your Linux system has been loaded, switch to a command-line terminal (tty5) by pressing **Ctrl+Alt+F5** and log in to the terminal using the user name of **root** and the password of **LINUXrocks!**.

2. At the command prompt, type `dnf install sysstat` and press **Enter**. Press `y` when prompted to complete the installation of the sysstat package.

3. At the command prompt, type `mpstat` and press **Enter** to view average CPU statistics for your system since the last boot time. What is the value for %user? Is this higher, lower, or the same as %system? What is the value for %idle? What should this value be greater than over long periods of time?

4. At the command prompt, type `mpstat 1 5` and press **Enter** to view five CPU statistic measurements, one per second. How do these values compare to the ones seen in the previous step?

5. Switch to tty1 by pressing **Ctrl+Alt+F1** and log into the GNOME desktop using your user account and the password of **LINUXrocks!**. Open several applications of your choice.

6. Switch back to tty5 by pressing **Ctrl+Alt+F5**. Type `mpstat 1 5` at the command prompt and press **Enter** to view five CPU statistic measurements, one per second. How do these values compare to the ones seen in Step 4?

7. Switch back to the GNOME desktop by pressing **Ctrl+Alt+F2** and close all programs.

8. Switch back to tty5 by pressing **Ctrl+Alt+F5**. Type `iostat 1 5` at the command prompt and press **Enter** to view five I/O statistic measurements, one per second. Note the block devices that are displayed and the I/O measurements for each one.

9. Switch to the GNOME desktop by pressing **Ctrl+Alt+F2** and open several applications of your choice.

10. Switch back to tty5 by pressing **Ctrl+Alt+F5**, type `iostat 1 5` at the command prompt. How do these values compare to the ones seen in Step 8?

11. Switch to the GNOME desktop by pressing **Ctrl+Alt+F2** and close all programs.

12. Switch back to tty5 by pressing **Ctrl+Alt+F5**, type `pidstat | less` at the command prompt, and press **Enter**. Examine the output. What processes are the most active on the system? Press `q` when finished to return to your command prompt.

13. At the command prompt, type `sar` and press **Enter**. What statistics are displayed by default? What times were the statistics taken?

14. At the command prompt, type `sar -q` and press **Enter** to view queue statistics. What is the queue size? What is the average load for the last minute? What is the average load for the last five minutes?

15. At the command prompt, type `sar -q 1 5` and press **Enter** to view five queue statistics, one per second.

16. Switch to the GNOME desktop by pressing **Ctrl+Alt+F2** and open several applications of your choice.

17. Switch back to tty5 by pressing **Ctrl+Alt+F5**, type `sar -q 1 5` at the command prompt, and press **Enter**. How do these values compare to the ones seen in Step 15?

18. Switch to the GNOME desktop by pressing **Ctrl+Alt+F2** and close all programs.

19. Switch back to tty5 by pressing **Ctrl+Alt+F5**, type `sar -W 1 5` and press **Enter** to view five swap statistics, one per second.

20. Switch to the GNOME desktop by pressing **Ctrl+Alt+F2** and open several applications of your choice.

21. Switch back to tty5 by pressing **Ctrl+Alt+F5**, type `sar -W 1 5` at the command prompt, and press **Enter**. How do these values compare to the ones seen in Step 19? Type `exit`, and press **Enter** to log out of your shell.

22. Switch to the GNOME desktop by pressing **Ctrl+Alt+F2**. Close all programs and log out of the GNOME desktop.

Project 14-2

In this hands-on project, you monitor system, memory, swap, and I/O performance using various utilities.

1. On your Fedora Linux virtual machine, switch to a command-line terminal (tty5) by pressing **Ctrl+Alt+F5** and log in to the terminal using the user name of **root** and the password of **LINUXrocks!**.

2. At the command prompt, type `top` and press **Enter**. From the information displayed, write the answers to the following questions on a piece of paper:

   a. How many processes are currently running?

   b. How much memory does your system have in total?

   c. How much memory is being used?

   d. How much memory is used by buffers?

   e. How much swap memory does your system have in total?

   f. How much swap is being used?

   g. What is the system load average over the last minute, last 5 minutes, and last 15 minutes?

3. Type **q** to quit the top utility.

4. At the command prompt, type `free` and press **Enter**. Does this utility give more or less information regarding memory and swap memory than the top utility? How do the values shown compare to those from Step 2?

5. At the command prompt, type `vmstat` and press **Enter**. Does this utility give more or less information regarding memory and swap memory than the top and free utilities? How do the values shown compare to those from Step 2?

6. At the command prompt, type `uptime` and press **Enter**. How do the load average values shown compare to those from Step 2?

7. At the command prompt, type `dnf install iotop` and press **Enter**. Press **y** when prompted to complete the installation of the iotop package.

8. At the command prompt, type `iotop` and press **Enter**. Which processes are using the most block storage device I/O? Press **Ctrl+c** when finished.

9. At the command prompt, type `dnf install ioping` and press **Enter**. Press **y** when prompted to complete the installation of the ioping package.

10. At the command prompt, type `ioping /dev/sda` and press **Enter**. After 10 measurements, press **Ctrl+c**. Note the average I/O values for your storage device. Why should you measure these values when the system is performing normally?

11. Type `exit` and press **Enter** to log out of your shell.

Project 14-3

In this hands-on project, you examine the services running on your Ubuntu Server 18 Linux virtual machine using the nmap utility and /etc/services file.

1. Boot your Ubuntu Server 18 Linux virtual machine and log into tty1 using the user name of **root** and the password of **LINUXrocks!**.

2. At the command prompt, type `apt install nmap` and press **Enter**. Press **y** when prompted to complete the installation of the nmap utility.

3. At the command prompt, type `systemctl stop smbd` and press **Enter**.

4. At the command prompt, type `systemctl stop vsftpd` and press **Enter**.

5. At the command prompt, type `nmap -sT 127.0.0.1` and press **Enter**. Note the services that are started and the port numbers listed. When did you configure most of these services? What is the service associated with port 631/tcp?

6. At the command prompt, type `grep 631 /etc/services` and press **Enter**. What is the full name for the service running on port 631?

7. At the command prompt, type `systemctl start smbd` and press **Enter**.

8. At the command prompt, type `systemctl start vsftpd` and press **Enter**.

9. At the command prompt, type `nmap -sT 127.0.0.1` and press **Enter**. What additional ports were opened by the Samba and Very Secure FTP daemons?

10. Type `exit` and press **Enter** to log out of your shell.

Project 14-4

In this hands-on project, you configure and use the sudo utility to gain root access on your Ubuntu Server 18 Linux virtual machine.

1. On your Ubuntu Server 18 Linux virtual machine, log into tty1 using the user name of **root** and the password of **LINUXrocks!**.

2. At the command prompt, type `useradd -m regularuser` and press **Enter**.

3. At the command prompt, type `passwd regularuser` and press **Enter**. Supply the password **LINUXrocks!** when prompted both times.

4. Run the command `vi /etc/sudoers`. Examine the existing lines within the file. Which two groups are granted the ability to run all commands by default on Ubuntu Server 18? Add the following line to the end of the file:

```
regularuser    ALL = (root) /usr/bin/touch
```

When finished, save your changes (you must use **:w!**) and quit the vi editor.

5. At the command prompt, type `su - regularuser` and press **Enter**.

6. At the command prompt, type `touch /testfile` and press **Enter**. Were you able to create a file under the / directory?

7. At the command prompt, type `sudo touch /testfile` and press **Enter**, then enter the password **LINUXrocks!** when prompted. Were you able to create a file under the / directory?

8. At the command prompt, type `ls -l /testfile` and press **Enter**. Who is the owner and group owner for this file? Why?

9. Type `exit` and press **Enter** to end your regularuser session, and then type `exit` again and press **Enter** to log out of your shell.

Project 14-5

In this hands-on project, you configure and test the netfilter firewall on your Ubuntu Server 18 Linux virtual machine.

1. On your Ubuntu Server 18 Linux virtual machine, log into tty1 using the user name of **root** and the password of **LINUXrocks!**.

2. At the command prompt, type `iptables -L` and press **Enter**. What is the default action for the INPUT, FORWARD, and OUTPUT chains? Also note that docker creates additional chains for use with containers.

3. At the command prompt, type `apt install apache2` and press **Enter**. Press **y** when prompted to complete the installation of the Apache Web server. Note that this step is unnecessary if you completed Discover Exercise 4 within Chapter 13.

4. Open a Web browser on your Windows host and enter the IP address of your Ubuntu Server 18 Linux virtual machine in the location dialog box. Is the default Web page displayed?

5. On your Ubuntu Server 18 Linux virtual machine, type `iptables -P INPUT DROP` at the command prompt and press **Enter**. What does this command do?

6. At the command prompt, type `iptables -L` and press **Enter**. What is the default action for the INPUT chain?

7. Switch back to the Web browser on your Windows host and click the reload button. Does your page reload successfully?

8. On your Ubuntu Server 18 Linux virtual machine, type `iptables -A INPUT -s IP -j ACCEPT` at the command prompt (where *IP* is the IP address of your Windows host) and press **Enter**. What does this command do?

9. At the command prompt, type `iptables -L` and press **Enter**. Do you see your rule underneath the INPUT chain?

10. Switch back to the Web browser on your Windows host and click the reload button. Does your page reload successfully?

11. On your Ubuntu Server 18 Linux virtual machine, type `iptables -F` at the command prompt and press **Enter**. Next, type `iptables -P INPUT ACCEPT` at the command prompt and press **Enter**. What do these commands do? At the command prompt, type

`iptables -L` and press **Enter** to verify that the default policies for all three chains have been restored.

12. At the command prompt, type `ufw enable` and press **Enter**. Next, type `iptables -L | less` and press **Enter**. Observe the additional chains and rules that UFW created within netfilter.

13. At the command prompt, type `ufw status verbose` and press **Enter**. Note the exceptions that UFW created for the services running on your computer. Next, type `ufw disable` and press **Enter**.

14. Type `exit` and press **Enter** to log out of your shell.

Project 14-6

In this hands-on project, you configure firewalld and test the results on your Fedora Linux virtual machine.

1. On your Fedora Linux virtual machine, switch to a command-line terminal (tty5) by pressing **Ctrl+Alt+F5** and log in to the terminal using the user name of **root** and the password of **LINUXrocks!**.

2. At the command prompt, type `iptables -L | less` and press **Enter**. Can you tell that firewalld is configured to set netfilter rules on your system? Press **q** when finished to quit the less utility.

3. At the command prompt, type `firewall-cmd --get-zones` and press **Enter** to view the network zones on your system.

4. At the command prompt, type `firewall-cmd --get-default-zone` and press **Enter**. What is the default zone on your system?

5. At the command prompt, type `firewall-cmd --list-all` and press **Enter**. Note the services that are allowed in your firewall within the current (default) zone. Why is the Apache Web server not listed?

6. At the command prompt, type `systemctl start httpd` and press **Enter** to ensure that the Apache Web server is started.

7. Open a Web browser on your Windows host and enter the IP address of your Fedora Linux virtual machine in the location dialog box. Is your Web page displayed?

8. On your Fedora Linux virtual machine, type `firewall-cmd --add-service=http` at the command prompt and press **Enter** to allow the http service in your firewall. Next, type `firewall-cmd --add-service=http --permanent` and press **Enter** to ensure that the http service is allowed in the firewall after the next boot.

9. At the command prompt, type `firewall-cmd --list-all` and press **Enter**. Is http listed?

10. Switch back to the Web browser on your Windows host and click the reload button. Did your page reload successfully?

11. On your Fedora Linux virtual machine, type `exit` and press **Enter** to log out of your shell.

Project 14-7

In this hands-on project, you configure and test account lockout on your Ubuntu Server 18 Linux virtual machine.

1. On your Ubuntu Server 18 Linux virtual machine, log into tty1 using the user name of **root** and the password of **LINUXrocks!**.

2. Run the command `vi /etc/pam.d/common-auth`. Add the following line above the line that contains the pam_unix.so PAM:

   ```
   auth required pam_tally2.so deny=3 onerr=fail unlock_time=3600
   ```

   When finished, save your changes and quit the vi editor.

3. Switch to tty2 by pressing **Ctrl+Alt+F2** and log into the terminal using the user name **regularuser** with an incorrect password of your choice. Repeat this process two more times. Was there a noticeable lag following the last login attempt before you were able to receive a new login prompt?

4. Attempt to log in one more time as **regularuser** using the password **LINUXrocks!**. Did your login prompt warn you that regularuser has been locked out of the system due to multiple invalid login attempts? Were you able to successfully complete the login process?

5. Switch back to tty1 by pressing **Ctrl+Alt+F1**. Next, type `pam_tally2` at the command prompt and press **Enter**. Is regularuser listed? How many invalid attempts were made in total?

6. At the command prompt, type `pam_tally2 --reset --user regularuser` and press **Enter**. Next, type `pam_tally2` at the command prompt and press **Enter**. Are any users listed?

7. Switch back to tty2 by pressing **Ctrl+Alt+F2** and log into the terminal as the user **regularuser** with the password **LINUXrocks!**. Were you successful?

8. At the command prompt, type `exit` and press **Enter** to log out of your shell.

9. Switch back to tty1 by pressing **Ctrl+Alt+F1**. Next, type `exit` at the command prompt and press **Enter** to log out of your shell.

Project 14-8

In this hands-on project, you troubleshoot SELinux enforcement on your Fedora Linux virtual machine.

1. On your Fedora Linux virtual machine, switch to a command-line terminal (tty5) by pressing **Ctrl+Alt+F5** and log in to the terminal using the user name of **root** and the password of **LINUXrocks!**.

2. At the command prompt, type `systemctl start httpd` and press **Enter** to start the Apache daemon.

3. Open a Web browser on your Windows host and enter **http://IP** in the location dialog box, where IP is the IP address of your Fedora Linux virtual machine. Is your Web page displayed?

4. On your Fedora Linux virtual machine, run the command `vi /etc/httpd/conf.d` `/userdir.conf`. Locate the following directives, and modify them as follows:

```
#UserDir disabled
UserDir public_html
```

When finished, save your changes and quit the vi editor.

5. At the command prompt, type `mkdir /home/bozoette/public_html` and press **Enter** to create a public_html directory within bozoette's home directory. Next, type `chmod 755 /home/bozoette /home/bozoette/public_html` and press **Enter** to ensure that the Apache daemons are able to access both directories.

6. At the command prompt, run the command `vi /home/bozoette/public_html` `/index.html`. Add the following lines:

```
<html>
<body>
<h1>This is a sample user homepage</h1>
</body>
</html>
```

When finished, save your changes and quit the vi editor.

7. At the command prompt, type `chmod 644 /home/bozoette/public_html/index.` `html` and press **Enter** to ensure that the Apache daemons are able to access bozoette's Web page.

8. On your Windows host, enter **http://*IP*/~bozoette** in the location dialog box of your Web browser, where *IP* is the IP address of your Fedora Linux virtual machine. What error do you receive?

9. On your Fedora Linux virtual machine, type `sestatus` at the command prompt and press **Enter**. Is SELinux enforcing the targeted policy on your system? Next, type `less` `/var/log/audit/audit.log` at the command prompt and press **Enter**. Did SELinux prevent access to the /home/bozoette/public_html/index.html file?

10. At the command prompt, type `ls -Z /home/bozoette/public_html/index.html` and press **Enter**. What type classification does the index.html file have? Next, type `ps -eZ | grep httpd` and press **Enter**. What type classification do the Apache daemons run as?

11. At the command prompt, type `getsebool | grep httpd | less` and press **Enter**. Examine the SELinux policy settings for httpd. What is the value of the httpd_enable_homedirs setting? Press `q` when finished.

12. At the command prompt, type `setsebool httpd_enable_homedirs on` and press **Enter**.

13. On your Windows host, enter **http://*IP*/~bozoette** in the location dialog box of your Web browser, where *IP* is the IP address of your Fedora Linux virtual machine. Do you see bozoette's Web page?

14. On your Fedora Linux virtual machine, type `exit` and press **Enter** to log out of your shell.

Discovery Exercises

1. Given the following situations, list any log files or commands that you would use when collecting information during the troubleshooting process.

   a. A USB device that worked previously with Linux does not respond to the mount command.

   b. The system was unable to mount the /home filesystem (/dev/sda6).

   c. A new database application fails to start successfully.

   d. All applications on a system open very slowly.

   e. You have installed a new network interface in the Linux system, but it is not displayed within the graphical Network utility within Fedora Linux.

2. For each problem in Exercise 1, list as many possible causes and solutions that you can think of, given the material presented throughout this book. Next, research other possible causes using the Internet.

3. You are the administrator of a Linux system that provides file and print services to over 100 clients in your company. The system uses several fast SSD hard disks and has a Xeon E3 processor with 128GB of RAM. Since its installation, you have installed database software that is used by only a few users. Unfortunately, you have rarely monitored and documented performance information of this system in the past. Recently, users complain that the performance of the server is very poor. What commands could you use to narrow down the problem? Are there any other troubleshooting methods that might be useful when solving this problem?

4. Briefly describe the purpose of a baseline. What areas of the system would you include in a baseline for your Linux system? Which commands would you use to obtain the information about these areas? Use these commands to generate baseline information for your system (for the current day only) and place this information in a folder on your system for later use. Next, monitor the normal activity of your system for three consecutive days and compare the results to the baseline that you have printed. Are there any differences? Incorporate this new information into your baseline by averaging the results. Are these new values a more accurate indication of normal activity? Why or why not?

5. You are a Linux administrator for your organization and are required to plan and deploy a new Linux file and print server that will service Windows, Linux, and macOS client computers. In addition, the server will provide DHCP services on the network and host a small Web site listing company information. In a brief document, draft the services that you plan to implement for this server and the methods that you will use to maximize the security of the system.

6. Add a virtual hard disk to your Fedora Linux virtual machine. Next, configure this virtual hard disk with a single partition that uses LUKS encryption and an ext4 filesystem. Ensure that the filesystem is automatically mounted at boot time to a mount point directory of your choice. Briefly describe situations in which LUKS encryption is commonly used.

7. On your Ubuntu Server 18 Linux virtual machine, create GPG keys for your user account and encrypt and digitally sign a file of your choice using GPG. Next, decrypt this file within another directory. Briefly describe situations in which GPG encryption is commonly used.

8. Install the `iperf` command on your Ubuntu Server 18 Linux and Fedora Linux virtual machines. Next, use the `iperf` command to test the bandwidth between your two virtual machines and interpret the results.

9. Examine the default AppArmor configuration on your Ubuntu Server 18 Linux virtual machine. Note the AppArmor profiles that are enforced, and their settings. Next, summarize the differences you noticed between exploring AppArmor and SELinux in a short memo.

CERTIFICATION

As technology advances, so does the need for educated people to manage technology. One of the principal risks that companies take is the hiring of qualified people to administer, use, or develop programs for Linux. To lower this risk, companies seek people who have demonstrated proficiency in certain technical areas. Although this proficiency can be demonstrated in the form of practical experience, practical experience alone is often not enough for companies when hiring for certain technical positions. Certification tests have become a standard benchmark of technical ability and are sought after by many companies. Certification tests can vary based on the technical certification, but they usually involve a computer test administered by an approved testing center. Hundreds of thousands of computer-related certification tests are written worldwide each year, and the certification process is likely to increase in importance in the future as technology advances.

> **Note** 📎
>
> It is important to recognize that certification does not replace ability, it demonstrates it. An employer might get 30 qualified applicants, and part of the hiring process will likely be a demonstration of ability. It is unlikely the employer will incur the cost and time it takes to test all 30. Rather, it is more likely the employer will look for benchmark certifications, which indicate a base ability and then test this smaller subgroup.

Furthermore, certifications are an internationally administered and recognized standard. Although an employer might not be familiar with the criteria involved in achieving a computer science degree from a particular university in Canada or a certain college in Texas, certification exam criteria are well published on websites and are, hence, well known. In addition, it does not matter in which country the certification exam is taken because the tests are standardized and administered by the same authority using common rules.

Certifications come in two broad categories: vendor-specific and vendor-neutral. Vendor-specific certifications are ones in which the vendor of a particular operating system or technology sets the standards to be met and creates the exams. Obtaining one of these certifications demonstrates knowledge of, or on, a particular technology product or operating system. Microsoft, Red Hat, and Cisco, for example, all have vendor-specific certifications for their products. Vendor-neutral exams, such as those offered by the Computing Technology Industry Association (CompTIA) and Linux Professional Institute (LPI), demonstrate knowledge in a particular area but not on any specific product or brand of product. Because Linux is a general category of operating system software that shares a common operating system kernel and utilities across multiple Linux distributions, vendor-neutral certification suits Linux particularly well. To certify on one particular distribution might well indicate the ability to port to and work well on another distribution, but with the varied number of distributions it is probably best to show proficiency on the most common features of Linux that the majority of distributions share.

Regardless of whether a certification exam is vendor-specific or vendor-neutral, the organizations that create them strive to ensure they are of the highest quality and integrity for use as a worldwide benchmark. Two globally recognized and vendor-neutral Linux certifications used by the industry are CompTIA's *Linux+* certification, and LPI's *LPIC-1: System Administrator* certification. This book covers the topics listed within the exam objectives for the 2019 versions of these two certifications.

> **Note** 📎
>
> Prior to 2019, CompTIA offered a certification called *Linux+ (Powered by LPI)* that was identical to the *LPIC-1: System Administrator* certification. Today, however, *Linux+* and *LPIC-1: System Administrator* are two entirely different certifications.

Linux+ Certification

CompTIA Linux+ is comprised of a single exam: XK0-004. You can take the exam at any participating VUE or Prometric testing center worldwide. The exam consists of a series of multiple-choice and simulation questions.

> **Note** 📎
>
> To learn more about the Linux+ certification exam and how to book one, visit the CompTIA website at *certification.comptia.org/certifications/linux*.

The following tables identify where the certification exam topics are covered in this book. Each table represents a separate domain, or skill set, measured by the exam.

1.0 Hardware and System Configuration

Objective	Chapter
1.1 Explain Linux boot process concepts	2, 6, 8
1.2 Given a scenario, install, configure, and monitor kernel modules	6
1.3 Given a scenario, configure and verify network connection parameters	12, 13, 14
1.4 Given a scenario, manage storage in a Linux environment	2, 3, 5, 6, 13, 14
1.5 Compare and contrast cloud and virtualization concepts and technologies	6, 13
1.6 Given a scenario, configure localization options	8

2.0 Systems Operation and Maintenance

Objective	Chapter
2.1 Given a scenario, conduct software installations, configurations, updates, and removals	11
2.2 Given a scenario, manage users and groups	2, 5, 7, 10
2.3 Given a scenario, create, modify, and redirect files	3, 4, 7, 11, 12
2.4 Given a scenario, manage services	8, 12
2.5 Summarize and explain server roles	1, 12
2.6 Given a scenario, automate and schedule jobs	9
2.7 Explain the use and operation of Linux devices	6, 8, 9, 10, 14
2.8 Compare and contrast Linux graphical user interfaces	8, 12

3.0 Security

Objective	Chapter
3.1 Given a scenario, apply or acquire the appropriate user and/or group permissions and ownership	2, 4, 10, 14
3.2 Given a scenario, configure and implement appropriate access and authentication methods	12, 14
3.3 Summarize security best practices in a Linux environment	12, 13, 14
3.4 Given a scenario, implement logging services	10
3.5 Given a scenario, implement and configure Linux firewalls	12, 13, 14
3.6 Given a scenario, backup, restore, and compress files	6, 11, 12, 13

4.0 Linux Troubleshooting and Diagnostics

Objective	Chapter
4.1 Given a scenario, analyze system properties and remediate accordingly	5, 12, 14
4.2 Given a scenario, analyze system processes in order to optimize performance	9
4.3 Given a scenario, analyze and troubleshoot user issues	4, 5, 14
4.4 Given a scenario, analyze and troubleshoot application and hardware issues	6, 11, 14

5.0 Automation and Scripting

Objective	Chapter
5.1 Given a scenario, deploy and execute basic BASH scripts	3, 7
5.2 Given a scenario, carry out version control using Git	7
5.3 Summarize orchestration processes and concepts	12, 13

LPIC-1: System Administrator Certification

There are two exams that comprise the LPIC-1: System Administrator certification: 101-500 and 102-500. You can take the exams separately, in any order; however, you must pass both exams to achieve the LPIC-1: System Administrator certification. As with CompTIA Linux+, you can take the exams at any participating VUE or Prometric testing center worldwide. The exam consists of a series of multiple-choice and short answer questions.

Note

To learn more about the LPIC-1: System Administrator certification exam and how to book one, visit the LPI website at *www.lpi.org/our-certifications/lpic-1-overview*.

The following tables identify where the certification exam topics are covered in this book. Each table represents a separate domain, or skill set, measured by the exam. Domains 101 through 104 are tested on the 101-500 certification exam, whereas domains 105 through 110 are tested on the 102-500 certification exam.

101 System Architecture

Objective	Chapter
101.1 Determine and configure hardware settings	5, 6
101.2 Boot the system	2, 5, 6, 8
101.3 Change runlevels/boot targets and shutdown or reboot system	2, 8

102 Linux Installation and Package Management

Objective	Chapter
102.1 Design hard disk layout	5
102.2 Install a boot manager	8
102.3 Manage shared libraries	11
102.4 Use Debian package management	11
102.5 Use RPM and YUM package management	11
102.6 Linux as a virtualization guest	6, 12, 13

103 GNU and UNIX Commands

Objective	Chapter
103.1 Work on the command line	2, 3, 4, 7
103.2 Process text streams using filters	3, 7, 11
103.3 Perform basic file management	3, 4, 11
103.4 Use streams, pipes, and redirects	7
103.5 Create, monitor, and kill processes	2, 9, 14
103.6 Modify process execution priorities	9
103.7 Search text files using regular expressions	3, 7
103.8 Basic file editing	3, 7

104 Devices, Linux Filesystems, Filesystem Hierarchy Standard

Objective	Chapter
104.1 Create partitions and filesystems	5
104.2 Maintain the integrity of filesystems	5, 6
104.3 Control mounting and unmounting of filesystems	5, 8
104.4 Manage disk quotas	5
104.5 Manage file permissions and ownership	4
104.6 Create and change hard and symbolic links	4
104.7 Find system files and place files in the correct location	4

105 Shells, Scripting, and Data Management

Objective	Chapter
105.1 Customize and use the shell environment	7, 10
105.2 Customize or write simple scripts	7, 9

106 User Interfaces and Desktops

Objective	Chapter
106.1 Install and configure X11	8, 12
106.2 Graphical desktops	8, 12
106.3 Accessibility	8

107 Administrative Tasks

Objective	Chapter
107.1 Manage user and group accounts and related system files	10
107.2 Automate system administration tasks by scheduling jobs	9
107.3 Localization and internationalization	8

108 Essential System Services

Objective	Chapter
108.1 Maintain system time	8, 13
108.2 System logging	10
108.3 Mail Transfer Agent (MTA) basics	1, 13
108.4 Manage printers and printing	10

109 Networking Fundamentals

Objective	Chapter
109.1 Fundamentals of Internet protocols	12
109.2 Persistent network configuration	12
109.3 Basic network troubleshooting	12
109.4 Configure client side DNS	12

110 Security

Objective	Chapter
110.1 Perform security administration tasks	2, 4, 5, 9, 10, 14
110.2 Setup host security	8, 10, 14
110.3 Securing data with encryption	12, 14

GNU PUBLIC LICENSE

A copy of the original GNU Public License referred to in Chapter 1 is shown in Figure B-1. This license and its revisions can be found at *www.gnu.org*.

GNU GENERAL PUBLIC LICENSE

Version 3, 29 June 2007

Copyright © 2007 Free Software Foundation, Inc. <*http://fsf.org/*>
Everyone is permitted to copy and distribute verbatim copies of
this license document, but changing it is not allowed.

Preamble

The GNU General Public License is a free, copyleft license for
software and other kinds of works.

The licenses for most software and other practical works are
designed to take away your freedom to share and change the works. By
contrast, the GNU General Public License is intended to guarantee
your freedom to share and change all versions of a program-to make
sure it remains free software for all its users. We, the Free
Software Foundation, use the GNU General Public License for most of
our software; it applies also to any other work released this way by
its authors. You can apply it to your programs, too.

When we speak of free software, we are referring to freedom, not
price. Our General Public Licenses are designed to make sure that
you have the freedom to distribute copies of free software (and
charge for them if you wish), that you receive source code or can
get it if you want it, that you can change the software or use
pieces of it in new free programs, and that you know you can do
these things.

To protect your rights, we need to prevent others from denying you
these rights or asking you to surrender the rights. Therefore, you
have certain responsibilities if you distribute copies of the
software, or if you modify it: responsibilities to respect the
freedom of others.

For example, if you distribute copies of such a program, whether
gratis or for a fee, you must pass on to the recipients the same
freedoms that you received. You must make sure that they, too,
receive or can get the source code. And you must show them these
terms so they know their rights.

Developers that use the GNU GPL protect your rights with two steps:
(1) assert copyright on the software, and (2) offer you this License
giving you legal permission to copy, distribute and/or modify it.

For the developers' and authors' protection, the GPL clearly
explains that there is no warranty for this free software. For both
users' and authors' sake, the GPL requires that modified versions be
marked as changed, so that their problems will not be attributed
erroneously to authors of previous versions.

Some devices are designed to deny users access to install or run
modified versions of the software inside them, although the
manufacturer can do so. This is fundamentally incompatible with the

Figure B-1   The GNU Public License

Source: Free Software Foundation, In. http://fsf.org/

aim of protecting users' freedom to change the software. The systematic pattern of such abuse occurs in the area of products for individuals to use, which is precisely where it is most unacceptable. Therefore, we have designed this version of the GPL to prohibit the practice for those products. If such problems arise substantially in other domains, we stand ready to extend this provision to those domains in future versions of the GPL, as needed to protect the freedom of users.

Finally, every program is threatened constantly by software patents. States should not allow patents to restrict development and use of software on general-purpose computers, but in those that do, we wish to avoid the special danger that patents applied to a free program could make it effectively proprietary. To prevent this, the GPL assures that patents cannot be used to render the program non-free.

The precise terms and conditions for copying, distribution and modification follow.

TERMS AND CONDITIONS

0. Definitions.

"This License" refers to version 3 of the GNU General Public License.

"Copyright" also means copyright-like laws that apply to other kinds of works, such as semiconductor masks.

"The Program" refers to any copyrightable work licensed under this License. Each licensee is addressed as "you". "Licensees" and "recipients" may be individuals or organizations.

To "modify" a work means to copy from or adapt all or part of the work in a fashion requiring copyright permission, other than the making of an exact copy. The resulting work is called a "modified version" of the earlier work or a work "based on" the earlier work.

A "covered work" means either the unmodified Program or a work based on the Program.

To "propagate" a work means to do anything with it that, without permission, would make you directly or secondarily liable for infringement under applicable copyright law, except executing it on a computer or modifying a private copy. Propagation includes copying, distribution (with or without modification), making available to the public, and in some countries other activities as well.

To "convey" a work means any kind of propagation that enables other parties to make or receive copies. Mere interaction with a user through a computer network, with no transfer of a copy, is not conveying.

An interactive user interface displays "Appropriate Legal Notices" to the extent that it includes a convenient and prominently

Figure B-1   The GNU Public License *(continued)*

Source: Free Software Foundation, In. http://fsf.org/

visible feature that (1) displays an appropriate copyright notice, and (2) tells the user that there is no warranty for the work (except to the extent that warranties are provided), that licensees may convey the work under this License, and how to view a copy of this License. If the interface presents a list of user commands or options, such as a menu, a prominent item in the list meets this criterion.

1. Source Code.

The "source code" for a work means the preferred form of the work for making modifications to it. "Object code" means any non-source form of a work.

A "Standard Interface" means an interface that either is an official standard defined by a recognized standards body, or, in the case of interfaces specified for a particular programming language, one that is widely used among developers working in that language.

The "System Libraries" of an executable work include anything, other than the work as a whole, that (a) is included in the normal form of packaging a Major Component, but which is not part of that Major Component, and (b) serves only to enable use of the work with that Major Component, or to implement a Standard Interface for which an implementation is available to the public in source code form. A "Major Component", in this context, means a major essential component (kernel, window system, and so on) of the specific operating system (if any) on which the executable work runs, or a compiler used to produce the work, or an object code interpreter used to run it.

The "Corresponding Source" for a work in object code form means all the source code needed to generate, install, and (for an executable work) run the object code and to modify the work, including scripts to control those activities. However, it does not include the work's System Libraries, or general-purpose tools or generally available free programs which are used unmodified in performing those activities but which are not part of the work. For example, Corresponding Source includes interface definition files associated with source files for the work, and the source code for shared libraries and dynamically linked subprograms that the work is specifically designed to require, such as by intimate data communication or control flow between those subprograms and other parts of the work.

The Corresponding Source need not include anything that users can regenerate automatically from other parts of the Corresponding Source.

The Corresponding Source for a work in source code form is that same work.

2. Basic Permissions.

All rights granted under this License are granted for the term of copyright on the Program, and are irrevocable provided the stated

Figure B-1   The GNU Public License (*continued*)

Source: Free Software Foundation, In. http://fsf.org/

conditions are met. This License explicitly affirms your unlimited permission to run the unmodified Program. The output from running a covered work is covered by this License only if the output, given its content, constitutes a covered work. This License acknowledges your rights of fair use or other equivalent, as provided by copyright law.

You may make, run and propagate covered works that you do not convey, without conditions so long as your license otherwise remains in force. You may convey covered works to others for the sole purpose of having them make modifications exclusively for you, or provide you with facilities for running those works, provided that you comply with the terms of this License in conveying all material for which you do not control copyright. Those thus making or running the covered works for you must do so exclusively on your behalf, under your direction and control, on terms that prohibit them from making any copies of your copyrighted material outside their relationship with you.

Conveying under any other circumstances is permitted solely under the conditions stated below. Sublicensing is not allowed; section 10 makes it unnecessary.

3. Protecting Users' Legal Rights From Anti-Circumvention Law.

No covered work shall be deemed part of an effective technological measure under any applicable law fulfilling obligations under article 11 of the WIPO copyright treaty adopted on 20 December 1996, or similar laws prohibiting or restricting circumvention of such measures.

When you convey a covered work, you waive any legal power to forbid circumvention of technological measures to the extent such circumvention is effected by exercising rights under this License with respect to the covered work, and you disclaim any intention to limit operation or modification of the work as a means of enforcing, against the work's users, your or third parties' legal rights to forbid circumvention of technological measures.

4. Conveying Verbatim Copies.

You may convey verbatim copies of the Program's source code as you receive it, in any medium, provided that you conspicuously and appropriately publish on each copy an appropriate copyright notice; keep intact all notices stating that this License and any non-permissive terms added in accord with section 7 apply to the code; keep intact all notices of the absence of any warranty; and give all recipients a copy of this License along with the Program.

You may charge any price or no price for each copy that you convey, and you may offer support or warranty protection for a fee.

5. Conveying Modified Source Versions.

You may convey a work based on the Program, or the modifications to produce it from the Program, in the form of source code under the

Figure B-1   The GNU Public License (*continued*)

Source: Free Software Foundation, In. http://fsf.org/

terms of section 4, provided that you also meet all of these conditions:

a) The work must carry prominent notices stating that you modified it, and giving a relevant date.

b) The work must carry prominent notices stating that it is released under this License and any conditions added under section 7. This requirement modifies the requirement in section 4 to "keep intact all notices".

c) You must license the entire work, as a whole, under this License to anyone who comes into possession of a copy. This License will therefore apply, along with any applicable section 7 additional terms, to the whole of the work, and all its parts, regardless of how they are packaged. This License gives no permission to license the work in any other way, but it does not invalidate such permission if you have separately received it.

d) If the work has interactive user interfaces, each must display Appropriate Legal Notices; however, if the Program has interactive interfaces that do not display Appropriate Legal Notices, your work need not make them do so.

A compilation of a covered work with other separate and independent works, which are not by their nature extensions of the covered work, and which are not combined with it such as to form a larger program, in or on a volume of a storage or distribution medium, is called an "aggregate" if the compilation and its resulting copyright are not used to limit the access or legal rights of the compilation's users beyond what the individual works permit. Inclusion of a covered work in an aggregate does not cause this License to apply to the other parts of the aggregate.

6. Conveying Non-Source Forms.

You may convey a covered work in object code form under the terms of sections 4 and 5, provided that you also convey the machine-readable Corresponding Source under the terms of this License, in one of these ways:

a) Convey the object code in, or embodied in, a physical product (including a physical distribution medium), accompanied by the Corresponding Source fixed on a durable physical medium customarily used for software interchange.

b) Convey the object code in, or embodied in, a physical product (including a physical distribution medium), accompanied by a written offer, valid for at least three years and valid for as long as you offer spare parts or customer support for that product model, to give anyone who possesses the object code either (1) a copy of the Corresponding Source for all the software in the product that is covered by this License, on a durable physical medium customarily used for software interchange, for a price no more than your

Figure B-1   The GNU Public License (*continued*)

Source: Free Software Foundation, In. http://fsf.org/

reasonable cost of physically performing this conveying of source, or (2) access to copy the Corresponding Source from a network server at no charge.

c) Convey individual copies of the object code with a copy of the written offer to provide the Corresponding Source. This alternative is allowed only occasionally and noncommercially, and only if you received the object code with such an offer, in accord with subsection 6b.

d) Convey the object code by offering access from a designated place (gratis or for a charge), and offer equivalent access to the Corresponding Source in the same way through the same place at no further charge. You need not require recipients to copy the Corresponding Source along with the object code. If the place to copy the object code is a network server, the Corresponding Source may be on a different server (operated by you or a third party) that supports equivalent copying facilities, provided you maintain clear directions next to the object code saying where to find the Corresponding Source. Regardless of what server hosts the Corresponding Source, you remain obligated to ensure that it is available for as long as needed to satisfy these requirements.

e) Convey the object code using peer-to-peer transmission, provided you inform other peers where the object code and Corresponding Source of the work are being offered to the general public at no charge under subsection 6d.

A separable portion of the object code, whose source code is excluded from the Corresponding Source as a System Library, need not be included in conveying the object code work.

A "User Product" is either (1) a "consumer product", which means any tangible personal property which is normally used for personal, family, or household purposes, or (2) anything designed or sold for incorporation into a dwelling. In determining whether a product is a consumer product, doubtful cases shall be resolved in favor of coverage. For a particular product received by a particular user, "normally used" refers to a typical or common use of that class of product, regardless of the status of the particular user or of the way in which the particular user actually uses, or expects or is expected to use, the product. A product is a consumer product regardless of whether the product has substantial commercial, industrial or non-consumer uses, unless such uses represent the only significant mode of use of the product.

"Installation Information" for a User Product means any methods, procedures, authorization keys, or other information required to install and execute modified versions of a covered work in that User Product from a modified version of its Corresponding Source. The information must suffice to ensure that the continued functioning of the modified object code is in no case prevented or interfered with solely because modification has been made.

Figure B-1   The GNU Public License (*continued*)

If you convey an object code work under this section in, or with, or specifically for use in, a User Product, and the conveying occurs as part of a transaction in which the right of possession and use of the User Product is transferred to the recipient in perpetuity or for a fixed term (regardless of how the transaction is characterized), the Corresponding Source conveyed under this section must be accompanied by the Installation Information. But this requirement does not apply if neither you nor any third party retains the ability to install modified object code on the User Product (for example, the work has been installed in ROM).

The requirement to provide Installation Information does not include a requirement to continue to provide support service, warranty, or updates for a work that has been modified or installed by the recipient, or for the User Product in which it has been modified or installed. Access to a network may be denied when the modification itself materially and adversely affects the operation of the network or violates the rules and protocols for communication across the network.

Corresponding Source conveyed, and Installation Information provided, in accord with this section must be in a format that is publicly documented (and with an implementation available to the public in source code form), and must require no special password or key for unpacking, reading or copying.

7. Additional Terms.

"Additional permissions" are terms that supplement the terms of this License by making exceptions from one or more of its conditions. Additional permissions that are applicable to the entire Program shall be treated as though they were included in this License, to the extent that they are valid under applicable law. If additional permissions apply only to part of the Program, that part may be used separately under those permissions, but the entire Program remains governed by this License without regard to the additional permissions.

When you convey a copy of a covered work, you may at your option remove any additional permissions from that copy, or from any part of it. (Additional permissions may be written to require their own removal in certain cases when you modify the work.) You may place additional permissions on material, added by you to a covered work, for which you have or can give appropriate copyright permission.

Notwithstanding any other provision of this License, for material you add to a covered work, you may (if authorized by the copyright holders of that material) supplement the terms of this License with terms:

a) Disclaiming warranty or limiting liability differently from the terms of sections 15 and 16 of this License; or

Figure B-1   The GNU Public License (*continued*)

b) Requiring preservation of specified reasonable legal notices or author attributions in that material or in the Appropriate Legal Notices displayed by works containing it; or

c) Prohibiting misrepresentation of the origin of that material, or requiring that modified versions of such material be marked in reasonable ways as different from the original version; or

d) Limiting the use for publicity purposes of names of licensors or authors of the material; or

e) Declining to grant rights under trademark law for use of some trade names, trademarks, or service marks; or

f) Requiring indemnification of licensors and authors of that material by anyone who conveys the material (or modified versions of it) with contractual assumptions of liability to the recipient, for any liability that these contractual assumptions directly impose on those licensors and authors.

All other non-permissive additional terms are considered "further restrictions" within the meaning of section 10. If the Program as you received it, or any part of it, contains a notice stating that it is governed by this License along with a term that is a further restriction, you may remove that term. If a license document contains a further restriction but permits relicensing or conveying under this License, you may add to a covered work material governed by the terms of that license document, provided that the further restriction does not survive such relicensing or conveying.

If you add terms to a covered work in accord with this section, you must place, in the relevant source files, a statement of the additional terms that apply to those files, or a notice indicating where to find the applicable terms.

Additional terms, permissive or non-permissive, may be stated in the form of a separately written license, or stated as exceptions; the above requirements apply either way.

8. Termination.

You may not propagate or modify a covered work except as expressly provided under this License. Any attempt otherwise to propagate or modify it is void, and will automatically terminate your rights under this License (including any patent licenses granted under the third paragraph of section 11).

However, if you cease all violation of this License, then your license from a particular copyright holder is reinstated (a) provisionally, unless and until the copyright holder explicitly and ?finally terminates your license, and (b) permanently, if the copyright holder fails to notify you of the violation by some reasonable means prior to 60 days after the cessation.

Figure B-1   The GNU Public License (*continued*)

Moreover, your license from a particular copyright holder is reinstated permanently if the copyright holder notifies you of the violation by some reasonable means, this is the first time you have received notice of violation of this License (for any work) from that copyright holder, and you cure the violation prior to 30 days after your receipt of the notice.

Termination of your rights under this section does not terminate the licenses of parties who have received copies or rights from you under this License. If your rights have been terminated and not permanently reinstated, you do not qualify to receive new licenses for the same material under section 10.

9. Acceptance Not Required for Having Copies.

You are not required to accept this License in order to receive or run a copy of the Program. Ancillary propagation of a covered work occurring solely as a consequence of using peer-to-peer transmission to receive a copy likewise does not require acceptance. However, nothing other than this License grants you permission to propagate or modify any covered work. These actions infringe copyright if you do not accept this License. Therefore, by modifying or propagating a covered work, you indicate your acceptance of this License to do so.

10. Automatic Licensing of Downstream Recipients.

Each time you convey a covered work, the recipient automatically receives a license from the original licensors, to run, modify and propagate that work, subject to this License. You are not responsible for enforcing compliance by third parties with this License.

An "entity transaction" is a transaction transferring control of an organization, or substantially all assets of one, or subdividing an organization, or merging organizations. If propagation of a covered work results from an entity transaction, each party to that transaction who receives a copy of the work also receives whatever licenses to the work the party's predecessor in interest had or could give under the previous paragraph, plus a right to possession of the Corresponding Source of the work from the predecessor in interest, if the predecessor has it or can get it with reasonable efforts.

You may not impose any further restrictions on the exercise of the rights granted or affirmed under this License. For example, you may not impose a license fee, royalty, or other charge for exercise of rights granted under this License, and you may not initiate litigation (including a cross-claim or counterclaim in a lawsuit) alleging that any patent claim is infringed by making, using, selling, offering for sale, or importing the Program or any portion of it.

Figure B-1 The GNU Public License (continued)

11. Patents.

A "contributor" is a copyright holder who authorizes use under this License of the Program or a work on which the Program is based. The work thus licensed is called the contributor's "contributor version".

A contributor's "essential patent claims" are all patent claims owned or controlled by the contributor, whether already acquired or hereafter acquired, that would be infringed by some manner, permitted by this License, of making, using, or selling its contributor version, but do not include claims that would be infringed only as a consequence of further modification of the contributor version. For purposes of this definition, "control" includes the right to grant patent sublicenses in a manner consistent with the requirements of this License.

Each contributor grants you a non-exclusive, worldwide, royalty-free patent license under the contributor's essential patent claims, to make, use, sell, offer for sale, import and otherwise run, modify and propagate the contents of its contributor version.

In the following three paragraphs, a "patent license" is any express agreement or commitment, however denominated, not to enforce a patent (such as an express permission to practice a patent or covenant not to sue for patent infringement). To "grant" such a patent license to a party means to make such an agreement or commitment not to enforce a patent against the party.

If you convey a covered work, knowingly relying on a patent license, and the Corresponding Source of the work is not available for anyone to copy, free of charge and under the terms of this License, through a publicly available network server or other readily accessible means, then you must either (1) cause the Corresponding Source to be so available, or (2) arrange to deprive yourself of the benefit of the patent license for this particular work, or (3) arrange, in a manner consistent with the requirements of this License, to extend the patent license to downstream recipients. "Knowingly relying" means you have actual knowledge that, but for the patent license, your conveying the covered work in a country, or your recipient's use of the covered work in a country, would infringe one or more identifiable patents in that country that you have reason to believe are valid.

If, pursuant to or in connection with a single transaction or arrangement, you convey, or propagate by procuring conveyance of, a covered work, and grant a patent license to some of the parties receiving the covered work authorizing them to use, propagate, modify or convey a specific copy of the covered work, then the patent license you grant is automatically extended to all recipients of the covered work and works based on it.

A patent license is "discriminatory" if it does not include within the scope of its coverage, prohibits the exercise of, or is conditioned on the non-exercise of one or more of the rights that are

Figure B-1   The GNU Public License (*continued*)

Source: Free Software Foundation, In. http://fsf.org/

specifically granted under this License. You may not convey a covered work if you are a party to an arrangement with a third party that is in the business of distributing software, under which you make payment to the third party based on the extent of your activity of conveying the work, and under which the third party grants, to any of the parties who would receive the covered work from you, a discriminatory patent license (a) in connection with copies of the covered work conveyed by you (or copies made from those copies), or (b) primarily for and in connection with specific products or compilations that contain the covered work, unless you entered into that arrangement, or that patent license was granted, prior to 28 March 2007.

Nothing in this License shall be construed as excluding or limiting any implied license or other defenses to infringement that may otherwise be available to you under applicable patent law.

12. No Surrender of Others' Freedom.

If conditions are imposed on you (whether by court order, agreement or otherwise) that contradict the conditions of this License, they do not excuse you from the conditions of this License. If you cannot convey a covered work so as to satisfy simultaneously your obligations under this License and any other pertinent obligations, then as a consequence you may not convey it at all. For example, if you agree to terms that obligate you to collect a royalty for further conveying from those to whom you convey the Program, the only way you could satisfy both those terms and this License would be to refrain entirely from conveying the Program.

13. Use with the GNU Affero General Public License.

Notwithstanding any other provision of this License, you have permission to link or combine any covered work with a work licensed under version 3 of the GNU Affero General Public License into a single combined work, and to convey the resulting work. The terms of this License will continue to apply to the part which is the covered work, but the special requirements of the GNU Affero General Public License, section 13, concerning interaction through a network will apply to the combination as such.

14. Revised Versions of this License.

The Free Software Foundation may publish revised and/or new versions of the GNU General Public License from time to time. Such new versions will be similar in spirit to the present version, but may differ in detail to address new problems or concerns.

Each version is given a distinguishing version number. If the Program specifies that a certain numbered version of the GNU General Public License "or any later version" applies to it, you have the option of following the terms and conditions either of that numbered version or of any later version published by the Free Software Foundation. If the Program does not specify a version number of the

Figure B-1 The GNU Public License (*continued*)

Source: Free Software Foundation, In. http://fsf.org/

GNU General Public License, you may choose any version ever published by the Free Software Foundation.

If the Program specifies that a proxy can decide which future versions of the GNU General Public License can be used, that proxy's public statement of acceptance of a version permanently authorizes you to choose that version for the Program.

Later license versions may give you additional or different permissions. However, no additional obligations are imposed on any author or copyright holder as a result of your choosing to follow a later version.

15. Disclaimer of Warranty.

THERE IS NO WARRANTY FOR THE PROGRAM, TO THE EXTENT PERMITTED BY APPLICABLE LAW. EXCEPT WHEN OTHERWISE STATED IN WRITING THE COPYRIGHT HOLDERS AND/OR OTHER PARTIES PROVIDE THE PROGRAM "AS IS" WITHOUT WARRANTY OF ANY KIND, EITHER EXPRESSED OR IMPLIED, INCLUDING, BUT NOT LIMITED TO, THE IMPLIED WARRANTIES OF MERCHANTABILITY AND FITNESS FOR A PARTICULAR PURPOSE. THE ENTIRE RISK AS TO THE QUALITY AND PERFORMANCE OF THE PROGRAM IS WITH YOU. SHOULD THE PROGRAM PROVE DEFECTIVE, YOU ASSUME THE COST OF ALL NECESSARY SERVICING, REPAIR OR CORRECTION.

16. Limitation of Liability.

IN NO EVENT UNLESS REQUIRED BY APPLICABLE LAW OR AGREED TO IN WRITING WILL ANY COPYRIGHT HOLDER, OR ANY OTHER PARTY WHO MODIFIES AND/OR CONVEYS THE PROGRAM AS PERMITTED ABOVE, BE LIABLE TO YOU FOR DAMAGES, INCLUDING ANY GENERAL, SPECIAL, INCIDENTAL OR CONSEQUENTIAL DAMAGES ARISING OUT OF THE USE OR INABILITY TO USE THE PROGRAM (INCLUDING BUT NOT LIMITED TO LOSS OF DATA OR DATA BEING RENDERED INACCURATE OR LOSSES SUSTAINED BY YOU OR THIRD PARTIES OR A FAILURE OF THE PROGRAM TO OPERATE WITH ANY OTHER PROGRAMS), EVEN IF SUCH HOLDER OR OTHER PARTY HAS BEEN ADVISED OF THE POSSIBILITY OF SUCH DAMAGES.

17. Interpretation of Sections 15 and 16.

If the disclaimer of warranty and limitation of liability provided above cannot be given local legal effect according to their terms, reviewing courts shall apply local law that most closely approximates an absolute waiver of all civil liability in connection with the Program, unless a warranty or assumption of liability accompanies a copy of the Program in return for a fee.

END OF TERMS AND CONDITIONS

How to Apply These Terms to Your New Programs

If you develop a new program, and you want it to be of the greatest possible use to the public, the best way to achieve this is to make it free software which everyone can redistribute and change under these terms.

Figure B-1 The GNU Public License (*continued*)

Source: Free Software Foundation, In. http://fsf.org/

To do so, attach the following notices to the program. It is safest to attach them to the start of each source file to most effectively state the exclusion of warranty; and each file should have at least the "copyright" line and a pointer to where the full notice is found.

<one line to give the program's name and a brief idea of what it does.> Copyright (C) <year> <name of author> This program is free software: you can redistribute it and/or modify it under the terms of the GNU General Public License as published by the Free Software Foundation, either version 3 of the License, or (at your option) any later version. This program is distributed in the hope that it will be useful, but WITHOUT ANY WARRANTY; without even the implied warranty of MERCHANTABILITY or FITNESS FOR A PARTICULAR PURPOSE. See the GNU General Public License for more details. You should have received a copy of the GNU General Public License along with this program. If not, see <*http://www.gnu.org/licenses/*>.

Also add information on how to contact you by electronic and paper mail.

If the program does terminal interaction, make it output a short notice like this when it starts in an interactive mode:

<program> Copyright (C) <year> <name of author> This program comes with ABSOLUTELY NO WARRANTY; for details type 'show w'. This is free software, and you are welcome to redistribute it under certain conditions; type 'show c' for details.

The hypothetical commands 'show w' and 'show c' should show the appropriate parts of the General Public License. Of course, your program's commands might be different; for a GUI interface, you would use an "about box".

You should also get your employer (if you work as a programmer) or school, if any, to sign a "copyright disclaimer" for the program, if necessary. For more information on this, and how to apply and follow the GNU GPL, see <*http://www.gnu.org/licenses/*>.

The GNU General Public License does not permit incorporating your program into proprietary programs. If your program is a subroutine library, you may consider it more useful to permit linking proprietary applications with the library. If this is what you want to do, use the GNU Lesser General Public License instead of this License. But first, please read <*http://www.gnu.org/philosophy/why-not-lgpl.html*>.

Figure B-1 The GNU Public License

Source: Free Software Foundation, In. http://fsf.org/

APPENDIX C

FINDING LINUX RESOURCES ON THE INTERNET

Open source development has made Linux a powerful and versatile operating system; however, this development has also increased the complexity of Linux resources available on the Internet. This bounty of resources can seem intimidating, but search engines and key websites make finding particular types of Linux resources easier.

Using Search Engines

By far, the easiest way to locate resources on any topic is by searching for a Linux-related key term using an Internet search engine. However, a single search may yield thousands of results. Consequently, it is important that you use advanced search features when using a search engine. Of the search engines available today, Google (*www.google.com*) provides the richest set of advanced search features. For example, when searching for multiple words within Google, the words listed to the left are given higher search weighting than the words listed to the right. For example, a search for `Linux filesystem repair` will display Linux-focused websites that list filesystem repair topics. Alternatively, a search for `filesystem repair Linux` will display websites that provide filesystem repair topics for any operating system, but mention Linux within their content. Consequently, it is important to start most search queries with the word `Linux` to ensure that the first page of search results contains Linux-relevant material only.

You can also add related words to a Google search using a tilde (~) character; this allows a related word to be given the same search weighting as the first word searched. For example to search for Apache configuration related to the Fedora Linux distribution, you could search for `Apache configuration ~Fedora` within Google.

Because Linux commands are case-sensitive, case sensitivity is also important within Google searches, as Google will match the case in your search, where possible. For example, the Secure Shell (SSH) technology within Linux is often capitalized within websites, whereas the related `ssh` command is lowercase. Consequently, a Google search for `SSH` will return general results for SSH, whereas a Google search for `ssh` will return specific results for the `ssh` command.

By default, the words that you enter within a Google search are interpreted by Google as separate, unrelated search criteria. However, you can surround search terms with double quotes to match results that have those exact words in the order that you specify. For example, a search for `"zpool create"` will return results that contain examples of the `zpool create` command, rather than results that have the words zpool and create somewhere in the webpage, but not necessarily together.

You can also use wildcards in a Google search. For example, to search for the smbd and nmbd daemons used by the Samba file sharing service on Linux, you could enter `Samba *mbd` within Google.

If the number of results returned by a Google search are too broad, you can re-run the search excluding unwanted keywords using the - character. For example, if your `docker containers` search displays too many results geared toward the Windows operating system, you could instead search for `docker containers -Windows` to omit any results that contain the word Windows.

Google can also narrow down results by time period. This is especially useful when searching for results that match newer Linux distributions, or problems that were recently discovered. For example, a search for `Ubuntu network configuration 2018..2020` would list webpages that discuss how to configure network settings on the Ubuntu Linux distribution that were created between 2018 and 2020.

To narrow your results to a specific website, you could add the prefix `site:website` (without spaces) to your Google search. For example, to search for Web pages on the wikipedia.org website related to the postgresql daemon, you could search for `site:wikipedia.org postgresql` within Google.

There are many other prefixes that you can add to Google searches. For example, to search for examples of SSH configuration files (that use a `.config` file extension), you could search for `filetype:config ssh` within Google. Similarly, to search for websites that have Linux security in their title and contain the term ssh, you could enter `intitle:"Linux security" ssh` within Google.

Useful Internet Resources

There are hundreds of websites dedicated to Linux and open source software. Many of these websites provide specific help with Linux commands, as well as host HOWTO documents, Linux software, user forums, or links to other Linux resources organized by topic. Table C-1 lists some Linux-related websites that you may find useful.

YouTube channels are also a great source of Linux information as they provide visual walkthroughs for Linux configuration, or Linux-related commentary that is easy to understand. Table C-2 lists some Linux-related YouTube channels.

Table C-1   Useful Linux-related websites

Website	Title	Description
opensource.com	The Open Organization	Maintains links to useful Linux resources by topic area. You can optionally enter your email address to receive weekly summaries of recent Linux articles within the community.
www.commandlinefu. com	Command Line Fu	Useful user-submitted Linux commands and command-line tricks.
explainshell.com	Explain Shell Commands	You can enter any Linux command on this site and receive an easy-to-read description of what each component of the command does.
fullcirclemagazine.org	Full Circle Magazine	An online monthly magazine that contains many easy-to-read articles focusing on the Ubuntu family of Linux distributions.
www.howtoforge.com	HowtoForge	This site hosts a large number of user-submitted, easy-to-read Linux tutorials on a wide variety of topics for many Linux distributions, as well as includes a forum where you can ask for help and discuss Linux-related topics.
kernelnewbies.org/ LinuxChanges	Kernel Newbies	This site explains the different Linux kernels available as well as the latest Linux kernel features in an easy-to-read form.
linuxappfinder.com	Linux App Finder	You can search this site for useful Linux programs by keyword or topic area.
www.linuxjournal.com	Linux Journal	An online magazine dedicated to Linux-related news that also boasts several how-to guides, blogs, software reviews, tips, and tricks.
lxer.com	Linux News	Provides a list of the latest news within the Linux and open source software community.
www.linuxpromagazine. com	Linux Pro Magazine	Contains a large set of Linux and open source articles and white papers divided by system administration topics (e.g., software, networking, administration, security, hardware, desktop).
www.linuxquestions. org	Linux Questions	This is an online forum where users, administrators, and developers can ask and answer questions on Linux topics. This website also hosts several Linux tutorials and articles.
linuxsurvival.com	Linux Survival	This is a free tutorial designed for people who have little or no experience with the Linux operating system. It covers the usage of the key commands that can jump-start a user into using Linux quickly.

(continues)

Table C-1 Useful Linux-related websites (*continued*)

Website	Title	Description
www.linuxvoice.com	Linux Voice	This is an online magazine that hosts several Linux-focused articles and podcasts. It also contains useful tutorials on the site, as well as an active forum discussing many key Linux topics.
linux.com	Linux.com	Aside from hosting Linux-related blogs and forums, this website contains a directory of popular Linux resources, including books, videos, software, Linux distributions, and community resources.
www.linux.org	Linux.org	This site hosts a wide variety of Linux resources (tutorials, how-to documents, links) for many Linux distributions. Additionally, it hosts forums that contain a large number of tips, walkthroughs, and information for Linux users and system administrators.
www.phoronix.com	Phoronix	Provides Linux hardware-related news and resources, including product reviews, and Linux hardware benchmarks by hardware category.
sourceforge.net	Source Forge	This is an online software and code repository for open source software. A wide variety of Linux software can be obtained directly from Source Forge by searching the available software catalog.
www.ss64.com/bash	SS64 BASH Reference	The site provides an easy-to-search reference for commands on various systems and programming environments.
www.tecmint.com	TecMint	Offers a comprehensive selection of Linux-related reference material, including information on different Linux distributions, Linux command references, BASH shell script examples, Linux tips and tricks, as well as several free guides and eBooks.
teknixx.com	Teknixx	Contains a wide range of online Linux usage and administration tutorials.
www.tldp.org	The Linux Documentation Project	This site is a central repository of HOWTO documents for specific Linux packages.
www.unixmen.com	UNIXmen	In addition to several useful UNIX and Linux tutorials, this site provides valuable reviews on different Linux distributions and open source software.
www.fsf.org	The Free Software Foundation	This website for the Free Software Foundation includes information about the free software movement and licensing, as well as contains links to valuable Linux and open source resources and websites.

Table C-2   Useful Linux-related YouTube channels

YouTube channel name	Description
Celebrate Ubuntu	Provides a wide range of tutorials and topics related to Ubuntu-based Linux distributions.
Nixie Pixel	Covers a wide range of topics that are security-related (Linux, Android, and iOS) as well as hosts a wide variety of Linux topics and tutorials.
Quidsup	Discusses various Linux-related topics, with an emphasis on Linux security and the Ubuntu Linux distribution.
Spatry	This channel is dedicated to Windows users who are considering Linux as an alternative, and contains useful Linux usage and support tips.
SysAdmGirl	Covers Linux system administration topics on a wide variety of Linux distributions and open source technologies.
The Linux Foundation	Discusses information on the development and features of the Linux operating system itself, including new features.
Theurbanpenguin	Contains tutorials on a wide variety of different Linux distributions and UNIX flavors, with a focus on certification.

Links to websites and YouTube videos are often shared on social media. As a result, following Linux-related accounts on social media is often an easy way to get the latest Linux news and tips. Twitter is one of the easiest social media platforms for obtaining technology-related information. Table C-3 lists some valuable Twitter handles that you can follow to obtain Linux-related information.

Table C-3   Useful Linux-related Twitter handles

Twitter handle	Name
@UbuntuForums	Official Ubuntu Forums
@Fedora	The Fedora Project
@Ubuntu	The Ubuntu Linux Distribution
@AskUbuntu	The Stack Exchange Network
@LinuxQuestions	LinuxQuestions.org Twitter Feed
@Linux_Pro	Linux Pro Magazine
@LinuxVoice	Linux Voice Magazine
@FullCircleMag	Full Circle Magazine

APPLYING YOUR LINUX KNOWLEDGE TO macOS

Recall from Chapter 1 that Linux is an open source evolution of the UNIX operating system. As a result, most of the concepts, commands, and files that we have discussed within this book apply equally to UNIX operating systems, including Apple macOS.

Unlike Linux, which is commonly used on a wide variety of different systems, from embedded hardware systems to cloud servers, macOS is used primarily as an end-user operating system only, and licensed exclusively for use on Apple computers. The majority of macOS is comprised of an open source version of the NeXTSTEP UNIX operating system called **Darwin**. Darwin uses a kernel based on NeXTSTEP MACH and BSD UNIX called **XNU** (which stands for "X is Not UNIX"). Apple combines Darwin with their closed source Aqua desktop environment and application frameworks to create macOS. Mojave (version 10.14) is the latest version of macOS at the time of this writing.

Because many organizations today purchase macOS systems, many Linux administrators often support macOS systems within their organization. This appendix outlines the similarities and key differences between Linux and macOS system administration.

The macOS Filesystem

Although earlier versions of macOS used Hierarchical File System Plus (HFS+), the default filesystem used by recent versions of macOS is the Apple File System (APFS). Both HFS+ and APFS use the same features and conventions as any other Linux or UNIX filesystem. Filenames may be 255 characters in length, and can contain uppercase and lowercase letters, numbers, underscores (_) and dashes (-). Hidden files start with a period (.), and each directory contains a reference to the current directory (.), and a reference to the parent directory (. .).

Because macOS supports the Filesystem Hierarchy Standard (FHS), it uses the same basic directory structure as Linux. However, macOS adds several other directories that begin with an uppercase letter to store key system and user files, as shown in Table D-1. Only the /Applications, /Library, /System, /User Information, and /Users folders are shown in the graphical desktop by default. All other directories are hidden, but can be viewed using a BASH shell.

Table D-1   Common macOS directories

Directory	Description
/Applications	Stores most user applications
/bin	Contains binary executables
/etc	Contains most system configuration
/Library	Contains app libraries, settings, & documentation
/Network	Contains remote libraries and information
/private	Contains OS information
/sbin	Contains superuser (root) executables
/System	Contains most OS & system configuration files
/tmp	Contains temporary files used by apps
/Users	Default location for regular user home directories
/User Information	Contains system documentation
/usr	Stores most executables & their documentation
/var	Contains log files and spool/content directories
/Volumes	Contains subdirectories for mounting devices to

Using the macOS Desktop

As shown in Figure D-1, the macOS desktop is very similar to the GNOME desktop in Linux. The application launcher along the bottom of the desktop is called the **Dock**, and is equivalent to the Favorites launcher at the left of the GNOME desktop. The leftmost icon in the Dock shown in Figure D-1 opens the **Finder** application, which can be used to explore the files and directories on the system. The cog wheel icon in the

Dock shown in Figure D-1 opens the **System Preferences** application, which can be used to configure all aspects of the macOS operating system. The menu bar at the top of the macOS desktop contains menus to control the foreground application, as well as icons that perform common system tasks such as connecting to a Wi-Fi network. By selecting the Apple icon menu at the far left of the menu bar, you can update your system software, view system information, force a running application to stop, as well as shut down or reboot your system.

Figure D-1   The macOS desktop
Source: Apple, Inc.

Using BASH within macOS

Unlike Linux, macOS does not support local terminals outside of the desktop environment. However, you can open the Finder application and navigate to /Applications/Utilities/Terminal in order to start the **Terminal** application that allows you to interact with a BASH shell. When you open the Terminal application, you are placed in your home directory (/Users/*username*), which contains a series of subfolders that allow you to store user content, as shown in Figure D-2.

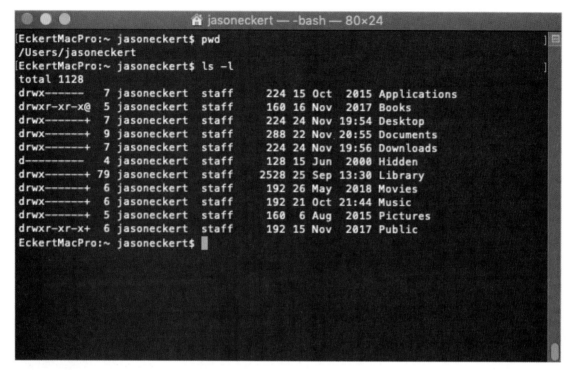

```
●●●                    🏠 jasoneckert — -bash — 80×24
[EckertMacPro:~ jasoneckert$ pwd
/Users/jasoneckert
[EckertMacPro:~ jasoneckert$ ls -l
total 1128
drwx------    7 jasoneckert  staff     224 15 Oct   2015 Applications
drwxr-xr-x@   5 jasoneckert  staff     160 16 Nov   2017 Books
drwx------+   7 jasoneckert  staff     224 24 Nov 19:54 Desktop
drwx------+   9 jasoneckert  staff     288 22 Nov 20:55 Documents
drwx------+   7 jasoneckert  staff     224 24 Nov 19:56 Downloads
d---------    4 jasoneckert  staff     128 15 Jun   2000 Hidden
drwx------+  79 jasoneckert  staff    2528 25 Sep 13:30 Library
drwx------+   6 jasoneckert  staff     192 26 May   2018 Movies
drwx------+   6 jasoneckert  staff     192 21 Oct 21:44 Music
drwx------+   5 jasoneckert  staff     160  6 Aug   2015 Pictures
drwxr-xr-x+   6 jasoneckert  staff     192 15 Nov   2017 Public
EckertMacPro:~ jasoneckert$ ▌
```

Figure D-2   The Terminal application

Source: Apple, Inc.

Note 📎

If you want to perform system administration as the root user, you must first enable the root user using the `dsenableroot` **command**.

All of the BASH features that you have used on Linux apply equally to macOS, including case sensitivity, shell metacharacters, redirection, piping, quotes, environment variables, environment files, and shell script constructs. Similarly, the Tab key can be used to expand commands and file paths, and the Ctrl+c key combination can be used to quit a foreground command.

Many of the same Linux commands and associated options that you are familiar with work identically on macOS. Table D-2 lists the Linux commands discussed within this book that can be used within a BASH shell on macOS. For Linux commands that are not listed in Table D-2, there is a separate command or process used to provide the same functionality within macOS. Table D-3 lists useful macOS-specific commands.

Table D-2 Linux commands available in macOS

Category	Commands
System documentation	`man, apropos, info, help`
File management	`pwd, cd, ls, file, locate, which, find, whereis, type, cp, mv, rm, unlink, rmdir, mkdir, ln, touch, chown, chgrp, chmod, umask`
Text tools	`cat, more, less, head, tail, pr, uniq, cut, paste, tr, split, nl, seq, sort, wc, diff, strings, od, grep, egrep, sed, awk, vi (vim), emacs, nano`
Filesystem administration	`mount, umount, fuser, fsck, df, du, quota, quotaon, quotaoff, edquota, requota, quotacheck`
Compression, backup, and software	`gzip, gunzip, zcat, zgrep, zmore, zless, compress, uncompress, bzip2, bzcat, bzgrep, bzmore, bzless, zip, tar, cpio, dd, make, gcc`
BASH management and scripting	`set, unset, export, env, alias, unalias, tee, xargs, read, printenv, history, expr, source, git, ulimit`
Process management	`ps, top, kill, killall, jobs, fg, bg, nice, renice, at, atq, atrm, crontab, pgrep, pkill, nohup, lsof`
User and group management	`who, w, whoami, groups, id, newgrp, chfn, finger, chsh, passwd`
Printing	`lp, lpstat, lpadmin, cancel, lpc, lpr, lpq, lprm, cupsaccept, cupsreject, cupsenable, cupsdisable`
Networking and security	`ifconfig, ping, ping6, whois, arp, netstat, route, traceroute, traceroute6, hostname, host, nslookup, dig, su, sudo, visudo, last, rsync, scp, sftp, ftp, curl, nc, ssh, ssh-keygen, ssh-agent, ssh-copy-id, curl, apachectl, mail, mailq, newaliases, showmount, brctl, kinit, klist, tcpdump`
System and miscellaneous	`shutdown, halt, reboot, date, cal, exit, echo, clear, reset, uname, uptime, mknod, chroot, dmesg, iconv, locale, logger, sysctl, screen, iotop, iostat`

Table D-3 Useful macOS-specific commands

Command	Description
`asr`	This is the Apple System Restore utility. It can be used to restore the system from a disk image.
`bless`	Sets volume bootability and startup disk options
`caffeinate`	Prevents the system from sleeping
`chflags`	This modifies the attributes of a file (e.g., immutable). It is equivalent to the `chattr` command within Linux.

(continues)

Table D-3 Useful macOS-specific commands *(continued)*

Command	Description
defaults	Sets macOS system preferences, such as the option to display hidden files
diskutil	Creates, formats, verifies and repairs filesystems
ditto	Copies files and folders
drutil	Interacts with and writes to CD/DVD devices
dscacheutil	Displays or clears the DNS name cache
dseditgroup	Edits, creates, manipulates, or deletes groups
dsenableroot	Enables the root user
dscl	This is the Directory Service command line utility. It is used to manage users and groups on the system.
fdesetup	Configures FileVault (Apple's equivalent to LUKS disk encryption)
hdiutil	Creates and manages ISO/DMG disk images
kextfind	This lists kernel extensions and is equivalent to lsmod on Linux systems.
kextload	This loads a kernel extension and is equivalent to modprobe on Linux systems.
kextstat	Displays the status of kernel extensions on the system
kextunload	This unloads a kernel extension and is equivalent to rmmod on Linux systems.
launchctl	This is used to load or unload daemons/agents. It is functionally equivalent to systemctl on Linux systems.
networksetup	Configures network interface settings, including IP information and wireless settings
newfs_type	This creates a filesystem on a slice identified by *type*, where *type* can be apfs, hfs, ufs, msdos or exfat. It is equivalent to mkfs on Linux systems.
nvram	Displays and modifies boot firmware parameters
open	Executes an application bundle
pkgutil	Query and manage installed macOS applications
plutil	Checks the syntax of .plist files, as well as converts .plist files to and from other formats
pmset	Configures power management options
say	Speaks an argument using a build-in system voice
screencapture	Takes a screenshot and saves it to the file specified as an argument
scselect	Switches between network locations
scutil	Creates and manages network locations
softwareupdate	Updates system software packages
security	Configures certificates and password storage (keychain) settings

Table D-3   **Useful macOS-specific commands** (*continued*)

Command	Description
spctl	Displays and configures XNU kernel security parameters used by SecAssessment (the macOS equivalent to SELinux)
sw_vers	Displays the version of the operating system
system_ profiler	Displays system information
systemsetup	Configures general computer and display settings
vm_stat	Displays memory and swap information

Administering macOS

User Administration

To add users on macOS, you cannot use the same useradd command that you use within Linux. Instead, you must use the **dscl command** or System Preferences application to create user accounts. User account information is stored in an LDAP database under the /var/db directory that is used for authentication. The /etc/shadow file does not exist and the /etc/passwd and /etc/group files exist only to provide information to other applications.

When you create a new user account within the System Preferences application, you can optionally choose the *Allow user to administer this computer* option if you wish to allow the user to perform administrative tasks on the computer. This option adds the user to the admin group, which is given the ability to run all commands on the system via the %admin ALL=(ALL) ALL line within the /etc/sudoers file. Members of the admin group can run any command using the sudo command, or change system configuration using graphical applications.

Filesystem Administration

On a Linux system, recall that the first SATA/SCSI/SAS hard disk or SSD is represented by the /dev/sda block device file, and the first partition on this device is represented by the /dev/sda1 block device file. On macOS systems, hard disks and SSDs typically contain a single partition that is divided into **slices**, and each slice can contain a filesystem. By default, the /dev/disk0 block device file refers to the partition on the first hard disk or SSD, and the /dev/disk0s1 block device file refers to the first slice within this partition. Because partition and slice operations cannot be performed using block device files in macOS, character (raw) device files are present for all block storage devices (e.g., /dev/rdisk0 and /dev/rdisk0s1). Block device files within macOS are primarily used for mounting filesystems.

The `diskutil` **command** can be used to create Apple disk partitions and slices, and the `newfs_apfs` **command** can be used to create a new APFS filesystem on a slice. To check and repair filesystems, you can specify the appropriate options to the `diskutil` command. However, the preferred method to create and manage Apple disk partitions and filesystems is using the graphical **Disk Utility** application (/Applications/Utilities/Disk Utility). The Disk Utility application can also be used to create disk images, burn CDs and DVDs, as well as manage RAID volumes.

> **Note** 📎
>
> If you accidentally change permissions on macOS operating system files, the system will report errors to the screen. Checking the disk for errors within the Disk Utility will reset the default permissions on these operating system files to remedy the issue.

Disk quotas are enabled differently in macOS, because macOS does not use the /etc/fstab file to specify mount options for filesystems at boot time. Instead, you must create two files (.quota.ops.user and .quota.ops.group) in the mount point directory for each filesystem that you wish to enable quotas for. Following this, quotas can be configured and managed using the same commands as on a Linux system.

Understanding macOS Applications

When you install an application on a Linux system using a package manager, the files that comprise the application are distributed across the filesystem in various directories, such as /etc, /bin, /opt, /usr, and /var. The package manager stores the location of these files, such that they can be queried or removed at a later time.

In macOS, all of the binary executable files, supporting data files, configuration information and other app-related information are stored in a single directory with a `.app` extension called a **bundle**. When viewed in the macOS Finder, bundles appear as a single icon (without a `.app` extension) that can be executed to run the associated application. To execute an application from a BASH shell, you can use the `open` **command** followed by the pathname to the bundle. For example, to open the Firefox Web browser, you could run the `open/Applications/Firefox.app` command.

To remove a macOS application within the macOS desktop, you can drag the associated bundle icon to the trash can icon in the Dock. To remove a macOS application from a BASH shell, you can supply the full path to the bundle as an argument to the `rm -Rf` command.

The configuration information and settings for macOS apps are stored within XML files that have a `.plist` extension within the associated bundle. When searching the Internet for a solution to a problem related to macOS or a macOS application, the solution often involves modifying a specific `.plist` file within an application bundle.

As with Linux applications, many macOS applications rely on shared libraries. However, in macOS these shared libraries are called **frameworks** and are stored within bundle files that have a `.framework` extension under the /System/Library/Frameworks directory.

Although you can compile apps from source code using the `make` command on macOS, most macOS applications are installed via an online software repository. You can search for and install applications from this repository by starting the **App Store** application. You can start the App Store application by selecting App Store from the Apple icon menu within the macOS desktop.

Alternatively, many macOS application vendors make their macOS applications available for download on their website. When you choose to obtain a macOS application from a website, an ISO image file that has a `.dmg` extension is downloaded to the Downloads folder in your home directory. When you open the `.dmg` file, the ISO image is mounted, and a shortcut is placed on your desktop. You can then open this shortcut and drag the application bundle within to the /Applications folder to install the application.

Managing macOS Devices

On Linux systems, most specialized hardware devices, such as network interfaces and video cards, have device drivers under the /lib/modules directory that are loaded into the Linux kernel at boot time. On macOS systems, device drivers for specialized hardware devices are called **kernel extensions** and are loaded into the XNU kernel from `.kext` files under the /System/Library/Extensions directory.

To view the currently loaded kernel extensions, you can use the `kextfind` **command**. Similarly, the `kextload` **command** may be used to activate kernel extensions, and the `kextunload` **command** may be used to deactivate kernel extensions. You can also use the graphical **System Information** utility (/Applications/Utilities/System Information) to view loaded kernel extensions.

macOS System Initialization

Modern Intel-based Apple computers use a UEFI BIOS that controls the loading of the macOS bootloader. To boot from a different storage device, you can hold down the Option key on the Apple keyboard (or the Alt key on a non-Apple keyboard) during system startup, and select the appropriate device when prompted.

You can also hold down the Command+v keys on your Apple keyboard (or Windows+v keys on a non-Apple keyboard) during system startup to view detailed information about the boot process as well as interact with the macOS boot process itself.

The macOS UEFI bootloader is stored in the /System/Library/CoreServices/boot. efi file, and loads XNU from the /System/Library/Kernels/kernel file. XNU then loads the **Launch Daemon** (/sbin/launchd), which is functionally equivalent to the Systemd daemon on modern Linux systems. The Launch Daemon proceeds to load all other system daemons to bring the system to a useable state via entries within the /Library/ LaunchAgents and /Library/LaunchDaemons directories, as well as any optional apps listed in the /System/Library/StartupItems directory. You can use the `launchctl` `command` to view, start, and stop daemons on your system after the system has started. For example, you can run the `launchctl list` command as the root user to view the status of daemons on the system.

Holding the Command+s keys during system startup instructs launchd to boot to single user mode, where you can perform system repair. Alternatively, you can hold the Command+r keys during system startup to start the **macOS Recovery Tool** that can be used to repair or reinstall the operating system.

macOS Installation and Updates

While Apple computers come pre-installed with macOS, you may need to reinstall macOS if the operating system files become corrupted. The easiest method to reinstall macOS is to use the macOS Recovery Tool discussed earlier. The macOS Recovery Tool allows you to download and reinstall macOS from the App Store, and will require network connectivity as a result. Alternatively, you can insert USB media that contains the macOS installation files, boot your computer while holding down the Option key, and select the USB media to start the installation.

Regardless of how to you choose to start the macOS installation, the installation program will allow you to perform different types of installations. A clean installation erases existing filesystems and all of the data within. However, you can choose to reinstall the operating system, while preserving system settings, applications, and user files. You can also choose to archive your current system to the /Previous Systems directory and install a new copy of the operating system, preserving applications and user files.

Following installation, you can obtain macOS updates using the App Store application discussed earlier, or the `softwareupdate` `command`. To see macOS updates that were successfully installed, you can use the `softwareupdate --history` command, or view the contents of the /Library/Receipts directory.

Log File Administration

As in Linux, macOS logs system events to files under the /var/log directory. For example, /var/log/install.log contains installation events, whereas /var/log/system.log records kernel events. While you can view many of these log files using text tools within a BASH shell, macOS provides a **Console** application (/Applications/Utilities/Console) that contains shortcuts to key system log files. You can use the Console application to sort events by severity as well as research solutions to problems, such as application crashes, online.

Managing macOS Processes

While you can use the same Linux process management commands to manage macOS processes, it is often easier to manage macOS processes using the graphical **Activity Monitor** application (/Applications/Utilities/Activity Monitor). Activity Monitor sorts processes by system activity and usage, as well as displays general system statistics. You can also view process information or kill problematic processes within Activity Monitor. If you encounter a rogue application that prevents you from opening Activity Monitor, you can use the Command+Shift+Option+Esc key combination to kill the foreground application, or right-click the associated application icon in the Dock and select Force Quit.

Network and Network Service Configuration

Network interfaces use a different naming convention within macOS. The first Ethernet network interface is called en0, the second Ethernet network interface is called en1, and so on. To modify the IP, DNS, and routing configuration for a wired or wireless network interface, you can use the Network section of the System Preferences application, or the `networksetup` **command**. To configure firewall settings, you can use the Security & Privacy section of the System Preferences application. If you want to use an authentication service, such as Active Directory, with macOS, you can specify the appropriate authentication service settings within the graphical **Directory Utility** application (/System/Library/CoreServices/Applications/Directory Utility).

To configure network services within macOS, you can use the Sharing section of the System Preferences application as shown in Figure D-3. Each service that you select within Figure D-3 configures a specific network service on macOS. For example, Screen Sharing configures a VNC server, File Sharing configures Samba, Printer Sharing configures IPP sharing using CUPS, and Remote Login configures the SSH daemon.

Figure D-3   Configuring network services in macOS

Source: Apple, Inc.

Key Terms

Activity Monitor	`dsenableroot` **command**	`networksetup` **command**
App Store	**Finder**	`newfs_apfs` **command**
bundle	**framework**	`open` **command**
Console	**kernel extension**	**slice**
Darwin	`kextfind` **command**	`softwareupdate`
Directory Utility	`kextload` **command**	**command**
Disk Utility	`kextunload` **command**	**System Information**
`diskutil` **command**	**Launch Daemon**	**System Preferences**
Dock	`launchctl` **command**	**Terminal**
`dscl` **command**	**macOS Recovery Tool**	**XNU**

GLOSSARY

*sum commands Used to verify the checksum on a file where * represents the checksum algorithm. For example, to verify a SHA1 checksum, you could use the `sha1sum` command.

/dev directory The directory off the root where device files are typically stored.

/etc/fstab A file used to specify which filesystems to mount automatically at boot time and queried by the `mount` command if an insufficient number of arguments are specified.

/etc/mtab A file that stores a list of currently mounted filesystems.

/proc/devices A file that contains currently used device information.

| A shell metacharacter used to pipe Standard Output from one command to the Standard Input of another command.

~ metacharacter A metacharacter used to represent a user's home directory.

< A shell metacharacter used to obtain Standard Input from a file.

> A shell metacharacter used to redirect Standard Output and Standard Error to a file.

1U server A rackmount server that has a standard height of 1.75 inches.

A

aa_status command Used to view the status of AppArmor and AppArmor profiles.

aa_unconfined command Lists processes that are not controlled by AppArmor.

aa-complain command Sets an AppArmor profile to complain mode.

aa-disable command Disables an AppArmor profile.

aa-enforce command Sets an AppArmor profile to enforce mode.

ab (Apache benchmark) command Used to obtain performance benchmarks for a Web server such as Apache.

absolute pathname The full pathname to a certain file or directory starting from the root directory.

access control list (ACL) The section within an inode of a file or directory that lists the permissions assigned to users and groups on the file or directory.

active partition The partition that a standard BIOS searches for an operating system on.

Activity Monitor The macOS application used to view and manage processes.

add-apt-repository command Used to add repository information to the DPM repository database.

Advanced Configuration and Power Interface (ACPI) A BIOS component that provides hardware and power management event functionality to an operating system.

Advanced Technology Attachment (ATA) See *Parallel Advanced Technology Attachment*.

agent A software component that is installed on a Linux system that communicates to another computer across the network.

agentless A term that refers to software that manages other computers using a native protocol, such as SSH.

aggregation See *bonding*.

AIX A version of UNIX developed by IBM.

`alias` **command** Used to create special variables that are shortcuts to longer command strings.

American Standard Code for Information Interchange (ASCII) A character set that provides character mappings for English characters.

ANDing The process by which binary bits are compared to calculate the network and host IDs from an IP address and subnet mask.

Android A mobile Linux-based operating system currently developed by Google's Open Handset Alliance.

Anything as a Service (XaaS) A blanket term that refers to cloud services that are not specifically identified as SaaS, PaaS, or IaaS.

`apachectl` **command** Used to start, stop, and restart the Apache Web server as well as check for syntax errors within the Apache configuration file.

App Store The macOS application used to download and install other macOS applications from an online Apple software repository.

AppArmor A Linux kernel module and related software packages that prevent malicious software from accessing system resources.

AppArmor profile A text file within the /etc/apparmor.d directory that lists application-specific restrictions.

application (app) The software that runs on an operating system and provides the user with specific functionality (such as word processing or financial calculation). Applications are commonly referred to as apps today.

`apt` **(Advanced Package Tool) command** Used to search for, install, and upgrade DPM packages from software repositories, as well as view, manage, and remove installed DPM packages.

`apt-cache` **command** Used to search DPM repositories for package information.

`apt-get` **command** Used to install and upgrade DPM packages from software repositories, as well as manage and remove installed DPM packages.

`aptitude` **command** Used to start the Aptitude utility.

Aptitude A utility that can be used to manage DPM packages using a graphical interface.

Arch A major Linux distribution known for its simplicity and customization features.

archive The location (file or device) that contains a copy of files; it is typically created by a backup utility.

arguments The text that appears after a command name, does not start with a dash (-), and specifies information that the command requires to work properly.

`arp` **command** Displays and modifies the MAC address cache on a system.

artistic license An open source license that allows source code to be distributed freely but changed at the discretion of the original author.

assistive technologies Software programs that cater to specific user needs.

asymmetric encryption A type of encryption that uses a key pair to encrypt and decrypt data.

`at` **command** Used to view, create, and manage scheduled tasks that run at a preset time in the future.

at daemon (atd) The system daemon that executes tasks at a future time; it is configured with the `at` command.

`atq` **command** Used to view a scheduled at job.

`atrm` **command** Used to remove a scheduled at job.

`audit2why` **command** Displays the description and purpose of SELinux log entries.

authentication The process whereby each user must log in with a valid user name and password before gaining access to a system.

Automatic Bug Reporting Tool Daemon (abrtd) A process that automatically sends application crash data to an online bug reporting service.

Automatic Private IP Addressing (APIPA) A feature that automatically configures a network interface using an IPv4 address on the 169.254.0.0 network, or an IPv6 address on the FE80 network.

B

`background` **(bg) command** Used to run a foreground process in the background.

background process A process that does not require the BASH shell to wait for its termination.

Upon execution, the user receives the BASH shell prompt immediately.

bad blocks   The areas of a storage medium unable to store data properly.

baseline   A measure of normal system activity.

BASH shell   Also known as the Bourne Again Shell, this is the default command-line interface in Linux.

Beowulf clustering   A popular and widespread method of clustering computers together to perform useful tasks using Linux.

Berkeley Internet Name Domain (BIND)   The standard that all DNS servers and DNS configuration files adhere to.

binary data file   A file that contains machine language (binary 1s and 0s) and stores information (such as common functions and graphics) used by binary compiled programs.

Binary Large Object (BLOB) storage   See *object storage*.

BIND configuration utility   A graphical utility that can be used to generate and modify the files that are used by the DNS name daemon.

biometric   A type of authentication that uses physical human attributes, such as fingerprints, to validate a user's identity.

BIOS (Basic Input/Output System)   The part of a computer system that contains the programs used to initialize hardware components at boot time.

BIOS Boot Partition   A small partition that is created by the Linux installation program to store information needed to boot the Linux operating system from a GPT hard disk on a computer that does not have a UEFI BIOS.

blade server   See *rackmount server*.

`blkid` **command**   Used to list UUIDs for filesystems and GPT partitions.

block   The unit of data commonly used by filesystem commands; a block can contain several sectors.

block devices   Storage devices that transfer data to and from the system in chunks of many data bits by caching the information in RAM; they are represented by block device files.

block storage   Storage made available by a cloud provider using a virtual hard disk file that contains a filesystem.

bonding   The process of combining two NICs on the same network to provide fault tolerance or load balancing.

boot loader   A program used to load an operating system.

Boxes   A virtual machine configuration and management tool included with the GNOME desktop.

branch   A separate section within a Git repository used to track changes made to files.

Brasero   A common disc burning software used on Linux systems.

`brctl` **command**   Displays and modifies Ethernet bridge configuration within the Linux kernel.

bridging   The process of merging two separate networks using the NICs on a server.

broadcast   A TCP/IP communication destined for all computers on a network.

BSD (Berkeley Software Distribution)   A version of UNIX developed out of the original UNIX source code and given free to the University of California, Berkeley by AT&T.

B-tree File System (BTRFS)   A filesystem that can be used to create fault tolerant volumes much like ZFS. It is currently still in development, but designed as a replacement for ext4.

`btrfs` **command**   Used to view and manage BTRFS filesystems.

BTRFS subvolume   A subdirectory on a BTRFS volume that can be mounted as a separate unit by BTRFS.

`btrfsck` **command**   Used to check and repair BTRFS filesystems.

buffer overrun   An attack in which a network service is altered in memory.

build automation   A process used within cloud environments that allow containers and virtual machines to be created quickly.

bundle   An application package within macOS.

`bunzip2` **command**   Used to decompress files compressed by the `bzip2` command.

bus mastering   The process by which peripheral components perform tasks normally executed by the CPU.

BusyBox DHCP daemon (udhcpd) A lightweight Linux daemon used to provide IPv4 addresses to other computers on the network.

`bzcat` **command** Used to display the contents of an archive created with `bzip2` to Standard Output.

`bzgrep` **command** Used to search and display the contents of an archive created with `bzip2` to Standard Output.

`bzip2` **command** Used to compress files using a Burrows–Wheeler Block Sorting Huffman Coding compression algorithm.

`bzless` **command** Used to display the contents of an archive created with `bzip2` to Standard Output in a page-by-page fashion using the less command.

`bzmore` **command** Used to display the contents of an archive created with `bzip2` to Standard Output in a page-by-page fashion using the more command.

C

`cancel` **command** Used to remove print jobs from the print queue in the CUPS print system.

`cat` **command** A Linux command used to display (or concatenate) the entire contents of a text file to the screen.

`cd` **(change directory) command** A Linux command used to change the current directory in the directory tree.

certificate A digitally signed public key file.

Certification Authority (CA) A server that digitally signs public keys used by other computers to validate their authenticity.

`cfdisk` **command** Used to partition hard disks; displays a graphical interface in which the user can select partitioning options.

`chage` **command** Used to modify password expiry information for user accounts.

chains The components of a firewall that specify the general type of network traffic to which rules apply.

character devices The storage devices that transfer data to and from the system one data bit at a time; they are represented by character device files.

`chattr` **(change attributes) command** A command used to change filesystem attributes for a Linux file.

`chcon` **command** Used to change the type classification within SELinux labels on system files and directories.

checksum A calculated value that is unique to a file's size and contents.

`chfn` **command** Used to change the GECOS for a user.

`chgrp` **(change group) command** A command used to change the group owner of a file or directory.

child process A process that was started by another process (parent process).

`chkconfig` **command** Used to configure UNIX SysV daemon startup by runlevel.

`chmod` **(change mode) command** A command used to change the mode (permissions) of a file or directory.

`chown` **(change owner) command** A command used to change the owner and group owner of a file or directory.

Chrony NTP daemon (chronyd) A daemon that provides fast time synchronization services on Linux computers.

`chronyc` **command** Used to query the state of an NTP server or client, as well as synchronize the system time with an NTP server.

`chroot` **command** Used to change the root of one Linux system to another.

`chsh` **command** Used to change a valid shell to an invalid shell.

Cinnamon A desktop environment based on GNOME and used by Linux Mint.

classless interdomain routing (CIDR) notation A notation that is often used to represent an IP address and its subnet mask.

cloning The process of copying a Git repository from another computer.

closed source software The software whose source code is not freely available from the original author; Windows 10 is an example.

cloud Another term for the Internet.

cloud platform A series of software components that are used to provide access to IaaS virtualized operating systems.

cloud provider   An organization that provides Internet access to resources in a data center.

cloud-init   A system that can be used to automatically configure a Linux virtual machine at boot time.

cluster   A grouping of several smaller computers that function as one large supercomputer.

clustering   The act of making a cluster; see also *cluster*.

command   A program that exists on the filesystem and is executed when typed on the command line.

command mode   One of the two modes in vi; it allows a user to perform any available text-editing task that is not related to inserting text into the document.

commit   A snapshot of files that are tracked by Git for version control.

Common Unix Printing System (CUPS)   The printing system commonly used on Linux computers.

Common Vulnerabilities and Exposures (CVE)   A system used to catalog security vulnerabilities.

Common Weakness Enumeration (CWE)   A system used to catalog security vulnerabilities.

compress command   Used to compress files using a Lempel–Ziv compression algorithm.

compression   The process in which files are reduced in size by a compression algorithm.

compression algorithm   The set of instructions used to reduce the contents of a file systematically.

compression ratio   The amount that a file size is reduced during compression.

concatenation   The joining of text together to make one larger whole. In Linux, words and strings of text are joined together to form a displayed file.

configuration management (CM)   A type of software that is used to automate the configuration of virtual machines and containers.

Console   The macOS application used to view log files.

container   A subset of an operating system that provides a unique service on the network.

continuous deployment (CD)   A process whereby developer apps are regularly sent to a cloud provider for testing.

counter variable   A variable that is altered by loop constructs to ensure that commands are not executed indefinitely.

cp (copy) command   A command used to create copies of files and directories.

cpio (copy in/out) command   Used to back up a wide variety of file types, as well as view and restore files from a backup.

cracker   A person who uses computer software maliciously for personal profit.

cron daemon (crond)   The system daemon that executes tasks repetitively in the future and that is configured using cron tables.

cron table   A file specifying tasks to be run by the cron daemon; there are user cron tables and system cron tables.

crontab command   Used to view and edit user cron tables.

cryptsetup command   Used to configure and manage LUKS.

CUPS daemon (cupsd)   The daemon responsible for printing in the CUPS printing system.

CUPS Web administration tool   A Web-based management tool for the CUPS printing system.

cupsaccept command   Used to allow a printer to accept jobs into the print queue.

cupsdisable command   Used to prevent print jobs from leaving the print queue.

cupsenable command   Used to allow print jobs to leave the print queue.

cupsreject command   Used to force a printer to reject jobs from entering the print queue.

curl (client for URLs) command   Used to download Web pages and files from the Internet.

cybersecurity   A term that refers to the technologies and processes used to provide security within a network environment and on the Internet.

cylinder   A series of tracks on a hard disk that are written to simultaneously by the magnetic heads in a hard disk drive.

D

daemon   A Linux system process that provides a system service.

daemon process   A system process that is not associated with a terminal.

Darwin   The open source operating system that macOS is based on.

data   In BTRFS terminology, it refers to the blocks on the BTRFS filesystem used to store data.

data blocks   A filesystem allocation unit in which the data that makes up the contents of the file as well as the filename are stored.

database   A file that contains data organized into tables.

Database Management System (DBMS) Software that manages databases.

Date & Time utility   A graphical utility within Fedora 28 that can be used to set the date, time, and time zone information for a system.

dd command   Used to create and restore image backups.

Debian   A major Linux distribution that is widely used worldwide.

Debian Package Manager (DPM)   A package manager used on Debian and Debian-based Linux distributions, such as Ubuntu Server.

decision construct   A special syntax used in a shell script to alter the flow of the program based on the outcome of a command or contents of a variable. Common decision constructs include `if`, `case`, `&&`, and `||`.

declarative configuration   A CM process whereby inventory members are configured using the attributes listed within a configuration file.

default gateway   The IP address of the router on the network used to send packets to remote networks.

depmod command   Used to update the module dependency database.

Desktop Bus (D-Bus)   A software component that allows programs running within a desktop environment to easily communicate with one another.

desktop environment   The software that works with a window manager to provide a standard GUI environment that uses standard programs and development tools.

developmental kernel   A Linux kernel that has been recently developed yet not thoroughly tested.

device driver   A piece of software containing instructions that the kernel of an operating system uses to control and interact with a specific type of computer hardware.

device file   A file used by Linux commands that represents a specific device on the system; these files do not have a data section and use major and minor numbers to reference the proper driver and specific device on the system, respectively.

Device Mapper MPIO (DM-MPIO)   The MPIO implementation used by Linux servers.

devop   A Linux administrator that manages the software that provides a CD workflow.

df (disk free space) command   Used to display disk free space by filesystem.

dhclient command   Used to obtain IP configuration for a network interface from a DHCP or BOOTP server on the network.

DHCP daemon (dhcpd)   The most common Linux daemon used to provide IPv4 and IPv6 addresses to other computers on the network.

diff command   A Linux command that compares the contents of text files to identify any differences.

differential backup   An archive of a filesystem that contains only files that were modified since the last full backup was created.

dig command   Used to resolve host names to IP addresses.

digital signature   Information that has been encrypted using a private key.

directive   A line within a configuration file.

directory   A special file on the filesystem used to organize other files into a logical tree structure.

Directory Utility   The macOS application used to configure authentication and directory services.

disk mirroring   A RAID configuration consisting of two hard disks to which identical data are written in parallel, ensuring fault tolerance. Also known as RAID 1.

disk quotas   The limits on the number of files, or total storage space on a filesystem, available to a user.

disk striping   A RAID configuration in which a single file is divided into sections, which are then written to different hard disks concurrently to speed up access time; this type of RAID is not fault tolerant. Also known as RAID 0.

disk striping with parity A RAID configuration that incorporates disk striping for faster file access, as well as parity information to ensure fault tolerance. Also known as RAID 5.

Disk Utility The macOS application used to manage storage devices and filesystems.

`diskutil` **command** Used to create and manage disks and filesystems on macOS systems.

distribution A complete set of operating system software, including the Linux kernel, supporting function libraries, and a variety of OSS packages that can be downloaded from the Internet free of charge. These OSS packages are what differentiate the various distributions of Linux.

distribution kernel A production Linux kernel that receives long term patch support for a particular Linux distribution.

`dmesg` **command** Used to list the information recorded by the Linux kernel at the beginning of the boot process.

`dmidecode` **command** Displays hardware device information detected by the system BIOS.

`dnf` **(Dandified YUM) command** A speed-improved version of the `yum` command used on modern Linux distributions.

DNS cache file A file that contains the IP addresses of top-level DNS servers.

Dock The application launcher used within the macOS desktop.

Docker The most common software used to create containers.

Docker client A program that can be used to create and manage Docker containers.

`docker` **command** Used to start the Docker client program.

Docker Hub An online repository of container images that can be used with Docker.

document root The directory on a Web server that stores Web content for distribution to Web browsers.

documentation System information that is stored in a file or log book for future reference.

Domain Name Space (DNS) The naming convention used by computers on the Internet.

dot (.) command Used to execute the contents of a shell script within the current shell, instead of using a subshell.

`dpkg` **command** Used to install, query, and remove DPM packages.

`dpkg-query` **command** Used to query installed DPM packages.

`dpkg-reconfigure` **command** Used to reconfigure the installation settings for an already-installed DPM package.

`dracut` **command** Used to generate an initramfs.

`dscl` **command** Used to manage users and groups on macOS systems.

`dsenableroot` **command** Used to enable the root user account on macOS systems.

`du` **(directory usage) command** Used to display directory usage.

`dump` **command** Used to create full and incremental backups of files on an ext2, ext3, or ext4 filesystem.

`dumpleases` **command** A command that can be used to obtain current DHCP leases from the BusyBox DHCP daemon (udhcpd).

Dynamic Host Configuration Protocol (DHCP) The protocol that is used to automatically obtain IP configuration for a computer.

E

`e2label` **command** Used to set a description label on an ext2/ext3/ext4 filesystem.

`echo` **command** Used to display or echo output to the terminal screen. It can use escape sequences.

`edquota` **command** Used to specify quota limits for users and groups.

`egrep` **command** A variant of the `grep` command used to search files for patterns, using extended regular expressions.

`eject` **command** Used to unmount and eject CD/DVD removable media.

Emacs (Editor MACroS) editor A popular and widespread text editor more conducive to word processing than vi. It was originally developed by Richard Stallman.

`env` **command**   Used to display a list of exported variables and functions present in the current shell.

environment files   The files used immediately after login to execute commands; they are typically used to load variables into memory.

environment variables   The variables that store information commonly accessed by the system or programs executing on the system; together, these variables form the user environment.

epoch time   The time format used by the Linux kernel; it is represented by the number of seconds since January 1, 1970.

escape sequences   The character combinations that have special meaning inside the `echo` command. They are prefixed by the \ character.

Ethernet   The most common media access method used in networks today.

`ethtool` **command**   Used to configure and display NIC hardware settings.

executable program   A file that can be executed by the Linux operating system to run in memory as a process and perform a useful function.

`exfatlabel` **command**   Used to set a description label on an exFAT filesystem.

exit status   A number that is returned by each command on a Linux system to indicate successful (0) or unsuccessful (1-255) execution. It can be used to provide the true/false functionality within shell script constructs.

`export` **command**   Used to send variables to subshells.

exporting   The process used to describe the sharing of a directory using NFS to other computers.

`expr` **command**   Used to perform mathematical operations.

ext2   A nonjournaling Linux filesystem.

ext3   A journaling Linux filesystem.

ext4   An improved version of the ext3 filesystem, with an extended feature set and better performance.

Extended Internet Super Daemon (xinetd)   A network daemon that is used to start other network daemons on demand.

extended partition   A partition on an MBR-based hard disk or SSD that can be further subdivided into components called logical drives.

F

facility   The area of the system from which information is gathered when logging system events.

`faillock` **command**   Used to view and modify user lockout settings.

`fatlabel` **command**   Used to set a description label on a FAT filesystem.

fault tolerant   Term used to describe a device that exhibits a minimum of downtime in the event of a failure.

`fdisk` **command**   Used to create and modify MBR and GPT partitions.

`fgrep` **command**   A variant of the `grep` command that does not allow the use of regular expressions.

Fibre Channel (FC)   A technology that transfers data across fiber optic or Ethernet networks.

field   An attribute used by records within a database table.

`file` **command**   A Linux command that displays the file type of a specified filename.

file descriptors   The numeric labels used to define command input and command output.

file globbing   The process of using wildcard metacharacters within a command to match multiple files or directories.

file handles   The connections that a program makes to files on a filesystem.

File Transfer Protocol (FTP)   The most common protocol used to transfer files across networks, such as the Internet.

filename   The user-friendly identifier given to a file.

filename extension   A series of identifiers following a dot (.) at the end of a filename, used to denote the type of the file; the filename extension .txt denotes a text file.

filesystem   The way in which a hard disk drive or SSD partition is formatted to allow data to reside on the physical media; common Linux filesystems include ext2, ext3, ext4, XFS, and VFAT.

filesystem corruption   The errors in a filesystem structure that prevent the retrieval of stored data.

Filesystem Hierarchy Standard (FHS) A standard outlining the location of set files and directories on a Linux or UNIX system.

filter A command that can take from Standard Input and send to Standard Output. In other words, a filter is a command that can exist in the middle of a pipe.

`find` **command** A command used to find files on the filesystem using various criteria.

Finder The graphical file browser application within macOS.

Firewall Configuration utility A graphical firewall configuration utility used on Fedora systems.

firewall daemon (firewalld) A daemon that can be used to simplify the configuration of netfilter firewall rules via network zones.

`firewall-cmd` **command** Used to view and configure firewalld zones, services, and rules.

firmware RAID A RAID system controlled by the computer's BIOS/UEFI.

flavor A term that refers to a specific type of UNIX operating system. For example, macOS and BSD are two different flavors of UNIX.

`foreground` **(fg) command** Used to run a background process in the foreground.

foreground process A process for which the BASH shell that executed it must wait for its termination.

forking The act of creating a new BASH shell child process from a parent BASH shell process.

formatting The process in which a filesystem is placed on a disk device.

forward lookup A DNS name resolution request whereby a FQDN is resolved to an IP address.

framework A shared library within macOS.

`free` **command** Used to display memory and swap statistics.

Free Software Foundation (FSF) An organization started by Richard Stallman that promotes and encourages the collaboration of software developers worldwide to allow the free sharing of source code and software programs.

freeware Software distributed by the developer at no cost to the user.

frequently asked questions (FAQs) An area on a Web site where answers to commonly posed questions can be found.

`fsck` **(filesystem check) command** Used to check the integrity of a filesystem and repair damaged files.

`ftp` **command** Used to interact with FTP servers using standard FTP. It can be found on most operating systems.

full backup An archive of all files on a filesystem.

fully qualified domain name (FQDN) A host name that follows the DNS naming convention.

function A special variable that can accept positional parameters and is used to store commands and constructs for later execution.

function library A file that contains multiple functions for use in other programs and shell scripts.

`fuser` **command** Used to identify any users or processes using a particular file or directory.

G

`gcc` **(GNU C Compiler) command** Used to compile source code written in the C programming language into binary programs.

`gdisk` **(GPT fdisk) command** Used to create and modify GPT partitions. It uses an interface that is very similar to `fdisk`.

gedit editor A common text editor used within GUI environments.

General Electric Comprehensive Operating System (GECOS) The field in the /etc/passwd file that contains a description of the user account.

Gentoo A major Linux distribution known for its focus on hardware and software optimization.

`getenforce` **command** Used to view whether SELinux is using enforcing or permissive mode.

`getent` **command** Used to display the entries within system databases, such as /etc/passwd, /etc/shadow, and /etc/group.

`getfacl` **(get file ACL) command** A command used to list all ACL entries for a particular Linux file or directory.

`getsebool` **command** Used to display SELinux settings within an SELinux policy.

Git A common open source version control program primarily used for software development.

`git` **command** Used to perform version control operations using Git.

Git repo   See *Git repository*.

Git repository   A collection of files and commits that are used by Git. Git repositories often represent software development projects.

GNOME Display Manager (gdm)   A program that provides a graphical login screen.

GNOME Shell   The graphical interface components within the GNOME 3 desktop environment.

GNU   An acronym that stands for "GNU's Not Unix."

GNU General Public License (GPL)   A software license, ensuring that the source code for any OSS will remain freely available to anyone who wants to examine, build on, or improve upon it.

GNU Network Object Model Environment (GNOME)   The default desktop environment on most modern Linux systems; it was first created in 1997.

GNU Privacy Guard (GPG)   An open source asymmetric encryption technology that can be used to encrypt and digitally sign files and email.

GNU Project   A free operating system project started by Richard Stallman.

GPG Agent   A daemon that can be used to store the private key passphrase used by GPG.

`gpg` **command**   Used to configure and manage GPG.

GRand Unified Bootloader (GRUB)   A boot loader used to boot a variety of operating systems (including Linux) on a variety of hardware platforms.

GRand Unified Bootloader version 2 (GRUB2)   An enhanced version of the original GRUB boot loader. It is the most common boot loader used on modern Linux systems.

graphical user interface (GUI)   The component of an operating system that provides a user-friendly interface comprising graphics or icons to represent desired tasks. Users can point and click to execute a command rather than having to know and use proper command-line syntax.

`grep` **command**   A Linux command that searches files for patterns of characters using regular expression metacharacters. The command name is short for "global regular expression print."

group   When used in the mode of a certain file or directory, the collection of users who have ownership of that file or directory.

Group Identifier (GID)   A unique number given to each group.

`groupadd` **command**   Used to add a group to the system.

`groupdel` **command**   Used to delete a group from the system.

`groupmod` **command**   Used to modify the name or GID of a group on the system.

`groups` **command**   Lists group membership for a user.

GRUB (GRand Unified Boot loader)   The most common boot loader used on Linux systems. It loads and executes the Linux kernel at boot time.

GRUB Legacy   The original version of the GRUB boot loader.

GRUB root partition   The partition containing the second stage of the GRUB boot loader and the GRUB configuration file; it is normally a partition that is mounted to /boot.

`grub2-install` **command**   Used to install the GRUB2 boot loader.

`grub2-mkconfig` **command**   Used to build the GRUB2 configuration file from entries within the /etc/default/grub file and /etc/grub.d/ directory.

`grub-install` **command**   Used to install the GRUB boot loader.

GTK+ toolkit   A development toolkit for C programming; it is used in the GNOME desktop and the GNU Image Manipulation Program (GIMP).

guest operating system   A virtual operating system that is run on a hypervisor.

GUI environment   A GUI core component such as X Windows, combined with a window manager and desktop environment that provides the look and feel of the GUI. Although functionality might be similar among GUI environments, users might prefer one environment to another due to its ease of use.

GUID Partition Table (GPT)   The area of a large hard disk (> 2TB) outside a partition that stores partition information. GPTs are used on most modern hard disks and SSDs.

`gunzip` **command**   Used to decompress files compressed by the `gzip` command.

`gzip` **(GNU zip) command**   Used to compress files using a Lempel–Ziv compression algorithm.

H

hacker   A person who explores computer science to gain knowledge—not to be confused with "cracker."

hard limit   A disk quota that the user cannot exceed.

hard link   A file joined to other files on the same filesystem that shares the same inode.

hardware   The tangible parts of a computer, such as the network boards, video card, hard disk drives, printers, and keyboards.

Hardware Compatibility List (HCL)   A list of hardware components that have been tested and deemed compatible with a given operating system.

hardware platform   A particular configuration and grouping of computer hardware, normally centered on and determined by processor type and architecture.

hardware RAID   A RAID system controlled by hardware located on a disk controller card within the computer.

hash   See *checksum*.

hashpling   The first line in a shell script, which defines the shell that will be used to interpret the commands in the script file.

`head` **command**   A Linux command that displays the first set of lines of a text file; by default, the `head` command displays the first 10 lines.

here document   A syntax used to perform multiline input redirection.

`history` **command**   Used to view previously executed commands within a shell.

home directory   A directory on the filesystem set aside for users to store personal files and information.

Host Bus Adapter (HBA)   A controller card that connects to FC storage.

`host` **command**   Used to resolve host names to IP addresses.

host ID   The portion of an IP address that denotes the host.

host name   A user-friendly name assigned to a computer.

host operating system   The operating system used to host a Type 2 hypervisor.

`hostname` **command**   Used to display and change the host name of a computer.

`hostnamectl` **command**   Used to change the host name of a computer as well as ensure that the new host name is loaded at boot time.

hot fix   A solution for a software bug.

HOWTO   A task-specific instruction guide to performing any of a wide variety of tasks; it is freely available from the Linux Documentation Project at *www.tldp.org*.

HP-UX   A version of UNIX developed by Hewlett-Packard.

`hwclock` **command**   A command that can be used to view and modify the system clock within the computer BIOS.

hypervisor   The software component that provides for virtualization.

I

`iconv` **command**   Used to convert data from one character set to another.

`id` **command**   Lists the UID and GIDs for a user.

`ifconfig` **(interface configuration) command**   Used to display and modify the IP configuration information for a network interface.

`iftop` **command**   Displays the bandwidth sent from the local computer to other hosts.

image backup   A backup that writes data block by block to an archive without maintaining file structure information.

imperative configuration   A CM process whereby inventory members are configured using the procedures listed within a script file.

incremental backup   An archive of a filesystem that contains only files that were modified since the last archive was created.

info pages   A set of local, easy-to-read command syntax documentation available by typing the `info` command-line utility.

Infrastructure as a Service (IaaS)   A cloud strategy that allows access to virtualized operating systems stored within a data center.

Infrastructure as Code (IaC)   See *infrastructure automation*.

infrastructure automation   A cloud practice that involves using both build automation and CM.

infrastructure services Services that provide TCP configuration, name resolution, or time synchronization to other computers on a network.

init command Used to change the operating system from one runlevel to another.

initialize (init) daemon The first process started by the Linux kernel; it is responsible for starting and stopping other daemons.

initramfs A disk image that contains Linux kernel modules that are needed by the Linux kernel during the boot process.

initstate See *runlevel*.

inode The portion of a file that stores information on the file's attributes, access permissions, location, ownership, and file type.

inode table The collection of inodes for all files and directories on a filesystem.

insert mode One of the two modes in vi; it allows the user to insert text into the document but does not allow any other functionality.

insmod command Used to load a module into the Linux kernel.

installation log files The files created at installation to record actions that occurred or failed during the installation process.

Integrated Drive Electronics (IDE) See *Parallel Advanced Technology Attachment*.

interactive mode The mode that file management commands use when a file can be overwritten; the system interacts with a user asking the user to confirm the action.

Internet Control Message Protocol (ICMP) A protocol used on the Internet to provide error messages and network-related information.

Internet Control Message Protocol version 6 (ICMPv6) A protocol used by computers to obtain an IPv6 configuration from a router on the network.

Internet of Things (IoT) A term that refers to the worldwide collection of small Internet-connected devices.

Internet Printing Protocol (IPP) A printing protocol that can be used to send print jobs across a TCP/IP network, such as the Internet, using HTTP or HTTPS.

Internet Protocol (IP) address A unique string of numbers assigned to a computer to uniquely identify it on the Internet.

Internet SCSI (iSCSI) A SCSI technology that transfers data via TCP/IP networks.

Internet service provider (ISP) A company that provides Internet access.

inventory The sum total of all virtual machines and containers that are managed by CM software.

inventory member An individual virtual machine or container that is managed by CM software.

ioping (input/output ping) command Sends input/output requests to a block storage device and measures the speed at which they occur.

iOS A mobile version of UNIX developed by Apple for use on iPhone, iPod, and iPad devices.

iostat (input/output statistics) command Displays input and output statistics for block storage devices on the system.

iotop (input/output top) command Displays the processes on a Linux system that have the highest number of associated input/output requests to block storage devices.

ip command Used to perform a wide variety of IP management tasks on a Linux system, such as viewing and manipulating the route table. It is part of the optional iproute2 package.

IP forwarding The act of forwarding TCP/IP packets from one network to another; see also *routing*.

IP set A list of hosts and networks that can be used within a firewall rule.

IP version 4 (IPv4) The most common version of IP used on the Internet. It uses a 32-bit addressing scheme organized into different classes.

IP version 6 (IPv6) A recent version of IP that is used by some hosts on the Internet. It uses a 128-bit addressing scheme.

ip6tables command Used to configure IPv6 rules for a netfilter firewall.

iperf command Used to measure the bandwidth between two computers.

ipset command Used to configure IP sets.

iptables command Used to configure IPv4 rules for a netfilter firewall.

iSCSI initiator A term that refers to the computer that connects to the iSCSI target within an iSCSI SAN.

iSCSI target   A term that refers to a storage device within an iSCSI SAN.

`iscsiadm` **command**   Used to configure an iSCSI initiator.

ISO image   A file that contains the content of a DVD. ISO images of Linux installation media can be downloaded from the Internet.

ISO-8859   A character set that extends ASCII to provide additional character mappings for non-English languages.

iterative query   A DNS resolution request that was resolved without the use of top-level DNS servers.

`iwconfig` **command**   Used to set and display the configuration of wireless network interfaces.

J

jabbering   The process by which failing hardware components send large amounts of information to the CPU.

jitter   The difference between time measurements from several different NTP servers.

`jobs` **command**   Displays background processes running in the current shell.

`journalctl` **command**   Used to configure journald, as well as to view log entries in the journald database.

journald   A system used to record (or journal) system events on modern Linux distributions.

journaling   A filesystem function that keeps track of the information that needs to be written to the hard disk or SSD in a journal; common Linux journaling filesystems include ext3, ext4, and XFS.

Just a Bunch of Disks (JBOD)   See *spanning*.

K

K Desktop Environment (KDE)   A Linux desktop environment created by Matthias Ettrich in 1996.

K Window Manager (kwin)   The window manager that works under the KDE Desktop Environment.

KDE Display Manager (kdm)   A graphical login screen for users that resembles the KDE desktop.

Kerberos   A network protocol used by most authentication services.

kernel   The central, core program of the operating system. The shared commonality of the kernel is what defines Linux; the differing OSS applications that can interact with the common kernel are what differentiates Linux distributions.

kernel extension   A kernel module within macOS. Each macOS device driver has a related kernel module.

kernel panic   A condition in which a system halts immediately after loading the Linux kernel.

Kernel Virtual Machine (KVM)   A hypervisor that is built into the Linux kernel.

`kextfind` **command**   Displays macOS kernel extensions.

`kextload` **command**   Activates a macOS kernel extension.

`kextunload` **command**   Deactivates a macOS kernel extension.

key   A unique piece of information that is used within an encryption algorithm.

Kickstart   A component of the Anaconda Linux installer that can be used to automate the configuration of a Linux installation.

`kill` **command**   Used to send kill signals to a process by PID.

kill signal   The signal sent to a process for use in terminating or restarting processes; different kill signals affect processes in different ways.

`killall` **command**   Sends kill signals to processes by process name.

`kinit` **command**   Used to authenticate to a Kerberos authentication service.

`klist` **command**   Used to view Kerberos authentication information.

L

label   An identifier that SELinux places on a file, directory, or process.

Launch Daemon   The macOS daemon that starts and stops other system daemons and system components. It is functionally equivalent to Systemd on Linux systems.

`launchctl` **command**   Used to view and manage the Launch Daemon.

`ldconfig` **command**   Used to update the /etc/ld.so.conf and /etc/ld.so.cache files.

ldd command   Displays the shared libraries used by a certain program.

less command   A Linux command used to display a text file page-by-page on the terminal screen; users can then use the cursor keys to navigate the file.

LightDM   A program that provides a graphical login screen on Ubuntu systems.

Lightweight Directory Access Protocol (LDAP)   An industry-standard protocol used to access directory service databases across a network.

Line Printer Daemon (LPD)   A printing system typically used on legacy Linux computers.

linked file   The files that represent the same data as other files.

Linus Torvalds   A Finnish graduate student who coded and created the first version of Linux and subsequently distributed it under the GNU Public License.

Linux   A software operating system originated by Linus Torvalds. The common core, or kernel, continues to evolve and be revised. Differing OSS bundled with the Linux kernel is what defines the wide variety of distributions now available.

Linux Documentation Project (LDP)   A large collection of Linux resources, information, and help files supplied free of charge and maintained by the Linux community.

Linux Mint   A major Linux distribution that is known for its small learning curve.

Linux server distribution   A Linux distribution containing packages that are geared specifically for Linux servers.

Linux Unified Key Setup (LUKS)   A technology that encrypts the contents of a Linux filesystem.

Linux User Group (LUG)   The open forums of Linux users who discuss and assist each other in using and modifying the Linux operating system and the OSS run on it. There are LUGs worldwide.

live media   Linux installation media that provides a fully functional Linux operating system in RAM prior to installation on permanent storage.

ll command   An alias for the ls -l command; it gives a long file listing.

ln (link) command   A command used to create hard and symbolic links.

load balancing   A feature of some network devices that allows requests for a service to be spread across several different computers for fault tolerance and performance.

local area network (LAN)   A network in which the computers are all in close physical proximity.

locale   The regional language and character set used on a system.

locale command   Used to display locale information.

localectl command   Used to view and modify locale information.

localization   The collection of settings on a system that are region-specific.

locate command   A command used to locate files from a file database.

lock an account   To make an account temporarily unusable by altering the password information for it stored on the system.

log file   A file that contains past system events.

logger command   Used to create system log entries.

logical drives   The smaller partitions contained within an extended partition on an MBR-based hard disk or SSD.

Logical Unit Number (LUN)   A unique identifier for each device attached to any given node in a SCSI chain.

Logical Volume (LV)   A volume that is managed by the LVM and comprised of free space within a VG.

Logical Volume Manager (LVM)   A set of software components within Linux that can be used to manage the storage of information across several hard disks on a Linux system.

login banner   A message that is displayed to users after logging into a system.

logrotate command   Used to rotate log files; typically uses the configuration information stored in /etc/logrotate.conf.

loop construct   A special syntax used in a shell script to execute commands repetitively. Common decision constructs include for and while.

lp command   Used to create print jobs in the print queue in the CUPS printing system.

lpadmin command   Used to perform printer administration in the CUPS printing system.

`lpc` **command** Used to view the status of, and control printers in, the LPD printing system.

`lpq` **command** Used to view the contents of print queues in the LPD printing system.

`lpr` **command** Used to create print jobs in the print queue in the LPD printing system.

`lprm` **command** Used to remove print jobs from the print queue in the LPD printing system.

`lpstat` **command** Used to view the contents of print queues and printer information in the CUPS printing system.

`ls` **command** A Linux command used to list the files in a given directory.

`lsattr` **(list attributes) command** A command used to list filesystem attributes for a Linux file.

`lsblk` **command** Used to display storage device information including type, size, major number, minor number, and mount point.

`lshw` **command** Used to list information about the hardware components on a Linux system.

`lsmod` **command** Used to list modules that are currently loaded in a Linux kernel.

`lsof` **(list open files) command** Lists the files that are currently being viewed or modified by processes and users.

`lsusb` **command** Used to display USB devices that are attached to the system, such as a USB flash memory drive.

`lvcreate` **command** Used to create LVM logical volumes.

`lvdisplay` **command** Used to view LVM logical volumes.

`lvextend` **command** Used to add space from VGs to existing LVM logical volumes.

`lvscan` **command** Used to view LVM logical volumes.

M

macOS A version of UNIX developed by Apple for use on Apple desktop computers and servers.

macOS Recovery Tool A graphical tool on macOS systems that can reset passwords, repair filesystems, and install or reinstall macOS.

`mail` **command** Used to check and compose email on UNIX, Linux, and macOS systems.

Mail Delivery Agent (MDA) The service that downloads email from a mail transfer agent.

Mail Transfer Agent (MTA) An email server.

Mail User Agent (MUA) A program that allows users to read email.

`mailq` **command** Lists email awaiting delivery, as well as any delivery errors.

major number When referring to device files, it is the number used by the kernel to identify which device driver to call to interact properly with a given category of hardware; similar devices share a common major number. When referring to kernel versions, it is the number preceding the first dot in the kernel version; it is used to denote a major change or modification.

man pages See *manual pages*.

manual pages The most common set of local command syntax documentation, available by typing the man command-line utility. Also known as man pages.

Master Boot Record (MBR) The area of a typical hard disk ($< 2TB$) outside a partition that stores partition information.

master branch The default branch in a Git repo.

master DNS server See *primary DNS server*.

MATE A desktop environment based on GNOME and used by Arch Linux.

`mdadm` **command** Used to configure software RAID on a Linux system.

Media Access Control (MAC) address The hardware address that uniquely identifies a network interface.

media access method A system that defines how computers on a network share access to the physical medium.

memory leak A condition whereby a process continually uses more and more memory within a system, until there is no more memory available.

memtest86 A common RAM-checking utility.

message digest See *checksum*.

Message Passing Interface (MPI) A system that is used on Beowulf clusters to pass information to several separate computers in a parallel fashion.

metacharacters The key combinations that have special meaning in the Linux operating system.

metadata In BTRFS terminology, it refers to the inode table on the BTRFS filesystem.

MINIX Mini-UNIX created by Andrew Tannenbaum. Instructions on how to code the kernel for this version of the Unix operating system were publicly available. Using this as a starting point, Linus Torvalds improved this version of UNIX for the Intel platform and created the first version of Linux.

minor number When referring to device files, it is the number used by the kernel to identify which specific hardware device, within a given category, to use as a driver to communicate with. When referring to kernel versions, it is the number following the first dot in the kernel version; it denotes a minor modification.

`mkdir` **(make directory) command** A command used to create directories.

`mkfs` **(make filesystem) command** Used to format (create) filesystems.

`mkfs.btrfs` **command** Used to create a BTRFS filesystem.

`mkinitrd` **command** Used to generate an initramfs.

`mkisofs` **command** Used to create an ISO image from one or more files on the filesystem.

`mknod` **command** Used to re-create a device file, provided the major number, minor number, and type (character or block) are known.

`mkswap` **command** Used to prepare newly created swap partitions for use by the Linux system.

mode The part of the inode that stores information on access permissions.

Modem Manager utility A graphical utility that can be used to configure modem settings on Linux systems.

`modinfo` **command** Used to list information about a module.

`modprobe` **command** Used to load a module, including any module dependencies, into the Linux kernel.

module A Linux device driver that is inserted into the Linux kernel in a modular fashion.

monitoring The process by which system areas are observed for problems or irregularities.

`more` **command** A Linux command used to display a text file page-by-page and line-by-line on the terminal screen.

`mount` **command** Used to mount filesystems on devices to mount point directories.

mount point The directory in a file structure to which something is mounted.

mounting A process used to associate a device with a directory in the logical directory tree such that users can store data on that device.

`mpathconf` **command** Used to configure DM-MPIO on a Linux system.

`mpstat` **(multiple processor statistics) command** Displays CPU statistics on a Linux system.

`mtr` **command** Used to trace the path an IPv4 or IPv6 packet takes through routers to a destination host.

multi boot A configuration in which two or more operating systems exist on the hard disk of a computer; the boot loader allows the user to choose which operating system to load at boot time.

multicast IP communication destined for a certain group of computers.

Multi-Category Security (MCS) An optional SELinux policy scheme that prevents processes from accessing other processes that have similar attributes.

multi-factor authentication The process whereby multiple separate mechanisms are used to validate a user's identity.

multihomed hosts The computers that have more than one network interface.

Multi-Level Security (MLS) An optional SELinux policy scheme that uses custom attributes.

Multipath Input Output (MPIO) A technology used to provide multiple redundant connections to a SAN for fault tolerance and speed.

Multiplexed Information and Computing Service (MULTICS) A prototype time-sharing operating system that was developed in the late-1960s by AT&T Bell Laboratories.

multitasking A type of operating system that is able to manage multiple tasks simultaneously.

multiuser A type of operating system that is able to provide access to multiple users simultaneously.

mutter window manager The default window manager for the GNOME 3 desktop environment.

mv (move) command A command used to move/rename files and directories.

N

named pipe file A temporary connection that sends information from one command or process in memory to another; it can also be represented by a file on the filesystem.

namespace A major section of an NVMe SSD that can be partitioned.

nano editor A user-friendly terminal text editor that uses Ctrl key combinations to perform basic functions.

ncat (net cat) command A network testing utility. It is often used to test the functionality of services on the network.

NetBIOS A protocol used by Windows computers that adds a unique 15-character name to file- and printer-sharing traffic.

netbooting The process of loading an operating system from across a network; it is often used to load Linux live installation media across a network for installation purposes.

netfilter The Linux kernel component that provides firewall and NAT capability on modern Linux systems.

NetPlan The software component that configures NICs on modern Ubuntu systems.

netstat command Used to display network information and active connections.

network Two or more computers joined together via network media and able to exchange information.

Network Address Translation (NAT) A technology that allows a router to obtain Internet resources on behalf of computers on the network.

Network Connections tool A graphical NetworkManager utility that can be used to configure additional network interfaces and related technologies, such as DSL.

Network File System (NFS) A set of software components that can be used to share files between UNIX, Linux, macOS, and Windows computers on a network.

network ID The portion of an IP address that denotes the network.

network latency A condition where replies to network requests are slow or intermittent.

network service A process that responds to network requests.

Network Time Protocol (NTP) A protocol that is used to obtain time and time zone information from servers across a network, such as the Internet.

Network utility A graphical utility in Fedora 28 that can be used to configure settings for the network interfaces on the system.

network zone A component of firewalld that defines the level of trust for network connections.

networkctl command Used to display and configure network interfaces using Systemd-networkd.

NetworkManager A software component that manages the configuration of network interfaces.

networksetup command Used to configure network interfaces on macOS systems.

newaliases command Used to rebuild the email alias database based on the entries within the /etc/aliases file.

newfs_apfs command Used to create an APFS filesystem on macOS systems.

newgrp command Used to temporarily change the primary group of a user.

newsgroup An Internet service that allows access to postings (e-mails in a central place accessible by all newsgroup users) normally organized along specific themes. Users with questions on specific topics can post messages, which can be answered by other users.

Next Generation Firewall (NGFW) Often used to describe a security appliance that performs multiple security functions.

nice command Used to change the priority of a process as it is started.

nice value The value that indirectly represents the priority of a process; the higher the value, the lower the priority.

nmap (network mapper) command Used to scan ports on network computers.

nmblookup command Used to test NetBIOS name resolution on a Linux system.

nmcli command Used to display and configure network interfaces using NetworkManager.

nm-connection-editor command Used to start the graphical Network Connections tool that is part of NetworkManager.

nmtui command Used to start a text version of the Network Connections tool that is part of NetworkManager.

nohup command Used to execute a child process without parent association.

Non-Volatile Memory Express (NVMe) A modern SSDs technology that allows for very fast data transfer directly to the PCIe bus on the computer.

nslookup command Used to resolve host names to IP addresses.

NTP daemon (ntpd) The daemon used to provide time synchronization services on legacy Linux computers.

ntpdate command Used to view the current system time as well as synchronize the system time with an NTP server.

ntpq command Used to query the state of an NTP server or client.

O

object storage Storage made available to Web apps run within a cloud provider. Web apps access object storage using an HTTP request.

octet A portion of an IPv4 address that represents eight binary bits.

od command A Linux command used to display the contents of a file in octal format.

offset The difference in time between two computers that use the NTP protocol.

offsite backup The process whereby an archive is copied to another computer across the Internet.

One Time Password (OTP) A password that is used to validate a user's identity once only.

open command Used to execute an application bundle on macOS systems.

Open Source Software (OSS) The programs distributed and licensed so that the source code making up the program is freely available to anyone who wants to examine, utilize, or improve upon it.

Open Virtualization Archive (OVA) A common virtual appliance file format.

Open Virtualization Format (OVF) A file format used to specify virtual machine settings.

openSUSE One of the most popular and prevalent distributions of Linux, originally developed in Europe.

operating system (OS) The software used to control and directly interact with the computer hardware components.

options The specific letters that start with a dash (-) or two and appear after the command name to alter the way the command works.

orchestration The process of arranging and coordinating the execution of automated tasks, ultimately resulting in a consolidated process, such as a CD workflow.

other When used in the mode of a certain file or directory, all the users on the Linux system.

overclocked Term used to describe a CPU that runs faster than the clock speed for which it has been rated.

owner The user whose name appears in a long listing of a file or directory and who has the ability to change permissions on that file or directory.

P

package dependencies A list of packages that are prerequisite to the current package being installed on the system.

package group A group of RPM packages that are commonly installed to provide a specific function on the system.

package manager A system that defines a standard package format and can be used to install, query, and remove packages.

packet A package of data formatted by a network protocol.

pam_tally2 command Used to view and modify user lockout settings.

Parallel Advanced Technology Attachment (PATA) A legacy hard disk technology that uses ribbon cables to typically attach up to four hard disk devices to a single computer.

parallel SCSI   The traditional SCSI technology that transfers data across parallel cables.

parent directory   The directory that is one level closer to the root directory in the directory tree relative to your current directory.

parent process   A process that has started other processes (child processes).

parent process ID (PPID)   The PID of the parent process that created the current process.

`parted` **(GNU Parted) command**   Used to create and modify MBR and GPT partitions.

partition   A physical division of a hard disk or SSD.

`partprobe` **command**   Used to request that partition tables be reloaded by the Linux kernel.

`passwd` **command**   Used to change user passwords.

PATH variable   A variable that stores a list of directories that will be searched in order when commands are executed without an absolute or relative pathname.

penetration test   The process whereby a CyberSecurity worker attempts to break into systems to test security functionality.

permissions   A list that identifies who can access a file or folder and their level of access.

persistent volume   See *block storage*.

`pgrep` **command**   Used to list the PIDs of processes that match a regular expression or other criteria.

physical extent (PE) size   The block size used by the LVM when storing data on a volume group.

Physical Volumes (PVs)   A partition that is used by the LVM.

`pidstat` **(PID statistics) command**   Displays CPU statistics for each PID on a Linux system.

`ping` **(Packet Internet Groper) command**   Used to check connectivity on an IPv4 network.

`ping6` **command**   Used to check connectivity on an IPv6 network.

pipe   A string of commands connected by | metacharacters.

`pkill` **command**   Used to send a kill signal to processes that match a regular expression or other criteria.

Platform as a Service (PaaS)   A cloud strategy that allows organizations to host custom apps and data within a data center.

Pluggable Authentication Module (PAM)   A component that provides authentication-related functionality on a Linux system.

Point-to-Point Protocol (PPP)   The most common WAN protocol used to send TCP/IP packets across a telephone line.

port   A number that uniquely identifies a network service.

positional parameter   An argument to a shell script or function.

Postfix   A common email server daemon used on Linux systems.

PostgreSQL   A common SQL server used on Linux computers.

PostgreSQL utility   The program used to perform most database management on a PostgreSQL server.

Power On Self Test (POST)   An initial series of tests run when a computer is powered on to ensure that hardware components are functional.

PPP over Ethernet (PPPoE)   The protocol used by DSL to send PPP information over an Ethernet connection.

`pppoeconf` **command**   Used to configure a DSL connection on Ubuntu systems.

`pppoe-setup` **command**   Used to configure a DSL connection on Fedora systems.

primary DNS server   The DNS server that contains a read/write copy of the zone.

primary group   The group that is specified for a user in the /etc/passwd file and set as the group owner for all files created by a user.

primary partitions   The separate divisions into which an MBR-based hard disk or SSD can be divided (up to four are allowed per hard disk).

print job   The information sent to a printer for printing.

print job ID   A unique numeric identifier used to mark and distinguish each print job.

print queue   A directory on the filesystem that holds print jobs that are waiting to be printed.

`printenv` **command**   Used to display a list of exported variables and functions present in the current shell.

printer class   A group of CUPS printers that are treated as a single unit for the purposes of printing and management.

Printers tool   A graphical utility used to configure printers on a Fedora system.

priority   The importance of system information when logging system events.

private cloud   A private data center hosted by an organization that is accessible to other computers across the Internet.

private key   An asymmetric encryption key that is used to decrypt data and create digital signatures.

proactive maintenance   The measures taken to reduce future system problems.

process   A program currently loaded into physical memory and running on the system.

process ID (PID)   A unique identifier assigned to every process as it begins.

process priority (PRI)   A number assigned to a process, used to determine how many time slices on the processor that process will receive; the higher the number, the lower the priority.

process state   The current state of the process on the processor; most processes are in the sleeping or running state.

production kernel   A Linux kernel whose minor number (the number after the dot in the version number) is even, therefore deemed stable for use through widespread testing.

program   A structured set of commands stored in an executable file on a filesystem. A program can be executed to create a process.

programming language   The syntax used for developing a program. Different programming languages use different syntaxes.

protocol   A set of rules of communication used between computers on a network.

proxy server   A server or hardware device that requests Internet resources on behalf of other computers.

pruning   The process of excluding files, directories, or filesystems from being processed by a command.

ps command   Used to obtain information about processes currently running on the system.

pseudo filesystem   See *virtual filesystem*.

psql command   Used to start the PostgreSQL utility.

pstree command   Displays processes according to their lineage, starting from the init daemon.

public key   An asymmetric encryption key that is used to encrypt data and decrypt digital signatures.

Public Key Infrastructure (PKI)   A system whereby a CA is used to validate the authenticity of public keys.

Putty   A cross-platform SSH client.

pvcreate command   Used to create LVM physical volumes.

pvdisplay command   Used to view LVM physical volumes.

pvscan command   Used to view LVM physical volumes.

pwconv command   Used to enable the use of the /etc/shadow file.

pwd (print working directory) command   A Linux command used to display the current directory in the directory tree.

pwunconv command   Used to disable the use of the /etc/shadow file.

Q

Qt toolkit   The software toolkit used with the K Desktop Environment.

queuing   See *spooling*.

Quick Emulator (Qemu)   A software component that provides fast virtual machine access to KVM.

quota command   Used to view disk quotas imposed on a user.

quotaoff command   Used to deactivate disk quotas.

quotaon command   Used to activate disk quotas.

quotas   The limits that can be imposed on users and groups for filesystem usage.

R

rackmount server   A thin form factor used to house server hardware that is installed in a server rack.

RAID-Z An implementation of RAID level 5 using ZFS, which uses a variable stripe that provides for better performance and fault tolerance.

reactive maintenance The measures taken when system problems arise.

`read` **command** Used to read Standard Input from a user into a variable.

record A line within a database table that represents a particular object.

recursive A term referring to itself and its own contents; a recursive search includes all subdirectories in a directory and their contents.

recursive query A DNS resolution request that was resolved with the use of top-level DNS servers.

Red Hat One of the most popular and prevalent distributions of Linux in North America, distributed and supported by Red Hat, Inc. Fedora is a Red Hat-based Linux distribution.

Red Hat Package Manager (RPM) A package manager commonly used on Linux distributions derived from Red Hat Linux, and the default package manager used on Fedora Linux.

redirection The process of changing the default locations of Standard Input, Standard Output, and Standard Error.

Redundant Array of Independent Disks (RAID) The process of combining the storage space of several hard disk drives into one larger, logical storage unit.

Redundant Array of Inexpensive Disks (RAID) A type of storage that can be used to combine hard disks together for performance and/or fault tolerance.

regexp See *regular expressions*.

regular expressions The special metacharacters used to match patterns of text within text files; they are commonly used by text tool commands, including `grep`.

relational database A database that contains multiple tables that are linked by common fields.

relative pathname The pathname of a target directory relative to your current directory in the tree.

`reload` **command** Used to reload the configuration files into memory for an upstart daemon.

Remote Authentication Dial In User Service (RADIUS) A service that provides centralized authentication, logging, and policy restrictions on a network.

Remote Direct Memory Access (RDMA) A technology used to allow hardware devices to communicate directly with each other without accessing the CPU of the system. It is often used by network technologies such as Infiniband.

`renice` **command** Used to alter the nice value of a process currently running on the system.

`repquota` **command** Used to produce a report on quotas for a particular filesystem.

`resize2fs` **command** Used to change the size of an ext2/ext3/ext4 filesystem after creation; it is normally used after an LV has been extended to include additional space.

resource records The records within a zone on a DNS server that provide name resolution for individual computers.

`restart` **command** Used to manually restart an upstart daemon.

`restore` **command** Used to extract archives created with the `dump` command.

`restorecon` **command** Forces SELinux to set the default label on system files and directories.

reverse lookup A DNS name resolution request whereby an IP address is resolved to a FQDN.

revision number The number after the second dot in the version number of a Linux kernel that identifies the release number of a kernel.

`rm` **(remove) command** A command used to remove files and directories.

`rmdir` **(remove directory) command** A command used to remove empty directories.

`rmmod` **command** Used to remove a module from the Linux kernel.

rogue process A process that has become faulty in some way and continues to consume far more system resources than it should.

root filesystem The filesystem containing most files that make up the operating system; it should have enough free space to prevent errors and slow performance.

`route` **command** Used to manipulate the route table.

route table A table of information used to indicate which networks are connected to network interfaces.

router A device capable of transferring packets from one network to another.

routing The act of forwarding data packets from one network to another.

rpm command Used to install, query, and remove RPM packages.

rpm2cpio command Used to convert an RPM package to an archive that can be accessed using the cpio command.

rsync (remote sync) command Used to copy files to and from Linux computers running the rsync service using SSH encryption. It is often used to copy archives to remote computers.

rules The components of a firewall that match specific network traffic that is to be allowed or dropped.

runlevel A UNIX SysV term that defines a certain type and number of daemons on a Linux system.

runlevel command Used to display the current and most recent (previous) UNIX SysV runlevel.

runtime configuration (rc) scripts Scripts that are used during the system initialization process to start daemons and provide system functionality.

S

sandboxing The process of running applications on a single operating system that are isolated from each other. Containers are the most common method used to sandbox apps.

sar (system activity reporter) command Displays various performance-related statistics on a Linux system.

scalability The capability of computers to increase workload as the number of processors increases.

scp (secure copy) command Used to copy files to and from Linux computers using SSH encryption. It is often used to copy archives to remote computers.

SCSI ID A number that uniquely identifies and prioritizes devices attached to a SCSI controller.

search engine An Internet Web site, such as *www.google.com*, where you simply enter a phrase representing your search item and receive a list of Web sites that contain relevant material.

secondary DNS server A DNS server that contains a read-only copy of the zone.

sector The smallest unit of data storage on a hard disk; sectors are arranged into concentric circles called tracks and can be grouped into blocks for use by the system.

secure boot A UEFI BIOS feature that checks files loaded during the boot process to ensure that they were not modified by malware.

Secure FTP (SFTP) A version of the FTP protocol that encrypts traffic using SSH.

Secure Shell (SSH) A technology that can be used to run remote applications on a Linux computer; it encrypts all client-server traffic.

security appliance A server that provides advanced security services on a network. Most security appliances run a custom Linux distribution.

Security Enhanced Linux (SELinux) A set of Linux kernel components and related software packages that prevent malicious software from accessing system resources.

Security Information and Event Management (SIEM) Software that is used to monitor security events and vulnerabilities on systems across a network.

segmentation fault An error that software encounters when it cannot locate the information needed to complete its task.

seinfo command Displays SELinux features.

self-signed certificate A certificate that was digitally signed by the computer that generated the public key within.

seq command Used to generate a list of sequential numbers.

Serial Advanced Technology Attachment (SATA) A technology that allows for fast data transfer along a serial cable for hard disks and SSDs. It is commonly used in newer workstation and server-class computers.

Serial Attached SCSI (SAS) A high-performance SCSI technology that is commonly used for hard disks and SSDs in modern server-class computers.

server A computer configured to allow other computers to connect to it from across a network.

server closet A secured room that stores servers within an organization.

Server Message Blocks (SMB) The protocol that Windows computers use to format file- and printer-sharing traffic on TCP/IP networks.

server services The services that are made available for other computers across a network.

`service` **command** Used to manually start, stop, and restart UNIX SysV daemons.

service unit A Systemd term that is used to describe a daemon.

`sestatus` **command** Displays the current status and functionality of the SELinux subsystem.

`set` **command** Used to display a list of variables and functions within the shell.

`setenforce` **command** Used to change SELinux between enforcing and permissive mode.

`setfacl` **(set file ACL) command** A command used to modify ACL entries for a particular Linux file or directory.

`setsebool` **command** Used to modify SELinux settings within an SELinux policy.

`sftp` **(secure FTP) command** Used to interact with FTP servers using SFTP.

shared library A file that contains executable code that can be used by multiple, different programs. It is the most common type of package dependency.

shareware The programs developed and provided at minimal cost to the end user. These programs are initially free but require payment after a period of time or usage.

shebang See *hashpling*.

shell A user interface that accepts input from the user and passes the input to the kernel for processing.

shell script A text file that contains a list of commands or constructs for the shell to execute in order.

`showmount` **command** Used to view NFS shared directories on a remote computer.

Simple Protocol for Independent Computing Environments (SPICE) A graphical remote access protocol commonly used to manage virtual machines; it is the default for Boxes.

skeleton directory A directory that contains files that are copied to all new users' home directories upon creation; the default skeleton directory on Linux systems is /etc/skel.

slave DNS server See *secondary DNS server*.

slice The area within a macOS disk partition that can contain a filesystem.

Small Computer Systems Interface (SCSI) A high-performance hard disk technology that is commonly used in legacy server-class computers.

`smbclient` **command** Used to connect to a remote Windows or Samba server and transfer files.

`smbpasswd` **command** Used to generate a Samba password for a user.

snapshot A virtualization feature that allows you to revert to a previous version of a virtual hard disk file.

socket file A named pipe connecting processes on two different computers; it can also be represented by a file on the filesystem.

soft limit A disk quota that the user can exceed for a certain period of time.

software The programs stored on a storage device in a computer, which provide a certain function when executed.

Software as a Service (SaaS) A cloud strategy that provides access to a service hosted on servers within a data center.

software mirror A software repository that hosts the same RPM or DPM packages as other software repositories for fault tolerance and load balancing of download requests.

software RAID A RAID system that is controlled by software running within the operating system.

software repository A server on the Internet that hosts RPM or DPM packages for download.

Software utility A program that can be used to install, update, and remove RPM packages within a desktop environment on Fedora 28.

`softwareupdate` **command** Used to update macOS systems.

solid-state drive (SSD) A type of disk drive that functions within a computer like a hard disk drive but instead uses fast flash memory chips to store data.

source code The sets of organized instructions on how to function and perform tasks that define or constitute a program.

`source` **command** Used to execute the contents of a shell script within the current shell, instead of using a subshell.

source file/directory The portion of a command that refers to the file or directory from which information is taken.

spanning A type of RAID level 0 that allows two or more devices to be represented as a single large volume.

special device file A file used to identify hardware devices such as hard disks and serial ports.

spooling The process of accepting a print job into a print queue.

SQL server A server service that gives other programs and computers the ability to access a database.

`ss` **(socket statistics) command** Used to display network connections.

`ssh` **command** Used to connect to a SSH daemon on a remote computer.

SSH host keys The asymmetric public and private keys on a computer running sshd. They are used to negotiate the symmetric key at the beginning of an SSH session.

`ssh-add` **command** Used to add SSH user keys to the SSH agent process.

`ssh-agent` **command** Used to start the SSH agent process.

`ssh-copy-id` **command** Used to copy SSH user keys to the home directory of a user on another computer to allow for simplified authentication.

`ssh-keygen` **command** Used to generate or regenerate SSH encryption keys.

staging The process of adding files to a Git index.

stand-alone daemon A daemon that is started without the use of xinetd.

Standard Error (stderr) A file descriptor that represents any error messages generated by a command.

Standard Input (stdin) A file descriptor that represents information input to a command during execution.

Standard Output (stdout) A file descriptor that represents the desired output from a command.

`start` **command** Used to manually start an upstart daemon.

`startx` **command** Used to manually start X Windows and the default window manager and desktop environment.

stateful packet filter A packet filter that applies rules to related packets within the same network session.

`status` **command** Used to view the status of an upstart daemon.

`stop` **command** Used to manually stop an upstart daemon.

Storage Area Network (SAN) A group of computers that access the same storage device across a fast network.

strata The levels used within an NTP hierarchy that describe the relative position of a server to an original time source, such as an atomic clock.

`strings` **command** A Linux command used to search for and display text characters in a binary file.

Structured Query Language (SQL) A language used by database servers to query, add, and modify the data within a database.

subdirectory A directory that resides within another directory in the directory tree.

subnet mask A series of four 8-bit numbers that determine the network and host portions of an IP address.

subnetting The process in which a single large network is subdivided into several smaller networks.

subshell A shell started by the current shell.

`sudo` **command** Used to perform commands as another user via entries in the /etc/sudoers file.

`sudoedit` **command** Used to edit text files as another user via entries in the /etc/sudoers file.

superblock The portion of a filesystem that stores critical information, such as the inode table and block size.

swap memory See *virtual memory*.

`swapoff` **command** Used to disable a partition for use as virtual memory on the Linux system.

`swapon` **command** Used to enable a partition for use as virtual memory on the Linux system.

symbolic link A pointer to another file on the same or another filesystem; commonly referred to as a shortcut.

symmetric encryption   A type of encryption that uses a single key to encrypt and decrypt data.

syncing   The process of writing data stored in RAM to a filesystem.

`sysctl` **command**   Used to view and modify files stored under /proc/sys.

system   In BTRFS terminology, it refers to the BTRFS superblock.

system backup   The process whereby files are copied to an archive.

System Information   A macOS utility that displays system information.

system initialization process   The process that executes the daemons that provide for system services during boot time and bring the system to a useable state.

System Log Daemon (rsyslogd)   The daemon that logs system events to various log files via information stored in /etc/rsyslog.conf and files within the /etc/rsyslog.d directory.

System Preferences   The graphical system configuration utility within macOS.

system rescue   The process of using a live Linux OS to access and repair a damaged Linux installation.

system service   The additional functionality provided by a program that has been incorporated into and started as part of the operating system.

System Statistics (sysstat) package   A software package that contains common performance-monitoring utilities.

`system-config-keyboard` **command**   Used on Fedora Linux systems to configure a keyboard for use by X Windows.

`systemctl` **command**   Used to view, start, stop, restart, and reload Systemd daemons, as well as configure Systemd daemon startup during the system initialization process.

Systemd   A relatively new software framework used on Linux systems that provides a system initialization process and system management functions.

Systemd Journal Daemon (journald)   A Systemd component that logs system events to a journal database.

`systemd-analyze` **command**   Used to view Systemd unit information.

`systemd-cat` **command**   Used to create system log entries in the journald database.

Systemd-networkd   A Systemd daemon that manages the configuration of network interfaces.

T

Tab-completion feature   A feature of the BASH shell that fills in the remaining characters of a unique filename or directory name when the user presses the Tab key.

table   A database structure that organizes data using records and fields.

`tac` **command**   A Linux command that displays a file on the screen, beginning with the last line of the file and ending with the first line of the file.

`tail` **command**   A Linux command used to display lines of text at the end of a file; by default, the `tail` command displays the last 10 lines of the file.

`tar` **(tape archive) command**   The most common command used to back up files to an archive. It can also be used to view and restore archives.

tarball   A compressed `tar` archive.

target   See *target unit*.

target file/directory   The portion of a command that refers to the file or directory to which information is directed.

target ID   See *SCSI ID*.

target unit   A Systemd term that describes the number and type of daemons running on a Linux system. It is functionally equivalent to the UNIX SysV term *runlevel*.

TCP wrapper   A program that can be used to run a network daemon with additional client restrictions specified in the /etc/hosts.allow and /etc/hosts.deny files.

`tcpdump` **command**   Used to display the network traffic passing through a network interface.

`telinit` **command**   Used to change the operating system from one UNIX SysV runlevel to another.

`telnet` **command**   Used to obtain a shell on a remote computer running a Telnet daemon.

Teredo   A protocol used to encapsulate IPv6 packets within an IPv4 network.

terminal   The channel that allows a certain user to log in and communicate with the kernel via a user interface. It is also the name of the graphical application that is used to obtain a BASH shell within the macOS desktop.

Terminal Access Controller Access Control System Plus (TACACS+)   A service that provides centralized authentication, logging, and policy restrictions on a network.

terminator   A device used to terminate an electrical conduction medium to absorb the transmitted signal and prevent signal bounce.

test statement   A syntax used to test a certain condition and generate a True/False value.

testparm command   Used to check for syntax errors within the Samba configuration file as well as display the current Samba configuration.

text file   A file that stores information in a readable text format.

text tools   The programs that allow for the creation, modification, and searching of text files.

thick provisioning   The process of using a virtual hard disk file that has a fixed size.

thin provisioning   The process of using a virtual hard disk file that dynamically expands as needed up to a maximum size.

time slice   The amount of time a process is given on a CPU in a multiprocessing operating system.

timedatectl command   Used to view and set time and time zone information for a system.

Time-To-Live (TTL)   The amount of time that a computer is allowed to cache name resolution information obtained from a DNS server.

tload command   Displays load average information for a Linux system.

Token Ring   A media access method commonly used by industrial networks.

top command   Used to give real-time information about the most active processes on the system; it can also be used to renice or kill processes.

total cost of ownership (TCO)   The full sum of all accumulated costs, over and above the simple purchase price of utilizing a product. Includes training, maintenance, additional hardware, and downtime.

touch command   A command commonly used to create new files. Its original intended purpose was to update the time stamp on a file.

tr command   Used to transform or change characters received from Standard Input.

tracepath command   Used to trace the path an IPv4 packet takes through routers to a destination host.

tracepath6 command   Used to trace the path an IPv6 packet takes through routers to a destination host.

traceroute command   Used to trace the path an IPv4 packet takes through routers to a destination host.

traceroute6 command   Used to trace the path an IPv6 packet takes through routers to a destination host.

track   The area on a hard disk that forms a concentric circle of sectors.

Transmission Control Protocol/Internet Protocol (TCP/IP)   The most common network protocol used on the Internet. It provides for reliable communication.

transport mode   A VPN mode whereby traffic is encrypted between two computers.

trapping   The process of ignoring a kill signal.

troubleshooting procedures   The tasks performed when solving system problems.

tshark command   Used to start a command-line version of the graphical Wireshark program.

tune2fs command   Used to modify ext2/ext3/ext4 filesystem parameters.

tunnel mode   A VPN mode whereby traffic is encrypted between two routers.

Type 1 hypervisor   A hypervisor that runs directly on computer hardware.

Type 2 hypervisor   A hypervisor that runs as a program within an operating system.

type command   A command used to locate executable files on the system; it returns the first alias or directory within the PATH variable for the command.

tzselect command   Used to locate the appropriate time zone file for a region.

U

Ubuntu A major Linux distribution that is widely used worldwide.

udev daemon A system process used to manage device files for block and character devices.

`udevadm` **command** Used to view and modify udev daemon configuration.

UEFI System Partition A small partition that is created by an operating system installation program to store boot-related files on a computer that has a UEFI BIOS.

`ufw` **(Uncomplicated Firewall) command** Used to configure UFW.

`ulimit` **command** Used to modify process limit parameters in the current shell.

umask A special variable used to alter the permissions on all new files and directories by taking away select default file and directory permissions.

`umask` **command** The command used to view and change the umask variable.

`umount` **command** Used to break the association between a device and a directory in the logical directory tree.

`unalias` **command** Used to remove an alias from shell memory.

Uncomplicated Firewall (UFW) A software component that can be used to simplify the configuration of netfilter firewall rules.

`uncompress` **command** Used to decompress files compressed by the `compress` command.

unicast IP communication that is destined for a single computer.

Unicode A character set that extends ASCII and represents characters used in most languages.

Unified Extensible Firmware Interface (UEFI) A feature-rich BIOS replacement used in modern computers.

Unified Threat Management (UTM) Often used to describe a security appliance that performs multiple security functions.

uninterruptible power supply (UPS) A device that contains battery storage and is used to supply power to computers in the event of a power outage.

Unity A GNOME Shell alternative focused on mobile devices.

Universal Access utility A graphical utility within Fedora Linux used to configure assistive technologies.

Universally Unique Identifier (UUID) A unique identifier given to a filesystem or GPT partition when it is created; it can be used to identify that filesystem or GPT partition afterwards.

UNIX The first true multitasking, multiuser operating system, developed by Ken Thompson and Dennis Ritchie, and from which Linux was originated.

UNIX SysV A UNIX standard that is used to provide the structure of the system initialization process on Linux systems.

`unlink` **command** A command used to delete files.

`unset` **command** Used to remove a variable or function from shell memory.

`unxz` **command** Used to decompress files compressed by the `xz` command.

`unzip` **command** Used to decompress files compressed by the `zip` command.

`update-rc.d` **command** Used to configure UNIX SysV daemon startup by runlevel on Ubuntu Linux systems.

upstart A recent version of the UNIX SysV system initialization process used on modern Linux distributions.

`uptime` **command** Displays system uptime and load average information for a Linux system.

user A person who uses a computer. When used in the mode of a certain file or directory, it refers to the owner of that file or directory.

user account The information regarding a user that is stored in a system database (/etc/passwd and /etc/shadow), which can be used to log in to the system and gain access to system resources.

User Datagram Protocol/Internet Protocol (UDP/IP) A less-reliable, but faster version of the TCP/IP protocol.

User Identifier (UID) A unique number assigned to each user account.

user interface The interface the user sees and uses to interact with the operating system and application programs.

user process   A process begun by a user and which runs on a terminal.

`useradd` **command**   Used to add a user account to the system.

user-defined variables   The variables that are created by the user and are not used by the system. These variables are typically exported to subshells.

`userdel` **command**   Used to remove a user account from the system.

`usermod` **command**   Used to modify the properties of a user account on the system.

UTF-8   A character set that allows programs to represent the characters in the Unicode character set using one to four 8-bit bytes; it is the most common character set used today.

V

variable   An area of memory used to store information. Variables are created from entries in environment files when the shell is first created after login, and are destroyed when the shell is destroyed upon logout.

variable identifier   The name of a variable.

version control   A system that keeps track of changes made to files by users.

Very Secure FTP daemon (vsftpd)   The default FTP server program used on modern Linux distributions.

VFAT (Virtual File Allocation Table)   A non journaling filesystem that might be used in Linux.

`vgcreate` **command**   Used to create an LVM VG.

`vgdisplay` **command**   Used to view an LVM VG.

`vgextend` **command**   Used to add physical volumes to an LVM VG.

`vgscan` **command**   Used to view LVM VGs.

vi editor   A powerful command-line text editor available on most UNIX and Linux systems.

virtual appliance   A file that contains virtual machine settings and a virtual hard disk file.

virtual filesystem   A special filesystem that is used by the Linux kernel for operating system use only; /sys, /dev, /run, and /proc are examples of virtual filesystems.

virtual machine   See *guest operating system*.

virtual machine host   An operating system that runs virtualization software.

virtual memory   An area on a hard disk or SSD (swap partition) that can be used to store information that normally resides in physical memory (RAM), if the physical memory is being used excessively.

Virtual Network Computing (VNC)   A cross-platform technology that allows users to connect to a graphical desktop across a network.

Virtual Private Network (VPN)   A virtual network that overlays an existing TCP/IP network. Any data sent on this virtual network is encrypted.

virtualization   The process of running several separate operating systems concurrently on a single computer.

virtualization software   A set of programs that can be used to concurrently run an operating system within another operating system.

`visudo` **command**   Used to modify the contents of the /etc/sudoers file.

`vmstat` **command**   Displays memory, CPU, and swap statistics on a Linux system.

VNC viewer   A program used to connect to a VNC server and obtain a graphical desktop.

`vncpasswd` **command**   Used to set a VNC connection password for a user.

`vncserver` **command**   Used to start the VNC server process for a user.

Volume Group (VG)   A group of PVs that are used by the LVM.

vulnerability assessment   The process whereby a cybersecurity worker scans computers and networks for security vulnerabilities.

vulnerability scanner   Software that is used to scan a system for known vulnerabilities.

W

`watch` **command**   Used to run a process repeatedly at the specified second interval.

Wayland   A new X server designed to replace X.org; it is currently still in development.

Wayland compositor   A windows manager that is used by the Wayland X server.

Web page hit   A single HTTP request that is sent from a Web browser to a Web server.

well-known ports   Of the 65,535 possible ports, the ports from 0 to 1023, which are used by common networking services.

`wget` **(Web get) command**   Used to download files from the Internet.

`whereis` **command**   A command used to locate executable files on the system; it returns any directories within the PATH variable for the command, as well as the location of associated man pages and info pages.

`which` **command**   A command used to locate executable files on the system; it returns any aliases and directories within the PATH variable for the command.

`whois` **command**   Used to obtain information about the organization that maintains a DNS domain.

wide area network (WAN)   A network in which computers are separated geographically by large distances.

wildcard metacharacters   The metacharacters used to match certain characters in a file or directory name; they are often used to specify multiple files.

window manager   The GUI component that is responsible for determining the appearance of the windows drawn on the screen by X Windows.

Wireless-Fidelity (Wi-Fi)   A LAN technology that uses Ethernet to transmit data over the air.

Wireshark   A graphical program used to display the network traffic passing through a network interface.

workstation   A computer used to connect to services on a server.

workstation services   The services that are used to access shared resources on a network server.

World Wide Name (WWN)   A unique name that can be assigned to a storage device. FC requires that each storage device and controller have a WWN.

X

X client   The component of X Windows that requests graphics to be drawn from the X server and displays them on the terminal screen.

X Display Manager (xdm)   A graphical login screen.

X server   The component of X Windows that draws graphics to windows on the terminal screen.

X Windows   The core component of the Linux GUI that displays graphics to windows on the terminal screen.

X.org   A common implementation of X Windows used in Linux distributions.

XFCE   A common lightweight desktop environment.

XFS   A high-performance journaling filesystem used in Linux.

`xfs_admin` **command**   Used to view and configure parameters for an XFS filesystem, including the description label.

`xfs_db` **command**   Used to view XFS filesystem information and parameters.

`xfs_fsr` **command**   Used to reorganize and optimize an XFS filesystem.

`xfs_growfs` **command**   Used to change the size of an XFS filesystem after creation; it is normally used after an LV has been extended to include additional space.

`xfs_info` **command**   Used to obtain usage information for an XFS filesystem; it can also be used to change the size of an XFS filesystem after creation.

`xfs_quota` **command**   Used to configure and manage disk quotas for an XFS filesystem.

`xfs_repair` **command**   Used to check the integrity of an XFS filesystem and repair damaged files.

XNU   The macOS kernel. It stands for "X is Not UNIX."

`xz` **command**   Used to compress files using a Lempel–Ziv compression algorithm.

`xzcat` **command**   Used to display the contents of an archive created with xz to Standard Output.

`xzgrep` **command**   Used to search and display the contents of an archive created with xz to Standard Output.

`xzless` **command**   Used to display the contents of an archive created with xz to Standard Output in a page-by-page fashion using the `less` command.

`xzmore` **command**   Used to display the contents of an archive created with xz to Standard Output in a page-by-page fashion using the `more` command.

Y

YAML (YAML Ain't Markup Language)   A data format based on JSON that is commonly used for configuration files.

yum (Yellowdog Updater Modified) command   Used to install and upgrade RPM packages from software repositories, as well as manage and remove installed RPM packages.

Z

zcat command   Used to display the contents of an archive created with compress, zip, or gzip to Standard Output.

zebra command   Used to configure routing protocols, such as RIP and OSPF, on a Linux system. It is part of the optional Quagga package.

Zettabyte File System (ZFS)   A high-performance filesystem and volume management software that is often used to create fault tolerance volumes from multiple storage devices on Linux and UNIX systems that are resilient to corruption.

zfs command   Used to configure ZFS filesystem features.

ZFS pool   A series of storage devices that are managed by ZFS.

ZFS subfilesystem   A subdirectory on a ZFS volume that can be managed as a separate unit by ZFS.

ZFS volume   A volume created from space within a ZFS pool that contains a ZFS filesystem.

zgrep command   Used to search and display the contents of an archive created with compress, zip, or gzip to Standard Output.

zip command   Used to compress files using a Lempel–Ziv compression algorithm.

zless command   Used to display the contents of an archive created with compress, zip, or gzip to Standard Output in a page-by-page fashion using the less command.

zmore command   Used to display the contents of an archive created with compress, zip, or gzip to Standard Output in a page-by-page fashion using the more command.

zombie process   A process that has finished executing but whose parent has not yet released its PID; the zombie still retains a spot in the kernel's process table.

zone   A portion of the Domain Name Space that is administered by one or more DNS servers.

zone transfer   The process of copying resource records for a zone from a master DNS server to a slave DNS server.

zpool command   Used to configure ZFS pools and volumes.

zypper command   Used to install and upgrade RPM packages from software repositories, as well as manage and remove installed RPM packages on SUSE and openSUSE Linux distributions.

INDEX